Praise for *Presidential Puppetry*

Andrew Kreig uses his decades of investigative journalism talent to unmask the characters who have manipulated our democratic institutions. His formidable sources and sophisticated insights will enable elected officials, journalists, professors, and voters to evaluate the power interests that were at stake in the 2012 elections and for the future.

This is a frightening book that challenges all of us to act bravely. We must rouse ourselves to prevent a small number of wealthy, cynical men from usurping the power that rightfully belongs to the American citizen. He identifies these men, reveals their motives, shows us how they intended to accomplish their goals, and thus puts all of us on notice in this powerful exposé.

- **Lillian McEwen**, author, D.C. Unmasked and Undressed

Andrew Kreig was for many years a respected reporter for the *Hartford Courant* and author of *Spiked*. He went on to lead with distinction the Wireless Communications Association and the Justice Integrity Project. These efforts help provide the intimate knowledge of the Washington, national, and global affairs required for such ambitious reporting.

- **Robert Ames Alden**, former president of the National Press Club, co-founder and former president of the National Press Foundation, and former *Washington Post* World News editor

Thought provoking. Controversial. *Presidential Puppetry* is sure to raise lots of eyebrows. One of those books that inspires readers to look deep beneath the surface.

- **John Perkins**, best-selling author of *Confessions of an Economic Hit Man* and other books

Four decades ago, I described shocking abuses of the troops and taxpayers when I went on-the-record with Jack Anderson following my resignation from CIA service in Indochina during the Vietnam era. The situation is far worse now.

- **John Kelly**, former news editor at NBC-TV and CBS-TV, and former CIA officer

Presidential Puppetry gives remarkable insight into how our Constitution has disintegrated at the hands of a few secret oligarchs who are calling the shots in domestic and foreign affairs. And if anyone should know the subject it would be the author, who is one of the best investigative journalists in the country.

- **John Edward Hurley**, Washington commentator, civic leader, and historian

Veteran investigative journalist Andrew Kreig delves deep into the underbelly of Washington politics, coming up with startling new revelations that are bound to shake up the status quo.

- **Dick Russell**, author, *The Life and Ideas of James Hillman, On the Trail of the JFK Assassins*, and other books

This is clearly the worst of times in many decades, perhaps since the Civil War. The problem that a writer has is that you can write this, explain it, argue it, prove it. But, in the end, the reader and friends have to do something about it.

- **Sam Smith**, *Progressive Review* publisher, DC Statehood movement co-founder, and author of books that include *Shadows of Hope, Captive Capital*, and *Why Bother?*

Andrew Kreig's keen investigative skills, outstanding authoring, and established track record make his aptly titled, *Presidential Puppetry*, a ready source of vital information.

- **Ron Fisher,** Captain, U.S. Navy (retired) and Chair, WeThePeopleNow.org

Andy Kreig is the man to see in Washington, DC to report the most important stories, and overcome media self-censorship.

- **Dana Jill Simpson,** progressive political analyst, and president, Election Protection Action

Andrew Kreig reveals the unvarnished truth about our political system, which we never get from the corporate media...A powerful indictment and a must read if you care about true democracy.

- **Richard Charnin**, author, *Matrix of Deceit*

National politics has never been a very wholesome game. But the odor of wholesale deception and cynical choreography has been ripening of late into an overpowering stench that our media seems hell-bent on spraying with Febreze. Kreig connects the myriad of dots, from corrupt and cynical jurisprudence, to the ruthlessly edited candidates' playbook, to outright computerized election theft. What emerges is a pointillist "big picture" of terrifying impact.

Imagine a Seurat rendition of "The Scream," and you'll get the idea. All of this is well researched and powerfully written. No book bearing 1,200 endnotes can be said to be a romp. But Kreig carries us on a wave-crest across an ocean of alarming, and often outraging, reality. *Presidential Puppetry* shows us our time, shorn of its crowd-pleasing decorations.

- **Jonathan D. Simon**, director, Election Defense Alliance and author, *Code Red*

As I read key portions of Andrew Kreig's book, I had the feeling that its insights could make good leaders better, and could give bad ones serious concern that their ongoing injustices have been exposed in a way that demands remedial public action.

- **Clifford Arnebeck**, public interest attorney challenging the integrity of recent Ohio elections

Presidential Puppetry provokes. It is not for those who can't handle the truth, or even entertain what might well be the truth. Andrew Kreig's legal and technical experience complements his fearless, well-documented investigative approach. What we get is a barrel of moist mortar to trowel between the bricks of what we thought we knew.

Have you found yourself wondering who really runs this country? Or what ever happened to Obama – or to Petraeus? Or what befell Eric Massa, a too-fresh freshman Congressman from upstate New York? Kreig provides much spicier food for thought than the pap "everyone knows." One strain running through the text is that lesser officials risk brutal reprisal should they offend the really powerful by digging into sensitive areas off limits to them.

The release of *Presidential Puppetry* could hardly be better timed, as we are freshly reminded by WikiLeaks of the take-no-prisoners approach of archetypical Establishment figure Henry Kissinger, quoted in a State Department cable as saying, "The illegal we do immediately; the unconstitutional takes a little longer."

Kissinger and the other power brokers featured in this book are the kind against whom the framers of the Constitution tried to put restraints, lest they end up running the place. They are the quintessential "upper crust," which my Irish grandmother defined as "a bunch of crumbs held together with a lot of dough." Read the book. You'll see.

- **Ray McGovern**, Steering Group, Veteran Intelligence Professionals for Sanity (VIPS)

A look behind the scenes in an uncompromising account of U.S. presidential politics. It's a must-read for international readers.

- **Eelco H. Dykstra**, M.D., chairman, International Katrina Project Europe, based in The Hague

Buy and read this book. You'll learn a lot more than you could have imagined, and you'll start seeing the world, politics, and the justice system in a very different, clearer, smarter way. This book exposes the puppet masters who pull the strings of leading officials in both major U.S. parties, including Obama and Romney. It's entertaining, cutting-edge reporting provides the kind of information that we in the independent press believe vital to informed decision-making.

As a publisher of Andrew Kreig's work, I confess to looking forward to publishing Andrew's postings, because he is an investigative journalist combined with constitutional scholarship extraordinaire. This book takes his investigations to the next level, connecting the dots to unveil a big picture that is startling yet not surprising at all.

The book goes into great depth, showing the connections behind the candidates. For example, I've written that Mitt Romney should be regarded as "Bishop Romney" because his experience in that LDS post is longer and more relevant to voters than his single term as governor. Kreig's book amplifies that theme into a full historical context found nowhere else regarding Bishop Romney and his ascendancy within the revamped, tea party-oriented GOP. The book applies similar treatment to President Obama and many more U.S leaders.

The author has been a respected OpEdNews contributor for years. So I am not surprised this book's revelations have enduring and even global significance.

- **Rob Kall**, publisher of OpEdNews.com, host of *The Rob Kall Bottom-Up Radio Show*, and blogger for Huffington Post

Presidential Puppetry:

Obama, Romney and Their Masters

Also by Andrew Kreig:

Spiked: How Chain Management Corrupted America's Oldest Newspaper

Cover Design and Graphic Images by Kyle Telman
Cover Photo by Len Bracken

Photos are courtesy of Dr. Cyril H. Wecht, the United States government, the State of Massachusetts, and license under Creative Commons.

Presidential Puppetry:

Obama, Romney and Their Masters

Andrew Kreig

Washington, DC
EagleViewDC.com

Eagle View Books

An imprint of Eagle View Capital Strategies LLC
Washington, DC
Copyright © 2013 by Andrew Kreig

First edition, June 2013
Library of Congress Cataloging-in-Publication Data TBD

Kreig, Andrew, 1949 –
Presidential Puppetry: Obama, Romney and Their Masters
Andrew Kreig—1st Eagle View edition

ISBN: 978-0-9886728-2-6

For information on lectures, interviews, bulk discounts, and excerpts, contact Eagle View: (202) 638-0070 and info@EagleViewDC.com.

For MA in memory of our parents' hopes and struggles

Table of Contents

Foreword

By Cyril H. Wecht, M.D., J.D

Presidential Puppetry: Obama, Romney and Their Masters is strongly recommended for every U.S. citizen. Andrew Kreig's new book presents a fascinating, no-holds-barred analysis of our national candidates within the context of a brilliant, courageous, factually documented discussion of the unethical, illegal, ruthless vendettas engineered by governmental agencies against various political figures in recent years.

The flagrant, unbridled abuse of governmental power by the DOJ and FBI in attempting to destroy an individual — (financially, professionally, socially, and sometimes physically) for personal and political reasons, and to an extent that is grossly disproportionate to any alleged act of criminality — is the hallmark of a totalitarian government.

Once a victim has been targeted, there are no limits to the amount of time, energy, money, and use of personnel that the Feds will employ to pursue and persecute that individual. No charge will be considered too petty or unimportant in their efforts to coerce the victim into pleading guilty to avoid the frightening possibility of a lengthy jail term.

"Select the victim / search for the crime" is a deplorable, dangerous prosecutorial tactic that all decent, fair-minded American citizens — liberal Democrats or conservative Republicans — need to let their voices be heard in denouncing, castigating, and rejecting.

This provocative exposé by Andrew Kreig is a clarion call for every American who firmly cherishes a belief of personal liberty within a just and democratic society.

Cyril H. Wecht, M.D., J.D., is one of the world's leading forensic pathologist/lawyers. He is the author or co-author of more than 40 scholarly and general interest books, including *A Question of Murder, Tales from the Morgue, and Mortal Evidence,*, and more than 550 professional articles. Dr. Wecht was the first independent forensics expert to examine President Kennedy's autopsy records. His long-held, well-known belief is that there was more than one assassin. He has served as president of both the American College of Legal Medicine and the American Academy of Forensic Sciences, and has appeared on many nationally syndicated television /programs. He serves on more than 20 editorial boards of professional journals.

Author's Preface

This book is for those who fear for the country's future. As President Obama embarked on a second term and Republicans regrouped to fight again, most Americans faced the same problems as before the 2012 elections. The majority are experiencing unnecessary austerity via a political process that works for the elite. The process appears broken only to those who fail to understand that decision-makers are intentionally gutting our basic democratic procedures and rights, such as voting, checks-and-balances, due process, other court oversight, the press, privacy, and many other safeguards we take for granted.

The core problem is that top officials posing as decision-makers instead are front men and women. They speak but do not inform. They listen, but do not hear. Their interests are not the public interest.

The following pages provide a tool-kit for those who want to address this problem. I connect the dots for the public about facts that are well known in specialized, elite circles. The just-completed 2012 elections provide a rare opportunity to illustrate vital matters neglected during the elections, which supposedly determine government policy. Instead, winners revert to the agendas of their powerful core supporters, whom I describe as puppeteers. The public has scant opportunity to influence this process without understanding it better.

This book's goal is help readers understand a new political reality: Our elected leaders are far less powerful than they used to be, or they seem. Their funders and other masters have changed the rules so that the public loses. As for the stakes in this new game? Some receive easy and often corrupt wealth, and low taxes. Others get lack of opportunity — or loss of job, savings, civil rights, health, or home.

The story in the pages ahead is like a mystery. Like other whodunits, everything seemed normal on the surface at the beginning for me as an observer aside from puzzling clues of potential danger, which arose in this instance with increasing frequency after 9/11. My perspective is from Washington, DC, where I worked more than two decades, primarily as an advocate for high-tech businesses. My job as president of the Wireless Communications Association from 1996 to 2008 was to foster the regulatory, financial, and other conditions that would enable a new wireless Internet industry. As such, a vital part of my job was monitoring public affairs and initiating opportunities, including in such post-9/11 government priorities as broadband initiatives for public safety, disaster remediation, homeland security, and warfare. At one convention in 2005, for example, we hosted important U.S. government and Iraqi leaders to describe in public for the first time how they had successfully deployed a nationwide public safety wireless network. My more typical work was helping foster deployments for consumers. For example, we featured as speakers CEOs of two of the world's leading spectrum holders. One of our group's members was Mexico's leading cable TV pioneer Ernesto Vargas, to my left in the photo below, and Dr. Jin Guojun of China, operator of the world's largest system and a former Beijing mayor.

While going about such work, I noticed what seemed like puzzling omissions in news coverage of U.S. public affairs. The omissions arose especially in the kinds of court cases I had worked on as a newspaper reporter and attorney early in my career. These irregularities proved to be disturbing upon further examination.

Three examples illustrate my concerns. One was the strangely low-profile federal probe of the post-9/11 anthrax attacks on journalists and U.S. Senators. These attacks had caused several  fatalities and transformed the federal business climate by requiring vastly greater security, especially on letters to government officials. Yet the public received only sporadic information about the investigation and suspects. The first "person of interest," Steven Hatfill, was exonerated in 2008. The second, Bruce Ivins, was found dead, reputedly by suicide.

Another case with obvious irregularities was the aggressive prosecution on prostitution charges of Jeane Palfrey, the so-called "DC Madam." She lived in California and was just days away from retiring to Germany before her prosecution. She faced massive charges and pretrial seizure of her assets, thereby limiting her defense options.

Also strange was the Bush federal prosecution on corruption charges of former Alabama Governor Don Siegelman, his state's leading Democrat. The Siegelman case fit a nationwide pattern that became apparent with the exposure of the Bush United States Attorney purge scandal in 2007. Federal prosecutors across the country launched politically motivated cases to keep their jobs as "loyal Bushies." The Bush administration fired nine of its other appointees in apparently unprecedented fashion, a process exposed in House Judiciary Committee hearings. In 2007, I met a Republican opposition researcher, Dana Jill Simpson, just as she was becoming nationally famous for exposing the scandals. I gave her advice, and she helped open my eyes in the years ahead to intrigues of global importance.

In mid-2008, I resigned after 15 years at the association. I became a legal reform advocate, strategic consultant, and research fellow with two universities. My research led to appalling discoveries about irregularities in the federal system. For example, investigative evidence and expert protests showed that Siegelman had been framed. I published many columns about it, and founded the Justice Integrity Project, a non-partisan legal reform group.

In researching those cases, I discovered sinister official conduct related to national security. These factors prevented the suspects from defending themselves fairly and the public from learning the facts. The research revealed plans to corrupt the democratic process, including presidential elections. This book reports my findings.

"What's it to you? Why should you care?" a friendly editor asked me in 2009 one day early in my research as we relaxed at the National Press Club. His was a logical question, especially from a thoughtful old hand who had covered vast numbers of speeches and charlatans during his three decades as a prominent journalist in the nation's capital.

"Journalists and lawyers don't seem to be doing their jobs. If what I'm learning is true we all need to know."

"If you feel that strongly," he replied, "write it up, and I'll see if I can help you get it out as an op-ed. Just make sure it's only 650 words."

I never went back to him. To be credible, the full story takes nearly that many pages, not words. Without a footnoted examination of the Cold War, for example, few readers are going to believe the Obama family had a national intelligence background. Similarly, few can appreciate without relevant history the importance of the Mormon religion to Mitt Romney. Each of these factors is vital also to understand whether Obama faced a *Seven Days in May*-style loyalty threat from the nation's military-intelligence complex. The inside story of the resignation of CIA Director David Petraeus is far different than the simple sex scandal peddled to the public. So is the Benghazi massacre. This book documents plots for massive election fraud in 2012. Second-term Obama appointments that affect jobs, pensions, health care, and the economy have been made without full disclosure. As of this writing, questions are arising unanswered about a potential CIA relationship with the family of the 2013 Boston Marathon bombing suspects. Separately, massive federal surveillance of Americans created new mysteries in June 2013 Should contractor Edward Snowden, age 29, have alerted the public by violating his CIA and NSA oaths?

Participate with me in this investigative process. Use your own power of imagination. Suppose you were minding your own business and living your normal life. Then you began seeing clues about seemingly sinister matters that few others seem to notice.

What would you do? Whom would you try to meet? What would you say? I faced those questions. The journey unfolds in these pages. I connect dots from significant events drawn from an entire century. The patterns seemed especially important after the 2012 election season. The public had every reason to believe the candidates were known after two years of campaigns. This book shows what was withheld. Candidates come and go. Puppet masters remain.

When I started this research, I had no idea it would lead me to assemble, bit by bit, a story that would suggest extreme treachery. At first, I thought I was assembling a gigantic jigsaw puzzle that would include missing information. With ever-greater excitement, I began to see patterns emerge. At this point, however, I realize the puzzle analogy is too simple. Assembling all the pieces provides an opportunity to visualize a scene, not truth. Someone of unknown motives created every scene we think we see in these political puzzles. They are created for us by master illusionists like Karl Rove, who once told a biographer that his generation of strategists could create a new reality. Thus, "completing" the jigsaw is never the end of the puzzle. We must update our understanding of who created each scene and why.

Some may regard the disclosures ahead as so depressing that no one can do anything. Please do not feel that way. I do not, and neither do my main sources. We are pointing out the potholes in the road, thereby easing our necessary journey to protect our heritage and future.

President Obama's second term could be far different from his first, especially if the public knew more about his strengths and vulnerabilities, and guided him and his opponents accordingly. One of my themes is "Knowledge is Your Power," drawn from the Biblical proverb. Hope without understanding does not lead to happiness.

A conversation with you as a reader is vital to each of our understanding. This book contains web-based tools for feedback and further discussion to unravel the mysteries confronting us. The book has more than 1,100 endnotes, nearly all with electronic links to sources. Use them to amplify, challenge, and share these revelations. Your future, like everyone's, may depend on it.

Andrew Kreig

Washington, DC
June 25, 2013

Part I: How Our Imperial Presidency Imperils Us All

"Since I entered politics, I have chiefly had men's views confided to me privately. Some of the biggest men in commerce and manufacture are afraid of somebody, are afraid of something. They know there is a power somewhere so organized, so subtle, so watchful, so interlocked, so complete, so pervasive, that they had better not speak above their breath when they speak in condemnation of it."

— President Woodrow Wilson
from his book *The New Freedom* (1913)

Chapter 1

Romney and Ryan: Apprentice Oligarchs

H erman Cain seems like a nice guy, but he's a puppet. That is what I thought to myself as I covered the biggest speech of his life and witnessed its relevance to what became the Romney-Ryan 2012 ticket.

Herman Cain was the GOP's 2012 front-running candidate in the polls when he took the stage of the National Press Club on October 31, 2011, a year before the election. The occasion was especially dramatic. Two score video crews covered his speech. The former Godfather's Pizza CEO had come from almost nowhere to lead that month's polls in the race to win the presidential nomination. On Sunday, October 30, however, the day before his long-planned press club speech, the insider tabloid, *Politico,* reported sexual harassment allegations against him. They came from two former subordinates from his tenure in the 1990s as CEO of the National Restaurant Association [1] Cain's press club lecture in the ballroom was his first full response to the allegations after he and his hosts had brushed them off at a different event earlier in the day.

At a VIP reception before the lecture, he flashed a big smile and effortlessly exchanged jokes. During the talk, he enthused about how a chauffeur's son, as he was, could ascend the success ladder to lead his party's presidential race. Naturally, he touted the "9-9-9" tax-cut plan as a cure-all for the nation's economy.

During the question-and-answer period, Club President Mark Hamrick posed tough questions to the candidate about the harassment claim, which arose from litigation by the women in the 1990s and became public despite a settlement deal forbidding disclosure. Cain denied the claims. He closed his talk with a deep-voiced, on-tune, and otherwise impressive *a Canella* rendition of the spiritual *Amazing Grace.*

"What did you think?" a friend asked me. She was the founder of a glossy magazine that covers the VIP and social scene for the metro Washington region. Her daughter, the publisher, listened for my answer from across the table. So did Cain's tall, friendly, and quite muscular bodyguard, sitting to my left. I ducked the question. I explained that I should refrain from an opinion because the press club had asked me to cover the speech for its web audience of readers.[2]

Within a few days, however, I voiced strong views for varied audiences on the web and radio, where commentary is not simply welcome but required.[3] "Cain as Front Man for Billionaires is a Consumer Issue" was my headline for the non-partisan consumer-oriented publication, Connecticut Watchdog. "GOP Presidential candidate Herman Cain," it began, "serves as front man for the billionaire Koch brothers in a way rarely, if ever, seen in modern times for a prominent U.S. major party candidate."

Cain's campaign soon imploded even though he and his backers gamely tried for several weeks to keep going.[4]

Backed by the Koch Brothers, Charles and David, Cain and his supporters suggested that feminists must have been attacking him because of his ideas.[5] His main idea, of course, was his "9-9-9" plan that, among other things, would save the Kochs and other elderly billionaires' vast amounts of money by eliminating inheritance taxes on the rich. Cain was a featured speaker at the annual convention of the Koch-funded Americans for Prosperity advocacy organization. "I am the Koch Brothers' brother from another mother and proud of it!" he told hundreds in the crowd at the Washington convention center, including David Koch.[6] Cain's helplessness when he went off-script was a factor in his demise along with the cascade of sex scandal claims and the candidate's obvious subservience to the Koch Brothers. Cain showed that he was not a serious candidate when he interrupted his campaign in the fall. He took a break to hawk his lightweight memoir, *This is Herman Cain!* at non-political book signings.[7] Even worse for his image was his devastating video interview in early November. He appeared pathetically unprepared to answer softball questions about foreign policy.[8]

The Cain candidacy solidified for me the central theme of this book: the concept of presidents and their top appointees as puppets, directed in their actions by those who prefer to operate unseen.

The pattern is obvious once you look for it and disregard the rhetoric from the conventional media (itself controlled by puppet masters in many ways) about how the president is "the most powerful man on earth." Perhaps that is true in a certain narrow sense, such as access to nuclear weapons. Yet any look at presidential candidates, aside from the Bushes (and perhaps Mitt Romney and Hillary Clinton), indicates that they are far from controlling the nation's true power centers. These control centers are, for the most part, privately held corporations, particularly in the financial, energy, and weapons sectors. Top government officials who theoretically provide oversight tend to be retainers or ideologues. They provide the illusion of independent control. In reality, they have far less freedom of action (or desire for it) than the public might imagine.

Romney, with his CEO bearing and estimated personal wealth of at least $250 million and perhaps vastly more, stood out from the pack of GOP rivals. That is no surprise. Most were implausible as world leaders. The party's establishment was secretly undermining several.

Yet even Romney, despite his wealth, two Harvard degrees, and a lifetime of connections, seemed a hat-in-hand aspirant to the real inner-circles. One of his backers, Las Vegas gambling tycoon Sheldon Adelson, committed to spending up to $100 million to help the GOP in 2012. One estimate is that Adelson would reap a $2.3 billion return from a Romney victory, given his investment and tax circumstances. This does not count the liability Adelson feared on corruption charges.[9]

Ryan, a supposed GOP leader of his generation, wilted under a simple request from a friendly interviewer for the time Ryan took to run the only marathon of his life.[10] Ryan, a fitness buff, claimed he ran more than 26 miles in less than three hours. His actual time was more than four hours – a huge difference, as he well knew. Similarly, he claimed to have climbed grueling Rockies mountain peaks 40 times. One report calculated the feat as impossible unless he spent all of his vacations for many years on the climbs.[11] These statements appear to illustrate the willingness of government leaders to mislead the public on even the simplest and most obvious matters. They proceed with even more shameless impunity on more complex matters important to their backers and to the public.

Similarly, President Obama has been a mere aspirant to real power until recently, as indicated in the following chapters. I was initially skeptical when one of Obama's top advisors told me in 2011 that they feared a "revolt" by the powerful if Obama sought to hold Bush-era personnel accountable for law breaking. What might that mean? Was the advisor's claim just an excuse for timid, ineffectual action? Those questions underlie much of this book's research and narrative.

This chapter introduces Mitt Romney and Paul Ryan. It focuses primarily on Romney and begins with a vital dimension of his thinking: his deep devotion to the Mormon Church, including its history, hierarchy, and beliefs. The conventional media touches only lightly on this sensitive topic even though his commitment to promote his church is crucial to understanding how his policies would have affected voters. The story of the fastest-growing church in the Western Hemisphere is fascinating in its own right and is a useful guide to how the nation would have changed under a Romney presidency. Most of the book draws a pattern between revelations about President Obama, his predecessors, and their supporters.

This book is based on years of research, and is being published on a fast track to provide voters with timely information in 2013 as the Obama second term takes shape.

A *Washington Post* headline about the only vice presidential debate of the campaign, "Biden and Ryan pull no punches," showed the tepid coverage readers received during the campaign. In fact, the two candidates debated under unspoken gentlemen's rules on October 12, 2012 in order to limit damage to each other's most vital interests. With the co-operation of a compliant media, the candidates avoided even mentioning most of their opponents' greatest vulnerabilities. Ryan, for example, failed to provide even a hint of the dishonest personal biography that President Obama has provided to the public. Why? Ryan is either too junior to know about it (a strange position for one of his ostensible stature), or he knows that disclosure will offend his own backers. The same thing goes for many Obama administration policies and actions that deserved specific, hard-hitting criticism from Ryan, instead of his vague, partisan complaints.

Biden, as well, held back from hitting as hard or effectively as he could have. Instead of making a great show of frowns and smiles, Biden could have simply looked at the camera and then at Ryan and said: "His ticket is proposing the same disastrous Bush-Cheney policies that wrecked the nation's economy and reputation."[12] Biden then could have said that until Ryan and Romney show their own commitment to the country by disclosing their tax returns, naming anyone in their family who has volunteered for overseas military service, and specifying which middle class tax deductions they would eliminate, all the rest of their promises were hokum. Biden, an accomplished politician, did not even undertake the basic gesture of looking into the camera and asking for the viewers' vote on November 6.

In the free-flowing debate format, Biden could have made such points repeatedly, with greater effectiveness each time. If he wanted variety he could have zeroed in on the hypocrisy of Ryan and his GOP colleagues in several major areas: One is their Republican war-mongering while so many of the macho proponents avoid military service themselves and neglect veterans issues, such as post-service jobs and health care. Another theme could have been the major effort by Bush operatives who were supporting the Romney-Ryan ticket to rig voting against Democrats by devious, secret methods.

An additional attack point for Biden could have been the national GOP effort, illustrated by the 2012 GOP platform and Ryan's longtime voting record, to oppose freedom of choice on conception and abortion when so many Republicans are predatory adulterers in private. One of the examples surfaced that week. A GOP "pro-life" congressman and physician from Tennessee reportedly pressured a patient, who was also the physician's lover, to obtain an abortion in order to hide their affair from the congressman's wife.[13] Most importantly, Biden could have attacked Ryan, his ticket-leader Romney, and their backers on the grounds of undermining the Constitution and fundamental legal system on a range of issues vital for both business and government. Examples constitute much of this book, and are too numerous to summarize here.

Biden, like such predecessors as Democratic nominees John Edwards in 2004 and Joseph Lieberman in 2000, did not undertake any such debate points. Why? It is not that they are unskilled. Each is an attorney steeped in politics. They do not want to attack too hard. Such debates are mostly for show. Each campaign spent a billion dollars on the presidential race alone. The conventional media, as indicated by the *Washington Post's* headline, is more than happy to keep up the drama. Everyone knows that gentlemen's rules prevail. Otherwise, opponents might hit back hard. Worse, the puppet masters would not approve so much information becoming available on air for ordinary voters.

With that introduction, we briefly examine the history of Mitt Romney's guiding faith, as well as the Romney and Ryan biographies.

Saints and Other Leaders

Mitt Romney's religion plays a powerful role in his life. He has been inspired to overcome opposition and even bigotry, and become the first member of his Mormon faith to win the presidency. This would have achieved a long-sought unification of church and state under the Mormon auspices. That was the vision of Mormon Prophet Joseph Smith when he ran for the United States presidency in 1844, before a lynch mob in Illinois ended his quest. The Romney family loyally supported Smith at the time, and carried on under his successors until current times. The family helped build the modern Latter-day Saints (LDS) Church to its current point: providing a largely satisfying community for its members and a powerful and hidden government in its regions of influence.

To learn about Mitt Romney in any depth, we need to go beyond his words. Even by the standards of a politician, Romney's speeches were filled with pieties, half-truths, and exaggerations. The prominent author-psychiatrist, Dr. Justin Frank, suggests that Romney's faith distorts his perceptions so much that he himself has difficulty knowing when he is lying.[14] This is because, in the mode of holy men from around the world, Romney believes his actions are directed by a Higher Power and for a greater good than the immediate needs of his audiences.[15]

Romney is a spiritual descendant of the prophet Joseph Smith, who founded a religion by announcing that he had Golden Tablets in an ancient Egyptian language that only he could decipher, and that he could edify the populace by the Book of Mormon, guaranteeing salvation and eternal life. Part of the new religion's attraction was that it drew on familiar Christian, Jewish, and even Muslim stories based in the Middle East to show that the future, as well as important parts of the past, centers on the United States and its expansion under God's guidance via Mormon prophets.

As summarized by, among others, the distinguished historian Fawn M. Brodie, herself a Mormon: In 1841, Romney ancestors joined Smith's flock in Nauvoo, located in Illinois on bluff overlooking a horseshoe bend of the Mississippi River[16] Nauvoo was a booming city comprised of Mormons located across the river from Indian Territory. By then, Smith had risen above his humble roots in rural Upstate New York and Vermont. Smith "detested the plow as only a farmer's son can."[17] Rather than pursue that kind of dreary labor, the charismatic young man charged fees to his neighbors to direct them in hunts for buried treasure. His setbacks included a misdemeanor conviction near his hometown in 1826 for being "an impostor" who charged his neighbors fees to use magic to find buried treasure.[18]

Undaunted, Smith proceeded to announce revelations from God, via the Mormon angel, Moroni. Among them: America had been settled by a lost tribe of Israel that evolved into Indian tribes populating the Americas; Jesus would return in a Resurrection in Missouri; and God's secrets were revealed to Smith. Smith went on to build an impressive following. In Nauvoo, Smith acquired the titles of mayor, general of a private army, and "king of kings." He practiced with fellow elders the secret rite of polygamy, also known as "plural marriage." Smith acquired forty-eight wives, some as young as age 15.[19] Smith also sought federal funds to expand his private army, the Nauvoo Legion, to rule the Indian territories from the Texas-Mexico border northwest through the Oregon Territory.

Mitt Romney's sense of confidence stems in part from his family's 170 years of involvement with top leaders of the Mormon Church. The conventional news media are reluctant to draw the connection between his secrecy, moneymaking, and religion. This book will connect for readers the power of the church and its doctrines over the candidate. This helps to explain Romney's focus on such seemingly disparate areas as empire building, tax shelters, and war. Smith, after all, described his own revelations from God as including such varied information as the locale in northwest Missouri where Jesus would appear for the Resurrection, as well as floor plans for Smith's residence in Nauvoo with instructions for followers to grant Smith lifelong free residency.[20]

Romney's faith should be a serious concern for those who are unaffiliated with the Mormon Church. The government of the United States often prosecuted Mormons and indeed Romney's own family for polygamy. United States law and ethical norms are often at odds with the Mormon faith. It is little wonder, then, that Romney often conflates his tax avoidance with his tithing for church. He seems to believe that support for the church is just as important as support for government. Perhaps it is more so in a sense. Yet it means in effect that those unaffiliated, especially children, the disabled and elderly, may be consigned to a hell on earth, as well as afterward.

In essence, Romney's words and deeds show that he believes that certain Americans are special and others deserve their fate. Ryan is a former aide to high-ranking political figures, a Roman Catholic, and a descendant from a prominent family in southern Wisconsin. He seems to share similar views. In sum, each man devotes himself to the pursuit of higher office and more government power despite an ostensible scorn for governing. Why? To what end?

Family Ties That Bind

Willard Mitt Romney was born in 1947 and was named for his father's best friend, the hotel entrepreneur Willard Marriott, and for Milton "Mitt" Romney, a cousin who once played quarterback for the Chicago Bears.[21] Mitt's father, George Romney, was born in Mexico. George's grandfather had established a polygamous colony with four wives before the family fled back to the United States in 1912 in fear of Mexican revolutionaries. In 1931, George persuaded a movie starlet to pass up a $50,000 Hollywood contract, convert to his religion and marry him. Without a college degree, George became CEO of American Motors and pioneered fuel-efficient cars during the gas-guzzler era. George became a three-term Michigan GOP governor and a leading 1968 presidential contender regarded as a moderate on race relations and the Vietnam War. Neither Democrats nor Republicans ever subjected George Romney because of his admitted foreign birthplace to anything remotely similar to the hate-filled, bogus "Birther" campaign ginned up against Obama, even though George Romney clearly was born in Mexico.[22] The disparity illustrates how hatred can be a powerful force in politics, especially when activated by well-funded partisans.

Mitt grew up in the posh Detroit suburb of Bloomfield Hills. He attended an elite prep school, where he met his future wife, who attended his prep school's female counterpart. Ann Davies, a non-Mormon, was the daughter of a wealthy industrialist and former mayor. Romney attended Stanford University and, after his freshman year, undertook 30-months of missionary service in France during the Vietnam War. In college, Romney had joined right-wing protests in favor of the war and against war critics. Nevertheless, he received student and missionary deferments during the peak of Vietnam War drafts. He failed to take any actions to serve in the war he supported, and drew a high enough number in the first draft lottery to avoid service.[23]

He later finished his degree at Brigham Young University. He persuaded Ann and most of her family to convert to his religion with its promise of salvation and access to God's secret revelations, and then married her. In 1972, Romney enrolled in a rigorous joint degree program at Harvard's law and business schools. Upon graduation, he readily found work at the Boston Consulting Group, a top-tier financial consultancy where his colleagues included future Israeli Prime Minister Benjamin Netanyahu, who became his close friend.

In 1977, Bill Bain, CEO of Bain and Company, hired Romney to join his Boston-based consultancy. Six years later, Bain persuaded Romney to lead a start-up affiliate, Bain Capital. Bain's plan was that the venture capital firm would invest in companies, not simply advise them.

Conventional wisdom is that Romney earned fabulous wealth by implementing the concept with such sterling personal qualities as his intelligence, education, vision, and hard work. *Vanity Fair* and others have alleged that additional success factors included unsavory startup funding of $2 million from British press lord and reputed Mossad operative Robert Maxwell, who disappeared overboard from a cruise ship in 1991 after he looted a company pension fund of hundreds of millions of pounds. Other seven-figure investments in the Bain start-up came from arguably disreputable El Salvador and Panamanian oligarchs associated with the CIA, according to a *Vanity Fair* report that alleged a variety of other unsavory business practices by Romney and his colleagues to amass their wealth and hide major parts of its offshore.[24] The reporter said he had no evidence of illegality. But he quoted a financial analyst as saying certain business tactics seemed "shocking" for a presidential candidate.

The Romney campaign would maintain strict secrecy during its years of campaigning, aside from releasing two years of tax returns. As a result, little definitive follow-up has occurred.

The potential relevance to Bain and Romney of the eccentric billionaire Howard Hughes is worth a mention here. Hughes was one of the most fascinating figures of his era before his death in 1976. He was, among other achievements, a major war contractor with top-secret CIA business. Below is a glimpse of his final years that was almost totally ignored during Romney's 2012 presidential campaign.

Romney's Bain Capital colleagues early on included Robert Gay, a Mormon. Gay would become managing director of Bain from 1989 to 2004 and a Mormon General Authority. The title is one of the church's highest-ranking offices, with roots extending back to the 1830s in a largely secret decision-making process launched by Joseph Smith. In recent years after moving on from Bain, Gay has also been managing director of Huntsman-Gay Global Capital, a billion-dollar financial firm.[25]

Gay was the son of William "Bill" Gay, the former CEO and president of Summa Corporation.[26] Summa was an umbrella group for the holdings of the secretive Hughes, one of world's wealthiest, most glamorous, and otherwise successful men.[27] Hughes built great companies, designed innovative airplanes and films, bedded movie stars, bested the Mafia, bribed presidents, and served as the front man for a secret $250 million CIA project in 1970 to salvage a sunken Soviet nuclear submarine.[28]

Bill Gay led what became known in business circles as the "Mormon Mafia" that ran the Hughes empire during the tycoon's last years. The obsessive and drug-deranged Hughes lived in seclusion on the ninth floor of the Desert Inn, the famed Las Vegas casino.[29]

Prominent recent Hughes biographers allege that Bill Gay systematically abused his boss's trust by fostering Hughes drug use so that Gay and other top executives could loot his holdings after Hughes discarded his previous chief.[30] Their allegation is not a passing reference. The biographers say Gay conspired with his brother-in-law, a physician of the Mormon faith, for Hughes to receive massive, unnecessary, daily drug doses for two years. They allege that Hughes was killed by this treatment, and that a billion dollars in his assets disappeared in mysterious circumstances.

The conventional media almost totally neglected these suspicions about Bill Gay in 2012 campaign coverage. For example, the most definitive biography of Romney is *The Real Romney*, a 400-page book in 2012 by two *Boston Globe* political reporters, Michael Kranish and Scott Helman.[31] The book, like nearly all campaign coverage, fails to mention Bill Gay, Howard Hughes, or Robert Gay's extraordinarily high rank in the Mormon Church. Instead, the book's focus on the Mitt Romney-Robert Gay relationship is based on what is portrayed as a heartwarming tale. This was how Romney closed down Bain Capital temporarily in Boston to deploy all personnel in a New York metro region search for Gay's missing daughter. She turned out to have embarked on a long weekend at a Rave concert. The story serves to humanize Romney as a caring executive. On reflection, however, his professional and charitable acts raise a question, entirely omitted in the book, of how much he would extend himself for those not within the inner-circle of his church and business. For Mitt Romney, helping Robert Gay was more like helping a brother than an act of true charity.[32]

To be clear, I have no evidence that any of the purportedly looted Hughes money found its way into Bain or Romney coffers. Yet even a one-step-removed association of Bain with such an exceptional business leader as Hughes adds a new dimension of sophistication and intrigue to the Bain-Romney saga. It is difficult to imagine that, at the minimum, the younger Gay did not learn useful business strategies from his father and from the Hughes track record of vision and success via astute investments. In his day, Hughes was like Warren Buffett, Charles Lindbergh, and Cary Grant (his fellow playboy pal and friend for four decades) — all combined into one person. Timid or unimaginative news coverage deprived readers and voters from learning about any of that during the 2102 campaign.   Even a mini-bio, as here, of Mitt Romney during the 1970s should touch on his personal life as a bishop in his church, and also on the rapid growth of the LDS church in the United States in terms of worshippers and overall influence. The church's overall growth during that period is charted in many places, including by the book, *America's Saints: The Rise of Mormon Power.*[33] President Nixon's appointment of George Romney to the cabinet as secretary of housing and urban development helped raise the profile of the church within Washington. So did the ascendancy within the intelligence community of LDS member Brent Scowcroft, national security advisor to Presidents Ford and the first President Bush. Scowcroft has been a protégé of the Rockefeller family and one of its leading Washington representatives, Henry Kissinger.[34] The CIA and FBI began heavily recruiting[35] LDS members during this period because of their clean-cut image, work ethic, and language skills acquired during missionary work. The Church's famed genealogy database is a unique trove of historical information on the nation's families. Also, the National Security Agency's $2 billion data center at Bluffdale Utah — scheduled for completion in October, 2013 — is part of the "Big Brother" surveillance controversy that erupted mid-year. James Bamford, the leading historian of the NSA, told set the scene this way in early 2012:

> Today Bluffdale is home to one of the nation's largest sects of polygamists, the Apostolic United Brethren, with upwards of 9,000 members....But new pioneers have quietly begun moving into the area, secretive outsiders who say little and keep to themselves. Like the pious polygamists, they are focused on deciphering cryptic messages that only they have the power to understand....Rather than Bibles, prophets, and worshippers, this temple will be filled with servers, computer intelligence experts, and armed guards. And instead of listening for words flowing down from heaven, these newcomers will be secretly capturing, storing, and analyzing vast quantities of words and images hurtling through the world's telecommunications networks. In the little town of Bluffdale, Big Love and Big Brother have become uneasy neighbors.[36]

Readers of conventional news reports during the campaign missed not simply the story of Hughes, the Gay family, Mormons, and their common involvement in the gambling industry. Almost always missing also was context of why the gaming sector threatens to corrupt public officials. Gambling poses unique dangers. It is a volatile, high-volume, cash business that is heavily regulated, and has a history of mob control. As a result, the industry has a long history of elaborate money laundering and tax-avoidance schemes. Six decades ago, beneficiaries of money laundering services included major Mexican narcotics dealers as well as the OSS and CIA, according to the experienced reporters Sally Denton and Roger Morris.[37] The motives for government involvement are too varied to list. For current purposes, however, the spirit can be summed up in the goodwill gesture made famous in *Casablanca*: "Your winnings, Sir!" In sum, the casino industry has a long history that did not end with Bugsy Siegel or Howard Hughes, no matter how family-friendly they make the tourist shows.

Getting Rich at Bain

The standard story is that Romney, a brilliant Harvard MBA with great instincts, and his colleagues all became rich because their talents identified spectacular successes among their approximately 100 deals during Romney's years leading Bain Capital. The pro-Romney tilt is that his successes, including as an early investor in Staples, the office supply company, show that he was a "job-creator." The fairer view is that company's purpose was wealth creation for its owners, a goal that sometimes led Bain Capital to build companies and sometimes to gut them, including via complex financial transactions leading to bankruptcy, plant closures and job losses. At other times, creating wealth meant investing in companies providing controversial services, such as off shoring jobs and disposing of medical waste that included aborted fetuses.[38] An article on the fetal medical waste is important because it shows that Romney was signing documents and running Bain- affiliated companies well after February 1999, when he and his 2012 campaign say he left the firm.[39]

First Steps in Politics

Romney became wealthy as CEO of Bain Capital, and politically prominent as an unsuccessful 1994 Senate rival to Ted Kennedy. Romney is widely credited with rescuing the 2002 Winter Olympics at Salt Lake City by stepping in as CEO with the backing of important Mormon leaders, such as Utah Governor Michael Leavitt. In 2002, Romney spent $6.3 million of his own money in a successful campaign as a reform-minded, pro-business, pro-choice, pro-gay rights GOP gubernatorial candidate in Massachusetts. His proudest accomplishment at the time was a universal health care law that would serve as the model for the "ObamaCare" law that he now opposes.

Romney's reversals in policy positions won him the nickname "Mr. Etch-a-Sketch." His changes have perplexed voters. He now opposes his previous positions on the social safety net, women's choice, and gay rights. He says his views have evolved. The question is why?

Conservatives fretted over his changes as their central issue during his GOP Presidential primary campaigns in 2007-2008 and 2011-2012. They asked whether Romney would revert back to his moderate positions if elected. *Presidential Puppetry* argues that, to the contrary, his previous positions were opportunistic choices made to advance his religion, career, and allies. He is operating on a level of history and destiny whereby these controversies are petty compared to his goal of winning office. A family friend of the Romneys told the *New York Times* that Mitt and Ann Romney decided he should run for president because they each "felt it was what God wanted them to do." What does a divine mandate mean in practice?

The VP Choice

Late on the Friday evening of August 3, 2012, Romney announced that Paul Ryan as his running mate. The choice confirmed that Romney's policies were cemented to a radical right agenda. The right had feared that Romney's moderate record in Massachusetts reflected closet-liberal principles to which he would revert in a presidency. Instead, his Massachusetts record was simply an effort to do whatever necessary in order to ascend in that time. Even before the 2012 primary contests, Romney formally endorsed the right's agenda at the Americans for Prosperity convention in Washington, DC. Charles and David Koch, the two billionaires who control Koch Industries, fund the event. They control 84% the nation's second largest privately owned company, and each hold assets valued at $34 billion.[40] "I'm tempted to say that Mitt Romney has found his inner Paul Ryan," wrote Jennifer Rubin, a neo-conservative blogger for the *Washington Post*.[41] "In today's speech before Americans for Prosperity and in the accompanying documentation he lays out, it is fair to say he's done something extraordinarily out of character — he's gone bold. The spending and entitlement plan Romney presents embodies a great many of the ideas that Ryan, chairman of the House Budget Committee, has laid out in his original 'Roadmap for America's Future' (on Social Security) and in his 2012 budget."

Thus, the far right had nothing to fear about Romney being an Etch-a-Sketch candidate. Romney's selection of Ryan confirmed that the head of the ticket would not deviate from the hard-right path. This would please the Koch Brothers, who were among the leading oligarchs seeking to defeat Obama. They made massive donations to advocacy organizations in hope of turning back the nation's social safety net, and gutting regulation and taxes.[42]

New York Times columnist Paul Krugman, a Princeton professor and Nobel Prize-winner in economics, wrote, "Mr. Ryan's true constituency is the commentariat, which years ago decided that he was the Honest,

Serious Conservative, whose proposals deserve respect even if you don't like him."[43]

Longtime GOP consultant Roger Stone spoke more bluntly. He claimed to have evidence from a confidential source that, during a meeting in July, David Koch offered Mitt Romney $100 million extra in 2012 campaign funding if he would pick Ryan for the ticket.[44] Stone is more likely than most to know such matters.[45] That sum of $100 million is modest for the two brothers, each of whom is well into their seventies and facing the prospect of inheritance taxes. Their wealth comes in significant part from the Kansas-based company founded by their father, Fred Koch.[46] Under a Koch-friendly Romney-Ryan government, the Koch dynasty would recoup a $100 million campaign investment many times over in savings on inheritance taxes and avoidance of regulation for an energy business with many regulatory battles.

Although a $100 million payment might have been illegal if sent with conditions, the donation could hardly lead to court if a Romney-Ryan government failed to investigate the allegations. Moreover, why would an investigation occur? Any probe would be difficult under the murky new campaign rules following the Supreme Court's 2010 Koch-friendly decision in *Citizens United v. Federal Elections Commission.*[47]

The Paul Ryan Family Saga

In 1970, Paul Davis Ryan was born in Janesville in the southeast corner of Wisconsin. He is from a fifth-generation family dwelling in that region just north of Chicago, with part of the family running a construction business. In addition, he has a compelling personal story of achievement through adversity. He was just 16 when his lawyer-father died, and so he relied on Social Security benefits for college. "At a very, very difficult time in our lives," he says, "Social Security was there for us."[48]

He won an internship in Washington with GOP Senator Bob Kasten, worked at Jack Kemp's "Empower America" advocacy center, and was a top staffer for the ultimate-conservative Kansas Senator, Sam Brownback, now governor. Like his mentors, Ryan's view is that privatizing Social Security is the best way to save it. An excellent campaigner, he won election in 1998 with 57 percent of the votes in a swing district encompassing his hometown. Voters have re-elected him since with margins well over 60 per cent.

Ryan has relied on government paychecks virtually his entire adult career. Thanks to his government jobs, Ryan draws on the excellent congressional health insurance plan, and has a lavish pension plan awaiting him.[49] He, Romney, and their backers draw the line, however, in policies helping those outside their partisan, religious, business, and social circles.

Pundits drew the battle lines in 2011, when Ryan led a tea party-fostered GOP House majority into approving a budget that deeply cut spending. "Ludicrous and Cruel" was liberal Paul Krugman's assessment.[50] "The conventional line of attack on Ryan's plan," responded conservative Charles Krauthammer, "is already taking shape: It cuts poverty programs and "privatizes" Medicare in order to cut taxes for the rich. Major demagoguery on all three counts."[51]

The Romney-Ryan Platform

The stakes were high for the 2012 election. With good reason, Democrats claimed that Mitt Romney and Paul Ryan threatened the jobs, health care, and savings of many millions of Americans. The GOP candidates advocated removal of 31 million Americans from health care coverage required under the Obama-backed Affordable Health Care Law, or "ObamaCare." The Republicans failed to describe any alternative, aside from stating that they would work with Congress. In the meantime, hospital emergency room care was available for those in dire need, they claimed. The GOP stand-pat approach was in a nation that spends at least twice that of other advanced nations on our unique private-controlled and thinly regulated medical care system, which delivers shockingly poor results: A major recent study ranked the United States last among 17 Western nations in life expectancy for men. The rank was second to last for women.[52]

An obvious question during the campaign on the health care issue was whether GOP success in overturning President Obama's health care initiative would cause vast numbers of premature deaths among the uninsured. In 2009, a study claimed that 45,000 excess deaths a year were occurring for lack of insurance.[53] Similar questions arose from the GOP plan to cut Medicare. Such an action would persuade more and more providers to withdraw from treating those who have relied on the program for their retirement. The Ryan-backed plan that passed the House of Representatives would have replaced guaranteed coverage with "vouchers" for the elderly that provide only the possibility of full coverage. The old and sick would need to make up the rest of out their own pockets at a cost estimated by Democrats as unaffordable. Implementation would certainly cause more deaths, mostly to the aged with limited options. Romney and Ryan thus wanted to victimize those who have faithfully paid taxes for many years in expectation of coverage. The claim that their proposal will affect no one over age 55 was bogus because cuts in funding to providers would prompt many to abandon the Medicare recipients.

More generally, Romney, Ryan, and their backers advocated the same jobs offshoring, bubble-economy, and war mongering that caused the nation's economic collapse.[54] The 2012 candidates advocated similar but more radical versions of the policies of their kindred spirits George Bush and Dick Cheney.[55]

Romney-Ryan programs seemed likely to provide far harsher restrictions on women's health choices and cutbacks in the social safety net, along with increased security to prevent protests. As typical in recent years, the 2012 Republican Platform took an extremely pious, right-to-life posture on reproductive health. It contained no exceptions in banning abortions, even in cases of rape or incest. In foreign affairs, the top Romney-Ryan foreign policy advisors represented the Bush foreign policy team that planned the Iraq, Afghanistan, and many other initiatives leading to horrific death totals and trillions of dollars of wasted spending.

A new wave of such Romney-Ryan policies could have led in time to widespread civic protests crushed by the recent massive increases in domestic federal agency and police firepower. These increases included bizarre reports, largely ignored by the mainstream media, of federal procurements of hollow-point bullet purchases.[56] Some beneficiaries of these increases were otherwise routine bureaucracies such as the Social Security Administration, the National Weather Service, and the Department of Homeland Security.[57] These non-law enforcement agencies would ordinarily not have a need for such deadly firepower.

Later chapters will show why Romney-Ryan policies offered little hope for ordinary citizens. Many of their policies were pure hokum designed by their backers to hide the hard times ahead for most Americans. These chapters also will show that the Obama administration was willing to take significant steps in its second term to advance these same Romney-Ryan policies. As a clue, the Obama deference was not simply because Romney declined to leave the scene. In 2013, he returned to Washington to demand further austerity, saying Obama was like "Nero fiddling while Rome burns."[58] It would be easy enough to ignore such comments. More valuable and instructive, however, is to understand the basis for the confidence of Romney and his supporters that he possesses solutions to the nation's problems.

Summing Up

The material above is a preface to more thorough portraits of Romney and Ryan later in the book. The candidates had many complexities that shaded their portraits. For example, part of the Mormon faith until 1978, including Romney's time as a missionary, was that blacks should not be permitted to participate fully in the church. Some argued that LDS theology decreed that black skin was a sign of diabolical ancestry.[59]

The following chapters will focus on the deceptions and scandals of Barack Obama, along with his predecessors in the White House and his current and recent colleagues in the federal government. By the end of that discussion, many readers might yearn for a more straightforward alternative. Should it have been Romney-Ryan? This introduction provides the clues, as in any mystery.

Chapter 2

The President's Hidden History
And Why It Matters

On the frigid morning of January 20, 2009, I joined vast numbers in Washington, DC and across the nation in celebrating the inauguration of Barack Obama as president. My front-row view of Pennsylvania Avenue came from the condo balcony of my longtime friends, Bill and Barbara Conklin.

Their balcony overlooked the Navy Memorial on Pennsylvania Avenue halfway between the Capitol, where the new president took the oath of office, and his destination, the White House. Years ago, Bill had designed the Memorial, with a plaza and adjoining museum at the foot of our building at the center of the city's oldest section of downtown. Bill was an architect, age 85, with a crew cut that suggested his military background. He and his former college sweetheart, Barbara, invited me to speak informally to a visiting student group from their *alma mater*, Doane College, located in Crete, Nebraska. I was thrilled to do so, especially on that historic day.[1]

For me, as for millions of others, the day was a celebration of a fresh start for the country after the nation's horrid hardships in the months and years previous. With history happening all around on that bitterly cold day, I was gratified to join the warm hospitality of the Conklins, my longtime neighbors and friends. We needed only to step from their tenth floor condo to their balcony to observe both the Memorial and a grand vista of the parade route.

The National Archives houses the nation's most treasured documents, just across the avenue. Next to the Archives is the headquarters of the United States Department of Justice. On our side of the street, the Navy Memorial adjoins the former site of Signatures Restaurant owned by the notorious Republican lobbyist Jack Abramoff. By then, Abramoff was imprisoned for his briberies, which symbolized what many thought were bad old days of Washington secrecy, duplicity, and insider corruption. To see an era of hope and change unfold before my eyes made me as happy as anyone could be.

Well, not quite anyone.

"He's getting out!" shouted Bill Conklin, excitedly pointing at Pennsylvania Avenue. "He's doing it!! I can't believe it! There's Michelle too. She's doing it too!!"

Just as Bill said, the president had emerged from his black limousine right in front of us, halfway between Seventh and Eighth Streets Northwest. He began walking toward the White House. So did the new First Lady, clad in her dazzling canary-yellow overcoat.

I raised my Canon Elf to record the moments, regretting I had not borrowed better equipment for the occasion or repaired my Pentax with its array of long-distance lenses. Nevertheless, there had been no reason to imagine in advance that personal photos of such a widely photographed occasion would have any unique value. My photo, above, shows the Justice Department at top right, with the Archives as the columned structure and the First Couple being pointed out to the right of the Navy Memorial flagpole at center.

Why was Bill Conklin so excited? Used to working with famous people (including Nelson Rockefeller), Bill had designed not simply the Memorial, but has had a long, distinguished career otherwise. His work had included a prominent a role in the redevelopment of the entire "Pennsylvania Quarter," thereby fulfilling a legacy request that Jacqueline Kennedy had made upon her husband's death to their friend Daniel Patrick Moynihan, the longtime New York senator. To fulfill his promise to JFK's widow, Moynihan fought hard for these projects as chair  of the Senate Finance Committee, and was a fixture himself with his wife, Liz, in their penthouse suite overlooking the Naval Memorial.

"Let me show you something," Bill told me just after the President's motorcade passed from view and the First Couple re-entered their limo (as we could see on television). Bill took me to his study and quickly found a copy of a letter he had written in November 2008 to the Obama Transition Team two weeks after the election. In it, he suggested that the new President could show his respect for the nation's veterans if he stepped out of his limo at that spot during his parade. Bill wrote the Obama team that such a gesture would be doubly significant because the President, as a former Constitutional law instructor at the University of Chicago, would also demonstrate his respect for the nation's founding documents, housed at the National Archives.

When Bill gave me a copy of his letter, I sensed a news story, even though I had no outlet. This seemed like a unique story angle even for an event millions were watching on television. I proceeded to write a blog that described the incident as well as the history of the neighborhood. I then made my first-ever submission to the Huffington Post in the hope that someone would like it enough to publish.

While I awaited results that evening, I attended one of the nearby Inaugural Balls six blocks from me at the Washington Convention Center. Early the next day, the Huffington Post front-paged my column.[2] The scoop facilitated my return to journalism, my first career after college before I became a DC-based lawyer and trade association leader. After the Obama column, I undertook a number of investigative reports published by the Huffington Post. The reports led to my deeper inquiries on Washington corruption and cover-ups, which provide the foundation of this book.

Less than a month after the Inauguration, my journey resulting in *Presidential Puppetry* began with a shocking discovery about Obama at the National Archives. It is sufficiently complex, if not inherently unbelievable, that I have waited until I could describe it here with book-length context.

Investigative reporter Wayne Madsen provided me the first clue. A friend of mine from the National Press Club in Washington, Madsen invited me to visit the Archives with him so he could show me procedures for inspecting sensitive documents. He is a political affairs commentator, author, and investigative reporter who publishes the *Wayne Madsen Report*, whose major scoops are embargoed behind a pay wall. Madsen spent fourteen years in the United States Navy. Ten years of it was as an intelligence officer, including a year detailed to the National Security Agency as an analyst.

Upon arrival at the Archives, Wayne instructed me on how to retrieve declassified documents. Then he started his search for materials relating to the Obama life story. While he worked on that, I tried out the system by looking up Colonel J. C. King. My late mother, Margaret Kreig, had mentioned King to me as her main secret CIA liaison when she was a globetrotting author/editor in the 1960s who occasionally briefed the agency on her observations.[3]

One of the first women to join the United States Marines in World War II, she became medical editor of *Parent's* Magazine. In addition, she wrote murder mysteries and many pioneering articles on crime, medicine, and other consumer topics, including circa 1950 the then-novel topic of drug abuse by middle class teenagers. One of her books was a first-person account of jungle exploration with Harvard researchers, entitled *Green Medicine: The Search for the Plants that Heal.*[4] The book became an international best-seller probing experiments with LSD and revealing the promise of folk remedies used by unschooled practitioners. Her other major book was *Black Market Medicine*, which drew on her exclusive access to federal records revealing how the Mafia and other crime syndicates endangered consumers by marketing counterfeited prescription drugs, including ones intended for life-saving purposes.[5]

Part of her work was as a volunteer working with federal agents. The federal undercover photo at right shows her helping them by pretending to be a madam seeking to buy pills for "my girls." The photo illustrates the risks reporters sometimes take to get the story, and also the level of hidden cooperation with authorities that sometimes enables access to the inside story angle. Based on the courageous reporting in the book, she testified in 1967 as the star witness in one of the first congressional hearings ever to focus on the Mafia.[6] This was before the first books and movies that made the secret society famous.[7]

Her work on medical topics enabled her to arrange an invitation from Communist leaders in China to tour the nation's medical facilities as a VIP honored guest at a time when Americans were forbidden to enter the country. Her visit in 1972 predated that of President Nixon, and she later briefed the CIA. My impression was that she regarded such briefings as a combination of a patriotic responsibility in wartime during the Vietnam era, and as a useful way to obtain access and information in return. In addition, the occasional *honoraria* (which I recall as sometimes being several thousand dollars) were helpful to free-lancer living in such an expensive locale as Manhattan.

At the National Archives with Wayne in 2009, I punched in the name of Colonel King. I saw declassified correspondence regarding his post as the longtime CIA leader of covert intelligence for the Western Hemisphere. The documents indicated that King had been involved in sensitive matters at the highest levels of intrigue and diplomacy, such as his work with CIA Director Allen Dulles to determine United States options following Fidel Castro's ascendance to power in Cuba. My later research turned up only sporadic references to him in published work. That is understandable, given his role as leader of covert operations.

"Colonel King" was not even his real name, according to his sparse and largely unsourced Wikipedia entry.[8] It states that Joseph Caldwell King (1900–1977) was the chief of the Western Hemisphere Division of the CIA in the 1950s and 1960s, and at times used the CIA code name of "Colonel J. C. King." A West Point graduate, he had been a vice president of a major pharmaceutical company early in his career, and then worked closely with the Rockefeller family and its interests before his government career. After his official retirement from the CIA, he became CEO of a CIA "front" company called the Amazon Natural Drug Company.

All of this tended to confirm my mother's contemporary recollections, revealed here publicly for the first time

While I was researching "Col. King" at the Archives, Wayne was at the computer next to mine undertaking parallel research on the Obama family that proved even more startling to me. My mother, who died in 1998, would have loved his findings, which paralleled some of her own experiences.

Wayne looked up Business International Corporation (BIC), a New York-based research company that was President Obama's first employer after his 1983 graduation with a bachelor's degree from Columbia University. The CIA archives revealed a *New York Times* article published in 1977 quoting the son of the owner of BIC as stating that that the organization was a CIA front company. The headline was, "CIA established many links to journalists at home and abroad." The article by John Crewdson and Joseph Treaster drew on 1970s public concern about CIA over-reaching to document extensive ties between journalists and the agency.[9] Here is an excerpt from the news article:

> The agency's long-standing relationship with American journalists was first called to public attention in 1973, when William E. Colby, then the Director of Central Intelligence, provided reporters in Washington with some of the details on a background basis.

> The organizations, which range from some of the most influential in the nation to some of the most obscure, include ABC and CBS News, *Time, Life*, and *Newsweek* magazines. The *New York Times*, the *New York Herald Tribune*, the Associated Press and the United Press International.

> Another who acknowledged a connection was Elliot Haynes. He and his father, Eldridge Haynes, co-founded Business International, a widely respected business information service. The newspaper quoted the younger Haynes as saying his father had provided cover for four CIA employees in various countries between 1955 and 1960.

Later in this book, I will explore the implications of this article. Whatever the facts, the most striking aspect is how few in the media or anywhere else even dare to ask questions publicly about Obama's former employer and other biographical information suggesting national intelligence ties by him and other United States political leaders. The reason undoubtedly relates to the extraordinary deference the major news organizations provide to the CIA. The *Times* story, for example, was a follow-up to a breakthrough, 25,000-word article by Carl Bernstein for *Rolling Stone*.[10] Bernstein and his editors entitled their opus, "The CIA and the Media: How Americas Most Powerful News Media Worked Hand in Glove with the Central Intelligence Agency and Why the Church

Committee Covered It Up." The Bernstein article was a direct challenge to the major media and a Senate investigation of CIA transgressions led in 1975 by Senate Democrat Frank Church. Clearly, the *Times* saw the Bernstein article as an implicit challenge. Going forward, however, the topics apparently remain of limited interest for subsequent generations of high-ranking assignment editors and their publishers.

Until this book, I have not reported what I saw at the Archives and my later research on the topic. It was Wayne's scoop. He published it on the Wayne Madsen Report (WMR), his subscription-only blog, under the headline, "Barack Obama's post-graduate CIA employment."[11] I knew also that he hoped one day to write a book about it, which he did in 2012 under the title, *The Manufacturing of a President.*[12] Furthermore, I was focused on my research regarding injustices in domestic law enforcement facilitated by Karl Rove, among others. When I began it, I erroneously regarded these injustices as distinct from BIC, the CIA, or the Obama life story. I now see many inter-relationships, described later in this book. I strongly suspect, for example, that the Obama administration has protected Rove from serious investigation because he provides ongoing utility not simply to the intelligence community but to powerful outside patrons who command respect from office-holders at the highest levels of both parties. Protection of Rove and his confederates has inevitably allowed continued suffering in prison of victims of their abusive prosecution tactics.

With that background, let's look at the 2009 Madsen column, which reported:

> For one year, Obama worked as a researcher in BIC's financial services division where he wrote for two BIC publications, *Financing Foreign Operations* and *Business International Money Report*, a weekly newsletter.
>
> An informed source has told WMR that Obama's tuition debt at Columbia was paid off by BIC. In addition, WMR has learned that when [sic] Obama lived in Indonesia with his mother and his adoptive father Lolo Soetoro, the 20-year-old Obama, who was known as "Barry Soetoro," traveled to Pakistan in 1981 and was hosted by the family of Muhammdmian Soomroa Pakistani Sindhi who became acting President of Pakistan after the resignation of General Pervez Musharraf on August 18, 2008. WMR was told that the Obama/Soetoro trip to Pakistan, ostensibly to go "partridge hunting" with the Soomros, related to unknown CIA business.

Does this really suggest that the future president had a suspicious relationship with the CIA or those involved in front activities? There is reason to be skeptical, as I suggested to Wayne. First, just because the company had served as a "front" in the 1950s does not mean that it was still involved two decades later, or that the young Obama might know anything about it. Second, why would the mainstream news media not have pursued the matter if there were anything significant to be found? The *New York Times* article is readily available for anyone.[13]

Most important for me at the time was that I was hot on the trail of reporting then-fresh abuses arising from the Bush administration's political purge of U.S. attorneys in 2006. In the time since then, I've researched other deceptions or omissions in the president's autobiography. More important, I have analyzed how they relate to his government decision making. The president's true history clarifies his decision-making on jobs, the economy, national security, war, health, justice, and the environment. The story that follows provides new understanding of Obama's 2012 re-election victory and his likely decision-making in his second term.

In this chapter, I summarize some of the people, locales, and topics that fill later pages. At the outset, I introduce myself as your tour guide. Soon, however, I will fade to the background and the story will tell itself. Next, we will explore how President Obama ascended so far, so quickly.

The research will show that most of our leaders have many attractive qualities. These usually include innate ability, charm, intelligence, and hard work. Readers here will not see one-dimensional attacks. I was reminded of this the evening of June 28, 2012 in observing Supreme Court Justice Clarence Thomas meet members of the Yale Law School alumni association at its annual dinner just a few hours after the court rendered its decision on the controversy over the Affordable Healthcare Act, also known as "ObamaCare." Although the substance of his comments was off the record, I can share that he was gracious in private greetings with all who approached, eloquent in his remarks, and very well-received with two standing ovations by virtually all attendees, including me in recognition of a fine message suitable for the occasion.

Nonetheless, we explore in these pages suspicions that too many of our leaders have dangerous tendencies even if they are impressive most of the time. This book raises questions, and provides evidence, much of it in the same sequence I researched it. I challenge readers to walk in my shoes, making a personal judgment at each step about what questions seem worth pursuing. This review provides a fuller history of both our heroes and villains.

Along the way, we encounter courageous and often colorful men and women. Some have outsize personalities. Madsen for example, is a free-lancer who risked his life to travel to Rwanda to write a book about genocide. Similarly, he went to Asia to probe sex trafficking, and to challenge suspects about whether they were perverts who had been involved. Back in Washington, he operated in the style of the now-vanished, old-time reporters. He often worked at the Press Club, where he might be seen in public areas reviewing stacks of sensitive government files, complaining about no-smoking rules, and fielding calls from sources. One was the DC Madam, Jeane Palfrey, who was looking for a way out of the unrelenting prosecution pressure she faced when wanted to retire to Germany. She entrusted him with her 20,000 phone call records of "dating service" clients. These records were doubtless at the root of her problem. As she explained to Madsen, the clientele included high-level and otherwise illustrious government officials, including those with repulsive perversions. As in the Mafia, there is no clear path to retirement in her line of work.

Another unique spirit energizing this book is Dana Jill Simpson, an Alabama lawyer from a rural town who for years worked with Karl Rove and others of stature on high-level Republican intrigues. In 2007, Simpson embarked on an oft-dangerous and nearly always frustrating crusade to find justice for victims of political oppression on matters that span the country. That morphed into revelations about hidden partisan owners of vote-counting companies key to the nation's 2012 elections.

Throughout this book, we shall see such civic heroes battling officials who are leading the country to ruin, sometimes by intention. The corruption and class war hurts the economy, jobs, health care, education, the financial sector, technological advances, the media, war, and peace. The book will show schemes to steal national elections by large-scale tampering with election machines. Most important, we shall begin to see by the end of this book why our leaders dare not lead, and why their misconduct must be exposed.

Chapter 3

Hidden Evidence in Plain Sight

On May 9, 2011, *New York Times* reporter Janny Scott lectured five blocks from the White House about her then-new biography, *A Singular Woman: The Untold Story of Barack Obama's Mother.*[1]

Scott, who joined the *Times* in 1994, had been part of its team covering the Obama presidential campaign in 2008. Building on her in-depth profiles for the paper, she took leave in 2008 to research the first book focusing on Stanley Ann Dunham. Primarily as a single mom, Ann reared the future president, and died from cancer in 1995. Scott's book culminated in a 2010 interview with the president in which he shared his recollections. She obtained one hour of the president's time for her unique project, undertaken with her strong mainstream media credentials. She felt  fortunate to receive so much time from the president; she told those of us attending her book-signing audience in 2009.

For similar reasons, I felt fortunate to hear her lecture. She is the best-known biographical research expert on the president's mother. "Exploring the many unknown chapters of Dunham's life," the book's jacket states, "Janny Scott travelled to Indonesia and Hawaii and across the continental United States." Her publisher summarized the book this way:

> [Scott] combed through archive, personal papers, photographs and letters. She interviewed nearly two hundred of Dunham's colleagues, friends and family members, including her children. She has woven that reporting into a powerful portrait of a woman whose grown children stand as striking testament to their mother's brave, unorthodox life.

Her research and reviews seemed impressive and I bought two signed copies, including one for Madsen to help his research. During the question period, I asked about a photo of Barack Obama Sr. that Wayne was displaying on his website. The photo above appears to show Ann Dunham's father, Stanley Dunham, welcoming Obama Sr. to Honolulu

International Airport from Kenya. In the photo, Dunham is the white man standing immediately to the right of the new student, Barack Sr., amid a crowd of other island well-wishers.

"What were the circumstances of the photo?" I asked Scott, the *Times* reporter. "Why would President Obama's grandfather attend this kind of welcome reception without his daughter? Was it in 1959 or 1960?"

"I've never seen it," responded Scott. "So I'm afraid I can't answer."

That was odd, I thought, reflecting on how Scott had described exhaustive research to obtain letters, draft research papers and other documents from Ann Dunham's friends, family and colleagues. As a staff writer at the *Times* covering Obama, Scott was in a position also to draw conveniently on the paper's vast library and on years of previous articles, photos, and books about him. No can know everything even about a specialized subject. Therefore, this omission by itself is not surprising.

Next, I bought a copy of *New Yorker* Editor David Remnick's much-praised Obama biography, *The Bridge: The Life and Rise of Barack Obama*.[2] Like many researchers, I sometimes take a detail, such as the welcome photo, and try to see how different authors treat the same matter. Remnick's upbeat account of the Obama family has no reference to the welcome. More generally, Remnick provides a brief description in the paperback edition's 660 pages (including footnotes and index) of how Barack Obama Sr. met his future bride and her family members. Remnick relied primarily on the account in Obama's un-footnoted, un-indexed, and episodic autobiography, *Dreams from My Father*.[3] Obama describes most of the characters in his autobiography with pseudonyms. Some are composites. This style curtails the research of biographers, journalists, and the rest of the public.

Biographers have few details about the Dunham-Obama romance, in part because of the brevity of the relationship and early death of the lovers. The gist is that Dunham, who began her freshman year at the University of Hawaii at age seventeen in 1960, was soon smitten by the brilliant, self-confident, and worldly Barack Obama, Sr. He was 26 and one of the few black students at the entire university. That account begs a basic question about the photo: why would Ann's father, ostensibly a furniture salesman, get involved in a welcome party for Obama, reportedly in 1959?

The answer, argues Madsen based on his Naval Intelligence experience and sources, is that furniture selling was a cover for Stanley Dunham's secret responsibilities. Based largely on confidential sources so far, Madsen makes the case that Obama, his parents, and his maternal grandparents had significant career ties to U.S. intelligence as part of an overall U.S. effort to combat communism in such former European colonies as Kenya and Indonesia.[4] By his account: Stanley and Madelyn Dunham, their daughter, Ann, and grandson, Barack, each worked in political intelligence while using a variety of retailing, banking, non-profit, foundation, and academic covers.

According to that interpretation, the Dunham family undertook United States government work unrecorded by conventional biographers. Their move to Hawaii coincided with the U.S. government's major funding of the East-West Center at the University of Hawaii to influence foreign policy in Asia. While Stanley ostensibly sold furniture and then insurance, Madelyn Dunham worked at the Bank of Hawaii.[5] Part of her work was facilitating highly sensitive U.S. government money transfers to Asia during the Vietnam War and related regional Cold War initiatives. Ann Dunham's Russian studies, romantic relationships, and her later work in Indonesia and Pakistan evolved from her parents' experiences. So Ann's work as a homemaker, crafts enthusiast, and anthropologist was, in part, a sincere expression of her interests – and was also partly the cover for intelligence work. This was, perhaps, much like the way in which my own mother's career of cutting-edge reporting co-existed with her occasional cooperation with authorities. Vast numbers of other examples exist, as described an upcoming chapter, "Cold War, Hot Climates."

Madsen portrays a dark side to Ann Dunham's role as a teacher and then researcher. He suggests her work in Indonesia helped identify rural leaders and social networks as the U.S.-backed Indonesian government consolidated power. Researchers do not necessarily know the ultimate uses of their work. It is usually best if they do not in sensitive matters. The historical record provides the general background: The hostilities resulted in the deaths of an estimated 500,000 or more people, most of them suspected leftists in rural areas.[6]

One might dismiss any one, two, or perhaps even a dozen of these examples with, "Not credible!" or "So what?" At some point, however, an important pattern arises.

The president and his staff have successfully hidden or kept unavailable his significant school and university records in a manner that is virtually unprecedented in modern times. His and his family's passport and similar records are unavailable. We know that Ann Dunham worked for the Asian Development Bank and U.S. Agency for International Development. She earned a doctorate for studies on rural culture. There are major gaps in her career timeline. Her life-story raises similar question about Barack Obama's, including his resolve to become a community organizer in Chicago. The conventional interpretation, especially from admirers, is that he was so idealistic that he wanted to serve the downtrodden. Opponents are convinced the decision illustrates his leftism. The evidence includes Obama's friendships with the Rev. Jeremiah

Wright, a radical preacher, and former terrorists Bill Ayres and Bernadine Dorhn.

An alternative explanation is that Obama's government handlers and advisors wanted him to immerse himself in the black community, and report back on important developments. This would be in keeping with the longstanding goal of federal law enforcers to monitor if not thwart radical black movements. Those in government worried about national security would want him at the heart of the action, not working at some bureaucracy and leading a Cub Scout troop in the suburbs. Moreover, Ayres and Dorhn, each from privileged backgrounds, may have been among the government moles and instigators populating the student and black protest movements in the 1960s.[7] I covered the protests and organizations efforts both as a student newspaper editor and briefly as a stringer for the *Chicago Tribune* during 1969 in my first paid newspaper work.

The concept of Obama as an intelligence "asset" — a cooperating individual not on staff — might seem preposterous. However, is the concept untrue, or merely unexamined?

I have seen no documents among declassified CIA documents at the National Archives or elsewhere mentioning Obama or his family specifically. The vast bulk of Dunham-Obama family records from a variety of institutional archives are reported as lost or sealed. The candidate's grandmother, Madelyn "Toot" Dunham, certainly could have provided perspectives with a unique historical and presumably popular value. The campaign shielded her from media interviews during the nearly two-year campaign before her death two days before her grandson's election in 2008.

In general, however, declassified CIA records and other authoritative sources illustrate a longstanding pattern of Cold War recruitment of personnel from precisely the kinds of schools Obama and his family favored: The East-West Center at the University of Hawaii, Occidental College, Columbia University, and Harvard Law School. The East-West Center, founded to fight communism, is the current employer of Maya Soetoro-Ng, Obama's half-sister and closest living relative.[8] Occidental College was a major recruitment center for the CIA during the late 1970s when the younger Obama began his college education there.[9] Despite Obama's decision to keep his college records sealed, persistent reports suggest that one of his professors or advisors at Columbia was former Carter Administration National Security Advisor Zbigniew Brzezinski. The professor was just then finishing his grand opus, *Power and Principle*, and remains highly influential in foreign policy and media circles.[10]

Records from Business International Corp, the future president's first employer after his Columbia graduation, indicate that it ran conferences featuring major world leaders, such as Spain's Generalissimo Francisco Franco. Such attendees were far above the stature of conferences run by most newsletters, or even major publications. Moreover, if Elliott Haynes admitted that BIC once served as a cover for the CIA, does that mean it never continued in any fashion? After all, longtime CIA executive Victor Marchetti defines the agency's term "limited hangout," most famously used as a Nixon administration strategy to quell public interest in Watergate, as a PR technique. Its goal is to deflect further research by providing limited information.[11] Was Haynes making a "limited hangout" in describing Barack Obama Jr.'s future employer as a CIA front? Probably.

Skeptics will surely say, "This can't be. If there were any truth to it, then the nation's major media would explore it." Apparently not, at least not by the leading authors. There was no such discussion in *Barack Obama: The Story*, a lively account of Obama's early years by *Washington Post* Associate editor David Maraniss, a Pulitzer-winning biographer of Bill Clinton and fellow of the Society of American Historians. The Maraniss book was published on June 19, 2012 after more than two years research. It mentions Obama's employment at Business International several times. But it fails to explore the claim by the owner's son to *New York Times* reporters that the company had been a CIA front.[12]

Similarly, Maraniss explores in considerable depth Obama's relationship with his lover, Genevieve Cook, during this period.[13] Maraniss explained in a lecture I attended shortly after book publication that it required extensive effort – "two and a half years" – for him and his research colleagues to find Cook and persuade her to share her story for the first time.[14] Her father, Michael J. Cook, ran Australia's Office of National Assessment, the country's counterpart to the White House National Security Council. Her stepfather, Philip C. Jessup Jr., was a prominent figure in art and formerly in Indonesian business under the Suharto regime, and was the son of the noted post-war U.S. diplomat and Columbia Law School professor Philip C. Jessup Sr.[15] Maraniss described the president's grandmother, "Toot," as "an alcoholic." Perhaps that was the rationale for keeping her away from media, as well as her advancing age and illness.[16] But even alcoholics and the otherwise ailing can usually be packaged for at least one interview. Her seclusion fits with an unusually secretive pattern whereby details regarding the Dunham-Obama Family have been limited or hidden so far as is possible with a presidential campaign and administration.

In sum, the key to this puzzle is Cold War intrigue, not today's headlines. So this story begins in what seemed like a simpler, more transparent age for most Americans. World War II veterans returning home focused on family, peace, and prosperity. Behind the scenes, however, U.S. government officials were fighting what they called Communist "Masters of Deceit."[17] Vital to the contest was to steer emerging colonies on the right path as new nations.

The CIA was prepared for that struggle, whether with "Quiet" or even "Ugly" Americans. These and other operatives gravitated to innocuous covers for their work. James Bond, for example, described himself as being in the "import–export business" and certainly not as an intelligence officer.[18]

Chapter 4

Cold War, Hot Climates

To understand the Obama family history, we first must appreciate the political climate for his parents on both sides as they came of age in the late 1940s and 1950s. This was America's Cold War Era. The Cold War especially involves also the life, work, and perspectives of the future president's maternal grandparents, Stanley and Madelyn Dunham, who played a key role in raising young Barack "Barry" Obama after his birth in 1961. The Cold War and colonial independence movement were vitally important also in Kenya and Indonesia for Obama's father and stepfather, respectively.[1]

In brief outline: The United States' interest during World War II was to encourage cooperation from then-European colonies for the greater goal of defeating the Axis Powers led by Nazi Germany, Fascist Italy, and Imperial Japan. President Franklin Delano Roosevelt was a Groton-educated patrician with many of the prejudices of his time toward non-whites. Yet he was also a practical politician of considerable experience, including in world affairs. He wanted to focus Allies and colonies alike in the use of their resources to defeat the Axis. During World War II, therefore, he courted Third World nationalists with vague statements encouraging their postwar aspirations for independence.

George Orwell pioneered the term "Cold War" in an essay for a London newspaper in 1945 as he separately published his dystopian novel, *Animal Farm*.[2] His follow-up, *1984*, predicted life in the future, including the concepts of endless war, mind-numbering austerity for the populace, pervasive surveillance, and rebel leaders who were secretly part of the establishment.

A World Wrought by Rockefellers, Rothschilds, and Friends

The Rockefellers and a few other leading financial families created the groundwork for today's American politics. Nelson Rockefeller was a four-term GOP New York governor and the nation's vice president in President Gerald Ford's administration. Rockefeller, or "Rocky" as he was called by the New York press, was best known to the public via elected politics, including several runs for president. He and his family were even more influential through their private work, which include strategic vision, placement of high-officials in government, and enduring institutions.

Nelson's brother, David, born in 1915 and still alive as of this writing, became president of the Chase Manhattan Bank. He earned a doctorate from the University of Chicago. Among many interests, he advised on the creation the CIA, and helped ensure BP's retention of Iranian oil contracts. He has been an enduring influence over many other major organizations. One is the Rockefeller Foundation, founded with the oil wealth of the family's ancestor, John D. Rockefeller. Like other foundations, it is a way to maintain tax-free within the nation's oligarchical leadership.

David Rockefeller has been a core leader of the three major elite and largely secret bodies of Western leaders. One is the Council on Foreign Relations (CFR).[3] Which now has some Another is the smaller Bilderberg Group, which has convened about 120 Western leaders in annual secret meetings since 1954. The first meeting was at the Bilderberg Hotel in a small Dutch town. The Queen of England and her counterpart from the Netherlands were among attendees. Growing out of later Bilderberg discussions, Rockefeller co-founded in 1973 the Trilateral Commission. Its first meeting was in Tokyo, with about 35 of its 65 North American members also CFR members.[4] Rockefeller was North American chairman from 1977 to 1991. Another co-founder was Zbigniew Brzezinski, the Columbia professor who would become National Security Advisor to President Carter.[5] Brzezinski is reputed to have attracted Rockefeller's attention in 1970 with his vision,[6] and later to have mentored Barack Obama at Columbia University in still-secret ways.[7]

The Ford Foundation is at least as important. This because of its bold innovations more than a half century ago and its continuing influence on current public life, including its role funding the careers of Ann Dunham and Barack Obama. The Foundation was created from the legacy of the brilliant carmaker Henry Ford. Early in his career, he pioneered high-worker pay. As his wealth increased, he moved into ultra-right politics and flirted with fascism.

In the 1960s, the foundation shifted major resources from traditional philanthropy into innovative political and social engineering under leadership of McGeorge Bundy, a former National Security Advisor to President Kennedy. Bundy was a self-confident Yale Skull and Bones member deeply implicated in the disastrous Vietnam War. As part of the nation's elite, however, he decided that the foundation would help empower blacks against racist attitudes by lower and middle-class whites. He thus increased the foundation's spending on minority rights from 2.5 percent in 1960 to 40 percent by 1970. Theoretically, this spending helped radical black reformers earn a living and reduce racism. But the strategy is at best misguided. Worse, it may be deliberately intended to fracture the remnants of the New Deal coalition by empowering wacko elements on the left and fostering a "Silent Majority" on the right.[8]

Ann Dunham was funded in Indonesia by the Ford Foundation, whose New York-based director of international grants was Peter Geithner, father of Obama's controversial Treasury Secretary, Timothy Geithner. Later, Barack Obama's community organizing effort in Chicago was funded in part via the Ford Foundation.

For perspective, let's examine the Rothschild Family, which became prominent in banking more than two centuries ago by close attention to public affairs during the Napoleonic Era. The Rothschilds sometimes provided vital financing to both sides of wars. Establishing family-run headquarters in the major capitals through the rest of the century, the Rothschilds helped Great Britain colonize South Africa, and extract diamonds under the leadership of Cecil Rhodes.

Rhodes had been educated at Oxford University, influenced in part by the vision of John Ruskin, who lectured on why British culture, institutions, and government should extend throughout the world. To this end, Rhodes is reported to have worked with the British government to concoct a phony atrocity in South Africa as an excuse to try extending British control in a then-famous, trumped-up "Jameson Raid," targeting German-backed Boer settlers. Most telling for current purposes is Rhodes' comment to then-prominent journalist Frank Harris. Rhodes told Harris that Ruskin had influenced him, as did his understanding of Darwinism. Harris wrote, "God's purpose, to [Ruskin], was to make the Anglo-Saxon race predominant."[9] Harris found that view appalling, even though he liked Rhodes personally as a man with relatively few "airs."[10]

Rhodes went on to become fabulously wealthy through diamond mining. Upon his death in 1902, he bequeathed his wealth to found the Rhodes Scholarships at Oxford and similar pathways to success for world leaders.[11] Like-minded banking and political leaders, including Sir Nathan Meyer Rothschild (1840-1915), helped use the bequest to found elite, secretive bodies to advance shared goals. Among the bodies arising from these roots are the Rhodes Scholarships to Oxford. Many in this group later founded Chatham House (also known as the Royal Institute of International Affairs) and a United States-based counterpart, the Council on Foreign Relations. Arguably most important of all was the Federal Reserve system, created in 1913 and now nicknamed "The Fourth Branch of Government." Such bodies presented a face to the world of promoting research, meritocracy, and peaceful diplomacy — while more secretly advancing the agendas of British and Anglo-American elites.[12]

This movement directly impacted American presidential politics when three of Wall Street's major financial consortiums, those controlled by the J.P. Morgan, Rothschild, and Rockefeller interests, agreed to split the 1912 Republican vote by backing former President Teddy Roosevelt against the isolationist incumbent, William Howard Taft. The plan was help Democratic nominee Woodrow Wilson. The understanding was Wilson would help create a Federal Reserve bank system and an income tax after his election, listen to his backers in creating his cabinet, and be mindful of the importance of intervention on behalf of the United Kingdom in case of world war with Germany.[13]

Wilson's unprecedented challenge in competing against an incumbent president and a popular former president was complicated by another factor from his past. As Princeton University's president and as New Jersey's governor, the married Democrat had been charmed by Mary Peck, a divorced mother and poet, on his visit to Bermuda in the company of such other celebrities as Mark Twain. Wilson later engaged in frequent and intimate correspondence with her in letters that started to fall into other hands and threatened to hurt his reputation if revealed more widely. "Forget the image of Woodrow Wilson as puritanical prude," as a scholarly biographer wrote. "The 28th president had hot blood in his veins."[14] Wilson later described his behavior as "indiscrete but not improper."

Whatever the case and whatever leverage anyone might have had on him, Wilson went from lecturing at Princeton to the presidency in just 30 months. His ascent was even more rapid than Obama's would be.

Once in office, Wilson implemented each of the four Wall Street goals in ways that resonate through history to the present. In essence, a Democratic presidential candidate did Wall Street's bidding through his top aide, Colonel Edward Mandel House, an advisor so close he lived in the White House.

The Wilson administration's role in working with Congress to create the Federal Reserve system is especially instructive. The consequences and parallels are apparent more a century later as the Obama second term began. The bank grew out of the financial panic of 1907 that ravaged the country. Some claim that Wall Street artificially induced the panic, leading in 2010 to a highly secret meeting in Georgia led by bankers to reestablish in the United States the kind of central bank that Democratic presidents Thomas Jefferson and Andrew Jackson had bitterly fought during the previous century.

Among attendees at the Georgia meeting were Colonel House and U.S. Senate Finance Committee Chairman Nelson Aldrich, a wealthy Republican leader from Rhode Island whose daughter would marry the only son of oil tycoon John D. Rockefeller. Aldrich's grandchildren included future United States Vice President Nelson Aldrich Rockefeller and financial titan David Rockefeller. The handful of influential bankers attending the planning meeting included representatives of Wall Street's leading companies, some of whom are reputed to have been controlled or otherwise influenced by European bankers who preferred to keep a low profile in the United States. One leader of the discussions was Paul Warburg, trained in finance in his native Germany. Wilson appointed Warburg to initial leadership on the board. Warburg, who described the operations as patriotic but necessarily confidential, helped enforce the bank's code of secrecy regarding its deliberations and ownership. The bank, governed by presidential appointees, is privately operated and owned for the most part despite the implications of its name.[15]

The reserve system's currency printing and other capabilities make possible the nation's modern financial system, for better and worse. One of its leaders after Warburg was Eugene Meyer, future owner of the *Washington Post*. Meyer was a Yale graduate who had advanced from Wall Street to chair Wilson's World War I Finance Board in 1918. Meyer was brilliant and hardworking — and had talents for money-making and public service. President Herbert Hoover named Meyer in 1930 to lead the Reconstruction Finance Board to fight the Depression at the same time Meyer led the Federal Reserve Bank. Strongly opposed to the New Deal, Meyer acquired the *Post* out of bankruptcy in 1933. He became the first chairman of the World Bank after World War II. In the course of these years, he and his descendants have fostered many relationships bridging Wall Street and the highest levels of governments. A full survey of the family's career suggest that Meyer's true calling was far more Wall Street than Watchdog, despite the reputation of the *Post* and its subsidiaries such as *Newsweek* and broadcast stations.

Meyer's daughter, *Post* Publisher Katharine Graham, focused on the personal qualities of her father and his circle in her award-winning memoir.[16]

Georgetown University's Dr. Carroll Quigley, by contrast, documented high finance and secret societies in *Tragedy and Hope: A History of the World in Our Time,* first published in 1966. Quigley was the famed foreign policy guru who would mentor Bill Clinton in the 1960s. "The most legendary course at Georgetown," Clinton recalls in *My Life,* "was Professor Carroll Quigley's Development of Civilizations, a requirement for all freshmen with more than 20 people in each class. Though difficult, the course was wildly popular because of Professor Quigley's intellect, opinions, and antics."[17]

Quigley was fascinated by secret societies and their influence. Not coincidentally, Bill Clinton went to work for Senate Foreign Relations Committee Chairman William Fulbright, a Democrat from Arkansas. A former Rhodes Scholar, Fulbright initiated legislation for the post-war Fulbright Fellowships, promoting international exchanges much in the same way Barack Obama Sr., who would find his way to the University of

Hawaii and Harvard. Clinton himself became a Rhodes Scholar. This put a young man from modest circumstances in Arkansas, born fatherless because of his dad's death, on a path first to Yale Law School and then a two-term presidency.

Quigley's book was 1,359 pages. Also, it was bold in revealing the secrets of secret societies — while also praising them as effective instruments for civic betterment. One of Quigley's observations was:

> The chief problem of American political life for a long time has been how to make the two Congressional parties more national and international...[Therefore] the argument that the two parties should represent opposed ideals and policies, one, perhaps, of the Right and the other of the Left, is a foolish idea acceptable only to doctrinaire and academic thinkers...**Instead the two parties should be almost identical, so that the American people can 'throw the rascals out' at any election without leading to any profound or extensive shifts in policy** (Emphasis added).[18]

The Dulles Brothers and the Cold War

The Cold War is often dated as 1947–1991, a period when the United States and Soviet Union emerged from World War II as reigning superpowers, but with deep differences.

The United States and Soviets each possessed devastating force. So, they tended to jockey for supremacy with "brinkmanship" in regional tests of strength that held the possibility of becoming "hot wars," such as those in Korea (1950–1953), Vietnam (1959–1975), and Afghanistan (1979–1989). More often, confrontations stopped short of war, as in the Berlin Blockade (1948–1949), the overthrow of Iran's prime minister (1953), the Suez Crisis (1956), the Berlin Crisis of 1961, the Cuban Missile Crisis (1962), and the "Able Archer" NATO military exercises (1983).

Under President Truman's overall leadership, Secretary of State George Marshall devised what became known as the Marshall Plan to reconstruct Europe after the war. In 1949, the North Atlantic Treaty Organization (NATO) was founded to help the United States thwart serious Communist efforts to expand into Western Europe. The Soviet bloc formed the Warsaw Pact in 1955. Some countries chose to remain neutral with the Non-Aligned Movement.

The widely published, University of Florida-based historian John Spanier maintained that American postwar foreign policy was so successful against the Soviets in Western Europe that it encouraged Communists and socialists to assist independence movements in the Third World, initially in Asia and then black Africa and elsewhere.[19] Prof. Spanier's estimate of the annual income in those places was about $40 to

$50 per person (including in the Mideast before many locales became known for oil deposits.)[20]

President Eisenhower's Secretary of State John Foster Dulles (1888-1959) espoused liberation of Communist regions, not simply "containment."[21] His brother, Allen W. Dulles (1893-1969), at right, was in the 1920s an early director and the secretary of the Council on Foreign Relations. Allen, like John Foster, was a partner of the Wall Street firm Sullivan and Cromwell. With occasional time out for government posts, they represented powerful financial houses, working closely with Harriman and Rockefeller interests. In the 1940s, Allen Dulles led a CFR initiative to create a private forerunner to the CIA. With the support of major financiers, he became the CIA's first civilian director.[22]

One of his first major CIA successes was to overthrow Iran's democratically elected leader, Mohammad Mossadegh, in 1953 after Iran's leader nationalized British Petroleum assets.[23] Kermit Roosevelt, Jr., grandson of former President Teddy Roosevelt and ostensibly a private businessman, secretly dispersed millions of dollars in CIA funds to topple Iran's prime minister. Roosevelt's role as a private citizen provided the U.S. government with deniability in case the operation failed or nearby Soviets objected. The short-term success paved the way for the United States government to use private citizens and groups on a secret basis to achieve the government's foreign policy goals.[24]

Kenya Connections

Anti-colonial movements blossomed in Africa after World War II. Colonial struggles evolved into long-term Cold War chess games. Emerging leaders sought support from the Soviet Union or, more rarely, other Communist nations.

The British colony Kenya was a leading center of rebellion. The Kenya Land and Freedom Army (called "Mau Mau" by the British) launched an uprising lasting from 1952 to 1960, with a British intelligence officer later confirming British complicity in smearing the nationalists as more violent than they were.[25] In 1953, British authorities convicted Jomo Kenyatta, a British-educated nationalist, of crimes in the uprising and imprisoned him for seven years at hard labor. Kenyatta remained so popular that he won a political election while imprisoned. Upon its independence in 1963, he won election as Kenya's first prime minister, and then as its president.[26]

During Kenyatta's prison term, Tom Mboya positioned himself as a nationalist and dynamic, pro-Western leader. Mboya was educated in Britain at Oxford. So his success in Kenya helped fulfill the original vision of Rhodes and his contemporaries in sustaining British influence. Mboya returned from Oxford to his native country in 1957. Declassified

CIA cables from the 1950s show that Mboya was among a handful of African leaders most trusted by the CIA as an information source on the continent and as a pro-Western ally.[27]

Mboya's pet project was to arrange scholarship financing from United States donors for African students from British colonies to study in the United States. Among the students he selected from Kenya was a brilliant fellow Luo tribesman and friend named Barack Hussein Obama, Sr.[28] The fellowship enabled Obama to attend the University of Hawaii, beginning in 1959. The Soviet Union also provided grants to prospective leaders of former colonies. Among the more famous recipients of Soviet largess was Kwame Nkrumah of Ghana.[29]

Another Soviet scholarship beneficiary was Patrice Lumumba, who later became the first legally elected prime minister of the Republic of the Congo. His fate illustrated Cold War pressures in Africa. In 1961, the military removed him just twelve weeks after he took office to govern the former Belgian colony. Lumumba denied being a Communist, and said he sought non-aligned status to advance a nationalist, non-aligned agenda. A firing squad assisted by Belgian soldiers shot him to death.[30]

In Kenya, a gunman assassinated Mboya in 1969. The killer told his defense attorney that Mboya "got what he deserved" for "selling us to the Americans." Kenya President Jomo Kenyatta's minions are suspected of assassinating Mboya,[31] as suggested here[32] and here.[33] The gist is that many of these scholarships and career paths involved hidden Cold War factors.

Ronald Reagan, Bill Clinton as FBI, CIA Assets

Meanwhile, the FBI and CIA infiltrated union, student, academic, business, non-profit, government and other centers of thought-leadership during the 1960s, both in the United States and abroad, according to many books, articles and reports of recent years.

A solid case has emerged that Ronald Reagan advanced his entertainment, union, and political careers in significant part because of his longtime secret cooperation with the FBI and its outside allies. Reagan, together with FBI leaders at the top of the agency, opposed suspected leftists in Hollywood, at the University of California, and elsewhere. Breakthrough documentation comes from Seth Rosenfeld's three-decades of litigation to obtain 300,000 pages of secret government documents. Rosenfeld published his award-winning book *Subversives* in mid-2012. It built on pioneering work also by Dan Moldea and Gus Russo . The latter two authors focused on Chicago family dynasties nationally powerful for decades, including the Pritzker family. Russo described Chicago-born Los Angeles "Superlawyer" Sidney Korshak, for example, as representing Al Capone's mob, and moving on to work comfortably with leaders both parties, top movie studio heads, other major corporate leaders, Jimmy Hoffa of the Teamsters, and Howard Hughes. They schemed in an ongoing saga extending over decades in ways that shaped our world.[34]

Secret Clinton links to law enforcement require more background here than the Reagan past that Rosenfeld documented.

In 1967, a small-circulation, leftish magazine, *Ramparts*, revealed that the CIA was laundering funding through foundations for left-leaning groups. These included the National Student Association, which had 400 schools as members at its peak.[35] The magazine described the CIA's motivation as fighting communism by maintaining influence with future leaders of varied political leanings. In return, the agency secretly provided funding for student leaders and their organizations that cooperated. In some cases, the agency quietly urged local draft boards to provide student deferments protecting the student leaders from the Vietnam War draft. The magazine quoted an association leader, Richard Stearns, as pleading with the magazine not to disclose CIA funding because it would be "disastrous for NSA." The article continued:

> It would put them in an awful political predicament. If they publicly admitted past CIA connections, it would tarnish NSA's image badly at home and abroad, and hurt its chances of receiving grants from other government agencies. NSA staff members also feared CIA retaliation, especially the loss of their draft deferments.

Stearns would later become a good friend of Bill Clinton at Oxford University when their time overlapped as Rhodes Scholars. They travelled through Europe together on a break, and Clinton nominated Stearns in 1993 to become a federal judge in Boston.

This background leads to evidence suggesting that Clinton became an intelligence asset while he was a Rhodes Scholar at Oxford from 1968 to 1970. Clinton opposed the Vietnam War. He sought to delay the threatened induction that would interrupt his studies and force him to fight. His strategies have been described in many places, and need not be repeated here. In this by-now-familiar tale, biographer Roger Morris cited sources to assert that Clinton created an additional option in the hopes of delaying draft induction and otherwise assisting his future. In *Partners in Power: The Clintons and their America*, Morris wrote: "'Bill Clinton's ties to the intelligence community go back all the way to Oxford and come forward from there,' says a former government official who claims to have seen files long since destroyed."[36]

Morris cited other evidence, largely circumstantial, to argue that United States intelligence authorities recruited Clinton to help monitor left wing and international developments. Morris writes that such recruitment by the CIA and FBI frequently occurred, sometimes in exchange for help deferring military service or similar benefits. Morris noted that Clinton undertook a 40-day trip to Russia and other Scandinavian countries during Oxford's winter break from 1969 to 1970, and later travelled also to Spain with Stearns, who would become one of his most politically influential friends after school. Sol Stern, primary author of 1967 *Ramparts* article, separately wrote in 2010 that available evidence suggests that Clinton became a CIA asset during his time at Oxford to help avoid the draft, and that Stearns was a likely recruiter.[37] The *Ramparts* author is not the only researcher with such a conclusion. The late *Vanity Fair* columnist Christopher Hitchens, a contemporary of Clinton's at Oxford, told a conservative columnist in 2003 that he believed Clinton informed on other anti-war activists.[38]

At the time, both of Clinton's roommates, Strobe Talbot and Frank Aller, were fellow Rhodes Scholars undertaking major research projects on the communist systems in the Soviet Union and China, respectively. Talbot, as a Yale undergraduate, had belonged to the elite St. Elmo society, and was engaged in one of the nation's most remarkable scholarly undertakings. At Oxford as Clinton's roommate, the future deputy secretary of state in the Clinton administration translated and edited *Khrushchev Remembers*, the memoirs of the former Russian premier, Nikita Khrushchev, published in 1970.[39] The overwhelming likelihood is that the CIA was involved. Aller, another roommate, had as his specialty study of the Chinese Communist revolution. Like many of his peers, Aller opposed the Vietnam War. But that does not mean that Aller and his elite group of roommates, including Clinton, were not of interest to authorities, who worked all sides of such Cold War controversies.

The high-level and bipartisan credentials of the biographer Morris enhance his credibility on this and other allegations in his well-received biography. Morris was born in 1937, and earned a doctorate in government from Harvard University. He served as a senior aide to such Democratic eminences as Dean Acheson, Lyndon Johnson, and Walter Mondale, and to Republican President Richard Nixon. Morris, a member of the National Security Council under Presidents Johnson and Nixon, resigned from the council in 1970 in protest over an expansion of the Vietnam War into Cambodia. He has written 10 books on prominent leaders, including Nixon, and foreign policy and intelligence gurus Henry Kissinger, Alexander Haig, and Robert Gates. In sum, this assertion that Clinton worked as a student with United States intelligence comes from an expert in the field.

The mainstream media, aside from Morris, have almost totally ignored this background on Clinton. The omission parallels the lack of news coverage of the intelligence agency ties to the Bush and Obama Families. Most striking is the similarity between Clinton and Obama.

Each was a highly talented, near-fatherless, and otherwise vulnerable young man from modest means. Each ascended to the presidency as a Democrat, while hounded by largely unwarranted claims of radicalism. True, significant differences exist in each story. Yet in a nation of more than 300 million, the names Rhodes, Oxford, Harvard, and Yale often crop up in the biographies of top leaders.

'Quiet Americans' in Asia

The CIA focused heavily on Asia in the two decades after its founding, most notably in the Korean and Vietnam Wars. American leaders feared direct war with China on both battlegrounds.[40]

They were concerned also about the vast island nation of Indonesia, a global leader among non-aligned nations. The United States feared Indonesia was blighted by socialist policies. Its leader was Sukarno, who used just one name. Sukarno advocated independence from the Netherlands after World War II, and became the nation's first president.[41] Sukarno led wars that rebuffed postwar invasions by Dutch and British troops that attempted to re-assert colonial control. He nationalized industry and natural resources, angering powerful interests in the West. By the late 1950s, the CIA began covert efforts to kill him.

Sukarno survived at least one serious assassination attempt. A coup overthrew him in 1965, following upheavals that the *New York Times* described as "a convulsion of mass bloodletting ... that took at least 500,000 lives."[42] The pro-Western leader, Suharto, replaced Sukarno and governed until 1998. Some estimates put the death toll much higher under Suharto. As might be expected, few reporters and historians could document the specifics. But the consensus is that most of those killed were suspected leftists in rural areas in Java.

So, this was Indonesia after 1965. It was a hellhole. But Ann Dunham took her young son, Barry, there to be with her husband, Lolo Soetoro. We'll examine their experiences, including those in the rural areas of Java, in the next chapter.

1970s Oversight of Intelligence Agencies

By the mid-1970s, the Vietnam War and Watergate scandals had fostered public concern that the CIA and other national intelligence agencies deserved far more oversight from Congress. In 1974, *The CIA and the Cult of Intelligence* examined the agency and became the first book in American history to be subjected to censorship prior to publication because of its disclosures.[43] Co-author Victor Marchetti was a CIA loyalist, but he nonetheless helped convey a sense of arrogance and failure within the agency.[44]

Senator Frank Church, a Democrat from Idaho, led a Senate investigation of the CIA that documented revelations of widespread CIA assassination plots against foreign leaders, illegal surveillance (including a longstanding program to open mail sent within the United States) and other irregularities little-known by Congressional oversight bodies, much less the public.[45] In 1978, former CIA officer John Stockwell published *In Search of Enemies*, which provided additional evidence of CIA complicity in covert actions.[46] Hence the long *New York Times* article of December 27, 1977 headlined, "CIA Established Many Links to Journalists in U.S. and Abroad, exposing agency ties to Business International Corporation."[47] The revelations led to oversight measures such as the Foreign Intelligence Surveillance Act (FISA) and Foreign Intelligence Surveillance Court (FISC). Also, the revelations prompted the replacement of CIA Director William Colby by former George H. W. Bush, the future president.

The Reagan-Bush administration strongly resisted such reforms. Its first CIA director was William Casey. A former spymaster, he went on to become a successful Wall Street financier and media tycoon. Casey controlled properties that included Capital Cities Communications, parent company of ABC-TV and such newspapers as the *Kansas City Star*. Upon taking the helm at the CIA in 1981, Casey pushed for aggressive and illegal ways to manipulate United States public opinion to support President Reagan's anticommunist interventions worldwide. Robert Parry was an Associated Press and then a *Newsweek* reporter at the forefront of breaking what became known as the Iran-contra scandal. He described Casey's role this way:[48]

Casey, a tall, stooped man whose quick mind was hidden by his inarticulate speech, had run spies and disinformation programs in World War II's Office of Special Services, the CIA's forerunner. At the core of his intelligence experience, he knew the value of effective propaganda, deception and political action.

Much more than the sexy paramilitary operations which attract most of the attention, covert political manipulations and the stock-in-trade of modern intelligence. The CIA had sponsored thousands of these covert operations in foreign countries over more than three decades: planting newspaper stories, secretly funding favored political groups, discrediting opponents, pulling off dirty tricks, and spreading rumors and lies.

But what made this operation different and more sensitive was that it would take place inside the United States – and would target not some foreign adversary but the American people. It would run counter to the legal prohibition against the spy agency conducting domestic operations. Indeed, President Reagan's own executive order on intelligence activities, numbered

12333, had prohibited CIA activities "intended to influence United States processes, public opinion . . . or media."

"But Bill Casey was never one to worry about fine print," Parry wrote. Casey's CIA and such White House staff as Admiral John Poindexter and Colonel Oliver North implemented an illegal plan to finance anti-communist "contra" rebellions in Central America with profits from secret arms deals with Iran. The trail led also to discovery that the CIA's allies, and arguably the CIA itself, were trafficking in narcotics. Casey died of brain cancer. Poindexter and North were among those indicted on multiple counts. President Bush pardoned them, thus foreclosing the kinds of further documentation that could have occurred at trial or upon an expanded investigation. Meanwhile, Parry and other reporters pursuing such stories encountered increasing resistance from management and media owners, who wanted to avoid antagonizing government officials. In fact, the reluctance of management to purpose such stories was not simply their expense or fear by media management of retribution by officials because of negative stories. Middle management might worry about that. But the more insidious problem as media conglomerates and their debt grew in the 1980s was that the media's ownership increasingly overlapped with government leadership, and the higher-ups who controlled by news organizations and government. Casey, at the cusp of such power, illustrated the overlap. .So, did my first book, *Spiked: How Chain Management Corrupted America's Oldest Newspaper.* The book was a case study published in 1987 about how conglomerate news managers killed or inflated stories. Specifics included revelations of deceptive investigative articles submitted for Pulitzer Prize public service awards.[49]

Parry believes that the era of reporter enterprise breaking a Watergate or Iran-contra-type story had evaporated in Washington by the early 1990s.[50] Instead, reporting of top-level events became largely pack journalism, or what he called CW or "conventional wisdom." Standard fare has been enlivened by occasional scandals and government-authorized leaks of information, such as secret disclosures by prosecutors. But independent investigative reporting fully backed by news organizations against top officials is in short supply. Hence the legend of long-ago Watergate continues, given the paucity of more recent mainstream success.

Parry details the evidence showing the intimate involvement in the Iran-contra scandal by Vice President George H.W. Bush and his staff, along with the reprisals officials and media organizations imposed on reporters who sought to inform the public. In sum, Parry provides two views of George H. W. Bush, the first former CIA director to run for president. Bush could be warm-hearted to his colleagues and members of the public. Those of us in Washington know many such anecdotes about Bush, who often seemed genuinely avuncular, as exhibited in his private papers. Yet it has been true also that reporters generally failed reveal even during the 1988 Bush presidential campaign the allegations that he and his team were instrumental in gun-running, drug-dealing and assassination plots.[51] Parry, stressing the importance of conventional wisdom as guiding the media into self-censorship, wrote:

> It is one thing for the CW to accept personal foibles of the rich and powerful – too much drinking, too much sex, too much extravagance. But it is another to suggest that the Washington elite cozies up to terrorists or drug traffickers.

Understanding "The" CIA, FBI, and Defense Department

The CIA long ago adopted the practice of working in part through non-government front groups, especially in foreign nations. In his best-selling *Confessions of an Economic Hit Man*, author John Perkins describes the process. As an example, he cited his own lucrative career: Early on, he worked in Indonesia as chief economist for Chas. T. Main, a Boston-based engineering company closely affiliated with intelligence officials and United States industrial and financial powers. The company built major projects worldwide. Perkins says he functioned as what he called an "economic hit man." He was expert in siphoning funds from Third World nations through complex loan agreements. By his account, these agreements were enforced with a background threat of violence against those few leaders not willing to be bribed to sell out their countrymen.[52]

As a parallel development, national security agencies recruited assets from journalism, academic, and non-government organizations (NGOs) to supplement their pay and help their country by providing specialized insights to our intelligence agencies. My mother, for example, was one such recruit. Further, the FBI, the Justice Department, the CIA, and many state and local police forces are well known, as are foreign counterparts, to hire *agents provocateurs* who pretend to be anti-government protesters.

Disputes arose during the 1960s within anthropology circles about these practices. The fear was that too many field workers were involved with intelligence agencies, thereby creating dangers for them and unwitting academics engaged in fieldwork. Dr. Ralph Beals, a University of California-Los Angeles anthropology professor,, led the American Anthropological Association (AAA). At the group's annual meeting in 1966, Beals and the rest of the group's officers harshly criticized collusion by anthropologists with intelligence agencies.[53] Madsen wrote: [54]

> Beals' significant report remains relatively obscure to those outside the field of applied anthropology but what it detailed is a critical indictment of the CIA

and Defense Department in co-opting young and inexperienced field anthropologists like Ann Dunham Soetoro to conduct "data mining" for CIA and Pentagon covert "counter-insurgency" operations. Dunham-Soetoro's receipt of funding from the Ford Foundation is a troubling aspect of President Obama's upbringing.

Additionally, evidence exists from multiple, authoritative sources that the CIA and similar intelligence bodies funded various leftish and even radical leaders and organizations. Former CIA executive Tom Braden told a CNN Crossfire audience in 1983 that the CIA funded the Communist *Daily Worker* newspaper in the 1950s.[55] Scott Stanley, editor of two John Birch Society publications and the featured guest on Braden's CNN show, protested the spending. "Our point for many years," argued Scott, the right-wing editor, "has been that people like Mr. Braden and the CIA put up the funds for half of the left-wing organizations in the world....Now he tells us they were even funding the *Daily Worker*. I'm not surprised at all."

"Well," Braden responded, "You don't know anything about fighting Communism....The CIA licked Joseph Stalin's last great offensive in Western Europe, and it did it by helping liberals, intellectuals, and socialists, which is to say conservatives, because socialism in France and Belgium is nothing but a sort of moderate Republicanism." Casey, Reagan's first CIA director, was another master of intrigue, as was Casey's trusted staffer, Graham Fuller, a Russian-language expert who specialized in fostering anti-Soviet dissidents before and after his retirement from the agency in 1988. Declassified CIA documents from the mid-1980s suggest an extraordinarily close relationship between Casey and Fuller on high-level planning to fight Communists, Russians, and other leftists worldwide.[56]   With that kind of activity behind the scenes, it's no wonder that many in the public are befuddled by the complex politics surrounding supposed left-wingers. These issues are still with us, as indicated in 2013 by long-hidden links of Fuller to the Chechen family of the suspected Boston Marathon bombers. Those ties unfold later in the book.

From Cold To Covert War

President Obama and his team have tried to transition Bush-era "hot wars" with combat troops in the Mideast to strategies that rely in significant part on CIA covert actions, drones, and other paramilitary capabilities.

A key leader in this change has been John O. Brennan, the Obama administration's counter-terrorism chief during its first term. Brennan was a behind-the-scenes presence in many high-profile events, including efforts to control militants in Libya before their fatal ambush of four

Americans in a temporary mission facility in the Libyan seaport of Benghazi. More than 100 Muslim militants by some estimates killed U.S. Ambassador to Libya Christopher Stevens and three American security personnel in a surprise attack. The story remains cloaked in secrecy because it involved, in part, unmentionable covert actions. Yet the deaths remained in 2013 a major hot-button political issue as a test of Obama's foreign policy.

Despite Benghazi and Brennan's previous leadership of controversial prisoner interrogation and drone programs, Brennan became the Obama nominee in 2013 to direct the CIA, where he had worked for a quarter of a century. The backgrounder below contains clues regarding his rise to power that rarely arose in public despite his contentious 2013 confirmation hearing. Such is the influence of the CIA.

Born in 1955, Brennan was a New Jersey native who attended Fordham University in New York with plans for the priesthood before he responded to a CIA recruitment ad for analysts before graduating in 1977. In 1980, he obtained a master's degree in public policy at the University of Texas at Austin. This enabled him to become immersed in Arabic culture and fluent in the language.

By coincidence, this was a period when the Houston-based Bush family patriarch, George H.W. Bush, a former CIA director, was enhancing his business relationships with the Saudi royal family and preparing for a presidential campaign in 1980. Bush's former Washington aide Karl Rove, moved to Austin in 1977. James A. Baker III, the top political guru of the Bush family, recruited Rove to serve in Austin as the only staffer for the political action committee of the 1980 presidential campaign.[57] Rove intermittently attended the university in Austin for years to obtain a public policy degree and teach. The official record reveals no interactions of note between Brennan, Rove and the Bush family that I could find. Yet a source who knows all the principals advises me not to underestimate the probability of enduring bonds between ambitious masters of intrigue in the same Texas oil orbit at the dawn of the historic alliance between the Bush and the Saudi dynasties.

Others, most notably author Craig Unger, have documented that dynastic relationship.[58] The essence of the deal was that the Bush family and its allies would use their ascendant political strength in the United States to help the vulnerable Saudi monarchy endure, along with its fabulous oil wealth. In return, grateful Saudis would fund sweetheart deals for worthy American benefactors. Baker was the facilitator. The future secretary of the Treasury and secretary of State descended from a Baker family that had played a similar role as far back as World War I. The opportunities then, much like now, involved the Bush family, their allies on Wall Street, along with oil, arms dealing, spy work, war, and other international intrigue at the presidential and cabinet levels.[59]

In that tradition, the 1980 presidential campaign featured an innovation, "Spooks for Bush," whereby former CIA covert operatives banded together to help the Bush campaign — thereby fostering a pattern revived in the 2004 "Swift Boat Veterans for Truth" group helping George W. Bush. "With James Baker as campaign manager and young Karl Rove in supporting role," wrote Russ Baker of 1980, "Poppy [Bush] began assembling a campaign organization full of former intelligence officials....At CIA headquarters, nervy employees even affixed Bush stickers to their cubicles. Nothing remotely like it had ever happened in the history of the agency, though surprisingly little was made of it in the press."[60]

Brennan, armed with his Texas degree and his sojourn in the oil-oriented culture in Texas, enjoyed a steady rise in the CIA during the Reagan administration. He served from 1996 to 1999 as CIA Saudi Arabia station chief. He became deputy CIA director under George Tenet with responsibilities that included briefing President Clinton each day. In the Bush administration after 9/11, Brennan became founding director of the national counter-intelligence center. The position involved supervision of terror suspect interrogation. This prompted controversy because of accusations of overly harsh methods, sometimes described as torture.

Brennan left the agency after 25 years in 2005 to become president of The Analysis Group, a federal security contractor founded in 2001 with strong Republican ties. Additionally, Brennan chaired the Intelligence and National Security Alliance, an association of intelligence professionals. He was a CBS news analyst on national security. Most important, he held an unpaid post as the top national security advisor for Obama's 2008 presidential campaign.

Brennan's background and his high-ranking Obama posts help underscore the absurdity of years of right-wing claims that Obama was a radical, leftist community organizer of dubious United States citizenship. The bogus claims have assumed a life of their own. They are an important part of the disinformation and propaganda that permeates public life. The confusion serves important interests by diverting public attention from real issues.

Passport record snooping is one such forgotten scandal that helps illustrate the superficial nature of traditional news coverage.

In March 2008, Brennan briefly appeared in the news because of his company's involvement with the notoriously sparse official records regarding the Obama family. At the time, then-Senator Obama was seeking to fend off Hillary Clinton's last hopes for victory in the Democratic primaries. Meanwhile, the State Department alerted authorities that private security contractors triggered an electronic alert system by improperly accessing records of Obama, Clinton, and presumptive GOP presidential nominee John McCain. Suspicion focused first on two employees of the Stanley Company. Authorities soon fingered also an unnamed employee of Brennan's company as the primary suspect.[61] The employee, working on a contract with the State Department, illicitly accessed the passport files of Obama during early 2008 when he was a Democratic contender.

The conservative outlets Newsmax, the *Washington Times* and Fox News suggested that Brennan may have been trying to purge Obama's files or hurt rival candidates. For example: "Sources who tracked the investigation tell Newsmax that the main target of the breach was the Obama passport file, and that the contractor accessed the file in order to "cauterize" the records of potentially embarrassing information."[62] What might such information entail? For years, Republican and defense sources have speculated that travel records of Obama and his mother might suggest patterns raising uncomfortable questions about the family. One persistent rumor that is that Obama used an Indonesian passport at times. If so, that would raise questions by right-wing Birther fanatics and, potentially, by those who know spy novels and movies.

Brennan denied any knowledge or other involvement in the passport scandal. The story died. The scandal's details were inherently secret during an investigation by the State Department's inspector general. In July 2008, the State Department issued a heavily redacted 104-page report.[63] The report buried the Obama incident within a comprehensive overview of improper viewings of hundreds of celebrity files by many government employees and contractors. The media largely ignored the State Department findings aside from routine coverage of prosecutions of various employees and contractors.[64] The ultra-right conservative media occasionally tried to revive the issue, but usually from the perspective that Brennan had been trying to cleanse Obama's records of radical taint.[65] The most thorough such report was by Jerome Corsi, a columnist for the conservative World Net Daily (WND). Corsi is best known for his "Birther" and "Swift Boat" best-sellers.[66] Corsi claimed Brennan's company sought to "sanitize" Obama's passport files.[67]

The sparse facts available regarding a potential Brennan role in the passport office scandal raise two different possibilities. One is happenstance: that Brennan had the bad luck to employ someone caught snooping. The alternative is best summarized in a saying by former baseball manager Yogi Berra, "That's too coincidental to be coincidence."[68] Brennan's company may have been helping Obama by trying to identify or purge damaging official records.

Before leaving behind the mystery of the passport snoops, let's reflect on curious incidents involving the watchdogs. Sherlock Holmes once solved a case by noting the curious "incident" that dog did not bark at a criminal in the night. That was, as it turned out, because the criminal was the dog's master.[69] In this instance, none of the top three candidates of the presidential campaign raised any significant outcry. Neither did members of the establishment media, or even the attorneys for small-fry bureaucrats and contractors later convicted and sentenced for other instances of snooping in State Department passport files.

I do not suggest these individuals conspired to keep silent. Instead, nearly all would probably find this account as new information. The significance of this incident is it helps illustrate that we should not assume that someone is going to ferret out for us the relevant facts about our government. We need to do a lot of it ourselves.

As for the bigger picture: One way or another, Brennan became White House counter-terrorism director for President Obama. At first glance, one might assume that Brennan was simply a qualified career expert liberated from years of Republican leadership. Or was there some other factor? Might Brennan be a designated representative for powers in the background? After all, the famed Dulles Brothers had pivoted into leadership posts in the 1950s when Republican election victories forced a lower public profile for their onetime client, Democrat Averell Harriman.

To explore these questions, we next examine the history of the Obama family and of the Bush family.

Summing Up

Clinton and Obama advanced their careers by cooperating in their twenties with intelligence agencies. They were not alone in this such efforts, as indicated by the 2012 book, *Subversives: The FBI's War on Student Radicals and Reagan's Rise to Power*. The book documents via more than 300,000 pages of FBI records how Reagan advanced his career by his decades of secret help to the FBI and its political allies. They sought to thwart the careers of liberals and other suspected left-wingers, including Communist sympathizers in Hollywood and elsewhere.

This chapter focused primarily on United States Cold War policy relevant to President Obama's family. Over time, the Soviet Union was experiencing powerful changes, including repercussions from the murderous and otherwise barbaric rule of Joseph Stalin.

In recalling that era for this book, I reviewed copies of the two-volume memoir published in 1970 and 1974 by Khrushchev (and edited by Strobe Talbot).[70] On the flyleaf of the 1970 volume, I found an inscription that seems apt for this story about life, death, history, and families. "For a historian's bookshelf" was the inscription from my late mother, as a gift of Khrushchev's memoir when I started my career. As it happens, my book is the first time anyone has ever publicly disclosed her CIA past. I think she was proud of it and would be ever more proud that its disclosure helps provide context to the Obama family saga.

Chapter 5

Barack Obama: The President's Family Tree

W ith Cold War intrigue as background, this chapter examines the mysteries surrounding President Obama's origins. The chapter starts with conventional wisdom about the Obama-Dunham family. Next follows the rest of the story, which augments the half-truths with missing information on how the Cold War helped propel Obama to the White House. As an overview, we know less about the life of Obama than of any other modern president. Why is that?

Part of the difficulty is the far-flung nature of the family, spanning the globe from Kenya to Kansas to Hawaii to Indonesia. More important, however, is the family's roots in secretive Cold War and Third World strategies. Thus, major gaps and irregularities exist in conventional accounts of the future president's birth, childhood, academic, and professional development.

Raising such questions neither answers them nor apportions blame. Furthermore, to research these issues is not to assume the belief that CIA masterminds anointed Obama specifically as a future ruler. That's a straw-man counter-argument to trivialize any attempt at research. Anyone knows, or can imagine, that leadership-training programs seek to nurture large numbers of ambitious politicos who span a range of demographics and viewpoints. This is nothing new. On a grander scale, the wealthy Democratic diplomat Averell Harriman could rest easy after 1952 elections installed Republicans. His longtime retainers Allen Dulles and Prescott Bush (forebear of two presidents) became CIA director and United States senator, respectively. Harriman himself went on to become New York's governor and ultimately to marry the vivacious socialite Pamela Harriman. Their Georgetown salon and donations would nurture new generations of aspiring politicos, including in the 1980s Bill Clinton.[1] Obama, like Clinton, was one of many aspiring politicians oligarchs helped with the hope, but no guarantees, that future leaders would be grateful to their enablers.

In the Cold War days, national security agencies recruited personnel from journalism, academic, and non-government organizations (such as foundations) who supplemented their regular pay with special bonuses to provide specialized insights. This is why my mother proved useful as a

51

CIA asset. She was a mainstream journalist and a book author researching indigenous cultures in remote societies.

Barack Obama: The Official Story

Wikipedia summarized Barack Obama's life this way in early 2012:

Barack Hussein Obama II (i/bə'ra:k hu:'seɪn oʊ'ba:mə/; born August 4, 1961) is the 44th and current president of the United States. He is the first African American to hold the office. Obama previously served as a United States Senator from Illinois, from January 2005 until he resigned following his victory in the 2008 presidential election.

Born in Honolulu, Hawaii, Obama is a graduate of Columbia University and Harvard Law School, where he was the president of the Harvard Law Review. He was a community organizer in Chicago before earning his law degree. He worked as a civil rights attorney in Chicago and taught constitutional law at the University of Chicago Law School from 1992 to 2004. He served three terms representing the 13th District in the Illinois Senate from 1997 to 2004.[2]

The text above is accurate. But it contains significant omissions that exist also in full-length biographies. These omissions raise substantial questions not simply about Obama's background, but about how he accomplished his 2008 victory. Was that victory to help ordinary voters, or more powerful enablers?

Roots: The Obama-Dunham Family

What did President Obama's forebears do for a living? That's a basic issue. Conventional wisdom is that his maternal grandfather Stanley sold furniture and insurance, his grandmother, Madelyn worked in a bank, his Kenya-born father Barack was an exchange student, his Indonesia-born stepfather Lolo was a businessman, and his mother Ann was an anthropologist specializing in Third World cultures, especially small businesses and crafts that could be enhanced by "microfinancing." Each thumbnail description is true, but omits vital information.[3]

Summarized below is more than a half century of the Obama-Dunham family saga along with a sample of significant questions and their implications. The treatment is necessarily brief, with suggestions for further reading in the footnotes. Whatever President Obama's secrets and power, he is one of the "Puppets" deserving attention.

Kenya Connections

Barack Obama Jr.'s paternal grandfather was Hussein Onyango Obama, born in 1895 in Kenya, a cook for British missionaries and colonialists.[4] Reared a Roman Catholic, he later converted to Islam. He was a member of the Luo tribe, one of the nation's two most important. Tribal ties would prove to be a valuable affiliation for his descendants.

His son, Barack Hussein Obama Sr., was born in 1936 and educated at a prestigious Christian school. In 1959, Tom Mboya, an emerging Kenyan leader, encouraged his fellow Luo tribesman, Barack Sr., to study in the United States. This was concurrent with a program that supported eighty-one students on what was called Mboya's "Airlift" from African to United States universities. The program's first eight thousand financial supporters included Harry Belafonte, Sidney Poitier, Jackie Robinson, and Elizabeth Mooney Kirk, a literacy advocate.[5] Obama cobbled together his first-year funding in several innovative ways outside the main program, and benefited indirectly from its growing prestige and funding. On July 26, 1960, Mboya met Democratic Presidential nominee John F. Kennedy in Hyannis Port to arrange a $100,000 donation from the Joseph P. Kennedy foundation.[6] This was eleven days after Kennedy received the nomination to run against incumbent Vice President Richard Nixon, illustrating the importance Kennedy ascribed to the program.[7]

The "Airlift" was more than a generous gesture. It was part of an overall foreign policy program that Kennedy, a senator, author, Harvard-trained member of the Eastern elite and a World War II war hero, well understood. Each of Kennedy's three books was relevant to the Cold War scholarship program, as much of his administration's overall foreign policy would be.[8] The Kennedy Foundation's gift to nurture a next-generation, pro-West leadership in Africa was congruent, in essence, with the Anglo-American initiatives illustrated years previously by the Rhodes-funded scholarships and councils.

Obama's destination, the University of Hawaii, was in the process of expanding under a United States Department of State appropriation of $10 million in initial funding for a new East-West Center advocated by Democratic Senate Majority Leader Lyndon B. Johnson.[9] GOP President Dwight D. Eisenhower signed funding into law before leaving office in early 1961. Thus, top United States leaders from both parties united to leverage the university's central Pacific location. This helped extend United States influence on Asian nations, including on the former French region of Indochina and the former Dutch colony of Indonesia. David Maraniss writes:

> With its opening on campus in January 1961, the East-West Center began bringing scholars from twenty-seven Asian nations, undergrads and grads students to Hawaii to further their studies in specific fields while also inculcating in them Western traditions of government, politics, history, and culture. An equal number of student and advanced scholars from American colleges were to attend the center to focus on Asian studies. East meets West

and vice versa. There was a second travel component to the program, as the Asian students eventually headed father east to the mainland and the Americans dispersed west to various Asian countries. As the cold war turned ever hotter in much of Asia, the United States government, which supplied more than half the money, saw the East-West Center as a useful resource in the struggle for the hearts and minds. Obama the African was not part of the center, but he quickly latched onto it and its students, many of whom were in his economics classes.[10]

Invisible to the public, Eisenhower authorized an unsuccessful coup against Indonesia's leader Sukarno, who had nationalized oil companies and had become a globally influential leader of nonaligned countries.[11] In 1965, Sukarno expelled the Peace Corps from Indonesia in April, and in August withdrew Indonesia from the World Bank, the International Monetary Fund, and INTERPOL.[12] That same month he became violently ill during an international meeting from a nonfatal poisoning that led to a successful coup against him.

The Dunham Family: Not in Kansas Anymore

The future president's forebears on his mother's side, Madelyn Lee Payne and Stanley Armour Dunham, met in Wichita, Kansas. In 1940, they eloped at age seventeen and twenty-two, respectively.[13] Standard biographies state that Stanley joined the Army after the attack on Pearl Harbor. Madelyn Dunham worked at a Boeing plant in Wichita. Stanley Ann, their only child, was born in 1942. Her parents named her "Stanley" after her father, who wanted a son. Ultimately using the name Ann, she spent her childhood in California, Oklahoma, Texas, Kansas, and Washington State.[14] Following Ann's teenage years in the Seattle suburb of Mercer, the family moved to Hawaii. Ann enrolled at the university in September, 1960.

Obama Sr. reportedly met Ann Dunham a year after his arrival in an introductory Russian-language course. That was an unusual first-semester selection for Ann, a then 17-year-old.[15] The brilliant, outgoing Obama impressed Ann, as often recounted in biographies. Pregnant, she married Obama Sr. on February 2 of the following year in a quiet ceremony. Some researchers, particularly with partisan hard-right view, believe that Ann and Obama may have had other romantic relationships. This would potentially confuse biographical research.[16]

Ann dropped out of school during the spring semester and gave birth to a son on August 4, according to official records. The mostly disingenuous "Birther" controversy about this would explode nearly five decades later. Part of the controversy stemmed from Obama's secretive tendencies, which generate legitimate suspicions because he and his supporters have now been caught hiding omissions, half-truths, and other irregularities in other parts of his biography, including references to his family's covert intelligence and foundation work. But many of his critics are far from truthseekers. They know their focus on "Birther" research fosters emotion-based racial and pseudo-patriotic animosity against a black Democrat, whatever the facts. Sustained, hate-filled "Birther" battles are unique to Obama in modern times, despite similar questions that could be raised about recent GOP candidates.[17] It's not out of the question either that the Obama camp prolonged the public dispute. It distracted opponents from his real secrets and vulnerabilities, and could always be resolved by release of documents through the administration of Hawaii Governor Neil Abercrombie, a Democrat.

Abercrombie, a friend of Ann Dunham at the University of Hawaii, has long been a go-to source for biographers seeking to sort through sparse data about the family. Abercrombie earned a doctorate at Hawaii, then gained political traction in the 1960s as a longhaired city councilman critical of the Vietnam War. He describes the Dunham-Obama family as one that overcame their challenges in a positive manner. For example, he recalled the Dunham grandparents' reacting to their African son-in-law as follows: "Stan worked hard at accepting Barack Sr. and he had had an instinctive reaction that life would be hard for Barack Jr. But he came to adore that child like nothing else."[18]

That is a charming story for today's audiences who, for the most part, want to hear about success in overcoming racial prejudice and other adversity. Only the more recent Obama biographies correct a misleading impression from his 1995 memoir, *Dreams from My Father.* The book implies that the parents remained together in Hawaii after his birth. Instead, Ann Dunham-Obama returned to Washington State several weeks after the 1961 birth to enroll in college.[19]

In June 1962, Obama Sr. received his degree with Phi Beta Kappa honors. He would soon move to Massachusetts to accept a fellowship at Harvard University rather than take a less prestigious scholarship at the New School in New York City that would have provided a scholarship sufficient to support his new family.[20] In the spring of 1963, Ann returned to the University of Hawaii to study anthropology at the university's new East-West Center.

Studies at Harvard complete, Barack Obama Sr. returned to his homeland in Kenya with a different wife than Ann. Obama benefited from his relationship with Mboya and so obtained a government post. However, he hurt himself seriously in a drunken-driving car wreck in 1965. He descended into career oblivion and alcoholism. His depression deepened after a gunman in 1969 assassinated his mentor, Mboya. During these years, Ann had little contact with her first husband aside from letters. She lived with her parents. Her father was listed in a city directory as manager of Pratt Furniture and her mother worked at the Bank of Hawaii, initially as a loan interviewer and then as vice president in charge of escrow accounts.[21]

Here is where conventional biographies diverge greatly from those of Wayne Madsen, left-wing author Webster Tarpley, and conservative author and professor, Angelo Codevilla. Madsen describes Stanley Dunham's furniture store job as a front congruent with the CIA's long-standing practices. Similarly, he says Madelyn's duties at the bank included transferring sensitive federal funding to Asian recipients, many of them involving ramped-up government operations for the Indochina wars and related business intrigues. This was not *Petticoat Junction*. As a broader context, Rockefeller interests owned a major share of the Bank of Hawaii. The bottom line is that Madelyn Dunham created an impressive career at the bank without a college education even before the feminist movement. For such reasons, she seems an unlikely vice president without an extra credential, such as a trusted track record in national security in tandem with her husband's work.[22]

As early as January 2008, the biographer Webster Tarpley wrote that Obama was the product of a CIA background at the University of Hawaii and Columbia University.[23] Tarpley holds a doctorate from Catholic University. He taught at Cornell University and worked for Lyndon LaRouche's *Executive Intelligence Review*. Tarpley wrote:

> [R]ight-wing critics try to portray Obama as a communist, when his pedigree is that of a controlled asset of the Ford Foundation and the Trilateral Commission, both important centers of coordination for the Anglo-American financial oligarchy. And the list is even longer: Not just Ford and Trilateral, but also Bilderberger, Council on Foreign Relations, Skull and Bones, RAND Corporation, Chicago School, Woodrow Wilson Center — all of them are backing Obama.[24]

Codevilla was a member of President-elect Reagan's transition teams. He earned a doctorate from Claremont Graduate School, and became a Boston University professor in 1995. A former staffer at the U.S. Senate, he has served as vice chairman of the U.S. War College Board of Visitors. He holds other prestigious credentials reflecting conservative perspectives. His published work parallels the conclusions of Madsen and Tarpley about the Obama family background. "Nothing small time, never mind hippyish," Codevilla wrote of Ann Dunham's foundation and government jobs, including five years in Pakistan. Surveying the rest of the family, the professor wrote: "In sum, though the only evidence available is circumstantial, Barack Obama, Jr.'s mother, father, stepfather, grandmother, and grandfather seem to have been well connected, body and soul, with the U.S. government's then-extensive and well-financed trans-public-private influence operations."[25]

These politically diverse researchers essentially made similar findings. Yet none of them could crack the news blackout by the conventional media on the Obama family history. Very few have heard of them or their findings. Why?

Media owners at the Bilderberg level do not want this kind of reporting, of course. Yet that is only a miniscule part of the answer. I have spent four decades in and about the media sector. Vast numbers of reporters exist who have never met the top corporate owners of their news organizations, and most would not consciously defer even if they did. Furthermore, I have probed the knowledge of prominent activists on both the right and left who would love to use the kind of findings here to bolster their varied advocacy. The vast majority have never heard of the suspicions, much less the facts, recounted here.

What's happened is that various straw-man conspiracy arguments divert virtually all public attention onto hoked-up debates signifying little except divisive themes. Recall the clever Miller Lite beer commercials of years back: The entire world (at least of sports audiences) was portrayed on TV commercials as divided between Miller Lite enthusiasts. Some fans would shout that they liked the beer because it was "Less filling!" Others would chant that they loved the beer because it "Tastes great!"

These days, many Americans, at least 15 percent and perhaps more, have been persuaded to despise the president because they suspect him of various radical, socialist, or Muslim schemes, and doubts his legitimacy because of various Birther-style allegations. Another minority of the population regards those allegations as bogus, and despises the haters.

That ongoing rivalry remains the country's main political story even for journalists and other commentators who have no idea that another research trail exists. For such reasons, the generally progressive Huffington Post has republished several times extending at least until late 2012 a 2010 photo essay of the "11 worst paranoid theories about Obama."[26] As a Huffington Post blogger myself, I am reasonably confident that no directive exists to suppress solid research efforts about the president's biography. Few know about that real bio, except a tiny few well-paid master manipulators hiding in the shadows and floating false rumors to the public, and alternative media audiences.

The conventional media tend to ignore, at least publicly, another type of political researcher. These are the opposition researchers who work in the background for private clients, or the major political parties. They develop reports on political candidates or other government officials. The information in these dossiers can kept in the background for the client's surreptitious influence, or it can be slipped into mainstream news outlets with no fingerprints to embarrass or even ruin an official, candidate or other target. My information is that this was the original source of the

"Birther" controversy. Bush operatives devised the concept to use against Arizona Senator John McCain, who was born while his parents were stationed in the U.S. Panama Canal Zone. Operatives mothballed the smear as unnecessary against McCain when he faltered in the primary season in 2000. Fees can reach hundreds of thousands of dollars in rare cases for such dossiers. For that amount, reports can include financial and sexual information, or simply connect the dots about otherwise obscure power relationships.

Opposition researchers from both the right and left have been especially interested for different reasons in two African Americans on the Hawaii islands in the 1960s. The two prompted especially strong interest on both the right and left. One is the left-wing journalist and poet Frank Marshall Davis. The other is former University of Hawaii basketball star Richard D. Parsons, future CEO of Citibank and more recently a volunteer economic advisor to President Obama. Standard biographies of Obama sometimes briefly mention Davis, and usually omit Parsons entirely. But each man is likely relevant to the Dunham-Obama story in ways that insiders can exploit.

Ultra-conservatives such as Cliff Kincaid of American Survival and author Paul Kengor have claimed that Frank Davis was a radical, left-wing corrupting influence on the future president. This is based in part on alleged Davis contacts with Ann Dunham in the 1960s. Yet there is virtually no evidence of any 1960s Dunham contact with Davis aside from alleged modeling photos, which could well be electronic fabrications used as disinformation. But evidence exists from Obama's memoir that he accompanied his grandfather during the 1970s to visit Davis in a bohemian section of Honolulu.[27] To assess the Davis impact on "Barry" Obama, Tarpley draws widely. He cites Kincaid, formerly of Accuracy in Media, along with several communist or leftish academics who have studied Davis. Tarpley's own view is that the Davis impact on the future president was profound and unhealthy, leading to insecurities and an authoritarian streak.[28]

As for Parsons, there's no evidence I have seen that Ann Dunham ever met him. But Parsons was prominent on campus, which fosters speculation that he was active in Dunham's East-West Center circles during his University of Hawaii student years from 1964 to 1968, and that he later helped Barack.

Parsons has enjoyed a success story that rivals Obama's record. Parsons was the grandson of a groundskeeper on the Rockefeller estate, and was mentored by the Rockefeller Family. Nelson Rockefeller hired Parsons for his staff as New York governor and then as vice president. Parsons became a partner at a top New York law firm, a bank president before age thirty, and progressed after that to become chairman of AOL Time Warner. He has long been active in such civic groups as the Council on Foreign Relations and, in general, has the reputation of a man who makes important things happen, usually working behind-the-scenes. Although a lifelong Republican, Parsons has been an advisor to Obama and may have helped him at early stages of his career. At the minimum, the stellar Parsons career illustrates that Madelyn Dunham's bank employer was not small-time. Decades later, the successor to Parsons at Citibank was the former CEO of the Bank of Hawaii.[29]

In sum, Davis and Parsons could hardly be more different aside from their African American heritage, residence in Hawaii, and speculation about their separate ties to Obama. Nonetheless, voters should know that some in politics make a good living researching such matters — and scheming how to leverage it.

The Years of Living Dangerously

In January 1964, Ann Dunham-Obama divorced Barack Sr. without protest by him.[30] Later in 1964, Ann married fellow East-West student Lolo Soetoro, who obtained a master's degree in geography that year. The East-West Center was undergoing an impressive period of expansion with more funding, programs, and new leadership. As part of this, Howard Palfrey Jones, the United States Ambassador to Indonesia from 1958 to 1965, assumed the East-West presidency in 1965.[31]

That same year, Indonesia's army summoned Lolo home during a general recall of students abroad to prove their loyalty and to help rebuild the country.[32] Several months later, on September 30, 1965, a coup killed six top military officers. Authorities blamed Communists for the mysterious developments that may have been a CIA-induced, false-flag operation. The military under pro-West General Suharto overthrew Sukarno, beginning a prolonged period of bloodshed costing at least 500,000 lives. Some estimates of the death toll are up to a million.[33] Many of those killed were of mixed Chinese-Indonesia heritage living in rural regions and suspected of loyalties to Sukarno or the Indonesian Communist Party (Partai Komunis Indonesia, or "PKI"). Suharto kept Sukarno under house arrest until his death in 1970 as the nation opened more fully to Western development. *The Year of Living Dangerously*, a 1982 film starring Mel Gibson, Sigourney Weaver, and Linda Hunt, later dramatized the terror for global audiences. The movie ends as the film's expatriate heroes escape the dangerous nation.

This was a destination for the Soetoro-Dunham family. In 1967, Ann and seven-year-old Barack joined Lolo in Indonesia. Juggling the roles of wife, mother, and careerist in a traditional society, she became an English teacher at the United States Embassy while Lolo advanced in his career to become a government lobbyist with the Union Oil Company. They enrolled Barack in St. Francis, a Catholic School, and later in a Muslim school. In 1970, Ann became an English teacher at the Jakarta-based Institute of Management Education and Development. That year, she gave birth to a daughter, now Maya Soetoro-Ng, who works at the East-West Center in Hawaii. Ann was also active throughout the period as a volunteer at a historical society and with other civic duties.[34]

As context, author John Perkins, former chief economist for a major U.S. contractor, Chas. T. Main, published a 2004 best-seller, *Confessions of an Economic Hit Man*. He described his 1971 assignment to Indonesia as part of a Western plot to subjugate the country economically through phony predictions of growth via massive economic development projects — with Indonesia's infrastructure as collateral to foster long-term control by the United States.[35] Perkins wrote two subsequent books on the same theme, describing with regret his role as an "economic hit man" abusing a number of Third World nations. Perkins said his luxurious life posing as a public-spirited economic analyst served in complementary fashion to real-life hit men, whom he did not meet in person. Their function, he said, was to terminate, sometimes by small plane "accidents," those Third World leaders, such as Panama's Omar Torrijos and Ecuador's Jaime Roldós, who declined bribes to sign over national assets under oppressive loan terms.[36]

In the Soetoro household, Ann's work outside the home reportedly grated on her husband, a heavy-drinking, golf-focused, status-conscious Muslim whose family and colleagues were uncomfortable with an independent-minded wife pursuing an active career after marriage.[37] That is the theme of most mainstream biographers, and it plays well with the important United States political constituency of moms struggling to balance work and provide a better life for their children. The portrayal emphasizes how Ann nurtured her son and carved out accomplishments of her own despite an increasingly estranged relationship with Lolo. To arrange the best available schooling, they chose Muslim schools. The schools may have required Indonesian citizenship. This led to sinister-sounding claims by the right that Obama was indoctrinated in a "madrassa."

Wayne Madsen has taken the lead in identifying more serious issues.[38] Based on a research trip to Indonesia in 2011, he suggests that Obama's parents renounced, at least for a time, their son's United States citizenship because of school requirements and Indonesia's hostility to dual citizenship. He believes the "Birther" issue of a birth in Kenya is a false trail that distracts from truly sensitive issues. The possibility that Obama may have had to re-establish United States citizenship is one potential cause, Madsen suggests, for the secrecy regarding Obama's official records.

Barry, Safe Back at Home

In 1971, Ann sent Barack to live with her grandparents in Hawaii after he completed the fourth grade. Grandfather Stanley, by then an insurance salesman, helped pave the way for Barack to attend the Punahou Academy, the state's most prestigious prep school and one whose founding by missionaries in 1841 made it the oldest of any kind west of the Mississippi. Barack adopted the name, "Barry," better to fit in as one of just three or four blacks in a school of more than 3,500 students on a 76-acre campus.[39] Madelyn, meanwhile, handled Bank of Hawaii escrow transfers between United States and Asian interests during a period of vast and sensitive operations that included the Vietnam War. In *Dreams from my Father*, Barry Obama describes frequent visits with his grandfather to a bar in Honolulu's red-light district where his hard-drinking grandfather would lose himself in card games as "the only white man in the place." A few critics have challenged this as a false lead away from the family's intelligence ties."[40] Whatever the implications of that, Maraniss says that Obama's mother "was an alcoholic," a not uncommon affliction of the time or in that family.[41]

Later in 1971, Barack Obama Sr. made an uncomfortable, month-long visit to Honolulu. The middle-aged man put up a proud and reasonably impressive front. Yet he seemed much diminished professionally and physically following his 1965 auto accident, heavy drinking, and the 1969 loss of his government job after Mboya's assassination.[42] Ann rejoined her son in the fall 1972, working at a Honolulu museum. Two years later, in 1974, she resumed her studies at the University of Hawaii en route to a master's degree in anthropology. Her focus was on Indonesia, an enormously complex nation comprised of 17,500 islands with 300 languages that would be governed by Suharto until the 1990s. She returned to Indonesia in 1975, during the last three of Barry's high school years at Punahou. She would pursue graduate fieldwork primarily in rural regions of Java that would lead to her doctorate in 1992 from the University of Hawaii and publication of her research.[43]

During the late 1970s and early 1980s, Ann's job titles involved development work with the Indonesian government, Ford Foundation, World Bank, and Bank Rakyat.[44] Declassified CIA documents indicate that United States authorities wanted to open up Indonesia to relationships with such elite development institutions as the World Bank.[45] Her Indonesian government job was in a program funded by the United States Agency for International Development (USAID), then, as now, a frequent front for CIA initiatives in the Third World.

The conventional view remains that Ann Dunham was a precursor of the 1960s do-it-all, independent woman.[46] That perception seems accurate as far it goes. Ann travelled during these years for largely unknown reasons to, among other places, Bangladesh, India, Nepal, the Philippines, Ghana, and Thailand.[47] Her work from 1981 to 1984 as a Ford Foundation grantee in Jakarta was under the overall supervision of New York-based Ford executive Peter Geithner, father of the future President Obama's controversial Treasury Secretary Timothy Geithner.[48] Neither one of the Geithners is referenced even in such lengthy and focused biographies as those by Remnick, Scott and Maraniss. The Dunham-Geithner relationship is virtually never mentioned in news coverage of the younger Geithner.

Summing Up School Years

Obama's two memoirs create composite characters, and have no indices or footnotes. Those omissions are unusual for a former law review editor and law school lecturer. The gaps have the effect, if not purpose, of keeping details obscure regarding Obama's family travels, professional goals, and other biographic details.

Even so, Obama appears to have cooperated with U.S. intelligence in his youth, like many of his peers ascending to the highest ranks of government. With his international background, he likely used more than one passport to maintain an innocuous international profile in travels, including his 1981 trip as a student to stay with the family of a future Pakistani president.[49] Pakistan, after all, was a key staging ground for U.S. intelligence regarding its fellow Muslim neighbors in Afghanistan and Iran during that tumultuous time.

Republican sleuths and foreign intelligence services would later become aware of Obama's intelligence background, and would use it try to gain leverage over him and his policies. My understanding is that knowledge extended as high as the Rove level among Republicans and Vladimir Putin's in Russia. Republicans used the Birther claim – that Obama was born in Kenya — as a reminder to Obama and his allies of their power to activate their GOP base against him even on a false narrative. The Birther allegations are bogus, and will always be confined to a belligerent minority in the public. The real political danger to Obama has been if his opponents discredited him as a deceiver to a much wider group, including his supporters. Foreign intelligence services, including the ever-resourceful ones in the Mideast, have varied agendas also, of course.

My question: Why should masters of intrigue be able to use such biographical information about our president for their selfish purposes while the facts are withheld from American voters?

In normal times, readers might be content with whatever scraps of information the Obama family has made available. But these persistent questions remain about the family's intelligence and banking ties, including Ann's work in remote areas during years of "living dangerously." Such complex issues cannot be fully resolved in this space, especially because truth depends on suppressed and lost documents and criminal penalties for government sources who talk to researchers. But the issues illustrate the suspicions that arise when government records disappear, and officials remain unavailable for comment. Public confidence is hardly enhanced when the president nominated in 2013 as his CIA director John Brennan, who ran a company accused in 2008 of scouring Obama's passport records. Also in 2013, leaders in the mainstream media realized that even the Associated Press and Fox News became vulnerable to reprisal for trying to report sensitive information. We examine those matters more fully later in this book.

For the reasons described in this chapter, the burden should fall on President Obama and his defenders to explain the mysteries about his mother's work and his early days as a student and first career steps. This book has amply documented United States-sponsored political and business intrigue in Indonesia through the decades, beginning in the late 1950s. Ann Dunham's career path is highly congruent with such work. So is the pattern of lost and withheld records about her life and her family's. The heart-warming image of her nurturing of him as a single mom struggling against the odds helped elect Obama.

Now, however, a simplistic view is inadequate given the disclosures resonating from critics on the right and left, and the tough decisions facing him in a second term.

The Geithner connection underscores why the Dunham-Obama past is not so far removed from its present, as indicated by many news stories during the summer of 2012 about Geithner and global banking scandals fleecing the public."[50]Obama kept Geithner as Treasury secretary for four years despite Geithner's ascendancy through the same Wall Street banking hierarchy that caused the 2008 financial collapse. As described in later chapters, Obama's administration is on a path (as are Republicans) to drastically reduce the United States domestic safety net in ways that will cause many premature American deaths and much greater poverty and hardship for all but the wealthiest. Similarly, he and Republicans alike are radically reducing historic constitutional freedoms as part of the hyped-up war on terrorism that Obama inherited and continued.

More generally, no reasonable person is going to blame Obama for the decisions his grandparents or parents made to advance themselves and their nations' goals. Their views appear to have been generally liberal but anti-Communist, and their methods appear to have included clandestine work. This was not a unique combination from what we now know of CIA and other government assets from the era. Cord Meyer was one of the Western world's most illustrious advocates for peace before he became head of the CIA's secret outreach program to the news media, as described in this book's "Cold War, Hot Climates" chapter. On a more personal level, my mother dropped out of college to join the Marines in World War II. As previously noted, she later took several modestly paid covert assignments for the CIA during the same years she worked as a journalist in the 1960s and early the next decade. Far from condemning that, I proudly describe it here. Nor would a reasonable person blame Obama or his relatives if they wanted to provide him, essentially a fatherless boy, with a path forward in life by using their experiences and contacts. That is what most parents do.

It is, however, Obama's decision and his alone to withhold what he knows about vital elements of the historical record.

The previous chapter, "Cold War Daze," summarized a few snapshots from a long history of intrigue by the United States and other nations. The Dunham-Obama story is another example. Looking ahead, the next chapter examines Genevieve Cook, Barack Obama's long-lost sweetheart while he was working for Business International. She turns out to have been the daughter of Michael Cook, head of Australia's version of the National Security Council from 1981 to 1989. No wonder she disappeared from the view of journalists and Obama biographers.

Chapter 6

Barack Obama: The Path to Power

Many of Barack Obama's early experiences have been widely reported and need not be repeated here.[1] But much remains obscure or entirely hidden. Among the matters deserving analysis are three separate sex scandals, involving other Chicago politicians, which cleared the field in 2004 for Obama to win his long-shot Senate victory, positioning him for the presidency. Most sensational and important were the revelations in June 2004 about Obama's handsome, wealthy, and accomplished GOP opponent Jack Ryan. Sealed court records were released during a crucial juncture of the Senate race showing that actress Jeri Ryan claimed that Ryan urged her to participate at a sex club while they were married. Predictably, this created an explosive scandal readily illustrated by file photos and videos of the beautiful actress and new footage of the flustered Republican, thereby forcing his exit.

To appreciate fully Obama's good fortune in this, we must chart his overall path from the beginning. This will include reports of suspicions about Obama that some readers here will find reprehensible even to mention. My view after working with a sampling of opposition researchers, however, is that the public needs to understand that candidates and elections are influenced by dossiers far more than commonly known. Further, some candidates, not necessarily Obama, are groomed for office *because* of their vulnerabilities, rather than *despite* their shortcomings. A track record of deceit makes a candidate more amenable to control. Therefore, the only antidote to political dirty tricks and sudden surprises is either more thorough reporting or the near-impossible task of recruiting only candidates proven pure in mind and deed throughout the lives, including resume-building, alliance-making, and fund-raising.

Prepping for a Future

In the 1970s, Barry Obama attended Punahou Academy, Hawaii's most prestigious prep school.[2] In the fall of 1979, he enrolled at Occidental College, a liberal arts school near Pasadena in California. He became active in politics and in world affairs. One such progressive cause was protest against investment in South Africa, whose white government enforced white supremacy over blacks. Also, Obama joined Students for Economic Democracy, a national student advocacy group. The founder was future California State Representative Tom Hayden, and his former wife, actress Jane Fonda, each famous (o notorious) for their protests against the Vietnam War. In 1962, for example, Hayden had authored, "The Port Huron Statement," the founding document of the Students for a Democratic Society, or SDS.

On the surface, Obama's involvement with diverse causes seemed to illustrate that his college experience awakened him to a life of advocacy for the downtrodden and commitment to public service.[3] Additionally, however, declassified CIA documents indicate that Occidental was one of the CIA's favorite campuses to recruit prospective operatives. One CIA internal report boasted that more than 70 students attended a recruitment briefing in 1979.[4] A separate internal report states that CIA recruiters regarded the University of Hawaii and Columbia University as among the top five universities for their purposes.[5] Documents also show a wide range of covert CIA programs involving universities, the media, and major private companies, as indicated in part through this book's previous chapter on Cold War recruitment.[6]

Therefore, recent conservative efforts to smear Obama because of his early contacts with leftist and his missing records could just as easily suggest that he was a government informant or similar asset being groomed by authorities for larger endeavors in the service of his country.

Much of the evidence, for example, in a 2011 conservative analysis of Obama's college years can be reinterpreted in this way.[7] The article claims in a derisive manner that Obama likely held an Indonesian passport as a memento of his years in that country. Yet an Indonesian passport for Obama could have made him a more valuable operative for the U.S. government in his early years by providing him more freedom to travel internationally to such Muslim nations as Pakistan. An alternative interpretation can be made also regarding another of the prize discoveries of conservatives. In Hawaii, the aging onetime Communist Frank Marshall Davis had developed an avuncular relationship with Obama on visits to the Davis home accompanied by grandfather Stanley Dunham. In the 1940s, Davis had been active in Chicago black journalism, civil rights, pro-labor, and Communist-linked organizations. One of his colleagues and friends at the *Chicago Defender* was Vernon Jarrett, a future *Chicago Tribune* columnist and father-in-law to Obama advisor Valerie Jarrett.

Conservatives assume, either for polemical reasons or from ideological certitude, that Davis must have advised the pre-teen Obama in Hawaii to become a radical leftist. A contrary possibility that fits better with the evidence is that Marshall was a burned-out bohemian by the time he met Obama. Davis also may have been an occasional government asset working with Obama's grandfather, Stanley. By most accounts, Stanley was a free spirit whose diverse friends included the famous former CIA covert strategist William Lederer, co-author of *The Ugly American* and a bar owner in his post-agency days.[8] In such a sphere, Davis may well have advised the young Obama to advance himself by working with the power structure, including the government, as best he could.

By comparison, Marshall's old friend, Vernon Jarrett, became in 1970 the first black syndicated columnist at the *Tribune*. The paper, the iconic conservative voice of the Midwest, had been founded in the 1850s by Joseph Medill, founder also of the Republican Party.[9] Medill's descendants included the *Tribune* Publisher Robert McCormick, one of the nation's most important conservatives for many years before his death in 1955. Their successors would hardly have recruited Jarrett, even as a columnist focusing heavily on black issues, if he fought management's core interests.

In 1981, Obama transferred from a four-year scholarship at Occidental to Columbia, which is located in New York City's island of Manhattan in the Harlem neighborhood.

During the summer before starting at Columbia, Obama drew on a Ford Foundation travel fund for dependents of employees to visit his mother and sister in Indonesia.[10] His mother had divorced Lolo Soetoro in 1980. Her travels took her to Africa and Pakistan, with the latter a hotbed of international intrigue following the overthrow of the shah in Iran and the Russian invasion of Afghanistan. Ann Dunham worked sporadically for years in Pakistan.

Obama's summer trip to Asia included three weeks in Pakistan that are seldom described in any detail by traditional biographers. Bloggers have stitched together a chronology that Obama stayed as an overnight guest at the home of a politically influential family, whose household head later served as Pakistan's president.[11] That region was of intense interest to the United States government. Former Carter National Security Advisor Zbigniew Brzezinski met with Osama bin Laden, for example, in discussions on how to fight the common threat of Russia in the region.

Obama's years at Columbia, much like other periods in his life, have frustrated biographers by gaps in standard records.[12] He has not authorized release of courses taken and grades, and many of his and his family's travel records are missing or secret. The sources of Obama's tuition and other expenses remain largely unknown. Biographers and reporters have cobbled together portraits of him based on anecdotal scraps in the absence of standard material on his school courses, grades, and professors. We do know that Obama began introducing himself as "Barack," not "Barry."[13]

Partisan audiences welcome even incomplete information. Thus, Democrats applaud the tale of a young Obama finding his calling at Columbia and later in community work that would help society. That is the message Obama emphasized in his memoir. "In 1983," Obama wrote, "I decided to become a community organizer. There wasn't much detail to the idea: I didn't know anyone making a living that way. When classmates in college asked me just what it was that a community organizer did, I couldn't answer them directly. Instead I'd pronounce on the need for change."[14]

By contrast, conservatives ridicule such statements as shallow, self-important, and otherwise inadequate.[15] Even Obama supporters, however, have reason to wonder about secrecy and lost records to a degree unusual for recent presidents.

I glimpsed the implications of Obama's propensity for secrecy and bombast in 2011 when I invited Wayne Allyn Root, an outspoken conservative-libertarian activist and up-by-bootstraps entrepreneur, onto my weekly public affairs radio show. Root's political polemics against Obama as a radical, left-wing menace to the public often emphasized Root's perspective as a Columbia classmate of the future president. In an off-air interview for this research, I asked Root to describe Obama from an up-close perspective. "I don't know," Root responded. "I never met him. What's even more remarkable, no one I knew ever met him, even though there were only about 700 students in our undergraduate class."[16]

Years of global reporting and scholarship have not penetrated much further. On the eve of Obama's first visit as presidential Israel in March 2013, an Israeli newspaper tracked down his classmates at Columbia in the class of 1983 to share their impressions. "Yet," the newspaper reported, "none of the 25 or so alumni of his class who are now living in Israel remember laying eyes on him."[17] In a similar research project, a commentator claimed lack of any evidence that Obama was present in New York or Columbia for his spring semester in 1982.[18] Then an Obama classmate laboriously reconstructed some of Obama's courses and professors at Columbia that have been revealed in bits and pieces. The incomplete data puzzled the author because Obama apparently took so few required courses in his major, political science.[19]

Obama's undergraduate courses need not be such a huge mystery, even if an administration that boasts of its transparency prefers to protect relevant records. I suspect that Obama took one or more independent study projects in his major field, perhaps combined with a semester abroad component during his junior year. If so, he doubtless performed well and pleased mentors who would help his future career. Details might raise undesirable questions about the nature of his studies, the background of his instructors (including any government service related to intelligence), and the locale of any countries he may have visited.

Perhaps not coincidentally, Columbia's faculty then as later included some of the nation's most distinguished federal officials specializing in foreign policy. Most prominent on the faculty in international studies was Zbigniew Brzezinski, a longtime professor at Columbia. As an example of clout, Brzezinski bragged in his memoirs how he helped Jimmy Carter become president by steering the Trilateral Commission to support him.[20] Carter named then named Brzezinski, nicknamed "Zbig," as his assistant for national security affairs.

Zbig had long been a trusted arm of the Rockefeller interests and their allies.[21] Brzezinski is of Polish descent and strongly opposes Russian power. He was pleased with Carter's responses to Russian ambitions in Poland. But the advisor struggled against what he perceived as a necessary commitment to oppose the Soviets in more remote areas.[22] Zbig's opponents in these disputes tended to be Secretary of State Cyrus Vance and CIA Director Stansfield Turner. Turner, a former admiral, had been a trusted friend of Carter since their days as Naval Academy midshipmen. Zbig wanted Turner's CIA to act as powerful covert force despite the post-Watergate reform spirit in the 1970s regarding CIA transgressions.

Republicans and top-level Carter administration officials, usually unnamed, are suspected of stretching out Iran hostage negotiations in 1980 with a goal of sabotaging Democratic President Jimmy Carter's re-election. A major source for this allegation is Dr. Gary Sick, who wrote *October Surprise*, a 1991 book centered on that allegation. Sick had been Carter's principal aide for the Iran crisis from 1979 to 1981. Sick held a doctorate from Columbia University, reached the rank of captain during his 24-year career in Naval intelligence, and served on the National Security Council staff of Ford, Carter and Reagan.

By 1991, Sick concluded that disloyal CIA, Defense Department and even fellow White House Carter staff wanted to help Republicans win in 1980. The federal employees did so by working with high-level Republicans and Iranians to promise secret arms deliveries to Iran if they would keep U.S. hostages until after the 1980 elections to make Carter look weak. Sick wrote that key non-government liaisons included Wall Street mogul and media tycoon William Casey. He was Reagan's campaign manager and later became the president's CIA director. Casey, a former intelligence officer who rose to control such entities as ABC News, exemplifies the "secret government" that falls outside constitutional and other good government principles. Sick has been an adjunct professor at Columbia following his government service. He wrote that evidence suggested complicity and disloyalty by Carter underlings arising virtually to the level of treason.[23] For that reason, he said he would not name disloyal government officials by name, only the circumstances and non-government players.

Such reports have percolated for decades in high-level foreign policy and national security circles. Sick has not named names. Others have suggested that Brzezinski's White House aide, Robert Gates, was among those deeply involved in undermining the president.[24] Carter's perceived weakness by not freeing the hostages provided the GOP presidential ticket of Reagan-Bush with one of its paths to victory. The supposed "tough" acumen of the Reagan-Bush team was confirmed by Iran's prompt release of hostages after the election. Not reported until years later, including in Sick's book, were secret arms shipments from the United States to Iran through Israel as an intermediary. Sick wrote that Casey and disloyal, Republican-leaning CIA officials reached agreement to arrange the shipment of arms to Iran while Carter was still president in August 1980 and after Carter had explicitly forbidden such sales in keeping with his foreign policy in the region. In mid-2013, new evidence prompted a leading congressional investigator to reassess his view that had cleared Casey from scandal.[25]

The allegations are important not simply as history, but as an illustration of this book's themes regarding financial and political interests with the power to determine foreign policy and heavily influence elections in ways beyond the control of an elected president. The scenario that Gary Sick and others have portrayed demonstrates also the difficulty of proving such charges and the courage it takes to make them. All the principal figures ignore or deny any claims irregularities.

Brzezinski, a far more senior member of Columbia's foreign relations faculty than the adjunct professor Sick, vouched in his memoir for Carter's successes. Carter similarly spoke well of their overall relationship, albeit noting at one point in his diary, "Zbig has been too much a part of the David Rockefeller community...."[26] From her perch at Columbia and other powerful institutions, Zbig became Obama's top foreign policy advisor in the 2008 campaign. The professor told Obama's biographer, David Maraniss, that he does not remember Obama as a student.[27] Gates became CIA director under President George H. W. Bush and Secretary of Defense under the second Bush administration. Gates continued in office as Obama's first secretary of defense until 2011.

That would come later.

The Graduate Finds His Calling

Obama's first post-college job was his year as a New York City-based researcher for Business International, as noted previously. Obama dismissed the work as boring. He does not name the company in his memoir.[28] His posture of boredom has deflected attention away from the company, which the London-based Economist Group bought in 1986 and merged into its Intelligence Group.

One of BIC's projects was to run conferences on global issues. The events strike me as astonishingly impressive. That perception is based on my years organizing large conventions for a global trade association, and sometimes partnering with other major players. Among BIC's speakers were several United States presidents, plus Konrad Adenauer, West Germany's chancellor from 1949 to 1967, Ethiopian Emperor Haile Selassie, and Spain's ruler, Generalissimo Francisco Franco, head of state from 1936 until his death in 1975.[29] Even more impressive, BIC roundtables attracted large retinues of the cabinet-level officials from the United States, Canada, Mexico, Japan, India and Indonesia who convened to hear their leaders and to network. Cabinet members usually meet behind closed doors in government offices, for obvious reasons.

BIC required considerable clout to attract such interest for its confidential speeches. There's no need to belabor the point. We know from the *New York Times* article in 1977 that BIC was a CIA front company. Further, we know from BIC conference brochures that Madsen discovered in CIA files that extremely important people wanted to meet under BIC auspices without news coverage.

Little has emerged about Obama's actual work with BIC. His University of Chicago bio stated that he worked at BIC from January 1984 to the following January. He wrote in his memoir that he wrote financial reports with "my own office, my own secretary, money in the bank" even as he yearned to become a community organizer because of "the importance of mobilizing the poor and giving back to the community."[30] Several former Obama colleagues say he inflated his status on such matters as supervising his own secretary.[31] The real question about his work, however, is what it portends for the policies his administration would pursue as president.

A previous chapter, "Cold War, Hot Climates," noted that Obama biographer David Maraniss spent more than two years finding Obama's long-lost lover from that era, Genevieve Cook, daughter of the director of Australia's version of the CIA from 1981 to 1988. Long unavailable to the media, she shared with Maraniss on an exclusive basis her memories of the young love she shared with Obama. Maraniss describes it as "the deepest romantic relationship of his young life."[32] He dramatized it as an interracial romance doomed to failure by his determination to pursue his black roots as his calling. Nonetheless, her father's background included work as a senior diplomat working in Indonesia during the *Year of Living Dangerously* era, and provides intriguing possibilities also for inquiry. The author and Cook skip the substance almost entirely.

In 1984, Barack left BIC to work for three months for what he calls "a Ralph Nader offshoot," the New York Public Interest Research Group.[33] In seeking something else beyond that, Barack spotted an ad for a community organizing position with the Chicago-based Calumet

Community Religious Conference. This was a coalition of churches on the city's South Side supported by the Gamaliel Foundation, an offshoot of the Ford Foundation.[34] In June 1985, Barack began three and half years work there under a plan to expand its mission from the depressed region surrounding the Calumet River on the South Side into a citywide Developing Communities Project.[35] Remnick describes Obama's boss as "a follower (more or less)" of the Saul Alinsky-style of organizing the poor. The method was to organize confrontations with the power structure around such issues as voter registration, and policies for police, housing, sanitation, and schools.[36]

My purpose here is to raise new questions for voter education, not to try to summarize all of the previous book-length treatments of Obama's life story, an impossible task. So, let's reflect on how Barack Obama's national security background transforms our understanding of his community organizing work. If his family business were intelligence and NGO work, his handlers would want him in the thick of the action, mingling with suspected radicals, community leaders, undercover agents, cut-outs, and otherwise proving his *bona fides*.

By all accounts, Barack immersed himself in his Chicago work. He lived in a sparsely furnished bachelor's apartment near the University of Chicago. One of his major community action projects involved the removal of dangerous asbestos from Altgeld Gardens, a nearly all-black housing development.

The Rev. Jeremiah Wright, pastor of the Trinity United Church of Christ on the South Side, became the young man's teacher and friend. Obama's memoirs portray the minister as a near-father figure. Obama's work and personal interest in civil rights required close relationships with the community's leading pastors. None was more prominent than Wright in Chicago. He was a fiery and popular orator who attracted a large congregation to his church with his radical sermons.[37]

Other Obama friends from this era included former Weatherman terrorists-turned-professors William "Bill" Ayres and his wife, Bernadine Dorhn. Ayres was the son of a wealthy Chicago utility executive. Dorhn, his companion since the 1960s, was a 1967 University of Chicago Law School graduate. She joined the National Lawyers Guild and Students for a Democratic Society (SDS) in the 1960s. Ayres also was an SDS leader. They helped create a split of SDS into a radical Weather Underground faction that took responsibility for bombings at the U.S. Capitol, Pentagon, and police stations. While fugitives, Ayres and Dorhn issued inflammatory statements that helped prompt the Nixon-era nationwide revulsion against leftist protests of all kinds. The two remained in hiding for much of the 1970s, living in Chicago under assumed names.

They resurfaced with two children in 1980. Ayres won dismissal of the charges after arguing that investigators violated his rights. Authorities dropped most charges from their investigation of Dorhn. She served a year in jail after refusing to testify against other radicals. Despite their past, the two became affiliated with several of the state's prominent institutions. The eminent law firm of Sidley and Austin hired Dorhn as a junior attorney in the 1980s. She went on to work for many years for Northwestern University's School of Law as a clinical director and professor. Ayres became a professor of education at the Chicago campus of the University of Illinois, and authored a largely-unrepentant memoir in 2001, *Fugitive Days*.[38]

Both volunteered extensively on civic issues and helped Obama professionally in his Chicago years in the 1980s and in the 1990s after his Harvard studies. Obama sometimes attended their soirees of writers and reformers in Hyde Park. They are reported to have helped him in many other ways, including through an Ayres-led foundation that hired Obama and his small law firm in the 1990s. Conservative WND columnist Jack Cashill wrote a book claiming to find literary clues that Ayres ghost-wrote Obama's memoir.[39]

Such right-wing critics often smear Obama as a radical because of ties to Ayres and Dorhn, whose public statements created an image as the most violent and otherwise repulsive of 1960s radicals. But it is logical also to explore whether Obama became close to those two either because the government handlers wanted him to keep an eye on them. Not implausible either is the possibility, indeed likelihood, that Ayres and Dorhn were government *agents provocateurs* from their start, or else flipped at an early stage to become government assets when they considered a life of long imprisonment. In the latter scenario, high-ranking government officials probably provided discreet (and as-yet unreported) recommendations of Ayres and Dorhn to employers in the 1980s.

On July 19, 2012, I attended the annual conference of ultra-conservative American Survival Group at the National Press Club and raised a question about Dorhn-Ayres post-Weatherman employment. One speaker was Lawrence Grathwohl. He has lectured to conservative audiences about his experiences in the late 1960s and early 1970s as a Cincinnati police officer assigned to infiltrate the Weathermen, and thus work closely with Ayres and Dorhn. He said he despised Ayres and Dorhn, whom he described as constantly urging others to take violent action but remaining safely insulated.[40] He described Dorhn as the most personally vicious individual he had ever met because she gloated over innocent deaths of bombing victims. From the audience, I asked him why eminent Chicago institutions such as Sidley and Austin had hired them. He responded that law firms and universities are filled with "leftists." I am not persuaded. Like Ayres and Dorhn, *agents provocateurs* urge others to commit crime. Whatever their own goals, their actions also fragmented the New Deal coalition nationally.

Many such situations occurred during the student movement, which I covered sporadically in the 1960s as a student newspaper editor.[41]

Others have thoroughly documented the use of agents, double agents, and even triple agents as a common tactic in intelligence circles worldwide, including by the CIA and FBI. *The Quiet American*, the most powerful and controversial of former British intelligence officer Graham Greene's novels, portrays an idealist, Harvard-trained U.S. intelligence operative (from the early 1950s era) who blows up a marketplace to create a political counter-reaction.[42] Any meaningful discussion of Obama and his Chicago "radical" friends needs to mention the possibility of covert status. But partisans on the left and right avoid it in order to focus on their standard scripts: Obama as an idealistic community organizer, or as a misguided and potentially dangerous radical.

Chicago to Harvard to Chicago

Barack Obama's path-breaking success at Harvard and Chicago, two of the nation's leading law schools, is an oft-told tale. It is therefore best summarized here with a focus on new material beyond the basics. Harvard Law School accepted Obama for admission in September 1988. He graduated in 1991 as president of the *Harvard Law Review*, with his success creating a vast array of professional options.

The law review presidency is very impressive. Harvard Law requires undergraduate grades, test scores, and recommendations far beyond the capabilities of the vast majority of top students for admission. Additionally, the nation's lawyers, academics, and government leaders often know two special factors about Harvard. First, Harvard educates nearly triple the number of students of what are normally considered the three other top law schools, noted here in alphabetical order: Chicago, Stanford, and Yale. Thus, Obama's election to run the law review implies success over many more competitors than he would have faced at other top schools.

Further, law schools tend to require rigorous qualifying criteria of top grades and/or impressive sample law review articles for editorships. That way, law review elections do not become popularity contests for the general student body, potentially elevating glad-handers. Moreover, law is virtually the only field in which student-run publications are the major forum for academic recognition for professors. Thus, the top job at a law review, and indeed any of the officer and editing posts, provides the opportunity for productive relationships with the nation's top legal and law-oriented policy experts. Also, the job entails very hard work, which must be completed in addition to school coursework. Finally, according to varied sources, Obama did an excellent job leading the law review.

So what's left to say about this stellar achievement?

The persistent problem of hidden records continues to plague Obama in this, as it should. What could possibly be the big secret that he wants to prevent the public from knowing about his Harvard, Columbia, and Occidental courses, grades, and other relevant background, such as professors and recommendations?

Almost certainly, affirmative action and white guilt played at least a small role in Obama's Harvard admission and some of his later success. So what? Obama has excelled at many endeavors. At this point, no one but a racist would care if he received affirmation action consideration, which was probably less significant than the extra consideration that many children of the wealthy alumni receive in college admissions. Most adults have never graduated from a college of any type, much less Harvard Law School. His tenure as editor is a landmark achievement no matter what his grades and courses. Beyond that, every indication is that he was a thoughtful and otherwise capable executive in the job.

The reason for the hidden records must be something else. In the 1950s, a popular book and movie gave rise to the expression, "Someone up there likes me."[43] Who are the guardian angels for Obama? Why are they motivated? My default position is that the secrecy about Obama's school records reflects extraordinary help from leaders in the nation's intelligence community and their many contacts on Wall Street and at Harvard and Columbia. Clues may be apparent in his grades, professors, and courses, including possible independent study. The trail might lead also disclosure of regarding his recommendations, tuition arrangements, and foreign travel. That is common sense, and also accords with the speculative views of Washington insiders, including Obama supporters.

A string of blog posts suggest that Percy Sutton, one of the nation's most prominent African-American politicians and entrepreneurs, recommended Obama to Harvard even though Sutton had never met the young man. More interestingly, media inquiries about the recommendations show how the Obama camp later humiliated Sutton to silence him. The probable reason is that the Sutton recommendation is the type of detail that connects Obama as a young "community organizer" at an improbably young age to rich, politically influential men.

What follows is the story assembled by conservative blogger Jack Cashill of WND under the title "Saudi billionaire did help Obama into Harvard."[44] World Net Daily (WND) published it in September with scant response outside of highly conservative circles. Two of my pro-Obama intelligence sources have since confirmed to me its essential features. Their concurrence after independently reaching similar conclusions shows how practitioners of the dark side political research and commentary can admire each other's successes even if they dislike the implications for their preferred candidate. Cashill wrote.

> In late March 2008, on a local New York City show called "Inside City Hall," the venerable African-American entrepreneur and politico, Percy Sutton, told host Dominic Carter how he was asked to help smooth Barack Obama's admission into Harvard Law School 20 years earlier.
>
> The octogenarian Sutton calmly and lucidly explained that he had been "introduced to [Obama] by a friend." The friend's name was Dr. Khalid al-Mansour, and the introduction had taken place about 20 years prior. Sutton described al-Mansour as "the principal adviser to one of the world's richest men." The billionaire in question was Saudi prince Al-Waleed bin Talal.
>
> Given the game-changing nature of this revelation when it surfaced in late August 2008, the Obama camp and its allies in the media, particularly Politico and Media Matters, shifted into overdrive to kill the story. Through a series of denials, lies and slanders about Sutton's mental health, they succeeded.

The Obama team portrayed Sutton as mistaken. This stance prompted embarrassing news coverage for the aging civil rights pioneer, who was portrayed as making up a long-ago connection to the future president. Sutton, former Manhattan borough president, was one of the nation's most prominent black political and business leaders before his death in 2009. Sutton took a lead role with Richard Parsons, for example, in rescuing Harlem's famed Apollo Theater from financial ruin.[45]

"The story, however, has come back to life," Cashill wrote during the 2012 election campaign:

> The elusive al-Mansour was a guest Sept. 19 on the BlogTalkRadio show "The National and International Roundtable." In his introduction, the host openly acknowledged that al-Mansour "made news in 2008 when it was revealed that he had been a patron of President Barack Obama and had recommended him for admission to Harvard Law School." The host went on to describe al-Mansour as "co-founder of the international law firm of al-Waleed, al-Talal and al-Mansour and special adviser to Saudi Arabian prince, His Royal Highness Prince Al Waleed bin Talal bin Abdulazziz."

Further:

> This meshed completely with what Sutton had said in 2008. According to Sutton, al-Mansour had asked him to "please write a letter in support of [Obama] … a young man that has applied to Harvard." Sutton had friends at Harvard and gladly did so.

The nation's celebrity-focused media gave the issue new vitality when Donald Trump offered to donate $5 million to charity if Obama would release his passport and college records, including recommendations.[46] "President Obama is the least transparent president in the history of this country," Trump said in a widely disseminated video. "There's never been anything like it." In a cursory response, the Obama campaign mocked the offer as a transparent campaign stunt by the Republican Trump.

Most important about the episode is that the long-running controversy about school records persists with so little attempt to connect the dots of what missing records might indicate. Conservatives cite radical statements by al-Mansour to suggest suspicions about Obama's college records. Much of this comes from the "Birther" chorus, which fosters a bogus image of Obama of appearing to be a radical who has been illegitimately elected as president. The more appropriate view is that Obama was the kind of foundation-incubated careerist worthy of early and strong nurturing by a top-echelon of national and world leaders. Thus, something as simple as the casual Sutton remark on a radio station led to a connection with the Saudi prince, who is reputed to be worth $16 billion and to hold a seven percent share of Fox News. Al Waleed and Sutton's ties include the Parsons. As noted previously, Parsons had been a University of Hawaii contemporary of Ann Dunham, a Rockefeller protégé, former Citibank chairman, and volunteer advisor to the Obama White House on economic issues. Obama's Columbia connections almost certainly include ties with the academic acolytes of Professor Brzezinski, chairman of Obama's department, if not directly with the former Carter advisor. The Democrat Brzezinski, like his Republican counterpart Henry Kissinger, are two Rockefeller-nurtured figures who still reign near the top of the nation's foreign policy establishment, which is itself a handmaiden to Wall Street and several key industrial sectors.

For public relations purposes, the Saudi prince, his billions and his peers are best kept in the background. From his perspective, he can better work his magic through a variety of investments in media companies and via other key venues. Sutton unwittingly blundered by providing a clue to an Obama link to Al-Waleed via his business and legal associate Al-Mansour, an American born under another name, a longtime attorney and author of 24 books. Similarly, the public's carefully nurtured perceptions about Obama as a former community organizer might be disturbed by any suspicions that anyone at the Al-Waleed-Parsons-Brzezinski level of influence would know about his law school application and subsequent advancement.

It is perfectly congruent with White House image-making for Obama these days as president to seek the counsel of Parsons, who rose as a Republican, and the Democratic eminence Brzezinski. The situation is near-perfect also for the nation's Trumps and other Birthers. They can grandstand all they want about seeking records. My prediction is they would find some material capable of embarrassing Obama, but on the whole would not like the implication that he was nurtured by the establishment.

Such relationships are relevant not simply to Obama's school applications, but also to his reputation as a constitutional scholar and Nobel Peace Prize winner. Most important, they would help explain a number of his presidential policies that have puzzled supporters focused primarily on his campaign rhetoric. One such policy is the Obama administration's eagerness to hire Wall Street bankers and regulators such as Timothy Geithner, despite their role creating the nation's 2008 economic collapse. Geithner, former leader of the New York Federal Reserve. That is a private bank despite its misleading name.[47] Geithner, a darling of Wall Street, was the only one of Obama's top economic appointees to continue through the first term until 2013. Geithner was needed to negotiate the White House its "fiscal cliff" settlement that broke Obama's 2012 campaign promise to raise taxes only on those making $250,000 per year.

Meanwhile, the Obama administration refused to prosecute banksters who caused the 2008 financial collapse. Instead, Obama's team aggressively sought to imprison government whistleblowers for long jail terms on spy charges. The Obama Justice Department has launched, for example, six current prosecutions of former-government employees on spy charges for leaking information to the media, a topic examined later in this book.

Dr. Randy Short was a student at the Harvard Divinity School from 1988 to 1991, years congruent with Obama's time at the law school. Short sees no contradiction between the Obama he first encountered at Harvard in 1988 and today's version. A committed black activist, Short is the son of a prominent evangelical preacher in the District of Columbia. Short says he witnessed the future president advance his own career by denigrating African-American activists and their organizations at a Federalist Society meeting at Harvard Law School. Short is now a social activist, columnist for *Black Agenda Report,* and a documentary filmmaker. Short recalls telling several African-American friends, minutes after the Federalist Society speech, that Obama was a careerist who "is going all the way" to success.

"He *has* gone all the way," Short now says. He claims that Obama's war, national intelligence, and economic policies, if properly understood, "have far more in common with those of Federalist Society than of the Harvard Black Law School Association."[48]

Sweet Home Chicago

During the summer of Barack's first year of law school, he worked at the prestigious Chicago law firm of Sidley and Austin (the same one that had hired Dorhn). Sidley, as it is known, assigned recent Harvard Law graduate Michelle Robinson to mentor him. She had grown up on Chicago's South Shore neighborhood in a solid African-American family. Her father, Frasier Robinson III, worked at the city's water works and served as a precinct captain in the Democratic political machine of Mayor Richard Daley's family. Michelle followed her older brother, Craig, a basketball star, to Princeton University for her undergraduate degree. One Sidley senior partner was Newton Minow, a Democrat and former Federal Communications Commission chairman who would later support Barack's political career.

After Barack's graduation from Harvard, he returned to Hyde Park to begin a two-year fellowship at the University of Chicago School of Law. This enabled him to work on the autobiography, *Dreams from My Father,* published in 1995. Obama also became a lecturer in constitutional law, a post he held from 1992 to 2004. Several polemicists, primarily from the right, have sought to undermine Obama's authorship of his *Dreams* memoir. One is Jack Cashill, a columnist for World Net Daily. In 2008, Cashill claimed in columns and in a book that Ayres secretly authored *Dreams*.[49] "This was a charge that, if ever proved or *believed* to be true among enough voters, could have been the end of the candidacy," Remnick later wrote.[50] Obama doubtless received editing help from many friends, probably including Ayres. Yet such help is very common among well-connected authors. Some even hire ghostwriters who receive no recognition, only money, for major contributions. Political figures seldom write by themselves entirely honest memoirs, especially in their early years.

More intriguing, therefore, are questions about Obama's academic scholarship, which has been subjected to withering attacks by conservatives. One attack came in a series by the *Washington Examiner*, which described him as largely uninvolved in law school matters aside from his teaching.[51] Another is Jerome Corsi, who holds a doctorate from Harvard University and who writes for *World Net Daily*. Corsi aptly wrote that Chicago's law faculty "is known for voluminous publishing."[52] I earned a *juris doctorate* from Chicago, graduating in 1990. So, I know first-hand that its relatively small faculty boasts of the highest output of scholarly works per professor of any of the nation's approximately 200 law schools. Corsi's goal, however, was not to praise Chicago, founded nearly a century ago with Rockefeller donations, but to disparage Obama. Thus, Corsi quotes a *National Review* researcher as stating:

The university offered Obama a full-time tenure-track position, an honor typically reserved for published instructors. Reporters have been unable to find any scholarly articles authored by him. Matthew Franck noted in the National Review Online, "A search of the HeinOnLine database of law journals turns up exactly nothing credited to Obama in any law review anywhere at any time." Frank was emphatic: Let me say that again. There appears to be not one single article, published talk, or comment of any kind, anywhere in the professional legal literature, under Barack Obama's name, notwithstanding an apparent eleven-year teaching career in constitutional law at a top-flight school[53]

Elena Kagan was a friend and contemporary of Obama's on Chicago's faculty. Her career illustrates the law school's rigorous requirements for publication. The future Supreme Court Justice served on the faculty from 1991 to 1995. But Kagan failed to receive a permanent teaching offer, reputedly on the basis of too little scholarly publishing. But she had published eight law review articles, including two in 1996, presumably underway in 1995, given the long gestation period of law review articles.[54]

At the time, Obama was contending with several personal issues aside from finishing his memoir. He led a major voter registration project in the months before the 1992 elections.[55] That same year, he married Michelle Robinson, with the Reverend Jeremiah Wright presiding. Michelle embarked on her own rapid career ascent after the well-connected Valerie Jarrett hired her to work at Chicago's City Hall. That began Jarrett's close friendship with the Obamas.[56] Barack, in the meantime, joined a small private law firm and enhanced his civic ties in various ways. One was as a paid director with Ayres of the Woods Fund of Chicago, which funded projects for the disadvantaged and hired Obama's law firm.[57]

Also, Obama had to deal with the death of his grandfather, Stanley, in 1992 and of his mother in 1995.[58] Before her death, Ann received her doctorate from the University of Hawaii. Her thesis, "Peasant blacksmithing in Indonesia: Surviving against all odds," was more than a thousand pages.[59] That's an impressive achievement, often cited by biographers. But it tends to over-emphasize her academic work, enabling biographers to overlook the rest of her work that paid the bills.

Amid these transitions, Michelle and her family helped provide a stable core. Assisting Michelle's career was Valerie Jarrett, the lawyer and strategist. Jarrett was born in 1956 in Iran, where her physician-father, Dr. James E. Bowman, worked as chief of pathology at a hospital just after the CIA secretly toppled the Iranian prime minister and installed a pro-West ruler, or shah. Bowman became a prominent professor and practitioner at the University of Chicago School of Medicine. His daughter, Valerie, earned degrees at Stanford and the University of

Michigan Law School. She served in 1992 as deputy chief of staff for Chicago Mayor Richard Daley. In 1991, she began helping Michelle and then Barack get established in Chicago. Jarrett would later work in the Obama White House as a senior advisor, a relatively low-key title. Her influence was arguably comparable to a chief of staff, but with a twist. Her duties were to channel important information to the president and serve as a sounding board, not so much to implement his goals. Her father's background suggested intelligence ties that paved the way for her success as a Chicago power broker. In the process, she appears to have been, behind her relatively modest title, one of the handlers modern presidents acquire for VIP liaison.[60]

On the Chicago faculty, Obama made important friends in addition to Kagan. One was future Obama White House regulatory "Czar" Cass Sunstein, who became the head of all federal regulation at the Obama Office of Management and Budget. Sunstein is widely regarded as a brilliant liberal, as is his wife, White House National Security Advisor Samantha Power. Conventional wisdom is that Sunstein stands outside of "Chicago School" free market conservatives, and is a potential Obama Supreme Court nominee in a second term after bringing new efficiency to government deregulation.[61] Similarly, his wife is in the forefront of fighting terrorism and genocide with innovative methods to foster intervention by the United States, overcoming traditional barriers to new wars.[62] But Sunstein also suggested, in a 2008 law review article, that the government secretly hire academics and journalists to thwart the spread of dangerous ideas.[63] Sunstein and his co-author floated their idea in regard to conspiracy theories involving national security. Yet the concept could have wide application. Obama installed Power and Sunstein in high-ranking administration posts, with Power initially an aide to Clinton at the State Department.[64] Then she moved to the White House on the National Security staff. Her specialty was identifying human rights violations in other nations as a rationale for United States actions to topple the offending government. This argument would become an extremely valuable tool in post-colonial statecraft.[65]

Presidents often create jobs for old friends. Nonetheless, Sunstein's elevation after what one pundit aptly called his "spine-chilling proposal" to hire secret government agents in academia and journalism was yet another sign of Obama's comfort-level with secret and ever-expanding presidential power. In sum, Obama and his Chicago friends, whatever their rhetoric and training, fashioned themselves as heirs to a CIA covert action tradition, not the constitutional, open-government, checks-and-balance system voiced on the campaign trail.[66]

Onward and Upward: State Senate

In 1996, Obama won election to a heavily Democratic state senate district on Chicago's South Side that encompassed the University of Chicago and as well as far more populous black neighborhoods. Obama ran unopposed in the 1996 Democratic primary but only because he successfully challenged the sufficiency of valid signatures on the nominating petitions of his rivals. One was progressive incumbent Alice Palmer, who resigned in an unsuccessful effort to succeed a congressman, Mel Reynolds, a Yale Law School grad ousted in 2003 from Congress because he was exposed as having sex with minors. Palmer, after failing to succeed Reynolds, challenged Obama as a write-in candidate for her seat. But he played hardball, and successfully challenged her signature totals.[67]

He fathered two daughters and appeared to exemplify an outstanding, family-oriented civic leader who used his talents for worthy causes, at least by the standards of constituents in his Democratic-majority city. Behind the scenes, Obama was friendly with Antoin "Tony" Rezko, a real estate developer and entrepreneur who specialized in winning minority-oriented contracts. Rezko hired Obama's law firm, donated to his campaigns, and otherwise befriended him, including in a land-deal that expanded Obama's property value.[68] In a 2008 trial, Rezko was convicted on 16 of 24 fraud counts and sentenced to ten years in prison without implicating Obama in any wrongdoing.[69]

Obama broke with the Rev. Jeremiah Wright in a major speech in 2008, and campaign supporters consistently rejected all such attacks as baseless or dirty tricks.

In 2000, Obama challenged incumbent congressman Bobby Rush in the Democratic primary, but lost by a two-to-one margin. In the state senate, Barack became chairman of the Health and Human Services Committee in 2003 after Democrats regained a majority. Obama is credited with helping lead unanimous, bipartisan passage of laws to monitor racial profiling by police by recording the race of drivers they detained, and by requiring that homicide interrogations be videotaped.[70] Obama also opposed the Iraq War in a 2002 speech to an audience of progressives, helping him to rally other progressives nationwide for his primary contest against Hillary Clinton in 2008.

To this standard political biography, we can note that his important financial backers grew to include Chicago heiress and real estate tycoon Penny Pritzker, an heir of Hyatt Hotels fortune. She earned her undergraduate degree from Harvard, with law and MBA degrees from Stanford. She would later become a member of boards of Harvard, Stanford, and the Council on Foreign Relations among other posts. Her innovative career held many successes, including membership on

Chicago's Board of Education. Her personal website summarizes highlights.[71]

An alternative view focusing heavily on her leadership the Superior Bank before its bankruptcy comes from investigative reporter Greg Palast, who holds an MBA from the University of Chicago after studying under famed free-market economist Milton Friedman. Palast describes the Obama-Pritzker relationship as follows:

> Less than three years before taking the presidency, he was in the Illinois state senate, a swamp of scammers, backhanders, and party machine tools — not a stellar launch pad for the White House. And then, one day, state Sen. Barack Obama was visited by his fairy godmother.
>
> Her name is Penny Pritzker. Penny's from Heaven? Pritzker's net worth is listed in Forbes as $1.8 billion, which is one hell of a heavy magic wand in the world of politics. Her wand would have been heavier, and her net worth higher, except that in 2001, the federal government fined her and her family $460 million for the predatory, deceitful, racist tactics and practices of Superior, the bank-and-loan-shark operation she ran on the South Side of Chicago. Superior was the first of the deregulated go-go banks to go bust -- at the time, the costliest failure ever. U.S. taxpayers lost nearly half a billion dollars. Superior's depositors lost millions and poor folk in Sen. Obama's South Side district lost their homes.
>
> Penny did not like paying $460 million. No, not one bit. What she needed was someone to give her Hope and Change. She hoped someone would change the banking regulators so she could get away with this crap. Pritzker introduced Obama, the neophyte state senator, to the Ladies Who Lunch (that's really what they call themselves) on Chicago's Gold Coast. Obama got lunch, gold and better -- an introduction to Robert Rubin. Rubin is a former Secretary of the Treasury, former chairman of Goldman Sachs and, when Robert met Barry, co-chairman of Citibank. Even atheists recognized Rubin as the Supreme Deity of Wall Street.[72]

Advancing to the U.S. Senate

The year 2004 was huge for Obama. Incumbent Republican U.S. Sen. Peter Fitzgerald announced that he was retiring after one term to run a bank in McLean, a prosperous Virginia suburb of Washington that is home to many government officials, the CIA headquarters, and government contractors.

A wealthy Democrat, Blair Hull, announced a plan to spend more than $10 million to replace Fitzgerald. But political consultant David Axelrod, a well-connected former *Chicago Tribune* reporter helping Obama, elicited from Hull information that in his youth he had been a cocaine user and abused his wife.[73] Release of Hull's information drove him from the race.

Something similar occurred to Republican nominee Jack Ryan, a wealthy former Goldman Sachs executive formerly married to Jeri Ryan, famous for her roles in *Star Trek* and *Boston Public*. Although both wanted their divorce records kept sealed, a Los Angeles judge granted the *Tribune's* request to open them. The records contained a claim by the candidate's wife that he once suggested she have sex in public at a swinger's club. This effectively ended the Ryan candidacy. Republicans searched frantically for a viable replacement but Obama won in a landslide, receiving 70 percent of the vote.

In the Senate, Obama served on a total of seven committees. His major responsibility was to chair the European Affairs subcommittee of the Foreign Relations Committee. That committee held no major hearings, reflecting Obama's low-key Senate record. He voted in a reliably Democratic manner, with a few bipartisan exceptions. One of the latter was his vote in 2008 to grant immunity from civil liability to major telecommunications companies complicit with NSA warrantless wiretapping operations. The measure was backed by Senate Energy and Commerce Chairman John D. "Jay" Rockefeller, a West Virginia Democrat. Representing a reversal of his public views, it stripped U.S. citizens of the right for any redress against massive, illegal privacy invasions by the nation's telecom providers on orders of the Bush national intelligence agencies. Obama also had campaigned against immunity, but promptly switched his vote to support the Bush-Rockefeller-CIA position as soon as he secured the Democratic nomination.

Race for Presidency

The specifics of the 2008 presidential campaign have been so frequently reported elsewhere that this account will focus only on a few incidents that foreshadow larger themes of this book, as-yet rarely explored.

On January 7, 2008, Bill Clinton responded to a question at a Dartmouth College speech with an off-the-cuff comment that would become one of the most controversial of the primary campaign. In retrospect, Clinton's remark was probably correct. He aptly illustrated a herd mentality of many political journalists who rushed to defend Obama. Here's what happened: Just after Hillary Clinton's third-place finish in the Iowa caucus behind Obama and John Edwards, Clinton conceded that her political advisor, Mark Penn, had made a clumsy post-caucus remark. Clinton then accused the media of creating a false narrative claiming for Obama superb political judgment. Clinton cited the media's heavy focus on Obama's 2002 speech against the Iraq war before an anti-war audience, and minimal focus on Obama's later remark that he did not know how he would have voted if he had been a United States Senator with a statewide constituency.[74]

"This whole thing is the biggest fairy tale I've ever seen," Clinton continued, as he reminded his audience that experienced politicians were instrumental in enacting the 1960s civil rights legislation advocated by courageous civil rights leaders. Hillary Clinton made a similar comment that same day. ABC's White House correspondent Jake Tapper and others framed her comment as a slam against such revered civil rights leaders as the Reverend Martin Luther King Jr., thereby creating a narrative that she and her husband were dissing blacks just before South Carolina's Democratic primary.[75] Democratic House leader James Clyburn of South Carolina, the highest-ranking black member of the House, used the controversy to signal that he would break his pledge to remain neutral in advance of his state's important early primary.[76]

More than four years later, the Clintons have been proven largely correct in their comments. At best, Obama had scant legislative accomplishment in either civil rights or foreign policy congruent with the high hopes generated by his campaign. Additionally, the Clyburn role in the crucial South Carolina victory represented yet another occasion when Obama scored an election victory after a seemingly self-inflicted wound by an opponent. Finally, Bill Clinton's comments are readily available on YouTube and other versions,[77] and are tame compared to the fierce, media-generated reaction against him and his wife prompted at the time.

Most of us who follow politics were at least dimly aware of the controversy regarding Bill Clinton's remarks. Yet hardly anyone except connoisseurs of the independent media (and not including me at that time) would have been aware of several developments far more intriguing in retrospect. One was that an employee working for a private contracting company led by former CIA executive John Brennan had been caught illegally accessing the State Department passport records of Obama, Hillary Clinton, and John McCain. Separately, McCain, buoyed by efforts to help a Rothschild-backed defense contractor win a $35 billion Air Force contract for a new generation of tanker planes, was enjoying a Rothschild-hosted fund-raiser in England. The event to benefit the McCain presidential campaign had the appearance of an illegal contribution by a non-citizen.

Reporters covering the Obama campaign became irritated one day in June 2008 when they were fooled into thinking the candidate was travelling by plane from Dulles International Airport in Washington to Chicago, when Obama actually stayed in the capital city. The Obama campaign mollified the media by saying Obama wanted private meeting time, and thus had met with Clinton at the home of California senator Dianne Feinstein. Campaign spokesman Robert Gibbs declined to provide details about Obama's schedule, including whether he had met with any others besides Clinton.

Alternative media on the left and right reported that both contenders had secretly attended the annual Bilderberg Group meeting.[78] That meeting occurred as usual during presidential election years at Westfields Marriott Hotel three miles south of Dulles Airport. The locale provided easy airport access to the 120 or so visiting potentates, government leaders, and media tycoons from North Atlantic nations.

In 2008, attendees included Netherlands Queen Beatrix, David Rockefeller, Henry Kissinger, *Washington Post* Chairman and CEO Donald Graham, and Investor AB Chairman Jacob Wallenberg, part of Sweden's most dominant billionaire family and a longtime Bilderberg leader. All of Bilderbergers, including media barons and their most trusted commentators, strictly abide by the group's secrecy even on presidential campaign issues far more important than the pablum their hirelings deliver to the public. In 2008, for example, Bilderberger James Johnson, vice chairman of the merchant bank Perseus Group among his many leadership posts, was assigned to pick Obama's vice presidential running mate. Johnson, former campaign manager for Democrat Walter Mondale in 1984, had led vice presidential selection in 2004. The choice that year was North Carolina Senator John Edwards following what alternative media reported as a well-received presentation by Edwards to the group.

Bilderberg attendees include so many prominent media owners and trusted commentators that their refusal to cover the secret meetings undercuts their credibility on other issues. To reduce suspicions, therefore, Bilderberg has begun releasing limited information on occasion, such as names of most attendees. Yet huge incentives exist for active U.S. political candidates to deny attendance for fear the public might dislike their participation.

It is not necessary to support the entire worldview of Obama critics to note their warnings. Madsen wrote:

> The nexus of Obama's alma maters Occidental, Columbia, and Harvard, as well as that of his parents, the University of Hawaii, in the CIA's mind-control, behavioral modification, and mass hypnosis projects is deeply troubling. The fact that Obama has failed to provide a full accounting of his past academic and professional employment history, coupled with the presence of a major CIA presence within his and his parents', grandparents', and stepfather's backgrounds opens up the real possibility that Obama was, to use the CIA's own term, "nurtured," for a higher calling[79]

Similarly, Tarpley wrote in early 2008 that the media coverage of Obama's Iowa primary victory on January 7 was so favorable to the winner that it suggested that the nation's most powerful interests wanted Obama to defeat Hillary Clinton.[80]

Why prefer Obama? A Democratic presidency was almost inevitable after the Bush administration's economic and war-making disasters. Republicans lacked credibility to undertake new wars and more wealth-shifting to the rich in 2008 after eight years of governance. In Tarpley's view, the nation's top decision-makers felt more comfortable with Obama, a malleable newcomer of lesser independent stature, than the centrist Clinton. In contrast to conventional wisdom that Obama was an anti-war liberal, Tarpley spotted at the beginning of 2007 that Obama might drop that role at any time. If so, the motive would be to repay his elite backers. How? By undermining New Deal safety nets, retaining low taxes, privatizing public assets, and agreeing to impose austerity on the public while a managing to retain his popularity in ways impossible for a Republican, or even Hillary.

To explore these suspicions, the next chapters examine a parallel story, how the Bush family created a political dynasty that led to fabulous success for itself and its allies.

Chapter 7

Prescott Bush: Roots of the Bushes

T he Bush and Walker families, forebears of President George Herbert Walker Bush, have been prominent in American life for many generations. The profile below shows that Bush, the nation's forty-first president from 1989 to 1993, is far more than the patriarch of the Bush family. Also, he is a descendant.

The analysis over the next three chapters covers multiple generations of the Bush Family. That way, the disreputable methods and dire consequences for the public are understandable as part of a pattern, not mere aberrations. As one example, both George H. W. Bush and his father, Prescott Bush, presented themselves as war heroes to help launch their careers, despite serious questions about the facts. This raises doubt about their ultimate loyalties, given the central role that war-making, armaments, and energy have played in advancing the fortunes of their families and their armies of business cronies.

To explore these long-neglected issues will not resolve them with unanimous agreement, of course. Yet disclosure of the Bush family's past helps make more understandable the Obama-Dunham family's CIA and other national intelligence relationships. If George H. W. Bush and, as we have seen, Bill Clinton, were secret CIA assets when they were in their early twenties, and if Jimmy Carter was a protégé of David Rockefeller and Zbigniew Brzezinski, why not Barack Obama?

The pages ahead augment the familiar Bush history in several new ways that reflect *Puppetry* themes of secret agendas, elite institutions, greed, and corruption behind the veneer of normal civic life and public service. This chapter focuses on the career of Prescott Bush, father of the future president.

The Family, Kitty Kelley's entertaining 700-page history, includes a valuable genealogical chart showing an impressive earlier generation: descendants of Samuel Prescott Bush (1863-1948) and George Herbert Walker (1874-1953).[1] As indicated by additional books, the family story is a fascinating tale of Wall Street-generated wealth, political success, media power, and high-level military intrigue.

The history of the Yale College secret society Skull and Bones is a good place to start. William H. Russell founded the society in the 1830s after observing a model for it during his studies in Germany.[2] Russell, who became a prominent educator and pro-union abolitionist, was a cousin of the wealthy Samuel W. Russell, a silk, tea, and opium merchant based in China for many years.[3] Skull and Bones, also known as "The Order," is incorporated as the Russell Trust Association and is exempt from Connecticut's normal requirements for annual reports. Several researchers suggest the secret status proved useful in 1961 for laundering payments to CIA-orchestrated Bay of Pigs invaders of Cuba.[4]

The Order traditionally invites fifteen of the school's wealthiest and otherwise most outstanding juniors to forge a lifelong mutual assistance bond. This includes a rite in the longtime headquarters, a windowless stone building called "The Tomb" in New Haven. Each initiate lies in a coffin to confide intimate sexual experiences. George H. W. Bush and his father were members, as was son George W. Bush. Author Alexandra Robbins summarized the society's importance as follows:

> The men called their organization the "Brotherhood of Death," or, more informally, "The Order of Skull and Bones." They adopted the numerological symbol 322 because their group was the second chapter of the German organization, founded in 1832. They worshipped the goddess Eulogia, celebrated pirates, and covertly plotted an underground conspiracy to dominate the world. Fast forward 170 years. Skull and Bones has curled its tentacles into every reach of American society. This tiny club has set up networks that have thrust three members to the most powerful political position in the world....Skull and Bones has been dominated by approximately two dozen of the country's most prominent families — Bush, Bundy, Harriman, Lord, Phelps, Rockefeller, Taft, and Whitney, among them — who were and are encouraged by the society to intermarry so that the society's power is consolidated. In fact, the society forces members to confess their entire sexual histories so that Skull and Bones, as a eugenics overlord, can determine whether a new Bonesman will be fit to carry on the bloodlines of the powerful Skull and Bones dynasties.[5]

Understandably brimming with self-confidence, Prescott found himself humiliated in 1918, a little more than a year after his Yale graduation. While Prescott was on his way to Allied front lines in the final months of World War I, his hometown newspaper in Columbus, Ohio printed a front-page story describing him as a hero acclaimed by three nations. The reason? Prescott, according the report, courageously used a "bolo knife" as a baseball bat to swat away an incoming shell, thereby protecting his unit.[6] In fact, he had not yet reached the front lines. The paper published this preposterous tale as a news story, and included such flattering biographical detail as his college leadership of the Yale Glee Club and his election to Skull and Bones. But the bolo knife as baseball bat yarn prompted ridicule. And so, four weeks later, the paper published on its front page a brief letter from Prescott's mother saying that the original story was in error.[7] Bush himself is reputed to have said the story arose because he wrote a humorous cable to a friend, who thought it was real and placed it in the paper.

The incident was all the more embarrassing because Prescott's father, Samuel P. Bush, was the United States official in charge of World War I purchases of small arms (including machine guns) and ammunition.[8] Details remain shrouded because of destroyed records.[9]

Samuel Bush's wartime post helped illustrate the kind of ongoing relationships between the nation's Wall Street, munitions, energy, and media tycoons that would endure through the generations. Bush's work buying ammunition and arms put him in a position to provide troops with goods from the Rockefeller-controlled Remington Arms, the nation's largest grossing arms dealer during the war. Bush worked directly under Wall Street's trusted Bernard Baruch, head of the War Industries Board. Baruch, a native of South Carolina, was nicknamed "The Long Wolf" because of his investment acumen but was reputed more quietly to be also to be an important liaison between Europe's Rothschild banking family and their United States partners. The nation's finances, including for war industries, were highly dependent also on the work of War Finance Chairman Eugene Meyer, the future *Post* owner who would cement friendships with the Bush and other major dynasties during this period of explosive federal growth.

After the war, Prescott Bush found marriage, and professional success through The Order and similar elite connections. He married Dorothy Walker, daughter of W.A. Harriman Brothers CEO and Co-founder Herbert "Bert" Walker, a private banker and sports fan whose successes included building Madison Square Garden, serving as New York State Racing commissioner and running the Belmont Race Track as president. But Bert Walker's main business was to help create support for U.S. entry into World War I, and postwar to build up Harriman Brothers. Other co-founders included W. Averell Harriman, a member of The Order from Yale's class of 1913. He chaired the firm and co-owned it with his younger brother, Roland "Bunny" Harriman. The latter was a Bonesman in the same Yale Class of 1917 as Prescott Bush. Bunny took the lead in arranging for Prescott to become the firm's vice president. Another co-founder was Percy Rockefeller, a Bonesman in the Yale class of 1900 and the family's controller of Remington Arms[10] Prescott's brother attended Yale, and both of their sisters married Yale men.

If this all seems cozy, that's because it was. And to a significant extent, it still is. Rather remarkably, for example, 2004 Presidential candidates George W. Bush and John Kerry were Yale Bonesmen in the mid-1960s, as were at least two of the leading news commentators on their campaigns.

Prescott Makes His Mark

Prescott Bush, tall and self-righteous, worked hard to advance himself and Harriman Brothers. Among his major early successes was helping William Paley obtain financing to buy CBS. Paley later ran CBS for many years as chairman, with Bush as a director. Like CBS, NBC and later ABC were spinoffs from the Radio Corporation of America (RCA), and thus had many overlapping relationships with banks, and other financiers.

At Harriman Brothers, Bush also created a strong United States financial base for the German industrialist, Fritz Thyssen. Thyssen used Harriman Brothers as an agent for his efforts in the United States. In 1926, Thyssen also became mesmerized by up-and-coming German politician Adolf Hitler and so became Hitler's leading financier.[11] Harriman Brothers was well-positioned for this business after being involved in global activities that included projects in Russia after World War I. In 1931, Harriman had merged with Brown Brothers, which had been the nation's major shipping line for the slave trade before the Civil War, thus enabling extensive overseas offices. The new company became Brown Brothers Harriman, the world's largest private investment bank.[12] Bush ran the New York office, and focused heavily on Thyssen and related business. That was among Harriman's biggest income sources as Hitler ramped up his country's development after seizing power in 1933. Meanwhile, a Depression stagnated much of the United States.

Given Hitler's warmongering and racist policies, however, Thyssen-related income became increasingly awkward for the firm. Thyssen himself broke with Hitler before the war, and fled to France in 1941, doubtless hoping his United States assets would remain available under the safekeeping of Brown Brothers Harriman. In 1942, the United States government seized some assets under the Trading with the Enemy Act. But Averell Harriman was one of President Roosevelt's top foreign policy advisors, with many henchmen installed in high places. Not surprisingly, the Hitler-Thyssen-Harriman-Bush matter was resolved discreetly, for the most part, until investigative reporting arose a half-century later. .

Prescott Bush survived the Nazi taint with relatively little damage to his reputation. He was elected as a U.S. senator representing Connecticut as a Republican from 1952 to 1963.[13] Bush's patron Averell Harriman, a U.S. ambassador to Russia during the war, continued to hold several of the highest federal foreign affairs positions under the postwar presidency of Harry Truman. Bush served on the Armed Services Committee, and fostered close friendships with President Eisenhower and other top officials.

During the 1940s, Bush and tobacco heir Gordon Gray, fostered a friendship and alliance between their families that would affect the nation's history for decades. Gray's son, Boyden Gray, would augment that tradition by helping lead a secret, decade long-effort by power brokers to create "the tea party," which was sold to the public as a spontaneous grassroots organization of patriots arising in 2009 to fight the Obama administration. The sham's historical roots are intertwined with the power of the nation's great dynasties:

Gordon Gray, an heir to the R.J. Reynolds tobacco fortune, was a Yale Law School graduate and newspaper publisher among his accomplishments. In the 1940s, he and his wife became leaders in the eugenics movement along with Prescott Bush. The Harriman and Rockefeller families heavily funded eugenics and sterilization, which later evolved into more socially acceptable Planned Parenthood organization and decades of U.S. Agency for International Development birth control programs for Third World nations. Gray and his wife helped lead a pilot program to reduce birthrates by sterilizing hundreds of black boys and girls who performed poorly on school intelligence tests. The trial project was in segregated Winston-Salem, North Carolina, where Gray published a newspaper.[14]

Gray became secretary of the Army in the Truman administration. Gray's interests would include the mind-control drug experiments by the fledgling CIA on unsuspecting test subjects whose reactions could be studied. Gray would go on to hold important national security positions under both Republican and Democratic presidents into the Ford administration during the mid-1970s.

In 1953, President Eisenhower appointed former Harriman lawyers John Foster and Allen Dulles to lead the State Department and CIA, respectively. Averell Harriman became governor of New York State for one term before losing reelection in 1958 to Nelson Rockefeller, a Dartmouth graduate. Rockefeller's many influential posts before his four terms as governor included one with the quaint title of Special Assistant to President Eisenhower for psychological warfare.

Gray became Eisenhower's national security advisor. Gray and Prescott Bush were frequent golfing companions with President Eisenhower, with Vice President Nixon often rounding out their foursome.[15]

Illustrating the capacity for political jousting even among the highest levels of the governing elite, Prescott Bush damaged the national aspirations of Nelson Rockefeller by savagely attacking the scion of his longtime financial allies for obtaining a divorce and remarrying.[16]

Prescott's tirade was doubtless in part because of Nelson's notorious reputation as a philanderer, with Rockefeller's staff regarded as especially vulnerable to his charms. Another motive for the sabotage was the Bush Family's increasing interest in working with oil-rich Texas conservatives who were reshaping the Republican Party toward perspectives shaped by Arizona Senator Barry Goldwater. [17] Prescott retired from the Senate in 1963, just as his son George's political career was beginning in Texas. Prescott resumed his post as Brown Brothers Harriman managing director until his death in 1972.

In 2004, *The Guardian* in the United Kingdom published an extensive investigation seeking to answer questions about Prescott Bush's role assisting Thyssen and Hitler. The series noted that Bush enjoyed success in public life after the war, and was never prosecuted. However, it quoted John Loftus, a former federal prosecutor in the nation's Nazi hunt that began in the 1970s, as arguing that he would have sought Bush's indictment as a war criminal if he were still alive.[18] *The Guardian* noted that the Bush Family had always declined to respond to such comments. The news story continued:

"There is no one left alive who could be prosecuted but they did get away with it," said Loftus. "As a former federal prosecutor, I would make a case for Prescott Bush, his father-in-law (George Walker), and Averell Harriman [to be prosecuted] for giving aid and comfort to the enemy. They remained on the boards of these companies knowing that they were of financial benefit to the nation of Germany."

Loftus said Prescott Bush must have been aware of what was happening in Germany at the time. "My take on him was that he was a not terribly successful in-law who did what Herbert Walker told him to. Walker and Harriman were the two evil geniuses; they didn't care about the Nazis any more than they cared about their investments with the Bolsheviks.

Chapter 8

George H. W. Bush: Poppy's Seed and Bitter Harvest

I n early 1976, Republican U.S. Senator Charles Mathias of Maryland announced on the Senate floor that he could not vote in good conscience for former Republican National Chairman George Herbert Walker Bush to become CIA director. The farsighted senator told his colleagues, "CIA power should be kept away from those who ascend to that post via partisan politics." Mathias lost the debate, and Bush was confirmed.[1] Worse, the senator's concerns about an ever-growing and increasingly politicized national security sector have all but disappeared from the Senate discussion in both parties. Indeed, the CIA's headquarters has been renamed "The George Bush Center for Intelligence," and is far from the vision President Truman had of an expert resource without partisan taint and without military capabilities uncontrolled by civilian authority.

From the Mathias comments, even the senator did not seem to suspect that Bush became a CIA asset in the agency's earliest days in the 1940s, and was enriched beginning in 1954 by running a CIA-front company undertaking Gulf of Mexico oil drilling.

The pages ahead augment the familiar Bush history in several new ways that reflect *Puppetry* themes of secret agendas, elite institutions, greed, and corruption behind the veneer of normal civic life and public service. The scandals include Iran-Contra, and a long-running Bush romantic affair. True, it is nearly impossible to know with certainty all the specific details of scandals, but official follow-ups were far less aggressive than warranted. This illustrates how a selective, politically-biased justice system affects elections and the rest of governance.

The nation's 41st president has many attractive personal qualities, to be sure. Among them are an ethic of hard work, strong loyalty to family, and instinctive graciousness to most of those whom he encounters, high and low. I accept the view of trusted friends that he is considerate on a personal basis above the norm. His published letters from 1942 to 1998 reflect that quality.[2]

Nonetheless, admirable qualities do not foreclose a sense of entitlement, a willingness to exploit others outside the inner circle, and a potential for evil deeds in secret on occasion.[3] Successful politicians are often attractive, both superficially and personally. And even those with good manners can sometimes exploit those outside the inner circle of family, friends, and the powerful.

Poppy's Progress

George H. W. Bush was born in 1924, and prepped in Massachusetts at Phillips Academy, often known simply as "Andover" because of the town of its 1788 founding. Bush acquired the nickname "Poppy" and by all accounts graduated as a popular, undistinguished student. His roommate and lifelong friend, Edward Hooker, was the stepson of Dimitri von Mohrenschildt, descendant of an oil-rich Russian family that was allied with the Rockefellers and Harrimans at high levels of international diplomacy. Dimitri's brother, George, also was a friend of Poppy. George de Mohrenschildt closely mentored Lee Harvey Oswald for six months ending the April before the 1963 assassination of President Kennedy. The relationship between the two Georges intrigued some researchers after Kennedy's death, in part because of evidence of CIA ties for both.[4]

After Pearl Harbor, George H. W. Bush postponed college and enlisted in the Navy on his eighteenth birthday in 1942. He bypassed the Navy's normal requirement of two years of college for those hoping to become aviators. In the Pacific war zone in 1944, he piloted a Grumman Avenger that was bombing the Japanese-held island of Chichi Jima. Japanese antiaircraft flak hit his three-man plane. Rather than attempt a water landing, Bush bailed out. His two crewmates died. The crew of the submarine *U.S. Finback* rescued Bush from the water. Bush emerged a hero with a Distinguished Flying Cross Award. He and those writing flattering accounts of the episode repeatedly claimed valor for him, thereby advancing his political career.[5]

Far less visibly, critics disputed Bush's claim that he could not have saved his crew-mates. In 1988, a rear gunner on a plane directly ahead of Bush's told the *New York Post* that Bush had been lying about the extent of damage to his plane before he bailed, and was not a hero.[6] The controversy paralleled similar ones regarding the war records of Prescott Bush and George W. Bush, including the latter's disappearance from duty during the Vietnam War and his "Mission Accomplished" self-promotion during the Iraq War. Thus, three generations of Bushes were considered war-heroes under dubious circumstances, and went on to successful political and business careers.

In 1945, George married Barbara Pierce, daughter of Marvin Pierce. Marvin would rise to the top at *McCall's*, publisher of several popular women's magazines. After marriage, Barbara dropped out of Smith College. George was following the family tradition of attending Yale and being tapped for Skull and Bones. Poppy captained an outstanding Yale baseball team. George Herbert Walker Jr., a Class of '27 Bonesman, attended every Bush game his final year. The adoring uncle on Bush's mother's side ran an investment company that funded Latin American and Caribbean sugar-related industries.[7] A star baseball player, Bush graduated in 1948 under a special program whereby veterans could receive a degree in less than three years. He received a Phi Beta Kappa key. Researchers say records documenting the achievement have never been available, much like the secrecy that surrounds Barack Obama's transcripts.[8]

Soon after graduation, George and Barbara moved to Texas. The attractive young couple landed in the western part of the state, launched a family, and overcame the same kind of adversities facing many fellow veterans and their wives. The conventional wisdom is that Poppy's family reaped the benefits from risk taking, hard work, and impressive decision making.[9] That's true as far as it goes, but their success could not have occurred without wealthy family friends such as Bert Walker (who lived from 1874 to 1953), George Herbert Walker Jr. (1905 to 1977), and sinister decision making that has shaped our world for the worse via assassination, war, and oppression.

With political and financial power shifting west in postwar America, the Rockefeller, Morgan, and Harriman-level dynasties and their lieutenants at the Bush-level could not reasonably continue their financial and political dominance if they remained heavily concentrated in the New York City-Boston financial corridor.[10] Rather sensibly, Poppy and Barbara established themselves in the oil boom region of Odessa-Midland. In this, they moved in advance of, for example, the Rockefellers, whose comparable generation commanded powerful positions in banking, foundations and the national government. Nelson become New York's governor, serving four terms beginning in 1959. His brother, Winthrop, almost single-handedly created a viable Republican Party in Arkansas as governor. Their nephew, Jay, a Democrat, ascended to his current position as senior U.S. senator for West Virginia and Senate Energy and Commerce Committee chairman.

In *American Dynasty*, mainstream biographer Kevin Phillips highlights evidence pointing to George Bush CIA connections while he was at Yale in the late 1940s, during the agency's initial stage of formation.[11] Phillips and other biographers suggest that early CIA connections were useful in many ways, including access to high-level contacts, their research data, and financial support. Bush also had family connections that were instrumental in persuading their business cronies to help him get his start in Texas with his first job, and then fund treasure chests for his business and political ventures. Among initial job offers for the recent grad was one from Wall Street legend Ray Kravis, who pioneered complex strategies whereby energy firms could reduce their taxes. Kravis, father of current Wall Street buyout king Henry Kravis, became part of the George Bush Texas business circle in the 1950s.[12]

George's work began modestly enough with jobs at Dresser Industries. This was a prominent manufacturer of oil field equipment reorganized by Harriman beginning in 1928. The firm installed Bonesman and Prescott Bush contemporary Neil Mallon as president and CEO.[13] Bush, who would name a son in Neil's honor, worked at Dresser until 1951. One job was as a "landman" persuading land-owners to sell oil-rights. Most sales positions have only a few dollars in play. By contrast, a successful landman leverages his employer's expert estimates about sub-surface deposits and drives a tough bargain with the landowner, many of them novices. It's excellent training for a child of privilege who needs to get serious about making money.

In 1951, Bush and fellow Yale-educated landman John Overbey formed a company to buy oil rights on a large scale. Funding came from, among others, Bert Walker, Prescott Bush and *Washington Post* owner and former World Bank President Eugene Meyer, who had entrusted Brown Brothers Harriman with his personal investment portfolio. Meyer was the father of Katharine Graham, whose husband Philip Graham was another Bush-Overbey investor. Their descendants still control the *Washington Post* and its affiliated businesses.[14]

Then as now, the government, the financial community, the media, and the rest of the private sector engaged in confidential plans and struggles of great importance and scant disclosure. Averell Harriman, a close friend of the Graham family, wrote a friend in government, "I have not supported *Newsweek* for 10 years through its grave difficulties to allow our hired men to use the magazine to express their narrow, uninformed or insidious ideas."[15] Harriman called the journalists "hired men" with the easy contempt that came naturally to the son of a railroad tycoon, even one who occasionally had to find public support for his visionary plans.

To systematize such thinking in a core group, the political elite and wealthiest CEOs of North American and Europe founded an annual secret conference. Lord Rothschild and Laurence Rockefeller hand-picked the 100 invitees, who included royalty from the United Kingdom and the Netherlands.[16] An investigative history of the Bilderberg Group, as it came to be called, says of its media-heavy membership.[17]

> The ideas and policies that come out of the Bilderberg annual meetings are used to generate news in the leading periodicals and news groups of the world. The point is to make the prevalent opinions of the Bilderbergs so appealing that they become public policy and to pressure world leaders into submitting to the 'needs of the Masters of the Universe.'

The Bilderberg Group has about 80 core members, with 40 others invited on occasion to locales kept secret even though many are owners or top columnists of the West's most prominent news organizations. The annual meetings provide a rare occasion for crowned heads of Europe to meet formally with other Western European and American leaders. Bilderberg gatherings are reputed to have generated momentum for such concepts as the Common Market, Euro, and North American Free Trade Agreement (NAFTA). The Bilderberg Group's membership overlaps with the slightly larger Trilateral Commission and North American Union, and the larger and older Council on Foreign Relations (CFR). The latter generations of the Bush family, particularly George W. Bush, do not appear to have been especially active as leaders. This distance may reflect a sense of Southwestern-style independence from the East Coast-Rockefeller-Rothschild roots of the organizations. Yet all United States administrations draw heavily from the groups, including almost all secretaries of war/defense, other top national security advisors, and military leaders.

In 1953, Poppy Bush co-founded Zapata Petroleum in order to obtain and develop leases. The next year, Bush founded an affiliate, Zapata Offshore, which he led as president to exploit oil concessions that the Eisenhower administration started making available in the Gulf of Mexico. Senator Prescott Bush was by then a close friend and golfing partner of President Eisenhower, whose aides opened the Gulf for such development as production began to decline at many Texas oilfields. Investors included the usual circle of Bush-Walker and Harriman business cronies. One Zapata Offshore co-founder and officer, Thomas J. Devine, was a former CIA officer who would later return to the agency in the late 1960s. Other founding investors or their children would resurface prominently in the 1980s on Wall Street as the Reagan-Bush administration unleashed speculative fever upon the nation.[18]

Zapata Offshore's leadership, funding and mission raised suspicions that the company was a CIA front.[19] *National Review* founding Editor William F. Buckley, a Bonesman and heir to a Texas-Mexico oil fortune, told his readers in 2005 that he became a covert CIA asset shortly after his 1951 Yale graduation. The assignment in Mexico was so secret that Buckley did not even initially tell his wife.[20]

Zapata Offshore was well-positioned commercially to help the major "Seven Sister" oil companies extract oil from off-shore sites, and also to act as an intelligence gatherer whose offshore work justified travel to a number of Caribbean locales of keen interest to the CIA, including Cuba. The Dulles Brothers were ramping up anti-communist and pro-business activity in the region. This included the CIA-fostered overthrow of Prime Minister Jacobo Arbenz in Guatemala. Separately, the CIA closely monitored of Cuba's Castro-led rebels. The United States initially supported the rebels in their fight against the corrupt incumbent regime. Zapata helped anti-Castro rebels prepare for the Bay of Pigs invasion in 1961, and later provided training and money-laundering for Watergate operatives.[21]

One of the more controversial aspects of the Bush life story involves suspicions that he was present and otherwise involved in the assassination of President Kennedy on November 22, 1963.[22] A photo, widely displayed on the Internet, shows a man closely resembling Bush leaning against the Texas Book Depository building shortly before the assassination. Bush has denied being there, and his wife provided an alibi. George de Mohrenschildt, the former Bush family friend who became Oswald's mentor, described Oswald as a "patsy" in an unpublished book before being found dead of a gunshot wound. But any such suspicions are so explosive that few in the conventional media dare mention them.

Resolving lingering mysteries about the Kennedy assassination is beyond the scope of this book. The number of suspects and motives is vast, with one set of Warren Commission evidence filling 26 volumes. My late friend Fred J. Cook authored a pioneering critique of the Commission's findings. The thoughtful actor Robert Ryan, father of a lifelong friend of mine, starred in *Executive Action,* which challenged the Commission Report.[23]

Since then more than 250 books have been published that question vital elements of the official theory blaming Oswald as a lone, leftist assassin. Among authors risking their professional reputations to argue that the assassination was part of a coup have been retired Air Force Colonel Fletcher Prouty, chief of special operations for the Joint Chiefs of Staff during the Kennedy years, and Dr. Cyril Wecht, the Pittsburgh-based coroner, medical school professor, author and consultant. "The murder of President was traumatic enough," Prouty wrote in 1996, "but the course of events that followed and that affected the welfare of this country and the world since that time has, in many ways, been tragic."

I discovered Prouty's book late in this research. Yet it seemed as if he were speaking to me from beyond the grave when I read that he named names of those angered by Kennedy's increasing disapproval of Cold War crusades and schemers. In 1962, the president fired CIA Director Allen Dulles, who later became by far the most influential member of the Warren Commission because of his expertise and freedom to work while most other commission members fulfilled official duties in other major posts. Also, Kennedy intended to draw down United States troops in Vietnam. Prouty would have known also of the long-classified "Operation Northwoods" plan by the Joint Chiefs to concoct a deadly pretext for the United States to invade Cuba. Summing up, Prouty wrote these chilling words regarding JFK's death:

> That assassination has demonstrated that most of the major events of world significance are masterfully planned and orchestrated by an elite coterie of enormously powerful people who are not of one nation, one ethnic group, or one overridingly important business group. They are a power unto themselves for whom these others work. Neither is this power elite of recent origin. Its roots go deep into the past.[24]

Questions have reverberated additionally about conventional wisdom regarding the assassinations of Robert F. Kennedy, Malcolm X, and Martin Luther King Jr., and the plane crash death of conservative Congressman Larry McDonald of Georgia. Some have questioned also official explanations of the assassination attempts against conservatives Ronald Reagan and George Wallace. The best course is for all of us to remain alert to a wide array of possibilities as the facts, including new evidence, might dictate.

Texas Politics, Bush-Style

Poppy Bush fathered six children. The oldest was the future president George, born in 1946. The next, Robin, died of leukemia in 1953, at age four. Barbara Bush says it turned her hair prematurely white.[25]

After the family moved to Houston in 1959, Poppy became active in Texas Republican politics. His initial post was as Harris County GOP finance chairman. This enabled him to leverage his financial contacts, and prepare for a losing Senate campaign against Democrat Ralph Yarborough in 1964. Bush aimed lower for his next campaign, and won a Houston congressional seat in 1966. By then a millionaire, he exited from Zapata Offshore by selling his shares to fellow Yale Bonesman Robert Gow.[26]

President Nixon persuaded Bush to run again for the Senate in 1970, and rewarded him after another losing effort with an appointment to become the United States ambassador to the United Nations. Bush became Republican National chairman in 1973, defending Nixon at first from Watergate charges but ultimately calling for his resignation. President Ford named Bush to be the nation's top representative to China for fourteen months, and then CIA director. Bush was disappointed that Ford did not pick him for the 1976 GOP vice presidential slot. He returned to Houston to create an investment banking business, with a specialty in fostering deals with oil-rich Arab nations. He prepared also for a 1980 Presidential candidacy — working with a young Texas-based consultant named Karl Rove, among others. Bush lost that race but emerged as vice president in the Reagan administration.

White House Years and Fears

Bush became one of the most powerful vice presidents in history during his two terms, from 1981 to 1989. From the outset of the Reagan administration, the pattern was so obvious that a UPI writer described Bush as "co-president" as early as March 10, less than two months after inauguration.[27]

Then came the March 30 assassination attempt on Reagan, followed by a lengthy recovery. Bush solidified his role even more during Reagan's recovery and the crucial early stages of the administration's decision making. Furthermore, Secretary of State Alexander Haig, a former general regarded as Bush's most capable rival for administration bureaucratic control, became an object of ridicule in the media. The scorn from colleagues and their media friends was ostensibly because of Haig's comment, "I'm in control here," after the assassination while the vice president was travelling.[28] Haig would be forced to resign a year later.

The back story is that Haig was targeted for elimination by Bush allies in the Brown Brothers Harriman/Skull and Bones network in Washington.[29] The former New York governor, Averell Harriman, and his younger bride, Pamela Harriman, presided over Washington thought-leaders from their Georgetown salon until his death in 1986. Similarly, Time-Life founder Henry Luce, a Bonesman and Bush friend of longstanding, once described as the nation's "most powerful private citizen," had picked editors in his image who strived to maintain traditions long after his death in 1967.[30] The focus on Reagan's valiant recovery, the crazy assailant John W. Hinckley, and perceived foibles by Haig largely obscured Bush's consolidation of power and the bizarre coincidence that Hinckley's brother, Scott Hinckley, had been scheduled to dine with Bush's son, Neil Bush, on March 31 in Denver.[31]

Bush's foreign policy agenda helped guide the Reagan administration to a more aggressive and covert outlook than existed in the Carter administration. Bush was also influential in deregulatory efforts helping those in the energy industry and related fields long-associated with the Bush dynasty and its cronies.[32] Ronald Reagan, to be sure, had the stature of a governor-turned president and a compelling presence as commander-in-chief. The former movie star and TV host of the *GE Theater* was fundamentally a pitchman-made-good, and was not himself a member of the ruling financial elite. Bush, while not especially wealthy, came from a different world. In it, his forbears ran the nation's largest private bank at

Brown Brothers Harriman, but some had lost vast fortunes, as Uncle Herbie had done when Fidel Castro nationalized their refineries and railroads in Cuba. Fighting communism was not an abstraction. It was deeply personal and financial. Bush readily transferred that mind-set during his 1989 to 1993 presidency to the fight to maintain power for the Mideast royalty, most notably in Saudi Arabia, Kuwait, and other oil-rich states that he and his family had long cultivated.

Bush leadership in the Iran-Contra scandal illustrates, among other things, the contempt that Bush and his peers held for any sense of accountability in a democratic society to Congress, the media, or anyone else. His supervision of the Reagan Administration's major deregulatory initiatives shows the ruthless impact of crony capitalism in an era of spectacular speculation that especially benefited two of his peers and diminished circumstances for many others. The Iraq War is already well-known ground, yet Saddam Hussein was originally a creature of the United States. Similarly, the CIA and its UK allies created today's radical Islam state of Iran, in effect, by overthrowing an elected prime minister in 1953 who governed in a manner that would be considered highly pro-West by comparison with today's Iranian leaders.

Iran-Contra

The Iran-Contra scandal erupted in late 1986, prompting the federal court appointment of Lawrence E. Walsh as an independent counsel to investigate. Bush said, "I was out of the loop."[33] A deeper look heavily implicates Bush in the scandal and cover-up, which involved a shift of the United States constitutional system to enable Executive Branch insiders to launch unaccountable covert action and war on a global scale.

The scandal's essence was that the Executive Branch violated its announced policies and clear congressional law and instead pursued an illegal foreign policy of arms smuggling to Iran and elsewhere. The administration also engaged in drug running, creating a moral blemish on the United States and a slush fund for illegal paramilitary activities, potentially causing vast harm to United States communities, especially those hurt by the drugs. All of this was obscured with systematic lies to the public and the creation of "terror" incidents to build up public support.[34]

The independent prosecutor Walsh found that Bush was involved, but with insufficient evidence to charge him criminally. This may have been in part because of Bush's cover-up, which included failure to deliver requested personal diaries. The Walsh report stated:

> Independent Counsel's investigation did not develop evidence that proved that Vice President Bush violated any criminal statute. Contrary to his public

pronouncements, however, he was fully aware of the Iran arms sales. Bush was regularly briefed, along with the President, on the Iran arms sales, and he participated in discussions to obtain third-country support for the contras. The OIC obtained no evidence that Bush was aware of the diversion. The OIC learned in December 1992 that Bush had failed to produce a diary containing contemporaneous notes relevant to Iran/contra, despite requests made in 1987 and again in early 1992 for the production of such material. Bush refused to be interviewed for a final time in light of evidence developed in the latter stages of OIC's investigation, leaving unresolved a clear picture of his Iran/contra involvement. Bush's pardon of Weinberger on December 24, 1992 preempted a trial in which defense counsel indicated that they intended to call Bush as a witness[35]

These same stalling and cover-up tactics are used by all administrations. But Poppy escaped accountability from especially serious violations, creating a leadership model that would encourage more abuses by his successors.

Deregulation

The central domestic purpose of the Reagan-Bush administration was to implement free market, free trade, and other deregulatory theories that supposedly hobbled the United States economy. As with Iran-Contra's radical cuts in constitutional checks and balances, Poppy Bush was at the center of the deregulatory changes that helped reposition the nation's economic structure to align better with the perceived golden age of fewer government restrictions, as in the Roaring Twenties.

By the end of the Roaring Eighties, the Reagan-Bush changes would transform much of the economy. This led to many new fortunes, especially among well-connected cronies, along with false hopes and complacency among many others too busy living their lives to notice long-term trends. Yet even insiders had difficulties foreseeing the financial future. The president's son, Neil Bush, became both a villain and a victim in the $2 billion Silverado Savings and Loan scandal. That bank's loss was a small part of the deregulatory debacle that cost taxpayers tens of billions of dollars in bailout funds.[36] Also ruined by bad investments was Democrat-turned-Republican John Connolly, the former Nixon Treasury Secretary and Bush rival regarded as the most astute politician of his generation next to LBJ. When the bubble burst a national recession and Ross Perot-led rebellion against free trade helped scuttle Poppy's 1992 reelection bid.

Like most, I observed these events from afar. In the 1970s, I recognized that conservatives were capitalizing politically on real abuses fostered by liberals. In my newspaper work, for example, I saw that the Carter-created Inspector General program was identifying scandalous examples of waste, fraud, and abuse in government, but Democrats ceded that issue almost entirely to Republicans. Similarly, I provided a favorable book review in 1978 to *The Antitrust Paradox*, a book by conservative University of Chicago legal scholar Robert Bork. He ridiculed conventional wisdom in antitrust enforcement as oppressive, over-regulatory, and otherwise ineffective.[37] In this way, the "Chicago School" economic theory of Bork, Milton Freedman, and a wide array of well-funded think tanks and editorialists, conservatives ascribed the late-1970s "stag-flation" to outdated Democratic policies. Republicans ridiculed the liberal hero from Massachusetts, Senator Ted Kennedy for social policies that seemingly tolerated or even encouraged a welfare culture, drugs, crime, and other abuses among the lower classes and minorities.[38]

The GOP victory in 1980 against Jimmy Carter launched a wave of what appeared to be exciting new financial investments, including the leveraged buyout (LBO) that enabled corporate "raiders" to use a company's own assets to acquire it and transform it, supposedly, into a more efficient model based on best practices. Three of the best-known LBOs had longtime links to the Bush Family and Texas oilfields. The national leader in this was Henry Kravis of KKR (Kohlberg, Kravis, Roberts), son of Ray Kravis, the Tulsa and Wall Street oil development genius who had offered Poppy his first job out of Yale. Another was Hugh Liedtke, a co-founder of Zapata who would go on to evolve it into Pennzoil Petroleum and win billions of dollars in remarkable litigation against Texaco, which led to the latter's dissolution. Another was T. Boone Pickens, who built his Mesa Petroleum raiding company with Liedtke's help.

I observed with alarm related developments in the sphere I best knew, the news business, and so published a case study in 1987 called *Spiked*.[39] After the book, however, I finished my legal education at the University of Chicago and began working in the Washington office of Latham and Watkins. Its clients had included Michael Milken of Drexel Burnham Lambert, the national leader in using junk bonds for acquisitions. One of the senior partners was Mark Fowler, who radically deregulated the communications industry as Reagan's first and only Federal Communications Commission chairman from 1981 to 1989. That fostered vast new opportunities for many in that sector, which I joined for two decades, extending to the date of this writing to some degree.

"There are a million stories in *The Naked City*," an announcer used to intone on a long-ago television show by that name. So it's pointless to provide more than a sample of them. My best effort at a conclusion is that the great financial experiments of the Reagan-Bush era helped many people in the 1980s, myself included. But they were too extreme even then. Now they are spinning out of control as the rich get richer and others are left to fend for themselves, without adequate warning.

We have seen that devastation can come very fast. Every American needs to consider thoughtfully the thesis of Naomi Klein's *The Shock Doctrine*, which argues that savvy politicians and industry leaders nefariously implement policies to profiteer from natural disasters, wars, and economic upheavals.[40] Disturbing as her theme might be, it is congruent with examples elsewhere, including in the remainder of this book.

Iraq War

In the Persian Gulf War two decades ago, President George H. W. Bush and his team demonstrated their contempt for public disclosure or other democratic procedures that might hinder their freewheeling approach to oil-based foreign policy. That policy, a disaster for the United States overall, has been highly lucrative for the Bush Family, its cronies, and its constituencies.

The war began with Iraq's invasion of its smaller neighbor Kuwait on August 2, 1990. A United States-led coalition of thirty-four nations retaliated in Operation Desert Storm. Aerial bombardments of Iraqi forces began January 17, 1991. A ground assault on February 23 quickly liberated Kuwait, and pulverized Iraq into surrender three days later.[41]

The victory temporarily sent President Bush's popularity ratings sky-high. That is like measuring victory for a baseball game by one inning's play, however. Bush and his team used phony public relations tactics to con the United States public into supporting a war against Iraq, a former ally. Overall, the Reagan-Bush years paved the way for vast death and destruction. Despite all of the lives and treasure the United States has spent in Iraq to foster pro-West support, that nation is now Iran's most important ally.

Keys to the Iraq disaster are the long-term business ties of the Bush-led, Texas-centered oil, banking, and arms sectors with oil-rich, Persian Gulf royalty. Most important of all are the business and government ties that the Bush Family has nurtured with Saudi Arabia. The United States helps protect a near-feudal monarchy through arms sales and other means in return for the profits from the arms sales, reasonable policies on oil sales, and other foreign policy partnerships. The United States-Saudi bilateral relationship is buttressed with similar understandings with other oil-rich royal rulers in the Persian Gulf states.

Several decades of private relationships exist between those royals and their United States counterpart, the Bush dynasty. In the 2004 book *House of Bush, House of Saud*, author Craig Unger documented $1.48 billion in payments by the Saudi royal family to four Bush officials and their affiliated entities. That is a tiny portion of the sums accruing to leaders of the military-industrial complex from Mideast wars of recent decades. The four officials were the two Bush presidents, the family's longtime advisor James Baker, and Dick Cheney. The entities included the Carlyle Group, a financier of weapons companies that boasts Bush and several of his former top aides as executives, and Halliburton, which Cheney formerly ran as CEO in the 1990s.[42] Poppy Bush cultivated Saudi relationships when he became a Houston-based banker and dealmaker in the 1970s following his CIA leadership and before his presidential run. Baker has alternated between government and private-sector deal making at the highest levels for decades. For the past decade, he has demonstrated his priorities, if not loyalties, by defending Saudi officials from a trillion-dollar damage suit filed in New York's federal court by families of 9/11 victims.

This is part of a long pattern, as we can recall from the beginning of this chapter. Harriman Family brothers Averell and Bunny worked with public relations impresario Bert Walker to encourage the United States to enter World War I, with Poppy's great-grandfather, Samuel Bush, presiding over the federal government's purchases of arms and ammunition from, not surprisingly, well-connected companies. Then Prescott Bush and his company, Harriman Brothers, made a fortune by serving as the main United States agent for Adolf Hitler's leading financier in the run-up to World War II. Warmongering and war profiteering have thus been the Bush Family business for nearly a century, not some off-the-cuff response to events while in public service.

During the 1980s, the Reagan-Bush administration generally supported Iraq's ruler Saddam Hussein in his horrific war with Iran that killed more than a million, counting deaths on both sides. United States officials knew of his brutal methods and dangerous goals, but regarded his nonreligious regime as a useful regional counterweight to the hard-line Shia Muslims running the much-larger Iran. Hussein caught the Reagan-Bush administration largely off-guard in July 1990 by planning retaliation against neighboring Kuwait for what he claimed as debts by the small, oil-rich, Sunni Moslem emirate. Iraq invaded on August 2, 1990. The Bush administration and key allies promptly concluded that Iraq must be stopped before it controlled too much of the world's oil and threatened the Saudis and Israelis.

More importantly, the Bush administration wanted a big American victory to make the country feel good about the president, the country and war in general following the "Vietnam Syndrome" of withdrawal from foreign engagements. How do we know such ambitions were pivotal? Because Iraq's dictator had extended unsuccessful offers to negotiate or withdraw from Kuwait, according to reporting by author Robert Parry, the intrepid former Associated Press and *Newsweek* reporter who had broken the Iran-contra story. The Bush administration kept the peace offers secret in the same way Washington's "conventional wisdom" conveniently shifted to make a villain of Hussein and heroes of the oligarchical Kuwaitis.[43]

The administration did not want to rely publicly on those points. Help for Israel might create Arab resignations from a war coalition the United States was leading. Also, the male-run religious Gulf States were not especially sympathetic as victims to the United States public. Instead, a phony Washington public relations strategy evolved. Kuwait, acting through front groups, hired a score of U.S. public relations agencies to build grassroots support for a U.S.-led military rescue mission also sought by Bush. Kuwait spent $10 million on Hill and Knowlton, alone, to bring the U.S. into the war. One of the agency's most effective stunts was to create dramatic testimony to Congress by an unidentified teenager describing how Iraq troops were killing babies in Kuwait by pulling them out of incubators. David Gergen, a Yale Bonesman and highly influential political commentator and former White House staffer, is typical of those who spread the story widely by decrying the invader's responsibility for twenty-two babies killed when they were pulled from hospital incubators.[44]

Babies were not killed. It was a hoked-up story. Among others, *Harper's* publisher John R. MacArthur reported in his 1992 book, *Second Front,* that the baby incubator story had been a hoax. It turned out that the heart-rending testimony before Congress had been by the daughter of Kuwait's ambassador. Postwar research found no evidence that Iraqi troops had endangered newborn babies in incubators.[45] These psychological operations are finely honed. Experts in perception management, propaganda, and mind control, believe that horror stories about rape and baby-killing, even if fraudulent, are especially effective in generating support for war, especially among women.[46]

The baby-killing story was only a small part of a massive propaganda campaign to stampede the American public into war. This job was outsourced to the private sector to prevent accountability to Congress and the media. In this, it was just like many sensitive foreign policy missions since the CIA used Kermit Roosevelt to overthrow Iran's elected prime minister in 1953. The main operatives were Washington's booming lobbying and public relations sector hired by the government of Kuwait through various front-group names to disguise government involvement. As documented by MacArthur and Susan Trento in her 1992 book, *The Power House*, the main player was Hill and Knowlton, Washington's highest-grossing lobbying and public relations firm. Its president was Craig Fuller, former chief of staff to Vice President Bush.

Even more important than Fuller as the hands-on chairman was Robert Keith Gray, an advisor to five GOP presidents extending from Eisenhower to Bush. Prior to taking on Kuwait as a client, Gray's extensive CIA ties helped him recruit the Bank of Credit and Commerce

International (BCCI) as a client. That was when the bank needed serious image polishing after it was exposed as undertaking massive illegal money laundering for the world's most notorious dictators, as well as the CIA. Hill and Knowlton helped out, just as it would for Kuwait. I came to know Gray during the summer of 2012 by inviting him on my weekly public affairs radio show to discuss his new book, an attack on Obama.[47] Gray seemed like a happy warrior, delighted as he approached his 90th birthday to be still in the political attack mode, even though he had much to hide in terms of professional and personal secrets.[48]

The experience underscored several axioms of public life in Washington. First, the enormous clout of the revolving door between government and business. Second, how much ostensibly independent major media are influenced by well-funded lobbyist/government relations companies, such as Hill and Knowlton. Finally, even those who are the masters of media manipulation, like Gray, can become genuinely frustrated at other's tactics — and even at "the media."

Most importantly, the tale of *sub-rosa* Bush effort to engage the United States in a Mideast war brings this chapter full circle to its beginning. We saw how Harriman-Walker initiatives helped to foster United States entry into World War I. This helped set the stage for arms deals and the postwar financing of Hitler that would help keep the clan (by then including the Bushes) and their cronies in wealth during repetitions of the cycle to current times.

The Rest of the Story

Among the many strands to the Bush career, one of the most important is George Bush's role in expanding American war culture and arms-dealing into the Mideast. A mainstream biographer wrote of Bush:

> ....no major American leader remotely matched his 1976-92 record of pouring weaponry into Afghanistan, co-opting Pakistani intelligence, liaising with the shah's Iranian police, making secret arms deals with Shiite ayatollahs, becoming near family to Saudi princes, rescuing undemocratic Kuwait, and helping to transform Peshawar – Kipling's mountain gateway to the Khyber Pass – into a CIA station and munitions dump.[49]

Curiously, Bush and his allies fund themselves repeatedly boasting of "A New World Order" even though the phrase had already been associated with foreign policy disasters extending back to Woodrow Wilson and the League of Nations. Bush used it for the major foreign policy address of his administration to a joint session of Congress in late 1990 after the collapse of the Soviet Union and shortly before the invasion of Iraq.[50] Although "New World Order" carries a certain bold resonance even to the unsophisticated, it could hardly have escaped Bush's speechwriters that the phrase s regarded as powerful code-language in certain circles. Skull and Bones has been more commonly known for more than a century as "The Order" to its secret initiates, who include not just the Bushes but many influential public affairs pundits.

Christian Broadcasting Network founder Pat Robertson published *The New World Order,* a best-seller in the election year of 1992. Those with only passing familiarity with conservative tele-evangelist might imagine he would seek to support Bush, whom Robertson identified as "a man of integrity."[51] Instead, Robertson — a Yale Law School graduate, son of a U.S. Senator, and the founder of Regent University — decried the danger that "one-world" secret societies run by elites posed for the United States. Robertson's main fear was the destruction of religious faith and national sovereignty. He traced dupes and danger from the Colonial era through the Wilson presidency, the aberration of Hitler, and through the Bush era, citing presidents ostensibly as different as the Republican Nixon and Democrat Carter.[52] Robertson's blunt conclusion was that each was beholden to behind-the-scenes players such as the Rockefellers, the Ford Foundation and what he called "the mind-boggling" role of the Council on Foreign Relations.[53] Robertson warned also against spiritual deterioration in Americans from the great Bush triumph of victory in the Gulf War, when, "for the first time since Babel all the nations of the earth acted in concert with one another."

Those warnings were three decades ago. I'll not seek to repeat all his fears and predictions. I merely note that even Republicans have had concerns about their party's most successful family dynasty.[54]

In 2004, author Craig Unger estimated that the House of Saud sent at least $1.477 billion "to the Bush family and its friends and allies over the years."

Even the powerful cannot always control events. In 1992, Arkansas Governor Bill Clinton, made George Bush a one-term president, ending a dozen Bush years in the White House. Clinton, born fatherless and poor, was groomed at elite institutions via a Rhodes scholarship, Oxford, CIA work, and Yale. His ascension was thus not so much a defeat for the old order, but a vindication of the economic elite's wisdom in fostering alternative avenues to ensure its own success no matter who prevails in elections.

Chapter 9

George W.: Shameless, Heartless, and Selected-Not Elected

This chapter describes how threats to 2012 elections are rooted in the frauds that enabled Bush's two terms and their disastrous governance. Corruption, zealotry, and incompetence helped devastate the nation's economy, foreign affairs, justice system, and constitutional protections. Yet key players on the Bush team quietly reassembled under the Romney banner with high hopes of governing the country once again, beginning in 2013. Voter suppression and other dirty tricks would be the secret weapon for 2012, just as it had been for previous victories.

A Connecticut Yankee in a Texas Hat

The GOP's 2000 nominee portrayed himself as a "compassionate conservative."[1] George Walker Bush, the first of his parents' six children, was born on July 6, 1946. New Haven was his birthplace as his father pursued a busy schedule at Yale. For his father, "Making money was crucial," according to biographer Kitty Kelley.

> "Assumptions to the contrary, George Herbert Walker Bush did not come from extraordinary wealth. Comfortably prosperous, his family was not of unlimited means and could not subsidize him."[2] Home was primarily in Texas following his family's move to Odessa-Midland in young W.'s earliest years. Then it was east to Houston. Barbara Bush, who had been from a Social Register family back in Rye, New York, later complained in her memoir that those early years were far from easy. At one point, a Bush apartment shared a hallway bathroom with a family of prostitutes.[3] Daughter Robin was her second-born and George's close playmate. She died of leukemia in 1953 at age four. The family kept the ailment secret from George, merely warning him not to play with her and informing him of the illness after she died.[4] It was a disturbing experience for young George by most accounts (including his own bland memoir, Decision Points).

The family became more prosperous, and young George attended prep school at Andover. He returned to New Haven in 1964 when he

110

enrolled in Yale, and was selected for Skull and Bones before graduation in 1968.[5]

Dr. Justin Frank, a Harvard-trained psychiatrist based in Washington, is the author of *Bush on the Couch,* a best-selling remote diagnosis in 2004. In evaluating Bush (albeit from afar), Frank saw dangerous signs in the young man's upbringing by a busy father and a cold, discipline-oriented mother.[6] Frank reports that George vividly recalled hearing of his sister's death from leukemia when he was six.[7] Frank found it significant that young George was never told she was ill, and that the family held no funeral for her. Frank's method of reading psychiatric significance into such events is controversial, to be sure. Even more so are his conclusions:

> At first, George W.'s attempts to rival his father's accomplishments were largely unsuccessful. His limited intellectual capacity doomed his chances of achieving the level of academic distinction his father achieved at Andover and Yale, and he had to settle for the cheerleading squad at the prep school where his father was a varsity star.[8]

Frank goes on to find evidence from other sources that young George's lifelong conflicts made him a deeply disturbed man. "Bush has a specific attitude to reality – he changes his perception of events, applying his internal spin system, and if that doesn't work he changes the rules by which reality itself is defined."[9] Remote "diagnosis" can be derided as suspect at the minimum. Frank's conclusions are similar to those of other critics in print and on the nation's airwaves.[10]

George, the Yale Bonesman, was also a member of the Delta Epsilon fraternity, a football team cheerleader, and a scoffer at the war protesters of the era. He was also a 1968 college graduate, making him highly vulnerable to the Vietnam draft as the government had abolished graduate school deferments to feed the war machine in Vietnam. Bush, an advocate of the war from a pro-war family, faced a decision.

Family connections helped Bush receive favored treatment and obtain a very difficult appointment to the "Champagne Unit" of the Texas Air National Guard. He also received almost unprecedented boosts with an officer's commissioner and pilot training without the normal prerequisites, as we know from authoritative reporting by Russ Baker and many others.[11] The preferences Bush received are especially shocking given the heavy casualties in Vietnam and Bush's subsequent delinquencies, including an apparently unpunished AWOL status. Instead of serving in Vietnam or even fulfilling his duties in his Texas unit, Bush proceeded to party and politick in Alabama, and then leave the service early to obtain an MBA degree at Harvard. [12] His record was not dissimilar to others' in his family, as previous chapters showed. Similar also to his forebears was George W.'s later record of boasting about his service and his war-mongering to advance his political career. There's little doubt that the CBS report in 2004 about the political preferences bestowed on Bush to avoid service and his disgraceful record afterward were essentially correct.[13]

The young man's lifestyle involved an unusual excess in drinking, drugs, and by some standards, premarital sex. This was a little over a decade after his grandfather, Prescott, had broken with longtime family ally Nelson Rockefeller over his divorce. Widespread lifestyle changes were affecting many families. Yet few had the Bush political profile, and the self-righteous demeanor.

To the rescue of George and his social and political viability came Laura Welch. She was a schoolteacher who joked that she was called at age 30 "the old maid of Midland" when she met Bush, "Midland's most eligible" bachelor, as he prepared for a congressional race in 1978.[14] She remembered him from two decades previously in the seventh grade, and described her attraction. She married him three months later in 1977. That was the year before he lost his congressional race for the district surrounding Midland as his opponent attacked him for having an elitist Andover-Yale-Harvard background. The twins, Barbara and Jenna, were born in 1981.

As George came of age to enter the family businesses of politics, a comparison with Lyndon Johnson's ascent is instructive. Johnson, reared in poverty in a Texas county named after a Johnson forebear, is the most notorious vote thief in American history, with the possible exception of George W. Bush.

Historian Robert Caro provides the most vivid account: Johnson refused to concede defeat in 1948 during his first Senate run when Election Day results showed him 854 votes behind Coke Stevenson, the state's incumbent governor. Several irregular changes narrowed the margins. Then Johnson's allies arranged a final adjustment that boosted the congressman to victory by 87 votes out of nearly a million cast. Senate colleagues gave Johnson the nickname "Landslide Lyndon" because of his victory.[15] The fraud was not an aberration. As a Texas congressman, Johnson ducked World War II service as long as he could, and then found a sinecure as a stateside lieutenant commander in the Naval Reserve. Upon coming under fire for thirteen minutes during his one combat flight, he leveraged the experience into a Silver Star. Beyond that, Johnson resented how he had not received greater recognition and that others in the nation less deserving shared the same award.[16]

Despite such selfishness, Johnson remained savvy enough to steer federal contracts to his top supporters, founders of the construction company Brown and Root. This favoritism helped the company become one of the nation's most important contractors before Halliburton acquired it in 1962.[17] Johnson also nurtured the new CIA created during his watch, and became its chief Senate benefactor in funding, which was inherently secret. Johnson, the most enthusiastic Washington wheeler-dealer of his era, was also smart enough to maintain a public image of a down-home man who preferred to relax at his Texas ranch whenever possible, away from Washington wickedness.[18]

George W. must have assimilated such lessons, even from the Democrat LBJ. George's career and image-building would follow the Johnson model in many respects. George assisted his father's political campaigns and business ventures funded by paternal friends.[19] Most failed despite funding from angels who would provide vital help for Bush throughout his career.[20] Bush received his biggest career break when wealthy Texans cut him in on a deal to leverage a government-funded stadium. This enabled the core group of insiders to acquire the Texas Rangers baseball team in Dallas-Forth-Worth. A key figure in arranging the baseball deal was former Texas State Representative Tom Schieffer, brother of CBS newsman Bob Schieffer.[21] They installed Bush as titular leader, thereby lining his pockets with a stock deal and allowing him to acquire a celebrity profile and reputation as a good businessman.[22]

Longtime family advisor Karl Rove helped inspire George to run successfully in 1994 against incumbent Texas Governor Ann Richards, a then-popular Democrat. Meanwhile, George's younger brother, Jeb, lost a 1994 race to become Florida governor. As governor, Bush cultivated a relatively moderate public image, aside from death penalty cases,[23] while preparing for a presidential run in 2000.[24] Part of George's preparation was to help Jeb become Florida's governor in 1998. Texans re-elected George that year by a large margin.

By Hook and Crook

This section on the Bush presidency focuses primarily on his election-fraud strategies, not the policies the frauds enabled, such as wars, tax cuts, and deregulation, along with increased government surveillance and political prosecutions that helped deter opposition. Election fraud was not an aberration in the policies of George Bush. Instead, it was part of the Bush revenue-generating machine for Bush backers, as indicated in the next few chapters. Similarly, W.'s war policies were patterned after those of his ancestors during World War I, who awarded contracts to their cronies at Remington Arms.

A second war against Iraq privately attracted W. as early in the late 1990s as he prepared for his presidential race. Bush and his team saw that such a war presented highly attractive domestic and international opportunities, according to authorized Bush biographer Mickey Herskowitz, a Houston newspaperman and prolific author.[25] Bush biographer Russ Baker summarized Herskowitz's recollections of his 1990s interviews with Bush on his career:

> Soon they were discussing what Bush hoped to achieve as president. While W. seemed somewhat hazy on specifics, on one point he was clear: the many benefits that would accrue if he were to overthrow Saddam Hussein. Herskowitz recalled that Bush and his advisors were sold on the idea that it was difficult for a resident to realize his legislative agency without the high approval numbers that accompany successful – even if modest – wars.[26]

To accomplish anything, Bush needed first to win the election. In 1998, Florida Governor Jeb Bush hired a ChoicePoint subsidiary to purge voter rolls in preparation for the 2000 elections. The subsidiary, Database Technologies, ostensibly sought to remove convicted felons from voter rolls congruent with GOP-backed legislation. Instead, the contractor, paid at two hundred times the rate of the previous contractor for the task, secretly removed 91,000 non-felons who were eligible voters. Most of them were Democrats and minorities. Forget about chads or Ralph Nader's third-party candidacy as the cause of George W. Bush's victory in Florida (and the nation) by a mere 200 votes. It was the software fraud by the private contractor that stole the 2000 presidential election for the Bush Family and its anointed son, George. The corrupt decision-making knocked probable Democratic voters off the rolls even before Election Day, and cost Democrat Al Gore an estimated 20,000 actual votes out of the 91,000 eligible voters.

That's the conclusion of author and BBC reporter Greg Palast in a series of reports for BBC and the *Guardian* he began publishing soon after the election. These reports led to important books.[27] His latest was *Billionaires & Ballot Bandits: How to Steal an Election in 9 Easy Steps* in September 2012. The book predicts that, unless the public becomes vigilant far beyond the level of past elections, Republicans are posed in 2012 to use the same techniques they ruthlessly used to steal the presidential race in Florida. Republicans reused the same scheme, Palast and others show, to steal the 2004 presidential election via an even more ambitious vote fraud scheme based in Ohio.[28] It relied on Florida-style voter suppression and also mind-boggling software fraud orchestrated by the Ohio secretary of state's office, as I believe also following my review of the literature and interviews of sources.[29]

The Bush theft of Florida's election was the most audacious effort of its kind in recent American history[30] and it caught the nation's watchdog institutions almost by surprise, with a few exceptions.[31] George W. showed no humility over stealing the presidency and losing the popular vote nationwide. Within weeks after taking office in 2001, his administration launched a massive new program to spy on Americans. Meanwhile, they ignored warnings about terrorism, whether from national security staff such as Richard Clarke or lower-level information sources.[32] The 9/11 attacks came after Bush spent much of August on vacation at his ranch in Crawford, Texas, emulating Lyndon Johnson.

In 2001, the Bush administration moved briskly after the 9/11 attacks to crack-down on civil liberties via the Patriot Act and otherwise.[33] As predicted by George Bush in his 1999 discussion with Herskowitz, the president won enormous popularity via a prompt and initially successful invasion of Afghanistan.[34] Gearing up for the Iraq investigation required more difficult marketing, as noted previously.[35] The dollars involved were so high that the Bush administration's main image-maker to foster the war was a former executive director of the Democratic National Committee.[36]

We now know also from such sources as the memoir of British Prime Minister Tony Blair, a Bush ally, that Dick Cheney was planning a series of Mideast wars. The goal, Blair recalled, was to reshape the largely secular but "rogue" dictatorships in Iraq, Libya, Syria, Lebanon, Sudan, Somalia, and Iran through United States "hard power."[37]

Bush went from 51 to 91 percent favorability in public opinion polls after 9/11. This enabled him to foster a radical foreign and domestic agenda, including appointments in the Democratic-controlled Senate. Tax cuts combined with war spending wiped out the Clinton-era budget surpluses, and made it more difficult for Democrats to argue for non-defense domestic discretionary spending despised by the conservatives. Various other initiatives such as easy credit and lax regulation of financial institutions fostered a bubble economy, financed in part by easy lending terms to consumers. Many of modest means spent freely, using second mortgages and credit card debt.[38] Bush signed into law the No Child Left Behind Act, the Partial-Birth Abortion Ban Act, and Medicare prescription drug benefits for seniors.

As Bush faced re-election in 2004, the Iraq War loomed as a festering problem. Military service and foreign policy expertise were at the forefront of Democratic nominee John Kerry's campaign, which focused on both his Vietnam combat experience and critique of Bush wars. Supposedly independent operatives countered that in part with "Swift Boat Veterans for Truth," an attack that put Kerry on the defensive.[39]

One threat to Bush came from a CBS news team led by producer Mary Mapes. Her CBS team in early 2004 revealed gross abuses supervised by Americans at the Abu Ghraib prison in Iraq. They followed up with months of research on W.'s disgraceful military record during the Vietnam War. Exposure of his AWOL status would inevitably focus more attention on the favoritism that enabled his appointment to a safe post while others were dying. Even worse, it would undermine his war-mongering in fomenting two wars where American troops were bogged down after initial successes.

With the stakes so high, the Bush team pulled off a brilliant, multi-front counter-attack. It now appears they sabotaged the CBS probe by putting a questionable reproduction of an actual document into the hands of a CBS source. Then they orchestrated a protest when CBS cited that reproduction given to the network by a source who lied about its origin.

The plot against the news team exploited two factors readily known to news industry and Washington insiders. First, that CBS Anchor and Managing Editor Dan Rather, like his peers, is dependent on his team more than is apparent to the casual viewer. The team, in turn, could well be professional without being immune to a deliberate ruse crafted by experts. Second, CBS News was a relatively insignificant part of Viacom, the parent company conglomerate controlled by CEO Sumner Redstone. Redstone, a code-breaker during World War II and brilliant Harvard Law grad, had become the nation's wealthiest man in the entertainment business. This was partly through his ruthless and other effective business tactics, often involving mergers subject to federal approval by such bodies as the Federal Communications Commission.[40] As it happened, two members of the commission had proved themselves worthy of regulating the nation's communications companies by running the Bush-Cheney Florida vote recount in 2000. One, the soon-to-become-FCC-chairman Kevin Martin, was a ruthless partisan who was married to Bush-Cheney Communications Director Catherine Martin. This was a particularly efficient arrangement: her job was to influence the nation's media, and her husband's job was to regulate it.

In other words, Viacom's leader had a clear choice: He could put Viacom's regulatory interests and profits first, or allow his CBS employees to pursue an embarrassing story about the Bush administration that important officials would hate. In those terms, the choice became easy, especially because few would know even that the issues exist if they are thinly reported.

After Bush loyalists concocted a fierce reaction against the CBS News story about Bush's AWOL status, the pieces fell into place for Viacom/CBS management to cave into pressure. Redstone, ostensibly a Democrat, promptly announced his support for Bush's re-election. Also, he had Mapes fired and Rather transferred out of the anchor chair. The network appointed the avuncular-sounding Bob Schieffer, whose brother had enabled Bush's career ascent, to replace Rather. That signaled to the White House and its allies how much the CBS cared about becoming Bush-friendly.

For experienced journalists around the nation, it signaled also the career consequences of probing too deeply into the nation's power centers, most notably the Bush Family and the AWOL story. Rather's supposed disgrace was confirmed by bogus investigating commission and parroted by craven pundits. His downfall was especially sweet revenge for the Bush team because of Rather's aggressive 1988 interview of Vice President George H. W. Bush on Iran-Contra allegations.[41]

In sum, the Bush team pulled off one of the great counter-attacks in recent political history. Few in the public were aware because the plot was enabled by Bush regulatory authority over increasingly timid and greedy corporate news organizations. Most importantly, Bush was re-elected, in part because news organizations were too frightened to use clearly valid evidence of Bush's Air Guard scandal. Just as important, every journalist in the country understood what could happen to even the most famous name, Dan Rather, at the "Tiffany Network," even after a CBS career that began in the 1950s following Rather's wartime service as a Marine.[42]

On other fronts, ordinary citizens took the lead in pointing out scandals in the administration. Purported Iraq war heroine Jessica Lynch, whose first public speech I attended upon her recovery from serious injuries, took pains to set the record straight, and go about her life in a modest manner.[43] The family of former football star Pat Tillman refused to stay silent when they suspected his death in 2004 in Afghanistan was the result of "Friendly Fire" prompted by the anti-war views that replaced his initial gung-ho attitude.[44] Countrywide Mortgage executive Eileen Foster unsuccessfully tried to warn against the massive mortgage fraud that would help to devastate the economy in 2008, causing many to lose their homes.[45] Meanwhile, the country's plutocrats in the energy, mining, and financial sectors benefited greatly from deregulation and sweetheart deals in the Jack Abramoff era.[46]

Along with profiteering came serious erosion in the nation's federal legal system. On close observation, this was especially obvious in the ethic of a professional, non-partisan Justice Department that provides due process via safeguards that have been a unique feature of the Anglo-American legal system since the time of the *Magna Carta* eight centuries ago. A few legal scholars, including those of such conservative backgrounds as Paul Craig Roberts, Kevin Philips, and Bruce Fein, began identifying this trend.[47] Roberts, for example, frequently wrote of "The Department of Justice (sic)," as if it were a clear-cut error to suggest that the department focused on justice.[48] But nearly all such voices were inevitably overshadowed by more timid if not cowardly news coverage.

As noted in this book's preface, I began researching in 2008 suspected political prosecutions across the nation arising from the U.S. attorney firing scandal of 2006.[49] New Mexico U.S. Attorney David Iglesias was one of nine Republican U.S. attorneys forced out of the 93 regional offices that year as part of what Republican Justice Department official, Kyle Sampson, described to Bush White House advisor Karl

Rove as an effort to retain "loyal Bushies" in the powerful Justice posts.[50] Iglesias believes he and others were forced out in an unprecedented manner, in his case for failure to misuse his powers to affect the 2006 elections. "All Roads Lead to Rove" was the title of the pivotal chapter in his memoir, *In Justice*, which invoked similar sarcasm to the Paul Roberts word-play.[51]

This proved to be especially true in the federal prosecution of former Alabama governor Don Siegelman, his state's leading Democrat. The Bush administration framed him on corruption charges and obtained a seven-year prison sentence. My three-year investigation of the case demonstrated sinister parallels in other Bush administration, political prosecutions of Democrats across the country, as well as craven behavior by judges, lawyers, Congress, and Obama successors regarding such injustices. This book's next chapter illustrates those themes.

In addition to injustice for defendants, Siegelman's experience illustrates the growing importance of electronic voting fraud in determining election outcomes. A test case for the new technology was Siegelman's re-election campaign in 2002 following his first term in Alabama. He went to bed on Election Day after an announcement that he had won re-election with a statewide margin of more than 3,000 votes. Upon arising, however, he learned that nearly 7,000 votes in rural Baldwin Country outside of Mobile had been dropped, and his Republican rival, Congressman Bob Riley, had been declared the winner statewide.[52] The never-investigated and therefore never-resolved shenanigans in Alabama emboldened Republicans for even more ambitious plans to ensure President Bush's re-election in 2004.

That re-election, as it turned out, depended on winning Ohio's 18 electoral votes. Ohio's Secretary of State Kenneth Blackwell co-chaired the state's Bush-Cheney re-election campaign. Therefore, he had the duel responsibility and the huge conflict of interests of ensuring fair elections while also advocating for Bush-Cheney. This was much like the conflict of interests held by Florida Secretary of State Kathleen Harris, co-chair of her state's Bush-Cheney campaign in 2000.

Republican IT expert Stephen Spoonamore said that the system Ohio devised was a viable method for corrupting the vote. Spoonamore, former IT director for the John McCain for president campaign, was one of the top expert witnesses for the plaintiffs, who said they represented Ohio voters deprived of their votes by authorities. The other main witness was Michael Connell, the Republican IT expert who set up the system. Connell, a reluctant witness, confirmed the logistics of the set-up in a pretrial deposition. He died in a mysterious small plane crash the next month. The lawsuit was dismissed before trial. Plaintiff co-counsel Bob Fitrakis, a law professor, and co-authors Harvey Wasserman and Steve Rosenfeld authored several books portraying their impressive evidence.[53]

My column for the Justice Integrity Project, "Cutting Through Hype, Hypocrisy of Vote Fraud Claims," analyzed (and listed with hot links) leading books, news articles, and allegations in this field. The conclusion was, "Recent events show why election theft deserves much more scrutiny than it receives from either government officials or news reporters."[54] Also, I advocated grand jury investigations for conspiracy, an end to the news blackout by traditional media, and a return to verifiable paper ballots.

I am far from alone in this. Fitrakis and Wasserman argued that the Romney campaign drew on Bush-Rove blueprints from the 2004 election to win the 2012 by voter suppression and electronic voting fraud.[55] Greg Palast, meanwhile, was doing everything possible to alert the public to the dangers of electronic voting fraud.[56]

As for George Bush, a man who had once reached 91 percent approval in the polls left office with a 22 percent rating. That is surely the greatest comedown in United States political polling history. He wrote a forgettable memoir, *Decision Points,* and raised funds for his presidential library.[57] His name and legacy were virtually ignored at the 2012 GOP National Convention in Tampa. Bush himself lives in a gated community in Dallas. He no longer pretends to enjoy cutting brush at his ranch in Crawford.

Karl Rove would carry on, however, with an election fraud scheme for 2012 so audacious that it loomed as Mitt Romney's greatest hope.

Part II: Romney Henchmen, Enablers, and Fellow Puppets

"We're an empire now, and when we act, we create our own reality. And while you're studying that reality — judiciously, as you will — we'll act again, creating other new realities, which you can study too, and that's how things will sort out. We're history's actors . . . and you, all of you, will be left to just study what we do."

— President George W. Bush's senior
White House aide, reputedly Karl Rove,
in mid-2002

Chapter 10

Karl Rove: A Frightening Fraud

As Election Day neared for the fall of 2012, Karl Rove emerged as the nation's most important Republican in public life, aside from the true money-men behind the scenes. Rove could tap into funding sources as well as anyone, and also carried a unique combination of media skills, government experience, and contacts along with the all-important passion to win. In the aggregate, Rove dwarfed the clout of Republican National Chairman Reince Priebus. In day-to-day terms, Rove has arguably surpassed in unpopularity the inactive and unpopular George W. Bush, and the flawed, mistake-prone aspirant Mitt Romney. Niccolò Machiavelli,[1] author of *The Prince*, was the world's first great political advisor, describing the world as it was, not as it should be. Yet the Italian died without seeing his insights implemented by a powerful leader. Rove, who has worked in 2012 to see his third president elected, is America's leading counterpart in the dark arts.

The Making of America's Machiavelli

Karl Christian Rove was born in 1950 in Denver, and reared in a broken home in Colorado and Utah.[2] A self-described "nerd" in high school in Utah, he attended several colleges without graduating. Unusually hard-working and creative, he found his niche in the early 1970s with College Republicans, a national group of fellow activists. Unger describes their style as follows:

> Nixon was president, and the College Republicans perfected the 'rat-fucking' techniques of the Watergate era, as Donald Segretti famously called them. There were false press releases or "leaked documents" bearing the names of Democratic rivals, jammed phone lines, spying on opponents, purloined speeches, hired "rioters" and activists planted in enemy camps, and push polls in which volunteer pollsters hunkered down in phone banks for hour after hour, disseminating disinformation and smears about opponents.[3]

Rove signed up to help the campaign of Illinois Democratic Senate candidate Alan Dixon. He purloined letterhead, and used it to disrupt an event by inviting hundreds of people to Dixon's new headquarters opening, falsely promising "free beer, free food, girls and a good time for

122

nothing."[4] Rove admits the trick in his 2010 memoir, *Courage and Consequence.*[5] In the Watergate days, that kind of concession of minor wrongdoing to deflect inquiries away from bigger scandals was known as "a limited, modified hang-out," a term borrowed from CIA spycraft.

The military draft and the wisdom of the Vietnam War were the nation's greatest national issues of the time. Rove, with no record of military service, devoted his energies to advocating for pro-war politicians. He dated and ultimately married a College Republican colleague, Valerie Wainwright. The leaders of College Republicans were mostly men. They forged bonds and developed candidate strategies (including family values and gay-bashing) that would keep many of them prominent in conservative circles for decades. This success occurred even though a high proportion of the group's leaders, even the married ones, are reported to have been active for years in Washington's gay and bisexual scene. The hypocrisy was kept hidden by the conventional media. In recent years, it has become a topic of vast commentary enabled by Internet communications as central figures became prominent righteous opponents of extra-marital sex, including during the Clinton impeachment.

Aspiring to become College Republicans chairman in 1973, Rove competed in a fiercely contested election against Terry Dolan.[6] Rove's campaign manager was Lee Atwater, who would go on to notorious national success as a master of dirty tricks. The election was so close and hard-fought that Republican National Chairman George H. W. Bush got involved after the *Washington Post* reported anonymous allegations of dirty tricks training by Rove.[7] Rove's rival, Terry Dolan, was suspected of the slur.[8] To teach the youngsters a lesson in not leaking to the press, Bush picked Rove to be both College Republicans chairman and to be his special assistant at the Republican National Committee.[9]

That year, Rove met Bush's son, George, who liked to be called "Dubya." Four decades later, Rove recalled Dubya on that first meeting as resplendent in an Air Guard flight jacket, boots and blue jeans, and possessing "more charisma than any one man should have."[10] Rove came from a difficult background, including an adoptive father who became an out-of-the closet gay. Rove fondly recalls in his memoirs the jocular young Dubya, who affected a down-home, Western macho swagger despite his Andover-Yale-Harvard pedigree. The fun-loving Dubya bestowed on Rove what became a lifelong nickname, Turd Blossom, in honor of the flowers that grow out of prairie cow pies.

Rove undertook GOP political work in Virginia after the senior Bush became U.S. ambassador to China and CIA director. Rove stayed in the Bush orbit, and moved to Texas. He worked on Dubya's unsuccessful 1978 congressional campaign, and helped the Reagan-Bush 1980 presidential success. He was deputy chief of staff for Texas Governor Bill

Clements, and opened the "Rove + Company" political consultancy in 1981. It would handle 75 campaigns for governor, congress, and the senate, including senate campaigns for out-of-state clients such as John Ashcroft of Missouri and Orrin Hatch of Utah. Rove's first wife divorced him. In 1986, he married Darby Hickson, an Alabama native who worked as a free-lance graphics designer for his firm.[11] Their son, Andrew, was born in 1989.

Rove is credited with helping Dubya defeat incumbent Democratic Texas Governor Ann Richards in 1994. In the new administration, Rove chaired Bush's political committee while he continued his consulting business. Rove holds a key role in transforming the nation's judiciary to an activist, pro-business instrument, especially in the Deep South and on prominent federal courts. Harper's columnist and prominent human rights lawyer Scott Horton describes the process this way:

> As Rove understands it, electoral politics has little to do with policy and everything to do with money—in particular with ensuring that his side has a massive advantage over its adversary. From early in his career, Rove's game plan was to tap the tills of corporate America by pushing "tort reform," which is to say, stacking the deck against tort lawyers by electing Republican judges in state court elections. In Alabama, Mississippi, Texas, and other states around the nation, this tactic served to fill the coffers of a flagging Republican Party and to bolster its electoral efforts across the board.[12]

Yet some of his methods and successes in Alabama would become so notorious that Rove would accord his Alabama work less than a sentence in his 500-page memoir, thereby deflecting attention.[13]

Bush's Brain[14]

In 2001, Bush appointed Rove to be senior advisor. The president later increased Rove's power by naming him deputy chief of staff. John DiIulio, White House director of Faith-based initiatives and community outreach, became the first senior aide to resign. A Bush loyalist, he had been a University of Pennsylvania professor and author before joining the administration. He quit out of frustration with what he called "Mayberry Machiavellis" who gauged decision-making on short-term politic impact.[15] Meanwhile, Rove clashed with Treasury Secretary Paul O'Neill, a prominent Republican businessman and former high-level official long close to Dick Cheney and other powerful players. O'Neill, far from liberal, saw government descend to what he regarded as a distressing level of short-term political goals bad for the country and needless intrigue. O'Neill was cut off from discussions normally within the sphere of the Executive Branch's third-highest-ranking official. He soon resigned, as described in *Price of Loyalty*, a biography published with his cooperation.[16] Its author, Ron Suskind, quoted a White House aide as bragging that the Bush White House could create its own reality because of its influence over the media.[17]

All administrations have their cronies and patronage scandals. But the pay-to-play culture reached new levels in the Bush White House, especially with the administration doling out vast sums in post-9/11 security contracts and war contracts.[18] Rove's assistant was Susan Ralston, former aide to the lobbyist Jack Abramoff, a lawyer near the center of wheeler-dealing. Before imprisonment on corruption charges, Abramoff often held court for free-loading government officials and aides at his restaurant, Signature's. It was located just downstairs from my office just across the street from both the Justice Department headquarters and the FBI headquarters. Despite such ties, Rove successfully avoided serious damage in the Abramoff scandals. They followed a familiar Washington formula: authorities identified a few scapegoats, such as Abramoff, and then punished them for the sins of the many.[19]

Rove was heavily implicated as a White House aide in two other major Washington scandals, but was never charged. First was the White House effort to expose Valerie Plame Wilson as a CIA covert agent, thereby risking her life and those of her family and colleagues. This was after her husband, former Ambassador Joseph C. Wilson, declined to find evidence supporting the administration's case for an invasion of Iraq.

Separately, Rove played a suspicious role when the Justice Department fired, for political reasons, nine of the nation's 93 presidentially appointed U.S. attorneys. The prosecutors, typically all loyal members of the president's party, have wide powers in their regions over criminal and civil cases but are supposed to use their powers in a non-partisan and otherwise fair manner.[20] The nine were dismissed in an unprecedented manner, mostly after the 2006 elections and with little explanation. Several were reluctant to leave office under suspicion of failure. Comparing impressions, they realized they had antagonized political bosses and the White House for failing to make unjust but politically useful prosecutions of Democrats or voter registrants.[21]

Detroit Congressman John Conyers resumed his longtime chairmanship of the House Judiciary Committee in 2007 following elections that restored Democratic control of the House of Representatives. Conyers ordered hearings and reports that kept the heat on Rove, Gonzales, and other Republicans.

In August 2007, Rove resigned from the White House. He denied being forced to resign, and said he wanted to return to private life and consulting.[22] Gonzales also resigned that month after he failed to stem criticism over the firing scandal and the massive federal wiretapping of

U.S. citizens contrary to federal law.[23] Conyers unsuccessfully tried to force testimony from Rove, and to obtain his full email correspondence.

The White House claimed "executive privilege," enabled the administration to prevent Rove from testifying, and claimed that many of Rove's emails were lost forever, being made on private Republican National Committee accounts via SmarTech, a Chattanooga IT firm with a controversial history described later in this chapter. The White House, at first, said only a few of the emails were missing. The total turned out to be an estimated 22 million, including nearly all of Rove's emails that were required to be preserved. No known action was ever taken against White House personnel, including Rove, or SmarTech. By contrast, my legal reform work has documented cases where the Justice Department has obtained multi-year sentences against targets that deleted even a few emails, backdated a check or omitted facts on a home loan application. The selective prosecutions illustrate author Harvey Silverglate's thesis that authorities can imprison or absolve almost anyone.[24]

In 2007, I met Dana Jill Simpson, an attorney who had worked as a volunteer on confidential Republican political projects, such as deep research on judicial appointments to meet Rove's political criteria. This timing was shortly after Rove's resignation and just as public interest in the U.S. attorney purge and political prosecution scandals was cresting. Reporter Wayne Madsen introduced her to me on the eve of her House testimony before staff. This was just before a separate interview by CBS for *60 Minutes*. She asked my advice on how to avoid being verbally mauled at a hearing.

I later learned that she had already obtained expert representation. But she was sabotaged anyway by various turncoat Democrats. They kowtowed in private to her critics, failed to seek corroborating witnesses, and steered her testimony away from such sensitive topics as her family's three-decade relationship with the Bush Family, judicial corruption, and huge military contracts. I later heard from her the story of how she came to know Madsen: During Rove's White House heyday, he asked her to probe who was funding Madsen to publish so many Jack Anderson-style muckraking reports. Simpson says her investigation found that he battled the giant forces in Washington fearlessly with scant income.[25] "So," she told me, "he was at the top of the list when I needed a reporter to tell the story."[26]

Several developments in 2009 reduced pressure on Rove. The Obama administration worked out a deal brokered by White House Counsel Gregory Craig for Rove and former White House Counsel Harriet Miers to testify in private under special rules. The testimony took place in July 2009. Committee questions were led by California Congressman Adam Schiff. With no known preparations interviewing such political prosecution victims as Siegelman or whistleblowers, Schiff failed to box in Rove with tight questions. Instead, he posed broad questions that Rove could duck. Schiff, a Harvard Law grad, thus failed to apply basic cross-examination techniques. Upon review of the specific questions that Schiff posed to Rove, I described the results as a whitewash, as did several other commentators.[27]

The White House deal with Republicans protecting Rove was just one of the ways constricting Conyers as he pursued the facts of the U.S. attorney purge scandal at the Justice Department. The Justice Department announced the indictment of Monica Conyers, the chairman's wife, less than two weeks before the long-touted interrogation of Rove on whether he and DOJ officials illegally conspired against innocent targets. Monica Conyers received a three-year prison term for bribery and conspiracy. Conyers himself labored under a threat of investigation for separate misconduct involving the kind of self-indulgent life-style common to office-holders but rarely prosecuted. That inevitably encouraged him to confine his oversight of the DOJ to anti-GOP rhetoric, especially once Democrats assumed control of the White House.

For perspective, the major case implicating Rove in wrongdoing was that of Siegelman. He was the former Alabama governor sentenced to seven years in prison essentially for asking a rich man to donate to a non-profit advocating for a state lottery to fund better education. Jack Abramoff alone generated $20 million in donations against Siegelman's 1998 and 2002 election campaigns, primarily from Indian casinos that regarded a lottery as a threat. In sum, Conyers had a ringside seat to see the vast power of prosecutors. Therefore, Conyers, ostensibly the nation's leading government watchdog protecting the public from misconduct in the courts, was all bark and no bite. The Senate took even less of a role. The senators approved abuses, cover-up, and the appointments of additional malefactors.

Escaping the Judiciary Committee's spotlight, Rove published his memoir, *Courage and Consequence.* It boasted of his accomplishments and attacked his critics. Rove, employed by Rupert Murdoch's empire as a columnist for the *Wall Street Journal* and commentator on Fox News, skillfully used those outlets to prepare for his next steps. A misstep, however, was his bullying and false claim in a *Journal* column in 2011 that Simpson was too cowardly to make her claims against him under oath.[28] The transcript of Simpson's 2007 testimony under oath and cross-examination is more than 140 pages.[29]

Rove's arrogance reminded me of Machiavelli's advice in Chapter XIX of *The Prince,* entitled, "That We Must Avoid Being Despised and Hated." Further, the great thinker warned against the dangers of conspiracies. He did not claim that conspiracies do not exist, only that participants risk exposure.

In 2010, the 5-4 U.S. Supreme Court decision *Citizen United v. Federal Elections Commission* found that corporations have civil rights comparable to individuals, and thus cannot be restricted any longer by campaign finance law.[30] Stewart Hall, a Rove ally with Alabama roots, promptly created American Crossroads.[31] An affiliate, Crossroads GPS, later provided the benefits of tax-exemption to donors seeking to win elections under IRS rules designed for non-partisan civic groups.[32] The Crossroads fundraising elevates Rove to a unique position of power. He does not simply counsel Republican candidates. He funds them in scope rivaling the Republican National Committee. As a political pundit, Rove was awarded press credentials to the Democratic National Convention, and his opinion is widely sought by all major news organizations.

Globally, Karl Rove and company were active in major countries around the globe on sensitive issues including national intelligence work.[33] For example, I helped break the story that Rove has for years advised the conservative, governing party in Sweden.[34] This is significant in view of Sweden's trumped-up investigation of WikiLeaks founder Julian Assange on claims by two Swedish women who say he crossed their boundaries after they invited him, separately, to sleep with them when he travelled Sweden to speak in 2010.

Sweden spent vast sums to extradite Assange for additional questioning without even formal charges. As feminist Naomi Wolf argues, such a manhunt is unparalleled globally and virtually inexplicable – except for the Swedish government's record of cooperation with the CIA, and the mutual goals of governments and traditional media to thwart unauthorized WikiLeaks revelations. As of this writing, Ecuador has provided Assange refuge in its embassy in London to avoid his extradition to Sweden and potentially from there to the United States.

Further research, however, suggests that the Assange and WikiLeaks stories are far more complicated than commonly believed by either his attackers or fans. He appears to have been an asset of Western intelligence at times in his career, putting into the public domain a mix of approved disinformation along with enough sensational revelations to make him vulnerable as a suspected cyber terrorist.[35] The full story is beyond this book's scope, but is worth exploring more deeply.

Chapter 11

David Petraeus: Revolt of the Generals

David Petraeus was the most honored United States military leader of his time. This chapter describes how Petraeus achieved such eminence, and how his ambitions led to a tragedy far more horrific than the public realized when he resigned as CIA director after the 2012 election.

David Howell Petraeus is shown above with his wife and Vice President Biden during his 2011 CIA installation ceremony. Petraeus was born in 1952 and grew up in Cornwall-on-Hudson. The small town, upstream from New York City on the Hudson River, rests just north of the United States Military Academy at West Point. His father was a Dutch seaman who commanded a Liberty ship in Russian waters during World War II and then immigrated to New York to work for a power company. His mother was a librarian. In a community housing a number of elite families, the future general won an appointment to attend West Point as a cadet.

While there, he married Holly Knowlton, a debutante and the daughter of the four-star general who commanded the academy. They raised two children. Petraeus described his politics as that of a "Rockefeller Republican" in honor of the nation's most financially dominant family. The Rockefeller brand of moderation and internationalism had a particular influence in the Hudson Valley. Kykuit, a hilltop paradise overlooking the river to the south of West Point, housed four generations of Rockefellers after its construction in 1913. Several of the Rockefeller brothers played immense roles in the nation's public life as Petraeus embarked on his military career in 1974. Nelson Rockefeller was the nation's vice president from 1974 to 1977 after serving as New York's governor from 1959 to 1973. Over a varied career, Petraeus developed a specialty in airborne operations. He earned a doctorate in military history at Princeton University. He also overcame two serious injuries from training accidents. The first was a gunshot wound to the chest and the other was a broken pelvis from a parachute jump. Upon recovery, Petraeus thrived into his 50s as a physical fitness buff who could run six-minute miles. In addition, he was a prominent advocate of the military's "spiritual fitness" movement that emphasized thinly disguised Christian fundamentalism.[1]

Petraeus distinguished himself in his first combat command in Iraq in 2003. Colleagues regarded Petraeus as unusually skilled in developing a practical knowledge of Iraq's culture. He trained security forces and helped supervise innovative plans encouraging economic development as a complement to military success. The public received highly positive reports of progress following the invasion.

During that period, my work in advanced technology led me to meet with experts who implemented advanced communications for military and civilian users in post-invasion Iraq, among other war zones and sensitive locales. One conference I organized in Washington, DC in 2005 featured government and private leaders who, for the first time, publicly described how they had built the first nationwide public safety network in Iraq's history.[2] My work also required me to stay up to date regarding concepts such as "Network Centric Warfare," an innovation of the era by which military experts sought to integrate advanced technology to maximize effectiveness.[3] Although I do not claim to be an expert in the field, I did work frequently with those who were. My conclusion was that whatever the wisdom of the U.S. long-term policy for Iraq, Petraeus appears to have been genuinely effective and admired by his peers as he implemented United States goals as directed.

In September 2005, Petraeus left his second duty tour in Iraq to assume command of much of the Army's training at Fort Leavenworth, Kansas. He augmented counter-insurgency techniques and became influential among opinion-leaders in the field. They included well-funded neo-conservatives who had advocated for a war with Iraq since the mid-1990s via their Project for a New American Century. Among them were American Enterprise Institute fellows Frederick Kagan, Richard Perle, and their neighbor in the same building, *Weekly Standard* Editor William Kristol. The same building on 17th Street in Washington housed the two groups PNAC and AEI along with the *Weekly Standard*. "In the fall of 2006, they saw their war in Iraq going down the tubes," wrote military historian Thomas Ricks.[4] Neo-cons influential in Washington believed the solution was more U.S. ground troops under Petraeus command.

In February 2007, the Bush administration promoted Petraeus to become the commanding general of the Multi-National Force in Iraq. He led "The Surge" of troops in Iraq that reduced civil strife during the late stages of the Bush administration from 2007 to September 2008.[5] Conservative, military, Republican, and Washington think-tank circles praised the scholar-warrior especially as he provided success stories that countered increased public disillusionment with the lingering wars in Iraq and Afghanistan. In sum, Petraeus had a rare ability to project a positive image for United States actions in Iraq and Afghanistan.

In October 2008, the Bush administration named Petraeus as the Florida-based commander of the U.S. Central Command (CENTCOM), which oversees U.S. military operations in Afghanistan, Pakistan, Central Asia, the Arabian Peninsula, and Egypt. Petraeus, based in Tampa and travelling frequently, enjoyed renown as the most honored war commander since the era of Joint Chiefs of Staff Chairman Colin Powell, the Desert Storm mastermind, and Allied Commander Norman Schwarzkopf.

Trouble loomed. The danger came via social-climbing twin sisters in Tampa who courted the commander's favor.

General Decorum

To evaluate the Petraeus career, we need to recall the nation's history of civilian leadership of the military. Every trained officer respects the civilian control in theory since the tradition derives from the Constitution, and is taught in the service academies and every other official venue.

That is the theory. In practice, men of war, like others, sometimes have their own ideas. One confrontation occurred during the Civil War when President Lincoln relieved Union commander George B. McClellan of his duties in 1862 for being "overcautious." Two years later, McClellan won the Democratic nomination to challenge Lincoln for the presidency. McClellan lost decisively, 212 electoral votes to 21. Another clash occurred at the turn of the century. As Army commander in the Philippines, General Arthur MacArthur managed to insult three Republican presidents or future presidents by asserting his authority and humiliating presidential envoy William Howard Taft. They relieved him of command in the Philippines and prevented his ascension to Army chief of staff. He and his wife raised a son, Douglas MacArthur, who carried a similar attitude in an illustrious career, and met a similar fate. President Harry Truman, a Democrat, relieved Douglas MacArthur of his posts in 1951 during the Korean War following a pattern of MacArthur's insubordination as supreme Allied commander in the Pacific.[6] The prominent military historian Eliot Cohen praised tradition's value in his *Supreme Command*, a case study of four British and United States civilian leaders who opposed positions of military officers in wartime.[7]

Several trends undermining civilian control come to a head during the Petraeus era. Beginning in the 1990s, presidents with no military combat service tended to duck responsibility for tough decisions by deferring to uniformed decision makers. Another pattern was the contempt that many in the military privately held for Democrats, whose leaders and supporters after the 1960s generally tended to be less supportive than Republicans of wars, military traditions, and defense budgets. Even more explosive was a propaganda campaign by zealots and GOP strategists to demonize (with an undercurrent of racism) Obama as an imposter, a foreigner, and a radical undeserving of the presidency, much as Bill Clinton had been attacked as a "draft dodger." Cohen, a professor at Johns Hopkins University, warned Bush administration civilian leaders, including President Bush, that their military leadership in Iraq was wrong during a December 2006 meeting. The Harvard-educated Cohen had been a founding member of the Project for a New American Century in 1996, and in 2001 he advocated with Iraq and Iran as part of the "World War IV" against terror. Cohen recommended the promotion of David Petraeus as the leader best able to adapt to current conditions.[8]

That both major parties have long sought to recruit military veterans as candidates plays a sort of wild card role. Recently, Republicans have had the greater success cases, including the presidential victories for former Civil War general Ulysses S. Grant and Allied European Commander Dwight D. Eisenhower. Republicans also endured great failures in candidate selection.

Today, the most relevant history repercussion of Republican candidate failure is that of General Douglas MacArthur. GOP supporters of MacArthur (who lived from 1880 to 1964), sought the general's nomination in 1948 to run against Truman. The failed GOP effort prompted enactment of the Uniform Military Code of Justice, which strictly forbids partisan political activity by federal military personnel. Case law and other tradition have since defined the ban as banning non-public expressions of criticism of civilian leaders. Some argue that it also forbids other acts of disloyalty such as entertaining while in service invitations to run for office.

CENTCOM and the Tampa Twins

Petraeus led the U.S. Central Command for nearly two years beginning in October 2008. The command oversaw operations in a score of nations in Asia, the Mideast, and North Africa, and is one of six United States regional unified commands. The headquarters is at MacDill Air Force Base, located on a peninsula in Tampa Bay. Along with the Central Command, the base houses USSOCOM, which oversees Navy SEALS and Army Green Berets. As commander, Petraeus had enormous responsibilities supervising wars in Iraq and Afghanistan while public support was dwindling. He won bipartisan support under those difficult circumstances, in part because he fulfilled the image of warrior-scholar with a successful track record delivering a message popular with power brokers.

His arrival coincided with the ascendancy of a family of social climbers who found great opportunities in the powerful but transient leadership of the base. The prime movers were Jill Kelley and her identical twin sister, Natalie Khawam. They were born in 1975 in Lebanon to a Catholic family of Syrian background that moved to the Philadelphia area when the girls were young. The parents were of modest means. Jill, whose birth name was Gilberte Khawam, married surgeon Scott Kelley. In 2008, Natalie, an attorney, married Grayson Wolfe, a Washington-based attorney who had been a prominent aide to United States leadership in Iraq. Wolfe had been a member of Paul Bremer's staff managing procurement in Iraq for the Coalition Provisional Authority in 2003. Wolfe reported to Bremer aide Dan Senor, who is the husband of former CNN anchor Campbell Brown. Senor, well-connected in Israeli and neo-con circles, would become the top foreign policy advisor in 2012 to the Romney campaign.

In the period after the Iraq invasion and as the Central Command's importance grew, Kelley and her husband became high-profile social enablers at MacDill. They threw lavish parties in public, and ran up huge debts in private. To the public eye, the events welcomed distinguished military leaders to the community, fostered better civic relations, relieved stress, and raised the profile of worthy causes, including a cancer-fighting charity run by the Kelleys. Their social friends included Central Command leaders John Abizaid and John Allen, and others at the highest levels. As is often the case, the social scene involved ambitious defense contractors and political operatives seeking to ingratiate themselves and their causes. Kelley won a "Friends of MacDill" government designation that allowed her access to the base and received the title of "honorary counsel" from the Republic of Korea. She was an unpaid volunteer, but one reputedly interested in a "finder's fee" for suitable introductions.

Petraeus enjoyed the pomp that came from his status and four-star lifestyle. For one party in 2010, he used a 28-motorcycle escort to travel six miles from the base in Tampa to the Kelley home.[9] His wife, Holly Petraeus, is a *summa cum laude* college graduate who complements her husband's positive image. The Obama administration named her to new position helping military families during times of stress.[10]

The Petraeus and Kelley couples sometimes socialized together with Natalie, who lived in a cottage on the Kelley property with her son after a bitter divorce. As a mark of their close relationship, Natalie obtained a letter of recommendation from David Petraeus to use in her unsuccessful custody battle. In 2011, the commander also arranged for the Joint Chiefs of Staff to award Jill Kelley the military's second-highest civilian medal for her work hosting emissaries from 60 nations.

Town and Country magazine portrayed the twins as social climbers, nicknamed "The Kartampians" by disapproving local matrons. According to the article, they manipulated Petraeus and other top military officers as gullible stooges at best. "Sisters Jill Kelley and Natalie Khawam invaded

Tampa society like twin buccaneers," wrote Vicky Ward. "They were hilariously over-the-top, stars of their own imaginary reality show. But as they climbed ever higher, the revelations became ever more disturbing...."[11]

A Congressman's Protest

In the fall of 2009, New York Congressman Eric Massa faced an ethical dilemma regarding Petraeus worthy of a *Mr. Smith Goes To Washington* dramatic treatment. At the time, Massa was not yet a year into his first term as a Democrat representing an upstate New York district. Massa, a graduate of the U.S. Naval Academy, had served 24 years as a naval officer. Massa became an aide to Army General Wesley Clark, who was NATO's supreme Allied commander from 1997 until retirement in 2000. Massa, a former Republican who became a critic of the Iraq war, was elected in 2008 to a Republican-leaning district stretching from Corning north to Rochester.

This is Massa's account, provided to me in several interviews during 2012.[12] Massa described his ill-fated effort to exercise congressional oversight on several issues including confidential complaints from uniformed officers about Petraeus:

In September 2009, four generals informed Massa that Petraeus had twice met with former GOP Vice President Dick Cheney. They discussed Cheney's suggestion that Petraeus compete in a weak field for the 2012 GOP nomination to oppose President Obama's re-election. The generals and Massa regarded even the discussion of such a candidacy as illegal under military law and arguably as treasonous for a commander in wartime because a battlefield commander has an especially sensitive role. Massa says his former boss, Wesley Clark, scrupulously avoided political conversations while in the military. Clark unsuccessfully ran for the presidency as a Democrat in 2004.

Massa was reluctant to criticize the popular Petraeus. Massa was a freshman congressman trying to focus on local issues and had no leadership clout. The generals, however, persuaded him to move forward as a patriotic duty because of his military background. Massa complied, and complained to Pentagon officials that same month in September 2009, while declining to name his informants. Pentagon officials were non-committal, but a civilian Defense Department appointee threatened Massa's congressional career for bringing forward such unwelcome allegations against Petraeus, who was extremely popular on a bipartisan basis in Washington for leadership of "The Surge" in Iraq that staved off U.S. withdrawal past the end of the Bush-Cheney administration.

Massa pressed on. Beginning in December 2009, he confided his concerns to *Esquire* Magazine. Meanwhile, Massa showed an independent streak unbecoming freshman on several other matters undercutting positions of his party's leadership. In November 2009, he voted with the Republican minority in 220-215 against the president's Affordable Health Care Act. Massa stood almost alone in either party to base his vote on the bill's lack of a public option, a progressive position. His opposition to the bill potentially endangered the narrow, largely party-line passage of the president's main domestic policy priority scheduled for the following spring.[13]

Massa argued several other policy positions that made him a pest to leaders in both parties.[14]

In late February 2010, the married Massa became the centerpiece of a bizarre series of allegations that he had made a lewd comment to a male staffer at the end of a widely-attended wedding party. Congressional Democratic leadership launched an ethics investigation, which was accompanied by many news reports on the allegations.

Massa, a then-50-year-old cancer survivor, cited health reasons initially in resigning his seat in March 2010. This ended the ethics investigation. His resignation came before the final health legislation vote, a reconciliation of House and Senate versions, and before *Esquire* published his allegations against Petraeus.[15] With Massa by then out of Congress, *Esquire* published a report that discredited Massa with a headline suggesting that he was "insane."[16] The coverage also included a denial via a spokesman that Petraeus had ever engaged in political activity forbidden by military law. Conventional wisdom in Washington was – and remains – that Massa must have done something terrible in his personal life to have merited such disgrace.

Yet the allegations against Massa raised more questions about his main accuser and the removal process than about the Congressman. Massa asserted his innocence to the House ethics and employment officials, arguing that a disloyal top staffer of homosexual inclinations and close connections to Democratic leadership trashed his credibility and orchestrated his removal. My review of the allegations and a hundred pages of related correspondence suggest that the charges against Massa were trumped up, especially in comparison with the significant evidence that almost never surfaces implicating other members of Congress in sex overtures to staff, consorting with prostitutes, and other debauchery. In sum, it appears that someone apparently targeted Massa in early 2010 in a massive hit campaign prompted by still-unknown reasons.

The Massa takedown thus illustrates a theme throughout this book. Elected representatives, far from being independent watchdogs, face reprisal if they dig into sensitive areas aside from occasional interludes of partisan *kabuki* theater on safe, narrow issues orchestrated by leadership. Executive Branch authorities can access congressional communications in almost undetectable ways without a warrant, just as they can retrieve emails and phone calls made by other citizens. Elected representatives risk disgrace or worse because many can be accused of fund-raising violations or sexual misconduct. Dossiers and blackmail did not go out of fashion with J. Edgar Hoover's death. Hoover's success merely showcased the effectiveness of the tool.

By mid-2010, Massa and his warnings about Petraeus had vanished from Washington as if they never existed.

Hero of the Afghan Surge

In June 2010, President Obama nominated Petraeus to succeed General Stanley McChrystal as commanding general of United States and NATO forces in Afghanistan. McChrystal resigned because a magazine profile portrayed him and aides mocking Obama administration civilian leaders.[17] Petraeus generated a can-do attitude in assuming command in Afghanistan. He fostered a mutually beneficial relationship with Washington thought leaders, especially pro-war neo-cons funded by the defense industry. The war industry helped fund many influential political and media leaders. The *Washington Post* is one of many influential news organizations that are heavily dependent on government contracts. Contractor ads in the media are one visible indicator of the deeper relationships surveyed in this book's "Cold War" chapter. More subtle and more important are more lucrative financial ties, such as the defense contracting business of the parent companies of the non-Fox television networks, ABC, CBS, and NBC, and the *Post's* Kaplan education affiliate that has provided nearly 60 percent of its revenue in recent year.

Soon after Petraeus assumed command in Afghanistan, the husband-and-wife team of Frederick and Kimberly Kagan obtained extraordinary status as embedded volunteer workers for Petraeus for nearly a year in Afghanistan. The two civilian military analysts were paid by their influential Washington think tanks to use top-level security clearances in Kabul to examine classified intelligence reports.[18] They "participated in senior-level strategy sessions and probed the assessments of field officers in order to advise Petraeus about how to fight the war differently," according to a 2002 report by the *Washington Post*.[19] The paper frequently published the Kagan pro-war columns and employed as a columnist Robert Kagan, Fred's brother. In effect, the Kagans were paid by war contractors who funded their think tank jobs. The Kagans had advocated for an invasion of Iraq as early as 1996, when they co-signed the Project for a New American Century manifesto calling for war. Petraeus and his policies became heroes of the right thanks to such initiatives. As the *Post* reported, long after the fact, "The extraordinary arrangement raises new questions about the access and influence Petraeus accorded to civilian friends while he was running the Afghan war."

The manner in which powerbrokers and their emissaries network with active duty military officers when useful is illustrated in a conversation between Fox News contributor Kathleen "KT" McFarland and Petraeus. McFarland approached Petraeus in Afghanistan for a private meeting in his office. McFarland was a former White House aide from 1970 to 1976 to National Security Advisor Henry Kissinger, among her other GOP posts. She offered Petraeus support from Fox News Chairman Roger Ailes for Petraeus either to lead the Joint Chiefs of Staff or run against Obama in the GOP 2012 presidential primaries taking shape that year.[20]

In the 90-minute conversation, McFarland said that Ailes might resign his Fox job to manage a Petraeus presidential campaign. [21] McFarland and Petraeus spoke also about the possibility that News Corp. Chairman Rupert Murdoch might "bankroll" the campaign. Petraeus declined the offers, saying he preferred to become Obama's CIA director. The president offered the job, and the Senate confirmed Petraeus for the CIA post in June 2011.

The McFarland-Petraeus conversation parallels the kind of warning that Massa, the congressman, had tried to raise previously.

Prelude To Scandal

Virtually all successful professionals network to advance their careers. The game is to curry favor with superiors and other power brokers early on. A leader must also develop trusted followers, and remain accessible to opportunities and to those who make them available, sometimes in devious ways. Unofficial contacts often begin innocently enough by a chance meeting at a professional lecture or a VIP reception, where smiles and business cards are exchanged.

Such was the case in 2006, when West Point graduate and Harvard grad student Paula Broadwell spoke to Petraeus after he delivered a lecture at the school. Evidence of romantic interest was reputedly available at that time to military colleagues.[22] Whatever the case on that, Broadwell persuaded the general to take a professional interest in her research. The married mother of two sons later became his biographer, *de facto* publicist, and running partner.

Born Paula Kranz, she had been a high school valedictorian, homecoming queen, and all-state basketball star growing up in Bismarck, North Dakota's capital city. She won an appointment to be a West Point cadet. During her military career, she focused on intelligence, especially regarding the Mideast. She experienced kibbutz life on a study program, and also studied Arab culture and language. She married Scott Broadwell after meeting him in 2000 when they were both active duty captains. She obtained a master's degree at the University of Denver's Korbel School of International Relations, and pursued graduate studies at Harvard. She obtained a Harvard master's degree and enrolled at Kings College in the United Kingdom after Harvard required her departure for failure to meet its coursework standards.[23]

She persuaded Petraeus to entrust her with his vision and confidences for her doctoral thesis. With the cooperation of her husband, she travelled to Afghanistan as an embedded journalist and landed a book contract. *Washington Post* editor Vernon Loeb performed much of the grunt work as co-author while she maintained access to Petraeus, in part as his partner in his rigorous running regimen.

In Afghanistan, she and Petraeus raised eyebrows among both United States and foreign leaders by her unusual access to him. Petraeus brought an "intriguing" young woman, presumed to be Broadwell, with him to a dinner with Yemen's ambassador to the United States at one event in early 2010, according to an investigation by Douglas Lucas and Russ Baker with the assistance of WikiLeaks. The Texas-based private intelligence consultancy Stratfor undertook extensive analysis and gossip with clients in emails later hijacked by hackers and published by WikiLeaks.[24] The timing of the beginning of an affair is significant. A documented affair before Petraeus retired from command in mid-2011 would be punishable as a crime. Also, an affair in a war zone raises dangers of blackmail or other intrigue, especially if known not simply by a private intelligence firm selling information to clients but also by a foreign power.

Meanwhile, Broadwell worked as a goodwill ambassador to a variety of audiences. As a model for the machine gun manufacturer KRISS Arms, for example, she provided sexy glamour for their deadly products.[25] As co-author of a biography of Petraeus, she could polish his image and advance in his reflected glory. In January 2012, she published her book, *All In*. She embarked on the lecture and talk show circuit as a proselytizer of the Petraeus story, most notably regarding his military successes in Iraq and Afghan Wars. Neo-con and Republican circles especially were happy to hear positive news about the wars. She told friends that she hoped to challenge Senator Kay Hagen, a Democrat, for North Carolina's U.S. Senate seat in 2014. Working the circuit, Broadwell, a lieutenant colonel in the Army Reserves, posed in uniform with Karl Rove in a break from their appearances at the National Conference of State Legislators, the main organization of the country's state legislators.

That spring, Broadwell moved into action against Jill Kelley. Broadwell used basic spycraft precautions to disguise her identity. In emails with the ominous inscription "Kelley Patrol," Broadwell warned Kelley to stay away from Petraeus. Broadwell also sent General John

Allen, a former second-in-command to Petraeus, a warning about Kelley. Broadwell described Kelley as the Tampa "seductress."[26] This was merely the prelude to the real drama.

.

Chapter 12

Michael Leavitt: On a Mission from God

Years ago, George Romney and hotel tycoon J. Willard Marriott served together on a Mormon Church commission to improve the church's image.[1] They doubtless suggested that the church groom moderate political leaders of proven loyalty to the church for display. The prototype is a leader much like Mitt Romney, his close ally Mike Leavitt, the transition director for a Romney presidency.[2]

In June 2012, Romney appointed Leavitt, a fellow Mormon and Utah's three-term former governor, to recommend presidential appointees during a transition period after November's elections.[3] This made Leavitt the front-runner to become chief of staff. With a wide array of duties, chief of staff can be an administration's most powerful post below the presidency.[4] Leavitt's appointment received positive coverage.[5] The corporate-owned news media have long accepted Leavitt at face value as a civic-minded expert.

In reality, Leavitt threatened the public. Leavitt was cut from the same cloth as Romney. They were not simply proud of their shared background, but seemingly wanted to replicate it throughout the government, which might be regarded as a minor affectation if they confined their pride to church or other private realms. Instead, Leavitt and Romney wanted to select the personnel and policies for the government of a diverse nation. Their conceit was dangerous. The religion was founded on principles of divine revelation to leaders, male supremacy, racism, and secrecy. It was based also on the supremacy of church over state, ends-justify-the-means ideology, and deep hostility toward the United States government.

Leavitt usually appointed a Mormon as his top aide. As Utah's governor, he required the state's top officials to include LDS teachings in government work. In several of his government posts, he schemed to perpetrate and gross financial irregularities to help himself, his family, and his cronies. Leavitt's record reflects badly on him, but also on Romney for failing to understand, even during a campaign, why naming cronies from his church raises concern.

This chapter reveals these problems in detail. It shows why the church's history is vital to understanding Romney and what his administration would have been like. The focus here is primarily on four men. Two of the men are the church's founding prophets, Joseph Smith and Brigham Young. They created the religion via divine revelations. The other two men are Michael Leavitt and Mitt Romney. They are the devout followers inspired by a religion whose history and central teachings combine church and state in ways foreign to mainstream constitutional history.

Romney and Leavitt aspired to hold the federal government's top two offices.[6] Both Romney and Leavitt have namesake ancestors prominently supporting the prophets Smith and Young in controversies that have counterparts today. The religion's founders are far from ancient figures. The founders have direct ties through their descendants and the institutions that created modern America.[7]

Before I recount the specifics, here is a brief reader guide. It is not my intention to distract from current events by providing full portraits of historic figures, including the positive traits that leaders tend to have. This chapter's endnotes suggest further reading on that. For the purposes of this chapter, newcomers to LDS should know that Mormon theology entails divine revelations to leaders in modern times. These sometimes eliminate previous mandates, such as those for polygamy and racial bias. The doctrine has the effect of creating top-down, secretive, unpredictable, and unaccountable decision making that is more appropriate for governing a church than a nation.

My research has elicited suggestions that I emphasize how many upstanding, civic-minded, family-oriented LDS church members exist around the country, and around the world. That is true, of course.[8] Yet the relationship of equals in a community is fundamentally different from that of ruler and governed. In the study, *America's Saints: The Rise of Mormon Power*, two social critics praised the LDS religion and its typical adherents. Yet the authors also explored higher-level decision making, such as the church's massive real-estate operations[9] and remarkable, almost obsessive emphasis on secrecy.[10]

Introducing Michael Leavitt

Like Romney, Leavitt is a crony capitalist, elitist heir, and loyal Bushie. His track record shows how he favors agendas helping puppet masters: loot the government, lower taxes on the rich, gut social programs, and waste money on war mongering. In sum, he would have helped Romney recreate the disastrous Bush era, except with more benefits flowing to coffers in Utah than under Bush.

Regarding the basics: Michael Leavitt served as Utah's governor from 1993 to 2003. He obtained his first Bush cabinet appointment as head of the Environmental Protection Administration, from 2003 to 2005. Leavitt was secretary of the Health and Human Services Department from January 26, 2005 to January 20, 2009. This encompassed virtually every day of the second George W. Bush administration. The HHS budget is the federal government's largest, exceeding (so far as the public knows) even that of the Defense Department. As shown below, Leavitt managed the department in a disgraceful manner that boded poorly for any larger responsibilities.

Michael Okerlund "Mike" Leavitt was born in 1951 in Cedar City, Utah. His ancestors include Thomas Dudley, the second colonial governor of Massachusetts, and Dudley Leavitt, one of the first Mormon pioneers in Utah arriving with Prophet Brigham Young.[11] Mike Leavitt spent six years in the Utah National Guard during the Vietnam War, with no reported Vietnam service.[12] He graduated from Southern Utah University in 1973 with a bachelor's degree in economics. His first job was with the Leavitt Group, a regional insurance company founded by his father, Dixie Leavitt, a Republican politician. Michael Leavitt expanded the company as president and CEO, and served on several influential business and university boards.

In 1992, he won election as Utah's governor. Voters gave him high margins in two re-elections. In 2002, the Winter Olympics scheduled for Salt Lake City faced a financial and public relations disaster after host officials were caught bribing other officials. To rescue the games, Leavitt orchestrated the appointment of Mitt Romney to lead the host committee.[13]

Leavitt's successes obscure the traits that should have disqualified him from being Romney's top aide. The track record shows that Leavitt has been a self-righteous self-server who has deplored the federal government while using it to help friends, supporters, relatives, and himself. Perhaps it is merely coincidence, but Leavitt's religion arose from leaders who distrusted, despised, and plotted against the United States. His ancestors and their religious leaders sought a grand alliance with the Confederate states against the Union, in hopes of a political map with a striking resemblance to today's Red-Blue divisions. Here is the background:

A Brief LDS History

In the 1820s, the tall, handsome, self-educated, and charismatic young Joseph Smith found a way to avoid many of the dreary rigors of farm work and canal digging in upstate New York. He persuaded his family and neighbors that he possessed supernatural powers which allowed him to locate gold and other treasure buried by Native Americans, whom he described as descendants of the Lost Tribes of Israel.

Authoritative books and a vast array of newspaper clippings document the account that follows. The research is indebted to the work of the historian Fawn Brodie in her 1945 biography of Joseph Smith, *No Man Knows My History*. The title comes from one of the prophet's last and most eloquent speeches, in which he says of his life, "If I had not experienced what I have, I could not have believed it myself." Here is part of that remarkable story, still vitally important today to Mormon and non-Mormon alike: [14]

Among many contemporary reports about Smith, Brodie cites an 1826 judicial verdict against him in Bainbridge, New York on criminal charges of "disorderly conduct" and "imposture" for charging gullible neighbors to tell them where to dig for treasure after he consulted his "magic stone."[15] Smith courted Emma Hale, the daughter of Isaac Hale. The father regarded Smith as a "cheap imposter."[16] Smith reputedly wed Emma by frightening her at age 23 with the threat of damnation if she did not elope with him.

Eight months later, the couple visited Emma's family. "You have stolen my daughter and married her," Isaac shouted to Smith in tears, according to a witness. "I had much rather followed her to her grave. You spend your time digging for money, and pretending to see in a stone – and thus try to deceive people."[17] Smith reputedly confessed he never had supernatural powers to know where money was buried.

Smith, after abandoning magic, increasingly focused on religion, including his announcement that an angel had shown him secret golden plates revealing a hidden religious history of the continent. In 1830, Smith obtained funds from a follower to publish *The Book of Mormon*. The book became popular. It combined evangelical excitement of the era with then-widespread fascination with discoveries of Native American artifacts in New York and of ancient scrolls in Egypt under British colonial rule.

In founding a new, America-centric religion, Smith described revelations based on a language called "reformed Egyptian," which no one but he could read.[18] The revelations described the migration of Israelis to America, and the death of their noble leader, the fair-skinned Mormon, at the hands of dark-skinned tribes who spawned modern Native Americans.[19] Smith's *Book of Mormon* and his other revelations established himself as prophet of a religion that built on traditional Biblical texts and popular ceremonies, including some that were similar to Freemason rites. Smith said that Jesus once lived in North America and would return for new resurrection in northwest Missouri. LDS members called the holy site Zion, near the current locale of Independence.

From the first, Smith's accounts attracted enthusiastic followings, as well as critics who called him a con man, adulterer, liar, counterfeiter, bank fraudster, and traitor to the United States. Smith persuaded his flock to move from New York to Kirtland, Ohio, east of current Cleveland. There he founded, among other entities, the Kirtland Safety Savings Society, a bank falsely claiming $4 million in assets while possessing just a few thousand dollars. Because the institution printed its own currency without a required state charter for institutions issuing bank notes, Smith cleverly called the money "anti-bank" notes to escape regulation. The bank crashed, making the notes worthless. This angered both victims and authorities.[20] At the suggestion of an eloquent convert, preacher Sidney Rigdon, they changed their religion's formal name to the Church of the Latter-day Saints (LDS) in order to avoid what they regarded as hated nickname, "Mormonites." However, the "Mormon" name has lingered almost interchangeably through the years.

Smith led his followers to Missouri to build communities to await the return of Jesus, which they predicted would occur in 1836. The region was so remote that it adjoined the vast Indian Territory extending west, beginning at the border of what became Kansas. In frontier conditions, the LDS soon encountered renewed controversy. Issues included Mormon land-acquisition and suspected polygamy. Smith organized a vigilante militia, the Danites. Professing a need for self-protection against bias, Danites fought other settlers.[21]

As part of the "The Mormon War of 1838," Missouri militia gunned down 15 Mormons who took refuge in a blacksmith's shop. "Nits will make lice," commented one militiaman before shooting a nine-year-old discovered hiding under a bellows in the head. In 1838, a militia general demanded that Mormons hand over the leaders, including Smith and Mitt Romney's ancestor Parley Pratt, to face treason charges.

Missouri's governor, Lilburn Boggs, issued an order requiring all other Mormons to leave the state or face execution and property seizure.[22] Smith and his followers escaped to Illinois and built a vibrant community in Nauvoo on a site overlooking the Mississippi River. In 1841, Smith prophesized that Boggs would meet a violent death within a year. Among the faithful, Smith's supernatural powers as a prophet were fortified when Boggs was left for dead in 1842 after being shot three times in the head by an unknown assailant. Further details from Fawn Brodie's research follow:[23]

John C. Bennett, a physician and onetime close ally of Smith, accused the prophet of the Boggs shooting via Porter Rockwell, Smith's notoriously tough bodyguard. Missouri authorities filed charges of attempted murder against Smith and Rockwell, but were never successful in asserting jurisdiction across state lines in Nauvoo.

Often in hiding during this period, Smith consolidated his power in Nauvoo by ousting Bennett from LDS leadership. Smith forced Bennett to sign a confession of wrongdoing at gunpoint. Bennett's many offices had included Nauvoo mayor, assistant president of the LDS church, brigadier-general of the Nauvoo Legion, chancellor of Nauvoo University, the chief LDS lobbyist to the state legislature in Springfield, and secretary of the LDS Masonic lodge. Smith and Bennett had made Nauvoo's Masonic chapter the state's largest, with 286 membership candidates within six months of creation. This membership exceeded the entire Freemason membership in the rest of Illinois — and horrified the state's other Masonic leaders, who kept the membership process selective in their lodges.

Yet Smith and Bennett had seen the opportunity to weave Masonic-style secret rituals into Mormon pageantry in ways that proved highly popular. The plan was brilliant in its own way. The recruitment policy provided the core LDS audience with the prestige of the Masonic membership and culture while persuading them that the similar LDS rites were even more authentic. Smith told his followers that their rites stemmed directly from Old Testament traditions and that faithful followers could advance to paradise. The secret rites involving temple garments, or sacred under-garments, came to the forefront during this period.[24]

Bennett, for all his titles, was a crass opportunist, especially in contrast to the elegant Smith. The prophet customarily dressed in a blue general's uniform with a sword and two long-barreled horse pistols on his hip. The foot-long pistols were so heavy that most men using them holstered them only on their horses, not on the waist. Smith enjoyed the ceremonies of his posts, and was hospitable to Nauvoo visitors, either friends or skeptics.

Contemporary authors argue that Bennett, whose medical practice included abortions, had been highly promiscuous, and reckless in failing to cloak his philandering with religious rhetoric. The break between Bennett and Smith occurred in 1842 as the two onetime close friends competed for the affections of Nancy Rigdon. She was the 19-year-old daughter of Sidney Rigdon, a righteous LDS leader who had been one of Ohio's top revivalists when he joined the younger Smith's church back in Kirtland. Sidney Rigdon was horrified to read Smith's letter to his daughter describing the importance of happiness in God's plan. Smith explained that he was merely testing the daughter's virtue. Bennett, angered by ex-communication and exile from Nauvoo, countered with a series of claims against Smith published in a Springfield newspapers and then in a book.[25] Bennett said he merely pretended to ally himself with Smith in order to undertake the research necessary for an exposé. Bennett accused Smith of being a murderer, swindler, and con man. The allegations proved to be so extreme that they rallied the faithful even more to the prophet.

1844: The First Mormon Presidential Campaign

Smith campaigned for the U.S. presidency in 1844 in hopes of adding that office to his titles as prophet, general, and King of the Kingdom of God. He wanted, among other things, to expand his private army to create a Mormon-run theistic empire through most of what is now the Western United States. Nauvoo became one of the largest cities in Illinois, populated in part by LDS converts from England. The emigrants included Mitt Romney's great-great grandfather, Miles A. Romney, an expert carpenter who became a strong supporter of Smith.

As part of the prophet's presidential campaign, he called for the federal government to confer enough funding for a huge army under Smith that would rule the Indian and Mexican territories from the Rio Grande region in what is now Texas north and west through what is now Oregon upon him and fellow LDS leaders. Some followers claim that Smith issued what came to be known as "The White Horse" prophecy, a prediction that an LDS leader would govern lands from the Atlantic to the Pacific. The church has denied that prophecy.[26]

During the 1844 presidential campaign, Dr. Robert Foster, a prominent LDS leader, caught his wife being wooed by Smith with his longstanding "plural marriage" vision. As indicated in the Rigdon tale, the secret practice by Smith, Bennett, and certain other LDS leaders was to persuade females as young as fifteen to demonstrate their faith by secret, carnal marriage rites. They courted these "brides" with promises of eternal bliss. They threatened those who failed to comply with eternal perdition. The LDS tradition of assigning large numbers of men away on missionary trips, sometimes as far as New York or London, left stay-at-home women lonely or otherwise vulnerable.

Foster became infuriated that his wife had been so courted by Smith. He joined with several other prominent Nauvoo Mormons to found the *Nauvoo Expositor*, a newspaper whose first issue exposed debauchery and other corruption by LDS leaders. In response, Smith persuaded the city to authorize the Mormon Danite forces to destroy the newspaper's printing press and burn the newspaper's only edition. The apostates fled to nearby towns. Foster, like Bennett before him, wrote that Smith had used his bodyguard to shoot Missouri's former governor, Boggs. Missouri authorities never solved that crime.

Tensions ran high in Nauvoo and surrounding communities after the newspaper allegations. Illinois authorities stepped in, jailing Smith and his brother Hyrum on charges of rioting. The makeshift jail was in Carthage, outside Nauvoo. Some gentiles were furious at Mormons for political and business reasons, aside from religion and polygamy. They regarded Smith as a tyrant and his supporters as anti-democratic because of their campaign tactics. One was Smith's adroit use of "block-voting" by Mormons in Illinois elections to win special deals for his followers. Meanwhile, Smith's followers, such as the Romneys, regarded their leaders as holy men voicing the word of God.

The militiamen defied orders from the state's governor, and broke into the Cathage jail on June 27, 1844. The Smith brothers, each armed with one pistol that had been smuggled into the jail, fought impossible odds. The militia gunned down Hyrum. Joseph fired back with all six of his shots. He was shot in the back as he tried to escape by jumping from a second-story window. Militiamen killed the dazed prophet with a fusillade while he lay wounded on the ground.

A delegation of Smith's followers, unaware of his death, formally nominated him for the United States presidency at a convention in Boston shortly afterward, with Sidney Rigdon as the vice presidential nominee.

Smith's Fellow Elder, Brigham Young, won a succession struggle against several others, including Smith's son, Joseph III. Smith's son returned to Missouri to lead a small group, the Reorganized Branch of LDS. Smith's widow, Emma Smith, remarried to an unbeliever, and always denied that her late husband had been a polygamist.[27]

A superb organizer, Young led most of the flock west from Illinois in 1847 to what became Utah, which was then part of Mexico. The pioneers, including the Romneys, reestablished the church in isolation on the frontier. Young inspired them by glorifying Smith, the Book of Mormon, and his own divine revelations. As a prophet, Young extolled polygamy, impugned blacks as descendants of the devil, and preached that non-Mormons left behind in the United States were unworthy of salvation.[28] He sought *de facto* independent status for his isolated community. The region became part of the expanse of territory Mexico ceded to the United States in 1848.

Meanwhile, the Mormon tradition of missionary work produced especially strong numbers of converts in the crowded slums of Britain. Missionaries helped arrange cheap passage to the open spaces of the United States. The British government condoned the missions to reduce population pressures and augment its presence in North America after losing two wars to United States. The LDS faith took hold also in Britain. Mormons numbered 35,000 in the United Kingdom by 1852 compared to 60,000 in the entire Utah territory.[29]

Meanwhile, the 1856 platform of the newly created Republican Party denounced polygamy and slavery as "the twin relics of barbarism."[30] In Utah, the Mormon colony under Young grew rebellious against such criticism. Young was pro-slavery, and regarded the United States government as a rival to an emerging LDS inland empire.

The Meadows Massacre

Brigham Young fostered a distinctive Mormon style of top-down, church-state governance. Young proudly announced polygamy as official church doctrine and fostered a long history of race bias against African Americans, who were barred from full church participation until 1978.[31] He and other LDS leaders plotted for a Confederate victory, which they foresaw providing maximum opportunity for Mormon growth.

The history of antagonism between Mormons and others led Mormon leaders in 1857 to authorize the massacre of a wagon train comprised of 140 pioneers, primarily from Arkansas. The pioneers, many from families named Fancher or Baker, travelled through Utah with 1,000 head of cattle, 200 horses, and a reputed $100,000 in cash. A band of Mormons disguised as Paiute Indians recruited actual Paiute as accomplices to plunder the goods. The attackers pounced as the settlers camped at Mountain Meadows, near the Santa Clara River in southern Utah.

Most Paiute fled after the settlers fought back with expert sharpshooting. The Saints then tricked the settlers into surrender and killed an estimated 120 men, women, and children in cold-blood. The killers spared 17 children under the age of five. The children were considered too young to be effective witnesses and were useful as Mormon-reared converts to help populate the frontier.[32] Author Jon Krakauer, like several other historians, implicates Mike Leavitt's ancestor, Dudley Leavitt, as a participant in the atrocity.[33]

The Meadows Massacre and refusal of Mormon leaders to investigate prompted decades of public outcry from the states back east, especially those in the North and the Arkansas-Missouri region. The Civil War temporarily diverted Union attentions.[34]

Polygamy and recruitment by missionaries helped Mormons expand their numbers south into Mexico and north into Oregon, Montana and Lower Canada. In 1867, Brigham Young ordered Miles P. Romney, son of the first Romneys in the United States, to join the church and help to expand it by taking a second wife. The prophet later appointed Romney, great-grandfather of the 2012 candidate, to lead Mormon advocacy to Congress to legitimize polygamy.[35]

Local and national resentments festered against the Mormons, even after the horrors of the Civil War. The reunified United States sought LDS compliance with federal law banning polygamy. Authorities also sought to prosecute LDS leaders for the 1857 Meadows Massacre. Mormons also faced hostility from non-Mormons in Arizona and other Western states appalled at polygamy. One Arizona newspaper urged its community to rise up and hang Miles Romney. He subsequently fled to Mexico in 1885. Three of his four wives and their children joined him.[36]

The more serious problem for Mormon leaders, especially as they considered the benefits of statehood, was continuing resentment back East over the Meadows Massacre and the rebellious, religious fanaticism it represented. Federal authorities sought justice to placate a fired-up public. As appeasement, Brigham Young secretly helped federal authorities convict in 1876 his adopted son, John Lee, commander of the attack. Lee, who had been a Smith bodyguard in Nauvoo, was the only person charged or convicted for the murders. Before a firing squad executed Lee in 1877, he wrote *Mormonism Unveiled*, which became a national best seller. Lee argued that he was a scapegoat for others, including Young.[37]

The continued notoriety of the 1857 massacre and rumors of greed and misogyny by LDS leaders helped prompt the young physician Arthur Conan Doyle to publish the first Sherlock Holmes mystery in 1887. "A Study in Scarlet" portrayed Sherlock Holmes as a brilliant, civic-minded private detective able to solve the London murder of a brutal Mormon. In the story, the victim had fled Utah in an unsuccessful effort to escape revenge after he forcibly married a young woman, confiscated her property, and murdered her father.[38] Much to the alarm of LDS leaders, the fictional Sherlock Holmes story captured popular imagination on both sides of the Atlantic, helping spawn a new literary genre: private detectives who fight villainy.

From Frontier to Statehood

In 1890, LDS Church President Wilford Woodruff, a successor to Young and an LDS minister in Ohio as early as 1833, issued a "Manifesto" renouncing the doctrine of polygamy.[39] Woodruff, with seven wives and 33 children, had lived in hiding from federal marshals for years. The U.S. marshals customarily prosecuted LDS men on charges of "cohabitating" rather than charges of polygamy, which were more difficult to prove. Woodruff's revelation created a schism. Mormon fundamentalists have continued to advocate polygamy into modern times. A small number of fanatics have occasionally turned to kidnapping, incest, and child rape.[40] The 1890 manifesto, however, helped to enable Utah's statehood in 1896.

Miles Romney, Mitt's great-grandfather, was still living in Mexico after his flight to escape federal marshals in 1885. Romney lived in Colonia Juárez, a valley 90 miles south of Mexico's Arizona border.[41] Seven years after the Manifesto, Miles took a fourth wife (not counting the one who had divorced him) in a household totaling 30 children.[42] Mitt Romney's grandfather, Gaskell, had just one wife, Anna. Her son, George, was born in Mexico. He would run for the United States presidency in 1968 with little question about his eligibility. George Romney's experience contrasts to the frequent questions about Barack Obama's eligibility. The difference suggests race-based animosity against Obama, as well as increased ability of well-funded political manipulators to create bogus issues. In 1912, Gaskell Romney's family was among about 2,300 of the 4,000 Mormon settlers from the United States to abandon the Colonia Juárez region of Mexico when threatened by Mexican revolutionaries.[43]

Prophet Joseph Smith's vision of an LDS church-state government across the continent remained relevant to modern times. The titles and ambitions that Smith assumed indicated his vision of a unified power centralized in one leader who would have minimal oversight by councils of church oligarchs. Smith and Young, as prophets, readily dismissed and even exiled members of the oligarchy. To be sure, the faithful remained confident that God oversaw the process, and communicated directly with the prophets and other elders. Nevertheless, a governance system handled largely by prophets hearing directly from God necessarily relied less on the constitutional and other temporal traditions developed elsewhere in the new nation.

Mitt Romney, a bishop in the Mormon Church for 10 years, and other LDS leaders argued during the 2012 campaign that their faith was irrelevant to their goals in building strong communities and a strong country. Furthermore, they insisted that their faith and its history were off limits for any discussion during the campaign. Yet the history recounted here is recent by the standards of major religions, and was undertaken by founders of the church to which Romney, Leavitt, and others owe not simply their total allegiance, but their hope of salvation.

One troublesome trait for the general public is the religion's extreme focus on moneymaking, often with a rationale that "ends justify the means". This is apparent both historically and in the news reports during the 2012 campaign. Deferential as reporters might be about Romney's faith, they constantly reported about his methods at Bain Capital, his secret tax shelters and tax returns, and his policy plans to protect the wealthy in tandem with his running mate, Ryan.[44]

True, the Mormon tradition has produced vast numbers of industrious, law-abiding citizens who have created better lives for themselves, their families and communities by hard work and creativity and, one could rightfully argue, more than a proportionate share of the population. By all accounts, family forebear Miles A. Romney fit the description of an upstanding Mormon citizen. He emigrated from Great Britain to Nauvoo in 1841 and became an expert carpenter who could handle significant building projects in growing communities.

The tradition of Romney industrial success continued in the family. Mitt's father George became CEO of American Motors, the nation's fourth-largest car manufacturer. George Romney lacked a college degree but had an innovative vision for a new kind of fuel-economy car, superior to the gas-guzzlers made by competitors in the 1950s.[45] Alongside that wholesome tradition, however, is a near-fanatic quest for dollars by high-level manipulations apparently orchestrated by leaders, not just lowly followers. The list begins with the gold digging and bank fraud schemes of the religion's founding prophet.

Faith in the Prophets

Leavitt and Romney are devout followers of relatively recent prophets who spoke with absolute certainty and constantly feuded with what they called "gentiles." Clearly, the church has changed certain doctrines. Brigham Young disdained women, predicted God's ruination of the Union and its populace, threatened to hang federal officials, and hated blacks and Jews. While those are not current issues, their time is not long past, and the disputed words and theories arc from the religion's prophets.[46]

Polygamy has been one of the most enduring disputes. These days, best-selling author Jon Krakauer estimates that 30,000 LDS fundamentalists still advocate polygamy, and foster "fanaticism and brutality" with scant fear of punishment.[47] In 1998, the usually smooth-talking Leavitt slipped up while discussing polygamy. To understand his gaffe, one needs to know LDS theology on what its founders described as "plural marriages" sanctioned by God. Upon Smith's death, Brigham Young openly advocated polygamy, as did the ancestors of Leavitt and Romney. Leavitt's great-grandmother had advocated polygamy to him before her passing, although he recalls telling her, even as a boy, that the church had changed its views.[48]

As Utah governor in 1998, Mike Leavitt described polygamy as a "religious freedom" issue. His statement promptly caused pushback, even in Utah.[49] The First Amendment protects religious practices that do not violate the law. Thus, the "Thug" cult in India that claimed religious motives when its followers murdered caravan travelers is not legally protected under Anglo-American law (or anywhere).[50]

The patriarchal view and legal ignorance implicit in Leavitt's statement made him ill-suited to supervise the entire federal workforce. Several other incidents from Leavitt's career similarly displayed why he was not fit to take the lead in staffing the personnel of a Romney administration.

In 1999, researchers discovered the remains of women and children in Southern Utah, left over from the 1857 Mountain Meadows Massacre.[51]

A backhoe accidentally uncovered the remains of at least 29 victims, primarily women and children, initially thought to have been killed with bullets. This created a conflict of interest for Leavitt. The Saints had believed themselves to be following a higher calling in resisting inquiries about the massacre. They felt secure in Utah, a largely self-governing territory of the United States until statehood.[52] Federal troops originally marked the gravesite in the 1800s but Mormons removed the commemoration, reputedly in compliance with Brigham Young's desires.[53] Here was Leavitt's problem in 1999: A state law required scientific analysis of the remains. Further research, however, might prove unflattering to the Leavitt family and the church. Forensic evidence of death by bullets would suggest killing by LDS members. Leavitt ordered prompt reburial, contrary to the state law. Destruction of physical evidence enabled alternative theories of the victims' death, either by the hands of Paiute or from disease.

Below are several other disturbing examples of Leavitt's *modus operandi.*[54] As governor, Leavitt ordered religious instruction for all state employees so that they would learn how to incorporate LDS teaching into governance. The *Salt Lake Tribune* reported on this as follows in 2007.

> Former Utah governor and current Cabinet secretary Mike Leavitt sought to infuse the lessons of his religion into his inaugural address and into state policy, conducting a series of "Early Morning Seminary" classes in which he and top advisers discussed how to incorporate "just and holy" Mormon principles into his governance, archival records show.

> The disclosure of those 1996 meetings, never before reported, comes at a time when the interface between God and government is dominating political dialogue and Republican presidential candidate Mitt Romney has been forced to take great pains to assure distrustful voters that his Mormon faith will not drive his policy decisions. Romney promised in his recent "Faith in America" speech [during his 2008 campaign] that, if elected, he would not take marching orders from his church leaders or doctrine —and pointed to his record as Massachusetts governor as proof.[55]

Among other investigative reports is one suggesting cronyism in Leavitt's recommendation that Romney lead the 2002 Winter Olympics.[56]

The clever way Leavitt exploited financial rules to win tax breaks is also documented in investigative stories. In one,[57] National Public Radio and the *Salt Lake Tribune* showed how the Leavitt family obtained massive tax deductions by donating to the Leavitt Family Foundation, which thereupon loaned money back to family enterprises. An independent critic called the practice disturbing but not illegal. Of course it's not illegal. Leavitt and those of his stature make the laws. Therefore, the laws include precisely this kind of legal loophole that enables perks for the powerful and their loyal servants. In the same spirit, the Leavitt tax avoidance strategy is much like what we know of the Romney methods including the Romney Swiss and Cayman Islands accounts as well as many years of secret tax returns that disguise how Romney benefits from such a low rate as 13 or 14 percent on income. Taxes are for suckers, his message seems to say, whereas government itself is for insiders to exploit.

Leavitt's leadership of the U.S. Department of Health and Human Services further illustrates the tax evasion point. His conduct in the department encompassed misconduct large and small. Most important is the fundamental conflict of interest involved in having the heir and former CEO of one of the nation's largest insurance companies lead the nation's biggest spending department. HHS regulations, grant-making, and other programs directly affect a company such as The Leavitt Group, which describes itself as the nation's eighth-largest insurance brokerage.[58] The chairman and CEO is Dane Leavitt, brother to Mike.[59] Mike Leavitt rarely discloses his family business in his policy statements that cite his government positions, with the implication that he is a neutral expert.

The role of Leavitt's deputy secretary Charles E. Johnson further reveals Leavitt's reliance on a close inner circle. Johnson is a Mormon who was Leavitt's chief of staff when Leavitt was Utah governor . He was CFO under Leavitt at the Environmental Protection Agency and before becoming deputy HHS secretary. He succeeded Leavitt as Acting HHS Secretary for the first months of the Obama administration.[60] He later rejoined Leavitt as partner at the Leavitt Group, which advises companies on health care issues.[61]

These ties suggest smooth-running crony capitalism. To assist their management of HHS, Leavitt and Johnson hired Johnson's niece during the Bush administration. Her title was director of the Office of Grants Modernization, a post in the Senior Executive Service.

That kind of cronyism is commonplace in government. One reason this particular instance is noteworthy is because it involved the transition chief of a 2012 major party candidate who campaigned on a platform of reducing government waste and other spending. Additionally, HHS involves lots of money. Although the niece's title seems boringly bureaucratic, her job is to supervise compliance for vast numbers of federal grants, some of which could involve political favoritism.

The whole process underscores nepotism, cronyism, and lack of accountability pervasive in Washington under both parties. The hypocrisy is especially striking for Republicans, however, because Romney and Ryan campaigned against federal employees. They sought to break down the social safety net implemented by agencies such as HHS. They especially wanted to reduce "ObamaCare," even though Obama modeled it on Romney's plan in Massachusetts to win GOP support. Money making always trumps policy, however. Therefore, Leavitt's consulting company, whose staffers include Johnson, advises companies to exploit "ObamaCare" and instructs them how to do so.

Summing Up

In Mike Leavitt's final Bush administration post, he engaged in a massive, ongoing conflict of interest that he rarely disclosed in meaningful ways. Similarly, once the Obama election forced Leavitt's departure, his trusted aide, Johnson, ran the department as acting secretary for many months under the Obama administration. Meanwhile, the public naively assumed that Obama appointees were delivering "change" via those like Johnson.

Finally, one more Leavitt initiative illustrates the stakes involved and how the system works (for the benefit of insiders, of course). National Public Radio and the *Salt Lake Tribune* exposed Leavitt for spending $700,000 in dubious travel costs so he could jet around the nation in 2005, sounding an alarm about the supposed epidemic of the then-looming avian flu. Leavitt helped panic the nation into fearing that the diseases might kill millions of people. Congress appropriated $8 billion for a massive prevention program.

The real scandal, in retrospect, is how this helped enrich former Defense Secretary Don Rumsfeld, a warmonger who resigned in 2004 after steering vast wealth to well-connected war contractors. As 2004 elections approached, Bush forced Rumsfeld's resignation so that he could serve as a major scapegoat for the Iraq War, thereby avoiding scrutiny for others. However, VIP circles still regarded him favorably as a loyal member of the inner circle, deserving of support. Rumsfeld adroitly positioned himself to be a major investor in Tamilflu, a vaccine against Asian flu. One analyst described the situation in 2005 as follows:

Against all scientific prudence and normal public health procedure, the world population is being whipped up into fear frenzy by irresponsible public health officials from the US Administration to WHO to the United States Centers for Disease Control. They all warn about the imminent danger that a malicious viral strain might spread from infected birds, primarily in Vietnam and other Asian centers, to contaminate the entire human species in pandemic proportions.

[...]

Rumsfeld stands to make a fortune on royalties as a panicked world population scrambles to buy a drug worthless in curing effects of alleged Avian Flu. The model suggests the parallel to the brazen corruption of

Halliburton Corporation, whose former CEO is Vice President Dick Cheney. Cheney's company has so far gotten billions worth of US construction contracts in Iraq and elsewhere.

Coincidence that Cheney's closest political friend is Defense Secretary and Avian Flu beneficiary Don Rumsfeld? It is another example of what someone has called the principle of modern US corrupt special interest politics: 'Concentrate the benefits; diffuse the costs' President Bush has ordered the US Government to buy $2 billion worth of Gilead Science's Tamilflu.[62]

From a big picture perspective, Rumsfeld had been effective within the revolving door of government to help others become rich. Now that it was his turn, it was time for the system to work for him. Mike Leavitt was there to do his part. Under a Romney White House run by Leavitt, every indication is that the system would have continued to work well in serving the rich in their quest to become richer.

Chapter 13

Big Brothers for Romney – and Us?

On September 11, 2012, Mitt Romney described the Obama administration's reaction to riots outside U.S. embassies in Egypt and Libya as "disgraceful.[1] The next day, Romney repeated his criticism of besieged U.S. embassy staff in Egypt. He did so after learning that an ambassador and three other embassy workers had been killed in Libya.[2] Mistaken on facts, Romney broke the tradition of remaining silent when the country fell under foreign attack.[3]

In the same spirit as George W. Bush, Romney liked tough-talking national security and foreign policy advisers. Romney drew more than two-thirds of his campaign team directly from the Bush administration.[4] He also picked former Bush Secretary of State Condoleezza Rice to be one of his major GOP convention endorsers and campaign surrogates.[5] To those who remember foreign affairs during the past decade, she was a peculiar example of an expert, particularly given the Romney campaign's focus in 2012 on the Benghazi deaths as one of its most specific issues. As National Security Advisor, she and Bush ignored pre-9/11 warnings about a prospective terror attack. She then claimed that no one could have imagined such an assault. Rice and her colleagues failed the public, aside from war contractors and the contractors' armies of advocates in Congress, universities, law firms, the media, and 'think tanks.'

To explore their world, this chapter examines the background of three members of the official Romney foreign affairs team: Michael Hayden, Robert Kagan, and Michael Chertoff.

Under Hayden, the Bush administration broke the nation's laws protecting the privacy of United States citizens from government surveillance. With the encouragement of Kagan and fellow neoconservatives, the administration concocted the Iraq War and pursued the destruction of enemies in Afghanistan. In multiple ways, Michael Chertoff helped gut the Constitution to prepare the way for a police state. In doing so, Chertoff co-authored the Patriot Act, and then advocated the spending of billions of dollars for intrusive, wasteful airport searches and scanning equipment for a federal government that neglected such real-life hazards as identity theft and hurricane disasters.

The government and a timid media tend to downplay the government's huge power to retrieve ostensibly private communications and enforce retribution against individuals. Spying, in other words.

Romney's Team

As of 2012, Hayden and Chertoff were advising Romney while also enriching themselves in the private sector through the vast spending required from the government policies they had advocated. Kagan, a scholar and *Washington Post* columnist married to the U.S. Department of State's top spokesperson, Victoria Nuland, personified the continuing bipartisan dominance of fear-mongers in Washington's highest circles.

With such success already, what more could they possibly want from a Romney administration?[6]Each of these three Romney foreign affairs team members possesses strong, distinct skills that keep dollars flowing into the war and national security sectors by fostering public fears. To be sure, they base their work in part on the country's genuine need for national security. So, each of these men doubtless sees a high-minded public servant in the mirror each morning. For others besides themselves and their supporters, however, there can be scant confusion despite the best efforts of media image-makers: Their policies, in general, create war and vast suffering, and undermine historic freedoms in America for scant purpose.[7]

The carnage of the Bush Mideast wars has made their advocacy more difficult. So has public resentment over intrusive, wasteful, and largely pointless security measures. This is most obvious at airports, but more importantly, involves the interception of virtually all of our phone calls and emails. Therefore, Romney's empty deference to experts illustrates his empty vision.[8] Hayden, Kagan, and Chertoff are supposed to be experts/seers/gurus. Let's take a closer look.

Michael Hayden: Our Nation's Big Brother

Air Force Lieutenant General Michael Hayden directed the National Security Agency (NSA) from 1999 to 2005, and then the Central Intelligence Agency (CIA) from 2006 to 2009. He violated the law by authorizing massive, secret, intrusive, and pervasive interception of U.S. citizen phone calls and emails.[9]  Under his leadership, the NSA also stored the material, retrievable on demand. Hayden helped authorize prosecution for Americans deemed suspicious under the 2001 Patriot Act and otherwise.

Hayden was born in 1945 in Pittsburgh. He entered active duty military service in 1969, and became a three-star Air Force lieutenant general assigned to the Clinton White House as liaison before his 1999 appointment to head the NSA.[10]

Targeting Americans

Since 2001, the federal government has drastically reduced the privacy protections that the public came to expect under law by the end of the 20th Century. Those within government seeking to fulfill their responsibilities to balance privacy and security include career professionals within Executive Branch military and intelligence agencies, Congress, the media, and individuals using social media and the Internet. Executive power enthusiasts have silenced many of these watchdogs, sometimes through prison threats or involvement in sex scandals. The crackdown potentially affects every United States-based reader because technology enables surveillance of everyone along with storage and retrieval of personal data. Retrieval capability carries the potential for personal reprisal against anyone. Such reprisal is not feasible against everyone, of course. Nevertheless, government pressure can be highly effective against opposition leaders and followers. Pressure against random targets can spread additional fear that government is all-powerful, and so protest is pointless.

The Bush Administration began its Big Brother initiative under Hayden in early 2001. Hayden and the rest of the administration later used the 9/11 attack to justify what they had already started: illegal interception, storage, retrieval, and review of billions of emails and phone calls between unsuspecting citizens who had a reasonable expectation of privacy. George Orwell long ago predicted such oppression in his novel, *1984.* Congress forbade such illegal surveillance in a 1978 federal law passed after revelations of CIA scandals.[11] In July 2008, Barack Obama reneged on his campaign promise to fight for the public on the issue and the government permitted hackers, some of whom were government contractors, to plot cyber-attacks on political critics of big business. All of this occurred with an unprecedented crackdown on concerned career officials who dared discuss it with the media.

Government Surveillance and Telecom Immunity

Michael Hayden, like most who attain such high rank, is not simply a military expert but is adept at public relations. To assist his career and the NSA's image, Hayden cooperated with author James Bamford on *Body of Secrets*, which Bamford published in 2001 as a sequel to *The Puzzle Palace*, a controversial book in 1982 revealing NSA's existence. The sequel disclosed, among other things, the shocking story of Operation Northwoods, a secret plan approved by each of the Joint Chiefs of Staff in the early 1960s to invade Cuba under the false claim that Cuba had killed

American travelers or a famous astronaut. Defense Secretary Robert McNamara irritated his top uniformed officers by repeatedly rejecting their plan for the U.S. government to kill its own citizens, or pretend to kill them. With Northwoods still secret, McNamara falsely testified in 1968 to the Senate Foreign Relations Committee — as it examined the Gulf of Tonkin Resolution enabling the Vietnam War — that it was "inconceivable" that U.S. military officials might conspire to provoke a war on a pretext. President Kennedy backed McNamara against the Joint Chiefs, a factor in any thorough assessment of whether it was Oswald or others who wanted JFK dead.[12]

Even though Bamford's book was a best-seller, his documentation for the long-secret Northwoods plan is relatively little known to the general public beyond the book audience. Instead, the NSA and the rest of the Bush administration came under intense and more widely reported public criticism beginning in late December 2005 after disclosure of massive illegal surveillance against Americans.

Bamford believes that Hayden should have fought harder for the Constitution he was sworn to uphold and defend.[13] Here is Bamford's account of that era in his 2008 book, *The Shadow Factory*, with relevant parts confirmed in my own, albeit more limited, reporting:

> The ramp-up stage of illegal government surveillance with the cooperation of major telecom companies is best understood through the experience of former Qwest Communications CEO Joseph Nacchio, the only CEO of the "Baby Bell" telecommunications giants who refused to comply with a request/demand by the new Bush administration to spy illegally on customers. Federal officials asked Nacchio in February 2001 shortly after the Bush administration assumed office to undertake massive illegal surveillance of Americans.[14] Nacchio, a New York City native, was aggressively seeking government contracts at the time. Even so, he believed the request to be illegal. He therefore avoided the cooperation that each of his peer telecom CEOs were providing to NSA.[15] For ostensibly separate reasons, authorities convicted Nacchio for securities fraud under a novel interpretation of the law. He is now serving a long prison term.[16] Several of my sources who worked in high-level Qwest posts believe, as Nacchio has alleged, that authorities trumped up the charges to teach him and others in the telecom business a lesson that they should cooperate with whatever requests the government makes to spy on the public.[17]

Meanwhile, unknown to the public, Hayden's methods and ambition alarmed senior career subordinates within NSA. Perhaps the most courageous and most thoroughly punished of these subordinates turned out to be Thomas Drake. Drake is a former Air Force officer. He learned advanced surveillance techniques, but always with the institutional motto that the NSA could never use the surveillance against ordinary

Americans. As a high-ranking NSA executive, Drake was appalled at the one billion dollars in what he regarded wasteful NSA spending on its "Trailblazer" surveillance project, advocated by Hayden. After failing to get NSA management's attention, Drake tried to save taxpayers money by alerting a *Baltimore Sun* reporter to the project in the hope of shedding light on more useless spending. In response, the NSA retroactively marked relevant documents as "Classified" and had Drake indicted on bogus spy charges that could imprison him for the rest of his life. Drake was represented by the Government Accountability Project's Jesselyn Radack, who was herself a former whistleblower. Drake was also fortunate to have drawn a fair judge, who required the government to produce its evidence. The government has sought in such cases to keep evidence secret under the theory the facts are too sensitive to reveal, even to defendants.[18]

A third critic of that Hayden era was Mark Klein, an AT&T engineer who worked in San Francisco during the years after 9/11. From a bottom-up perspective, Klein discovered, almost by accident, at an AT&T switching center that Hayden's NSA had built a secret room where AT&T, on behalf of NSA, was illegally intercepting billions of phone calls and emails of ordinary citizens. Klein was a technician by training and an employee concerned about layoffs in a consolidating industry sector. In addition he was a citizen who knew about the privacy protections for the public embedded in the Constitution and federal law. Concerned about law-breaking, Klein undertook extraordinary outreach to find a journalist, public interest group, or public official courageous enough to take an interest in his discovery. Klein ultimately interested the Electronic Frontier Foundation, *Wired* magazine and *New York Times* reporter James Risen.[19] The *Times* sat on the story for nearly a year. Risen forced its publication and made it memorable in his important 2006 book, *State of War,* as well as in newspaper reports co-authored with Eric Lichtblau.[20]

Citing his book, authorities threatened Risen with prison during years of litigation against him and the newspaper. As part of a crackdown on leaks, the Justice Department pressured Risen to testify against former CIA analyst Jeffrey Sterling. The government categorized Sterling as a spy, not a whistleblower, and undertook a half dozen such prosecutions, including one against former CIA analyst John Kiriakou. Kiriakou was an ABC-TV analyst who had authored a book describing harsh interrogation methods by the CIA, *i.e.* torture.[21] In 2012, authorities indicted Kiriakou on spy charges potentially carrying 45 years of prison time as part of an aggressive crackdown on former government employees.[22]

In the midst of this, I covered an important forum on the case co-sponsored by the nation's two most important press clubs, based in

Washington and New York City.[23] Speakers stressed that traditional reporting on government is winding to a close if federal authorities can imprison former federal employees who talk to reporters. This would curtail comments except on themes helpful to officials. Kiriakou, who had not been critical when describing waterboarding to a reporter, accepted a guilty plea and a 30-month prison sentence in October 2012 rather than face the rest of his life in prison.[24] The prison sentence for Kiriakou illustrated the huge potential danger when a reporter or anyone else asks an informed source a question about national security issues.[25] That thwarts, for example, follow-ups on this book's issues.

Kiriakou's evident relief at accepting such a long sentence raised issues far beyond his own case. As noted in a previous chapter, one of the Romney campaign's major issues had become the deaths of Christopher Stevens, U.S. ambassador to Libya, and three American security personnel from an attack on September 11, 2012. Those paying close attention could discern that CIA personnel were responsible for security in significant part, but with their role hidden from the campaign debate and the public. Scattered reports suggested that some security personnel failed to perform, while others died heroically. Potential reasons for security failures included the Obama administration's extreme incompetence[26] or, alternatively, desire by disloyal Romney supporters to create a campaign issue.[27] A partial additional explanation for either theory would be the inherent hazard of the work in a war-torn region. Persistent reports also suggest that Stephens, an expert in Arab relations, was engaged in dangerous, ultra-secret efforts to facilitate radical Muslim armed support for the rebel insurrection in Syria. This would have been with the knowledge of his superiors but in violation of public U.S. policy. Therefore, CIA activity and complicated state secrets permeated the situation. The secrecy helped make authoritative independent reporting professionally dangerous and otherwise difficult except for information provided by government officials. As Kiriakou learned, a misstep, even by a former official, in communicating with a reporter could mean a long prison sentence and ruinous legal expense for both parties.

During the Bush administration, it seemed that hardly any Republicans, and just a handful of Democrats in Congress, spoke out about the government's crackdown on civil liberties. The beginning of the Obama administration also had the effect of silencing most Democratic advocates of civil liberties. During the summer of 2012, I wrote:

One notable exception has been Senator Ron Wyden (D-OR, a member of the Senate Intelligence Committee. Wyden continues a lonely battle to generate discussion and accountability where there is virtually none. Among his concerns are how Executive Branch officials resist providing meaningful estimates of whether it is only a few Americans — or vast numbers — who are being monitored without warrants. For example, while the public is generally aware that judges authorize limited numbers of wiretaps each year, it remains largely in the dark about newer and far more prevalent techniques, such as the routine use of cell phones as sophisticated tracking devices. Wyden's most recent effort involves placing a "hold" on the Senate's reauthorization of the Foreign Intelligence Surveillance Act (FISA) court system—until he is able to learn more about how, post-9/11, the Executive Branch is using its powers. [28]

When Wyden gave a speech to the libertarian Cato Institute on these themes, urging the audience to back his efforts in the Senate, he said he was constrained from detailing his concerns by secrecy provisions. Wyden, a three-term senator, was the third-highest-ranking senator on a committee controlled by his party. The chair is California Democrat Dianne Feinstein, whose husband, Richard Blum, has made a fortune as a financier. The second-ranking Democrat is West Virginia Senator Jay Rockefeller, scion of the oil tycoon

In a hallway after the speech, I asked Wyden why he did not arrange for diverse experts such as Nacchio and Drake (who attended Wyden's talk) to fill in the blanks for the public as witnesses before his Intelligence Committee. I knew from prior contacts that Klein and Drake would appreciate a chance to share their warnings with the public and I suspected from study of Nacchio's statements that he would also. Seemingly uncomfortable with my suggestion, Wyden rushed off after telling me neither he nor other senators besides the chair has any control over witness invitations. In fact, virtually all of the committee's hearings during recent years are secret. There are almost no announced witnesses, much less any who are willing to describe the government's threats to the public.

9/11, Anthrax, and the Patriot Act

Elected officials support war and homeland security programs in part to avoid seeming weak in the post-9/11 environment. Two major official investigations probing the 9/11 attacks called for reform. One body was the National Commission on Terrorist Attacks upon the United States, also known as the 9/11 Commission, chaired by New Jersey Republican Thomas Kean.[29] The other was the joint probe by the Senate and House Intelligence Committees, co-chaired by the committee chairs, Florida Democratic Senator Bob Graham and Florida Republican Congressman Porter Goss.[30]

The 2001 anthrax attack against Congress provoked a major change in the nation's lawmaking process. Beginning a week after the 9/11 attacks in 2001, someone mailed deadly anthrax to prominent officials and journalists. The mailings killed several men and women who had been exposed. The deaths then panicked many others in government and journalism. The specific anthrax was later described as the "Ames strain." The military lab at Fort Detrick, Maryland had studied the Ames strain.[31]

The panic enveloped Washington on the eve of debate and passage of the Patriot Act in 2001. Two of the few letters containing anthrax went to two Democratic leaders overseeing the Patriotic Act legislation: Senate Majority Leader Tom Daschle of South Dakota, and Senate Judiciary Committee Chairman Pat Leahy of Vermont. Anthrax also somehow sickened three staffers of Democratic Senator Russ Feingold of Wisconsin, a member of the Intelligence Committee who had criticized the intelligence agencies. For whatever reasons, Daschle and Leahy helped facilitate the prompt passage of the Patriot Act, which granted the Executive Branch vast powers unreviewable by courts and unsupervised by Congress aside from secret briefings to a few leaders.

Authorities first cast suspicion for the anthrax attack on a former federal scientist, Steven Hatfill, by calling him "a person of interest in 2002."[32] He sued to clear his name. Early on, I suspected something strange about his case, in part because I was professionally acquainted with his attorneys, whose clients included several of the nation's largest corporations. I thought it unlikely that they would depart so much from their normal practice unless they had spotted a major injustice. As it turned out, they won what has been reported as $5.8 million in settlement in 2008. Bruce Ivins, a researcher at the United States Army research labs at Fort Detrick, came under investigation and was subsequently found dead in 2008. He was later pronounced guilty by authorities.[33] Questions remain,[34] and the matter should be investigated in far greater depth.

2008 Telecom Immunity Kills Public Protection

In June 2008, Barack Obama won the Democratic presidential nomination following Hillary Clinton's concession. Promptly thereafter, Obama changed his progressive campaign position opposing telecom immunity for privacy violations. He voted for the more CIA-friendly, ostensibly conservative position to support immunity legislation, which quickly passed into law without a hearing. That immunity blocks civil lawsuits, which served as the only method by which members of the public could learn details and obtain compensation for the violation of their privacy. Authorities will not hold public hearings and, if questioned, will cite "national security" for withholding information.

Obama's capitulation to a secrecy agenda prompted most other Democrats to join him and Republicans in suppressing any redress for privacy invasions. Those seeking to enforce the nation's historic Constitutional requirements for warrants suffered repeated defeats in the courts and Congress, with scant public debate, news coverage, or protest.

Shortly after Christmas in 2012, for example, the Senate reauthorized warrantless surveillance 73 to 23.[35]

From Langley, With Love

Little known to the public, Michael Hayden took command of the CIA at a time when sex scandal at high levels threatened damaging revelations about the morals of the agency's leadership. The problem was that CIA personnel were among high-level government employees who had used prostitutes for personal gratification and also as an operational tool for intelligence-gathering and blackmail. This situation, a staple of spy agencies everywhere, is far more attractive in glamorized, fictional movies than in newspaper specifics. But Hayden faced the latter problem with the so-called "DC Madam" case.

The CIA is based in Langley on a campus in Northern Virginia separated from the Potomac River by a highway with an unmarked exist ramp. The lack of a sign implies, appropriately enough, that casual visitors are not welcome. The founders of the nation's premier modern spy agencies had extraordinary sexual appetites, an important part of the tradition that has carried forward to the present. The CIA's forerunner was the Office of Special Services (OSS), whose founding director during World War II was William "Wild Bill" Donovan. A Buffalo lawyer, Donovan had acquired his nickname for exploits during the First World War. Soon thereafter, Donovan became a Justice Department executive who acquired an implacable lifelong rival in fellow corruption fighter J. Edgar Hoover, the future FBI director. For nearly three decades, Hoover would secretly catalogue and disseminate damaging information about the married Donovan's dalliances, in part to prevent his rival from post-war appointment to a CIA leadership position.[36] Given Hoover's homosexual tendencies, his Donovan dossier was primarily a tool of the trade in power politics, not a means to enforce conventional morality.

The pattern of sex scandal slander used as a weapon has continued in investigative agencies up to the present. "As Harry Truman well knew," writes author Joseph Trento, "CIA Director Allen Dulles was an inveterate womanizer and he set the example." Trento wrote "station chiefs and base chiefs were turned into pimps when 'Uncle Allen' came to visit." He quotes Dr. William Corson, a high-level intelligence aide to four presidents, as saying, "Allen Dulles would screw anything that wasn't tied down. That was guilty knowledge that men at the top of the CIA shared: Did I sleep with the same woman as Dulles? Those were the real secrets these men had."[37]

Several historical snapshots illustrate a continuing pattern established by Dulles, the longest-serving intelligence chief. Any one person's marriage fidelity might hardly seem worth noticing in a world with billions of people. Examination is justified, however, when the subjects are those who maintain powerful posts in part through false images of rectitude, and abuse their organizations and other powers to expose and punish others for conduct similar to their own.[38]

The story of George H. W. Bush and his purported longtime affair with an aide rarely appeared in print even when Washington insiders discussed the matter as if it were common knowledge. Susan Trento, an author married to Joseph Trento, finally broke the story in her 1992 book about influence peddling in Washington.[39] Bush, a former CIA director, denied an affair.[40] His son, George W., denied the allegation also.[41] That marked an end to mainstream news coverage, except in books and by word of mouth.[42]

Later developments illustrate how misconduct at Washington's top levels sometimes results in career-ending scandal. Thus, Clinton-era CIA Director Dr. John Deutch resigned in 1996. Authorities revealed that his home computers used for work included X-rated pornography as well as classified material. Deutch, who said he did not know how some of the materials appeared in his sometimes unattended office, faced potential criminal charges before President Clinton pardoned him in 2000.[43]

In contrast, Bush CIA Director Porter Goss resigned in May 2006 with little adverse news coverage after he and a top aide, Kyle "Dusty" Foggo, were reputed to have attended lewd poker parties with prostitutes at the famed Watergate apartment complex.[44] Goss was well connected. As a Yale undergraduate, he was a member of the Book and Snake secret society before undertaking a career as a CIA intelligence officer. Upon leaving the service, the ardent Republican became a Florida mayor and congressman. Goss was chairman of the House Intelligence Committee before his appointment to lead the CIA in 2004. News coverage of his resignation cited his efforts to "reform" its operations as his primary reasons for stepping down. This reputedly antagonized an old guard at the CIA who was allied with the White House Director of National Intelligence John Negroponte. Negroponte, a fraternity brother of Goss at Yale, fought Goss in turf battles over resources and succeeded in winning Hayden's appointment as successor to Goss. Relatively unscathed, Goss, who was already a member of the Council on Foreign Relations, went on to become chairman of the Office of Congressional Ethics, which is staffed by non-members.[45]

Foggo, however, was sentenced to prison in 2009 for a massive bribery and prostitution scandal. Foggo was a former San Diego policeman and CIA officer whom Goss elevated to the agency's No. 3 position, running its day-to-day operations. Foggo's crimes were exposed in the wake of newspaper investigations documenting the corruption of Randy "Duke" Cunningham, a former Vietnam War hero and eight-term congressman sentenced to prison in 2005. I attended Foggo's sentencing in Virginia's federal court to see how the court system and news media would handle a major scandal with ties to the DC Madam and Jack Abramoff cases. The judge was James Cacheris, a Reagan-appointee who also serves on the highly-secret federal FISA court ratifying virtually all government requests for secret wiretaps. The senior judge, living up to his reputation as a CIA friendly jurist, imposed a three-year sentence with a minimum of public disclosure of the underlying offenses. Newspapers provided only partial coverage of the long-running poker parties at the Watergate that reputedly included CIA personnel, occasional VIPs, and prostitutes.[46]

In this book's Preface, I wrote that gaps in news coverage regarding the arrest and trial of the Jeane Palfrey, the DC Madam, struck me from afar as incomprehensible and potentially important. As I resumed journalistic work, I learned more about her case from a variety of well-informed sources. These included two of the main investigative reporters in whom she confided, Dan Moldea and Wayne Madsen, as well as two members of her defense team, attorney Montgomery Blair Sibley and researcher Matthew Janovic, as well as two female confidantes of Palfrey's closely familiar with her line of work.[47] Palfrey distributed a list of 20,000 customer phone numbers in a frantic attempt to raise money and media allies.

My interest was in the big picture although I respect recent research suggesting the value in gossip.[48] Sibley and Janovic each wrote books concluding that Palfrey had provided prostitutes to government VIPs and also to government allies (such as foreign visitors) whom the government wanted to entertain.[49] Sibley's 593-page *Why Just Her?* concluded that authorities unleashed a brutally unfair prosecution on Palfrey to thwart her retirement from California to Germany, as she had planned just before her arrest. Janovic's 622-page treatment concurred on the point.

There's more to the story, however. Palfrey's ordeal exposed widespread corruption in the nation's capital. The significance was the horrifying failure of due process and of the fair press. One of many examples of procedural failure was the unexplained replacement of the trial judge, Gladys Kessler after she ruled that the defendant could subpoena evidence from national security agencies. Federal judge James Robertson, a former member of the secret FISA court, assumed control of the case. He reversed Kessler's rulings, protected agencies and male clients, and presided over gruesome courtroom humiliations of the escorts, most of whom were part-timers with middle class jobs.[50]

The Palfrey tale and those like it illustrate several themes relevant to the ascendance of Michael Hayden and David Petraeus at the CIA. First, powerful officials, whatever their marital status or other outward appearance, can succumb to temptation. In fact, some scholars suggest that the powerful are more likely than others to pursue affairs.[51] Second, national security agencies and law enforcers have a long history in Washington, as elsewhere, of using "honeytraps" and similar stings to elicit information for police or federal dossiers. A defense lawyer in a major New York City prostitution case protested in 2012 that the prosecutors appeared far more interested in obtaining his client's customer list than in bringing appropriate charges.[52] In other words, the public can reasonably suspect a hidden agenda, at least some of the time, when a public official is exposed in a scandal.

Meanwhile, for the public, the big danger is the government's uncontrolled collection of data.

Meet Holly Weber, and Beware

Does all of this seem abstract and far removed from your daily life?

You may believe your own activities have nothing to do with the high-level intrigue described above. Even so, you may encounter Holly Weber, shown here, or others posing as friendly faces,  posting on Facebook, Twitter, and Linked-In. etc. You might even share your interests with someone like Holly, including your opinions on politics or a hobby, or mention of friends. Be careful, whatever your views. As I reported during 2011:

> New evidence has emerged in Washington of sophisticated avatar, phishing and similar surveillance plots. The snitch scams were reportedly run by government-affiliated IT contractors to obtain personal information from those who criticize federal officials or key members of the U.S. Chamber of Commerce.

Holly Weber, the lovely University of Denver alumna, for example, apparently does not exist except as an avatar. Computer security firm HB Gary Federal worked in a program to create and manage "sock puppet" Internet users like her to infiltrate websites. The goal, apparently, was to collect data from the public, create confusion, and propagate disinformation. HB Federal was a government contractor working for private clients as well as the government, and thus accountability is mysterious.

Think Progress reporter Lee Fang took a lead on the story. He drew on 50,000 emails stolen by the pro-WikiLeaks hackers group Anonymous from HB Gary Federal to report that several major companies were conspiring to destroy those who might support WikiLeaks. The hacked emails suggested that CIA-linked startup Palantir Technologies also participated in a proposal with HB Gary to the law firm Hunton and Williams to help the Chamber of Commerce (a client of the law firm) and the chamber's prominent member Bank of America use deceptive social media strategies to hurt Think Progress, Salon columnist Glenn Greenwald, and reporters for the *New York Times* and *Guardian*, among others. Palantir, founded in 2004 by former PayPay executives and Stanford graduates, held a particularly interesting status. The CIA's venture capital arm, IN-Q-TEL, invested $2 million to help start the IT company in 2004.

As a follow up, Greenwald described how government involvement worried him the most about the scandal. Officials at the Justice Department and elsewhere had recommended the private contractors to the chamber's law firm for the political and high-tech sabotage against critics. Greenwald wrote:

> The very idea of trying to threaten the careers of journalists and activists to punish and deter their advocacy is self-evidently pernicious; that it's being so freely and casually proposed to groups as powerful as the Bank of America, the Chamber of Commerce, and the DOJ-recommended Hunton & Williams demonstrates how common this is....And because the U.S. Government is free to break the law without any constraints, oversight or accountability, so, too, are its "private partners" able to act lawlessly.[53]

The scandal promptly disappeared from public view. Neither officials nor the media demonstrated much interest.

In retrospect, the reasons doubtless involved government complicity, as well as public apathy about loss of privacy. By contrast, insiders and thought-leaders — such as the Bilderberg Group attendees who include the *Washington Post* and National Security Agency leaders nearly every year — fully understand the high value of data-mining consumer information.

The dangers of government surveillance became more widely known in the late spring of 2013, when Greenwald broke the story in the *Guardian* that the NSA was secretly data-mining vast amounts of personal consumer information from Facebook, Microsoft, Yahoo, Google, PalTalk, AOL, Skype, YouTube and Apple. He reported the government's tool as a powerful Internet-scanning program called PRISM. The companies denied the accuracy of reports. Huge questions remained about the scope and legality of the spying, with no clear path for public understanding because the facts, law and court decisions are secret. Greenwald's report, soon followed by *Washington Post* coverage using the same key source, came on the eve of the 2013 annual Bilderberg secret conference. Palantir Co-Founder and CEO Alex Karp, whose company by then reported $5 billion in annual revenues, would take his place among approximate 100 other Western leaders from government and industry. The 2013 assemblage included top executives of the *Post,*

Facebook, Google, Amazon.com, and such other potentates as David Rockefeller. [54]

The pages ahead recount how insiders earn fabulous wealth and power from government-supervised violations of your privacy. As one lesson: most of us have fewer friends than we might imagine. We cannot count on even an avatar as friendly as Holly Weber.

Hayden Moves Up, Advises Romney

After retirement from the Bush administration, Michael Hayden went to work for the Chertoff Group, the security and defense consultancy founded by former Homeland Security secretary Michael Chertoff. War and fear do not foreclose opportunity. Hayden mocked critics for asserting that no useful intelligence comes from torture.[55] Yet his argument was undermined when he cited the superficial 9/11 Commission report as evidence, and then said, in essence that he could not discuss matters in depth because of "national security" concerns. By contrast, former Senate Intelligence Committee Chairman Bob Graham, co-chair of the Congressional Joint Inquiry into 9/11, has called for a new investigation on 9/11 because the first probe was so inadequate and so many questions remain.

A precious American legacy of privacy rights has now been discarded.[56] An important case decided by the Supreme Court during its 2012-13 term illustrates the danger.[57] The court ruled 5-4 against plaintiff journalists and other civil liberties advocates who tried to oppose surveillance. The all-Republican majority ruled that the plaintiffs have no right to litigate because they could not prove at the outset that the secret techniques harmed them.[58]

Hayden became a Romney advisor,[59] Unlike Romney and many of the other neocons, Hayden had military experience. This helped Hayden envision the full horror of all-out war with nations such as Iran.[60]

Robert Kagan: Fearless Chickenhawk

Robert Kagan, his brother, Frederick, and their father, Donald, were at the forefront of those neo-conservative warmongers who began advocating for renewed United States warfare against Iraq in the 1990s.[61] In 1996, Robert co-founded, with *Weekly Standard* editor William Kristol, the Project for a New American Century, which advocated for the aggressive foreign policy that the Bush administration later implemented in Iraq and Afghanistan, with disastrous results.[62] Other founding members included a Who's Who of the neocon movement, including former Reagan Navy Secretary John Lehman and former Bush United Nations Ambassador John Bolton.[63]

For many years, Donald Kagan has been an eminent professor of history at Yale.[64] His sons, Robert and Frederick, earned their undergraduate degrees at Yale before obtaining advanced degrees, serving conservative government officials, authoring books, and working at quasi-academic "think tanks." Frederick, a former professor of military history at West Point, is credited with devising the "surge" (i.e., escalation of the war) in Iraq.[65] Robert, a Bilderberg attendee, is a fellow at the Brookings Institution and writes a foreign affairs column for the *Washington Post* as a part-time contributor. 66 His wife, Victoria Nuland, is a longtime State Department executive who was an aide to Vice President Dick Cheney and was the Bush-appointed U.S. Ambassador to NATO. The Obama administration appointed her as spokesperson for the State Department.[67] This created the not-uncommon situation in Washington whereby a government official's job was to influence the media while the official's spouse or other family member was a major policy advocate in the same field.[68]

Neither of the younger Kagans nor Nuland list military service on their biographies despite their frequent advocacy of war around the world. This fits an increasingly common pattern of thought leaders who, backed by the financial power of the military-security complex, create innovative rationales for more government military and security spending.[69] They claim to be independent analysts. One favorite argument is that the president may authorize preventive wars or choose sides in civil wars if he finds a sufficient humanitarian basis for concern, as in Bosnia, Libya, and Syria.

Clearly, the Iraq and Afghanistan policies were humanitarian tragedies and policy follies on a historic scale.[70] By rights, the Kagan family should end its claims of expertise and undertake such community service disabled veterans at hospitals many hours a week. Instead, both Romney and Obama, to different degrees, welcomed them and their "expertise" In asserting U.S. power in the Mideast and Central Asia. *Foreign Policy*, a prestigious specialty publication owned by the *Washington Post*, is among those who repeatedly underscore the family's wisdom and continuing influence.[71] Those connections also served as a reason for Romney to seek Robert Kagan's advice.

Ultimately, the decision to declare war is the most serious the nation can make. That is why it was entrusted by the nation's founders solely to Congress, the people's most direct representatives. Timid elected representatives, dependent on the support of the war and security sectors, have gradually ceded that power to presidents, who increasingly lack any military experience and therefore cede responsibility to their panels of experts while largely confining themselves to scoring political points.

Shortly before the 2012 elections, this process came into clearer focus when Mitt Romney appeared on CBS's *60 Minutes* to reiterate his view, before the United Nations convened, that the United States should have a stronger policy on Iran. Romney did not, however, suggest what that policy should be aside from more deference to the views of Israeli Prime Minister Benjamin Netanyahu, who shared an office with Romney when they began their careers at Boston Consulting Group. Obama responded, "if Governor Romney is suggesting that we should start another war, he should say so."[72]

Michael Chertoff: Marketing Fear

Michael Chertoff used his government positions to create a horrific legacy of fear and radical cutbacks to the nation's long-treasured civil rights. In doing so, he served his political patrons. They, in turn, rewarded him with offices enabling him to capitalize on fear mongering to boost all of their political and financial fortunes.

Michael Chertoff was born in Elizabeth, New Jersey. A high-ranking student at Harvard Law School, he became a Supreme Court law clerk and then a successful federal prosecutor in New York City under U.S. attorney Rudy Giuliani. Chertoff parlayed courtroom victories into a 1990 appointment (in 1990) as the U.S. Attorney for New Jersey. The Clinton administration retained him in office as the only Republican in the nation invited to remain in the 93 Presidentially appointed posts. Senate Republicans then hired him to become a special counsel investigating Whitewater. A decade later, New York Senator Hillary Clinton resented his abusive partisan tactics against young White House staffers called as witnesses during his probes, putting them deeply into debt for legal bills at the beginnings of their careers. She cast the only Senate vote opposing his confirmation as a top Justice Department executive during the Bush administration in 2001, and then as a federal appellate judge in 2003.

Shortly after 9/11, the Bush administration proposed the Patriot Act, co-authored by Chertoff, to Congress. The Patriot Act created exemptions from law for the Homeland Security Department in the name of "national security."[73] As noted above, the Democratic-controlled Senate passed the law. Senate Judiciary Committee Chairman Pat Leahy of Vermont was frightened after his office received an anonymous letter containing deadly anthrax, later traced to U.S. Army labs. The office of Democratic Senate Majority Leader Tom Daschle also received anthrax by letter. Congress was not in session and its members were largely dispersed at the time. Hence, the Judiciary Committee passed the Patriot Act without the normal hearings and other investigative procedures. With Daschle's encouragement, the full Senate promptly passed the law.

The government ostensibly needed the Patriot Act to fight terrorists presumed to hold al-Qaeda or similar foreign loyalties. In practice, some of its most startling applications have been against United States citizens, including those in federal service feared to be potential whistleblowers. Chertoff and his Justice Department colleagues used the act for harsh retribution against federal workers as to enforce discipline.

One reprisal was against Jesselyn Radack, a 1995 Yale Law School graduate and respected ethics expert at the Justice Department. In December 2001, Radack was assigned to advise FBI agents who grilled John Walker Lindh, a California native who had been found in an Afghanistan prison after being captured by a local warlord in the early stages of the post-9/11 allied attack. Radack advised the FBI to not interrogate Lindh further because his parents had asserted his right to counsel. Later, she protested to superiors when she learned that the Justice Department was submitting a false chronology of events to a federal court preparing to try Lindh in the nation's first major post-9/11 terrorism case. She resigned under pressure in 2002. As recounted in her powerful book, *Traitor*, the Department forced her dismissal from her next job, sought her disbarment, and put her on its "No Fly" list at airports to prevent travel.[74]

FBI translator Sibel Edmonds has a similar tale of encountering suspicious conversations, reporting them to superiors, and finding herself forced out.[75] So does Kenneth Ford, a former White House Secret Service officer and NSA national security analyst who wrote a memo in 2003 concluding that Iraq had no weapons of mass destruction. Ford found himself serving a six-year prison sentence on what appear to be trumped-up federal charges that he purloined two boxes of NSA documents.[76] Similarly, authorities illegally revealed the identity of CIA Clandestine Service Officer Valerie Plame Wilson to punish her and her family after her husband, former Ambassador Joseph Wilson, failed to find WMD evidence in early 2003 to support the Bush argument for war against Iraq. Their story, including the fear that the retribution was life-threatening to their family and intended to send a message to other federal employees, is now well-known thanks to their books.[77]

Chertoff helped to create a climate for reprisals with the Patriot Act and his work as a top aide to Attorney General John Ashcroft. By 2003, however, he was a federal appeals court judge. Again, New York Senator Hillary Clinton, was the only Senator to oppose his confirmation. In January 2005, President Bush successfully nominated Chertoff to become Homeland Security Secretary. This exemplified, among other things, a relatively new trend whereby political operatives received judicial appointments, and then returned to political battles with that title on their resume.[78] Chertoff's wife, Meryl, was a legislative affairs advocate for the department. She then became a lobbyist, selling security equipment to government, and later the Aspen Institute's homeland security program director. Thus the revolving door spun constantly for the Chertoffs, as for many other power couples of both parties. They especially prosper from Washington's fastest-growing industry of the past decade: solutions against "terror."

Chertoff also presided over the epic disaster known as Hurricane Katrina. The House Republican majority and Democratic minority reports sharply criticized Chertoff for his role.[79] Democrats reported, "As the majority findings make clear, Secretary Chertoff provided ineffective leadership at a time of great crisis. We therefore recommend his replacement." In spite of these condemnations, Chertoff suffered no apparent career setback, doubtless because of his professional alliances and because many of the Katrina victims were poor and disorganized.[80] As Homeland Security Secretary, Chertoff ramped up airport security, fear mongering, and intrusive search procedures that helped pave the way for a police state.

At the end of the Bush administration, Chertoff founded the consultancy, the Chertoff Group, splitting his time with other pursuits such as his law practice at Covington and Burling. That law firm supplied the Obama administration with Attorney General Eric Holder and Criminal Division leader Lanny Breuer. Chertoff has become one of the leading advocates for increased airport security. This was most apparent when he took to the media airwaves in December 2009 to advocate for vast new spending in the wake of the United States' capture of the so-called "Underwear Bomber," a Nigerian Islamist of limited mental capacity who had boarded an airplane in Europe with a primitive explosive device concealed in his shorts.[81] The arrest has little value in justifying billions of new spending for airport security. The defendant was waved through European security without even standard paperwork by a mysterious official who wanted the defendant on that airplane.

Former Reagan administration assistant Treasury Secretary Paul Craig Roberts is among those who have debunked the Nigerian's arrest as a bogus justification for wasteful federal spending that prepares the public for police state procedures.[82] Others protest more publicly. "Groping people at the airport doesn't solve our problem," said GOP Texas Congressman and 2012 Presidential contender Ron Paul."[83] Former Minnesota Governor Jesse Ventura made a similar comment.[84] Several columns, including my own, are listed below about lesser-known victims and critics. One was a Libertarian commentator amplifying Paul's theme the devices target passengers, not terrorists.[85] Another focused on a rape victim who was arrested at a Texas airport after refusing a search.[86]

Unfazed, the Chertoff Group successfully represented Rapiscan Systems, a provider of new body scanners that were approved for nationwide installation following the panic over the Underwear Bomber. Authorities later ordered them removed from all airports, at vast cost to taxpayers.[87] Chertoff also invested in a company that markets a special luxury pass that VIPs can use to avoid airport security measures. Thus, Chertoff is among the first in line with moneymaking schemes after having helped foster the vast time, waste, and expense of largely needless high-tech airport precautions. Many former officials at the government's anti-terrorism agencies have been enriched by proceeding through the revolving door.[88] It is a way of life in Washington, but one getting worse for the public.[89]

As a postscript, federal authorities announced in early 2013 that they were pulling all of the Rapiscan machines out of airports because they revealed spectral naked forms of passengers, including children. The intrusiveness of the images, the "Don't touch my junk" controversy, and lingering concerns over radiation and the machines' effectiveness added up to a colossal boondoggle. "It's another disappointing chapter," said one congressman, "and the taxpayers are going to take it on the chin."[90]

Summing Up

During the 2012 presidential campaign, Mitt Romney asked the country to accept, as he does, the leadership of the three Bush veteran foreign policy advisers: Hayden, Kagan, and Chertoff.

The problems were not limited to those three, however. Romney's team personified the Bush-era theme of transferring vital government services to private corporations primarily answerable to political operatives in the White House. This would have removed vital checks-and-balances in the government. *Family of Secrets* author Russ Baker provides one useful indicator: "The growing role of the corporate world in spying was underlined in 2007, when the government revealed that 70 percent of its intelligence budget was contracted out to private firms. In essence, the Bush administration was putting the most secretive part of the government into outside hands with little oversight."[91]

Also in this chapter, we saw how Bush-appointees admired by Romney oversaw retribution against career government officials who dared point out false statements or illegalities. This created not only appalling hardships for the federal victims, but a chilling atmosphere throughout the rest of the government as honest workers were crushed and colleagues learned the lesson of "go-along, get-along" with lawbreakers at the top.

More broadly, Romney partisans echoed Bush themes of government spending cuts along with increased defense spending and war-mongering threats that can quickly turn into new conflicts. However, if these advisers were serious about getting more services for less federal spending, they would have dropped the charade that hiring "Beltway Bandit" private contractors to replace salaried civil servants improves results. Outsourcing is not intended to save the government money, but instead to enable government officials to award contracts and grants to reliable political allies in the private sector. Private contractors that are largely immune from government oversight can then repay their patrons with campaign contributions and "Revolving Door" post-government employment.

This chapter illustrates how government surveillance aimed against the domestic as well as global populations permeated the Bush-Cheney administration and its successors in the Romney-Ryan campaign. The majority that selected Obama might think, based on his campaign, he would implement much different policies. Not so, as it turned out.

Obama, behind his low-key demeanor and civil rights rhetoric, shared a bipartisan zealotry for advancing the goals of military-security sector. From the beginning of his first term, the president whitewashed probes of his predecessors and fostered surveillance of government whistleblowers and the media. He and his Justice Department ramped-up prosecutions of opponents in ways that would explode into controversy early in his second term with revelations his Justice Department was spying on Associated Press and Fox News reporters and sources, among others. Obama's actions would prompt critics from the mainstream, right, and left to denounce him as eroding First Amendment freedoms in ways matching or exceeding Richard Nixon. I describe the specifics in a later chapter. For now, the important point is that the candidates and their policies are remarkably similar on such core issues as expansion of presidential power, including secret surveillance of the United States population and other expanded security powers. Obama and Romney were trained in the law at Harvard, only a few miles from the site of the original Boston Tea Party. Both candidates and their advisors, whatever their differing rhetoric for campaign purposes, prioritized "national security" over protecting the public's privacy and freedom.

Chapter 14

Probing 2012 Voting Schemes

A labama attorney Dana Jill Simpson had big news for me about election fraud looming in 2012 as we met at the National Press Club in the nation's capital. The Friday night in late September was just six weeks before the elections. A former Republican, the high-energy political opposition researcher wanted to reveal what she described as Republican plans orchestrated by Karl Rove to manipulate election results to achieve a GOP win.

I had met her five years earlier, on the eve of her House Judiciary Committee testimony. In testimony to staff, she revealed how Bush loyalists corruptly prosecuted Alabama's leading Democrat, former Governor Don Siegelman. That scandal cost the jobs of major perpetrators Rove and Attorney General Alberto Gonzales.

They faced no sanctions otherwise, however, for a nation-wide pattern of frame ups targeting political opponents. Simpson had hoped her testimony might lead to further accountability. Canny Republicans and craven Democrats failed to follow through with investigations. Monstrous national abuses of the justice system escaped any sanction. Meanwhile, virtually all the prosecution misconduct victims and their families continued to suffer under the Obama administration. Simpson, from rural Rainsville in Alabama's northeast mountainous region, had her own ordeals after she abandoned her political roots in an attempt to bring peace to victims and justice to their oppressors. Her law practice temporarily suffered, the Bush administration initiated an unwarranted investigation of her, and a suspicious fire burned a substantial part of her home.

In 2012, at the century-old press club, Simpson and her colleague, IT consultant Jim March, revealed their findings to me. March, in addition to his IT work, was a volunteer election monitor in Arizona, and a board member of the civic group Black Box Voting.[1] Working under grants from the Free Press and Obama supporters, they described their research trip and predictions of how a "Rove election fraud empire" would attempt to corrupt the 2012 election.

This chapter explores threats to fair elections. It shows why Rove's career, in particular, illustrates a pattern of under-handed campaign techniques that a better-informed electorate should protest. The gist is that private contractors performing government work are protected by political favoritism and claims of national security even when they are suspected of participating in crimes.

On a global scale, it appears that two of the Bush Family's major financial backers are behind several of the world's most important vote verification companies and partisan Republican IT companies. Foreign connections raise questions. One is whether foreign interests are affecting United States elections. Conversely, are abuses festering in the United States because our authorities do not want to disrupt exports of voting technologies? The ultimate question is whether voters can be confident of election-day voting security that is financed in significant part by Republican-financed machines sold via Rove-assisted election officials and vendors.

Simpson is a knowledgeable researcher. I remained in close touch with her even when she largely withdrew from any public comments following the Obama administration's unwillingness to re-examine Rove-orchestrated Bush frame ups of Democratic politicians. She remained adamant in her original claims in 2007 that she first met Rove three decades ago in Texas via the Bush Family, and then worked with him and other Republicans as a volunteer on secret projects, loosely defined as "opposition research."

Simpson and other investigators have convinced me that Republican electronic voting machine software manipulation stole the 2002 Alabama gubernatorial election from Siegelman. The Alabama election provided a test-run for similar GOP operations used nationally, including 2004 voting fraud in Ohio determining that year's presidential election.

Grassroots activists appalled at official complicity in fraud have spent years warning the public. Meanwhile, the nation's political reporters, most working for outlets that profit handsomely from political ads spent by campaigns, ignore evidence of fraud. As a result, grassroots researchers are for the most part confined to small press books and blogs.

One of the most labor-intensive blogs is by Richard Charnin, an author and retired mathematician who once held expert posts in the government space and Wall Street financial sectors. He argues that exit polls in presidential elections since 1988 prove that Republicans have made overwhelming use of election machine fraud. In an October 26 daily report before the 2012 elections, he argued that polling data showed a large electoral vote margin for Obama.[2] Charnin is one of at least six voting integrity advocates who published books in the weeks before the 2012 elections claiming that election machine software and tabulation companies posed threats to fair voting counts.[3] Political reporters have shown little interest in the issue. They regard the entire topic too complex, adversarial or "conspiratorial" to investigate.[4]

Charnin, Simpson, March, and other critics of electronic voting machines believe that a knowledgeable software expert can change vote counts, thwarting the entire process of campaigns and elections. Individual voters and local election oversight volunteers have no meaningful way to detect software fraud. Those who want to change election results need to control voting machine contractors, and make sure that winning margins do not differ too greatly from final poll results without some plausible explanation preventing in-depth investigation. "If there's more than a three percent margin in the final polls," Simpson told me that Rove once informed her, "we probably can't win an election" with software shenanigans.

Rove has denied ever meeting Simpson, much less discussing any conspiracies. He called her "a nut" on Fox News in June 2012 while repeating his previous denial in his *Wall Street Journal* column and in his memoir, *Courage and Consequence*.[5] Rove coupled his denials, however, with several clearly untrue statements about her, such as a claim that she never dared provide sworn testimony. Craig Unger examined their opposing claims extensively in his 2012 book, *Boss Rove*. The book focused heavily on voting software fraud and concluded that Simpson is more credible than Rove.[6]

More generally, Rove was riding high in the fall of 2012. He and his allies were ready to spend $300 million to help GOP presidential nominee Mitt Romney and other federal candidates win November elections.[7] Behind the scenes, Republicans schemed to manipulate the outcome in shocking and potentially illegal ways, combining several of the worst recent dirty GOP tricks with new ones. Just before the election, there was good reason to suspect the following from Republicans:

■ **A Rove-enabled voting fraud empire.** Karl Rove and his allies have created a dangerous, integrated system of allied campaign finance and database companies, fund-raisers, and elected officials that select voting tabulation companies, according to abundant evidence. The actions fostered election fraud.[8]

■ **Partisan registration and voting suppression efforts against minorities**. Republican officials in swing states clearly intended to reduce voting by minorities, urban voters, and other likely Democrats by improper restrictions on registration and voting hours, forcing some voters to wait on line up to seven hours.[9]

■ **The Plot To Swift Boat Obama**. Republicans plotted how to create a Swift Boat-style campaign to portray Obama as weak in the Middle East, using the familiar Swift Boat strategy used against John Kerry in 2004. The arguments also echoed successful GOP attacks against Jimmy Carter in 1980 during the Iran hostage crisis.[10]

This chapter's survey of election procedures begins with a snapshot from history leading straight to President Obama's second-term cabinet.

Introduction: Hagel, Voting Machines, Silent Watchdogs

The mainstream media ignore the importance of election machine software and voter databases. Investors with a partisan interest in the political results do not make that mistake.

Voting machine executive Chuck Hagel became a United States senator via two upset election victories in 1996 using machines from his former company. Hagel advanced to become Obama's Secretary of Defense. His past as a voting machine executive is little known in 2013 even though Hagel's Republican opponents fought his nomination bitterly on other issues, including a filibuster threat in mid-February. Vote tabulation, it would appear, is a forbidden topic for much of the political class and mainstream media.

Charles "Chuck" Hagel is from a modest, small-town background in North Platte, Nebraska. He and his younger brother, Tom, began combat duty in the Vietnam War as enlisted men, a rare combination of siblings serving together in recent times. Chuck Hagel was seriously injured twice in combat. He and his brother saved each other's lives, winning admiration in their community and beyond.

Postwar, Chuck became active in Republican politics. The Reagan administration named him to a Veterans Administration post in Washington. Upon return to the private sector, he acquired cellphone licenses in the federal spectrum giveaways that helped solidify him among the well-connected insiders who became multi-millionaires. At that time, federal regulators awarded licenses to those deemed to be serving "the public interest," an inherently political and subjective standard.

In 1996, Hagel won an upset victory in Nebraska's Senate primary against a GOP opponent. In the general election, Hagel beat incumbent Nebraska Governor Ben Nelson, a heavily favored Democrat. After the election, rumors percolated that Hagel had been chair and CEO of American Information Systems (AIS), a vote-counting company that tabulated votes in Nebraska elections, among other places. Hagel's official biographical materials and disclosure statements gave scant mention of that role. Later, critics were unable to interest the Senate, or almost any other regulator or news reporter, in demanding fuller disclosure or otherwise probing the matter. In 1997, Hagel's former company changed its name to Election Systems and Software (ES&S). That company is now the nation's largest voting machine company by far.

In 2003, election activist Bev Harris published *Black Box Voting,* a pioneering look at dangers that election machines pose to the democratic process. More specifically, she warned against secret procedures for tabulating votes on proprietary software. She wrote that machines from Hagel's former company counted more than 80 percent of votes for his 1996 elections. The following account draws from her research:

Robert Urosevich and his brother Todd founded the Omaha-based company. Hagel chaired American Information Systems from 1992 to 1995 until his resignation two weeks before he announced his Senate campaign. The company has a complicated, evolving and secretive ownership structure that has included stakes by the parent company of the *Omaha World-Herald,* Nebraska's largest newspaper. Warren Buffett's Berkshire Hathaway Corp. has been an investor in the newspaper and voting machine company. In addition, the billionaire Buffett is a board member and major shareholder in the *Washington Post.* According to his authorized biography, he was a lover of the paper's owner, the late Katharine Graham.[11] The nation's largest voting machine company thus has overlapping ownership with the major local and national media that would normally be expected to play a watchdog role during campaigns. These are tight, mutually supportive, elite circles.[12] Other investors include the McCarthy Group, an investment company led by Hagel's former campaign finance director, Michael McCarthy. Hagel has seven-figure investments with McCarthy-led funds, as indicated by ethics disclosure statements.[13]

Since 1997, the company has been known as Election Systems and Software (ES&S). Its acquisitions have included some of the assets of Diebold Systems, another major company. Diebold's equipment, widely used in Ohio in 2004, became controversial after an executive urged a Bush-Cheney victory that year.

Hagel's voting machine work received virtually no news coverage from mainstream news outlets during his Senate campaign and subsequent career even though critics sent complaints alleging a conflict of interest to 3,000 journalists. "This is not, ultimately, a story about one man named Hagel," Bev Harris concludes. "It is a story about a rush to unauditable computerized voting using machines manufactured by people who have vested interests."[14] Currently, ES&S counts the votes for about half of the country's jurisdictions.[15]

Other election machine critics besides Harris believe serious problems exist across the nation with the vote tabulation and oversight process: The software in the machines can be adjusted to provide phony results, and the process is overseen by election officials or those beholden to officials who may be biased. Outside experts cannot monitor the process because the equipment and software are privately owned for the most part. Well-intentioned election day volunteers can perform traditional duties in monitoring registration lists on the local level. However, they cannot reliably certify high-tech tabulations on software screened from their view.

In the fall of 2012, longtime voting fraud public interest journalist, professor, lawyer, and Green Party candidate Bob Fitrakis and co-author Gerry Bello broke discoveries on their Free Press news site in Ohio under the headline, "Vote counting company tied to Romney."[16] They wrote of how Bain Capital alumni were heavily investing in the electronic voting machine business. They described the importance of the electronic voting machine network across the nation and the ownership of major companies by investors connected to Romney or the Bush Family. It focused, for example, on Hart InterCivic, whose machines are used "in all 234 counties of Texas, the entire states of Hawaii and Oklahoma, half of Washington and Colorado, and certain counties in swing state Ohio." The company responded that it has a diverse ownership structure, and has performed without irregularities.

A Rove-Enabled Voting Fraud Empire

The ownership stakes illustrate suspicious investment and management ties that undercut claims that the companies could not possibly affect voting. If that were true, why would partisans be so interested in investing and control?

Broadly speaking, the election industry sector includes both voting tabulation companies and those that provide ancillary services, including web hosting, backup and data mining to help campaigns target likely voters.

An alliance of Karl Rove-linked Republican companies was ready to repeat their previous vote-switching frauds in 2012. That was the claim of Simpson, March, and Ohio attorney Clifford Arnebeck at a news conference that I moderated on October 24 at the National Press Club. Arnebeck is a 1970 graduate of Harvard Law School who represented corporate and primarily Republican candidates in Ohio for many years in election law and related fields. He began representing public interest groups challenging the legality of the 2004 election after he researched serious disputes about voter suppression and vote theft in the 2004 presidential election.

At their 2012 news conference, Arnebeck and his co-panelists unveiled a chart alleging a Rove vote-fraud "empire" exists and courts must prevent authorities from secret vote switching.[17]

They announced their group, ElectionProtectionAction.org, whose site has a video describing their presentation.[18] Also speaking at the news conference was Dana Siegelman, daughter of imprisoned former Alabama Governor Don Alabama. She provided gripping descriptions of the real-world consequences of election software fraud her father had experienced in the 2002 gubernatorial election. This not only cost her father an election, but dramatically changed the state's public policies because Siegelman was a rare Democrat who could win statewide elections in Alabama.

Looking at such situations nationally, Simpson and March recounted how they had traveled the country for six weeks before the news conference in order to document the eco-system of election-tabulation companies. Simpson guided them based on her past as a volunteer GOP operative directly under Rove. They announced what they called the first "big picture" outline of a "total election fraud network... at least as connected to Karl Rove (which is most of it)." A video excerpt of their press conference can be found here.[19]

The essence of their message, echoing that of other election system critics, was that canny political operatives have achieved the ability to adjust election results by hidden influence in the campaign, vendor selection, and vote tabulation process. Big-dollar donors recruit, train and fund candidates for the state offices empowered to run elections. Data-mining companies use sophisticated techniques to compile information about the public to help these candidates.

It is not possible to replicate all such allegations (which form the core of several books) or the rebuttals. For further reading, I recommend "Cutting Through Hype, Hypocrisy of Vote Fraud Claims," my summary of a decade's major articles and books. My column argues that election theft deserves much more scrutiny than it receives from either government officials or news reporters, and in a dramatic move, it reported on how a federal judge had released the 2008 testimony of GOP IT guru Michael Connell. He died in a mysterious plane crash in 2008 after anonymous warnings that he would be killed if he testified about his work with those helping the Bush-Cheney ticket win in 2000 and 2004.[20] I updated the research report several times at the end of the 2012.[21]

As for the other side of the story, all those suspected of misconduct deny any wrongdoing. The defense to the lawsuit filed by Arnebeck and his colleagues on behalf of voters in Columbus, Ohio is a convenient summary of their denials.[22]

Out of all the materials now available concerning voting fraud, three topics are particularly important to treat. First is the heavy investment by two prominent Bush family patrons in the Rove-linked SmarTech. Second is the related issue of why voting machine companies have important international implications, both in terms of accuracy of domestic vote counting and in terms of American foreign policy. Finally, we explore the lack of oversight in this sector from regulators, academics, and the media.

Prominent Patrons. In *Boss Rove,* Unger extensively examines the history and importance of the Chattanooga-based SmarTech and its partners.[23] The company evolved from innovations by broadband pioneer, Michael Cunnyngham. After a bankruptcy, Cunnyngham's start-up transformed under new leadership into a little-known but powerful player in Republican politics.

Simpson describes SmarTech and its affiliates as controlled by two longtime Bush Family allies, Cincinnati hedge fund speculators William O. DeWitt Jr. and Reynolds Mercer. In *Family of Secrets*, Russ Baker reported the vital role that DeWitt and Mercer provided in helping George Bush in the 1980s with investments early in his business career. Bush later rewarded Mercer by naming him U.S. ambassador to Switzerland. Bush named Dewitt as a member of the highly secret and influential Foreign Intelligence Advisory Board.[24]

SmarTech hosted massive voter databases and outreach capabilities, as well as election security services. At the White House, Rove and a number of other senior officials used Republican National Committee accounts hosted by SmarTech instead of government accounts. When the House Judiciary Committee subpoenaed emails regarding the U.S. attorney purge, the White House said that most of the requested correspondence had been lost. SmarTech and other contractors lost 22 million emails, including nearly all of Rove's for extended periods, conveniently thwarting investigations.[25]

SmarTech subcontracted with GovTech, a company founded by Ohio resident Michael Connell, another IT pioneer with strong Republican connections. GovTech held IT contracts for congressional, White House, Florida, and Ohio work. Connell also controlled New Media, which served clients such as the two Bush-Cheney campaigns, the Republican National Committee, the Republican Governor's Association, and Republican Party units in at least thirty-one states.[26] In 2003, GovTech also received a $132,000 contract from Ohio Secretary of State Kenneth Blackwell to create a "mirror site" for Ohio election returns in 2004, with the data hosted, as usual, by SmarTech in Chattanooga.[27] Blackwell also co-chaired the Bush-Cheney re-election committee.

"There is a fundamental conflict of interest in having someone whose loyalty is not exclusively to the government," says Arnebeck, the Ohio attorney. "It's essential that there be a Chinese wall that would completely bar potential conflicts of interest."[28]

Simpson and public interest litigators from Ohio regard investment relationships as important. Mercer, for example, was chief fund-raiser for the Bush campaign in 2004 in Ohio. Arnebeck has for years claimed in litigation that SmarTech was instrumental in 2004 vote-switching in Ohio that helped enable the Bush-Cheney presidential victory that year.

Defendants denied wrongdoing, and the litigation was dismissed pre-trial on technical grounds. More currently, his clients and colleagues at the Free Press in Ohio published extensive reports on Romney investments in the election machine sector.[29]

Foreign Entanglements. The high-level posts that President Bush awarded to Mercer and DeWitt underscore the global dimensions to advanced voting technology. Most significant to election integrity critics are the unregulated aspects of the MOVE Act, a 2009 federal law more formally titled Military Overseas Voting Enhancement. The law's purpose was to make voting more efficient for overseas military, diplomatic, contractor, and other business employees. The act specified new federal funds for new systems to support the MOVE Act, which requires that these voters have the option to register to vote and vote electronically over the Internet

"No security provisions were put in – at all," Simpson and March reported in their prepared statement opening the news conference. "Worst of all, states are not allowed to put in security provisions stricter than the MOVE Act specifies if it slows down the 'efficiency goals' of the MOVE Act in any way." Their suspicions focused heavily on Scytl, based in Spain. The company describes itself as the developer of the world's most secure form of electronic balloting.[30] Grassroots voting security advocates say Scytl has gained contracts to oversee vote counting in more than 900 United States jurisdictions representing 25 percent of the nation. The company also received a Department of Defense appropriation for $800,000 to assist foreign-based military and other U.S. citizens in voting. That kind of funding to private companies is now pervasive in federal operations to replace core functions of the civil service with private contractors that have little accountability to the public.

In September 2012, Simpson and Jim March visited what they believed were Scytl's two main offices in the United States.[31]. One office appeared to be the private home of Hugh Gallagher, a Scytl officer who lived in a Richmond suburb. The other was a "virtual office," rentable by the month as a glorified mail drop with a group secretary, in a Baltimore office building. The office was the workplace of David Campbell, the company's general manager for United States operations.[32]

In response to news reports arising from the Simpson and March work, Scytl wrote me a denial of any irregularities and emphasized that its workforce was United States based and adequate to handle its core duties facilitating overseas balloting and assisting local officials.[33]

The United States intelligence community plays a disturbing role in the company's ownership, according to research by the Free Press and its parent organization, the Columbus Institute for Contemporary Journalism in Columbus, Ohio.[34] Scytl denied any irregularities about its company. It noted that is has a subsidiary based in Tampa, SOE Software.

More generally, many thousands of volunteers work in good faith on election days to enable accurate and otherwise fair elections. One of them, a good friend of mine who has been a senior elections official in a Washington suburb for many years, has assured me that it would be impossible for any non-local official or contractor to change or otherwise affect a vote submitted under the MOVE Act. That view is conventional wisdom.

Scant Oversight. Conventional wisdom and complacency lead to the current situation whereby almost no one is looking for problems, must less solving them. Thus, voters worried about election fraud can expect little help.

Election commissions are being kept weak by political leaders who want the freedom to skirt rules without consequences. The two major federal agencies should be in the forefront of fighting for honest elections. Instead, they have little mandate, vigor, or visibility. At the Federal Election Assistance Commission, all five commissioner posts were vacant during the 2012 campaign. The Obama administration failed to overcome Republican obstructions to staffing and funding.[35] A similar situation existed at the Federal Election Commission, where the terms of five of the six commissioners expired by the end of 2012. The commission, which focuses on funding, brought just a tenth of the number of official actions during the year compared to 2008.[36]

Frauds reliant on electronic means are unknowable to most voters and most poll-watchers. Under a national spotlight in 2012, GOP officials repeatedly cheated Texas congressman Ron Paul and his supporters during the 2012 primary battle and national convention arrangements. Procedures to reduce Paul's vote-counts were brazen, low-tech, and otherwise obvious. Even so, the Paul supporters had n recourse and little media coverage for their complaints.[37] If a presidential candidate cannot obtain coverage, ordinary voters can expect much less.[38]

In a deregulated, privatized, partisan political environment, election "regulators" and legislators have neither the desire nor capability to probe. Those deficiencies are even more glaring for the conventional news media. The media tend to have financial problems as well as huge conflicts of interest in scrutinizing a campaign committee that pumped well over a billion dollars into media advertising in 2012 alone.

Similar dysfunction and apathy occurred at the state level. The 2013 winter conference of the National Association of Secretaries of State had little visible discussion of election problems. That is not surprising since the association is comprised of those who run elections and those who sell the enabling equipment. Keynote speaker Chuck Todd, for example, had gone on record during the 2012 campaign to Tweet, "The voting machine conspiracies belong in the same category as the Trump birther garbage."[39] Three months later, Todd, NBC's political director and chief White House correspondent stood by that opinion, winning warm applause from a convention of vote-counters and sales workers.[40]

"That's just stretching the bounds of reality," Todd told the group in response to a question on vote-tampering claims. "That's feeding the conspiracy." Todd's spouse, like those of many other top political commentators, works for political campaigns. Like many situations in Washington, this appears to be a case of one hand washing the other — and so everyone looks clean.

Other examples abound of watchdogs that supposedly overlook the topic of election machine fraud. Heather Gerken, Yale Law professor advising the Obama campaign on election law, told a lecture audience in the spring of 2012 that there has never been a significant federal election decided by such fraud. Upon hearing her, I passed along my comprehensive article of relevant books and articles. [41] I introduced her to Jonathan D. Simon, head of the Election Defense Alliance and author of a book on electronic election fraud.[42] Simon sent her data on gross irregularities in electronic vote tabulation. I received in reply a brief email thanks, and Simon heard nothing back. My impression is that even experts have limited interest in the topic. By contrast, election integrity proponents argue that *prima facie* evidence already exists, with further evidence virtually impossible if no one reports or investigates.

I later checked with Simon shortly before the 2012 election on whether he had heard back from the professor or the Obama campaign. Simon described the professor as one of many highbrow "polite denialists" who have no apparent interest in forensic data suggesting criminal tampering with the elections process. Regarding the forthcoming election, Simon opined:

> The inside scoop I've heard is that the additional infrastructure (see SmarTech) has been installed in key swing/Senate states to "process" votes on off-site servers a la Ohio 2004. I have no doubt that Rove could rig-to-win pretty much anything he chose this year. The questions, however, are of reward/risk ratio, passing the smell test (*Citizens United* and Voter ID, whatever their impact-in-fact, will make that a lot easier than it would otherwise be), and long-term strategy (it may well suit to let Obama twist, collect the backflow in 2014, and have it all neatly wrapped in 2016).[43]

Rove thus stands at the center of suspicions. His American Crossroads and Crossroads GPS organizations help disburse hundreds of millions of dollars. The source of most of the money is cloaked because of the vagaries of election and tax law.

Mainstream news reporters have ignored the evidence for the most part. One of the most important reporters assigned to cover the Ohio claims of fraud told me privately that editors did not want a story unless the reporter provided absolute proof of fraud because it might shake public confidence in elections. Editors do not impose that standard of proof on other political stories.

The news conference on October 24 at the National Press Club also featured Dana Siegelman, daughter of the imprisoned former Alabama governor. Dana Siegelman said that the Alabama Attorney General William Pryor, Jr., now a federal appellate judge, threatened to arrest anyone who tried to investigate the vote-switch. Therefore, Don Siegelman simply focused on trying to prepare for the 2006 election, but was framed on corruption charges instead.

Jill Simpson told the audience that she was involved in machinations against Don Siegelman that were so unfair that she decided to speak out in 2007. Simpson has testified that Republicans went on to frame the former governor on corruption charges, in part by picking a corrupt federal trial judge, Mark Fuller of Montgomery, even before the defendant was indicted in 2005. The chief federal judge for Alabama's middle district secretly controlled Doss Aviation, a federal military contracting company, as a 44 percent shareholder. The company received nearly $300 million in Bush contracts from 2006 to 2009. The Bush funding of Judge Fuller was unknown to Siegelman and his defense attorneys before Simpson spoke up.[44]

The documented frame up of Siegelman underscores the radical nature of those willing to rig elections and courtrooms. The thievery also highlights the lack of protection for the public, including the direct victims such as Siegelman and the constituents robbed of their votes, leaders, and public policies.

Parker Griffith, a former GOP congressman from Alabama, highlighted all these themes during a 2012 radio interview in which he described Siegelman's seven-year sentence as a "political assassination." Griffith said of the victim, "There was not a finer man that wanted to do more for the state than Don Siegelman." He said that authorities unfairly convicted the former governor in what appeared to be a Karl Rove-orchestrated plot concocted with the help of Fuller. The former congressman described Fuller as a weak man ready to do what he could to please the Republican power structure.[45]

Griffith and Simpson were hardly alone in criticizing the Siegelman frame-up. U.W. Clemon, the initial federal judge to hear charges against Siegelman in 2004, later wrote the Justice Department in an unsuccessful effort to seek an investigation of what the judge called the most baseless case he had observed in nearly three decades on the federal bench.[46] Also,

113 former state attorneys general made an unprecedented yet unsuccessful petition to the U.S. Supreme Court to review Siegelman's corruption convictions in 2012. The bipartisan group of former chief law enforcers from more than 40 states argued that the defendant broke no law in his main convictions for reappointing a man to a state board in 1999.[47] The Supreme Court declined to hear the case, and Siegelman, at age 67, was ordered returned to prison on Sept. 11, 2012 for six more years regarding conduct that occurred in 1999.[48]

The Siegelman prosecution may seem far removed from election theft, perhaps as much as election theft seems different from this book's introduction by Dr. Cyril Wecht focusing on unjust prosecutions. In fact, however, election fraud and prosecutions with Rove fingerprints are parts of the same story. In it, we see the same man hounded for over a decade, so far, by outrageous, well-documented abuses. Meanwhile, watchdog institutions show virtually no interest in investigating.

If that weren't bad enough, there is the harm inflicted on his state by the deprivation of its elected leader, transforming it into a one-party fiefdom for the near future. I have a strong suspicion that this manifest injustice is the work of puppet masters with a keen interest in securing government contracts and casino gambling revenue.[49]

Overall, Rove was well positioned to help Mitt Romney become president in 2012. Romney's best hope for victory rested on the disreputable campaign tactics linked to Rove and his allies.

The two Crossroads funds drew great attention because of Rove's leadership and their heavy spending. In addition, Crossroads GPS claimed it is primarily an educational group, not a political advocate, and it claims tax exemption for its donors.[50] Robert Bauer, counsel for both the Obama re-election campaign and the Democratic National Committee, challenged the exemption in June 2012.[51] In a Fox News interview with Greta Van Susteren on June 20, Rove defended the tax-exempt status.[52]

The merits of the challenge to Crossroads' tax-exempt status remained an issue for IRS staff to resolve after the elections.

Suppressing Eligible Votes

In Chapter 9, I described the Florida GOP's successful 2000 Florida strategy whereby ChoicePoint's subsidary eliminated some 91,000 eligible Florida voters without warning shortly before the Bush-Gore election.[53] That effort relied on crude techniques of vote suppression. The tricksters use more sophisticated techniques these days to make voting more difficult for Democratic constituencies.[54] The Bush Justice Department and Fox News created a false public alarm that ineligible Democrats were stealing elections.[55]

The concept is preposterous on reflection. Nonetheless, partisan state legislatures enacted vote suppression legislation under the guise of preventing voting fraud.[56] Early voters complained harshly in Florida and Ohio, the two biggest swing states for the presidential race. Each state was run by a Republican governor suspected of trying to suppress votes in Democratic areas so that Republican Mitt Romney would win their state's electoral votes, and thus the presidency, as Bush had done in 2000 and 2004. Republicans mounted daring efforts to restrict the vote in new ways, right up to the 2012 elections.[57]

The Republican initiatives prompted court challenges in response.[58] The Democratic Party and the corporate-owned media belatedly focused on the vote suppression campaign.[59]

The Obama Justice Department challenged a number of the state laws. Those challenges achieved some successes but were far short of the major coordinated response required to prevent a fundamental assault on the right to vote. A GOP former Florida official admitted after the election that the "vote-fraud" scare tactics were designed to reduce Democratic turnout.[60] Yet the ordeal was a big joke three months later to three Fox and Friends hosts. They mocked a 102-year-old woman who waited three hours to vote because Obama honored her during his State of the Union address.[61]

The Plot To Swift Boat Obama

Two of the greatest recent Republican triumphs from successful presidential campaigns involved foreign affairs.

Republicans created an image of Democratic weakness on foreign affairs that doomed Jimmy Carter's 1980 reelection campaign against Ronald Reagan. President Carter's inability to persuade Iran to free United States hostages before the 1980 election made him look weak.

The other great success was the Swift Boat Veterans for Truth, a group of veterans who smeared 2004 Democratic nominee John Kerry regarding his war record.[62] The campaign fits into a familiar pattern of Rove and GOP-linked partisan sabotage designed to attack an opponent's supposed strength. In Kerry's case, the target was his medal-winning record of valor in Vietnam, as opposed to George Bush's questionable Air Guard if not AWOL status.

We can now reconstruct Republican efforts to replicate these "Carter" and "Swift Boat" strategies against Obama in 2012. On March 8, 2012, a new group called OpSec (standing for "Operational Security") obtained a domain name for its website.[63] OpSec had direct ties to longtime Republican IT experts who had formed the by-then defunct Swift Boats group. That is the account, which was provided to me exclusively for this book by an investigative team assembled by the Ohio-based Free Press. The team included Alabama attorney Jill Simpson, Arizona IT expert Jim March, and Ohio attorneys Clifford Arnebeck and Bob Fitrakis.

They told me that GOP IT consultant Rebecca Donatelli secured the domain name. She was principal in the firm Connell-Donatelli that succeeded Michael Connell's company. Soon afterward, Rove set the stage of an OpSec recruitment campaign in his *Wall Street Journal* column on March 21 by criticizing Obama foreign policy campaign themes.[64] SmarTech previously hosted the Swift Boat website as well as sites for many Republican campaigns and the Bush-Cheney White House. SmarTech began hosting the OpSec account on March 26.[65]

In June 2012, OpSec distributed a video to former SEALs and other elite members of the military and security community. The video portrayed President Obama as taking unwarranted credit for bin Laden's death in the 2011 raid and sought support from the military community in shaming the president for making the raid a centerpiece of the his reelection message. As expected, the OpSec video generated support from some recipients who opposed the president. The video was so extreme in its attack, however, that it also generated protest to the Pentagon. Authorities there secretly began an investigation of whether the video indicated that military and former military personnel were becoming involved in partisan campaigning in an illegal manner.

A few weeks later, an unknown person launched on YouTube another video, "The Innocence of the Muslims." Billed as a movie preview, the amateurish video portrayed the Prophet Mohammad as a pervert. The producer clearly intended to create controversy. The distribution on YouTube apparently attracted few views, yet the nasty anti-Muslim crusade had the effect of undercutting United States policy and personnel in Muslim nations.[66]

In mid-August 2012, the OpSec group of former commandos and intelligence operatives contacted news organizations to announce their group.[67] OpSec, formally known as the Special Operations OpSec Education Fund Inc., unveiled a 22-minute, documentary-style video featuring interviews with former spies and U.S. Special Forces commandos. Comprised largely of former Navy SEALs and other former military operatives, the speakers reiterated their anti-Obama claims. Reuters reported:

> Leaders of OpSec said it is nonpartisan and unconnected to any political party or presidential campaign. It is registered as a so-called social welfare group, which means its primary purpose is to further the common good and its political activities should be secondary. 68

Similarly, the *New York Times* reported that OpSec leader Chad Kolton, the spokesman for the director of national intelligence in the Bush administration, said the group had raised nearly $1 million since June and intended to run ads in swing states.[69] The 22-minute OpSec video, called "Dishonorable Disclosures," was "aimed squarely at the president, echoing charges made previously by Republicans." Another leader of the group, unsuccessful GOP congressional candidate Scott Taylor, described Obama as a "braggart" regarding the bin Laden raid. The *Times* also reported:

> Mr. Kolton rejected the comparison with the Swift Boat advertisements, saying they reflected narrow differences of opinion about Mr. Kerry's war record. He said the OpSec group had a broader purpose in speaking out against leaks and the politicization of the Navy SEALs and the CIA, and it hoped to keep working after the election. No one who was involved in the Swift Boat campaign is working with the OpSec group, he said.[70]

During the summer of 2012, the Defense Intelligence Agency (DIA), a body so secret that most Americans do not know it exists, undertook an investigation of OpSec. The group's recruitment efforts inevitably led investigators to Petraeus and his circle. Petraeus had commanded personnel in Tampa linked with special operations, and was known to have entertained invitations from Republicans to run against Obama in 2012, as previously described.

Any effort to use the inherent credibility of the military to foster emotional appeals against Obama, the military's commander-in-chief, is of particular concern to investigators in wartime. As background, Petraeus was a hero to the tea party and other angry Americans. Many believe with a passion that Obama holds office illegitimately and with a dangerous agenda. Investigators feared that the former military personnel featured by OpSec might breach confidentiality restrictions in force even for retirees. If so the perpetrators would violate special operations obligations and traditions. That said, any such investigation is itself affected by the views of authorities, and thus political.

Defense Department concerns also included longstanding suspicions that David Petraeus and his circle might want to help the Republican ticket in 2012 in order to foster the CIA director's political career later. Candidacies do not arise out of thin air. A candidate typically must provide vision and demonstrated loyalty to wealthy and otherwise highly influential supporters, not simply a resume and reputation. OpSec's creation, including the all-important step of creating contact lists of potential sympathizers, was fostered according to my information with the help of the Petraeus circle of supporters.

Syria, Libya, and the Benghazi Attack

By 2012, John Brennan and the Obama administration faced big problems in the Middle East and North Africa. The "Arab Spring" revolts the previous year had targeted autocratic regimes, including those in Egypt and Bahrain central to United States military strategies.

The complex tasks required expert analysis and covert operations, backed up by security and other paramilitary capabilities. The term "CIA" is often used to encompass these functions for convenience. More than a dozen United States intelligence agencies now have at least some overlapping responsibilities. The CIA itself has expanded from its roots as an analytic and covert agency to included drones and paramilitary work that overlaps with traditional functions of the Department of Defense. Therefore, an expert White House coordinator is vital for any hope of success.

In the long term, United States has sought to contain Soviet and Russian influence in the Mideast (broadly defined to include Arab North Africa and Muslim Central Asia). Most of the time, the United States works closely with its allies in Israel and the oil-rich Sunni Muslim Gulf monarchies, most notably Saudi Arabia, Kuwait, Qatar, and the United Arab Emirates. Iran, since its 1979 revolution, has been a United States opponent. Iran's leaders voice anti-Western and anti-Israel rhetoric tied to their Shia version of the Muslim faith that creates bitter rivalries also with Sunni adherents. The United States has also long opposed the governments of Syria and Libya. Each nation's rulers granted rights to the Soviet Union to operate naval bases on the Mediterranean Sea. The Soviets closed their base in Benghazi two decades ago, but Russia retains a base in Tartous, Syria, its sole installation on the sea.

Those United States major alliances and opponents have remained relatively stable for at least three decades. In the meantime, the United States has sought to advance its goals in temporary alliances with a number of other nations and interest groups. The United States, for example, supported the Taliban, Osama bin Laden, and Saddam Hussein to thwart Soviet and Iranian goals in Central Asia in the early 1980s, and then attacked these three former allies.[71] American leaders showered military aid to prop up leaders in Egypt and elsewhere for years. Then, "The Arab Spring" of street protests in 2011caught State Department and intelligence services relatively unaware. Secretary of State Hillary Clinton, for instance, called Egyptian President Hosni Mubarak a close friend shortly before widespread hatred of his regime ended with his imprisonment and replacement by the once-banned Moslem Brotherhood.

Here is the gist of the dramatic interventions in Libya and Syria, and why they are important to American foreign policy.

The North African street protests provided an opportunity to overthrow Libya's longtime director, Moammar Gaddafi. Players included his opponents, such as radical militants as well as Gulf monarchies and NATO allies. Benghazi, a city of 600,000 on the Mediterranean Sea near Egypt, was the center of the rebellion. With the help of a NATO "No-Fly Zone" amongst other allied support, the rebels captured and executed Gaddafi on October 20, 2011.

After the dictator's death, his vast arsenal of weapons fell into the hands of rebel leaders, some of them militants radicalized from anti-Western fighting in Iraq and Afghanistan. One of these was the group Ansar Al-Sharia based near Benghazi, led by Sufyan ben Qumu (aka Abu Sufian Bin Qumu). Allied forces had captured Qumu in Pakistan in 2002 and imprisoned him in Guantanamo Bay for suspected terrorism in working for bin Laden in the Sudan. The United States sent Qumu to Libya in 2007, where he was liberated three years later. Such a reprieve for a well-connected suspected radical raises the possibility that Qumu became a double agent. Yet a double agent might become a triple agent, or at least act against American interests on occasion.

Overall, the situation in Libya created *Casablanca*-style intrigue, but with far more firepower on the streets than shown in the World War II film. Scores of violent attacks against Westerners occurred in Libya in 2012, with more than 50 of them in Benghazi.

Meanwhile, in Syria, many in the Sunni Muslim majority were rebelling against President Bashar al-Assad. His family had governed since 1970, enforcing government favoritism for those in their Alawite faith. The rebellion began with street protests in early 2011 and escalated by mid-2012 into full-scale civil war abetted by mercenaries, jihadists, and other fighters from many nations. Turkey and the Sunni Gulf monarchies visibly helped the rebels, with NATO helping more in the background. Iran assisted Syria. So did Russia and China, who made maneuvers at the United Nations to resist the kinds of NATO interventions that doomed Gaddafi. The lingering Syrian war not only became a humanitarian disaster, but also a political threat to the West and Israel. Jihadists who hated the West were gaining power among the rebels the longer the fighting raged.

In this delicate situation, United States officials in Washington and Libya sought to help friendly forces in both countries and punish opponents without creating undue animosities. The United States has described its interest in toppling Assad as humanitarian. Therefore, our country has helped rebel forces comprised primarily of Sunnis, including some radical Muslims from other nations. Libya provided a convenient base for certain U.S. operations, including the surreptitious recruitment of arms and fighters for Syria. However, U.S. personnel faced many hazards and a command split between U.S. civilian, military, and intelligence leaders. Additionally, Congress cut more than $400 million from the State Department's security requests over a two-year period. Ongoing budget stalemates in Congress along with bureaucratic procedures at the State Department kept security planning in flux.

Such was the dangerous situation when U.S. Ambassador Christopher Stevens visited Benghazi on September 10, 2012, his first trip to the city in more than a year. An Arab expert, Stevens was a career foreign service officer after an early career as an attorney. He sought to foster a stable, pro-Western, and popular government. That work required him to meet with local and international power brokers.

On his visit to Benghazi, Stevens stayed in a "temporary mission facility." The compound was far less secure than a fortified embassy or consulate. A British private security company provided five unarmed, poorly-trained Libyan guards in front.[72] The compound lacked physical barricades against intruders used by more permanent installations. A companion facility for CIA paramilitary personnel was several minutes' drive away in order to keep up a public image that State employees and CIA worked separately. Five American security guards employed by the State Department were at the compound with Stevens and a communications aide, Sean Smith.

The next evening, Stevens retired around 9 p.m. local time. About 40 minutes later, an armed mob of more than 100 people unleashed a surprise attack. The unarmed Libyan security guards vanished at the first sign of trouble. The ambassador and Smith, a former Air Force sergeant, retreated to a safe room. They were smoked out and killed. The remaining State Department security contractors held off the mob for several hours and radioed for help. At dawn, mortar fire killed two former Navy SEALs, Tyrone Cobb and Glen Doherty. Each was a CIA independent security contractor who had rushed to the scene as part of a rescue effort, albeit too late to save Stevens and Smith. Remaining American personnel evacuated the battle scene and the city shortly after Cobb and Doherty died. Ten Americans were wounded, and 32 were evacuated along with the four corpses.

That and most of the rest of the following chronology is primarily based on official reports by the State Department and Senate. [73] The chronology and findings of fault are largely undisputed. Brandon Webb and Jack Murphy, two Special Operations veterans, have supplemented those reports with an electronic book, *Benghazi: The Definitive Report,* published by the Murdoch-owned subsidiary Morrow/HarperCollins.[74] The book, based on a dozen confidential interviews, names more of the participants than the official reports and otherwise provides more dramatic and interpretative detail. Brandon Webb is a former U.S. Navy SEAL who served combat deployments to Iraq and Afghanistan. He co-authored a 2010 book with Doherty, whom he describes as his best friend and a hero who would not want any sympathy for doing his job.[75] In addition, Webb is editor-in-chief of SOFREP.com, a website for Special Operations veterans and personnel from all four service branches. The other co-author is Jack Murphy, a former U.S. Army Ranger with multiple combat deployments in Iraq and Afghanistan. He is the co-founder and managing editor of the SOFREP.[76]

They describe how Cobb was among a half dozen CIA Global Response Staff (GRS) commandos who rushed to the State Department mission in two Toyota Land Rovers. A firefight lasted for hours, closely monitored by United States personnel in the region and in Washington. Doherty, at a CIA base in Tripoli, helped lead a team that bribed a local pilot to fly seven United States CIA commandos to Benghazi, where they arrived at 5 a.m. for a fight still in progress. The authors wrote:

> Contrary to the many media myths about Benghazi, requests for help were not denied by the Obama administration. It appears as if every informed agency and organization tried its best to give whatever help it could during the attack. As you will soon see, this would also be true at the smallest unit level, where several American patriots in Tripoli would do anything to rally to the aid of their fellow countrymen.[77]

Despite the assessment above, Romney and other Republicans unleashed an immediate, all-out, and unrelenting attack on Democrats blaming them for the deaths. The blame-throwing began even before the final two Americans, Cobb and Doherty, were killed on September 11. The criticism of Obama and his personnel continued far beyond the campaign. Some independent journalists claimed as early as mid-September 2012 that Republicans facilitated the attacks for vile partisan purposes.

Elections Enforcement Breakdowns

Republicans have been highly successful in fostering public fears of Democratic-led voter registration fraud. Author John Fund is a leading fear-monger of that illusory problem.[78] The real problem is election machine fraud, which receives little attention in mainstream news accounts aside from those published in the United Kingdom by BBC reporter Greg Palast. He predicted that Rove and his co-conspirators would try to repeat their previous successes in 2012.[79] Other warnings came from Craig Unger, who previewed his book with a *Vanity Fair* column.[80] The timing was bad for Rove. The book assembled little-known threads of his life for easy reference in case anything big went bad.

Simpson, a major source for Unger, wanted to prevent the kind of systemic voter fraud she believes Rove helps implement both in the United States and internationally.

Injustice remains because authorities have not been willing to ask high-level suspects to testify under oath. My research suggests that this failure stems in part from CIA and other national security connections. These relationships immunize them, in effect, no matter what they do. There are, of course, certain Constitutional and public relations obstacles to freewheeling investigations. The Fifth Amendment protects against self-incrimination. However, in the case of the voting fraud cases, no one ever dares even initiate serious investigations aside from citizens groups. But civil litigants do not possess the investigative power of government.

My goal, like that of my sources, is to alert the public and elections administrators that these problems will fester in future elections. Government officials and the news media must stop being so timid about exposing the most ruthless of the nation's elections thieves.

A Whale of A Battle

The Romney campaign was optimistic for 2012 success with its expensive "Project Orca." Orca was a high-tech GOTV ("Get out the vote") computerized operation based at Romney campaign headquarters in Boston. The project drew information on voting from 34,000 volunteers deployed in swing states. Data went to sophisticated software at Romney headquarters, which could then generate response instructions, including instructing field workers on how to turn out more voters before the polls closed.

As early as 2008, GOTV campaigns had become very sophisticated. By 2012, better technology and higher spending made the efforts vastly more pivotal than ever before. Shortly prior to an Election Day conference call, Romney GOTV staff revealed how Romney planned to preside at the Orca "inner war room" on Election Day. "The governor loves seeing data, he loves seeing numbers and he's a very strategic person; he's a very smart man," a campaign official told volunteers in the call heard by the Huffington Post. "So he actually loves being inside these war rooms, seeing the data come in and seeing exactly what's going on out there, so we can all put our heads together and say, 'Okay, we need to move resources here. We need to shift resources from here.'"[81]

Deeply hidden from view, even from Romney volunteers and the vast bulk of staff, was another use for the data aside from standard GOTV work. According to my sources, operatives could electronically manipulate votes in key jurisdictions if needed.

Orca is the name for killer whales. They are the largest members of the dolphin family, and grow to a length of up to 30 feet. Obama's grassroots operation was in San Francisco. The Obama team was called "Operation Narwhal" after a species of whales in Arctic regions that have a long tusk, and sometimes fight the much larger Orcas.[82]

Whales live much of their lives below the surface. So do important parts of political campaigns, as the 2012 el
ection would suggest.

Part III: The 2012 Challengers

"Well, Doctor, what have we got — a Republic or a Monarchy?"

"A Republic, if you can keep it."

— Attributed to Benjamin Franklin as
his response to a question at the close of
the Constitutional Convention of 1787

Chapter 15

Paul Ryan: Killing Us Softly...

As the stock market and nation's economy collapsed in September 2008, GOP House Budget Committee leader Paul Ryan sold shares of Citibank and Wachovia, and bought Goldman Sachs stock. The ranking Republican member of the House Budget Committee,[1] Ryan held a position that afforded him rare if not unique information on the financial situation of the stock market and government plans to bail out selected companies.[2] As millions of Americans were losing their savings and ultimately their jobs and homes, Ryan's committee needed to support any bailouts.

Ryan, a member of the House Republican leadership, had superb information, which allowed him to predict the outcome of the vote on bailouts. Party leaders conduct secret tallies before each major legislative vote and Ryan knew that House Republicans were in full revolt. On September 29, 133 of 198 House Republicans voted against the bailout proposal along with 95 Democrats, forming a 225-member majority.[3]

Ryan showed neither leadership nor ethics by attempting to profiteer for his personal portfolio amidst the banking crisis, thereby making money at someone else's expense. Ryan regarded these gains as his right, his entitlement. One day before the first bailout, after being alerted to a private briefing for Congressional leaders by session of Congress from Federal Reserve Chairman Ben Bernanke and Treasury Secretary Henry Paulson, Ryan made his moves.[4] The weight of evidence tilts against Ryan even if his campaign and some independent observers excused his conduct.

This behavior, although legal under the lax laws Congress imposed on itself, made Paul Ryan a poster boy for the public's 7 to 10 percent House approval rating in many 2012 polls. Instead of making trades, Ryan should have been protecting the public.

He was not the only member of Congress to trade based on inside information during the 2008 financial meltdown.[5] However, he was the only member who ran for vice president in 2012 on a platform of harsh austerity for the public.

Ryan, like the others profiled in *Puppetry*, possesses attractive qualities, of course. Those who groom the nation's future leaders obviously prefer those who can obtain positive responses from the public. Ryan, tall, slim, and wide-eyed, skillfully delivers his team's talking points and generates favorable responses from most in his intended audiences. In terms of the specifics here, Ryan and his defenders rebut criticism with confidence. For one thing, few in the public have the time to probe complicated policies in any depth. More important, core supporters of Ryan and virtually all of others from both parties portrayed in this book tend to dismiss any criticism by responding that leaders in the opposition party are worse, and that their man at least advances sound policies for civic betterment. Such circular logic is emotionally gratifying, almost indisputable, and thus widespread and otherwise powerful. Therefore, the Ryan profile, like others to follow, sheds new light on a familiar face but without presuming that it is the only possible perspective.

Mitt Romney's happy-looking campaign photos with Ryan made them look like the best of friends. In fact, they did have a common tie beyond most running mates. As Massachusetts governor, Romney presided over state contracts awarded to a marketing company controlled by Ryan's brother, Tobin Ryan, a former Bain and Company partner. Bain Capital funded Tobin Ryan's marketing start up. Ryan profited when it was sold for $230 million in 2005, according to a major investigative article published by a London newspaper.[6]

Many such situations involving huge sums of money arise in business and government. Few come to any significant public attention. This chapter reveals the source of Ryan's extremist political philosophies, the masters he serves, and the dangers that Ryan poses to nearly every American, even after he lost the 2012 vice presidency. He simultaneously ran for the Wisconsin congressional seat. He prevailed and remained as House Budget Committee chairman.

This chapter describes also the overall dishonesty of the Ryan platform, including the fiction that Ryan is an expert. "Apprentice Oligarchs," this book's first chapter, sketched Ryan's background as a Wisconsin-born political junkie. Now, we examine his development as a creature of the Washington bureaucracy and advocacy world. He has enriched himself by parroting the anti-government slogans of the one percent of the wealthiest so deftly that he has ascended to the government's highest levels. Ryan's financial practices show that he, despite his homilies about shared sacrifice, regards federal office as an opportunity to exploit the government for the benefit of fellow insiders. Finally, this chapter illustrates how Ryan and his colleagues blocked Democratic efforts to improve the economy. Many of the Democratic proposals were half-hearted and tainted by special interests. Nevertheless, the GOP reaction was far worse. They sought to sabotage remedial measures for the economy, and many other facets of government, so that they could then argue in the 2012 elections that Obama had not succeeded.[7]

The Ryan campaign threatened the living standard of vast numbers of Americans and the actual lives of more than a few.[8] Many of the most vulnerable fail to understand the gravity of these threats. For both Ryan and Romney, the 47 percent of Americans who pay no federal income tax are the pathetic discards of society, to whom they as leaders owe no obligation to represent. At a private Florida fundraiser, Romney described his view on the matter to his wealthy supporters.[9] The speech, secretly taped, was at the mansion of tycoon Marc Leder, a co-owner of the Philadelphia 76ers and CEO of Sun Capital, a leveraged buyout company that operates much like Bain Capital.[10] Leder is also known for his wild parties.[11] Romney showed that he was committed to governance by and for the nation's elite, speaking for nearly an hour at Leder's mansion. Overall, Romney came across as "a sneering plutocrat."[12]

Romney later professed that he would fight for "the 100 percent," but by October 16 everyone knew what Romney thought in private. Republican strategist and Romney surrogate Mary Matalin referred to the 47 percent as "parasites."[13] The candidates and their strategists aimed for a narrow 51 percent victory through massive vote suppression. They did not care about the facts: The 47 percent who do not pay federal income taxes include large numbers of retirees, students, disabled, active duty military, and working poor benefitting from GOP-initiated tax breaks. Like politicians everywhere, Romney and Ryan said what they needed to say to their largest donors. This chapter explores how the plutocrats whom Ryan serves and aspires to join play a rigged game. They win and the rest of the public loses.[14]

Ryan's Roots

Paul Ryan is an heir to a family fortune arising from his great-grandfather, who became wealthy in railway and road construction. The company is Ryan Incorporated Central. It grew rapidly through government contracts as a part of the transcontinental railroad. By the 1950s, the company had switched to road building. The company won federal contracts to build portions of the interstate highway system, part of a massive federal spending program launched by the GOP and Eisenhower administration.[15] The federal government has been good to the family, and to Paul Ryan in particular. This background allowed Ryan to spend most of his life in politics, advocating for those who have accumulated great wealth. One might think Ryan's family company might make him an advocate of public works and transportation projects, a type of work that creates well-paying jobs for hundreds of thousands. Instead, Ryan complains about stimulus projects when proposed by Democrats. He lauds them as job-creation tools in private when he is seeking funding.

Ryan's daily life demonstrated his hypocrisy and overall contempt for the public. These traits make it easier to assess his more abstract and futuristic financial scenarios as bogus. Ryan received a $2 million inheritance in 2010, but neglected to list it on his congressional financial statement for two years until he knew he would fall under extra scrutiny as the GOP vice presidential nominee.[16]

The man who forgot to declare a seven-figure inheritance is a House leader who slept on an office cot in Congress so he would not have to pay local rent and taxes of the kind his interns pay.[17] He has been on a federal payroll virtually his entire career except for training time at the Empower America conservative think tank led by Jack Kemp. Ryan took a pro-growth attitude from Kemp, but neglected to pick up Kemp's humanity.[18] Similarly, Ryan likes to cite the free market principles of the iconic economist Adam Smith, and ignore Smith's warnings about the limitations of his theory.[19]

Ryan's residential use of his office to save money is a habit considered gross on Capitol Hill because of the cramped offices in the historic buildings, the ubiquitous presence of eager and mostly youthful staffers, and the necessity of keeping personal grooming gear in an office environment. In normal circumstances, free residential lodging is a taxable benefit. Yet the politically powerless residents of the District of Columbia, prevented from having elected representatives with voting power, have no effective way to enforce that taxation requirement on their masters in Congress. The IRS presumably knows better than to tangle with congressional overseers on such a matter, especially since Ryan is following a precedent set by former House Majority Leader Dick Armey, who also used to sleep in his congressional office.

In 2010, Ryan joined with two GOP congressional colleagues, Eric Cantor of Virginia and Kevin McCarthy of California, to co-author *Young Guns*, a book outlining their harsh prescriptions for cutbacks in the social safety net.[20]

As a congressional leader, Ryan has not had to follow rules. He helps make them. He successfully proposed a House tax plan that (if enacted into law) would have required fat cats such as Mitt Romney to pay less than one percent of their income in federal taxes.[21] This amount would have been a significant cut to the already-tiny 14 percent Romney actually paid under his most recent filing announced during the 2012 campaign. Because of special tax provisions available to Romney and his peers, Romney could amend his 2011 filing after the 2012 election. Those changes can bring Romney's rate down to 10 percent, according to experts, now that his need for disclosure is over. With tax proposals like that, no wonder Romney wanted Ryan on his ticket.

The media rarely presented what should have been an obvious point: If Romney's money was in a blind trust, why should he benefit from a host of tax breaks? The investments were not risk-taking if he does not know what they are. These tax breaks helped keep his basic rate at 15 percent, a level far below the average member of the middle class.

Much of the nation became familiar with Ryan's penchant for lying about simple matters when he was caught exaggerating his speed in the only marathon of his life. Anyone who has run even one mile, much less 26 in a row, knows the vast difference between a sub-seven-minute per-mile pace, and a plus-minute-minute pace. So did Ryan. Nevertheless, he clearly did not care about the truth when he bragged about a false time to admiring right-wing radio host, Hugh Hewitt. This was not an aberration. The super-macho Ryan has also been caught boasting about climbing 40 high-peak mountains, an endeavor estimated to take all of his vacation time over the course of two decades.[22]

The Romney-Ryan campaign "ramrodded their way" into a religion-based Ohio soup kitchen for 15 minutes during the presidential campaign so that Ryan and his wife, Janna, could be photographed washing dishes as if they were working volunteers. This was after the kitchen closed and the pots were already clean. Every successful politician at times seeks "photo ops," and sometimes, as here, without permission from an organization's leader. Yet this was especially phony and hypocritical because the Ryan political agenda represents an assault on the poor and middle class that would, if enacted, cause vast suffering and premature death.[23]

Inspired by Rand, Empowered by Voters

Russian-born novelist Ayn Rand lived from 1905 to 1982.[24] An emigrant to the United States in 1926, she wrote three major novels that hold cult-like appeal for young conservatives. Her themes extol independent entrepreneurs, professionals, and tycoons who dare to despise conventional wisdom. Ryan was one such fan, and reportedly assigned interns in his congressional office to read the Rand works that he so greatly admired.[25] According to Ryan, "Rand makes the best case for the morality of democratic capitalism."[26] The 1,200 pages portray an America "where many of society's most productive citizens refuse to be exploited by increasing taxation and government regulations and go on strike."[27] To her, these productive citizens are the "makers, not the takers," as in modern America's "47 percent." She failed to note that inherited wealth, nepotism, conformity, and nasty business practices could also be paths to wealth, and that unpredictable health issues cause most bankruptcies.

Ryan is not alone in his admiration of Rand and her philosophy. Other fans have included longtime Federal Reserve Chairman Alan Greenspan[28] Another admirer of Rand was Christopher Cox, a former California congressman who presided over the deregulatory prelude to the Wall Street and mortgage industry collapse during his tenure as the Bush-appointed chairman of U.S. Securities and Exchange Commission. Their libertarian philosophy of economics rests on the removal of government restraints on the private sector. As a result, they unleashed financial scamsters who, in effect, destroyed the savings and home equity of many in the middle class.

Greenspan became embarrassed over the Bush-era economic collapse on his watch. Greenspan, in the twilight of his career, could afford to admit mistakes without suffering from the wrath of right-wing overlords. Ryan maintained his anti-regulatory rhetoric but backed away from his early praise for Rand, an atheist who deeply admired greed and sociopaths.[29]

Ryan exemplifies a longstanding weakness in the political system whereby a few members of congress wield enormous political power even though few of them face serious re-election challenge because of gerrymandering and the corrupt financial power of incumbency. Ryan, to his credit, won his first race in a swing district in southeastern Wisconsin. Since then he has been able to coast to easy victories. Only in political and partisan circles might he be regarded as an expert. He holds a bachelor's degree in political science and economics, and is not a published authority. He wants, in effect, socialism for the super-wealthy and their government enablers, and survival of the fittest for the rest.

A Program for America

During the 2012 campaign, MSNBC displayed videos of two speeches on the House floor by Paul Ryan in which he argued for opposite policies, depending on whether his proposal provided a political advantage to his leaders. In 2002 when the Bush administration sought $120 billion in stimulus funds even though it would worsen the deficit, Ryan argued that Keynesian economics justified the spending. In specific language, he explicitly supported unemployment insurance and healthcare. In 2010, when Democrats sought stimulus funds for jobs, Ryan claimed that Keynesian economics could not work.[30]

For such reasons, Ryan threatens the lives and living standard of vast numbers of Americans. Many of those who are financially vulnerable fail to understand the gravity of the threat that Ryan represents to their well-being. He has large, seemingly sympathetic eyes, and can flash a smile. He is physically fit, whatever his bogus accomplishments. He is skilled at voicing benign words. Watching his buoyant attitude, one can visualize a happier and more productive America. That America is hard for the younger generation to see under Presidents Obama and Bush. Instead, Americans have, in recent times, seen a major shift in wealth from the middle classes to the already wealthy. Few remember the lessons of the Depression and its resolution aside from a few old-timers and scholars.

Those willing to read this far already know what you need to know about Ryan and his ideas. He is a chiseler, an opportunist, and a deceiver. He has no independent stature aside from that provided him by the politics he professes to despise. He is in the pocket of tycoons who want to pay fewer taxes and obtain more from other taxpayers, whether by direct federal contracts or by raiding such once-safe safety nets as Social Security and Medicare funding. Genuine experts, such as Paul Krugman, have written on such topics many times, pointing out the lack of "loopholes" to close under the Ryan and Romney tax-cut promises.[31] For those who want to examine Ryan's program in more depth, it has been available in his own words on the Romney-Ryan website and his congressional site, both available via Wikipedia.[32]

Summing Up

Some who hear about Ryan sleeping in his congressional office, then think of him as a humble family man who loves his work and needs to save money. Smiles do not equal generosity and compassion. Sleeping in the office as a millionaire is eccentric, not admirable. "It's disgusting," one longtime Hill staffer told me. "I rented an apartment when I was making $13,000 a year on the Hill, and so should he."

The real Ryan, like the real Romney, favors programs and policies based on a rewritten history, adapted to achieve the goals of wealthy patrons. Ryan is a front man for crippling, "shock doctrine" economics that have little or nothing to do with the middle class. He merrily created a Medicare program that would price many seniors out on the first year, and would cut more each year after that. Ryan, a fitness buff famed for his workouts in the congressional gym, will not experience the guaranteed suffering and premature death that results from severe rationing and withdrawal of medical care. He has taxpayer-paid medical care and a generous pension.

Ryan said during the campaign that he and Romney would balance the federal budget while giving the super-wealthy huge tax breaks. But he and his running mate refused to describe any existing tax loopholes that would produce revenues to offset the money lost by their tax cuts. Independent analysts said that even drastic cuts to major deductions for home mortgages, charitable giving, and state and local taxes would not close the deficit. Furthermore, Romney and Ryan sought to change the rules for middle class taxpayers who bought homes anticipating deductions, and would devastate charities just at the time they would be expected to make up for the collapse of safety nets on local and state levels.

The Ryan and Romney vision offered a bold new world characterized by the most extreme politics and leadership in the nation's history. Ryan presented himself as a charming, fit, and capable young man. In fact, he was and is a front man for oligarchs such as the Koch Brothers, who are intent on delivering their version of complete freedom for those at the top of the financial pyramid and on sending the rest down a road to serfdom.[33]

The oligarchs and their minions were undaunted in achieving a hostile takeover of the government even after their 2012 election losses. Ryan lost the vote in his hometown of Janesville and in the Wisconsin statewide totals for the presidential race. He did win re-election in his district, which was reconfigured in 2000 and 2010 to provide a safe margin for Republicans. The same pattern occurred nationwide, where Republicans retained control of the House even though Democrats won the popular vote by a 52-48 percentage in congressional races.

Ryan's theories are economically harmful to most Americans. What would happen if they were enacted and protests arise? Big Brother from *1984*, not *Atlas Shrugged*, points the way to today's threat.

Chapter 16

Mitt Romney: The Prophet of Profit

T he public heard plenty about Mitt Romney's "47 percent" speech during the fall of 2012, but not enough. That is because Romney's secret speech to wealthy Florida donors the previous May defined not simply the candidate, but also today's GOP and the potential collapse of the country's democratic institutions.[1]

To recap, *Mother Jones* Washington Bureau Chief David Corn obtained a surreptitious video from a 38-year-old bartender at hedge fund financier Marc Leder's $50,000-per-person Romney fund raiser.[2] Bartender Scott Prouty thereby showed, among other things, that an individual can have an enormous impact on public life. In words worth recalling yet again, Romney told the group of fellow fat cats at Leder's mansion:

> There are 47 percent of the people who will vote for the president no matter what. All right, there are 47 percent who are with him, who are dependent upon government, who believe that they are victims, who believe the government has a responsibility to care for them, who believe that they are entitled to health care, to food, to housing, to you-name-it. That that's an entitlement. And the government should give it to them. And they will vote for this president no matter what...These are people who pay no income tax....[M]y job is not to worry about those people. I'll never convince them they should take personal responsibility and care for their lives[3]

Romney displayed his ignorance of the factors that may cause people to not pay federal income tax (including active duty military service). He also exhibited a remarkable lack of self-awareness. The records of the two federal returns that he has released show that he paid 13 or 14 percent rate on his millions of dollars of income. He refused to disclose more than two years of his returns. Obviously, he feared damaging revelations. Critics, including Senate Majority Leader Harry Reid, a Democrat from Nevada, speculated that the returns might disclose even lower tax rates, offshore holdings, and other embarrassing transactions. Romney avoided vast amounts of taxes by taking advantage of a massive loophole. According to a Bloomberg report, Romney sheltered income as if it were a charitable donation to the Mormon Church.[4]

Romney tried to minimize the impact of his remarks after the disclosure of his disdain for the "47 percent" in September. He ended his second presidential debate on October 16 by saying he would fight for "the hundred percent" of the population. That line provided Barack Obama with the opportunity for an unrebutted debate closing. The president reminded the national television audience that Romney had previously written off nearly half the nation as outside his responsibility if elected.

Later that week, two longtime investigative commentators separately reported explosive revelations confirming the worst suspicions that Romney was an unscrupulous, deceitful manipulator working with others of that ilk to capture the presidency in order to advance crony capitalism and a bellicose policy in the Mideast.

"Mitt Romney's opposition to the auto bailout has haunted him on the campaign trail, especially in Rust Belt states like Ohio," Greg Palast and the *Nation* reported. "But Romney has done a good job of concealing, until now, the fact that he and his wife, Ann, personally gained at least $15 million from the bailout – and a few of Romney's most important Wall Street donors made more than $4 billion. Their gains, and those of the Romneys, were astronomical – more than 3,000 percent on their investment."[5] Palast, the New York-based BBC reporter who broke the most important vote suppression stories regarding the 2000 Bush-Gore presidential race, went on to report that Elliot Management hedge fund had made $1.28 billion via its usual practice of acquiring distressed bonds in advance of a rise in the value. Palast had previously bird-dogged the career of the fund's director, Paul Singer, in a 2012 book that described Singer as a ruthless "vulture capitalist," proud of his skills in gouging governments.[6]

Independently, the iconoclastic historian Webster Tarpley wrote that the September 11 assassinations of four United States personnel in Libya stemmed from intrigue that implicated a rogue asset of the CIA. "Romney campaign, CIA Mormon Mafia both responsible for Benghazi attack" was the title of Tarpley's report. He reported that the chief suspect in the killing, Sufyan Ben Qumu, a former Osama Bin Laden chauffeur and Guantanamo Bay detainee, was by now probably a CIA operative. Tarpley suggested that Qumu might have been advancing a Republican plot to win the November elections by an assassination that would embarrass Obama.[7]

Tarpley had been writing extensively in the weeks since the attack about what he regarded as plots by neo-cons, Mormons, and ultra-Zionists to create foreign policy embarrassments for Obama during the late stages of the 2012 campaign. Tarpley compared the actions to the Republican-CIA plot to make Jimmy Carter look weak for failure to obtain the freedom of United States hostages kidnapped in Iran. The failure devastated Carter's

1980 re-election campaign and fostered the term "October Surprise," arising in 1972, to denote major foreign policy developments suspected as concocted to affect United States presidential elections.[8]

Furthermore, Tarpley wrote that GOP congressmen had inadvertently confirmed during their clumsy handling of an October oversight hearing that the CIA had a strong presence at the murder scene. Tarpley built on such little-reported revelations to suggest high levels of intrigue. His thesis proposed that rogue factions of the United States national security community, both in and out of government, had initiated and exploited the events leading to the "terror" assassinations.[9]

The Real Romney?

The next two chapters summarize the dangers of the Romney-Ryan domestic and foreign policy approach. The two men stood for little aside from their hope of election success, which would mandate their attempts to further enrich their enablers and cronies, and then impose an austerity regime on much of the rest of the population. Romney's selection of Ryan cemented his leadership of the ticket, overshadowing what the radical right had feared was only vague adherence to its agenda. The Romney-Ryan plans would unravel safety nets and replace freedom of health care choices for women with religious pieties promulgated largely by men.[10] More generally, Romney, Ryan, and their backers want to worsen the policies devised by their recent kindred spirits in the presidency, George Bush and Dick Cheney.

It's Even Worse Than It Looks: How the American Constitutional System Collided with the New Politics of Extremism is the title of a 2012 best-seller by Norman Ornstein of the American Enterprise Institute and Thomas Mann of the Brookings Institution, two leaders of the Washington thought-leader establishment.[11] The congressional scholars offered practical solutions to what they described as a serious breakdown in governance. Former Reagan Administration Assistant Treasury Paul Craig Roberts offers a much more dire assessment of the state of the government. "The United States has collapsed economically, socially, politically, legally, constitutionally, and environmentally," writes Roberts, a scholar and onetime associate editor of the *Wall Street Journal*. Formerly in charge of the opinion pages of the nation's most important conservative media outlet, Roberts now denounces oligarchs in both parties. "The country that exists today is not even a shell of the country into which I was born," Roberts continued in a 2012 column. Still an adherent of Reagan fiscal and foreign policy, Roberts documented, "America's descent into poverty," and the misery that craven politicians needless inflict upon the public.[12]

Reflecting on such voices, I seek to connect the dots on the Mitt Romney story to show why the public should have had little confidence in his word, his intentions, or his commitment to the welfare of the overall population.

The material below shows that Romney considers himself a figure destined by history and by God to lead a nation unified under Mormon leadership into a church-state theocracy, as Mormon founder Joseph Smith himself envisioned before his assassination during his 1844 presidential candidacy. Romney, as a church leader whose family support of Smith reaches back to that first presidential campaign in 1844, is driven by a historical and eternal vision that make the temporal promises and position-switches far less important to him than to his audiences. What political pundits might report as policy switches or false statements, Romney and his backers apparently believe to be routine tactics to achieve power. In this way, they have sought such goals as religious advancement, moneymaking, and the ability to bestow charity, war, and government contracts upon those whom they regard as most deserving.

To illustrate this pattern, I will first show how Romney's favorite campaign speech reveals his antiquated dream of empire building, along with his subservience to the power brokers that dominate his thinking. Next, we will explore how his core support largely stems from the Confederate and Mormon territories that were allied a century and half ago against the United States. Even now, the states that tend to support him against Obama share antipathy to what they regard as different values of the former Union states. Those were, of course, the states in the Northeast and Midwest that produced Prophets Joseph Smith and Brigham Young, and ultimately expelled them.

The Mormon Church is an America-centric religion. Church leaders interpreted sacred texts as incorporating much of the story of Jesus and the Old Testament into a hybrid faith. Joseph Smith and his fellow General Authorities and other founders presided over their flocks with a powerful combination of spiritual and governmental power.

The work culture fostered by the church reveals the benefits of brilliant alliances with secretive moneymen such as Howard Hughes. These stepping stones led directly to Romney's rapacious work at Bain Capital and his bold cover up of his past and future plans. The evidence also shows how most of the inconsistencies that preoccupied the media and interest groups during the campaign, such as his changes in position on policy issues, were essentially irrelevant to a man of destiny like Romney. Romney is preparing for eternal life. In his mind, vast numbers of gentiles, not just those "the 47 percent," are destined for oblivion while the Saints are saved.

Some LDS dissidents do speak out, to be sure. However, they are virtually unnoticed. The mainstream media does not address spiritual matters except in a superficial fashion. Religion helps explain Romney's shifting policy positions, his zeal for moneymaking, his tax avoidance, and his charitable instincts. Most importantly, it provides a roadmap to a Romney-led theocracy that would transform the America that Colonial-era religious leader John Carroll and other Constitution-drafters envisioned. Many of the tea party advocates extol patriotism and other civic virtues, but lack the relevant facts about Constitutional history, the real Romney, and the real Obama.

For these reasons, tea party and Ron Paul supporters in particular should recall how the Romney-led, Rove-affiliated GOP establishment systematically cheated Paul and other Romney-rivals during the primary season. Abusive vote-counting tactics received only scattered media coverage. The Republican establishment excluded primary candidates Buddy Roemer and Gary Johnson, each a former GOP governor, from all debates. Romney rivals such as Herman Cain imploded, seemingly by accident. Paul's tribulations in trying to obtain fairness, even under the eyes of thousands of so-called reporters covering the GOP convention, were especially stark and unreported.

Particularly relevant to all Americans and to the world community is the disclosure of how Bain, Romney, and Rove-influenced voting machine companies, radio stations, vote suppression, and propaganda campaigns geared up to control the 2012 general election, especially in the pivotal states of Ohio, Florida, and elsewhere in the Upper Midwest.

Even reasonably well-informed voters lack important facts about Romney, despite his five years of campaigning for the presidency beginning in 2007. Other candidates and the media were too timid to assess his greed and religion in blunt terms. They overlooked the accumulation of his wealth and his tax avoidance because he kept his tax returns secret. This secrecy was unprecedented for a recent presidential candidate. Romney's father released ten years of tax returns. W. Mitt Romney complied with John McCain's 2008 demand that all potential vice presidential nominees provide him with 10 years of tax returns for his review. Romney himself required 10 years of returns from Paul Ryan, demonstrating his knowledge that a wider range than the two years he released is vital and expected. He simply did not want to disclose his holdings.

Romney's Democratic opponents raised the issue at times, but they failed to reach the logical conclusion that Romney was hiding his disreputable methods of moneymaking and tax avoidance. Furthermore, he advocated policies that enable other oligarchs to do the same. He presented the rest of the public with hokum instead of solutions as he pursued his destiny as the nation's first Mormon president, uniting church and state. Senate Majority Leader Harry Reid, a Nevada Democrat, stepped forward in mid-summer 2012 to challenge Romney's integrity on tax returns. As noted, this chapter argues that Romney's devotion to a religion founded on prophecies and moneymaking schemes was vital voter information. A candidate's religion can affect policy unless the candidate assures voters otherwise, not simply with words but with actions. Therefore, we explore the importance of myth making in Romney's thinking. One leg of this exploration is the examination of his self-image as an empire-building man of destiny. Another involves a look at his apparent goal of serving as a religious leader and as God's instrument to unite the country under Mormon leadership, just as the Joseph Smith sought to do with in the 1844 election. Finally, we examine how Romney's ambitions to accumulate wealth and power violate the morality of most religions.

Men Who Build Empires

During the summer of 2012, Mitt Romney revealed that his favorite poem was recommended to him by one of the Koch brothers. The poem is, "Men To Match Our Mountains." Written in 1894, this is an ode to macho empire building, authored by Sam Walter Foss. Romney recited the poem at most campaign stops for more than a year. In public, the candidate had always attributed his acquaintance with the work to an unnamed "householder" until finally confiding to Texas petroleum executives in August 2012 that the "householder" was one of their own. Romney came into contact with the poem through William Koch, an heir to the family energy services fortune.[13] Koch was a noted philanthropist and big thinker, as well as a tycoon.[14]

Clearly, Romney realized throughout his campaign that identifying one of his masters so publicly before an election would hurt his image.[15] But the story held further embarrassment for the candidate. Romney and his running mate, Paul Ryan, are war advocates who lavishly praise generals and war after avoiding military service themselves.[16] Unsurprisingly, Romney's favorite poem is stridently macho.[17]Here is the poem that Romney was reputed to recite at nearly every stop in his New Hampshire campaign:

Bring me men to match my mountains,

Bring me men to match my plains.

Men with empires in their purpose,

And new eras in their brains.

The poem is controversial because it lauds self-aggrandizement, male superiority, and superhuman feats, not simply men who braved a wilderness. It is so out of place for today's times that in 2003 the Bush-era Air Force removed it from a prime location at the entrance to the U.S. Air Force Academy.[18] Its removal was the Air Force command's direct response to revelations that 12 percent of female cadets were reported raped at the academy. Vastly more women than 12 percent reported sexual harassment and other misdeeds as part of the academy's chauvinistic culture.[19] The poem had no place in military service in 2003, and had no place as a model for a 2013 government under a Romney-Ryan administration.

A New Confederacy: States' Rights, Tycoons, and Money

A glance at the 2012 electoral map, or those electoral maps of other recent years, shows a striking pattern. The Red States are primarily those of the rebellious slave-state Confederacy. This core is for the most part augmented by Western regions with significant Mormon populations whose religious founders once allied their populations with Confederates, against President Lincoln and his Union supporters from the North and Midwest. There are a few anomalies, most notably Wheat Belt states that largely came into existence opposed to slavery (aside from divided opinion in "Bloody Kansas") and supported the then-new Republican Party's opposition to Democratic Southern plantation oligarchs. Maryland, a former pro-slave state, has lost its Southern sensibilities. In addition, the Appalachian regions from New Hampshire to Alabama and the Ozark populace of Arkansas and southern Missouri have retained the nearly age-old independence of mountain people. They have increasingly abandoned New Deal Democratic loyalties to become part of the GOP coalition. That's true even in Arkansas and Tennessee, which voted in 1861 to remain in the Union until Fort Sumter inflamed pro-Confederate passions, and in West Virginia, which broke away from Virginia during the Civil War to stand by the Union.

President Lyndon Johnson predicted much of this when he told the Rev. Martin Luther King that the Civil Rights legislation they backed would lead to Republican control over the once Solid South. Karl Rove, as much as anyone, helped transform the South by his consulting work, transforming politics first in Texas, and then in nearby states such as Alabama and Florida. Articulating part of this theme was *Esquire* columnist Charles Pierce, who bemoaned the lack of such historical perspective by Democratic leaders at their 2012 national convention.[20] Pierce wrote:

There is no question in my mind anymore that the Republican Party has reconfigured itself as a Confederate party. Not because it is so largely white, though it is. Not because it is largely Southern, though it is that, too. And not because it fights so hard for vestigial accoutrements like the Confederate battle flag. The Republican Party is a Confederate party, I think, because that is its view of what the government of the United States should be. It is written quite clearly in the party's platform that the Republicans adopted last week in Tampa: "The Republican party stands for the rights of individuals, families, faith communities, institutions — and of the States which are their instruments of self-government."

Instead, Pierce continued, the Republican Party is now embracing the States' Rights philosophies of leading slave-era Southern apologists, such as South Carolina congressional leader John Calhoun.[21]

We, the living, owe it to those founders to recall what they actually wrote, not the spin whether voiced by Confederates or their modern counterparts.

No one advocates slavery or even poll taxes, of course, or banishment of religious and racial minorities from office. Nonetheless, modern equivalents to blatantly racist methods of the Segregationist South are being used to thwart the political power of minorities and other Democratic-oriented groups. One example is the long-running and irrational hate campaign against Obama on the claim he was foreign-born, a socialist, a Communist, a Muslim, etc. At least some conservatives know about the evidence in this book that Obama came from a CIA, foundation, NGO, and corporatist background. However, they found political advantage in stirring up groundless racial concerns, thereby cynically widening the divide between white voters and minorities.[22] These GOP tactics had the effect of fostering public perceptions that Obama and the Democrats were responsible for the economic and civil rights privations caused by Bush-era tax-cuts, wars, and civil rights erosions.

The 2012 campaign saw the rollout of a massive voter suppression tactics to discourage voting by minorities, the working class, Democrats, and the elderly in targeted electorally important regions such as Ohio and Florida. Voter suppression is the equivalent of the unconstitutional poll tax in the segregationist Deep South. Many Northern swing states captured in 2010 by GOP governors implemented suppression. The alternative press reported a bogus advertising campaign by unknown donors to warn prospective voters in minority neighborhoods in Ohio that they could be prosecuted for fraud in the 2012 elections. Billboards announcing such a prosecution effort might not foster fear in otherwise self-confident citizens.[23] Low-income voters do not have the resources to fight even unjust accusations. On the other hand, Ann Coulter and Mitt Romney are among those accused, without indictment, of voting in the wrong states. They face no serious investigation. Even so, the modern GOP has created a massive national campaign founded on the theory that blacks and other minorities vote illegally and must be prosecuted and otherwise thwarted.[24]

Behind that bogus crusade are indications that the campaign was enabled by Romney's former company, Bain Capital. In 2007, Bain Capital bought a major interest in Clear Channel Communications. The media conglomerate's holdings included the billboard company displaying the vote suppression message in Ohio.[25] Clear Channel owns more radio stations than any other company does by far. It heavily promotes on them a who's who of right-wing vote suppression advocates, including Rush Limbaugh and Sean Hannity.[26] Clear Channel seemed to want more than advertising dollars. Clear Channel (like many media outlets) slyly exerts content control to ban some messages.[27] At other times, it allows similar ads that advance the owners' political agendas.[28]

Many similar Jim-Crow tactics exist, including the political and prosecutorial targeting of effective minority House members for removal via actual or presumed scandals (hence the utility of "loyal Bushie" prosecutors). Conversely, Republicans secretly enjoy the continuation of a scandal-plagued minority congressman in office, such as Harlem's Charles Rangel, because his presence fires up the GOP base and prevents the emergence of a leader with a clean record who might be more effective on behalf of constituents. The refusal of both parties to create a compromise solution to enable congressional voting power for residents of the nation's capital, the District of Columbia, is an ongoing disgrace. Republicans and Democrats could easily resolve the supposed Constitutional problem, but neither side values the input of the city's heavily-minority population.[29]

Religion, Government, and Theocracy

For the most part, Mitt Romney and his LDS colleagues stonewalled inquiries about how his religious beliefs might affect his government leadership. That posture should no longer be acceptable to the public. The church's history, power, activist inclinations, and secrecy created great cause for concern. So did Romney's questionable moneymaking, crony capitalism, and tax avoidance policies. The candidate's enthusiasm for military adventures provided additional reason to dig deeper despite his protests.

During the campaign, for example, the public was entitled to know if Romney truly believed that he would achieve eternal salvation through his secret works and activities. How much, in his view, does his salvation depend on knowing the words and beliefs withheld from others? The public should know whether these matters govern his attitudes toward the "47 percent" or whatever other populations might potentially be despised, disparaged, or doomed to damnation.[30]

To explore such topics is to invite scorn, accusations of bigotry, and potential reprisal. My view is that no one has a right to the presidency. The Constitution forbids a government-imposed religious test for office but not private inquiry. If someone is offended by the examination that unfolds below, I would respectfully inquire if they would be offended also regarding a similar inquiry undertaken if a presidential candidate were a Jew, Muslim, Scientologist, atheist, etc., or were a former Catholic or Protestant missionary and bishop. Almost certainly, the answer would be that such a candidate would be immediately disqualified from consideration unless he or she made extraordinary disclosure about religious beliefs and their potential impact on government policy.

The country's main experience so far with a presidential nominee who was not a Protestant was with John F. Kennedy, who was bluntly criticized and scrutinized for his beliefs and eloquently responded with a major speech that has no parallel in the seven years of Mitt Romney's presidential quest. To borrow a phrase, I make no apology for embarking on this research.[31] Blogger Jacob Weisberg eloquently stated the need for such research in 2007 during the launch of Romney's first campaign.[32]

Weisberg's thoughtful, albeit controversial, 2007 column about these issues should have triggered more mainstream inquiry during the ensuing five years of Romney's presidential campaigning. Instead, the major media largely confined themselves to conventional feature stories and opinion pieces describing the LDS church and Romney's role. This book's footnotes list several representative examples of mainstream coverage of the campaign's religion issues.[33] Many are from the *Washington Post*.[34] The most vibrant commentary on this issue, as in many important matters, comes from blogs. One blog post by former LDS member Richard Packham describes why he left the church.[35] In another post, Packham reveals the most closely-held LDS church sacraments and argues why Romney presidency would be bad for the country.[36]

Susan Emmett, a direct descendent of Brigham Young and an officer with Packham in the group Ex-Mormon, gave a rare interview in a similar vein. She said the LDS church subordinates women in ways incongruent with modern society. In addition, she said that Romney would make a "frightening" president.[37] Retired Air Force General Michael L. "Mikey" Weinstein also attacked Romney's hypocrisy in claiming to understand the 42-year-old Glen Doherty, one of the security guards murdered in Libya on September 11, 2012. Weinstein wrote that Romney's words were insulting because the victim's passion was to reaffirm the nation's historic separation of church and state in the military.[38]

Romney's pro-war stance extends back nearly a half century. In 1965, he undertook pro-war protests against those seeking draft deferments from the Vietnam War, later availing himself of deferments that avoided service. In 2012, he embraced Israel's plan for American foreign policy.[39] Yet Romney's convention acceptance speech contained not a single word about veterans. His "47 percent" speech to wealthy donors lumped active military, jobless and under-employed vets, plus all their dependents into the category of moochers who pay no federal income taxes. Only "the real Romney," a man deluded by his own sense of destiny, could talk like that to his donors for an hour. He knew that neither he nor any of his sons have served, and that he has obtained so many tax breaks himself that he dared not reveal them to voters.

Summing Up

Before moving ahead from this segment on Romney and the church to address Romney's professional career, two important points remain.

My hope, perhaps quixotic, is that you will not regard this analysis as an attack on the church and its millions of worshippers. The vast majority of them know as little about the intrigues mentioned here as the average Democrat knows about Obama's national security ties. Most LDS members obviously find great value in their faith. Romney's commencement lecture at Liberty University in May 2012 was his major campaign speech on religion. Nevertheless, he failed to address relevant and material religious questions about his candidacy. Instead, he pandered to his evangelical audience by emphasizing his opposition to women's choices on sexual issues. The Mormon Church is highly centralized in its decision making and authority. This foreshadows an oppressive public policy that he failed to address.

John F. Kennedy faced similar challenges as the nation's first major party Roman Catholic candidate. Nevertheless, he was able to assure voters that his religion was not going to impact public policy. His thoughtful 1960 campaign speech to a convention of Protestant pastors in Houston described his independence from the Vatican.[40] This allayed fears of a church and state union replacing separation of church and state.

The need for a more expansive Romney speech was obvious. First, the Catholic Church was a well-known entity by 1960, with many centuries of tradition. Second, the Kennedy family held no leadership position in their church. Indeed, family members routinely and notoriously violated their marriage vows. In 2012, for example, a former White House intern published a credible memoir describing how JFK casually deflowered her, while married to Jackie Kennedy.[41] Little in Kennedy's church affiliations, observances, or conduct suggested that his faith would determine public policy. The opposite seems true for Romney.

The question arises whether Mitt Romney has proved to be the kind of public face for the LDS Church that his father, George Romney, and Willard Marriott yearned for so long ago. Did he become — as heirs, CEOs, religious leaders, and politicians sometimes do — unrepresentative of what is inspirational about his heritage? Most members of the LDS church are well regarded for traditions of civic service and global charitable work, as well as business success. The next chapter explores his record of accomplishment in these areas.

Chapter 17

Mitt Romney: Going for the Gold

There are many ways for government leaders to act rapaciously. From the beginning, Mormon Prophets Joseph Smith and Brigham Young focused on wealth acquisition for themselves and their church. They lied, when necessary, to deceive LDS faithful and gentiles alike. They sought to destroy those unlikely to support the leaders' full secret agendas.[1] These are not simply heroes to Mitt Romney, but holy men in his eyes. Romney's words and actions suggest that he wants to go to heaven by emulating them and their successors, and nothing will stop him from doing so.

This section summarizes allegations of greed and sharp business practices that were widely overlooked during the campaign. These episodes suggest the kind of trouble that gentiles and "the 47 percent" could expect from a Romney administration.

Bain Beginnings

Under Romney, Bain Capital began with a vital infusion of money from Salvadoran families linked to Death Squads that killed more than 10,000 men, women, and children to protect the elite.[2] The $9 million investment, 40 percent of Bain Capital's start-up funding, was crucial to the firm's creation. Most Bain Capital initiatives were not as dramatic as the company's initial fund raising, of course. Some moments were even fun, at least for the Bain team.[3] *Boston Globe* authors Kranish and Helman wrote a biography that takes readers through the mostly prosaic cycles of a financial capital firm, including what the authors called Romney's "finest hour at Bain." They describe his leadership in a successful effort to save the over-leveraged parent, Bain & Company, from bankruptcy in 1991.[4]

Krugman provides a stark and compelling contrast between the ways that George and Mitt Romney made their money, paid their taxes, and revealed their finances. Krugman wrote:

> Mr. [Mitt] Romney didn't get rich by producing things people wanted to buy; he made his fortune through financial engineering that seems in many cases to have left workers worse off, and in some cases driven companies into bankruptcy.

And there's another contrast: George Romney was open and forthcoming about what he did with his wealth, but Mitt Romney has largely kept his finances secret. He did, grudgingly, release one year's tax return plus an estimate for the next year, showing that he paid a startlingly low tax rate....Put it this way: Has there ever before been a major presidential candidate who had a multimillion-dollar Swiss bank account, plus tens of millions invested in the Cayman Islands, famed as a tax haven?[5]

Romney's CEO experience at Bain was his chief credential for his campaign along with the Massachusetts governorship whose highlights he rejected. *Washington Post* reporter Thomas Hamburger aggressively reported financial information about Bain.[6] Nonetheless, details of Romney's work remained wrapped in mystery and controversy for most voters.[7] One such dispute centered on the date of Romney's resignation from Bain management. That seems like a relatively simple matter, especially since Romney has insisted that the date was February 1999. Yet disputes still linger, and lead to much deeper controversies. As previously noted, legal documents suggested that Romney was active in Bain management much later than his official departure date, and perhaps as late as 2002.[8]

The distinction was important because it involved the basic honesty of the candidate and his campaign. Few can understand complex campaign promises about future budgets. Anyone can understand a job departure. In addition, a potential difference of up to three years in Romney's departure time would mean that he held at least some management responsibility for the company's controversial actions during those periods.

Vanity Fair explored those controversies in depth.[9] Then *Rolling Stone* published a cover story, subtitled, "How the GOP presidential candidate and his private equity firm staged an epic wealth grab, destroyed jobs – and stuck others with the bill."[10] The concept of looting companies via bankruptcy is so complicated in its particulars that almost no one who is not directly financially involved examines details. That is why the chaos of bankruptcy is such a lucrative field for canny lawyers and business vultures. I came to appreciate this as a young newspaper reporter covering bankruptcies in Connecticut. A litigant's best hope is that a vigilant, hard-working, and honest judge will oversee these procedures. Yet that is not always the case.[11] Even judges with distinguished credentials can become corrupt. Such cases prompt protests from relatively small timers in this system. They have a financial interest in the litigation, and so have an incentive to research the issues.

One such person is Steven "Laser" Haas, a liquidator of bankrupt assets by trade. His nickname is a relic of his long-ago basketball-shooting prowess in New York City's playgrounds. For the past 11 years, he has virtually dedicated his life to exposing machinations in bankruptcy cases by the Romney/Bain team. His focus is on the collapse of eToys, a major online toy distributor that, by his account, owed him millions of dollars under a contract to liquidate its inventory. he. Courts have repeatedly rejected his filings. Unlike most such litigants that I have encountered via the Justice Integrity Project, he spends most of his time on legal reform volunteering to help others he perceives as similar victims in complex financial cases. Most significant about his reform efforts is that he regards Romney and Bain Capital as the main perpetrators. He especially protests certain activities in 2000 and 2001 after Romney announced his retirement from Bain in 1999.[12] *Mother Jones* reported during the campaign that Romney had been deeply involved in Bain decision making in the SteriCycle medical waste/fetus disposal investment after 1999. The news report appeared to vindicate Haas in his similar arguments that Romney remained in power at that the company during the period when it allegedly looted the assets of eToys by forcing it into an unnecessary shutdown.[13]

The Haas argument is contained in many years of his *pro se* court filings in Delaware's state court.[14] Haas regards Romney as the primary villain in this saga, and as a deeply dangerous vulture capitalist who profits from destroying companies and jobs. Haas has also complained about the prominent Delaware law firm MNAT (Morris, Nichols, Arsht and Tunnell, LLP). In court filings and blog posts, he accuses the firm of improperly enabling Bain's machinations.[15] MNAT was the primary representative of Summa Corporation, the Howard Hughes umbrella company controlling the billionaire's global empire. As reported earlier in this book, the late Bill Gay, father of Romney's partner, Bob Gay, led Summa for many years. The elder Gay was the leader of the so-called "Mormon Mafia" alleged to have pillaged the Hughes estate during the addled billionaire's later years.[16]

All targets of Haas accusations have denied his claims and have prevailed in court so far. Their victories include a court order forbidding him from filing anything more. Furthermore, they can point to him as a man without a college degree, a company, or significant assets. The defendants, in other words, are powerful and wealthy, and he is neither. That is typical in these cases, as is my reaction:

Even if each defendant is correct that he or she has operated within the law and within normal business practices that should not foreclose the public from learning that disputes exist. Here, the controversy was about a presidential nominee who apparently played word games about the year when he left the main job on his resume. More interestingly, few seem to know about the dissembling aside from readers of *Rolling Stone* despite tens of thousands of news reports about the campaign.

Onward and Upward

Romney served as Massachusetts governor from 2003 to 2007. It was an impressive achievement for a Republican in a heavily Democratic state. Yet his ambitions, mania for secrecy, and contempt for the public's right to knowledge are illustrated by his decision to spend an estimated $100,000 in taxpayer funds to sanitize government computers of his work product.[17]

Mitt Romney's political career has been especially opportunistic, even by the standards of ambitious politicians. Since high school, for example, Romney has advocated aggressive military policies. He has never served in the military. Neither have any of his five sons. His mantra was that his missionary work in France was the equivalent of Vietnam War combat. Yet Romney's instinct from college to the present has been to advocate more war, more troops, and more deference to the military.

Mitt Romney's position as a "moderate" Republican governor in Massachusetts was a stepping stone toward a hard-right campaign as he secured his party's 2012 nomination. His first try in 2008 was too soon. The Republican base did not know him well enough to trust him and he had to compete against GOP warhorses waiting for their run after two Bush terms. The next campaign was different. Drawing on his Bain-enabled fortune, Romney had four years to make alliances while his competition prepared only sporadically because most needed to work regular jobs.

In the bigger picture, Republicans could try to blame the docile Obama for all the Bush-era failures that cascaded upon the Democratic majority in 2009. Then Republicans could double down on the process in 2013 with a pseudo-moderate Romney. This would be just like when the Rove-groomed George W. Bush came into office in 2000 with the campaign theme that he was a "compassionate conservative" and a "uniter, not a divider."

By the fall of 2012, Romney had made it clear that he was insisting on a nearly-unprecedented level of secrecy concerning his tax returns. This seems to have been not simply his preference, but an absolute necessity for his campaign's survival, especially after his robotic performance as a self-entitled candidate. He may have needed to hide his Swiss bank and Cayman Islands accounts, which suggested he was betting against America and shirking tax responsibilities (presumably in legal ways not available to most voters). Perhaps he was not paying substantial taxes because of arcane write-offs. Another possibility is that he was not properly computing his tithe to the LDS Church, or conversely contributing such a high percentage of his charitable donations to the church that the pattern underscored his disdain for gentiles. Given what we now know about his habit of lying and Bain's sharp business practices, the possibility exists that his returns might have disclosed serious wrongdoing, which would create a litigation trail leading to business, associates if not to the candidate himself. The public is entitled to speculate about worst-case scenarios given his refusal to comply with normal disclosure.

One indication that such problems existed was the trove of Romney and Bain-related documents that Gawker obtained during the summer of 2012. Reporter John Cook synthesized them:

> Mitt Romney's $250 million fortune is largely a black hole: Aside from the meager and vague disclosures he has filed under federal and Massachusetts laws, and the two years of partial tax returns (one filed and another provisional) he has released, there is almost no data on precisely what his vast holdings consist of, or what vehicles he has used to escape taxes on his income.
>
> Gawker has obtained a massive cache of confidential financial documents that shed a great deal of light on those finances, and on the tax-dodging tricks available to the hyper-rich that he has used to keep his effective tax rate at roughly 13% over the last decade.
>
> Today, we are publishing more than 950 pages of internal audits, financial statements, and private investor letters for 21 cryptically named entities in which Romney had invested—at minimum—more than $10 million as of 2011 (that number is based on the low end of ranges he has disclosed—the true number is almost certainly significantly higher).
>
> Almost all of them are affiliated with Bain Capital, the secretive private equity firm Romney co-founded in 1984 and ran until his departure in 1999 (or 2002, depending on whom you ask). Many of them are offshore funds based in the Cayman Islands.
>
> Together, they reveal the mind-numbing, maze-like, and deeply opaque complexity with which Romney has handled his wealth, the exotic tax-avoidance schemes available only to the preposterously wealthy that benefit him, the unlikely (for a right-wing religious Mormon) places that his money has ended up, and the deeply hypocritical distance between his own criticisms of Obama's fiscal approach and his money managers' embrace of those same policies.
>
> They also show that some of the investments that Romney has always described as part of his retirement package at Bain weren't made until years after he left the company[18]

Other reports indicated Romney's schemes to pass money on to his children through a tax dodge,[19] and to connive with Bain and gambling czar Sheldon Adelson.[20] The Bob Gay, Bain, "Mormon Mafia," and

Howard Hughes histories serve as reminders of the colorful circle involving Hughes, his aides, and their methods.

Crony capitalism exists as a central factor in the decision making of both parties. Obama reported more campaign donations from Bain employees than Romney. Financial intrigue works on many levels, however.

Romney denied the public the basic information needed to assess his Bain record and his policy promises on jobs, taxes, and protection of the social safety net. He failed to meet the minimum standards of disclosure required of one seeking office. A little-reported but especially clear-cut example of Romney's dishonesty, arrogance, and perverse family values arose in court just before the 2012 election. A Boston judge released sealed testimony showing that Romney lied in a 1988 hearing in order to cheat the wife of one of his business associates during a divorce. Romney swore that the stock of Staples was worth just one-tenth of a cent prior to its public offering when he had previously claimed it was worth $1.30 per share.[21] The episode illustrated Romney's contempt for the normal standards of truth in court, especially if he could help a business crony cheat a wife.

Romney's record also fell short regarding his policies. In October, Mitt Romney decisively won the first of his three 2012 presidential debates on style points. He vehemently denied that his longstanding plan to reduce taxes by 20 percent, or $5 trillion, would favor the rich or require higher taxes for others.[22] Credible experts disputed Romney's description of the fact.[23] Those who denied his claims included the leading non-partisan tax research center, a Bloomberg News columnist, and a Moody's analyst who has been generally favorable to Romney.[24] They concluded that Romney's plan could not remain budget-neutral, even if it drastically hurt the middle class by taxing company-paid health insurance and cutting home mortgage interest and charitable deductions. The Romney-Ryan campaign confused the public by arguing that a half dozen "studies" prove them right. Four of these "studies" turned out to be blogs and op-eds. The remaining two studies were similarly weak in academic-substance.[25]

Romney's sudden shift in position during an October presidential debate seemed to contradict his prior statements and non-partisan bean counting. Romney's change left Obama ineffective. So did Romney's refusal to specify any proposal for making up the revenue shortfall for the federal budgets, and his failure to address the health needs of an estimated 40 million men, women, and children who would be left uninsured if he repealed and/or failed to enforce "ObamaCare."

Romney and Ryan asked the public to trust them and a Republican-led Congress on these and a host of other issues, including the privatization of Social Security for those under age 55 with a vaguely-described optional alternative. The Republicans wanted to steer the population toward a system of Medicare vouchers in a plan similar to the one the public rejected during the George W. Bush administration.

More immediately relevant to all members of the population over age 55, the Romney-Ryan cuts in Medicare would have persuaded more providers to abandon the program in the short run. The elderly and infirm would therefore find it increasingly difficult to find a doctor as their mobility, income, and options decrease. begin to affect society. Meanwhile, anti-abortion zealots in Republican-led legislatures made it extremely difficult for doctors to provide a full range of health care options for women.

Ultimately, the Ryan-backed plan that passed the House of Representatives would replace guaranteed coverage with "vouchers," which would provide only the possibility of full coverage. The aged and ailing would have to make up the rest of out their own pockets. Imagine a sick woman with cancer, age 78 or so, trying to negotiate a good deal on the private insurance market, or find a job to earn extra money for a better plan. The GOP plan would certainly cause excessive death to the aged with limited options. With their planning, Romney and Ryan sought to victimize those who have faithfully paid taxes for many years in expectation of coverage.

Our Nation's Fate

The advantage of being a man of destiny, as Mitt Romney apparently imagined himself to be, is that he can be confident that God is directing his path to heaven along with his relatives. Conversely, most of those whom such a man encounters are inferiors in his eyes, unworthy of much consideration except during an election campaign.

There are many good reasons to attack Romney for his hour-long "47 percent" speech. As a factual matter, those who do not typically pay federal income taxes include many active duty soldiers, disabled people, working poor, and retirees. The speech was a disgrace for reasons beyond Romney's hypocrisy. Here was a grandmaster in the skills of avoiding taxes and military service pretending that federal tax payments should be the one-dimensional standard of a human being's moral worth. The speech was at the home of a fellow fat cat financier notorious for hosting wild parties.[26] Thus Romney's piety and planned restrictions on women's reproductive freedoms further his hypocrisy. The bartender who surreptitiously filmed the event at the risk of his career put it best in saying, "I didn't think the public should have to pay $50,000 to learn what a presidential candidate thinks."[27]

Shortly before the 2012 election, the author Paul Craig Roberts published another of his powerful columns describing how greed has destroyed the American economy.

In the 21st century the opportunity society has disappeared. Middle class jobs are scarce. Indeed, jobs of any kind are scarce. To stay even with population growth from 2002 through 2011, the economy needed about 14 million new jobs. However, at the end of 2011 there were only 1 million more jobs than in 2002 [citation].

Only 426,000 of these jobs are in the private sector. The bulk of the net new jobs consist of waitresses and bartenders and health care and social assistance....As for manufacturing jobs, they not only did not grow with the population but declined absolutely. During these nine years, 3.5 million middle class manufacturing jobs were lost. Over the entire nine years, only 48,000 new jobs were created for architects and engineers.....

The cause of all of the problems is the offshoring of Americans' jobs....Jobs offshoring is driven by Wall Street, "shareholder advocates," the threat of takeovers, and by large retailers, such as Wal-Mart. By cutting labor costs, profits go up.[28]

Assurance that Romney truly wanted the economy to work for the wider public — as opposed to his corporate partners, co-religionists, and political allies — was missing from the campaign. Romney's elitist orientation became readily apparent from his campaign gaffes and lifestyle. His stay-at-home wife and five clean-cut boys provided a superficially attractive image for the nation's still majority-white electorate, especially to voters dismayed over changing voter demographics and afraid of an Obama "class war."

Meanwhile, Ryan fostered an image as a budget balancing "deficit hawk" and "growth" politician. However, the actual budget passed by the House under his plan would have vastly increased federal deficits by giveaways to the rich for at least another decade. The only growth assured in his plan is the growth of the tax savings allotted to his puppet masters. The Romney-Ryan ticket advocated the preposterous "trickle-down" theory that the rich are prevented from sharing more of their wealth via job creation and other investment in the United States by taxes. Romney's own ruthless profit seeking at Bain Capital, job off-shoring, and hidden personal assets off-shore constitute strong evidence to contradict the "trickle-down" theory.

Among the more offensive characteristics of the Republican duo were their self-righteous sneers at the ordinary citizens who rely on government support. The Romney-Ryan ticket was eager to strip away these "entitlements," leaving those who have dutifully paid taxes for

Social Security, Medicare, and Medicaid without a safety net that has existed since the New Deal and Great Society.[29]

Meanwhile, Romney repeatedly displayed arrogance. One social gaffe on his 2012 summer trip to Israel revealed an especially appalling level ignorance about world affairs and diplomacy. Romney wanted to raise funds and show his support for the country, and for Prime Minister Benjamin Netanyahu, Romney's former colleague as a consultant. Caught up in the excitement of the occasion, Romney gushed that Israel's gross domestic product was double that of Palestinian areas because of Israel's superior culture. As a factual matter, the Israeli standard is approximately twenty times higher. That was not simply a number, but a proportion that any reasonably well-informed college student might guess, much less a presidential candidate and former CEO of a global company. Beyond that, of course, anyone with a serious interest in world affairs or common sense would recognize that United States foreign aid to Israel, Israel's occupation of Palestinian lands, and control over foreign trade in the occupied territories would factor into the substantial economic gap.

Furthermore, even if Romney fervently supports Israel and disdains Arab nations it was hardly dignified or effective for a presidential candidate to disparage the Arab world quite so bluntly in the midst of United States military actions in at least a half dozen Mideast nations.[30]

Romney's best-known gaffes to the American public were on his wealth, estimated at $250 million and perhaps much more. Among his classics, chronicled in the primary campaign by the *Wall Street Journal*, were these quotations: "I have some great friends who are NASCAR team owners," his annual speaking income of $370,000 is "not very much," and "I'm also unemployed."[31]

His wife chimed in, saying, "You people" already have all necessary financial information about the Romney family.[32] Recall how the utterance of "you people" by 1992 independent presidential candidate H. Ross Perot before the NAACP national convention in Nashville cost him potential African-American votes merely because of the use of those two patronizing words. Perot's entire comment was, "Financially at least, it's going to be a long, hot summer . . . Now I don't have to tell you who gets hurt first when this sort of thing happens, do I? You people do, your people do. I know that, you know that."[33] Although Perot seemed well intentioned, he was slayed in the press for using "you people" before the NACCP. Even with their huge, well-funded political organization behind them, the Romneys and their campaign apparatus appear to be politically tone deaf.

Romney-style tax avoidance was a core problem, as was his notion that he deserves a low tax rate of 15 percent at the most, because his investment income is somehow linked to "job creation." That is an absurdity. How could he be a job-creator if his full-time focus has been in politics since at least 2002, living off what he calls a blind trust of investments?

In the end, the media had a final opportunity to define the "Real Romney" after the election. They did so in a self-interested way. Nine news organizations that had covered the Romney campaign wrote that they were putting a hold on reimbursements because they felt the campaign had gouged them on costs, such as the $745 per person fee to attend the vice presidential debate "viewing party."[34]

Inspiring Multitudes

This portrait illustrates how Romney typifies the office holders who treasure their own entitlements and help their large-dollar backers avoid taxation and civic responsibilities. Meanwhile, they sneer at the legitimate expectations of ordinary citizens who believe they deserve the protection of their "entitlements" (better described as "taxpayer-paid benefits") after years of taxation and promises.

As it turns out, Rove's Crossroads groups went higher than initial estimates and spent more than $300 million on the presidential ticket and on other candidates. One reason for the big money advertisements is the vast financial upside for such executives as the Koch Brothers in a low-tax, deregulatory Republican administration. They have every incentive to invest in friendly political parties, much like their kindred spirits in the tobacco industry avoided massive court settlements with cancer victims by investing in GOP politicians and judges who opposed large verdicts. These industrialists funding tea party and similar efforts behind the scenes increasingly ally with voters from the religious right who care little about shortcomings in their heroes because they are more focused on Biblical Revelations than news cycle revelations.

The LDS church was able to downplay its interest in a Romney presidency. Similarly, many top evangelical leaders were willing to lay aside past rivalries with the Mormon Church in order to build a grand alliance against Obama and Democrats. Karl Rove attended high school in Utah, and was thus more familiar with Mormon culture than most Americans.[35] Rove was in a position to help foster smooth relations between different factions of the party.[36]

The research of Chris Hedges illustrates the strength of the Romney-Ryan ticket in another way. Hedges was a Harvard Divinity School graduate before he became a Pulitzer-winning foreign correspondent for the *New York Times*. In 2006, he published *American Fascists*, his findings from extensive reporting among the Christian right.[37] In immersing himself in their experiences, he described the evangelical right's love of tradition.[38] In addition, he wrote of "The Cult of

Masculinity" to illustrate the powerful appeal of preachers who advocate war.[39] Further, he described the immensely popular Christian novelist, Timothy LaHaye, as "The guru of the End of Times movement." LaHaye has sold more than 62 million books providing "graphic details of raw mayhem and cruelty that God will unleash on all non-believes when Christ returns and raptures Christians into heaven.[40]

Rapture and everlasting perdition compel attention for obvious reasons. They compete for public attention while the mainstream media focuses on comparing politicians in ways that are often boring or otherwise unsatisfying. The possibility of spending eternity in heaven or hell is, in other words, a far more powerful attention grabber than a typical news story.

Ironically, one of Mitt Romney's most animated discussions of his religion came up at the end of the campaign. Yet the discussion was supposed to be secret. The occasion was Romney's 2007 interview with Jan Mickelson, a conservative Iowa broadcaster. Romney, believing he was off-air, described and vigorously defended his beliefs. A studio camera captured the discussion and His tirade surfaced as an internet video during the last stages of the 2012 campaign and went viral, with more than two millions views.[41]

Summing Up

Romney went through Election Day so confident that he failed to write a concession speech. A man of destiny need not trifle with such details.

Part IV: Impact→ From the White House to Your House

"Boys forget what their country means by just reading 'The Land of the Free' in history books. Then they get to be men. They forget even more. Liberty's too precious a thing to be buried in books."

— Senator Jefferson Smith, a former boy scouting leader, as portrayed by James Stewart in *Mr. Smith Goes to Washington* (1939)

Chapter 18

Joseph Biden: When the Smiling Stops

Vice President Joe Biden took the stage in Charlotte, North Carolina, to renominate President Obama on September 6, 2012, the final night of the Democratic National Convention. Expectations were modest, at least from me after reading the advance coverage and researching him for this book. Biden has held high federal office since 1973, longer than almost anyone else in the United States government.[1] His public image remains mixed. Major public opinion polls in 2012 put him slightly in the negative, especially in comparison with his GOP rival, Wisconsin congressman Paul Ryan.[2]

When Biden spoke to a crowd roaring in approval, he was personal, focused, passionate, and effective in making gut-level connections. He spoke movingly about the importance of job holding for his father, a used car salesman who struggled financially. Biden contrasted his father's experience with that of the Romney family, whose patriarch, George Romney, had been CEO of a major car manufacturer. Biden described how Obama and Democrats saved the auto industry by emergency loans because they knew the importance of jobs for the middle class, whereas Romney opposed the loans because of ideology.[3]

"I don't think he's a bad guy," Biden said of Mitt Romney. "I'm sure he grew up loving cars as much as I did. But what I don't understand, what I don't think he understood: I don't think he understood that saving the automobile worker, saving the industry, what it meant to all of America, not just auto workers. I think he saw it the Bain way. Now, I mean this sincerely. I think he saw it in terms of balance sheets and write-offs."

Bingo, I thought at the time. There goes Michigan, Ohio, and the election to the Democrats unless the Republicans succeed in massive vote fraud and suppression, or an October surprise.[4] True, relatively few people watch a convention speech, much less are influenced by it. Biden, however, had a message that would make a difference in the swing-state, Rust-Belt campaign. Biden held important chairmanships in the Senate, but faltered on several major issues. *Politics in America*, a longtime reference for Washington insiders, provides this thumbnail description:

The son of a Scranton, PA, automobile dealer, Biden overcame a childhood stutter and often speaks with charming self-deprecation. But what has made him a compelling political figure are the tragedies and dramas of his private life. As a 29-year-old county councilman, Biden in 1972 summoned the brashness to challenge Republican Sen. J. Caleb Boggs in a campaign run by his sister. Running on a dovish Vietnam platform and accusing the incumbent of being a do-nothing, Biden won by 3,162 votes.[5]

The personal tragedy came five weeks later when Biden's wife, Neilia, and their infant daughter, Amy, were killed in an automobile accident. Their two sons, Beau and Hunter, were critically injured.

Biden at first said he would not take the job he had just won. Persuaded by Democratic Leader Mike Mansfield of Montana, Biden was sworn in at the bedside of one of his sons. Biden later remarried, had another child and commutes by train from Wilmington to Washington every day[6]

Biden's second wife, Jill Biden, holds a Ph.D. in education, and has been an educator for over two decades. She currently teaches at a DC-area community college. Beau Biden, the oldest of the vice president's three children, serves as Delaware's attorney general. During the campaign, he returned home from Iraq, where he served as a captain in the Delaware National Guard. Hunter is an attorney who, like his brother, is fully recovered from their 1972 accident. Ashley, Biden's daughter by Jill, is a social worker. She encouraged her father to be the Senate's leading advocate of police training programs to defend women from violent attacks.[7]

Biden's first Senate victory came during the same 1972 elections in which the President won re-election by an overwhelming national margin.[8] Biden's upset was also impressive because he won as an insurgent in Delaware, whose politics have long been conservative. Delaware is the state of incorporation for more than half of Fortune 500 companies because of its business-friendly laws. DuPont, a prominent defense contractor during the Vietnam War as well as a manufacturer of consumer products, has been especially influential in Delaware for generations because its business operations were Delaware-centered. In this environment, Biden averaged 60 percent of the vote in his re-election campaigns.[9]

Biden became well known in the Senate for tough attacks and for his ability to work privately with opponents. He also remains notorious in political circles as a plagiarist for having quoted another politician's speech without attribution one day in Iowa.

Upon closer examination by biographer Jules Witcover, however, Biden's culpability turns out to have been greatly inflated by the political press. During Biden's unsuccessful 1988 campaign, he used a favorite passage from a speech by British Labor Party leader Neil Kinnock without giving Kinnock credit. Biden had previously quoted the speech many times, always attributing it. An aide to Biden rival, Massachusetts Governor Michael Dukakis, persuaded top reporters from the *New York Times* and *Des Moines Register* to portray the Iowa incident as a scandal. This led to a media frenzy of "gotcha" attacks on other Biden speeches and on his school records, eventually leading to Biden's withdrawal from the race.[10] In retrospect, the supposed scandal suggests less about Biden than it does about presidential news coverage. Examples abound of the national media elevating trivial incidents and planted news stories into major public dramas. These hoked-up incidents supposedly reveal the candidate's character. Meanwhile, issues that affect millions of lives are ignored.[11]

Biden's career shows a mixed record on his top priority issues. The 2002 resolution authorizing the Iraq War, passed when he chaired the Foreign Relations Committee, and marked a low point in his effectiveness. He voiced misgivings along with other Senators. However, he could not prevent a majority of other Senators from authorizing the war. Thus, Biden held the top Senate post and boasted of expertise while failing to prevent one of the most horrific disasters in recent world history.[12] Biden's problems continued after he flip-flopped on the issue of whether it should be an impeachable offense for a president to bomb a country without Congressional authorization.[13]

Biden's leadership of the Senate Judiciary Committee as its chairman during the confirmation hearing for Bush Supreme Court nominee Clarence Thomas in 1991 marked another failure. After Anita Hill's accusations against Thomas of sexual harassment, Biden and other Democrats could have examined the matter more thoroughly. Biden's staff knew then that Lillian McEwen, the committee's counsel a few years previous, had dated Thomas for years because he had visited the offices during her service with the committee.[14] Therefore, they were aware that she had special insights into his veracity and capabilities. It turns out that the committee never interviewed McEwen, much less invited her to testify. Biden was intimidated, in part because Thomas was black and the senator fell into the GOP-trap of not wanting to appear unduly judgmental against a black man.[15]

In addition, the conservative group, Citizens United, ran pro-Thomas TV ads attacking Biden as a plagiarist and a hypocrite. Biden caved when he should have fought back. The Senate thereupon confirmed Thomas by a 52-48 vote. From his lifetime perch, Thomas would reward his friends and punish his enemies, in part by providing the deciding fifth vote in the

2010 Supreme Court decision *Citizens United vs. Federal Election Commission*. Biden was pained by his role, even though polls suggested that he emerged from the confirmation hearing with a better reputation than most.[16]

As another misstep, in the early 1980s Biden argued for the public benefits of expanding federal power to seize private property without a hearing in criminal "forfeiture" actions. As Senate Judiciary Committee chairman, Biden said that such seizures of businesses, homes, cars, etc. without trial would curb the financial power of drug dealers. However, government agents can now seize property merely on suspicion under nearly 500 different federal laws. These procedures fatten the federal treasury and make a mockery of due process under the law. Now authorities can target political enemies and dupes alike, with hardly any due process protections, causing great suffering.[17]

In terms of overall career assessment, an official biography of Biden from the White House can be found here[18] and an alternative view from a conservative pundit can be found here.[19]

In 2007, Biden campaigned for the presidency but soon dropped out for lack of support.[20] After Obama secured the nomination he sought vice presidential recommendations from Eric Holder, the future attorney general, and JFK's daughter Caroline Kennedy, an early endorser of the candidacy. Biden appeared on a short list containing just three other names: Indiana Senator Evan Bayh, Kansas Governor Kathleen Sebelius, and Virginia Governor Tim Kaine. Biographer Richard Wolffe described the criteria for Obama:

> He was poor at attack politics, and needed someone to take the fight to McCain. He lacked experience, and needed someone who knew Washington and the world. He had struggled in the primaries with white, working voters of the old Rust Belt states. In sum, he needed to play offense and defense at the same time[21]

Biden's great fighting test would come during the campaign of 2012. Biden's convention speech helped position Democrats for victory across the Rust Belt. Democrats also desperately needed his help in the vice presidential debate on October 10, following the president's diffident performance a week earlier in the first presidential debate. As the next chapter suggests, those debates may have had behind-the-scenes drama that could put them in the forefront of American history.

What we can say now with reasonable certainty is that Joe Biden, for years derided as a verbose plagiarist suckered on the Iraq War and Clarence Thomas votes, rose to the occasion in 2012 to become an effective verbal assassin. With that, his past shortcomings became largely moot. His smile was a dagger, wielded, at least for key moments, on stage.

Chapter 19

Barack Obama: The President as Performer

President Obama's first 2012 debate with Mitt Romney on October 3 was a fiasco for the incumbent. Romney repeatedly interrupted the president to get in the last word, often to make a misleading comment. Yet the president did not counter-punch with tough points of his own. Obama also failed to demand specifics from Romney on his tax cut plans or his own tax returns. He failed to mention Bush-generated wars and debts, Wall Street bankster fraud, the GOP vote suppression program, and the Romney "47 percent" slur on nearly half the country.

Romney ridiculed the president for bailing out financial institutions. The president even boasted several times that he shared policy views with Romney, including on one of Obama's strongest, poll-tested favorable issues. "You know," said Obama, "I suspect that, on Social Security, we've got a somewhat similar position." This brief comment revealed the core of Obama's internal struggle. He was telling those millions who rely on Social Security and Medicare that it made little difference if they voted for Romney's austerity agenda.[1]

Obama was suitably deep-voiced and at times seemed authoritative during the debate, yet he performed like a robot rather than a leader fighting for the public. Obama lacked passion. He could have attacked his opponent's obvious deceptions and defended himself.[2] One conventional explanation for Obama's shortcomings was that he was out of practice after setting modern records for ducking the media.[3] Deeper reasons existed in the background. He failed in part because he was felt threatened in a relatively novel way.[4] Obama had enjoyed early success in a CIA, foundation, and Harvard culture with helpful mentors. In 2007-2008, he had Wall Street backing his role as America's champion of peace and prosperity for the common people. Once in office, he repeatedly deferred to the real power players. Obama endured false claims that he was a radical leftist, a Muslim, and an otherwise unworthy occupant of the office. He governed by policies that further enriched the wealthy and their organizations, and avoided rigorous regulation, investigations, and prosecutions.

By the fall of 2012, however, a significant part of Wall Street and other oligarchic support had shifted to Republicans. By then, Obama was less necessary to them to provide a different face for the economic, foreign policy, and civil rights disasters of the Bush era. Therefore, by the time of the first presidential debate, Obama had reason to worry about whether important "friends" were loyal.[5]

Obama's debate performance was so beneath his abilities that former Senate counsel, Biden aide, and retired judge Lillian McEwen suggested to me shortly after the debate that the president seemed like a man dazed from a sudden threat upon his life. Her observation was prescient. A reliable source with strong national intelligence and political ties later told me that on the day of the debate, Obama was informed by military aides of a plot against him and the country. Such a plot would be one of the darkest chapters in American history, rivaling Aaron Burr's empire-building schemes of yore.[6] The details are the primary focus of this chapter.

As the world knows, Obama rebounded from his first debate to best Romney in the two remaining contests and win a clear-cut Election Day victory. By conventional wisdom, Romney failed to answer the central questions about his candidacy during the rest of the campaign, and so he lost. Mainstream post-election analysis further suggested that blatant GOP voter suppression techniques encouraged a much higher than expected turnout of Democrats in swing states. Obama won all of those nine battleground contests except for North Carolina.

The inside story is far more complicated and sinister.

Pre-election litigation in Ohio alerted Ohio's Secretary of State, Jon Husted, that he was under courtroom scrutiny for his secret plan to install software on 80 percent of the state's voting machines just before the election.[7] This time, litigation in advance of the election provided a vital deterrent effect in the high-stakes election.[8] I played a small role in thwarting voting fraud by urging litigants to file legal actions before the election in order to put the media on notice and warn potential miscreants that their secret plan would ultimately have to be explained under oath.[9]

Official results showed that Romney received 47 percent of the national vote, the same percentage he had disparaged during the campaign[10] After the election, Romney blamed his loss on "ObamaCare" and other "gifts" the president supposedly handed out to African Americans, Hispanics, and other core supporters.[11] Romney's comments reminded even those in his own party that he was prone to speak in an elitist and otherwise clumsy fashion. Nonetheless, some Romney supporters were encouraged that President Obama invited Romney to a post-election, post-Thanksgiving luncheon at the White House on November 29. Romney was living in his high-tone beach house in La

Jolla, California, where his wife was reported to have undergone crying jags over their loss.[12] Speculation percolated in Washington that Obama might resume bipartisanship by offering Romney a major Cabinet post. As it turned out, the main announcement was that Obama had offered Romney turkey chili for lunch. With millions eating holiday leftovers, the invitation suggested a snide welcome for the loser.

Republican insiders quickly consigned Romney to the political graveyard, in part because he held no office, stood for so little, and had run such an expensive losing campaign. Tagg Romney, the candidate's son and campaign manager, exemplified the family's oafish manner, much as he had during the campaign when he boasted of wanting to punch the president after the second presidential debate. Tagg had invested funds into the Texas vote tabulation company Hart InterCivic and watched his father campaign more than seven years for the presidency in a billion-dollar campaign. Yet Tagg voiced a classic "sour grapes" response, apparently unaware that Aesop's fable has resonated across cultures for more than 2,500 years.[13] Tagg claimed to the public that his father, "wanted to be president less than anyone I know."[14]

In assessing the race, the candidate likeability factor was important. In Obama's case, he has had to overcome a solid core of haters and doubters. However, he has done reasonably well with the rest of the population, as even his critics on policy would concede. A 2010 video of the president playing basketball with CBS sportscaster and former NBA player Clark Kellogg illustrates the reasons for Obama's popularity, especially in a youth-oriented culture. The president, dressed in a business shirt and tie, is shown making several long shots and joking comfortably. Obama has specialized also in putting a positive face on "ugly and discredited policies" of the elite, as commentator Glenn Greenwald describes. "The CIA presciently recognized this as a valuable asset back in 2008 when they correctly predicted that Obama's election would stem the tide of growing antiwar sentiment in western Europe by becoming the new, more attractive face of war, thereby converting hordes of his admirers from war opponents into war supporters."[15]

Looking back, GOP strategists realized that Paul Ryan had failed to resonate nationally even if he remained popular with the party's base. A polling group found that Romney won 79 percent of the white Christian vote (which also constituted 80 percent of his support). The analysts concluded that the 2012 elections were America's "last" in which a white Christian strategy be considered a plausible path to victory.[16]

Inevitably, some speculated that Jeb Bush in 2016 should run to restore the Bush Dynasty. In early 2013, Bush and his aides took steps to become active, thereby establishing himself as the front-runner for the GOP's 2016 nomination.[17] His fluency in Spanish, wealthy Mexican-born wife, and his book on immigration helped burnish his credential along with fading memories of his brother's presidency.[18] Allegations of Jeb's serious drug use in his younger days passed virtually unnoticed even with made by a former GOP congressman and school contemporary.[19] So have questions about the stolen presidential vote in 2000, and also about his alleged involvement in Iran-contra and savings and loan scandals in the 1980s.[20] A Bush candidacy aided by a supposedly independent Rove-led Crossroads GPS operation would revive the well-oiled Texas-Saudi-Wall Street federal contracting colossus focused on energy, banking, and war making. A Bush has appeared on every successful Republican presidential ticket since 1972.

Many questions remain unasked also about the prospective Democratic front-runner for 2016, Hillary Clinton. We must examine the recent past, however, to predict the future, including preposterous claims that meaningful action to help the public must await the results of the 2014 elections.

Lessons from the Obama First Term

Obama's background as a CIA/foundation-nurtured asset raises doubt over whether his true loyalties are to his elite enablers, or to "the 100 percent" of the country that he ostensibly supported during the 2012 campaign. Obama illustrated his ambivalence during his first-term policies. The pattern of deference to his powerful enablers was clear on jobs, health care, war-making, torture, due process in the justice system, and consumer protections against the financial sector and polluters. Yet Obama has an opportunity in a second term, especially if he no longer hides his past. He can rise above his false history and provide the leadership that he promised the country during his campaigns.

The scandals erupting at top levels the defense and intelligence communities in the week after the 2012 elections added new leverage to Obama's power to break free from his past and chart a more independent course in his second term. To recap:

CIA Director David Petraeus, a favorite of conservatives and the rest of the Washington establishment, resigned after the White House announced November 9 his affair with his biographer, Paula Broadwell.[21] Jill Kelley, a Tampa socialite, had complained about anonymous threats that were discovered to be the handiwork of Broadwell. The email trail led to Petraeus and to General John R. Allen, Petraeus' successor as commander of United States and NATO forces in Afghanistan.[22] The White House forced Petraeus to resign, a step he had not intended to take even after his affair was outed.[23] The Petraeus resignation, along with a delay in Allen's expected promotion to NATO commander in Europe, coincided with several other forced resignations and demotions, including those of military flag officers and other high-level security officials.

These steps, taken just after the election, seemed to suggest that President Obama would act more decisively during his second term, even with the military.

Backing Off at the Beginning

Just before Barack Obama took office in 2009, one of his comments foreshadowed the overall shortcomings of his first term as well as his failure in the first 2012 presidential debate. In an exclusive interview on national television, Obama said that his Justice Department would "look forward, not backward" on allegations of Bush-era law breaking.[24] Obama's comment focused upon the United States torture of Mideast detainees and the subsequent cover-up. The president-elect's words soon symbolized, however, the broader story of how his administration was failing to investigate, much less prosecute, a wide range of Bush-era crimes, including Wall Street bankster fraud, torture, political prosecutions, perjury, elections fraud, and illegal surveillance of the general public.

Corrupt officials sometimes commit multiple different crimes. For example, many whistleblowers, public interest attorneys, and independent journalists have documented the horror behind the nation's most notorious Bush political prosecution, that of Don Siegelman. It is worth repeating that authorities prosecuted Siegelman not simply because he was Alabama's leading Democrat. Vast gambling interests were involved. Jack Abramoff said that his casino clients alone contributed $20 million, through various conduits, to defeat Siegelman. The casino donors' goal was to prevent state-sanctioned gambling from competing with their private casinos. Casinos, as opposed to lotteries, can have especially nefarious social consequences. One such aspect is the ease of money laundering, which facilitates political bribes, unreviewable "black budgets" for any agencies involved, the cover-up of drug profits, and other serious societal ills. The relationship between gambling and money laundering is one of the reasons why even an industrial mastermind such as Howard Hughes did not neglect the profits available from casinos, even if they necessitated bribery.[25] Yet authorities considered Hughes to be a vast improvement in morality over his predecessor owners from the mob.

Siegelman's opponents also wanted to get him out of the way of other money-making opportunities. They wanted to secure a $35 billion Air Force tanker-refueling contract. Siegelman's trial judge, Mark Fuller, controlled an Air Force refueling company tied to Iran-Contra operations and received some $300 million in Bush contracts. The judge's company boasted of refueling Air Force One, and training Air Force and international pilots. In December 2011, Fuller and the handful of other owners sold the company, Doss Aviation, to one controlled by one of Mitt

Romney's leading supporters, former Navy Secretary John Lehman, a prominent neo-con.

In the fall of 2011, one of President Obama's top advisors described to me how the transition team preparing the Obama administration in 2009 had feared a "revolt" if the new administration tried to prosecute law breaking by Bush officials. University of California at Berkeley Law School Dean, Christopher Edley Jr., had been the sixth-highest-ranking official of the transition team. Edley did not specify to me precisely what form a "revolt" might take in his mind. However, the context of his comments suggested their fear that senior defense and national security officials and their outside patrons might undertake violent reprisal in some fashion. My column on the transition team's fear was widely read and republished on several websites.[26]

The president's actions and Edley's explanation seemed craven and politically opportunistic to me and to many of my readers who left comments.[27] After all, Obama was commander-in-chief and had won the election with promises of reform and a majority in the House and Senate. By the time of my correspondence with Edley, the administration had clearly fallen far short of public claims that they would govern in a just and transparent fashion regarding sensitive law enforcement, security, and whistleblower cases.

Yet my research has been a continuous learning process. I now suspect that Edley had a solid basis for his fears. In fact, Obama privately cited to friends the assassination of the Rev. Martin Luther King, Jr. as good reason to fear reprisal in the fight for social justice, according to a retired CIA analyst who had previously prepared daily briefings for presidents.[28] Knowledgeable sources confide that the president's 2013 security provisions have been enhanced in ways I shall not specify. The changes were to protect him against the extraordinary hatred that opponents generated during his first term by bogus claims of radicialism, birth in Kenya, and so forth. We now know also that 19 Republican congressional leaders held a summit meeting at the posh Caucus Room restaurant in Washington on the night of Obama's first-term inauguration. The conspirators vowed that night to obstruct Obama's first-term agenda no matter what he proposed, even if he sought their support for their own ideas.[29]

The nation was in the midst of the worst economic crisis since the 1929 Stock Market Crash and the Depression. Vast numbers of people across the country were losing their jobs, life savings, health benefits, and homes. The Bush administration was clearly responsible for most of the disaster following its eight years of governance. The public had just handed Obama and the Democrats a mandate for change, including change via control of Senate and the Houses. Yet on the very night of what should have been a joint national resolve to solve problems, GOP leaders conspired for four hours on how best to block any effective response for the next four years.

The GOP's secret meeting took place in the heart of the city, across the street from the FBI and three hundred yards from the site of Lincoln's assassination at Ford's Theater. Former lobbyist and Republican National Committee Chairman Haley Barbour cofounded the restaurant, but was not at the meeting. He was Mississippi's governor, with his 2002 election enabled by a series of Bush Justice Department frame ups of leading Democrats comparable to the Rove-inspired political prosecution of Siegelman in Alabama.[30] Instead, GOP image consultant Frank Luntz ran the restaurant meeting with congressmen, Paul Ryan of Wisconsin, Eric Cantor of Virginia, and Kevin McCarthy of California. Their ferocity in protecting their funders encouraged their peers to bestow an affectionate nickname upon them: "The Young Guns"

Meanwhile, the Nobel Peace Prize Committee was preparing to award Obama one of the world's most prestigious life achievement honors less than 10 months after he took office. The five-member Norwegian selection committee comprised of political leaders began deliberations in February to bestow the prize on behalf of the estate of Swedish industrialist Alfred Nobel, inventor of dynamite. The group made its formal announcement in early October 2009 that Obama had been chosen from among 205 nominees "for his extraordinary efforts to strengthen international diplomacy and cooperation between peoples." Council of Europe President and former Norwegian Prime Minister Thorbjørn Jagland was an important advocate for Obama on the committee, facilitating its unanimous decision in his favor.[31] The decision gratified Obama's supporters and puzzled if not irritated his detractors.[32]

The next four years would illustrate why power-brokers would want Obama to achieve the image of a man of peace.

First Term Track Record

The court system is the best place to begin a brief survey of the first term of the Obama presidency because actual or threatened legal action is integral to government policy. The president named his close friend Eric Holder, Jr. as attorney general, supervising the Justice Department. Holder, former deputy attorney general during the Clinton administration, became wealthy during the Bush administration at the Washington-based law firm Covington and Burling, from which he drew partner Lanny Breuer to lead the Justice Department's criminal division under Obama. Their firm is well known in Washington for hiring outstanding lawyers and representing well-funded clients. The firm defended the tobacco industry for many years from claims that its products induced illness.

Holder's clients included a major food importer accused of hiring assassins in Colombia.[33]

Holder's Justice Department continued the Bush administration's most notorious political prosecutions, according to my reporting for the Justice Integrity Project. Many victims of blatant Bush-era injustice endured unmerited additional suffering while perpetrators continued their machinations unexamined and, of course, undeterred.

Former Alabama Governor Don Siegelman, for example, began serving the last six years of his seven-year term at age 67 on September 11, 2012. This was after Justice Department had used sexual blackmail to threaten a young homosexual with 10 years in prison on an unrelated crime if he did not provide the testimony needed to frame Siegelman.[34] Authorities interrogated the witness 70 times at a military base before trial. Nearly all of the interrogations took place without the required disclosure to the defense.

Siegelman's sentence was by the tainted federal trial judge Mark Fuller. Former GOP Alabama Congressman Parker Griffith called the prosecution a "political assassination" orchestrated by Rove with a "weak judge." Griffith's comments came in a powerful video featuring other statements to similar effect.[35] Especially in the post-Willie Horton era, however, politicians in the White House and elsewhere across the nation remained far too fearful of political fallout to exercise their constitutional responsibilities for clemency. They avoided clemency in almost any criminal case, much less in those cases that might antagonize powerful interests.[36]

One of the few major Bush-era prosecutions that the Obama administration vacated on the grounds of fairness was the corruption convictions against former Republican Senator Ted Stevens of Alaska.[37] That case was replete with special circumstances, including the presiding judge's strong protest of Justice Department law breaking. Holder approved whitewash investigations set up by the Bush administration that cleared CIA officials of destroying evidence of torture.[38] The department failed to bring major criminal cases to court in the 2008 Wall Street and mortgage financial collapses[39] and failed to press serious charges against leaders of the BP/Deepwater Horizon Gulf of Mexico oil-drilling disaster. The Justice Department did sue several states to prevent state-initiated vote suppression abuses scheduled for the 2012 elections. The DOJ ignored the more sinister problem of election software fraud.

Obama's Supreme Court nomination of his friend, Elena Kagan, an executive power enthusiast and former Harvard Law dean, demonstrated anew his deference to those with elite credentials helpful to the goal of expanded presidential power. Kagan, a one-time consultant to Goldman

Sachs, had argued at the Justice Department against Supreme Court review of the obvious injustices in the Siegelman prosecution.

For oversight of the economy, Obama appointed a Wall Street-friendly economic team.[40] Many of them were involved with companies and policies that led to the economic collapse of 2008.[41]

As previously noted, Obama appointed Timothy Geithner to the post of Treasury Secretary. Geithner had been chairman of the New York Federal Reserve during the prelude to the financial crisis and was thus one of the nation's most important failed regulators.[42] Background reviews revealed that Geithner, the prospective head of the Internal Revenue Service (a unit of the Treasury Department), neglected to pay some $35,000 in federal self-employment taxes in the years prior to his nomination. He corrected that oversight with retroactive payment, an option available to some but not all other taxpayers.

The nominee's background provides clues to his inner-circle status. His father, Peter Geithner, had been head of the Ford Foundation's Asian program decades previous, and thus the boss of Ann Dunham in Indonesia when she undertook her micro-finance work.[43] Early in his career, Geithner worked for Kissinger & Associates, placing him in the Rockefeller orbit. He ascended to become a member of the Council on Foreign Relations and the Bilderberg Group.[44] Geithner went on to serve the entire first term as one of Obama's main advisors, including in negotiations with Republicans on compromise solutions to the so-called "fiscal cliff."

Both parties heavily rely on the financial industry. White House visitor logs during the first years of the Obama administration showed strong traffic from financial sector lobbyists.[45] As Obama navigated the first two years of his administration, his support for those struggling after the nation's 2008 financial collapse followed a pattern of deference to elite groups. Overall, he provided appointments to centrists such as Geithner and denied them to those such as consumer protection advocate Elizabeth Warren, who was regarded as too vigorous in identifying solutions for victims of the financial meltdown.

For military leadership at the Defense Department, Obama continued Bush Secretary of Defense Robert Gates, who had been the CIA director during the first Bush administration. Gates was a career government official aside from a stint as president of Texas A&M University, which houses the George Bush Presidential Library and Museum.[46] Gates had been a member of the Carter administration's National Security Council staff in 1980 under Brzezinski.

Some have accused Gates of being a mole who hurt Carter by tipping off the Reagan-Bush campaign that year about details of the Carter administration's unsuccessful negotiations with Iran to release United

States hostages. Carter's lack of success created an image that he was "weak," and helped cause Carter's defeat.[47] The Gates appointment by Obama followed a long pattern whereby Democratic presidents named Republicans to lead the Defense Department. Sold to the public under the claim of "bipartisanship," the practice is better understood as a way for the country's behind-the-scenes rulers to ensure that their agenda is implemented even if Democrats win an election. For Obama to pick Gates, given the Iran hostage and Iran-Contra controversies, shows how well he understood his limited prerogatives as president.

Obama's Secretary of State, Hillary Clinton, continued the trend, set by Madeleine Albright and Condoleezza Rice, of putting a female face on the department's mixed message of promoting democracy and of fighting "terror" by covert actions, drones, and other unaccountable war-making. The "Arab Spring" of 2011 presented an especially difficult challenge to the United States mission of serving as policeman to the world. This was because some of the activists challenging old regimes in North Africa were Islamist fundamentalists (including al-Qaeda) whom the United States would likely find hard to control. The oil-rich monarchies in Saudi Arabia and Qatar, allied with the United States, encouraged the radical activists who toppled the Mubarak government in Egypt and received United States help in overcoming Gaddafi in Libya. Yet "success" brought new challenges, including a free flow of arms to uncontrollable factions in Egypt and Syria, two nations that adjoined Israel, the main United States regional ally.

Leon Panetta, former Clinton administration chief of staff, was CIA director for two years until his appointment as defense secretary. As an example of the agency's public relations intrigues under Panetta, it devised a classified plan published by WikiLeaks in 2010 describing how the government could count on voter apathy to continue unpopular wars in Afghanistan.[48]

On such public relations and business regulation issues, Obama could rely on his friend Cass Sunstein, whom he appointed to lead federal regulatory efforts at the White House Office of Management and Budget. As a Harvard Law professor, Sunstein had proposed during the 2008 campaign that the government secretly hire academics and journalists to thwart the spread of ideas condemned by government. Such secret counter measures confirm the willingness of government officials to block transparency. Did the government secretly hire academic and journalism allies on still-classified disputes? It is hard to provide a comprehensive answer before of the secrecy restrictions. Yet we do know that Dr. Jonathan Gruber of the Massachusetts Institute of Technology was a grant-winner from the Obama administration at the time he was being widely quoted by the media as an independent expert.[49]

Sunstein, an engaging former professor of mine at Chicago, was best known in Washington for his Republican-friendly deregulatory theme to eliminate inefficient regulations. The plan offended liberals who regarded eight years of Bush control of the bureaucracy as already curtailing excessive regulation in such areas as environmental, consumer protection, and election law. Republicans gave Sunstein little credit for adopting some of their own themes. During the summer of 2012, he resigned to return to Harvard and publish a book on his accomplishments.

The Affordable Health Care Act, aka "ObamaCare," was the administration's proudest domestic policy achievement, and yet it is a deeply flawed plan. Its claims of cost containment and of extending insurance to more than 40 million uninsured Americans by 2014 are well-known by now. I reported on the law's debate and passage. As part of the research for these reports, I observed at close hand how traditional liberals such as Michigan Congressmen John Conyers and John Dingell (the two longest-serving members of Congress) can be eloquent in advocating simpler, cheaper, and fairer solutions. Conyers illustrated this as he co-presided over the only congressional hearing to invite patients to testify on the possibility of a public option during the long debate over a new law. He co-chaired the hearing with Texas Congresswoman Sheila Jackson Lee, also a Democrat.[50]

One of the first witnesses was cancer survivor Harriet Fulbright, widow of the Arkansas Senator J. William Fulbright, whose televised Vietnam War hearings helped to change the national opinion about the war four decades ago. "I can think of no subject more important," she testified, "than health care for every citizen of this country."

Independent-film-maker Natalie Noel, another witness, showed her work with Robert Corsini portraying the ravaged health care services in New Orleans and the helplessness of officials post-Katrina. She and Corsini began work in 2007 on their film "Reinventing Paradise." The movie was about post-Katrina recovery problems in Gulf of Mexico states. An Alabama native, she recounted how she later discovered that she had Stage Three cancer, which exhausted her ability to pay for treatments or even to continue to pay her insurer, which was Alabama's dominant carrier. With no options for life-saving care in Alabama and without the ability to work, she moved to Pennsylvania, where the state provided twice-weekly treatments toward her full recovery. Noel concluded her testimony by asking those present to consider: "What would happen if you were suddenly struck by your own personal Katrina?"[51]

At the hearing's conclusion, the Rev. Walter Fauntroy, a former congressman and an organizer of iconic Civil Rights marches in the 1960s, made an eloquent call for action. Fauntroy sought to put the issue of health care for those who might otherwise die into perspective. In the style of old-time preachers, he spoke of the curse of subjugation, the blessing of hard work and abundance, and the cycle of apathy and renewed subjugation in the rise and fall of civilizations. On that day in 2009, he sought to rekindle the passion that inspired his generation five decades ago at a time now often praised but seldom imitated. Immediately afterward, Conyers described his career-long fight for a "public option" and single-payer health care system in a video interview. This chapter's endnotes contain links to powerful video excerpts from the hearing.[52]

The Conyers hearing had no impact on the larger debate, and scant follow up. The powerful industry players opposed any discussion of a public option, as did the Obama administration. The ineffectual organization of the hearing by its leaders compounded that problem.[53] Much worse, Conyers, while eloquent on the topic, labored especially under the cloud of corruption tarnishing many members of Congress because his wife had recently pled guilty to bribery while holding office on Detroit's City Council.[54] These factors combined to prevent the advance of lower-cost health care solutions.

Obama's failure to fight harder against Republicans to establish a major jobs program was another central failing of his first term. In 2009, Obama had an election mandate to redress brutal economic trends that destroyed jobs, savings, home ownership, and pensions. Instead of mobilizing his majority to stimulate the economy with meaningful jobs programs, the president took modest steps that were too weak to have substantial impact, and with the small steps he did take had inherent flaws that undermined his reputation. Thus, the stimulus package he sought was too small. Yet the Obama plan also contained excessive funding for what became crony-marred boondoggles such as the Solyndra project. Moreover, the Obama plan contained giveaways that reinforced conservative stereotypes of big-spending Democrats. Instead of creating Works Progress Administration-style jobs in the proven New Deal success formula, the Obama Band-Aid approach kept up the dole over vast periods for others.

Handouts, which are ostensibly seen as a liberal measure, undermine public confidence in government for non-recipients because hardship is widely prevalent. "Between 2007 and 2010, the median net worth of U.S. households fell by 47 percent, reaching its lowest level in more than forty years, adjusted for inflation," according to a report in the *Atlantic* magazine. "In other words, middle class wealth virtually evaporated in this country. A good chunk of the population got sucked through a financial wormhole back to the sixties."[55] That is an astonishing degree of devastation.

Neither the president nor other major party leaders confronted the real problems in ways that would have seriously disturbed the patrons controlling both parties.[56]

Fat Cats and Their 'Tea Party' Hoax

The tea party and Occupy movements also arose during Obama's first term, as did hate groups that made vicious attacks on the president.

The tea party movement allowed an angry sector of the nation to organize with many legitimate grievances in a patriotic setting that was seemingly distinct from the tarnished brand of the Bush-led Republican Party. The nation's media portrayed the tea party as a spontaneous, grassroots effort by patriotic citizens insisting on traditional values, balanced budgets, and other austerity measures.

In reality, the movement was a decade in development funded by barons of traditional industries seeking to harness the energies of patriotic, religious, but otherwise low-information aging whites to serve as the drones for most wealthy Americans in political battles. "A new academic study confirms that front groups with longstanding ties to the tobacco industry and the billionaire Koch brothers planned the formation of the Tea Party movement more than a decade before it exploded onto the U.S. political scene," according to an academic study. "Far from a genuine grassroots uprising, this AstroTurf effort was curated by wealthy industrialists years in advance." [57]

FreedomWorks organized the movement from their headquarters in Washington. Dick Armey, a former Texas congressman and GOP majority leader, was among those running FreedomWorks. Another was C. Boyden Gray, an R.J. Reynolds tobacco heir and former White House counsel during the 1980s administration of the first president Bush. These dynastic ties and goals of social manipulation go back even further.

With that kind of pedigree, the tea party in achieved striking success in dominating the 2010 elections. Meanwhile, the Obama administration was extremely passive and otherwise ineffectual in mobilizing any warning to the public, much less opposition to a resurgence of the Bush-era dynastic interests in a new guise. One might think that activist groups in the private sector might also raise alarm. To do so, however, would endanger many of their funding sources from foundations and elsewhere.

Tea party enthusiasm helped restore GOP majorities in Congress and in state legislatures that promptly created gerrymandered congressional districts in force for the next decade. Tea-party-inspired victories also lead to the Republican control over most state offices. These are the officials who oversee elections, including the choice of private vote-counting contractors, thereby providing Republicans a huge advantage for the 2012 presidential elections.

Those disillusioned with both parties organized the Occupy movement in protest of both major parties. They sought to avoid being co-opted into normal political deal making. For example, Occupy Washington's encampment on Pennsylvania Avenue one day shouted down an offer of free bottled water from a union because the union offered the water only on condition that the campers support an Obama jobs proposal before Congress.

Inevitably, government officials cracked down on the encampments across the country. Occupy activists ran out of funds, patience, and enthusiasm, or rechanneled their energies into traditional parties. Kevin Zeese, one of the major organizers in Washington, termed the effort a success. He told me, "Our goal was not to occupy land permanently, but to make a statement." Documents released in December 2012 indicate that the FBI and other authorities worked closely with other federal agencies, local police departments, and bankers to disrupt Occupy encampments nationwide. The seizure of camping gear and multiple arrests ended the protests, which authorities themselves described as peaceful. *Guardian* columnist Naomi Wolf illustrated why the scope of the crackdown endangered a tradition of peaceful protest against what she called: [58]

> ...a terrifying network of coordinated DHS, FBI, police, regional fusion center, and private-sector activity so completely merged into one another that the monstrous whole is, in fact, one entity: in some cases, bearing a single name, the Domestic Security Alliance Council.

> And [litigation] reveals this merged entity to have one centrally planned, locally executed mission. The documents, in short, show the cops and DHS working for and with banks to target, arrest, and politically disable peaceful American citizens.

Several months previously, I had a more personal experience with the way the nation's civil liberties environment had deteriorated in recent decades. On 12th street in Washington's northwest quadrant, I spotted a white-haired, frail-looking man in a dark blue suit walking with a cane in the direction of the Occupy DC encampment a block away.

"Pardon me, but are you Senator John Warner?" I asked.

"I'm what's left of him!" was the cheerful response from Virginia's U.S. Senator from 1979 to 2009.

"Are you taking a look at the Occupy DC protest down the street?" I asked the World War II veteran. As a Republican, he had served as Navy Secretary from 1972 to 1974 during the Nixon administration.[59]

"No," Warner replied, stopping for a few moments, "but I support their right to do it. That is what I told President Nixon when the kids were out during those anti-war protests during the Vietnam War. Constitutional rights make our country different from the rest."

Four decades ago, vigorous peace, civil rights and union movements provided visible balance to the inherent power of the establishment. The movements collapsed for many reasons, including the end of the draft and the most obvious forms of segregation, along with the decline of unions. This coincided with excesses in the drug and welfare cultures, racial riots, and a well-funded promise by conservatives of a society filled with opportunity.

As indicated above, even the Democrat Obama focused federal law enforcement on non-violent Occupy protests against banks and Wall Street. His administration neglected groups that thrive far from most political and media centers, which rendered their factual-false, emotion-laden messages extremely powerful to susceptible voters. Attacks on Obama during his first term — claiming that he was born in Kenya, that he was a Muslim, a hater, a socialist, a communist, and that his mother was a model for a pornographer, etc. — helped foster an underlying fear and hatred of him among a significant minority of the population.

Obama and his top supporters avoided confronting the claims head-on for the most part. He had a strategy of projecting a non-partisan image during his first term. This preserved his likeability rating with the majority of voters. In addition, Obama doubtless feared, like Bill Clinton before him, that he might antagonize his base by revealing his own youthful national security credentials.

As part of my research for this book, I met repeatedly with proponents of bizarre theories about Obama. I invited several of them to amplify their theories on the radio show I co-hosted, and probed them both on air and privately. In general, I found their arguments unpersuasive. However, several had considerable media and other financial power behind them, and thus were able to spread their messages and reap strong financial returns. Puppet masters and disinformation specialists provide many book, lecture, and fellowship positions for these authors. Moreover, messages of hate and conspiracy resonate powerfully among niche audiences once given a platform. Many white voters, in particular, are furious at losses of middle class jobs, savings, and overall quality of life from causes that the national media tend to keep obscure.

Consumer and public interest groups clearly cannot match the firepower of special interest in general. Even in book publishing, which is theoretically a channel of bottom-up advocacy in the marketplace of ideas, strong barriers exist. In fact, few books and articles make money. Many of those providing political commentary are published and promoted to advance careers or the views of gatekeeper organizations.

One of the most important decisions that Obama and his team made during his first term was to conserve his political capital for a centrist re-election effort in 2012. Thus, Obama refrained from vigorously contesting the tea party movement and Republicans in the mid-term elections in 2010. As noted, Republicans thereby won huge victories at the federal and state level. The state victories were especially damaging to long-term

Democratic prospects. Republicans were able to gerrymander congressional districts for the next decade.[60] "A new analysis," one reporter wrote, "finds that even if Democratic congressional candidates won the popular vote by seven percentage points nationwide, they still would not have gained control of the House."[61]

In addition, the GOP controlled many state governments, including those in Upper Midwest states that were normally core centers of Democratic strength. In the 2012 elections, for example, Republicans won 13 congressional seats in Pennsylvania compared to five for Democrats, even though Democratic candidates received a million more total votes in the 18 contests.[62] Grassroots Democrats who track such patterns were left to wonder why their White House and other party leaders were so ineffectual.

Those few who understand the nature of modern political power realize that many topics are "forbidden" from any discussion by mainstream media. Professional comedian and political blogger Bob Somerby had mocked the "liberal" media for more than a decade on the issue. Somerby's theme is that legions of journalists who aspire to work at the *Washington Post* and *New York Times* and to appear on television news shows dare not mention topics deemed unsuitable by the leading news organizations.[63] Somerby, much like fellow humorists Jon Stewart and Stephen Colbert, mocks what he sees on a daily basis.

In essence, most broadcasters, publishers, and reporters have clear-cut incentives to overlook certain stories, namely the kinds reported here.

Information Gate Keepers

This survey of Obama's first term shows how he usually responded to pressure by governing from positions much farther to the right than the policies he had advocated during his first campaign. At the 2009 *Netroots* convention run by Daily Kos, presidential advisor Valerie Jarrett told Bush frame-up victim Don Siegelman that it was his job to win his freedom, not the president's job to intervene.[64]

One of Obama's oldest friends in government, Federal Communications Commission Chairman Julius Genachowski, helped to illustrate the deference that Democrats retain for the powerful, even the news empire of Murdoch that has been unrelentingly hostile towards Democrats and contemptuous of normal standards of news professionalism (as in the courtship of Petraeus for a presidential race).

Genachowski had been a contemporary of Obama at both Columbia University and Harvard Law, and he served as Obama's campaign chairman in the successful race for election to the *Law Review* presidency at Harvard. I knew and respected him from my time in the communications industry. In deference to major incumbent carriers, the regulator backed away from Obama campaign promises on "net neutrality" regulations, thereby baffling some of his core supporters. I was not totally surprised since any regulatory system would be complex, as well as opposed by powerful companies. More surprisingly, Genachowski proposed to waive cross-ownership regulations to assist the sale of Tribune assets in late 2012. The Koch Brothers and Rupert Murdoch's News Corp were reputed to be likely bidders for Tribune media outlets, thereby increasing media control by fabulously wealthy propagandists.

The FCC proposal was worse for the public than the horrific plan that the Bush FCC imposed in 2007 to enable GOP supporter and real estate tycoon Sam Zell to acquire the Tribune media conglomerate. The properties of the conglomerate included my first employer, the *Hartford Courant* newspaper, as well as Connecticut's Fox news stations and the state's three main alternative weeklies, thus illustrating the dangers of media control. As predicted by dissenting FCC Democrats in 2007, Zell soon destroyed the journalistic integrity of his properties.

In Connecticut, for example, Zell's management team of Fox television executives ran a combined TV/newspaper regional powerhouse. The *Courant* showed its standards when it fired one of its most senior editor/columnists, George Gombossy, after he reported a story that reflected badly on the paper's biggest advertiser, the mattress company Sleepy's. Gombossy reported that the State Attorney General Richard Blumenthal had announced that he was investigating consumer complaints alleging that Sleepy's was selling used mattresses as new, including one mattress allegedly containing bedbugs. Zell papers showed their journalistic values in other ways, including the exploitation of low-paid workers based in the Philippines caught making up local news stories under phony bylines for the flagship paper, the *Chicago Tribune*. Along with such journalistic outrages, Zell exploited financial rules to cause untold employee suffering by using an employee pension plan in a tax-avoidance scheme to bankroll his folly.[65] He then fired massive numbers of employees as the parent company fell into bankruptcy proceedings. Thus, some employees were victimized in multiple ways, having their pensions used without consent to finance Zell's folly and then being fired by a disreputable management.

Beyond that, Murdoch and News Corp. had been thoroughly discredited in the United Kingdom as a corrupt organization heavily involved in "hacking." Revelations indicated that Murdoch's employees trafficked in the illegal surveillance of celebrities, crime victims, and politicians. Executives used illegal electronic surveillance for many years in what became, in effect, a political blackmail operation targeting government officials in the United Kingdom. That was a theme of "Murdoch's Scandal," a compelling investigative report broadcast by *Frontline* on the Public Broadcasting System (PBS).[66]

In sum, the thoroughly documented Murdoch scandal in the United Kingdom focused on precisely the kind of antitrust conflicts that the FCC cross-ownership ban had been designed to prevent. The ban restricted excessive media concentration that can dominate the political process by biased news coverage, much less blackmail.

Weighing in favor of an FCC waiver were the financial difficulties of the mainstream media, including the Tribune properties. As always, there are competing arguments. However, smaller news organizations face the same economic climate and cross-ownership rules. Additionally, the Zell and Murdoch news organizations have been among the most prominent voices in the nation calling for accountability, sacrifice, and self-sufficiency for others. Yet these organizations shamelessly claimed victimhood from poor finances as their basis for exemption from the FCC's rules banning cross-ownership of newspapers and television stations within the same market.

The Obama FCC followed Bush precedent in helping Murdoch. That cave-in generated strong protest from Obama allies, including that of retired Democratic FCC Commissioner Michael Copps. Copps, a professor of history and Senate aide before his illustrious service on the commission, strongly attacked his former colleague's waiver proposal.[67] Copps wrote:

> President Obama's first term has come and almost gone. Important national priorities have been tackled and major legislative and executive milestones have been achieved. Reforming media policy was not among them. Now comes the second term and the opportunity to deliver on his earlier approach by tackling the declining state of America's news and information ecosystem. This essential infrastructure of democracy has suffered the same kind of collapse as so much of America's physical infrastructure — witness the sorry state of our bridges, highways, streets, public transportation, airports and public utilities.

> So, too, in media. Private sector consolidation led to the closing of hundreds of newsrooms and the firing of thousands of investigative reporters who should be combing the beats to hold the powerful accountable. Instead journalism has been hollowed out as badly as those rust-belt steel mills. Investigative journalism hangs by a slender thread, replaced by vapid infotainment, bloviating talking heads, and a dry well of facts and real-world analysis.

The Copps essay is about the Tribune Company, the successor to the company that I described in my first book, *Spiked: How Chain Management Destroyed America's Oldest Newspaper*. Copps, whose eloquence and genuine dedication to the public interest makes him a hero in my view, continued:

The public sector is at least equally culpable because government — especially the FCC where I served for more than a decade — blessed just about every media merger and acquisition that came before it. Then it proceeded, over the better part of a generation, to eviscerate almost all of the specific public interest guidelines that had been put in place over many years to ensure that the people's airwaves actually serve the people.

Fast forward to 2012. Oh, wait! Are we back in 2007? Isn't the current FCC about to vote on pretty much the same proposal loosening the newspaper-broadcast cross-ownership rule that the majority voted for back in 2007? Shockingly, the new proposal goes even beyond the 2007 proceeding by actually permitting more radio-TV consolidation, too — putting diversity-owned radio stations at greater risk of take-over by the media giants....

President Obama is less than half-way through his Presidency. I believe he understands that some of the issues he cares about have not yet had a fair hearing. I am not ready to believe that he will close the door on this issue that goes to the very ability of our media to nourish and sustain the kind of informed civic dialogue on which the course of American self-government depends.

Dire Deeds and the Fear Factor

In Dr. Justin Frank's 2011 best-seller, *Obama on the Couch,* the clinical professor of psychiatry argued that the president's turbulent childhood created a powerful need for consensus and aversion to conflict. [68] Frank described Obama as having "an obsessive bipartisan disorder" that remains his primary psychological defense.[69] This helps explain why Obama would refuse to investigate Bush-era crimes, and would cave into oligarchic pressure on a range of other vital issues without obtaining concessions. Furthermore, Obama would have to be super-human to not harbor at least some self-doubt when directly attacked by Romney, the new favorite of Wall Street and other oligarchic interests who provided him with decisive support in 2008, first against Hillary Clinton and then against John McCain. Romney, prepared by his sense of birthright to take control, found it relatively easy steamroll over Obama in the first presidential debate.

We cannot ignore the physical attacks on United States leaders in modern times as an additional factor in explaining Obama's behavior. Official inquiries after the attacks almost always determined that crazed assassins and would-be assassins acted entirely on their own to commit the crimes. Most of us are far too busy to research, much less dispute, these official findings.

The research for this book, however, has required me to look deeply into the workings of the justice system, particularly into intrigue and cover-up concerning assassination attempts on leaders, and provocations that can lead to war. The most prominent assassination is, of course, that of President John F. Kennedy in 1963. Questions also remain about 9/11, various border conflicts that have led to wars, and the deaths of other American civic leaders. According to many books and articles, suspicious circumstances surrounded the deaths of Robert Kennedy, Martin Luther King, Malcolm X, and Alabama federal judge Robert Vance. Similarly, a great deal of skepticism has been raised about official accounts of the attempted assassinations of George Wallace, Gerald Ford, and Ronald Reagan, as well as the events of 9/11, and the deaths of numerous foreign leaders. Investigators with a conspiratorial streak argue that airplane sabotage represents a significant threat to leaders. Officials tend to travel often and can seldom undertake all necessary protections on every trip.

Any summary of the vast literature on this topic as well as any attempt to reach conclusions are beyond the scope of this book. However, a brief commentary on research methods is appropriate: Experts on spycraft and related fields define several types of recurring players: patsy, *agent provocateur,* handler, informant, mole, cut-out, media stooge, and hit man (or "jackal").[70] They have real-life representatives in many nations and many eras.

As for conclusions, it is clear without going into all the specifics that authorities are often reluctant to make the information available to the public in a reasonable manner. For example, polls indicate that tens of millions of Americans believe that the public does not yet know everything important about President Kennedy's assassination. In 1964, the Warren Commission publicly released 26 volumes of evidence regarding the JFK assassination. Critics and commentators have doubtless exceeded that by now. Books continue to explore new theories and limitations of original investigators. In 2012, for example, the son of a CIA executive published a book documenting how the CIA and *Washington Post/Newsweek* withheld from the public the diary of Mary Meyer, President Kennedy's lover before his death, in 1964. Mary Meyer was the ex-wife of former CIA media liaison Cord Meyer and the sister-in-law of *Newsweek* executive Ben Bradlee.[71]

In sum, the public interest is served by vigorous scrutiny of the Warren Commission process. By now, the public has a vastly greater understanding of the goals and limitations of the original investigators.[72]

Similarly, it is not crazy for George Wallace supporters to wonder if he would have been elected president had he not been shot in 1972. He ran on a platform arguing that there was "not a dime's worth of difference" between the leading candidates of the two major parties, and won Democratic primaries in Michigan, Florida, and Maryland. He withdrew because of the paralysis resulting from his shooting injury. What might have happened if he, Martin Luther King, or Robert Kennedy had been politically active just a year or two longer?

Fast forward to 2012, and the anniversary date of September 11. Former U.S. Senate Intelligence Committee Chairman Bob Graham of Florida wrote a column calling for a reopened 9/11 joint Senate-House inquiry, which he co-chaired. He and co-author Sharon Premoli, a 9/11 survivor, wrote a column for the Huffington Post, saying:

> The passage of time since September 11, 2001, has not diminished the distrust many of us feel surrounding the official story of how 9/11 happened and, more specifically, who financed and supported it. After eleven years, the time has come for the families of the victims, the survivors and all Americans to get the whole story behind 9/11. Yet the story of who may have facilitated the 19 hijackers and the infrastructure that supported the attacks — a crucial element of the narrative — has not been told. The pieces we do have underscore how much more remains unknown.[73]

Their column has several extraordinary features, even aside from the former senator's stature and his obvious commitment to risk his reputation by pursuing such a controversial topic. Clearly, Graham's column and his previous two books on the topic indicate that he could not achieve the investigative results he sought when he was office.[74] I know that more from personally hosting him on my radio show and meeting with him. His assertion that other influential leaders and former leaders share his concerns was similarly striking. So was Graham's selection of a web-based forum, the Huffington Post, to voice his concerns. Graham, after all, is the brother of former *Washington Post* publisher Philip Graham, and uncle to current *Post* Chairman Donald Graham.

Bob Graham is a Harvard Law School graduate who went on to a highly successful business career as a real estate developer and a Florida governorship before his three-terms in the Senate and his best-selling books. Moreover, the 9/11 topic is precisely the type of thing that Sunstein, like others who dominate public discourse with name-calling, derided in the "Conspiracy Theories" essay. Many others mock calls for reopening the 9/11 investigation.[75] Yet Graham has a lifetime of relevant civic service and accomplishment.

I had a similar experience later in 2012 with best-selling author John Perkins. On September 29, I shared a two-hour dinner with Perkins in Georgetown. In attendance was a friend of mine whose father, former Panamanian leader Omar Torrijos, was the hero of Perkins' most recent book, *Hoodwinked*. Perkins formerly worked as chief economist for Chas. T. Main, a Boston-based consulting company with 2,000 employees, before it closed. Perkins describes the company as having national intelligence ties as it undertook Third World projects whereby nations obtained loans based on Perkins' financial projections.

Perkins confessed that he made fraudulent financial projections early in his career in order to advance by helping his employer, allied bankers, and intelligence agencies. The goal was to trigger debt foreclosures upon the debtor nations' core assets. Perkins describes his work as that of "an economic hit man" who was willing, in his heyday, to bribe leaders such as Torrijos to sell out the national assets of their countries as collateral under unreasonable loan terms.[76]

In the book, Perkins argued that unknown jackals killed Torrijos via a 1981 airplane crash while Torrijos was negotiating for the Japanese excavation of a potential new and larger canal to rival the United States controlled canal.[77] Perkins said, both in his book and during our dinner with friends in Georgetown, that Torrijos had warned him that United States "hit man" tactics used to privatize Latin American resources would prove so lucrative that the perpetrators would use them against United States citizens. He thus quoted Torrijos as saying the United States people were "hoodwinked" in starting that process. Perkins experienced a spiritual awakening induced by 9/11. Since then, he has devoted himself to reform efforts, including attempts to foster sustainable economies without such tactics.

The morning after our dinner, I attended the Red Mass at St. Matthew the Apostle Cathedral. This is the annual ceremony to inspire the nation's legal community. Usually, six or seven Supreme Court justices attend the ceremony. As I walked across the sidewalk and up the steps, I wondered if I was crossing the spot where John F. Kennedy Jr. had saluted his father's casket in the iconic photo from the 1963 ceremony at the cathedral. A few years after that photo, I sometimes used to see "John-John" in Central Park with his mother, Jacqueline Kennedy Onassis, and a bodyguard watching the practices of my football team, which played for Collegiate School. The young man later enrolled in that same school. In 1999, JFK Jr.'s Piper Saratoga crashed off of Martha's Vineyard, causing his death and that of his wife and sister-in-law. The deaths ended what might have been promising next steps in his career that, like Don Siegelman's, had presidential potential.[78]

Obama did not need to read spy novels about such matters to imagine the possibilities. His transition team's fear of a potential "revolt" in 2009 took on a special meaning. Yet the proper response is more transparency, not secrecy and fright.

This analysis further suggests why neither the CIA nor other national defense and law enforcement agencies are all-powerful monoliths. As we have seen, Obama, Clinton, George H. W. Bush, Rove, and possibly the younger Bush and Romney were all CIA-affiliated on their way up. That does not mean that they were predestined for success or controlled after success arrived. The CIA link simply means that a relationship existed unknown to the public. The relationship is a baseline, and events proceed from there on their own dynamic. Once in office, these presidents have appointed and even fired CIA directors. It is worth recalling that President

Kennedy, for instance, fired the long-serving CIA Director Allen Dulles, originally a minion of Harriman-Rockefeller interests, whose allies included the Bush family. Thus, Kennedy was in charge of the government hierarchy until his death. Even a president at the height of his governmental powers, however, cannot control hidden policies.

The mainstream media are extremely reluctant to report on such questions, or even such mysteries as how voting machines work.

Joe Lauria, the *Wall Street Journal's* intrepid United Nations correspondent, provides as an exception to the rule. He wrote the following for Consortium News, an alternative site, "What's left of American democracy is on the Nov. 6 ballot, with the Republicans hoping that a combination of voter suppression and attack ads bought by billionaires will secure the White House and Congress," Lauria wrote in advance of the vote. "The news media tend to concentrate on the horserace rather than the complicated issues surrounding how the winner will be determined. But the public is evidently interested."[79]

Two Voting Keys To Obama's 2012 Victory

In November 2012, President Obama won re-election by an Electoral College margin of 332 to 206. He prevailed with a strong reported popular vote margin and a Democratic gain of two Senate and eight House seats. Republicans retained their House majority through gerrymandered districts while losing the popular vote nationally by more than a million votes. Nine in ten members of the U.S. House and Senate who sought new terms in office were successful, even as public approval of Congress sank to all-time lows. In 2012, several conservative pundits and pollsters were so wrong in their predictions that they lost clout and jobs, at least temporarily.[80] A national poll, announced in January 2013, found that Congress had a 9% favorability rating with 85% of voters viewing it in a negative light, ranking below cockroaches and traffic jams in Americans' esteem.[81]

Obama captured an impressive mandate, especially compared to George Bush margins in 2000. Bush lost the popular vote, purloined his Electoral College margin in Florida, and governed, at times, with just 50 Republicans in the Senate. Yet he claimed a mandate, and imposed a radical conservative agenda on the country.

Post-election, the mind-boggling cost of the 2012 elections became apparent. Each side reported spending more than one billion dollars on the presidential contest alone.[82] This made it by far the most expensive election in American political history.[83] Mega-donors and "super" political action committees spent massive sums of money in the final weeks. One report said that casino magnate Sheldon Adelson -spent nearly $150 million.[84] That is a modest sum for a man reported to be worth $26.5 billion, placing him on the Forbes list of the richest billionaires.[85] Another report disclosed that Rove's Crossroads group sought to deceive the IRS in 2010 when it claimed that it deserved designation as a "social welfare group" conferring special tax-free status for donors because only a small part of the Crossroads work would involve political activity.[86] In a confidential 2010 filing, Crossroads GPS, the dark money group that spent more than $70 million from anonymous donors on the 2012 election, told the Internal Revenue Service that its efforts would focus on public education, research, and shaping legislation and policy. The group's application for recognition as a social welfare nonprofit acknowledged that it would spend money to influence elections. "Any such activity," it continued, "will be limited in amount, and will not constitute the organization's primary purpose."

By now, readers have digested this kind of conventional overview of the election. The *Washington Post* published an attractive collection of its coverage, including several photos.[87] What remains largely unexplored, except in isolated blogs, is how Obama's team handled the challenges described in this book's Chapter 11, "Probing the 2012 Vote Counters."

Step One: Overcoming Vote Suppression

The Justice Department and civil rights groups successfully challenged the most obvious vote suppression initiatives by Republican state officials. Several courts ruled that the restrictions were too unfair to implement for 2012, but could be used in the future. Corrupt state officials nonetheless imposed huge burdens on targeted populations. Ostensibly blaming of tight budgets, authorities made some voters wait many hours to vote whereas others could zip through the polls in two minutes. One study showed that 49,000 voters in central Florida gave up their votes because of long lines.[88] After the election, the Obama administration gave scant indication that it wanted to fight these abuses.

The Romney campaign's expensive Boston-based vote-getting effort, Project Orca, was a GOP disaster on Election Day. The mainstream media reported that technical foul ups caused the problem. "Orca turned out to be toothless, thanks to a series of deployment blunders and network and system failures," one commentator wrote. "While the system was stress-tested using automated testing tools, users received little or no advance training on the system. Crucially, there was no dry run to test how Orca would perform over the public Internet."[89] The Democrats' Narwhal was a big success, according to several in-depth treatments.[90] Narwhal was based in San Francisco, with offices in all 50 states. It became a huge advantage for the Obama campaign. "How on earth," one conservative wrote, "did Barack Obama, the community organizer, harness the power of data in the 2012 election like a Bain Capital numbers-cruncher, while

Mitt Romney's data-mining effort crashed and burned like, well, Solyndra?"[91]

An alternative view, voiced only in the independent media, was that hackers sabotaged Orca. The motive? At least in part to prevent it from being used for election fraud in addition to its ostensible sole purpose of getting out the legitimate vote. "Anonymous," a shadowy group sympathetic to WikiLeaks, claimed in a video to have disrupted Orca. Their purpose, they claimed, was to thwart a purported Karl Rove-inspired plot to use Orca capabilities to shift votes in several battleground states if needed. Here is what happened, as described by radio host Thom Hartmann and co-author Sam Sacks:

> In the video released prior to Election Day, Anonymous warns Karl Rove that he is being watched. "We know that you will attempt to rig the election of Mitt Romney to your favor," a black-robed figure in a Guy Fawkes mask says in the video. "We will watch as your merry band of conspirators try to achieve this overthrow of the United States government."
>
> The figure then warns Rove that Anonymous is "watching and monitoring all your servers," and goes on to say, "We want you to know that we are watching you, waiting for you to make this mistake of thinking you can rig this election to your favor....If we catch you we will turn over all of this data to the appropriate officials in the hopes that you will be prosecuted to the fullest extent of the law."[92]

After the election, those at Anonymous claimed that they prevented Rove's attempt to steal the election for Romney.[93] An intentional disruption of Orca did occur as described above, according to two sources of mine. Such a disruption would be illegal. The lack of a GOP request for a prosecution suggests that Republicans do not want a full probe of whatever they themselves planned at Orca on Election Day.[94] This underscores how elections are heavily dependent on private manipulators, not necessarily voters.

Step Two: Combating Electronic Vote Fraud

Obama overcame massive election day fraud, according to some election integrity analysts. "A landslide was denied, just as it was in 2008," wrote researcher Richard Charnin.[95] "In 2012, Obama won by 4.97 million recorded votes, a 51.03-47.19% share (51.95% two-party). In the True Vote Model, Obama won all plausible scenarios." He continued:

> There are some who are convinced that Election Fraud is systemic, but was thwarted in 2012 by Anonymous or government oversight. It is possible that the threat of an investigation in Ohio may have prevented late vote-rigging. But vote switching algorithms were in effect throughout the day in most

states. Exit pollsters always assume that both prior and current elections are fair and the exit poll samples biased. So they adjust exit poll weights and vote shares to match the sacrosanct recorded vote. They never consider the possibility that their samples were good and the elections were fraudulent.

A software expert's testimony on Election Day in Ohio may have thwarted a plot to flip many of the electoral votes needed to secure a victory for GOP Presidential nominee Mitt Romney. Building on years of research about Ohio's suspicious record with voting machines, election integrity activists presented software expert Michael Duniho to testify in Ohio's state court. Duniho had been a highly regarded computer expert for NSA before his retirement. Duniho doubtless frightened any potentially corrupt state officials in Ohio by testifying on Election Day that software they had secretly installed on Ohio machines could enable officials to flip enough votes to select different statewide winners than those chosen by voters.[96] The judge denied an injunction but said he would allow more extensive litigation if he suspected wrongdoing regarding the tabulation of the day's results.

Chapter 20

A Petraeus Betrayal?

T hree days after Election Day, the White House announced that CIA Director David Petraeus had just resigned because of his affair with his biographer Paula Broadwell. The White House said that the FBI had discovered the scandal by tracing anonymous and abusive emails that Broadwell had sent to the Tampa socialite Jill Kelley the previous spring. The chronology leaked to reporters was:

Kelley complained in fear to FBI special agent Frederick Humphries II about the anonymous emails. Humphries is a social acquaintance of hers famed for helping thwart a terrorist attack on the Los Angela airport in 1999. He pursued an aggressive investigation before the FBI replaced him. Authorities traced the emails to Broadwell. The probe then unearthed Broadwell's correspondence with Petraeus. On Election Day, the FBI disclosed its investigation and the results to James Clapper, the White House national security director. President Obama met Petraeus two days later and obtained his resignation. The resignation was effective later in the month. Before resigning, Petraeus testified in private before Senate and House inquiries concerning the Benghazi killings[1] and the results of his secret evaluation trip in October to Libya.[2]

Immediately after the resignation on November 9, *Newsmax* Washington Bureau Chief Ronald Kessler, a conservative, drew on his extensive sources to challenge the White House account.[3] "There are several cover-ups going on here," Kessler wrote. "One is the claim that the President Obama was not aware of what was going on with the FBI investigation. Is there any way the FBI would launch an investigation on the CIA Director without telling the president? The second cover-up was the fact that the FBI was told to hold off on this until after the election." Republican Congressman Peter King of New York also said the White House story did not make sense.[4]

Despite these early alarms, the facts of the Petraeus scandal remained hidden for the most part even after release of official reports. That is because the full story tarnishes players in both parties. Those with evidence or subpoena power saw no partisan advantage in full disclosure.

Furthermore, mainstream news organizations have been losing the ability to cover much beyond official viewpoints on national security stories, even if they use unattributed sources. The National Press Club and Overseas Press Club co-hosted an important conference on that theme in May 2012. The forum by the nation's two leading press clubs featured speakers from mainstream news outlets saying that their reporting on United States national security issues was becoming professionally dangerous.[5]

The reason? An unprecedented crackdown by federal authorities seeking to imprison relevant government officials who talk to reporters in an unauthorized manner. For example, *New York Times* reporter James Risen, a Pulitzer Prize winner, described how the danger applies not only to sources but also to reporters and, ultimately, their readers. Risen said that he had labored for several years under a threat of jail time for declining to testify against a source. He noted the vast expense that his situation cost the *Times* the danger that this control of information presses upon the kind of reporting that the public expects from American news organizations. Speakers did not know of the Petraeus scandal, of course.[6]

The real scandal in the Petraeus affair was that part of the CIA's top echelon was dangerously disloyal, or at least gave the appearance of disloyalty, to the country's democratically elected leaders. The evidence suggests that Petraeus and those acting in his name sought to use his position, first as a military leader and then as CIA director, to entertain discussions on how to thwart President Obama's re-election in 2012. The payoff for Petraeus under this scenario would have been continued support from grateful leaders of the military-industrial complex for his career aspirations. This would include help for the vast financing needed if he sought to join a presidential ticket.

Presidential puppet masters do not control every action of their creations, especially in the high-stakes crisis atmosphere of a presidential campaign in wartime. The control process tends to be long-term. Moreover, many power brokers might be trying to pull the strings in somewhat different directions, especially when campaigns require a billion dollars in fund-raising.

By now, you doubtless recall the official story about the Petraeus resignation. Now comes the rest of the story:

Setting the Scene

The preceding chapter described how Obama's 2008 transition team worried about a potential "revolt" by military personnel and their private sector enablers. As feared, Republicans repeatedly invited Petraeus to betray his commander-in-chief by running against him in 2012, even while Petraeus was a uniformed wartime commander. These events are outlined in Chapter 11, "David Petraeus: Revolt of the Generals," and Chapter 14, "Probing 2012 Voting Schemes."

The stakes were potentially high even though most facts remain hidden. The Uniform Code of Military Justice Code requires obedience. It provides drastic criminal penalties for violations. True, the case law is unclear for the apparently unprecedented situation involving Petraeus. He heard repeated invitations to campaign against his commander-in-chief, yet did not campaign against Obama. Whether or not Petraeus' conduct rose to the level of legal culpability, he clearly seems to have been disloyal by personal and political standards.

Clouding the issue further, the Obama administration would not want to publicly challenge such a popular neo-con favorite as Petraeus. Obama's team would not want a fight on the hot-button issue of loyalty, especially during the 2012 campaign.[7] Therefore, the White House needed to find evidence of private disgrace that would justify dismissal from the CIA. The good news for investigators is that they can almost always find an offense that can be invoked against a political target. As the head of Stalin's secret police is reputed to have said, "Show me the man, and I'll show you the crime."[8]

With that general background, the following chronology comes from both mainstream and independent sources. I invited Petraeus, Broadwell, Kelley, and their representatives to comment. None did so aside from Kelley, who said through her counsel that the media had subjected her to flawed reporting and privacy invasions merely because she protested threats against her.

The Plot Thickens

As CIA director beginning in the fall of the 2011, the fast-rising Petraeus sought to initiate significant change. Like his predecessor, Leon Panetta, Petraeus implemented an expansion of the agency's paramilitary capabilities that complemented its original analytic and covert expertise. The CIA's expansion using both fulltime staff and contractors included security for dangerous in-country operations as well as drone warfare whereby CIA personnel, under White House overall direction, could kill targets in Muslim nations. The White House oversight was led by John Brennan, who spent a quarter of a century at the CIA before becoming a private contractor and then chief of counter-terrorism under Obama.

Each of these expansions of CIA authority created foreseeable problems that Petraeus was expected to help resolve. The drone program could be construed domestically as, in effect, a replacement for the Petraeus surge strategies using large "boots-on the-ground" troop commitments that he and his neo-con supporters advocated. Drones created separate problems, including protests when the United States launched them without clear United States or international legal authority and killed innocent bystanders.

Petraeus found the civilian CIA culture, which includes many Democrats and those of scientific/analytic backgrounds, more resistant to change than his compliant subordinates in the military. He created further resistance by what some regarded as an aloof manner and an unseemly interest in the perks and politics of the job. Old-timers found that his management style contrasted that of his more political predecessors, including the well-liked George H.W. Bush. As illustrated by his collected letters among other materials, Bush had worked hard at maintaining an affable *persona* to obscure his patrician roots and often ruthless tactics.[9]

Petraeus could at least find comfort with his biographer Paula Broadwell, to whom he reportedly wrote of his enthusiasm for a fondly remembered tryst under his office desk. In January 2012, Broadwell published *All In,* her highly flattering biography of Petraeus. Through her, his legacy could remain vibrant even if the administration kept his public statements limited to a few sycophantic reporters. Broadwell promoted the biography on television and in speeches as the election campaign heated up.

In Chapter 14, we traced the developments by which the GOP-linked group OpSec recruited support from ex-SEALs and other former military who were believed to be hostile toward Obama, thereby prompting a Defense Department investigation. The Defense Department probe was concurrent with the early stages of the separate complaint by Kelley to the FBI about abusive, anonymous emails.[10]

OpSec was an effort to politicize public interest in special operations. That interest, most famous in the Rambo film series, had grown to include the career of former SEAL Jesse Ventura, as well as organizations and books of other special operations veterans. Yet the political partisan wants to capture that kind of tradition of patriotism, like anything else, and transform it into political capital. Thus OpSec was well financed and otherwise well positioned to provide a quasi-military echo chamber for any attacks on Obama by the Romney campaign and other Republicans. Recall that the 1980 presidential campaign had a "Spooks for Bush" group, even though the civil service is supposed to be non-partisan by law.

During the Republican National Convention in August, the Romney campaign argued that conditions remained far more dangerous in the Mideast than Obama claimed. The Romney campaign, in other words, had a clear vested interest in United States calamities in the Mideast.

After the Republican convention but just before September 11, "Sam Basile" surfaced to promote the *Innocence of the Muslims* hate video to major news organizations. The Egyptian-born ex-convict claimed that "100 Jews" had financed the video, a statement clearly intended to provoke maximum publicity and offend Muslims. The video's promotional boost provoked riots in Egypt and several other North African and Mideast nations on the date of the 9/11 anniversary.

The Benghazi Attack

In Libya, CIA personnel were interrogating, recruiting, and/or imprisoning suspected radicals. The operation doubtless fostered antagonism from local militants.[11] U.S. personnel at the site had asked for increased security, which the State Department failed to implement following denial by Congress of $400 million proposed increases in diplomatic security spending over the previous two years. Diplomatic and embassy security in Libya, as elsewhere, was administered by officials who had held high rank in the same posts under the Bush administration.[12]

The CIA, Brennan's counter-terrorism office in the White House, and perhaps Stevens himself were engaged in especially dangerous outreach to jihadists. The conservative commentary site World Net Daily (WND) has reported that Stevens and his colleagues "played a central role in recruiting jihadists to fight Bashar al-Assad's regime in Syria."[13] This report is congruent with previous ones cited in this book but almost never mentioned in the mainstream back-and-forth political punditry about the attack.

> WND has filed numerous reports quoting Middle East security officials who describe the mission in Benghazi as a meeting place to coordinate aid for the rebel-led insurgencies in the Middle East...Middle Eastern security sources further described both the U.S. mission and nearby CIA annex in Benghazi as the main intelligence and planning center for U.S. aid to the rebels that was being coordinated with Turkey, Saudi Arabia and Qatar.

> Many rebel fighters are openly members of terrorist organizations, including al-Qaida.

> Among the tasks performed inside the building was collaborating with countries, most notably Turkey, on the recruitment of fighters – including jihadists – to target Assad's regime, the security officials said.[14]

On September 10, U.S. Ambassador Stevens arrived in Benghazi to meet with a Turkish official in the temporary facility. Its perimeter guards were Libyans armed with only bats. A small British company under a State Department contract had hired the guards to protect Americans in one of the world's most dangerous locales. This kind of private security service was a direct result of the prevailing bipartisan Washington culture to privatize core government functions. The British former intelligence officer hired the local guards with money from United States taxpayers, placing operational control and accountability in private hands.

On September 11, 2012, Petraeus attended a private showing of *Argo,* the CIA-assisted film. The production celebrated intrepid work by a joint CIA-Canadian team in 1970 to rescue six American hostages from Iran. The movie is an action entertainment flick on a patriotic theme. Although not overtly political, it inevitably reminds the public of the horrible hostage crisis that hurt Democrats so badly during the 1980 elections.

On the evening of September 11, scattered news reports surfaced of protests across the Mideast in reaction to an excerpt from *The Innocence of Muslims.* The video's portrayal of the prophet as a pervert understandably provoked outrage from Muslims. Who would gain from such protests? The most serious attacks turned out to be at a United States facility in Benghazi that served as a lightly guarded adjunct to the main U.S. facility, a CIA operations center. As if on cue, Mitt Romney attacked President Obama that night, calling him weak. Romney thus violated a bipartisan United States tradition against political attacks on the White House when the nation is under foreign military attack. To Romney and his advisors, tradition obviously meant little compared to the potential of gaining political momentum.

Romney repeated his criticism of Obama the next morning even after he learned of the American deaths. The Romney campaign and its Capital Hill allies fomented a major campaign issue out of the attack on the consulate, but for the most part avoided criticizing the CIA and Petraeus. Their strategy achieved success when Republicans portrayed United Nations Ambassador Susan Rice, a surrogate for Obama, as falsely describing the attack on television talk shows. As a political appointee, her talking points were prepared by intelligence officials, including Petraeus. Close examination of her remarks indicates that she recited the substance to reflect well on the administration, as diplomats commonly do. She also repeatedly noted that the cause of the attack remained under investigation.[15] Nonetheless, Republicans pilloried her and Obama on largely false claims that the administration ruthlessly failed to save the murdered men and then orchestrated a cover-up on Sunday talk shows that flatly denied that the killers were extremists. The Democrats' motive was supposedly to deny that radicals remained a threat in the Mideast.

Immediately after the deaths, throughout the campaign, and continuing until publication of this book in the late spring of 2013, Republicans attacked Obama, Rice, and Hillary Clinton for Rice's talking points. Yet those points were drafted by the CIA, according to emails ultimately released[16].   Meanwhile, reporters unmasked the videographer "Sam Basile" as Nakoula Basseley Nakoula, a Christian born to Egypt's Coptic minority. He lived on modest means in California, owing $970,000 to fraud victims. He was on parole from a prison sentence for a series of bank frauds using stolen identification. A California judge promptly sentenced him to a year in prison as a parole violator. Considering his criminal past and disruptive global ambitions, authorities revealed surprisingly little about his finances, allies, and motivations before locking him up.[17]

Mysteries remained that were not easily resolved during the campaign season, especially given the inherent secrecy of law enforcement and national security. The CIA's ability to fend off a second attack in Libya provided a glimpse of a secret security force created after the Sept. 11, 2001 attacks in New York.[18] The *New York Times* reported that the evacuees after the Benghazi attack included a dozen CIA operatives and contractors."[19]

With reports during the campaign of CIA involvement largely secret, Republicans blamed Obama for being unprepared for riots in Libya and Egypt on September 11, and for being weak in his responses. This was the 1980 Iran hostage crisis and the 2004 Swift Boat smears rolled into one.

Craig Unger reported that a GOP source had revealed to him a "Jimmy Carter Strategy" to make Obama seem weak on defense in the campaign's final month.

> According to a highly reliable source, as Mitt Romney and President Barack Obama prepare for the first presidential debate Wednesday night, top Republican operatives are primed to unleash a new two-pronged offensive that will attack Obama as weak on national security, and will be based, in part, on new intelligence information regarding the attacks in Libya that killed U.S. Ambassador Chris Stevens on Sept. 11.

> The source described the Republicans as chortling with glee that the Obama administration 'definitely had intel' about the attack before it happened....The source declined to reveal the names of the GOP operatives who were present. Nevertheless, he said, 'These were the top guys in the party.[20]

Later, Qumu, the Ansar Al-Sharia leader and suspected double or triple agent, was suspected of responsibility for the attack.[21] If fault for the deaths might rest with disloyal figures within the United States government, this would not be the 2012 film, *Argo*, but instead *Seven Days in May* from the Cold War era.[22]

Shortly before the first 2012 presidential debate between Obama and Romney on October 3, Obama learned from loyal sources in the administration their confirmation of their suspicions during the summer that his political opponents were ramping up their plans to use Mideast disturbances to sway the electorate against him and Democrats. Obama, according to my information and independently published sources, heard that his CIA director, or those close to him, were involved.[23] The president and his team could hardly air such suspicions against a Beltway and neo-con hero during a presidential campaign, however. All they could do was quietly dig deeper into the relationships of Petraeus and his circle. In this, they were able to use the secret scandal of the Petraeus affair with Broadwell.[24]

Obama faced extreme pressure from Israeli Prime Minister Benjamin Netanyahu. In a way highly unusual for the leader of a United States ally, Netanyahu made public his preference for Romney to become United States president. Netanyahu's tilt was potentially harmful to Obama with Jewish and evangelical voters.

Security issues led to a Republican narrative all during the fall that Obama and his team were weak on Mideast policy and security. In late October, Fox News and *Weekly Standard* Editor William Kristol attacked Obama with the theme that he was trying to "throw Petraeus under the bus." The critics also blamed Obama for failing to rescue doomed personnel despite their "desperate requests" for help in Benghazi.[25]

Overplaying the Hand

Romney and his allies went too far, however. Even Romney advisor Michael Hayden, the former CIA and NSA director, objected to war with Iran. Beyond that, a House hearing in October designed to embarrass the Obama administration on Benghazi ended up accidentally disclosing that the compound housed at least seven CIA personnel during the massacre. Utah Congressman Jason Chaffetz tried to obscure the GOP slip up, but it had already been broadcast on C-SPAN.[26]

Separately, both Broadwell and the FBI agent Humphries stepped up their advocacy. In October, Humphries gave an unauthorized private briefing to Republican Congressman Dave Reichert of Washington, who passed along the information to House Majority leader Eric Cantor of Virginia. Such a private update to Republicans during the campaign was an astonishing breach of the FBI and Justice Department chain of command. Similarly, on October 26, Paula Broadwell revealed the layout and purpose of normally secret CIA activities at Benghazi during a lecture at her *alma mater* in Denver. Going beyond the *New York Times* report, Broadwell said that the CIA had been holding local militants as prisoners. Her disclosures during the height of the campaign in a swing state prompted official investigations into her information sources, as well as a raid on her Charlotte, North Carolina home to seize her computer.

Near the top of the White House organizational chart was Director of National Security James Clapper, a retired general who had led the Pentagon's Defense Intelligence Agency in many sensitive assignments over a career spanning a half century. Clapper and his deputy, career CIA executive John Brennan, were in a position to know Obama's true background of intelligence work and support him. Even some conservatives outside the administration who saw Obama in action believed he showed keen interest in aggressive intelligence and defense strategies, albeit not so much as those reliant on ground troops. Christopher Ruddy, president and CEO of Newsmax and still an inquiring reporter, summed up this iconoclastic view in a remarkable column in August 2012 that was both prescient and doubtless alarming to some of his conservative readers:[27]

Two years ago, I thought an Obama presidency would be a redux of the Jimmy Carter years. Remember them? The Soviets invaded Afghanistan and cracked down on Poland. Armed communist guerillas were prevalent throughout Latin America and Africa. Iran fell into the hands of the ayatollahs.

But I was wrong. Obama has, in fact, offered an engaged foreign policy, backed up with a strong military hand. I hear, from time to time — on talk radio, for instance — that Obama is weak on national security and that he's dismantling the U.S. military (I am being mild here about how Obama is described).

Recently, I was in Washington and talked privately with one of the nation's highest military officers, a member of the Joint Chiefs of Staff. I asked him for the Pentagon take on Obama. He told me bluntly that Pentagon officials that worked under Bush and Obama believe them "both to be very good" on national security matters.

He added that the Obama White House has been extremely supportive of the Pentagon and its initiatives. Rarely do they have disagreements, and when they do, Obama usually comes down on the side of the Pentagon brass. In fact, the officer said Obama had been engaged and supportive in ways that had amazed many in the upper ranks.

Ruddy's appraisal is relevant as a reminder that important perspectives can come from diverse and unpredictable sources.

Payback

Upon Obama's re-election in November, Clapper and his team were ready to deal with Petraeus and others suspected of improper activities. The White House outed Petraeus and Broadwell as adulterers, thwarting any looming Petraeus' political career. Petraeus flatterers in the Beltway soon moved on from the scandal, hoping to salvage at least his reputation for military success with large deployments of troops. One such headline was "Petraeus's behavior is no scandal."[28]

As some had suggested from the start, the White House seems to have been dissembling when it reported that it learned of the FBI investigation for the first time on Election Day.[29] Obama would not want to confide to the public during a wartime election campaign that he was dealing with a loyalty crisis. Hence, his White House emphasized that the FBI had probed a sex scandal, not a loyalty scandal. Further, national security concerns prevented Obama from describing all factors in the massacre. He would hardly confess during the campaign that his team was secretly recruiting fighters and munitions from Libya to help the rebels in Syria in violation of U.S. non-interference policy.

The State Department's internal report found a variety of shortcomings, as previously noted, but did not expose and assess the most secret and politically sensitive secrets.[30] One controversy rarely mentioned in mainstream media was the continuing skepticism in some quarters about the official accounts of the Osama Bin Laden raid in 2011. The raid was a centerpiece of the president's first-term foreign policy achievements. Dissection of the raid is beyond the scope of this book, except to note that critics claimed irregularities in official accounts. These included the sequence of events, the reluctance to interrogate the suspect, and the high level of secrecy involved in the aftermath. Prolonged debate on any of those points was highly unattractive to the administration, which doubtless preferred a *Zero Dark Thirty* narrative for the public.[31]

The gist was that the Benghazi massacre had political downsides for the Obama administration and Republicans alike.

A Post-Petraeus Purge and White House Warning

Shortly after Petraeus resigned, the White House announced its review of the legal and ethical status of senior officers.[32] This came in the wake of multiple high-level resignations in mid-November by senior military officers with responsibilities in the African region.[33] These resignations and disciplinary actions raised the question of whether the ostensible reasons for the resignations were accurate, or whether a purge was occurring in the military for hidden reasons.

The administration warned against disloyalty by dangerous but unnamed "insiders" working in the federal government.[34] "These threats," the White House said, "encompass potential espionage, violent acts against the Government or the Nation, and unauthorized disclosure of classified information, including the vast amounts of classified data available on interconnected United States Government computer networks and systems."

On its face, the White House warning against disloyal employees seems to have covered the kinds of issues that became suspected during the 2012 presidential elections. The announcement to all federal department heads generated virtually no news coverage or commentary aside from a book by Madsen, *L'Affair Petraeus*.[35] Virtually alone among commentators, Madsen noted that Congressman Eric Massa had warned of a Petraeus betrayal as early as 2009. From the left came other complaints that Petraeus should have been fired years earlier.[36] Tarpley reported that neo-cons, Mormons, and Netanyahu backers close to Petraeus had tried to "Carterize" Obama to help Romney.[37] Others demanded an investigation of Petraeus with a special focus on the CIA's role in the security breakdown.[38] Petraeus also had his backers, including a revisionist view that he was the victim of resentful CIA colleagues.[39]

No Watergate for Woodward This Time

In December, Bob Woodward of the *Washington Post* published a major scoop.[40] He obtained a 90-minute secret tape recording showing that Petraeus seemed gratified in 2011 by an offer of support from Fox News Chairman Roger Ailes for a 2012 presidential run.[41] As noted in Chapter 17, Fox News contributor Kathleen McFarland conveyed that offer to Petraeus. She also suggested that News Corp. Chairman Rupert Murdoch, head of the parent company, might be willing to bankroll a campaign.[42]

The *Post's* placement of Woodward's scoop in its Style section instead of onto the paper's front-page prompted criticism from Carl Bernstein, Woodward's former Watergate partner at the *Post* during the early 1970s. Writing for the *Guardian*, Bernstein also wondered, why his former paper did not pursue the Murdoch angle more aggressively.[43] Bernstein wrote, "The Murdoch story — his corruption of essential democratic institutions on both sides of the Atlantic — is one of the most important and far-reaching political/cultural stories of the past 30 years, an ongoing tale without equal."[44]

Extending that theme more broadly, another international commentator, Jonathan Cook, commented:

> What Bernstein cannot understand is why his media masters don't see things the way he does. He reserves his greatest dismay for "the ho-hum response to the story by the American press and the country's political establishment, whether out of fear of Murdoch, Ailes and Fox -- or, perhaps, lack of surprise at Murdoch's, Ailes' and Fox's contempt for decent journalistic values or a transparent electoral process."

Cook continued:

> The Petraeus story is disturbing to the media precisely because it tears away the façade of US democratic politics, an image carefully honed to persuade the American electorate that it chooses its presidents and ultimately decides the direction of the country's political future.
>
> Instead, the story reveals the charade of that electoral game, one in which powerful corporate elites manipulate the system through money and the media they own to restrict voters' choice to two almost-identical candidates. Those

candidates hold the same views on 80 percent of the issues. Even where their policies differ, most of the differences are quickly ironed out behind the scenes by the power elites through the pressure they exert on the White House via lobby groups, the media and Wall Street.[45]

Nothing To See, Just A Sex Scandal

In December 2012, Defense Secretary Leon Panetta beguiled a National Press Club lecture audience by explaining that the administration required Petraeus to resign because his emails would have been embarrassing upon revelation.[46]

On reflection, the secret emails of such a high-ranking CIA official as Petraeus do not inevitably become public. Neither does history suggest that a White House promptly dismisses every government official in a sensitive post caught having an affair. Dalliances have long been part of the CIA's culture, in particular. During what some may idealize as a far more moral era than today, OSS Director William Donovan and CIA Director Allen Dulles each became notorious adulterers, as described in Chapter 13. Honey traps, madams, and prostitutes have been longstanding tools of the trade in CIA covert operations, as for the spy agencies of other nations. We can conclude with confidence that Washington sex scandals, in general, usually become public by accident or because the target has antagonized a powerful opponent, not simply because Washington officials despise immorality.

Instead of Panetta's portrayal of a transparent and pious spy agency, the real story is that the Obama administration wanted to disgrace Petraeus. Those actions fit a long tradition, much as the Clinton administration is reputed to have used pornography and possession of secret documents as a public relations cover for its decision to remove CIA Director John Deutch.

The Meaning of the Mysteries

In reviewing all of this material about Petraeus, I owe readers a few more words about the allegations against him to underscore that much of the evidence against him aside from that pertaining to the sex scandal is source-based, circumstantial, politically generated, or otherwise subject to rebuttal. Even so, readers deserve to know the allegations, collected here for the first time in such detail.

Yet the claims involve military, CIA and political matters that are inherently secret. Most of us would have difficulty researching everything that even a family member does. The research challenge becomes greater in the case of a high-level public figure. Definitive proof on all matters is almost unknowable except via the results of an official investigation with subpoena power. For instance, how much should we ascribe the actions of subordinates to a leader such as Petraeus? Petraeus undoubtedly had some staff assigned to him not of his choosing. Staff perform the dirty work inherent in any large organization, with or without the boss's knowledge. That complexity regarding guilt is one of the meanings behind the sign that used to reside on President Truman's desk, "The Buck Stops Here."[47] The same rule must apply to Petraeus.

In the spring of 2013, Petraeus launched his career comeback with an apology for his affair, his appointment to teach at two major universities, and his chairmanship of the KKR Global Institute, a Wall Street investment body whose parent company, KKR, has been valued recently at $64 billion.[48] KKR is a pioneer in the leveraged buyouts that have transformed the nation after the first ones in the mid-1950s. Deals sometimes become notorious for breaking up long-established companies via spinoffs, offshored jobs, and other layoffs.

Recall from Chapter 8 that KKR's co-founding name partner is Henry Kravis. He is the son of the first man who offered George H. W. Bush a job following college graduation and who was a hero to the oil energy for helping keep its taxes extraordinarily low. Henry Kravis is a prominent Republican leader listed by *Forbes* in 2012 as the eighty-eighth richest American, with nearly $4 billion in personal assets. His wife serves on the board of the American Friends of Bilderberg with David Rockefeller, Henry Kissinger, Donald Graham, and billionaire funder of PayPal, Peter Thiel, who was also the biggest donor by far to 2012 GOP presidential candidate Ron Paul. They attended the 2013 Bilderberg secret conference in the United Kingdom in June, as did Petraeus. Not surprisingly, Petraeus completed his transition to high-level corporate raider while maintaining an image as a scholar with his university posts. This saga illustrates yet-again the long-term, dynastic roots of the Wall Street, energy sector, military-security complex — and how it takes care of its loyal servants as they rotate through government service.

We can draw at least three more general lessons from this tawdry tale.

First is the ruthless, selfish, and utterly unpatriotic mentality of the president's opponents and at least some of his own onetime puppet masters. Despite all the secrecy, we can now discern what they were trying to do in order to defeat Obama. They connived against him even though Obama's career and his foreign policy were direct products of their CIA-foundation-Chicago School roadmap. Only a few of Obama's opponents would have been aware of the full scope of the plot described here, of course. However, anyone could have assembled the outline of the tale documented in this book's endnotes.

Obama's failure in Benghazi derived directly from the high-risk mission advocated by both his team and that of his GOP opponents:

American micro-management of Muslim nations to control the region's politics and resources. This was the CIA/Kermit Roosevelt strategy beginning in Iran. That strategy inevitably brings about failures and short-term successes. Was the 1953 overthrow of the Iranian government a net gain for the United States in installing a monarchy that opposed nationalization of oil resources until its overthrow in 1979? That calculation is beyond this book's scope. Nevertheless, any reader can start making that kind of cost/benefit assessment as long-simmering issues arise during Obama's second-term.

A second lesson from the Petraeus saga is that even the nation's leading power brokers are not unified in their goals. The "One Percent" controls a Rhodes / Harvard / Yale / Columbia / Princeton / Chicago leadership training and funding process that produces at least initially attractive Democratic candidates such as Obama, whom some splinter groups then try to destroy. Up to a point, the puppet master concept is a useful tool for understanding our politics and politicians. Keep in mind, however, the image of puppeteers pushing each other around in a greedy frenzy while trying to grab the strings, ultimately creating chaos on stage.

Finally, we see a president, at times almost on his own along with his core supporters, having to overcome in secret one of the most monstrous Constitutional challenges since Thomas Jefferson repelled the 1806 empire-building of his former vice president, Aaron Burr. Obama's hero, President Lincoln, had to defeat his former Union general George McClellan, a Democrat, in the 1864 presidential election. Little known to the public, a loyal former Marine general, Smedley Butler, helped President Franklin Delano Roosevelt overcome a 1934 coup attempt by bankers associated with the American Liberty League who sought to fund a 500,000-man army of veterans to be equipped with Remington weapons for a march on Washington and a coup. In 1951, President Truman confronted the insubordination of General Douglas MacArthur.

We know of those long ago struggles thanks to historians. In the same way, we can now begin to assess Obama's fight to overcome the long-feared "revolt" by our era's law breakers and their patrons.

Chapter 21

Planning a Second Obama Term

On January 21, President Obama delivered an eloquent, hard-hitting inaugural address to launch his second term. On a day filled with pageantry, Obama orated one of his presidency's most liberal speeches, aside from those he gave to supporters during the election season. The second-term agenda surprised opponents and supporters alike. Everyone had seen him compromise on his campaign promises, including in the year-end "fiscal cliff" negotiations.

The implacable GOP opposition to Obama throughout his first term and the transition seemed to toughen his outlook, as a reaction. Republicans would pay the price for using over-the-top methods to win the White House.

Or, maybe not. The president's bold words and Reaganesque talent for rhetoric may have been as much a part of the Inauguration show as the lip-synching by featured performer Beyonce.

This chapter describes my revelations so far on the second-term's implications for the public. We are experiencing challenges living standards — jobs, health care, economic growth, and the rest of the safety net — as well as to Constitutional rights that the president is sworn to uphold. The president's hidden past affects his policies on these and other issues. The survey that follows is not intended to be comprehensive. Many other topics deserve your scrutiny. Use the lessons here to understand the hidden factors on the issues most vital to you. I fear that you will find serious disloyalty by officials not simply on foreign affairs and voting issues, but also on the economic and environmental safety nets that we take for granted.[1]

We begin by examining major cabinet appointments. Then we proceed to economic issues, such as the recommendation by the president's favorite business group that age 70 become the new standard for Social Security eligibility. Next come due process, privacy, and other basic civil rights that we take for granted even though each is at risk now that so much power is unified in the federal government and the presidency.

Until this juncture, I have tried to let the story unfold without intruding my views. A more personal perspective may help expedite our journey's final stages. Economic, national security, and civil rights issues, important though they are, can be difficult terrain without a suggested roadmap. Power brokers spend vast amounts of money to confuse the issues. "Did you know," a friend and successful economist once asked me over lunch in Washington, "that economics is the only profession without a code of ethics? It's just fine to lend your name to whatever the client wants."

To share my political compass enables me, if nothing else, to keep these final two chapters relatively brief.

The New Deal created a massive historical and theoretical record showing that budget balancing during a deep recession leads to disaster for the economy. Similar policies today are "cruel and stupid," in the words of Paul Krugman. [2]

In terms of balancing national security and civil rights, "I like Ike," as I used to say as a child growing up in the 1950s in an Illinois Republican household. The general led Allied troops to victory over Hitler and contended against the nuclear-powered Soviets. He nominated California Governor Earl Warren to the Supreme Court. And, as one of his greatest gifts, he described the "Military Industrial Complex" in his 1961 Farewell Address as the greatest threat to the nation's democracy. Eisenhower knew about balancing strength and peace. That era of 91 percent marginal income tax rates was the time of the country's greatest prosperity.

Yet fair resolution of any issue ultimately depends on a just legal system, not simply the safety net and foreign policy.

Presidential Appointments

After re-election, Obama drew on his inner circle for cabinet appointments. Many of his picks fit the familiar Washington revolving-door pattern whereby office holders rotate into lucrative posts in the private sector. In general, the rewards tend to be so high that they are best understood as fostering long term loyalty from officials and former officials, not simply ordinary payment for work.

A few of those employees typically serve as liaison between government decision makers and the power-centers on the outside. To the public eye, these Executive Branch employees, whether in the White House or in the departments, are mere minions of the president. However, a few secretly carry much stronger clout because they help implement messages from private sector titans. These staffers are, in effect, the "strings" of the puppet masters.

My analysis may seem overly speculative when applied to new personnel, for whom we lack all the facts concerning their confidential relationships. History clarifies the process. Colonel Edward House, President Wilson's top advisor, served in such a role a century ago. With

House's help, Wilson had swept to victory on a progressive platform that seemingly took hard positions against the financiers who were secretly supporting Wilson. Their improbably strategy succeeded.[3] In 1919, House resigned after a falling out with the ailing president.

For Obama's second term, he tried to promote United Nations ambassador Susan Rice to succeed Hillary Clinton as secretary of state. Rice was regarded as close to Valerie Jarrett, who continued as a senior advisor for external relations. By virtue of position and background, the well-connected Jarrett is a likely "puppet string" in the tradition of the President Wilson's Wall Street minder, Colonel House. Her specialties include the Chicago financial and political community, as well as the African-American media elite that provides political cover for the president's political maneuvers.

Rice, an African American career diplomat, would have kept up a recent tradition of naming women and minorities to the post. Others illustrating the pattern include Rice's godmother, Madeleine Albright, and the two of Bush secretaries, Colin Powell and the unrelated Condoleezza Rice. Such diversity has symbolic value both globally and domestically. Minorities in foreign policy posts have become especially important as the government justifies military actions and covert actions around the world as advancing democracy, women's freedom, and other civil rights.[4] A female member of a racial minority is thus the optimal United States spokesperson for the nation's relatively recent legal position that it has the option to launch military action — including drones, no-fly zones, or trade blockades — at any country such as Libya, Yemen, or Syria suspected of human rights violations or "terror."

A closer look suggests that Rice, aside from her race and gender, was a largely interchangeable cog in the military-security complex. The former Rhodes Scholar is married to a wealthy Canadian. Skilled in rhetoric about democracy, human rights, and peace, she was a friend to dictators and a strong advocate of Western military interventions into the Third World.[5] Also, she and her husband had up to $600,000 invested in TransCanda, the Canadian tar sands developer whose plans needed approval by the secretary of state to proceed in the United States on its $7 billion, 1,700-mile pipeline.[6] That huge conflict of interest did not hurt her nomination. Few in the public read of the financial conflicts and few of her fellow multi-millionaires in government seem to care. Instead, Republicans scapegoated her with bogus criticism regarding Libya, thereby forcing her to disclaim interest in the post.

The job went to Senate Foreign Relations Chairman John Kerry, the Massachusetts Democrat. Via marriage, the former Yale Bonesman and Vietnam War critic had become one of the nation's wealthiest office holders. Moving beyond his protest of the Vietnam War upon his return from combat duty, Kerry became a go-along, get-along member of the establishment. In the 2004 presidential election, Kerry had endured Swift Boating and the Ohio vote theft almost without protest. After that hazing, he proved he was unlikely to rock boats of any kind.

Upon taking office, his State Department promptly issued a report to reject the environmental challenge to the tars sands pipeline.[7] In addition, the one-time peace protester continued his evolution into a military activist by calling for more United States involvement in Syria's civil war, which followed his previous support for U.S. bombing campaigns in Serbia, Afghanistan, Iraq, and Libya. "Once war was considered the business of soldiers, international relations the concern of diplomats," C. Wright Mills wrote of the U.S. over 50 years ago in *The Power Elite*. "But now that war has become seemingly total and seemingly permanent...Peace is no longer serious; only war is serious."[8]

A longer fight occurred over the president's nomination of Republican former Senator Chuck Hagel of Nebraska to succeed Leon Panetta as secretary of defense. As described in a previous chapter, Hagel had won election to the Senate in 1996 as a Vietnam War hero and successful businessman with a largely hidden background in the election machine industry. According to several of my sources, Hagel's voting machine expertise was a positive factor in the eyes of the Obama team that selected him as defense secretary.[9] Here is the story:

Obama officials became increasingly aware during the campaign of the potential for abuse by election software, with scant meaningful oversight. Federal oversight is broken. In New York State, for example, the state Board of Elections had no investigators to handle any abuse of campaign finance or election law as of January 2013.[10] NSA and U.S. Cyber Command Director Keith Alexander, among others, became concerned that foreign investors were too prominent at companies counting votes. As one example: Saudi Prince Al-Waleed bin Talal, one of the world's richest men, is reputed to be a major investor in Election Systems and Software (ES&S). The prince's company was also reported to be a seven percent shareholder in News Corp. among other major communications companies.[11]

The fact that the Obama administration sought better understanding of the election software business is significant given the traditional hidden control of that sector by Republicans and the possibility of irregularities in the defense sector. The votes of military personnel stationed overseas present a particularly problematic vote-reporting issue. Under 2009 federal legislation, the Defense Department collects the votes of military personnel as well as the votes of other U.S. citizens living overseas. ES&S and Scytl lead this program. Vote tabulation is performed by local officials, but none of them is in a position to assure the public of transparency at all stages of the vote collection and tabulation process, especially involving remote military locations and the electronic aggregation of materials.

Republicans in the Senate maintained strong opposition to Hagel before failing to stop him in a near-party line vote, 58-41. Some argued that his experience as a combat veteran made him too resistant to war. In Hagel's biography, he had written, "Not that I'm a pacifist — I'm a hard-edged realist, I understand the world as it is — but war is a terrible thing. There's no glory, only suffering."[12] That kind of common sense would seem to deserve deference, especially coming from a former combat hero. Republicans were willing to attack him for his combat views, but never raised the sensitive issue of his past work in the election machine business.

After the Petraeus resignation from the CIA, the president emphasized loyalty along with experience in several remaining high-profile cabinet nominations. Thus, he nominated Chief of Staff Jack Lew, a two-time Office of Management and Budget director, to succeed Geithner as Treasury Secretary. Upon leaving office in 2013, Geithner accepted a fellowship at the Council on Foreign Relations to write a book.

Lew's confirmation process revealed disturbing patterns of how the revolving door between government and the private sector enriches and perhaps influences officials in ways that are entirely legal. Lew rose as a federal employee to be White House budget director during the Clinton administration. He was executive vice president of New York University from 2001 to 2006 at a reported salary of $700,000 to $800,000 a year.[13] Upon his departure to work for Citigroup, the University awarded him an unusual $685,000 severance. Citigroup is an affiliate of Citibank, and received a huge federal bailout. The company awarded Lew a nearly $950,000 bonus shortly before he rejoined the government in the Obama administration. The bonus contained a suspicious-looking provision that allowed it to be paid only if Lew returned to government.[14] This generated criticism. A more innocent explanation seems likely: that Lew negotiated the bonus provision to compensate for his reduced base pay at Citigroup.[15] Whatever the case, big-dollar perks are so common that senators confirmed Lew as Treasury secretary.

The president also retained Attorney General Eric Holder and Health and Human Services Secretary Kathleen Sebelius. Their retention foreclosed the need for contentious confirmation hearings and also maintained cabinet diversity, which was reduced by the replacement of Hillary Clinton. Denis McDonough, 43, former deputy national security advisor, became chief of staff. He was regarded as one of Obama's closest aides and friends. His appointment suggested that the second-term leadership would be "a band of brothers" more than the first-term "team of rivals."[16]

An obvious plant in the White House of someone with unknown clout involved Benjamin Rhodes, age 35, the President's second-term speechwriter for national security issues. Investigative reporter Russ Baker raised the issue of why a young novelist of Republican sympathies like Rhodes would have been picked at age 24 to draft the 9/11 report in 2002, and then would reach the White House in a meteoric ascent to craft a Democratic president's words on some of the world's most sensitive matters. Ever most interestingly, Baker asks, why would a major *New York Times* profile of Rhodes overlook such questions? Baker's clear implication is that Rhodes has powerful, unknown, non-political connections who seek input on the president's words — and that experienced White House news correspondents and their editors would know that probing too deep is not news fit to print.[17]

Most intriguing of Obama's appointments was that of Deputy National Security Advisor John Brennan as CIA director. Recall that Brennan's CIA work had included strong roots in both the Clinton and Bush administrations, as well as the extraordinary coincidence of his company's role in illegally inspecting (or sanitizing?) Obama passport records. At the time, Brennan led not simply his own company but also the trade association for the nation's security contractors. That was no small honorific when the nation was engaged in two overseas wars heavily reliant on contractors and was ramping up its enormous Homeland Defense sector. Brennan, in sum, would be my bet as the most likely "puppet string" conduit between the White House and the nation's military-industrial-security complex.

During the first-term of the Obama administration, Brennan helped Obama implement two controversial military tools in order to reduce reliance on American ground troops for Mideast wars. He ran "Terror Tuesdays," weekly meetings to decide which Middle East people should be nominated as drone targets for presidential authorization to kill. This put him at the center of the debates on whether such "kill lists" are legal and otherwise wise in undeclared wars, such as those in Pakistan, Yemen, and Somalia. The practice also increasingly arrayed Brennan and the Obama administration against neo-cons who continued to support ground troop commitments in Iraq, Afghanistan, and additional battlegrounds such as Libya and Syria long after most public support had dwindled.

Brennan, drawing on his extensive Saudi experience, fostered a recruitment strategy for ground troops in Libyan and Syrian battlefields that was popular with the president. This strategy involved recruiting local fighters, in cooperation with monarchies, dictatorships, and other forces friendly to the United States. This seemingly adroit "solution" developed the same problems as a similar U.S. technique used three decades previously against Russian troops in Afghanistan: the most committed rebel freedom fighters were likely to be Muslims so radical as to become difficult for the United States to control in the long run. More generally, the United States needed to keep the intrigues secret. Visible help to those who might seem like Taliban or al-Qaeda counterparts would not be good public relations for U.S. voters.

More generally, the evolving Obama strategy created the bizarre situation whereby the United States was helping Muslim firebrands in some countries but trying to kill them in other nations with drones. There is an uncomplicated, but rarely reported explanation for this mystery. Libya and Syria constituted special cases of Muslim nations whose dictators had flirted with Russia through the years. Syria's President Bashar al-Assad, for example, was the only leader on the Mediterranean to provide a military port for Russian ships after the Russians closed their base in Libya. The oil-rich monarchies had their own reasons to sponsor rebellions. They are highly undemocratic, and thus fear rebellion. The demise of Libya's Gaddafi, a secular tyrant, reaffirmed the Islam *bona fides* of the Sunni Muslim rulers who funded his opposition. Similarly, the Sunni monarchies were pursuing an age-old religious rivalry in funding a rebellion against Assad. Sunnis consider Assad's Alawite faith, like Shiite beliefs of his allies in Iran, as heresy.[18]

Brennan, in sum, was well positioned to help Obama implement a Mideast strategy via a CIA expanded to wield paramilitary powers. Furthermore, neo-cons frustrated over troop drawdowns knew that they could not oppose Brennan vigorously without exposing state secrets. The Senate confirmed Brennan, and yet he faced the possibility of prosecution on torture charges if he followed precedent and travelled widely overseas.[19]

In terms of foreign policy, Obama is hardly the naïve "community organizer" described by his worst critics. His first trip to Pakistan in 1981 coincided with U.S. support for the Taliban fighters against Soviets in nearby Afghanistan. More important, his family heritage grew out of intelligence intrigues involving emerging nations, as documented in this book's early chapters. After his 2012 election victory, his choice of proven-loyal colleagues for his second term's foreign affairs team signaled a new direction. He was going to defer less to his opponents after discovering the dark disloyalty shown him by previous appointees and their non-government mentors. His choices also showed that the powerful elite are not necessarily unified on every policy issue. They control the top personnel of both parties, but sometimes differ among themselves on strategies, such as the desirability of new United States wars in Syria and Iran.

The importance of such revelations regarding the Obama second-term leadership team is not that the new information should necessarily disqualify the nominees. Their work histories paralleled those of many previous office holders. The real significance is that the traditional news media raised so few of these issues, or did so (as in the case with some of the partisan criticism of Hagel and Lew) with selective reporting. Anyone wondering why some of the issues about candidates raised early in this book have not been brought to the public's attention can see from the 2013 confirmation battles that little has changed.

To review 2013 pocketbook issues, we next examine the outlook for pensions, jobs, health care, and civil liberties.

Raising the Retirement Age to 70

The 2012 GOP economic platform rested on several ideas disproven by history, rejected by voters, and yet continued to be touted by party leaders in 2013 as core principles. Leaders advocated radical plans for lower taxes, reduced taxpayer "entitlements" to Social Security and other social safety nets, deregulation, increased defense and national security spending, free-trade, off-shoring, gutting the civil service, and privatizing formerly public services and assets.

Even the most radically right of the nation's vulture capitalists and other oligarchs can recognize their program as unpopular and otherwise unlikely for enactment without careful strategies. One such strategy for the second term has involved distracting the public from money issues with divisive, high-emotion social issues such as abortion, gays, guns, welfare, and immigration. Another strategy involved co-opting Democrats into the program, making the ostensible opponents ineffective.

Many Democrats, including President Obama, understood the clout of the powerful elite and the public's lack of relevant information. So the politicians have been willing to go along with as much of the program as they could without alerting and antagonizing voters. The purpose of the puppet-training program for recruits such as Obama, is to foster precisely that kind of manageability.

Much of the rest of this chapter examines as a case study how the Obama administration handled the "fiscal cliff" negotiations at the beginning of his second term. Readers can extrapolate the results to other issues, which are too many to explore at this level of detail.

Social Security, Medicare, and Medicaid are core New Deal and Great Society programs. For Democrats (or indeed Republicans) to undercut the programs requires changing the frame of the debate. One widely promoted fallacy is that the government should act like a small business or a family by saving enough money to balance the budget during hard times. The United States government, however, is different from a family, in part because it can expand revenues by investment in creating jobs (and thus tax revenues) and, up to a point, cover shortfalls by expanding the money supply. We know that spending works, in part because of the Depression experience. Government cutbacks, in contrast, worsened the economy circa 1937, causing a new recession. Even so, polls show that the public accepts the often-repeated, false claim that the United States government must balance its budget each year, as if it were a small.

History also disproves the "trickle down" theory that lowering taxes on the wealthy encourages them to work harder to create opportunities that seep down to help lower classes. The expert, non-partisan Congressional Research Office issued a report in late 2012 stating that no evidence exists for the claim that trickle-down economics stimulates the economy.[20] Marginal tax rates in the United States were at least 91 percent during the 1950s, an era of great strength for the nation's economy even as unions reached their greatest power.[21] The "fiscal cliff" discussion regarding the 2013 economy was whether taxes should revert from the "temporary" Bush level of a maximum of 35 percent to the Clinton-era maximum rate of 39 percent. The Clinton era clearly prompted sustained growth, as well as budget surpluses.

Nonetheless, during the 2012 campaign, Republicans urged permanent tax cuts at Bush-levels and the abolition of all inheritance taxes even though such taxes affect only a few of the wealthiest. Inheritance taxes also undermine equal opportunity, especially if budget shortfalls force cuts in pre-school programs, college scholarships, and other opportunities for ambitious young people.

Here are the stakes: The "average" American family has lost 47 percent of its assets over a 40-year period, including an astonishing collapse in 2008 at the end of eight years of Bush rule.[22] In the face of such devastating losses of savings, jobs, and benefits such as employer-paid health insurance, GOP lawmakers sought reductions in Social Security, Medicare, Medicaid, and the elimination of ObamaCare with no replacement legislation.

Democrats better safeguarded the safety net, but also proved more than willing to go along with the overall cost-cutting themes of Republicans and the powerful special interests governing both parties. Thus, Democrats postponed collection of the payroll tax that funds Social Security for two years, and then complained that Social Security might run a shortfall one day. Democrats also joined with Republicans in avoiding an increase in the $110,000 annual limit on taxable income for the program.

The common denominator in many of these decisions was to ignore history and target the least powerful for sacrifice. The U.S. Chamber of Commerce and its President Thomas Donohue, a close Karl Rove ally, is blatant about its intentions. Even the Business Roundtable, regarded as a comparable group that is more bipartisan, voiced a remarkable campaign in 2013: "U.S. CEOs push plan to raise full retirement age to 70."[23]

An influential group of business CEOs is pushing a plan to gradually increase the full retirement age to 70 for both Social Security and Medicare and to partially privatize the health insurance program for older Americans.

Fiscal Cliff, Taxes, Spending, and Safety Net

Obama won the election on a platform of no new taxes on those making under $250,000 annually, with no cuts to the safety nets of Social Security, Medicare, and Medicaid. The president faced the challenge of either living up to his promises or caving in to the inept and unpopular Republicans.

Obama held strong cards because in 2001 Congress agreed to revert tax rates to Clinton-era levels on January 1. Opinion polls indicated that the public would blame Republicans for any tax increases and any other harm to income and the economy. In addition, if budget deficits were really the country's main problem, as claimed, Obama could afford to take a temporary hit to the economy early in his term to curtail deficits and blame Republicans until they either caved in to his terms, or faced a rout leading up to 2014 that would wipe out their majority and their obstruction.

In conventional political terms, Republicans could not thwart virtually every constituency aside from the one in a thousand earning more than a million dollars in taxable income annually. The tax increase for this elite group would be quite low by historical standards. The president had special powers if he wanted to use them to educate the veterans, elderly, farm, and other traditionally Republican constituencies on how the Republican plan would hurt them especially.[24] One study indicated that half of nine million veterans live almost exclusively on Society Security.[25] Yet many in the public did not know the basic facts of the matter, in part because politicians sometimes lied and reporters were sometimes too lazy to frame the issues. Some reporters, for example, erroneously described Obama's tax proposals as targeting "millionaires." That claim is wrong as a factual matter and it obscures the fact that an increase was planned for those annually *earning* a million dollars, a much smaller group than those possessing such sums in property or otherwise.

A Second-Term Sell Out?

Late on New Year's Eve, Obama reached what appeared to be an unwise "fiscal cliff" deal with Senate Republicans.[26] The Senate approved the New Year's Eve deal 89-8. The House voted for approval 257-167, with most of the approvals by Democrats.[27] The manufactured crisis and late-night voting showed an arrogant and highly undemocratic decision-making process tailor-made for lobbyists and their clients. No hearings were held on the proposals.

The deal included sweetheart provisions for insiders.[28] For the left, billions of dollars were spent to extend unemployment benefits for two million long-term unemployed for another year. The government also renounced an estimated $205 billion in expected tax revenue for special interests that included Goldman Sachs, NASCAR investors, rum manufacturers, and the Disney company.[29] One of the special deals sacrificed $500 million in revenue to help just one company, Amgen. Almost no one knew at the time of passage about the arrangement helping a company fined $762 million in a criminal case two weeks previously. Depriving the government of necessary tax revenues is part of the ongoing assault by the wealthy cabal on the rest of the public. It is all perfectly legal because the cabal controls the lawmaking process, regulators, and courts.[30] Overall, the foregone federal revenue represented a third of the expected $600 billion in new tax revenue. These were dead-of-night, sweetheart deals. Republican policy gurus have long vowed to "starve the beast" of the federal government by denying it revenue, and thereby return the country to an idealized past before New Deal regulations and social safety net programs.

"Just a few years ago," the *New York Times* reported, "the tax deal pushed through Congress on Tuesday [January 1] would have been a Republican fiscal fantasy, a sweeping bill that locks in virtually all of the Bush-era tax cuts, exempts almost all estates from taxation, and enshrines the former president's credo that dividends and capital gains should be taxed equally and gently."[31] More specifically, Obama extended Bush tax-cuts to individuals making less than $400,000 per year. As a result, the president renounced an estimated $4 trillion in revenue over the next decade. The deal postponed threatened deficit cuts of one billion dollars for two months. This put pressure on Democrats when Republican-led deficit hawks targeted Social Security, Medicare, and other domestic programs under the threat of a new manufactured crisis in late February: the expiration of the federal debt limit coinciding with a scheduled $500 billion in defense cuts on March 1.

My view was that Obama had wasted his overwhelming bargaining advantage and thereby sold out both his backers and the larger public. Obama understood why the Republican plan was bad for most of the GOP base, even if they did not. Other commentators also wrote that Obama's deal previewed a more momentous cave-in later in the year.[32] "Even Mitt Romney could never have accomplished for the Republicans what Obama has just done for them," commented Professor Jeffrey Sachs of Columbia University. Paul Krugman wrote a similar article on the matter, found here.[33]

Unexpectedly, Obama announced after the deal that he would not negotiate with the House over raising the debt ceiling. He said paying for debts already approved was not budget reduction. House Republican leaders agreed to a two-month extension even as they vowed that there would be no new taxes and that massive "entitlement" cuts would be made in negotiations in the spring.

As Inauguration approached, the public seemed to understand the grave threats, as indicated by opinion polls. "Dark mood casts a poll on big day," was the featured front-page story in one of Washington's major inside politics tabloids for its Inauguration Day edition in 2013. "A new poll for *The Hill*," it reported, "finds that 60 percent of voters are unsure or pessimistic about their immediate future."[34]

On January 21, President Obama delivered an eloquent, hard-hitting address to launch his second term. In a day filled with pageantry, Obama provided one of his presidency's most liberal speeches. He had reason to be proud, especially since the anniversary fell on the Martin Luther King holiday. Obama's reelection marked just the third time in American history that a Democrat had won two terms with a majority vote. He won with margins far higher than many other recent presidents, including his two predecessors, Bush and Clinton. Obama's achievement was all the more remarkable after the vicious attacks on his legitimacy, GOP obstruction in Congress, and election dirty tricks.

The president won a mandate, not just a reason to be proud.[35] His second-term to-do list surprised opponents and supporters alike who had seen him repeatedly compromise on his first-term campaign promises. Obama's stronger, more confident stance had its roots in the implacable GOP opposition to him throughout his first term and continuing into the transition. Obama could not complain about Republican campaign maneuvers during the campaign without sounding like a whiner. But Republican excesses steeled him to map out an ambitious agenda.

The possibility remained, however, that Obama's speech was just for show, and would be shelved as quickly as the Democrats' recent vow to undertake meaningful reform of the filibuster tactic.[36] As the administration moved forward in 2013, the likelihood grew loomed that the president's rhetoric would lull supporters before he negotiated away their future with last-minute concessions on safety net programs. That pattern would parallel his secret, first-term deal with pharmaceutical manufacturers in 2009 to scuttle a public option in the health care legislation.[37]

In early 2013, the editors of *Black Agenda Report* warned:

> Our black political class, from the president down to sheriffs, evoke the struggles and victories of the fifties and sixties, but have nothing to show for the seventies, eighties, nineties or the new century except their own careers. They are utterly unprepared to fight or even assist in the fight for economic justice, peace, and rolling back the prison state.[38]

"We are in the most anemic recovery in modern history," wrote former Labor Secretary Robert Reich in a similar critique, "yet our political leaders in Washington aren't doing squat about it. In fact, apart from the Fed — which continues to hold interest rates down in the quixotic hope that banks will begin lending again to average people — the government is heading in exactly the wrong direction: raising taxes on the middle class and cutting spending."[39] The conservative economist Paul Craig Roberts concurred:

> Officially, since June 2009 the US economy has been undergoing an economic recovery from the December 2007 recession. But where is this recovery? I cannot find it, and neither can millions of unemployed Americans....
>
> Despite recovery's absence and the lack of job opportunities for Americans, Republicans in Congress are sponsoring bills to enlarge the number of foreigners that corporations can bring in on work visas. The large corporations claim that they cannot find enough skilled Americans. This is one of the most transparent of the constant stream of lies that we are told. Foreign hires are not additions to the work force, but replacements. The corporations force their American employees to train the foreigners, and then the American employees are discharged. Obviously, if skilled employees were in short supply, they would not be laid off. Moreover, if the skills were in short supply, salaries would be bid up, not down, and the 36% of those who graduated in 2011 with doctorate degrees in engineering would not have been left unemployed.[40]

After the sequester took effect on March 1, conventional wisdom became that the president had offered up concessions for scant apparent gain. The president had traded away most of his advantage in return for only half of the revenue he had been seeking, wrote the insider tabloid *Roll Call*.[41] Thus, the president had no easy way to force more. So, he told Senate Democrats to be prepared to cut Social Security and Medicare as part of a budget deal.[42]

Paul Ryan, the House Budget Committee chairman, then proposed a budget calling for the elimination of ObamaCare and the slashing of other domestic programs.[43] It was as if the November elections had never occurred. Yet Ryan's proposal was a logical response to Washington's hidden, permanent government of financial backers, and not to voters. These financial titans and their mercenaries like Ryan may experience a temporary setback on election day from time to time when proven tools such as gerrymandering, disinformation, and voter suppression fall short. Washington's mercenaries (in both parties) can be confident, however, they retain funding for warfare to resume promptly after elections.

Meanwhile, many in the majority supporting Obama kept waiting for him to fight back more effectively on behalf of his majority coalition. Missing from such analysis is any understanding that the president, the "good cop" to Ryan's "bad cop," is playing a predetermined role to please his backers by splitting the difference with the GOP's Ryan on an austerity budget.

Game over. Checkmated. Or, if you prefer, hoodwinked.

Keeping It Classy

Our government-employed marionettes and their largely unseen manipulators have set the stage for an austerity regime for the United States, just as Panama's Omar Torrijos predicted. The results may prove deadly and otherwise harsh. Tens of millions are utterly dependent on Social Security and Medicare, for example. Decision makers provide voters with platitudes and promises at election time and promptly reverse themselves, as Obama did. Meanwhile, savings and home values are vanishing along with good jobs. The environment is hurting so badly in so many places that safety and sustainability are treated like an impossible dream in Washington.

The manipulators and profiteers have targeted a number of historically taxpayer-funded areas for cutbacks or privatizations. Among them are pensions, schools, water supplies, utilities (including the New Deal's Tennessee Valley Authority), and highways. The effort to destroy the promise of Medicare for the aged is especially dire because it affects so many who are vulnerable. In addition, they/we have paid years of taxes to achieve security through a system far more economical in terms of low administrative overhead than a system of private insurance.

Soon after Obama's retreat on his 2012 promises, the *Washington Post* urged him to keep funds available for war contractors and other favored groups by reducing "entitlements" for the public. Thus, the paper called for Medicare recipients to pay for 35 percent of the cost of their premiums "for physician and other outpatient services."[44] Where were the elderly supposed to find that money? Why they should be victimized by the ruinous deficits created by the Bush administration and continued under Obama? These questions are left unanswered by the Washington political elite and their backers.

Congress, Senate, and House members did little once elected in 2012 except postpone meaningful actions and blame each other for delays in early 2013. Republicans adopted the role of budget cutters. Democrats positioned themselves as seeking more taxes along with budget cuts. No one in leadership strongly supported the proven solutions from the Depression.[45] President Roosevelt and Congress spent enough money to create meaningful jobs on worthwhile projects, thereby ultimately providing the dignity of work along with increased consumer spending and more income tax payers. One of the few areas of bipartisan action appeared to be agreement on immigration "reform" that would continue to flood the job market with low-wage immigrants in the name of humanitarian principles notably absent from much of the rest of public policy. A sign of corporate pressure helping prompt the policy was a Senate vote to dramatically increase the number of foreign "HB-1" visas of high-tech employees when 36 percent of those receiving U.S. engineering doctorates in 2011 were reported as unemployed.[46]

These days, the public sees a "good cop/bad cop routine." Fueled with hatred of Obama as a radical leftist, Republicans played the role of insults, threats, and hyper-aggressive policies to enforce austerity with no new revenues. The non-partisan Congressional Budget Office predicted that the "sequester" of automatic budget cuts beginning March 1 would cost 750,000 American jobs, most of which would be lost as a direct effect of the cuts. Obama, by contrast to Republicans, sought with limited success to maintain his image as a voice of reason during early 2013. He maintained traction with core supporters and independents as a sympathetic protector for the public.

Predictably, Obama and his team of Wall Street/Chicago School Democrats are preparing for a time of fear and growing panic over a worsening economy. The president could then argue that the public did not deserve all of its entitlements and so must sacrifice to prevent the greater harms threatened by Republicans. In practice, that means sacrifices like the $130 billion reduction in Social Security increases over the next decade that the Obama team has already suggested as one of its planned deals with Republicans.[47] The point of that process is to take away earned benefits expected by old people who have paid their taxes, and see that the money remains available, either in unpaid taxes or new government spending, for the goals of those with political savvy and clout. The elderly are far from the only victims. Paul Roberts, the conservative economist, underscored the plight of young job seekers and others whom the powerful elite needlessly deprives of opportunities.[48] Even though different times call for different heroes, a public appetite for patriotism remains constant in our culture. Showman and political leader Phineas T. Barnum, among others, launched his career on the public's hero-worship and hunger for novelty. Barnum, born in 1810, at first edited an abolitionist newspaper in Connecticut. He turned to show business at the age of 25 when he purchased a black slave, Joice Heth, and exhibited her as the 161-year-old nurse of George Washington.[49] By understanding the public's desire for entertainment, Barnum built a fabulous career in show business, politics, and philanthropy.

My ambulations often bring me past the scene of one of his most notorious displays. Two blocks from my office, Barnum charged 25 cents per person for a glimpse at a supposed camel-horse-elephant captured during a California expedition by the greatest war hero of the era, Colonel John C. Fremont. In his best-selling 1855 memoir, Barnum boasted of cheating the public at the exhibit on Pennsylvania Avenue. By coincidence, or simply because of the nature of the nation's capital, the Barnum site adjoins the current headquarters of FreedomWorks, which one decade ago secretly hatched the plan to create a tea party movement that would look spontaneous to the most gullible in the public.[50]

In early 2013, the Academy Awards ceremonies focused heavily on two CIA-friendly blockbusters, *Argo* and *Zero Dark Thirty*, each created with administration help. *Lincoln*, a drama about Obama's role model, was another major movie up for awards. At the dramatic climax of the three-hour ceremony, First Lady Michelle Obama appeared by video as a surprise presenter to announce the best picture of the year. She was resplendent in a strapless sequined gown, and had an impressive backdrop at the White House of a military honor guard. With suitable fanfare, she announced *Argo* as the winner. Her poised performance enthralled many observers. The gala combination of newsmakers from Hollywood and the Potomac generated, as usual, wide news coverage.

Wayne Madsen., the former Navy intelligence officer, recapped the hidden CIA history of President Obama and his family members. A national celebration of *Argo* was fully congruent with Obama-Dunham tradition and the launch of the president's own career with a CIA front company three decades earlier. Furthermore, we can make an educated guess that White House staffer John Brennan is likely to be functioning in a dual role as the president's staffer and handler.[51]

Little did I imagine when I attended Barack Obama's first Washington presidential campaign fund raiser in March 2007 that I would write a book such as this. Whatever brought me there now requires me to unmask him and raise dark questions about the implications for the public.[52]

For any still skeptical and perhaps without time for the endnotes, I ask you to reflect a moment on the president's past and our future. Barack Obama lived in Indonesia as a boy during one of the worst genocides of the century. He then attended a prep school in Hawaii so beautiful and luxurious that some have described it as being like "paradise."

Ignore for a moment all the disinformation and confusion about records. How often has the president discussed any reflections on the political situation in Indonesia aside from relatively brief descriptions in his memoir? The Ford Foundation, one of his mother's employers, was among the entities that opened doors for the family. The opportunities ranged from the travel stipend, whereby as a college student he stayed at the home of a future president of Pakistan, as well as untold other possibilities still obscured by silence, secrets, and lost records. In a book, the distinguished *New York Times* financial columnist and author Gretchen Morgenson ranked Tim Geithner at the top of her list of the

"Feckless Regulators" who enabled the 2008 market crash during the Bush years, thereby wiping out the savings and jobs of millions.[53]

Living in genocide-plagued Indonesia, Barack Obama learned early on that life is a struggle. But he also learned that an escape route was available for him, his family, and their allies if they played their roles. Fine for him. What is in store for the public?

As the year 2013 began, all but the most ideological Republicans could privately gloat in their success of making "permanent" most of the Bush tax cuts they had rammed through the Senate on a 51-50 vote more than a decade earlier during flush times of budget surplus, with no need then for a filibuster-proof, 60-vote margin.

Hardship, Despair, Anger, Police Power

Politico, one of Washington's insider newspapers, published a profile in early 2013 of Tom Cotton, a tea party-backed Republican recently elected to represent southern Arkansas in Congress. The profile's purpose was to show why House members have scant interest in compromising with Obama on any issue. It described Cotton as "a veteran of two wars with a pair of Harvard degrees." The Club for Growth, an anti-tax group funded by the wealthy, enabled his election in a low-income district with $300,000. In gratitude, Cotton vowed to vote against raising the debt limit unless a raise coincided with massive cuts to non-defense spending hurting his own constituents.[54] The gist was that such a congressman in a low-income area best ensures his success by implementing the goals of his funders, not voters or even Republican party leaders. With the support of billionaires, Cotton can reliably expect to guide his district's future for many years as he works his way up the congressional ladder to become nationally influential in the manner of Paul Ryan and other austerity advocates.

Because of Cotton's fine education, he probably knows deep down that debt default is not a practical or moral way to reduce spending. In practical terms, default would force the United States to spend vast new sums in higher interest costs. Regarding the morality of a default, Congress has already authorized the money, which has promptly been spent for the most part. Default is akin to running up a credit card spending spree and then declaring bankruptcy. That would be considered either civil or criminal fraud by a company or an individual.[55] That is because the purpose and effect would be to con trusting dupes, as did Ohio's Kirtland Safety Savings Society in the 1830s and the Wall Street banksters in the run-up to the 2008 financial crisis.

Even the most sincere deficit hawks, however, should fear the ugly combination of austerity, job loss, reaction, and police state crackdowns that have been growing in the United States, especially after the

September 11 attack in 2001. The aged can be hurt badly, but tend not to fight back except by voting. A second vulnerable group is the African-American community, already devastated by an unemployment rate double the national average.[56] Out-of-work combat veterans facing joblessness are also deeply at risk. So far, victims tend to be too time-pressured and otherwise frustrated to seek out information about the true causes of their pain.[57]

In recent times, the social safety net has allowed many American to absorb, albeit with difficulty, their loss of savings, jobs, health insurance, and homes during the recession beginning in 2007. The next time may be far more horrendous. Not only is the safety net disappearing, but so is a spirit of a shared future. Legislators in drought-stricken Kansas opposed disaster aid for Hurricane Sandy victims in the Northeast in early 2013.

Expect such catastrophes and policy logjams to worsen and public despair to turn to anger and violence in some quarters. Americans no longer know how to grow food, as many of our predecessors did during the Depression. A nation of gun-owners will not include many people who are willing to sit starving by a roadside, as is commonly the case in the Third World.

Authorities are likely to respond with crackdowns. At that point, legal rights will seem more of a luxury than a pre-condition for a vibrant society.[58] To imagine how much farther such powers have grown, kindly look at the preliminary signs. I summarized them in my year-end 2012 round-up about police state enforcement across the United States.[59] Sadly, such a collection of harsh, un-American tactics did not take me long to compile. Neither did it take long to augment with accounts of the near unprecedented police lockdown of a major city in April 2013 to find the Boston Marathon bombing suspect. That manhunt by paramilitary teams occurred amid pleas by Senators to try the suspect in secret before a military tribunal, which would have created yet-another exception to Constitutional protections.

Especially powerful in my compilation of videos was a speech by former NSA executive Thomas Drake describing how every American communication is now subject to warrantless interception, storage, and use for prosecution — all unnecessary actions in gross violation, he states, of our Constitutional heritage. Drake expanded upon those dire themes with me during a five-hour discussion following his eloquent address in March 2013 at the National Press Club. Drake, a patriot in the *Mr. Smith Goes to Washington* mold, feared that our country is in a "pre-fascist" stage with a Constitution, courts and Congress gutted, and ripe for a locally produced dictator to assume power in the Oval Office.[60]

Watch also the video showing Texas police ordering two apparently middle-class women out of their car near Dallas and subjecting them to warrantless vaginal and anal searches at night on the roadside. Why? Police suspected that the car's occupants threw one or two cigarette-butts out of their car window while driving at night. That is far from the worst video. Look at a jail video of a Mississippi man beaten to death by guards for no apparent reason after being booked on misdemeanor charges. Guards cuffed his hands behind his back and attached his wrists to his ankles, totally incapacitating the prisoner. Then they beat and face-smashed him long enough to kill.

What else occurs among the nation's two million prisoners not on camera? Who oversees the process when prisons are awarded to private contractors, as is the current trend? The growth of for-profit privately operated prisons opens the door to vast potential abuse difficult for the public to monitor. This law enforcement process, like each of these policies, relies on elected officials to implement faithfully the goals of their puppet masters. Finally, I want to share the video of former Obama White House Counsel Gregory Craig and other experts describing how the nation's system of presidential clemency no longer functions in practice in the federal system and in most states despite constitutional enshrinement and nearly two decades of use.[61] The end of those protections effectively doomed Don Siegelman of Alabama and many others unfairly prosecuted. As Dr. Cyril Wecht wrote in his Foreword to this book, a suspect once accused faces vast hardship to avoid conviction. Once imprisoned, the prisoner has, in essence, no hope from a political system that is broken for the ordinary person.

The Democrats' high-handed actions in turning their backs on their 2012 election mandate provides an apt ending point for this book. Even Republicans should be concerned that President Obama and his White House have undermined the electoral process by his deceptive biography and his pretense of catering to voters instead of the ruling class that he and many of his top political cronies obviously aspire to join. Ordinary voters will never affect governance so long as they continue to believe that Obama's ascent occurred because he was a "constitutional scholar," eloquent speaker, and "community organizer."

Voters can do little via the ballot. Courts trashed campaign finance law, federal agencies have virtually ended meaningful oversight, and Republicans have gerrymandered House seats. Furthermore, it is far from clear that President Obama would provide his presidential campaign's database to Democratic candidates in 2014.[62] The result is that Democrats have little ability to gain more seats in the 2014 elections because of recently gerrymandered districts.

My original intention in drafting this book was to include revelations and analysis about why the courts, our ultimate safeguard for political and legal rights, fail to do so. In fact, I compiled so much evidence of horrid injustices that they would have distracted from the more timely revelations about our presidential candidates. *Courtroom Puppetry* will, in a separate book, present revelations about the justice system. In the meantime, previous books illustrate the larger themes. Among the best are those by Harvey Silverglate, Glenn Greenwald, Bruce Fein, Paul Craig Roberts and his co-author Lawrence Stratton.[63]

Most of those authors come from politically conservative and scholarly backgrounds. Their books are, in effect, cries from the heart about why our legal system fosters injustice. They illustrate the root causes of the problems that the Justice Integrity Project reports on a daily basis in our investigative reports and round-ups of appalling situations investigated by other authors.[64] The law can be a tool of oppression as well as liberation, a reality that must be recognized with specifics extending to the top before real reform can occur.

Experienced legal experts often voice comforting bromides upon encountering clear-cut injustice. They provide hope that a better legal argument on appeal or another conventional tactic can correct the wrong. Similarly, those committed to campaign politics — either as professionals or partisans — point us to the next election for reform.

Yet the game is fixed in increasingly obvious ways. Elections feature presidential candidates with deceptive bios. Scandals erupt in campaign financing, voter registration, and vote counting. Those obstacles to the democratic practice corrupt honest governance. They thwart the kind of civic commitment prompting you to read this far and to seek a better way.

Presidents, Pundits, and the Boston Bombing

In traditional plays, actors often assemble for a last big scene. That pattern occurred on the national political stage in the late spring of 2013. The Bush dynasty brought forth Jeb, who promptly became the favorite for the 2016 GOP nomination. As a prelude, Poppy Bush republished his 1999 best-seller *All My Best*, a sanitized collection of his correspondence illustrating his attractive qualities. Also, the opening of the George W. Bush Presidential Center underscored how the younger former president's popularity ratings had risen to nearly equal Obama's.

Hillary Clinton emerged as the early Democratic favorite for 2016 with Bill quietly lining up support in strict confidence. Joe Biden waited in the wings in case something happens that enables his stardom. Mitt Romney, Dick Cheney, and even Herman Cain found themselves once again in demand as keynote speakers before civic and business groups. Romney revealed to the *Wall Street Journal* that he would actively campaign for Republicans leading up to the 2014 elections. The same week in late May, *Time* magazine obtained from Michael Leavitt's 500-member transition team the specifics of its secret plan after the election to run the United States as a business. As House Budget Committee chairman, Paul Ryan reigned as his party's top economic guru. KKR's appointment of David Petraeus as chairman of a new hedge fund ensured that he would become wealthy and also stay prominent as a professor at the City University of New York and the University of Southern California.

President Obama, still under fire in June for Benghazi plus a series of perceived civil rights violations involving the Justice Department and IRS, responded in part by picking the Bush Justice Department's second-in-command for a 10-year term as the next FBI director. For one of the most important appointments of Obama's two-terms, the supposed "radical" president yet again turned to an establishment choice, former Bush Deputy Attorney General James Comer, a lifelong Republican and career prosecutor. Comer had left the Justice Department post in 2005 to become enriched as a senior executive of Lockheed Martin and then at the $75 billion hedge fund Bridgewater Associates. Those posts and others fostered Comer's close ties with the military-security, banking, and academic communities. This revolving-door tradition for government servants has included, as we have seen, Averell Harriman, Allen and John Foster Dulles, and vast numbers of other government servants for at least the past century.[65]

More generally, partisan leaders on all sides continued to enrage or otherwise energize their audiences with time-tested emotional or religious appeals and half-truths. Many in the public find inaccuracies difficult to detect, especially when the topics involve secret, life-and-death national security issues. Rick Wiles is a conservative Christian broadcaster who illustrated this pattern with such 2013 programs as his "Muslim Marxist in the White House posing as the president." Wiles argued during one show, "Barack Obama has now criminalized Christianity in the U.S. military." Like a journalist, Wiles tied his report to recent events. But he provided only the sketchiest of facts and sources. The omissions doubtless left listeners fearful, suspicious, angry, and in a poor position to make informed decisions. Such messaging carries powerful cumulative impact, especially in communities where the themes are replicated without rebuttal. The misinformation hurts all national discourse because the mainstream media primarily relies on politicians and other experts who advocate private agendas, not the public interest. Thus, the so-called "scandals" erupting during 2013 involving Benghazi and the IRS turned out to be far more complicated on examination than seemed apparent in the first news reports. Reporters and commentators parroted for the most part partisan officials and other experts unwilling or unable to cut to the real issues.[66]

By this point, *Puppetry* readers can be confident that the nation's power structure would never install a "Muslim Marxist" in the White House. Instead, behind-the-scenes manipulators plunder at will when the public focuses its attention on phony issues. Stock market indices more than doubled since Obama took office, exceeding a Dow Jones average of 15,000 by the late spring of 2013. True, the stock market is only a rough measure of wealth, even for the rich. Neither does the market reflect trillions of dollars in lost savings, jobs, home values, student debt, and retirement security because of the 2103 sequester/austerity measures — nor cancer clinics turning away thousands of patients across the nation for sudden lack of funding.[67] Still, the obvious growth of stock prices raises a question regarding the motives and judgment of those who describe Obama as ruining the country because he is a socialist, supposedly with loyalty to another country.

Obama, like virtually all of our other recent presidents with the arguable exception of Bill Clinton, has been a part of the federal military and security apparatus beginning in his twenties. The specifics are widely known regarding most presidents, especially those in the World War II generation extending from Dwight Eisenhower to George H. W. Bush. The younger George Bush was part of this pattern of military service and culture also as an Air National Guard member, and son of a CIA director.

Some recent presidents have also had less visible relationships the national security apparatus. Strong evidence exists, as we have seen, that Clinton served at least briefly as a CIA informant in 1969. More scattered evidence not yet fully explored suggests that Mitt Romney helped build Bain Capital with disreputable sources linked to international spying and military intrigue.[68] Reagan's service to the FBI as a longtime confidential informant on sensitive issues before he became president parallels the Obama history. Reagan's secret role is now well documented. But few knew about it until late 2012.[69]

Obama's government service thus fits a norm for presidents, although presidents and their handlers increasingly keep such affiliations secret from the public instead of boasting about the connections. As for journalists, reporting on these matters does not make money or win friends for the news organization. Most reporters and editors like to produce scoops. But relatively few readers will notice if such news does not appear. Sports, other entertainment, celebrities, and partisan political commentary fill up newspapers and broadcasts without antagonizing sources, regulators, and powerful patrons.[70]

As a case study, the *Washington Post* illustrates why its Watergate investigation and many other reportorial triumphs do not necessarily typify its coverage on the kinds of issues reported here.

A history of the paper quotes 1950s publisher Philip Graham, grandfather of the current publisher, as describing the *Times* of London as his model for a great newspaper. The reason? The *Times* aimed its coverage at decision-makers and worked closely with the British Foreign

Office to shape elite public opinion.[71] This was, of course, the same *Times* that Georgetown's Carroll Quigley had described in 1949 as engaging in a "really terrifying" secret cabal dominating British public life for nearly five decades until 1945. The plan, Quigley wrote, was for the major players — the *Times*, the Foreign Office, other officials, Oxford professors, and prestigious societies such as Chatham House and former grant winners in key posts around the Commonwealth and allied nations — to hide their relationships. Those relationships included common funding, initially from the fabulously wealthy Cecil Rhodes, and other mutual professional and intellectual support to sustain for more than four decades generally similar ideas, supposedly derived from independent professional positions and experiences.[72]

In the style of his role models, Graham was a brilliant wheeler-dealer who helped promote Eisenhower to the presidency. Souring on the Republican, Graham drafted his friend Lyndon Johnson's presidential campaign announcement in 1960, and then brokered with John F. Kennedy, another close friend, agreement for the winning Kennedy-Johnson ticket.[73] In those days, Graham and his wife, Katharine, dined once a week with CIA Covert Operations Chief Frank Wisner and his wife, Polly. Wisner's team worked closely with the media to influence coverage as part of what Wisner called a "Mighty Wurlitzer" able to arouse public opinion favorable to the CIA.[74] Yet no one is master of the universe forever. In 1965, Wisner shotgunned himself in a suicide similar to Graham's two years previously. Graham's widow, son, and granddaughter continued to run the *Post and* remain active in such elite bodies as the Bilderbergs.

In late 1963, former President Harry Truman protested what he regarded as a dangerous growth in the CIA's power just 16 years after he and Congress created it. A month after President Kennedy's assassination in 1963, Truman published a column in the first edition of *Post* urging, "Limit CIA Role to Intelligence," The newspaper pulled the column from its later editions and other media ignored the former president's words.[75] Undeterred, Truman wrote the following year to the editor of *Look* Magazine to rebuke it for what he regarded as an erroneous (and favorable) article about the agency's clandestine role. "The CIA was set up by me for the sole purpose of getting all the available information to the president," Truman wrote. "It was not intended to operate as an international agency engaged in strange activities."[76]

Any readers still unconvinced that the mainstream media might ignore youthful CIA and FBI connections of recent presidents should study carefully the 2013 coverage of the fatal Boston Marathon bombings. Obvious coverage gaps occurred even on such an important story. News outlets relied heavily on anonymous law enforcement sources who leaked background to friendly reporters, who then wove together seemingly thorough chronologies. The *Washington Post*, for example, published one story with more than two full pages of runover material about the two suspects, the brothers Tamerlan and Dzhokhar Tsarnaev.[77] The front-page story credited 12 *Post* reporters with the research. From this and similar reporting in the *Post* and elsewhere, the public obtained what seemed to be a comprehensive portrait of brothers who committed the atrocity with no warning because of their previously unknown radical Muslim, anti-American beliefs.

Yet Russ Baker, founder of the WhoWhatWhy investigative site, later summarized lingering questions, many of which had been reported on the web or overseas. "We've been disappointed," Baker wrote, "that the [U.S.] media have failed to demonstrate healthy skepticism while passing along, unchallenged, the (self-serving) assertions of 'the authorities.'"[78]

The mainstream media, for example, proved highly reluctant to report anything about the 1995 marriage of the brothers' uncle, Ruslan Tsarni, to Samantha Fuller, the daughter of longtime CIA executive Graham Fuller. As noted in Chapter 4, Fuller is a Harvard-educated Russian and Asian expert who worked closely in the 1980s with the CIA's director to oppose Communist governments and advance opportunities for dissident, pro-West civic groups and supportive business interests. Fuller retired from the agency in 1988 after serving as deputy director of its National Security Council and becoming implicated in the Iran-contra scandal. Fuller has remained prominent as a pundit, author, and security consultant for such employers as the Rand Corporation. His daughter met Tsarni, then using the name Tsarnaev, when they worked for USAID in the Caucasus region. In 1996, Tsarni incorporated the Congress of Chechen International Organizations, a group opposed to Russian control over Chechnya. With the couple living in Fuller's Maryland home, Fuller lent his home address to the Chechen group for a year to cite as its headquarters. Samantha and Ruslan divorced in 1999. The Chechen group existed for 17 years until 2012 under a Washington address.

Fuller and Tsarni live in the Washington suburbs and are prominent in business and the media. Tsarni has held an impressive array of executive posts at United States-based energy companies with operations near the Russian border. Yet virtually none of those details was reported except on web-based, independent media. Wayne Madsen wrote a pioneering early report and then obtained extensive documentation from CIA files of Fuller's high-profile spy work at the agency in fostering Asian opposition to Soviet rule.[79]I reviewed those documents, whose details had been sanitized via the CIA declassification process. Despite the sparse language, I sensed that Fuller and Bill Casey were not merely paper-shuffling bureaucrats. Let's just say I suspect they each thoroughly enjoyed watching James Bond's successes portrayed in *From Russia With Love*.

To provide his side of the Tsarni story in his only known interview, Fuller picked an establishment journalist working for a start-up web publication. Fuller described as "absurd" any suggestion of a CIA tie to Ruslan Tsarni, even though Fuller's record of fostering dissidents in that region is well-documented.[80] The print and broadcast media ignored the entire matter even after Fuller confirmed the family ties. I mention this not to suggest any plot in what remained a thoroughly mysterious situation. Instead, it illustrates the self-censorship prevalent in the media even on basic information that might embarrass law enforcement authorities regarding a major crime.

Another oddity mostly ignored by the mainstream media was a report by *Izvestia* that the Washington-based Jamestown Foundation helped sponsor a 2012 training course attended by Tamerlan Tsarnaev.[81] The Fund for the Caucasus reportedly ran the workshops in cooperation with Jamestown in Dagestan, a region bordering Chechnya. Then-CIA Director Casey, the former Wall Street tycoon, helped found the Jamestown Foundation in 1984 to promote freedom in such regions Soviet Union.[82] The Jamestown Foundation's board currently includes former CIA and NSA Director Hayden, and it previously included Brzezinski.

The Jamestown Foundation is one of many groups based in Washington that describe themselves as "non-government organizations" (NGOs) promoting democracy, press freedom, free trade, and human rights around the world. Many are widely suspected of receiving CIA or other federal government funding, either directly or via grants to allied, innocuous sounding groups that then pass along money in ways almost impossible to trace. The NGOs deny any improper government influence, and often deny that they receive government funding at all. Russia and India expelled several in 2013 from their nations as part of the ongoing political jousting.

The Marathon bombing coverage also helps illustrate little-known the challenges for web-based reporting. NGOs, think tanks, similar non-profits and web-based journalists have undertaken much of the nation's thought leadership on public policy issues. Some are well-funded, and most are proficient in web-based outreach at modest cost.

Yet many also have the same kinds of internal political conflicts as conventional newspapers and broadcasters, including agendas that are more activist and intrigue-filled than apparent on their mission statements. Those groups with reader comment sections are especially vulnerable to hackers or paid trolls who might disrupt discussions in the manner that H.B. Gary was planning in the "Holly Weber" plot examined here in Chapter 13.

In addition to paid executives or even saboteurs of web discussions, many ideologues effectively exert influence in other surreptitious ways. Some popular sites on the left maintain a blackball list, which includes Madsen. All bloggers or readers are forbidden to mention, even in a reader comment, the names or reporting of anyone on such blackball lists. The punishment for violations is a permanent ban from such sites, helping enforce a common approach to issues in what are ostensibly open discussions. Those running private organizations have the right, of course, to set rules. But the rest of us should not imagine web discourse as more open than it is.

A parallel procedure leading to similar results can erupt on short notice when minders denounce fellow bloggers for mentioning facts that could be used in a "conspiracy theory." This happened on one of the few widely read, left-oriented sites where a reader dared post basic biographical information about Tsarni and Fuller at the height of interest in the Marathon bombing investigation.[83] The trolls complained that any mention of Fuller carried an implied assumption that government-linked authorities were somehow involved in planning attacks.

Yet many other possibilities exist, and tight information control makes sense only to those with agendas beyond solving the crime and informing the public. That was one theme of Michael Springmann, an author, attorney, and former State Department Foreign Service officer. He argued in the Foreign Policy Journal, a web publication, that the Fuller interest in the region is part of a more benign but still newsworthy pattern of how United States security personnel try to stay close to potential dissidents. Cold War skirmishes begun decades ago, he wrote, leading to many "foreign policy blunders." The process continues. "It would be good to see the real story unfold," Springmann continued, "especially the close links between the CIA, the Tsarnaevs, and the strife-torn regions of the Soviet Union."[84]

I note the Marathon bombings for the limited purpose of illustrating that unknowns persisted even for such a newsworthy atrocity. My purpose is not to not to suggest a plot or answers to any mysteries. My goal instead is the obvious but little mentioned point that few in authority and only a few in the media seemed interested in questions unanswered by their prominent sources.

Further, I do not mean to impugn the media's judgment or professionalism *en masse*. The vast majority would like to do a good job, and do not have the luxury of time and job security to ponder such issues. I have many friends in relevant jobs, and know that few suspect even a small part of this.

This is a situation whereby the public cannot rely on the average journalist or frightened government source, but only on those at the front lines. Recall the comments of Tom Drake, for example. He is the patriot and former NSA executive who overcame the threat of spending the rest of his life in prison on spy charges for emailing a reporter about an unclassified matter. Less than a month after the bombing, the revelations of massive Obama administration surveillance of Associated Press reporters and their news sources further illustrated why so many mainstream journalists, their sources, and readers no longer dare deal with sensitive matters.

More generally, the *New York Times* counsel who litigated the Pentagon Papers case published a book arguing that only President Nixon in recent history has exceeded President Obama in attacks on the public's right to know. James Goodale said Obama, elected in part as constitutional law expert, might soon exceed Nixon in abuse of the free press. Senate Minority Leader Mitch McConnell of Kentucky, however, defended the Obama Justice Department's leak investigation of the Associated Press. The nation's most senior Republican elected official thereby illustrated how leaders of both parties, whatever their occasional populist rhetoric, disdain the public right to know.[85] When it comes to information control, oligarchs and puppets from both parties share the same inclination to control information and build prosecution cases.

Yet as a sign of hope regarding the hunger I sometimes encounter for information and freedom, I point to a powerful column in 2013 by *American Conservative* Publisher Ron Unz. He condemned the Iraq War as "the greatest strategic disaster in America's history." Without the partisan slurs that typify political magazines, Unz wrote: "Prominent journalists across the liberal and conservative spectrum eagerly published the most ridiculous lies and distortions passed on to them by anonymous sources, and stampeded Congress down the path to war." He begged the public to stop enabling war perpetrators in ongoing efforts to ignite new tragedies, and to scrutinize the major media more closely.[86]

Bottom Line

In the political world, President Obama, his team, and their opponents provide proof that they have beguiled us with sham biographies and rhetoric. With their fiscal cliff votes and proposed austerity budget in the spring of 2013, they have done more than I ever could to prove the thesis of this book: leaders of huge corporations and foundations with unaccountable power control leaders of both parties.

Following President Obama's re-election, he obtained the opportunity to focus his energies on productive policies rather than hiding his past and dealing with phony claims that he was a Marxist or born in Kenya. The real Romney, on the other hand, would have been tougher to influence if he had won. Romney is, at core, an elitist who has been trained to believe that he is destined to rule over a warlike American empire governed with a church-state unity. Like the founders of his church, Romney envisioned himself as a righteous man destined for a much higher calling than responding to constituents. His techniques for wealth-building raise further questions about his fitness for the public control he and his backers so eagerly sought.

Readers here should be absolutely certain that key leaders know the real outlines of the Obama life story. That includes those like Karl Rove and John Brennan, Rove's contemporary at the University of Texas at Austin. The major players who do not know are the concerned citizens of both right and left, including tea party foot soldiers and "Obama-bots" convinced that his career goal has been community organizing. I leave aside the information gate-keepers in the media. Very few of them in Washington know the facts, based on my observation and conversation. They easily could learn more by following up leads in this book and elsewhere. Yet they would face job reprisals unless an aroused grassroots forces their initiative.

As I finished final edits on this book in the spring of 2013, Ralph Nader encompassed many of these themes in a dinner speech to two dozen journalists and activists at the National Press Club. Nader recalled that he had begun his career in the 1960s working as a consumer advocate based in a tiny office at the club following his graduation from Harvard Law School. In those days, Congress was responsive to public pressure, generated in part by independent journalists such as Drew Pearson and Jack Anderson. Nader played a leading role in the recall of millions of unsafe consumer products, as well as vastly improved regulation of the environment, workplace safety, and transportation safety. Now, he concluded, every major watchdog institution in the capital city is controlled by corporations and their lobbyists, even though the Constitution and other founding documents do not mention the word "corporation." Lobbyists, "who are not here just to look at the Washington Monument," now outnumber consumer advocates by more than 100 to one, he said. There was a bittersweet quality to the reminiscences of the crusading attorney, who has been named by The *Atlantic* as one of the nation's 100 most influential figures and by *Time* and *Life* as one of the last century's most important figures. A club committee had determined Nader's prospective comments were not newsworthy enough to justify a sanctioned event. So, an alternative group provided a room to hear him. Nader's hopes remained with an energized and informed citizenry forcing members of Congress to do their jobs.[87]

Forceful and articulate as always, Nader specified the ways that corporations gut Congress, the courts, the executive branch, and the media, of any real effectiveness to accomplish their ostensible goals. Yet even with his grim conclusion, I found kernels of hope. We each do so in a personal way, and so kindly let me share in conclusion something I learned that evening.

Claire Nader, the speaker's sister, happened to sit to my left during at the long, rectangular dinner table. She is a vibrant, slender, retired social scientist with a doctorate from Columbia University. She looks and acts vastly younger than someone born in 1928. I was gratified — and extremely surprised — that she remembered me from my first book, *Spiked*, more than a quarter of a century previous. The case study on the decline of media under conglomerate ownership focused heavily on my first employer, the *Hartford Courant*, which she and her siblings had read as youngsters in northwestern Connecticut. "You were thinner then," she added, as nicely as possible. I laughed at myself for letting things slide in an obvious way, and said I hope to resume healthy living in the spirit of her family's healthy eating tradition following my latest research project.[88]

I previewed with her *Presidential Puppetry's* major findings. What I found most interesting was that even she, who shares her brother's activism and concern about unresponsive leaders, was not aware of the main revelations I mentioned. This is not unusual. I have tried out the findings with several reporter friends working for major media, and have learned they have not had time to explore even leads that fall directly into their specialties.

I have kept the research findings secret until this point to prevent the kind of literary sabotage that I occasionally observed growing up in a writing family in Manhattan and since then in Washington. Yet the explanations here for many recent failures in government leadership are based on 1,200 endnotes, most previously published. These sources, almost all on the record and available for follow-up by others, connect the dots. Startling facts and implications are apparent in history and current events. The Wilson administration, for example, has eerie parallels to the Obama presidency. Yet modern government has enormously more power than in the past because of the increase in the federal budget and decline of other branches.

Puppetry shows that the United States government is no longer entrusted to its citizens. Power over government is concentrated in a few executives, families, and institutions that advance their ideologies and other interests. The result is job loss, evaporation of the safety net, deficit spending, terrorism, financial instability, and partisan gridlock. Voters must take their power back by rejecting the puppet masters. The ABC-TV show *Scandal*, launched in 2012, focuses on important topics in a politically acceptable way: by fictionalizing them and portraying as the star "Olivia Pope," a former presidential advisor whose consulting firm specializes in containing scandals.

That is better than the mainstream media's all-too-frequent practice of ignoring major issues entirely. But it would be better still if the facts behind actual events were revealed. We need citizen Truth Patrols to hold elected and appointed officials accountable, and to demand answers from leaders. Let's pose tough questions for those seeking comebacks, such as Mitt Romney and David Petraeus — or those preparing themselves for 2016, such as Jeb Bush and Hillary Clinton.

President Obama, in my view, is following the path of accommodation that was his best opportunity growing up as a fatherless boy. He and his team might be open to change if it is presented in the right way. Shame is one possibility. Now that Obama has won a second term, the public can apply pressure to him in targeted ways in hopes of more positive results. Shorn of his pattern of deception, the president can at last, like Pinocchio, become a real person and a true leader accountable to the public.

Chapter 22

Next Steps

B efore the end of this book's long and mostly grim journey, we should meet at least some of the puppet masters, and learn how to beware of others. Then we should refresh ourselves by once again encountering this book's heroes. They are the women and men who fight for a better country even without holding any civic post, aside from what Supreme Court Justice Louis Brandeis described as the nation's highest office: Citizen.[1]

Who Are the Puppet Masters?

The public needs to be able to identify those who wield hidden power over our top public officials for selfish motives. The decision makers often lurk in the background, difficult to spot. They have enough money to keep up their images as honorable members of the community. With the advantage of wealth (sometimes for generations), many of the power players are well bred and well spoken, good-looking, personable, philanthropic, and otherwise prominent in community life. Their capacity for self-serving goals and ruthless methods can be hidden beneath such façades.

This overview suggests several ways of understanding the identities of these rulers. The real powers tend to have family fortunes of at least a half billion dollars and stay active in such policy groups as the Bilderberg Group or its overlapping bodies, the Trilateral Commission and the much larger Council on Foreign Relations.[2] The well-bred leaders of these overlapping groups were capable of humor on the rare occasions when they answered questions about their secret deliberations. "The Trilateral Commission doesn't secretly run the world," wrote Sir Winston Lord, a Bonesman and onetime assistant U.S. Secretary of State. "The Council on Foreign Relations does that."[3] Lord was also a former president of the Council on Foreign Relations. The meetings most likely resemble high-toned policy seminars, with much smaller groups actively implementing the most secret and controversial plans.

One irrefutable and immensely important fact is that media titans, heavily funded by Wall Street of course, are charter members of these exclusive groups and invite their most trusted pundits — and never report on the proceedings. That fact tells the rest of us exactly what we need to know about the most exclusive and powerful of these bodies. Whatever they are doing in these meetings, they don't want their media audiences to learn about it. In June 2013, the group convened at the luxury Grove Hotel in the village of Watford northwest of London for its annual meeting, which has been attracting unprecedented scrutiny from critics raising questions about the group's purpose. In response, Bilderberg has begun announcing a partial guest list and selected topics of discussion, but little else. The 2013 attendees included leaders or funders of such new media companies as Google, Amazon.com, Facebook, and Palantir, along with the usual group of financiers and high-level national security officials and former officials from varied nations.

The conference coincided with two important developments. First came news reports described in Chapter 13 regarding NSA and CIA secret surveillance of the global public (including all those in the United States). The system stores virtually all significant electronic communications by U.S. citizens and as many foreigners as possible for potential retrieval by government employees and the private contractors that currently control much of the operational function of the federal government on sensitive matters. As private companies (albeit supported by taxpayers), contractors are able to work outside normal oversight and also support their political allies in government. On June 9, a *Guardian* team including Glenn Greenwald revealed as a source Edward Snowden, a 29-year-old NSA-contractor. The *Washington Post*, which had also been using Snowden as a source, followed up shortly afterward. A former CIA employee, Snowden had been working the previous four years for the NSA via such outside contractors as Booz Allen Hamilton and Dell. The *Guardian* wrote of Snowden:

> The *Guardian*, after several days of interviews, is revealing his identity at his request. From the moment he decided to disclose numerous top-secret documents to the public, he was determined not to opt for the protection of anonymity....Snowden will go down in history as one of America's most consequential whistleblowers, alongside Daniel Ellsberg and Bradley Manning. He is responsible for handing over material from one of the world's most secretive organisations — the NSA.

> In a note accompanying the first set of documents he provided, he wrote: "I understand that I will be made to suffer for my actions," but "I will be satisfied if the federation of secret law, unequal pardon and irresistible executive powers that rule the world that I love are revealed even for an instant."

Snowden said his work for the CIA in Geneva had first prompted him to think about exposing government secrets. He refrained because he

did not want hurt individuals, who are the major focus of CIA probes —
and because he believed Barack Obama would reform abuses if elected in
2008. Later, Snowden observed as an NSA contractor that "Obama
advanced the very policies that I thought would be reined in." The main
lesson for Snowden was that "you can't wait around for someone else to
act. I had been looking for leaders, but I realized that leadership is about
being the first to act." He said NSA and CIA had the power to intercept,
store, and retrieve virtually all electronic communications involving the
president, members of Congress, and ordinary citizens, thereby putting the
nation on a path where the right of privacy is virtually over.

"Thousands of technology, finance and manufacturing companies are
working closely with U.S. national security agencies, providing sensitive
information and in return receiving benefits that include access to
classified intelligence, four people familiar with the process," Bloomberg
then reported. "In addition to private communications, information about
equipment specifications and data needed for the Internet to work —
much of which isn't subject to oversight because it doesn't involve private
communications — is valuable to intelligence, U.S. law-enforcement
officials and the military."[4]

Ellsberg described Snowden as a "hero" in the most significant
national security leak in history. Ellsberg noted that the younger man was
rare if not unique among the best known national security whistleblowers
in disclosing his identity and actions before authorities knew of them.
Snowden made his revelations from a hotel room in Hong Kong. United
States officials promptly demanded his extradition to face federal trial on
the spy charges that the Obama administration had been using against
other leakers. Senate Intelligence Committee Chair Dianne Feinstein, a
California Democrat whose husband is a major federal contractor,
adjudged Snowden guilty of "treason." But Hong Kong snubbed the
United States by describing the charges as unworthy of extradition. It
allowed Snowden to leave as a free man, seeking political asylum.

Separately, the Syrian government was achieving military successes
against U.S.-supported rebels that threatened to solidify a four-nation
"Shia Crescent" extending from Iran to Lebanon on the shores of the
Mediterranean Sea. Syria's gains despite U.S. public denunciations and
largely secret CIA and other military help for rebels raised the possibility
of the first United States military-strategic defeat since the Vietnam War.

Such a result would not be because Obama sought to fulfill campaign
promises to ordinary voters who had supported him and his much-
discussed opposition to the Iraq War. Instead, Obama had tried through
largely covert actions to implement a regime-change strategy in Syria
sought by many in the power elite. Obama responded by claiming Syrian
use of chemical weapons to authorize on June 13 U.S. delivery of arms
and ammunition to rebels. During a time of supposed austerity for

Americans, the new U.S. aid augmented more than $500 million reported in previous U.S. spending for the insurgents, many of whom were reported to be foreign fighters from more than a dozen nations lured into Syria by a billion dollars in aid from the fiercely Islamist and anti-democratic Gulf monarchies. Obama's administration justified the new war making on humanitarian grounds despite a video of rebel cannibalism and other atrocities, and reports of rebel leadership by Al Qaeda militants in significant part. The U.S. public face of the Obama's crusade seemed likely to become Obama's second-term team of female militants at the United Nations, White House and CIA. Yet the Obama initiative occurred without any formal United Nations or similar mandate. The potential false flag rationale for more war recalled such previous pretexts as Gulf of Tonkin to ramp up the Vietnam War. More recently, the nation saw phony claims of Iraqi "murder" of Kuwaiti babies in incubators in 1989 to rile up American women against Saddam Hussein, and the notorious "Weapons of Mass Destruction" propaganda before the 2003 invasion.

With that dramatic backdrop at mid-year 2013, we return to our survey of the United States oligarchs who helped propel Obama into office in 2008 before many withdrew support. By 2012, Obama's centrist policies were no longer so vital for their goals after the Bush-Cheney years faded from the public's memory. Personally, I found it striking during this book research to read of how many in the American public remained incensed about the 1857 Meadows Massacre in Utah for more than two decades after the killings, even with the Civil War's distractions and during an era of lower literacy.

Has much of the nation lost the will to fight? Or has it become harder to remember those events and core beliefs that are worth a fight? The issue, to be clear, is not the merits of Obama compared to his predecessors. Instead, the central battle is about jobs, prosperity, honor, honest government, and other self-interest in the face of hostility from both of the two corporate, globalist political parties. Jesse Ventura appeared on my radio show with co-host Scott Draughon in mid-June at the height of the scandals to argue that both political parties are so corrupt that any marginal reforms are hopeless. The former Minnesota governor said intensive airport searches and massive surveillance are primarily designed to condition Americans to give up their rights, not to improve security. Ventura said could not understand why Obama went along with such measures unless he had studied the JFK assassination — and realized that the killing threatened him and all other future presidents. Patriots must speak out, Ventura said.[5]

Do-gooder reform groups and political reporters focus primarily on political contributors to assess accountability for elected officials. *Politico*, the Washington-based insider tabloid, compiled running lists of "mega-donors" during the 2012 campaign. The lists of both Republicans and Democrats can be found here.[6] Las Vegas-based casino owner Sheldon Adelson attracted more attention than did any other donor. He made the largest individual contributions in the nation's campaign history, nearly $150 million, and said he planned to double that spending in 2016. He boasted of self-serving goals beyond what the Koch Brothers would specify. Adelson's fortune originally came from running high-tech conventions and magazines, including the huge *Comdex* show that dominated the high-tech field for years. Then he moved primarily into the legalized gambling sectors in Las Vegas and elsewhere. Also, he became involved with related businesses such as hotels, including The Sands in Las Vegas. Adelson's spending in the 2012 elections was nearly six times the previous record, $34 million in support for Democrats from George Soros in 2004.[7]

Adelson was clear about what he sought. Aged 79, he wanted the Justice Department and Securities and Exchange Commission to drop investigations concerning whether he bribed Chinese officials in order to operate his casino in Macau.[8] In a rare two-hour interview, Adelson explained how he believed that Romney would provide more support for Israeli Prime Minister Benjamin Netanyahu than would Obama.[9] An analyst writing for the Huffington Post calculated that an investment of $100 million in the 2012 Romney campaign could provide Adelson with a return of $2.3 billion in various benefits in the event of Romney's victory.[10]

The public should be grateful to Adelson for being so explicit about his goals. His words clearly illustrated flaws in the system. Offer $20 to a meter maid to void a parking ticket and you might go to jail. Offer $150 million to the right party to avoid prison? Well, that is our political system in action, more or less. Anything goes if no one who has the power to prosecute is offended. *Politico* printed Adelson's comments in early September. The top political pundits, law enforcement authorities, and political candidates, including Obama, generally refrained from any public response about his desire to exchange a campaign donation for immunity. Romney, who had cleverly avoided huge tax bills in the 1990s with donations to his church in a manner that is now illegal, was not going to protest against his major donor.[11] Both parties know full well how the justice system works in deference to the wealthy, with rare exceptions.

More generally, crusaders for morality in public life, including Romney, show little public concern about Adelson's legalized gambling empire, the source of his money. Gambling is the source also for the funding from many other major donors to the political parties.

Let's reflect generally about gambling, without reference to Adelson specifically.[12] The overview below is based on the public record, which I know from years covering the Mafia and other organized crime. Gaming holds a unique position in the nation's political system because it is a cash-based business with large transactions. The sector attracts participants who want to launder money from crime, often involving major narcotics sales. Influence peddlers also use gambling cash for convenient, hard-to-detect payoffs to politicians and staff. These factors partly explain the attraction of invitation-only VIP gaming rooms and cruises. Organizers sometimes hire prostitutes with actual or pretended legitimate careers (including college study) to glamorize the surroundings and, on occasion, lure VIPs into sex that may even end up on videotape.

Blackmail and the false suspicion of wrongdoing are sometimes part of the operation. Consorts are not necessarily female. Their involvement with public figures as "honeytraps" or as ambitious lobbyists on the make provides their sponsors with leverage. Many Washington officials and staff of both parties, including household names at high levels of power, are reputed to be secretly gay or bisexual. The extraordinarily high number of such reports raises the question of whether these men and women advanced in public life despite what would seem to be a political handicap — or because VIP backers prefer to support office-holders who are vulnerable to exposure.[13]

In sum, abuses and harms from gambling show why religious leaders and law enforcers have long wanted the industry to be closely regulated, or even banned. The inordinate influence of gambling tycoons betting with serious dollars on the 2012 election outcome vastly expanded a trend. Secret funding of campaigns from casino money was dangerous enough during the Abramoff years. Abramoff says he raised $20 million in relatively small, undetectable sums from gambling interests to help defeat Siegelman and his lottery proposals in Alabama.[14]

Analysis of campaign financing provides useful disclosure up to a point. But many of the most important players hold influence far beyond a campaign donation check. "Vulture capitalists" comprise one such group. They are the modern-day opportunists who make fortunes out of others' misery. Naturally, they have a huge incentive to help deepen that misery and thereby increase their profiteering. The legal, financial, and political strategies are far too complicated for the media or the typical regulator to oversee, even if such watchdogs were permitted to investigate. Yet some windows into this world exist. One is provided by investigative reporter Greg Palast, the former private detective who earned an MBA degree from the University of Chicago studying under Milton Friedman, among others. Palast has helped define the concept of the "vulture capitalist" through his profiles of Paul Singer, among others. Singer is a secretive billionaire who profits on Third World debt and, more recently, on the U.S. government's bailout of the auto industry.[15]

Far more important than Singer or Adelson is Peter Peterson, the billionaire investor who fronts for the nation's true power structure.

Peterson has spent hundreds of millions of dollars to generate momentum to impose an austerity economy upon the United States. Peterson was born in 1926 in Nebraska to a family of Greek immigrants. His father ran a diner. With an MBA also from the University of Chicago, Peterson advanced in the business world to become chair and CEO of the movie company Bell and Howell. He chaired an important government commission on philanthropy in 1972. Later, Peterson made a fortune on Wall Street through Lehman Brothers and the Blackstone Group, and succeeded David Rockefeller as chair of the Council on Foreign Relations. He recently chaired the Peter Peterson Foundation, which he funded with a billion dollars.

Peterson is the author of several books on the need for cutbacks in federal spending.[16] His most effective work is that done behind the scenes, through proxy groups. So, his movement looms much larger than his personal profile. He and his foundation have provided much of the momentum behind public fear of a "fiscal cliff" and a need to cut back on what are now known as the public's greed for "entitlements," such as Social Security. I saw him up close from a front row table at a conference in December 2012. The still-dynamic philanthropist spoke in compelling, modest, and disarming fashion about the need for the American people to make sacrifices on their entitlements and otherwise for the good of the nation.[17]

The manipulators know how to showcase attractive public personalities from within their own ranks for the occasions when they need a public face. It takes a Palast to drag the more repulsive social planners like Singer into view.

On the Democratic side, George Soros is a powerful force. He is an investor and philosopher born in 1930 in Hungary currently worth more than $20 billion. That net worth is in the same range as Adelson's.[18] Soros has used his wealth to fund many progressive groups and causes, with a special focus on the human rights, civil liberties, and freedom of expression. His support burnishes his image, of course, among those seeking funding. Nevertheless, Soros has generated critics on both the left and right. *New York Times* columnist Paul Krugman, for example, has suggested that Soros-like figures can generate extraordinary profits by anticipating, if not provoking international crisis situations.[19] Others have praised Soros as focused primarily on philanthropy and humanitarian causes, and not as active in markets as earlier in his career.

Whether benign or acquisitive, Soros has few, if any, rivals in terms of influence on liberal and Democratic-oriented causes in the United States. Some of his efforts are so intertwined with foreign policy that they receive significant funding from taxpayers via Congress. A full analysis of his influence and motives would require a book in itself. For current purposes, it is sufficient to state that he is despised by conservatives for helping Democrats and civil libertarians, and praised by most of the latter for those same acts.

Another power broker vital to Obama's ascendance was Penny Pritzker, who helped Obama to receive national political recognition. With her financial scandal fading from memory by 2013, she was on track to become Commerce Secretary even after understating her income from offshore fees by $80 million.[20]

Several additional wealthy policy crusaders have emerged from the traditional obscurity of the think tank and foundation world. Two of the most prominent, as noted in this book's first chapter, are Charles and David Koch, heirs of the family-owned Koch Industries, based in Wichita, Kansas. They built the company into the nation's second largest privately held company. Also, they have funded many influential conservative policy centers, including the Cato Institute, the American Legislative Exchange Council (ALEC) and Americans for Prosperity. Perhaps their greatest triumph in the political arena was their role in planning the launch of the supposedly grassroots tea party to transform America, or at least to block Democrats and other opponents from meaningful action in Washington. In 2013, revelation of the secret tea party planning prompted Al Gore to protest to little avail.[21] The greatest frauds in public life are nearly invulnerable to consequences. Like P.T. Barnum and Lyndon Johnson, the great deceivers even boast about their frauds at times.[22] Such bragging reinforces their reputation for power and expertise, and causes opponents to give up hope.

Under the guise of fighting "voting fraud," ALEC is leading the national effort to curtail voting by blacks, students, Hispanics, urban-dwellers, and others in state legislatures perceived likely to be Democrats. In 2013, one party controlled the legislative and executive branches of 37 state governments. Republicans ran 25 of those states. The Koch-affiliated groups have also made progress in several states to abolish an incomes tax in order to shift taxing to a regressive consumption tax that will fall more on the poor and middle class. The Koch Brothers are each in their seventies. They and their organizations, not surprisingly, oppose estate and capital gains taxes. In the spring of 2013, they were reputed to have aspirations of increasing their clout over public policy by buying the Tribune nationwide media empire.[23] The cost of this venture would be relatively trivial compared to their potential estate tax bills if the nation's public officials do not continue to follow their lead on tax policy.

Richard Mellon Scaife, a Pittsburgh-based heir to the Mellon fortune, has long been another major funder of Washington-based conservative organizations.[24] News Corporation Chairman Rupert Murdoch deserves inclusion despite his modest levels of official donations. He instead leverages the power of his media corporations to help candidates. This is most obvious from their biased news coverage and political crusades.

Murdoch's henchmen, however, have also shown their sinister and partisan agenda through their illegal recordings of politicians in the United Kingdom that were used for improper pressure on policy, such as the merger approvals necessary to expand their media empire.[25]

More Masters of Our Disaster

Readers will find relatively little additional value if I list many more of the nation's power brokers, especially those with obscure public profiles. Print encyclopedias are becoming outmoded. I shall better serve you by focusing upon two general categories of largely secret opinion shapers whose power is not readily disclosed by campaign donations data or other traditional news coverage. These players include fabulously wealthy international power brokers with a keen interest in United States policies. Technically, foreign citizens have long been forbidden to contribute to United States candidates. When there is wealth but scant enforcement, however, money can find its destination via willing intermediaries. Recent legal changes in the United States, including the *Citizens United* decision, have made such donations easier by enabling what is in effect money laundering via corporations.[26]

International influence of the kind I am describing is not measured in donations, which any millionaire can muster. Powerful non-citizens have much better ways to influence American leaders and voters, such as the news media. Although some restrictions for foreign influence apply, the rules are devised and enforced in ways that permit heavy foreign influence on United States media. Thus, the Rothschild banking family has long been an influential investor in the esteemed Reuters news service, along with other leading opinion shapers.[27] Mexico's telecom tycoon, Carlos Slim Helu, is ranked first on the *Forbes* 2013 list of the world's top billionaires. His estimated $73 billion in assets, included a reported 17 percent of non-voting New York Times stock.[28] In addition, the Saudi Prince Al-Waleed bin Talal, another *Forbes* top 20 billionaire, has been invested in several United States-based communications organizations, including News Corporation, Apple, and Twitter.[29] His assets have been estimated at $16 billion. Important though he is, the grandson of Saudi founder Ibn Saud is reputed to be a front man for other Mideast investors.

Secrecy is important to the operations of the media, government, and every other sector that matters. Perhaps we can agree by now that the concept that ownership does not affect news coverage is a fool's paradise. News consumers are going to see stories of human rights violations by the secular government of Syria that the United States and Saudi Arabia want to topple, not rights violations of women, Christians, and vast numbers of contract workers in allied monarchies such as Saudi Arabia.[30]

The second and most important category of hidden government influencers is that of the nation's corporations, foundations, universities, churches, unions, and government entities (including their grant and investigative units). A few examples will suffice to illustrate the financial power of these players, whose aggregate power dwarfs that of donors like Adelson or even most of the major "bundlers" of donations.

David Rockefeller is the grandson of the richest man in the United States and, born in 1915, was still alive as of the spring of 2013.[31] Rockefeller does not need to write a check to be influential with a candidate. Like his peers at the top of the pyramid, he has armies of minions who by now know what to do without even being told.

Those elevated through the Rockefeller empire wield powerful influence, including occasional public service. Paul Bremer, became a managing director of Kissinger and Associates before returning to government as the Bush civilian envoy leading the United States presence in Iraq from 2003 to 2004.[32] Former Citibank and AOL CEO Richard Parsons largely remains out of the limelight, but is extraordinarily influential and carries an oft-hidden Rockefeller "brand" along with the more public corporate titles he has held. Most influential of all of Rockefeller's acolytes, with the possible exception of Parsons, has been former Secretary of State Henry Kissinger and Bush aide Brent Scowcroft. Scowcroft's advancement through the elite political world was a landmark achievement for Mormons in Washington, much like that of Parsons has been in the corporate world for African-Americans.

This brief survey suggests how high-level policy is integrated with the revolving door in ways far beyond the dollar amounts of compensation. The controls reach into almost every sector. Critics, aka troublemakers, can find themselves ousted from jobs, health insurance, and indeed careers, with devastating financial and self-esteem losses for themselves and their families. The nation's capital is, in some ways, like a factory town. Employees and their families are beholden to the company.

Even for my small-scale legal reform efforts, I have received friendly advice from Democratic sources that the Justice Integrity Project might receive important support if it withdrew its opposition to Democrat Elena Kagan's confirmation to the Supreme Court, and dropped the controversial currency trader and philanthropist George Soros from this list of key behind-the-scenes political players.

On September 12, 2012, I greeted former Republican National Chairman Michael Steele at a brunch following the annual Red Mass at the Cathedral of St. Matthew the Apostle in Washington. The mass and brunch are organized by the John Carroll Society, a Roman Catholic lay group named in honor of the Constitution framer who fought hardest for the provisions separating church and state. Carroll later became the first

Vatican-appointed Catholic archbishop for North America. The Red Mass ceremonies typically attract two-thirds of the Supreme Court and many Catholic leaders prominent in law.

Steele is now a frequent political commentator on cable television. I invited him to comment on this book's themes. With a short laugh and a smile, he responded, "There's plenty of puppet masters in Washington!"

No doubt about that.

How To Change History

At this point, I suggest we stop imagining the political world in terms of puppets and puppet masters. The "show" would not exist without an audience. We must take responsibility for whatever we do not like.

Maybe you just want to tune out after reading about all this duplicity by powerful decision makers and their organizations. That would be a natural reaction, but a mistaken one. These stories may seem like they are about the White House, but they are in fact about your house. We are on our own in protecting our jobs, health, homes, savings, rights, votes, and everything else.

Hope and courage are the best reaction to the book's disclosures. Leaders deserve hard questions, and the electorate deserves forthright answers. Candidates should respond or disappear. The truth sets them free — free from blackmail, free from greed, free from shame, and free, finally, to do the jobs required by their office oaths. In the end, the winners of 2012 and future elections are less important than a fully informed public and our demand for much better performance.

This will not happen without major campaign and election reform. Shortly before this book went to press in 2013, I attended a seminar on campaign finance reform sponsored by the Cato Institute, a think tank promoting free market policies. A range of experts included the former counsel for President Obama's 2012 campaign and a GOP Federal Election Commission member. C-SPAN's video of the three-hour event is worth watching. The panelists dispel notions that current laws or likely reforms are likely to be effective.[33]

Panelist Lawrence Lessig outlined in vivid terms the kind of problems I have sought to address in this book. Lessig is a Harvard Law School professor and author who has founded two reform groups in recent years, Change Congress and Rootstrikers.[34] To illustrate congressional dysfunction, he described how legislative leaders increasingly rely on temporary laws (such as fiscal cliff and debt limit measures) to keep the public in limbo on vital issues and thereby extort campaign contributions from lobbyists. Furthermore, he quantified the role of wealthy campaign contributors as follows: No candidate can aspire to become a legitimate candidate without passing muster with major donors to win a nomination.

Lessig calculated that 159 major donors provided the same total of $313 million as all of the nation's "small" donors put together for the 2008 presidential election, the last election for which figures were available.

These donors exercise largely hidden veto power over candidates and policies, by this analysis, with vast power exercised not by "the one percent" but by "the .000042 percent." The power over the nomination process was never envisioned by those who created our constitutional system, and it now threatens to destroy the country's ability to govern itself in a way even remotely related to democratic principles.

Realistically, however, it is easy to lose hope of making a difference. *Why Bother?* aptly summarizes the reasons to continue the fight for democracy, due process, and freedom. *Why Bother?* was written by my friend Sam Smith, founder of the *Progressive Review* in Washington, DC. He has been a perceptive and intellectually courageous observer of national politics for nearly five decades. To answer the question posed by his title, he wrote:

> Someone has been careless, cruel, greedy, stupid. But it wasn't us, was it? We were inside, just watching. It all happened without us – by the hand of forces we can't see, understand or control...
>
> What safety we have, the privilege of the cocoon, comes from those who, at much greater danger and with far less chance or choice, climbed that wall, insisted on being human, fought despair, suppressed fear, and denied themselves the illusion of detachment. Some were only a generation or two away and carried our name, some were more distant. Our present safety is built upon their risks, on their integrity, rebellion, and passion, and upon the courage that propelled them.[35]

In terms of concrete reform actions, Smith aptly recommends:

> If we wish to change events there is no better place to start than to change our own reaction to them, to declare that a politics lacking justice, equity, decency, and compassion is no longer acceptable. Economics, efficiency, perception, and brutish power calculations no longer suffice. The bottom line has bottomed out. The most radical act of individualism in which one can engage today is to come together with other individuals – as church, neighborhood, city and organization – in order to uncover the biggest secret our leaders keep from us – that we are not alone.

There are other such brave spirits among independent journalists. Most eke out modest incomes with blogs, video blogs, photos, or even mainstream work (despite the difficulties of addressing certain issues disclosed here). I have elsewhere in this book cited many of those I have found most insightful, including acknowledgements. Revelations about complex topics are ultimately based on sources, however. Informed sources should be protected, but instead they are ruthlessly punished.

Many pages ago, you and I began this exploration with clues in a mystery case. By now, I hope much of it is resolved. But what's next for us? Bottom-up research and self-help can go only so far. Reform requires leaders reasonably independent of the power elite, many of whose leaders are quietly waging class war against the public in the guise of governance.

Finding leaders who are effective and widely respected is a challenge for every national civic project these days, as is my effort to conclude this book with hopeful words. Washington faces an unprecedented breakdown in governance. That is the theme of an important new book by the leading congressional scholars Norman Ornstein of the conservative American Enterprise Institute and Thomas Mann of the more centrist Brookings Institute.[36]

Identifying would-be leaders worthy of respect is a longstanding problem. Friedrich Nietzsche wrote of it in *The Use and Abuse of History*, published in 1874. "When one speaks to men of truth and justice," the German cultural critic wrote, "they will ever be troubled by the doubt whether it be the fanatic or the judge who is speaking to them."[37] That is true now, as then. The public perceives, rightfully in many cases, that thought leaders of all kinds are more likely than not to be charlatans.

Nietzsche provided a useful tool to distinguish between a fanatic and a "judge," which is his term for an honest historian. His criteria is whether the would-be historian or social critic is willing to apply the same legal and philosophic criteria to fellow partisans as to opponents. "The search for truth is often thoughtlessly praised," he continued. "But it has something great in it only if the truth-seeker has the sincere, unconditional will for justice."

That worthy aspiration is difficult maintain even in professional circles, much less for busy citizens who realize the country faces grave problems but who are unlikely to agree on the identity of the most credible social critics. I hope it has been helpful, therefore, to have cited in this book commentators from quite different political, ethnic, and social backgrounds who find common ground in identifying our system as massively corrupt and guided by unseen hands.[38]

In conclusion, I draw on the words of Washington Archbishop Donald Cardinal Wuerle as he concluded the same fall 2012 Red Mass in which I had met former Republican National Chairman Michael Steele. The archbishop said our times today require a new spirit of evangelism, comparable to those of the past. He meant renewals of the Catholic faith shared by the vast majority of his audience. Yet his words also have a non-religious meaning that is congruent with tradition of Constitution framer John Carroll, as well as the faith in honest rule of law common to many public policy reformers today.

"Renew our own faith," the archbishop counseled. "Have confidence it is true." Then, he said, "Share it."

Appendix: Reform Resources

You might despair after reading of how elites and their political operatives impose flim-flams and austerity on those regarded as dupes.

I hope not. The materials in this book empower reform when used with today's new developments in media. For the first time, we have the ability to bypass corporate-controlled gatekeepers. We can publish, at least for now, the kind of suppressed information essential for civic control under constitutional principles. True, we have already experienced the "Hope and Change" campaign that solidified its message with web-based tools enrolling tens of millions of followers. That was a top-down process whereby the leadership kept many secrets.

Now, we can make civic organizations of all kinds perform more closely to their ostensible missions.

My recommendations below are drawn from specialized experts I have sought out through the years. I suggest you do the same by being active in civic, school, church, and professional groups. A 2013 seminar hosted by the National Geographic Society shared practical tips about how they are transforming their magazine's unique content into exciting interactive and video formats. The society's mantra is, "Tell memorable stories in a meaningful way." It is a non-political mass membership society so its techniques cannot serve every need for reformers. Still, some of their innovations build online communities.

My work through the years has heavily focused on communications. As president of a global high-tech association, I organized many conventions that each showcased 80 or more expert speakers with a story to tell. More recently, I have arranged for more than 200 authors, public officials, and other newsmakers to appear on *Washington Update*, the weekly public affairs radio series that I have co-hosted for seven years with My Technology Lawyer network founder Scott Draughon.[1] I sometimes arrange lectures to help the most interesting guests visiting the nation's capital. If you have a compelling message, write us a brief query or call in to the show. The process is free and uncensored.

If you have read this far you care about the future, and doubtless receive many requests for your help. OpEdNews founder Rob Kall, an expert on "bottom-up" reform, recently questioned the value of many such requests. "Demonstrations may look grassroots, but they're really top down," he wrote. "A handful of organizers set the time and place and they hope people will show up. Sometimes a handful of powerful or famous people will show up to give talks. It's not that demonstrations don't work at all, but they are so inefficient and usually ineffective…"[2]

Kall's experience matches my observations of Washington protests. Neither the media nor public officials deign to notice most initiatives. Why would they? Many civic groups have become controlled, co-opted, or otherwise neutered. Some groups are frauds funded from the start by manipulators who want to confuse the public. Petitions, marches, letters to the editor, and donations to congressional candidates are unlikely to create much impact unless they advance a goal that opinion leaders already want, such as austerity for the public.

Many leading progressive reform groups dare not deliver blunt messages to officials for fear of losing the access necessary for what has become their true mission: fund-raising. Similarly, conservatives who know about Obama's intelligence background will not disclose it. They do not want to antagonize their base of supporters who have been trained to regard him as a leftist radical. Both major parties cut elected officials off from party support if they fail to support leaders. All of this fosters self-censorship and public ignorance, to the great harm of our country.

Do not give up. My goal is to advise on potholes in the road, not to warn against the journey to reform. Here are my suggestions:

- Find allies from the groups and authors cited in *Puppetry*. Pick an issue that drives your passion. Use this book's Bibliography and Notes sections to find kindred spirits among the authors and groups cited. Introduce yourself. Promote their work, or critique it.
- Join, and guide organizations. Opinion leaders pay attention to groups, not individuals. Help fundraise, pick speakers, and otherwise organize meetings. You can have huge impact.
- Become 'The Media.' Voice your own views via social media and reader comments on websites. If you are more ambitious, I have found a sequence that is particularly effective with traditional media: Get invited to speak at a meeting, and then use that appearance to obtain a radio interview. That combination is often sufficient for local newspaper coverage. Then seek local TV, cable, and additional radio interviews.
- Create your own 'official inquiry.' We must do so because hard-hitting oversight hearings are increasingly rare without a partisan or otherwise narrow agenda. Find a hall and recruit speakers (including officials). Then invite the media for coverage.

In that spirit, I organized and moderated a pioneering forum at the National Press Club in 2009 revealing investigative findings about U.S. political prosecutions. C-SPAN covered the entire three-hour, 13-speaker event. This broke a *de facto* media blackout on portraying victims of Bush-Rove political prosecution plot across the country.[3] As another example, I saw how the lack of big-money organizational support seemed likely to thwart visibility for the only congressional hearing to focus on victims of today's health care crisis. I suggested a compelling witness and persuaded Robert Corsini, a public-spirited videographer from Los Angeles, to record highlights of the hearing (described in Chapter 19). You can do the same things locally or nationally on issues that matter to you.

I hope I can count on your support to explore the themes of *Presidential Puppetry* that gatekeepers want secret. Your feedback is vital, whether public or private, pro or con. Please contact me or make your comments through social media. Your reaction and news tips help me sharpen the message in my interviews, lectures, and debates. Would you like me to speak with a group or media audience in your area? I can discuss topics from the book and related issues of concern to you. The best way to contact me for book subjects is via the *Puppetry* site (www.presidentialpuppetry.com). My legal reform work can be found via the Justice Integrity Project (www.justice-integrity.org).

We confront problems of a scale that require both self-help and group action. Use these tools. Let's make the puppets and their masters do what they are supposed to do. Remember, it is your stage, not theirs. Demonstrations have a purpose once we know our true objectives. In the words of the Rev. Walter Fauntroy, the 1960s civil rights leader: *"You* can do it!" he said recently, with a knowing smile. "*We* can do it — if we put our hearts and our minds to it. *Let's* go do it!"[4]

Acknowledgements

The chance to thank loyal friends, mentors, and volunteer warriors — each an inspiration — is the most gratifying part of this project. I fear I may omit someone important or, worse (given the controversial nature of this book) include someone who suffers reprisal. That is not a theoretical exercise now that certain large employers are telling employees how to vote, and sophisticated databases make surveillance widespread.

Recognizing that the spirit of freedom burns strong in those with long civic service, I first thank the fearless and expert directors of the Justice Integrity Project: Robert Ames Alden, John Edward Hurley, John Kelly and Ronald Fisher. Much of the early work in this research was done under the project's auspices, leading to deeper and darker themes that required this separate project. Vital to the work were a number of courageous sources who stepped out of their daily lives to provide valuable information about irregularities in the justice system. That led directly to this book: Among those I most admire are, in alphabetical order, Phil Fleming, Roger Shuler, Dana Jill Simpson and others I'll identify by initials BB, DW. LW, PBW.

Others were targeted victims of the system, who fought back hard to save both themselves and others, and in doing so broadened my understanding of the system: Kenneth Ford, Isidro Garza Jr., Robin Head, Susan Lindauer, Louis Manzo, Don Siegelman, and Charles Spadoni, and several others currently vulnerable whom I cite by initials: BK chief among them. I have a special category also of those whom I have not met because of their imprisonment but whom I believe are serving at least part of their sentence for selective prosecution when they declined to break one of their core principles. One is Joseph Nacchio, the former Qwest CEO who declined to go along with the illegal surveillance program in 2001. The other is Richard Scrushy, who (whatever else he may have done) refused to lighten his burdens by providing false testimony against Don Siegelman. Therefore he paid a deep price.

I thank also several organizations with which I have long worked and thereby benefited. Several are alternative news and commentary organizations that published early findings in this research, most notably OpEdNews (especially its fiery leader Rob Kall), Huffington Post, Connecticut Watchdog, Professors Blog, and Nieman Watchdog. None is in any way responsible for the final, major conclusions, which are presented initially in this book. Similarly, I thank the ownership and staff of the weekly public affairs radio show, *My Technology Lawyer /*

Washington Update, which I have co-hosted for more than six years. Show founder, producer and co-host Scott Draughon, a thoughtful conservative, has exhibited through discussions a genuine commitment to free inquiry while advancing his own ideas in compelling fashion. He has no responsibility for this book's material. Neither do our more than 200 news making guests. Yet I cannot overlook mention of their insights helping my journey in this research.

I am grateful also to several insightful readers who made insightful suggestions on portions of the manuscript, including Michael Collins, Priscilla Black Duncan, James Chapman French Jr., Gene Gaines, Lillian McEwen, Wayne Madsen, and old friends AB, GW, MN, SC, and new friends CK, CW, and MS. Len Bracken generously shared his insights and a stunning photo of the White House used on the cover. I thank also those literary, design and other production talents who shared their skills and insights, including web designer Marie Mauel, cover designer Kyle Telman, as well as book editors, designers, and proof readers CH, DB, EJ, KK, SMK, TGB, and TJC.

Special thanks go to my longtime friend, advocate, and literary advisor, Lewis Chambers of the Bethel Agency in New York City, for his extraordinary help in this multiyear project. In addition, my love and thanks go to my family, some of whom will not like all the conclusions here, but whose experiences, insights, and criticism I greatly value in the process of unraveling the mysteries around us.

Bibliography

Presidential Puppetry

Abramoff, Jack. *Capitol Punishment: The Hard Truth about Washington Corruption from America's Most Notorious Lobbyist*. WND, 2011.

Ackerman, Bruce. *The Decline and Fall of the American Republic*. Belknap / Harvard University, 2010.

Ackerman, Bruce, and Ian Ayres. *Voting with Dollars: A New Paradigm for Campaign Finance*. Yale University, 2002.

Agee, Philip. *Inside the Company: CIA Diary*. Bantam, 1989 (1975).

Albarelli, H.P. Jr., *A Terrible Mistake: The Murder of Frank Olson and the CIA's Secret Cold War Experiments*. Trine Day, 2009.

Alberts, David S., John J. Garstka, and Frederick P. Stein. *Network Centric Warfare: Developing and Leveraging Information Superiority*. Department of Defense Command and Control Research Program, 2003.

Alford, Mimi. *Once Upon a Secret: My Affair with President John F. Kennedy and Its Aftermath*. Random House, 2012.

Allen, Thomas B. *George Washington, Spymaster: How the Americans Outspied the British and Won the Revolutionary War*. National Geographic, 2004.

Alter, Jonathan. *The Promise: President Obama, Year One*. Simon & Schuster, 2010.

Anderson, Christopher. *Barack and Michelle*. William Morrow, 2009.

Anderson, Jack. *Confessions of a Muckraker*. Random House, 1979.

——— *Washington Expose*. Public Affairs, 1967.

Andrews, Lori. *I Know Who You Are and What You Did*. Free Press / Simon & Schuster, 2012.

Atkinson, Rick. *In the Company of Soldiers: A Chronicle of Combat*. Henry Holt, 2004.

Ayers, Bill. *Fugitive Days: A Memoir*. Beacon, 2001.

Bagley, Will. *Blood of the Prophets: Brigham Young and the Massacre at Mountain Meadows*. University of Oklahoma, 2004.

Baker, Russ. *Family of Secrets: The Bush Dynasty, America's Invisible Government, and the Hidden History of the Last Fifty Years*, Bloomsbury, 2009.

Bamford, James. *The Shadow Factory: The Ultra-Secret National Security Agency from 9/11 to the Eavesdropping on America*. Anchor / Random House, 2009.

——— *A Pretext for War: 9/11, Iraq, and the Abuse of America's Intelligence Agencies*. Anchor, 2005.

——— *Body of Secrets: Anatomy of the Ultra-Secret National Security Agency*. Anchor / Random House, 2002.

——— *The Puzzle Palace: Inside the National Security Agency, America's Most Secret Intelligence Organization*. Penguin, 1983.

Bartlett, Bruce. *Imposter: How George W. Bush Bankrupted America and Betrayed the Reagan Legacy*. Doubleday, 2006.

Bartlett, Donald L., and James B. Steele. *Empire: The Life, Legend, and Madness of Howard Hughes*. Norton, 1979.

Belzer, Richard, and David Wayne. *Hit List: An In-Depth Investigation into the Mysterious Deaths of Witnesses to the JFK Assassination*. Skyhorse, 2013.

———— *Dead Wrong: Straight Facts on the Country's Most Controversial Cover-ups.* Skyhorse, 2012.

Benedict, Jeff. *The Mormon Way of Doing Business.* Business Plus, 2008.

Bennett, John C. *The History of the Saints, or an Exposé of Joe Smith and Mormonism.* Leland & Whiting, 1842.

Berens, Charlyne. *Chuck Hagel: Moving Forward.* University of Nebraska, 2006.

Blair, Tony. *A Journey: My Political Life.* Knopf, 2010.

Blum, William. *Killing Hope: US Military and CIA Interventions Since World War II.* Common Courage, 2008.

Borjesson, Kristina, ed. *Into the Buzzsaw: Leading Journalists Expose the Myth of a Free Press.* Prometheus, 2002.

Bowen, Russell S. *The Immaculate Deception: The Bush Crime Family Exposed.* America West, 1991.

Bowman, Matthew. *The Mormon People: The Making of an American Faith.* Random House, 2012.

Bracken, Len. *The Arch Conspirator.* Adventures Unlimited, 1999.

Bravin, Jess. *The Terror Courts: Rough Justice at Guantanamo Bay.* Yale University, 2013.

Bremer, L. Paul. *My Year in Iraq: The Struggle to Build a Future of Hope.* Simon & Schuster, 2006.

Bringhurst, Newell C. *Reconsidering No Man Knows My History.* Utah State University, 1996.

———— *Fawn M. Brodie: A Biographer's Life.* University of Oklahoma, 1999.

———— *Brigham Young and the Expanding America Frontier.* Little, Brown, 1986.

Briody, Dan. *The Iron Triangle: Inside the Secret World of the Carlyle Group.* Wiley, 2003.

Broadwell, Paula, with Vernon Loeb. *All In: The Education of General David Petraeus.* Penguin, 2012.

Brock, David. *The Republican Noise Machine.* Crown, 2004.

———— *Blinded by the Right.* Crown, 2002.

———— *The Real Anita Hill.* Free Press, 1994.

Brodie, Fawn M. *No Man Knows My History: The Life of Joseph Smith.* Vintage, 1995 (1945).

Brooks, Juanita. *The Mountain Meadows Massacre.* University of Oklahoma, 1991.

Brown, Peter Harry, and Pat H. Broeske. *Howard Hughes: The Untold Story.* Da Capo, 1996.

Bryant, Nick. *The Franklin Scandal: A Story of Powerbrokers, Child Abuses and Betrayal.* TrineDay, 2009.

Brzezinski, Zbigniew. *The Grand Chessboard.* Basic, 1998.

———— *Power and Principle: Memoirs of the National Security Adviser 1977-1981.* Farrar, Straus, Giroux, 1983.

Bugliosi, Vincent. *The Prosecution of George W. Bush for Murder.* Vanguard, 2008.

Bugliosi, Vincent, and Gerry Spence, *The Betrayal of America: How the Supreme Court Undermined the Constitution and Chose Our President.* Nation, 2001.

Burdick, Eugene, and William J. Lederer. *The Ugly American.* Norton, 1999 (1958).

Burke, Richard E., with William and Marilyn Hoffer. *The Senator: My Ten Years with Ted Kennedy.* St. Martin's, 1992.

Burleigh, Nina. *A Very Private Woman: The Life and Unsolved Murder of Presidential Mistress Mary Meyer*. Bantam, 1999.

Bush, Barbara. *Barbara Bush: A Memoir*. Scribner, 1994.

————— *Reflections*. Scribner, 2003.

Bush, George H. W. *All the Best: My Life in Letters and Other Writings*. Touchstone / Simon & Schuster, 1999.

Bush, George H. W., and Brent Scowcroft. *A World Transformed*. Knopf, 1998.

Bush, George, with Victor Gold. *Looking Forward*. Doubleday, 1987.

Bush, George W. *Decision Points*. Crown, 2010.

————— *A Charge to Keep*. William Morrow, 1999.

Bush, Laura. *Spoken from the Heart*. Scribner, 2010.

Cain, Herman. *This is Herman Cain! My Journey to the White House*. Regnery, 2011.

Calabresi, Guido, with Philip Bobbitt. *Tragic Choices: The conflicts society confronts in the allocation of tragically scarce resources*. Norton, 1978.

Cannon, Carl M., Lou Dubose, and Jan Rein. *Boy Genius: Karl Rove, The Architect of George W. Bush's Remarkable Political Triumphs*. Public Affairs, 2005.

Cantor, Eric, Paul Ryan, and Kevin McCarthy. *Young Guns: A New Generation of Conservative Leaders*. Threshhold, 2010.

Carney, Timothy P. *Obamanomics: How Barack Obama is Bankrupting You and Enriching His Wall Street Friends, Corporate Lobbyists, and Union Bosses*. Regnery, 2009.

Caro, Robert A. *The Passage of Power*. Knopf, 2012.

————— *The Years of Lyndon Johnson: The Master of the Senate*. Knopf, 2002.

————— *The Years of Lyndon Johnson: Means of Ascent*. Knopf, 1990.

————— *The Years of Lyndon Johnson: The Path to Power*. Knopf, 1982.

Carter, Jimmy. *White House Diary*. Farrar, Straus & Giroux, 2010.

Cashill, Jack. *Deconstructing Obama: The Life, Loves, and Letters of America's First Postmodern President.* Threshold, 2009.

Chaudhary, Arun. *First Cameraman: Documenting the Obama Presidency in Real Time*. Times, 2012.

Charnin, Richard. *Matrix of Deceit*. CreateSpace, 2012.

Cheney, Dick. *In My Time: A Personal and Political Memoir*. Threshold, 2011.

Chernow Ron. *The House of Morgan: An American Banking Dynasty and the Rise of Modern Finance*. Atlantic Monthly, 1990.

Clark, Wesley. *Winning Modern Wars: Iraq, Terrorism, and the American Empire*. Public Affairs, 2003.

Clarke, Richard A. *Against All Enemies: Inside America's War on Terror*. Free Press, 2004.

Clinton, Bill. *Back To Work: Why We Need Smart Government for a Strong Economy*. Knopf, 2011.

————— *My Life*. Knopf. 2004.

————— *Between Hope and History: Meeting America's Challenges For the 21st Century*. Times. 1996.

Clinton, Bill, and Al Gore. *Putting People First: How We Can All Change America*. Times Books. 1992.

Clinton, Hillary. *Living History*. Scribner, 2003.

————— *It Takes a Village*. Simon & Schuster, 1996.

Cloud, David, and Greg Jaffe. *The Fourth Star: Four Generals and the Epic Struggle for the Future of the United States Army*. Random House, 2009.

Cohen, Eliot A. *Supreme Command: Soldiers, Statesmen, and Leadership in Wartime*. Anchor, 2003.

Coll, Steve. *The Bin Ladens: An Arabian Family in the American Century*. Penguin, 2008.

Collier, Peter, and David Horowitz. *The Rockefellers: An American Dynasty*. Holt, Rinehart & Winston, 1976.

Conason, Joe, and Gene Lyons. *The Hunting of the President: The Ten-Year Campaign to Destroy Bill and Hillary Clinton*. Thomas Dunne Books, 2000.

Corn, David. *Showdown: The Inside Story of How Obama Fought Back Against Boehner, Cantor, and the Tea Party*. William Morrow & Company, 2012.

Corsi, Jerome R. *Where's the Birth Certificate: The Case that Barack Obama is Not Eligible to be President*. WND Books, 2011.

——— *The Obama Nation: Leftist Politics and the Cult of Personality*. Simon & Schuster, 2008.

Crier, Catherine. *Patriot Acts: What Americans Must Do to Save the Republic*. Threshold, 2011.

——— *Contempt: How the Right Is Wronging American Justice*. Rugged Land, 2005.

Curran, Eddie. *The Governor of Goat Hill*. I Universe, 2010.

Curtis, Clint. *Just A Fly On The Wall*. Clint Curtis, 2004.

Davis, Deborah. *Katharine the Great*. Sheridan Square, 1991. (1983, Harcourt Brace Jovanovich, withdrawn.)

De Bellaigue, Christopher. *Patriot of Persia: Muhammad Mossadegh and a Tragic Anglo-American Coup*. Harper, 2012.

Dean, Howard. *Howard Dean's Prescription for Real Healthcare Reform*. Chelsea Green Publishing, 2009.

——— *You Have the Power: How to Take Back Our Country and Restore Democracy in America*. Simon & Schuster, 2004.

Dean, John. *Conservatives Without a Conscience*. Viking, 2006.

——— *Broken Government: How Republican Rule Destroyed the Legislative, Executive, and Judicial Branches*. Viking / Penguin, 2007.

DeLozier, Abbe Waldman, and Vickie Karp. *Hacked! High Tech Election Theft in America — 11 Experts Expose the Truth*. Truth Enterprises, 2006.

Denton, Sally. *The Plots Against the President*. Bloomsbury, 2012.

——— *American Massacre: The Tragedy at Mountain Meadows, September 1857*. Vintage, 2004.

——— *The Bluegrass Conspiracy: An Inside Story of Power, Greed, Drugs and Murder*. Doubleday, 1990.

Denton, Sally, and Roger Morris. *The Money and the Power: The Making of Las Vegas and Its Hold on America*. Vintage, 2002.

Dershowitz, Alan. *Supreme Injustice: How the High Court Hijacked Election 2000*. Oxford University, 2001.

Dickson, Paul. *Sputnik: The Shock of the Century*. Walker, 2001.

Domhoff, William G. *The Higher Circles*. Vintage, 1971.

——— *Who Rules America? Challenges to Corporate and Class Dominance*. McGraw-Hill, 6th ed., 2009 (1970).

Dorgan, Byron L. *Take This Job and Ship It: How Corporate Greed and Brain-Dead Politics are Selling Out America*. Thomas Dunne / St. Martins, 2006.

Douglas, William O. *Go East, Young Man: The Early Years*. Delta / Dell, 1974.

———— *The Court Years: 1939-1975*. Random House, 1980.

Douglass, James W. *JFK and the Unspeakable*. Orbis, 2008.

Doyle, Arthur Conan, with annotations by Leslie S. Klinger. *The New Annotated Sherlock Holmes: The Novels (A Study in Scarlet, The Sign of Four, The Hound of the Baskervilles, The Valley of Fear)*. Norton, 2005. *A Study in Scarlet* was first published in magazine form in 1887, and as a book in 1888.

D'Souza, Dinesh. *The Roots of Obama's Rage*. Regnery, 2010.

Duffy, Michael, and Dan Goodgame. *Marching in Place: The Status Quo Presidency of George Bush*. Simon & Schuster, 1992.

Dulles, Allen W. *The Craft of Intelligence: America's Legendary Spy Master on the Fundamentals of Intelligence Gathering for a Free World*. Lyons, 2006.

Dunham, Ann S. *Surviving Against the Odds: Village Industry in Indonesia*. Duke University Press, 2009.

Edmonds, Sibel. *Classified Woman, The Sibel Edmonds Story: A Memoir*. Boiling Frogs, 2012.

Engelhardt, Tom. *The United States of Fear*. Haymarket, 2011.

Estulin, Daniel. *Deconstructing WikiLeaks*. TrineDay, 2012.

———— *The True Story of the Bilderberg Group*. TrineDay, 2009.

Evans-Pritchard, Ambrose. *The Secret Life of Bill Clinton*. Regnery, 1997.

Evelyn, Douglas E., and Paul Dickson. *On This Spot: Pinpointing the Past in Washington, DC*. Capital, 2008.

Fang, Lee. *The Machine: A Field Guide to the Resurgent Right*. New Press, 2013.

Fein, Bruce. *The American Empire Before The Fall*. CreateSpace, 2010.

Ferguson, Niall. *The House of Rothschild: Money's Prophets 1849-1999*. Viking, 1999.

———— *The House of Rothschild: Money's Prophets 1798-1848*. Viking, 1998.

Firstbrook, Peter. *The Obamas: The Untold Story of an African Family*. Crown, 2011.

Fitrakis, Bob, and Harvey Wasserman. *How the GOP Stole America's 2004 Election & Is Rigging 2008*, Columbus Institute for Contemporary Journalism, 2005.

Fitrakis, Bob, Steve Rosenfeld, and Harvey Wasserman, eds. *Did George W. Bush Steal America's 2004 Election? Essential Documents*, Columbus Institute for Contemporary Journalism, 2005.

———— *What Happened in Ohio: A Documentary Record of Theft And Fraud in the 2004 Election, New Press,* 2006.

Foskett, Ken, *Judging Thomas: The Life and Times of Clarence Thomas*, William Morrow/Harper Collins, 2004.

Foster, Craig. *A Different God? Mitt Romney, the Religious Right, and the Mormon Question*. Greg Kofford, 2008.

Frank, Justin A. *Obama on the Couch: Inside the Mind of the President*. FreePress, 2011.

———— *Bush on the Couch Inside the Mind of the President*. HarperCollins, 2004.

Frazier, Mondo. *The Secret Life of Barack Hussein Obama*. Threshold/Simon & Schuster, 2011.

Freeland, Chrystia. *Plutocrats: The Rise of the New Global Super-Rich and the Fall of Everyone Else*. Penguin, 2012.

Freeman, Steven F., and Joel Bleifuss. *Was the 2004 Presidential Election Stolen?: Exit Polls, Election Fraud, and the Official Count*. Seven Stories Press, 2006.

Frum, David, and Richard N. Perle. *An End to Evil: How to Win the War on Terror*. Random House, 2003.

Fuller, Jack. *What Is Happening To News: The Information Explosion and the Crisis in Journalism*. University of Chicago, 2010.

Fund, John. *Stealing Elections: How Voter Fraud Threatens Our Democracy*, Encounter, 2008.

Gellman, Barton. Angler. *The Cheney Vice Presidency*. Penguin, 2008.

Gerken, Heather K. *The Democracy Index: Why Our Election System Is Failing and How to Fix It*. Princeton University, 2009.

Goeglein, Timothy S. *The Man in the Middle: An Inside Account of Faith and Politics in the George W. Bush Era*. B& H, 2011.

Goldsmith, Jack. *Power and Constraint: The Accountable Presidency After 9/11*. Norton, 2012.

———— *The Terror Presidency: Law and Judgment Inside the Bush Administration*. Norton, 2007.

Goodale, James C. *Fighting for the Press: The Inside Story of the Pentagon Papers and Other Battles*. CUNY Journalism, 2013.

Goodwin, Jan. *Price of Honor: Muslim Women Life the Veil of Silence on the Islamic World*. Penguin/Plume, 1994.

Gore, Al. *Earth in the Balance: Ecology and the Human Spirit*. Plume, 1992.

Gottlieb, Robert, and Peter Wiley. *America's Saints: Rise of Mormon Power*. Harvest / HBJ, 1986.

Gould, Lewis J. *The Most Exclusive Club: A History of the Modern United States Senate*. Basic Books, 2009.

Graham, Bob. *Keys to the Kingdom*. Vanguard, 2011.

———— *Intelligence Matters: The CIA, The FBI, Saudi Arabia, and The Failure of America's War on Terror*. Random House, 2004.

Graham, Katharine. *Personal History*. Knopf, 1997.

Gray, Robert Keith. *Presidential Perks Gone Royal: Your Taxes Are Being Used for Obama's Reelection*. New Voices. 2012.

Green, John Robert. *The Presidency of George Bush*. University Press of Kansas, 2000.

Greider, William. *Who Will Tell the People? The Betrayal of American Democracy*. Simon & Schuster, 1992.

Greene, Graham. *Our Man in Havana*. Penguin Classics, 2007 (1959).

———— *The Quiet American*. Penguin Classics, 2004 (1955).

Greenwald, Glenn. *With Liberty and Justice for Some*. Metropolitan, 2011.

———— *Great American Hypocrites*. Three Rivers, 2008.

———— *A Tragic Legacy: How a Good vs. Evil Mentality Destroyed the Bush Presidency*. Crown, 2007.

———— *How Would a Patriot Act? Defending American Values from a President Run Amok*. Working Assets, 2006.

Griffin, David Ray. *9/11: When State Crimes Against Democracy Succeed*. Olive Branch, 2011.

———— *Cognitive Infiltration: An Obama Appointee's Plan to Undermine the 9/11 Conspiracy Theory*. Olive Branch, 2011.

Grof, Stanislav. *Beyond the Brain: Birth, Death, and Transcendence in Psychotherapy*. State University of New York, 1985.

Grossman, Mark. *Political Corruption in America: An Encyclopedia of Scandals, Power, and Greed*. ABC-CLIO, 2003.

Gugliotta, Guy, and Jeff Leen. *Kings of Cocaine: An Astonishing Story of Murder, Money and Corruption*. Harper and Collins, 1990.

Hamburger, Tom, and Peter Wallsten. *One Party Country: The Republican Plan for Dominance in the 21st Century*. Wiley. 2006.

Harr, John Ensor, and Peter J. Johnson. *The Rockefeller Conscience: An American Family in Public and in Private*. Charles Scribner's Sons, 1992.

———— *The Rockefeller Century: Three Generations of America's Greatest Family*. Charles Scribner's Sons, 1988.

Harris, Bev, with David Allen. *Black Box Voting: Ballot-tampering* in the 21st Century. Plan Nine, 2003.

Harris, Frank. *My Life and Loves*. Grove, 1963, (1925).

Harris, Shane. *The Watchers: The Rise of America's Surveillance State*. Penguin, 2011.

Hartmann, Thom. *Screwed: The Undeclared War Against the Middle Class – And What We Can Do About It*. Berrett-Koehler, 2006.

Harwood, John, and Gerald F. Seib. *Pennsylvania Avenue: Profiles in Backroom Power: Making Washington Work Again*. Random House, 2008.

Hastings, Michael. *Panic: 2012 -The Sublime and Terrifying Inside Story of Obama's Final Campaign*. BuzzFeed/Blue Rider, 2013.

———— *The Operators: The Wild and Terrifying Inside Story of America's War in Afghanistan*. Plume, 2012.

Hedges, Chris. *American Fascists: The Christian Right and the War on America*. Free Press, 2006.

Heilemann, John, and Mark Halperin. *Game Change: Obama and the Clintons, McCain and Palin, and the Race of a Lifetime*. HarperCollins, 2010.

Herrnson, Paul S., Niemi, Richard G., Hanmer, Michael J., Bederson, Benjamin B., Conrad, Frederick C., and Traugott, Michael W. *Voting Technology: The Not-So-Simple Act of Casting a Ballot*, Brookings Institution, 2008.

Hersh, Seymour M. *The Samson Option: Israel's Nuclear Arsenal and American Foreign Policy*. Random House, 1991.

———— *The Price of Power: Kissinger in the Nixon White House*. Summit, 1983.

Herskowitz, Mickey. *Duty, Honor, Country: The Life and Legacy of Prescott Bush*. Rutledge Hill, 2003.

Hettena, Seth. *Feasting on the Spoils: The Life and Times of Randy "Duke" Cunningham, History's Most Corrupt Congressman*. St. Martin's, 2007.

Hettman, Seth. *Feasting on the Spoils: The Life and Times of Randy "Duke" Cunningham, History's Most Corrupt Congressman*. St. Martin's, 2007.

Hewitt, Hugh. *A Mormon in the White House? 10 Things Every American Should Know About Mitt Romney*. Regnery, 2007.

Hines, Phillip. *Mitt Romney in His Own Words*. Threshold, 2012.

Hoover, J. Edgar. *Masters of Deceit: The Story of Communism in America and How to Fight It*. Henry Holt, 1958.

Hopsicker, Daniel. *Barry & 'The Boys': The CIA, the Mob and America's Secret History*. Trine Day, 2006.

———— *Welcome To Terrorland: Mohamed Atta & The 9-11 Cover-up in Florida*. Mad Cow Press, 2004.

Hyams, Joe. *Flight of the Avenger: George Bush at War*. Harcourt, Brace Jovanovich, 1991.

Iglesias, David, with David Seay. *In Justice: Inside the Scandal that Rocked the Bush Administration*. Wiley, 2008.

Isikoff, Michael, and David Corn. *Hubris: The Inside Story of Spin, Scandal, and the Selling of the Iraq War*. Broadway, 2007.

Issacson, Walter. *Kissinger*. Simon & Schuster, 1992.

Jacobs, Sally H. *The Other Barack: The Bold and Reckless Life of President Obama's Father.* Public Affairs, 2011.

Janovic, Matthew Henry. *Let the Dead Bury the Dead: A DC Madam Account.* Trithemius, 2012.

Janney, Peter. *Mary's Mosaic: The CIA Conspiracy to Murder John F. Kennedy, Mary Pinchot Meyer, and Their Vision of World Peace.* Skyhorse, 2012.

Jarlett, Franklin. *Robert Ryan.* McFarland, 1990.

Jeffords, James M., with Yvonne Daley and Howard Coffin. *An Independent Man: Adventures of a Public Servant.* Simon & Schuster, 2003.

Johnston, David Cay. *Perfectly Legal: The Covert Campaign to Rig Our Tax System to Benefit the Super Rich, and Cheat Everybody Else.* Portfolio, 2003.

Kagan, Robert. *The World America Made.* Knopf. 2012.

Kahin, Audrey R., and George McT. Kahin. *Subversion As Foreign Policy. The Secret Eisenhower and Dulles Debacle In Indonesia.* New Press, 1995.

Kaiser, Robert G., *So Damn Much Money: The Triumph of Lobbying and the Corrosion of American Government.* Knopf, 2009.

Kantor, Jodi. *The Obamas.* Little, Brown, 2012.

Kaplan, Fred. *The Insurgents: David Petraeus and the Plot to Change the American Way of War.* Simon & Schuster, 2013.

Keisling, William. *The Midnight Ride Of Jonathan Luna.* Yardbird, 2005.

Kelley, Kitty. *The Family: The Real Story of the Bush Dynasty.* Doubleday, 2004.

Kelly, Tom. *Imperial Post.* William Morrow, 1983.

Kengor, Paul. *The Communist: Frank Marshall Davis: The Untold Story of Barack Obama's Mentor.* Threshold, 2012.

Kennedy, John F. *A Nation of Immigrants.* Harper Perennial, 2008 (1964, expanded from a 1958 treatise).

———— *Profiles in Courage.* Harper Perennial, 2006 (1955).

———— *Why England Slept.* Harper Perennial, 2008 (1940.

Kerik, Bernard B. *The Lost Son: A Life in Pursuit of Justice.* ReganBooks, 2001.

Kert, Bernice. *Abby Aldrich Rockefeller: The Woman in the Family.* Random House, 1993.

Khrushchev, Nikita, with Edward Crankshaw, Jerrold Schecter, and Strobe Talbot. *Khrushchev Remembers: The Last Testament,* Little Brown, 1974.

———— with Edward Crankshaw, and Strobe Talbot. *Khrushchev Remembers,* Little Brown, 1970.

Kimball, Penn. *The File.* Harcourt Brace Jovanovich, 1983.

Kiriakou, John. *The Reluctant Spy: My Secret Life in the CIA's War on Terror.* Bantam, 2010.

Kitson, Frank. *Low Intensity Operations: Subversion, Insurgency, Peace-Keeping.* Shoe String, 1974.

Klaidman. Daniel. *Kill or Capture: The War on Terror and the Soul of the Obama Presidency.* Houghton Mifflin Harcourt, 2012.

Klein, Edward. *The Amateur.* Regnery, 2012.

Klein, Mark. *Wiring Up the Big Brother Machine...And Fighting It.* Booksurge, 2009.

Klein, Naomi. *The Shock Doctrine: The Rise of Disaster Capitalism.* Metropolitan, 2007.

Klepper, Michael and Robert Gunther. *The Wealthy 100: From Benjamin Franklin to Bill Gates: A Ranking of the Richest Americans, Past and Present.* Citadel, 1996.

Koch, Charles G. *The Science of Success: How Market-Base Management Built the World's Largest Private Company.* Wiley, 2007.

Koszczuk, Jackie and Martha Angel, editors. *Politics in America*, Congressional Quarterly Staff, Congressional Quarterly, 2007, *et seq.*

Krakauer, Jon. *Where Men Win Glory: The Odyssey of Pat Tillman.* Doubleday, 2009.

———— *Under the Banner of Heaven: A Story of Violent Faith.* Doubleday, 2003.

Kranish, Michael and Scott Helman. *The Real Romney*, Harper, 2012.

Kreig, Andrew. *Spiked: How Chain Management Corrupted America's Oldest Newspaper.* Peregrine, 1987.

Kreig, Margaret. *Black Market Medicine.* Prentice Hall, 1967.

———— *Green Medicine: The Search for the Plants that Heal.* Rand McNally, 1963.

Krugman, Paul. *End This Depression Now!* Norton, 2012.

———— *The Great Unraveling: Losing Our Way in the New Century.* Norton, 2009.

Kunen, James Simon. *The Strawberry Statement: Notes of a College Revolutionary.* Avon, 1970.

Kurtz, Howard. *Media Circus: The Trouble with America's Newspapers.* Times Books, 1994.

Lane, Mark. *Plausible Denial: Was the CIA Involved in the Assassination of JFK?* Skyhorse, 2011 (1991).

Larsson, Stieg. *The Girl with the Dragon Tattoo.* Random House/Vintage, 2008.

Lazarus, Edward. *Closed Chambers: The Rise, Fall and Future of the Modern Supreme Court.* Times Books, 1998, Penguin, 1999.

Lederer, William J. *A Nation of Sheep.* Norton, 1961.

Lehr, Dick, and Gerard O'Neill. *Black Mass: The Irish Mob, the FBI and the Devil's Deal.* Public Affairs, 2000.

Lessig, Lawrence. *Republic, Lost: How Money Corrupts Congress--and a Plan to Stop It.* Twelve, 2011.

———— *The Future of Ideas: The Fate of the Commons in a Connected World.* Random House, 2001.

Lewis, Charles, and the Center for Public Integrity. *The Buying of the President 2000*, Avon, 2000.

———— *The Buying of the Congress.* Avon, 1998.

Lichtblau, Eric. *Bush's Law: The Remaking of American Justice.* Pantheon, 2008.

Limbaugh, David. *Crimes Against Liberty: An Indictment of President Barack Obama.* Regnery, 2010.

Lindauer, Susan. *Extreme Prejudice: The Terrifying Story of the Patriot Act and the Cover-ups of 9/11 and Iraq.* Create Space, 2010.

Lipton, Bruce H., and Steve Bhaerman. *Spontaneous Evolution: Our Positive Future and a Way to Get There From Here.* Hay House, 2010.

Loftus, John, and Mark Aarons. *The Secret War Against the Jews.* St. Martin's Press, 1994.

Loughman, Brian P., and Richard A. Sibery. *Bribery and Corruption.* Ernst & Young LLP, 2012.

Lyons, Gene, and the Editors of Harper's Magazine. *Fools for Scandal: How the Media Invented Whitewater.* Franklin Square Press, 1996.

MacArthur, John R. *The Selling of Free Trade: NAFTA, Washington, and the Subversion of American Democracy.* University of California, 1992.

———— *Second Front: Censorship and Propaganda in the Gulf War.* University of California. 1992.

Madsen, Wayne. *L'Affaire Petraeus: The Benghazi Stand-down and the Plot To "Carterize" Obama.* WMR / Lulu, Dec. 5, 2012.

——— *The Manufacturing of a President: The CIA's Insertion of Barack H. Obama, Jr. Into the White House.* WMR / Lulu, 2012.

——— *Decade of Death: Secret Wars and Genocide in Africa 1993-2003.* WMR/Lulu, 2012 (Edwin Mellen first edition, entitled, *Genocide and Covert Operations in Africa, 1993-1999,* 1999).

——— *Jaded Tasks: The Blood Politics of George Bush & Co.* Trine Day, 2006.

——— *Forbidden Truth: U.S.-Taliban Secret Oil Diplomacy, Saudi Arabia and the Failed Search for bin Laden.* Nation Books, 2002.

——— *Handbook of Personal Data Protection.* Macmillan, 1992.

Mahoney, Tom. *The Story of George Romney: Builder, Salesman, Crusader.* Harper, 1960.

Mann, James. *Rise of the Vulcans. The History of Bush's War Cabinet.* Penguin, 2004.

Mann, Thomas E., and Norman J. Ornstein. *It's Even Worse Than It Looks: How the American Constitutional System Collided with the New Politics of Extremism.* Basic, 2012.

Mansi, Stephen. *The Mormonizing of America: How the Mormon Religion Became a Dominant Force in Politics, Entertainment and Pop Culture.* Worthy, 2012.

Mapes, Mary. *Truth and Duty: The Press, the President and the Privilege of Power.* St. Martin's / Griffin, 2006.

Maraniss, David. *Barack Obama: The Story.* Simon & Schuster, June 19, 2012.

——— *Bill Clinton: First in His Class.* Touchstone / Simon & Schuster, 1996.

Marchetti, Victor, and John D. Marks. *The CIA and the Cult of Intelligence.* Knopf, 1974.

Martin, Al. *The Conspirators: Secrets of an Iran-Contra Insider.* National Liberty, 2002.

Mayer, Jane. *The Dark Side: The Inside Story of How the War on Terror Turned Into a War on American Ideals.* Random House/Anchor, 2009.

Mayer, Jane, and Jill Abramson. *Strange Justice: The Selling of Clarence Thomas.* Houghton Mifflin, 1994.

Mazzetti, Mark. *The Way of the Knife: The CIA, a Secret Army, and a War at the Ends of the Earth.* Penguin, 2013.

McCain, John, and Mark Salter. *Worth the Fighting For.* Random House, 2002.

——— *Faith of My Fathers.* Random House, 1999.

McEwen, Lillian. *DC Unmasked and Undressed.* TitleTown, 2011.

McGehee, Ralph W. *Deadly Secrets: My 25 Years in the CIA.* Sheridan Square, 1983.

McGinniss, Joe. *The Rogue: Searching for the Real Sarah Palin.* Crown, 2011.

Mendell, David. *Obama: From Promise to Power.* Amistad/Harper Collins, 2007.

Merida, Kevin, and Michael Fletcher. *Supreme Discomfort: The Divided Soul of Clarence Thomas.* Broadway, 2008.

Merriner, James. *The Second Fraud: How Does the Government Clean Up a Multi-Billion Dollar Mess?* Hillside Productions electronic-book and video, 2010.

Miller, Mark Crispin. *Fooled Again.* Basic Books, 2005.

Miller, Mark Crispin, ed. *Loser Take All: Election Fraud and The Subversion of Democracy, 2000 – 2008.* IG Publishing, 2008.

Millegan, Kris, ed. *Fleshing Out Skull & Bones: Investigations into America's Most Powerful Secret Society.* Trine Day.

Mills, C. Wight. *The Power Elite.* Oxford University, 1956.

Mintz, Morton, and Jerry S. Cohen. *America Inc.: Who Owns and Operates the United States.* Dial, 1971.

Minutaglio, Bill. *The President's Counselor: The Rise to Power of Alberto Gonzales*. Harper Collins, 2006.

———— *First Son*. Times Books, 1999.

Mitchell, Elizabeth. *W -- Revenge of the Bush Dynasty*. Hyperion, 2000.

Mitgang, Herbert. *Dangerous Dossiers: Exposing the Secret War Against America's Greatest Authors*. Ballantine, 1989.

Minnite, Lorraine. *The Myth of Voter Fraud*. Cornell University, 2010.

Morgenson, Gretchen, and Joshua Rosner. *Reckless Endangerment: How Outsized Ambition, Greed and Corruption Led to Economic Armageddon*. Times, 2011.

Moldea, Dan. *Dark Victory: Ronald Reagan, MCA, and the Mob*. Viking Penguin, 1986.

Mollenhoff, Clark R. *Washington Cover-Up*. Doubleday, 1962.

———— *The President Who Failed: Carter Out of Control*. MacMillan, 1980.

———— *George Romney: Mormon in Politics*. Meredith, 1968.

Moore, James, and Wayne Slater. *The Architect: Karl Rove and the Master Plan for Absolute Power*. Crown, 2006.

Morris, Richard B., ed., *Encyclopedia of American History Bicentennial Edition*. Harper and Row, 1976.

Morris, Roger. *Partners in Power*. John McRae / Henry Holt, 1996.

Multon, Joyce. *The First Partner: Hillary Rodham Clinton*. William Morris, 1999.

Nader, Ralph. *The Seventeen Traditions*. HarperCollins, 2007.

———— *The Good Fight: Declare Your Independence and Close the Democracy Gap*. HarperCollins, 2004.

Naifeh, Steven, and Gregory White Smith. *The Mormon Murders: A True Story of Greed, Forgery, Deceit, and Death*. St. Martin's, 1988.

Napolitano, Andrew P. *Constitutional Chaos: What Happens When the Government Breaks Its Own Laws*. Thomas Nelson, 2004.

Ney, Robert W. *Sideswiped: Lessons Learned Courtesy of the Hit Men of Capitol Hill*. Changing Lives, 2013.

Norquist, Grover Glenn. *Debacle: Obama's War on Jobs and Growth and What We Can Do Now to Regain Our Future*. John Wiley, 2012.

———— *Leave Us Alone: Getting the Governments Hands Off Our Money, Our Guns, Our Lives*. Morrow, 2008.

Obama, Barack. *The Audacity of Hope: Thoughts on Reclaiming the American Dream*. Crown, 2006.

———— *Dreams from my Father: A Story of Race and Inheritance*. Crown, 1995.

Ogden, Christopher. *Life of the Party: The Biography of Pamela Digby Churchill Hayward Harriman*. Little, Brown, 1994.

O'Neill, John E., and Jerome R. Corsi. *Unfit for Command: Swift Boat Veterans Speak Out about John Kerry*. Regnery, 2004.

Orwell, George. *Animal Farm*. 1945. Secker and Warburg, 1945 (United Kingdom).

Orwell, George. *1984*. Secker and Warburg, 1949 (United Kingdom).

———— *The Collected Essays, Journals and Letters* (Four Vols.), Harcourt, Brace & World, Inc., 1968.

Overton, Spencer, *Stealing Democracy: The New Politics of Voter Suppression*. Norton, 2006.

Palast, Greg, with Comics by Ted Rall and Introduction by Robert F. Kennedy, Jr. *Billionaires and Ballots: How To Steal An Election in 9 Easy Steps*. Seven Stories, 2012.

Palast, Greg, *Vultures Picnic: In Pursuit of Petroleum Pigs, Power Pirates, and High-Finance Carnivores*. Dutton, 2011.

—— *Armed Madhouse*. Dutton, 2006.

—— *The Best Democracy Money Can Buy*. Plume / Penguin, 2004.

Parks, Sheila. *While We Still Have Time: The Perils Of Electronic Voting Machines and Democracy's Solution* — Publicly Observed, Secure Hand-Counted Paper Ballots Elections. Create Space, 2012.

Parmet, Herbert S. *George Bush: Life of a Lone Star Yankee*. Lisa Drew/Scribner, 1996.

Parry, Robert, Sam Parry, and Nat Parry. *Neck Deep: The Disastrous Presidency of George W. Bush*. Media Consortium, 2007.

Parry, Robert. *Secrecy & Privilege: Rise of the Bush Dynasty from Watergate to Iraq*. Media Consortium, 2004.

—— *Lost History: Contras, Cocaine, the Press & "Project Truth."* Media Consortium, 1999.

—— *Fooling America: How Washington Insiders Twist the Truth and Manufacture Convention Wisdom*. Morrow, 1992.

Perloff, James. *The Shadows of Power: The Council on Foreign Relations and the American Decline*. Western Islands, 1988.

Perkins, John. *Hoodwinked: An Economic Hit Man Reveals Why the World Financial Markets Imploded — and What We Need to Do to Remake*. Crown Business, 2011.

—— *The Secret History of the American Empire: Economic Hit Men, Jackals, and the Truth about Global Corruption*. Dutton, 2007.

—— *Confessions of an Economic Hit Man*. Penguin, 2004. Plume,2006.

Perot, H. Ross. *United We Stand: How We Can Take Back Our Country*. Hyperion, 1992

Peterson, Peter G. *Running on Empty: How the Democratic and Republican Parties Are Bankrupting Our Future and What Americans Can Do About It*. Picador, 2005.

Petraeus, David H., and James F. Amos. *U.S. Army U.S. Marine Corps Counterinsurgency Field Manual*. Edited by John C. McClure. Signalman, 2009.

Phillips, Kevin. *American Dynasty: Aristocracy. Fortune. And the Politics of Deceit in the House of Bush*. Viking, 2004.

Polmar, Norman, and Thomas B. Allen. *Spy Book: the Encyclopedia of Espionage*. Random House, 2004.

Powell, Colin, with Joseph E. Persico. *My American Journey*. Random House, 1995.

Power, Samantha. *A Problem From Hell: American and the Age of Genocide*. Perseus /Basic, 2002.

Press, Bill. *The Obama Hate Machine: The Lies, Distortions, and Personal Attacks on the President —and Who Is Behind Them*. St. Martin's Griffin, 2012.

Priest, Dana, and William M. Arkin. *Top Secret America: The Rise of the New American Security State*. Little Brown, 2011.

Prouty, L. Fletcher. *JFK: The CIA, Vietnam, and the Plot to Assassinate John F. Kennedy*. Skyhorse, 2011 (1996.).

—— *The Secret Team: The CIA and Its Allies in Control of the United States and the World*. Skyhorse, 2008 (1973).

Quigley, Carroll. *Tragedy and Hope: A History of the World In Our Time*. Angriff, 1975.

—— *The Anglo-American Establishment*. G S G & Associates, 1981.

Quinn, D. Michael. *Early Mormonism and the Magic World View*. Signature, 1998.

Radack, Jesselyn A. *Traitor: The Whistleblower and the "American Taliban."* Whistleblower, 2012. (Previously published as *The Canary in the Coalmine*.)

Rand, Ayn. *The Fountainhead*. Signet, 1996 (1943).

Rather, Dan, with Digby Diehl. *Rather Outspoken: My Life in the News.* Grand Central, 2012.

Reagan, Ronald. *Ronald Reagan: An American Life.* Threshold/Simon & Schuster, 1990.

Redstone, Sumner, with Peter Knobler. *A Passion to Win.* Simon & Schuster, 2001.

Reed, Terry Kent, and John Cummings. *Compromised: Clinton, Bush and the CIA.* Shapolsky, 1994.

Reich, Cary. *The Life of Nelson A. Rockefeller: Worlds to Conquer 1908-1958.* Doubleday, 1996.

Remnick, David. *The Bridge: The Life and Rise of Barack Obama.* Knopf, 2010 (Vintage, 2011).

Rich, Frank. *Greatest Story Ever Told: Decline of the Truth from 9/11 to Katrina.* Penguin, 2006.

Richelson, Jeffrey T. *The US Intelligence Community.* Westview, 2011 (Sixth Ed.)

———— *A Century of Spies: Intelligence in the Twentieth Century.* Oxford University, 1997.

Ricks, Thomas E. *The Generals American Military Command from World War II to Today.* Penguin, 2012.

———— *The Gamble: General David Petraeus and the American Military Adventure in Iraq, 2006-2008.* Penguin, 2009.

———— *Fiasco: The American Military Adventure in Iraq, 2003 to 2005.* Penguin, 2007.

Risen, James. *State of War: The Secret History of the CIA and the Bush Administration.* Free Press/Simon & Schuster, 2006.

Roberts, Paul Craig, and Lawrence M. Stratton. *The Tyranny of Good Intentions: How Prosecutors and Law Enforcement Are Trampling the Constitution in the Name of Justice.* Forum/Prima, 2000.

Roberts, Robert North, and Marion T. Doss. *From Watergate to Whitewater: The Public Integrity War.* Greenwood, 1997.

Robbins, Alexandra. *Secrets of the Tomb: Skull and Bones, the Ivy League and the Secret Paths to Power.* Back Bay, 2002.

Robinson, Linda. *Tell Me How This Ends: General David Petraeus and the Search for a Way Out of Iraq.* PublicAffairs, 2008.

Rodriguez, Felix, and John Wiseman. *Shadow Warrior.* Simon & Schuster, 1989.

Robertson, Pat. *The New World Order.* W Publishing, 1992.

Rodriguez, José A. *Hard Measures: How Aggressive CIA Actions After 9/11 Saved American Lives.* Threshold/Simon & Schuster, 2012.

Rogers, Toby. *Ambushed: Secrets of the Bush Family, the Stolen Presidency, 9-11, and 2004.* TrineDay, 2004.

Rollins, Ed. *Bare Knuckles and Back Rooms.* Broadway, 1996.

Romney, George W. *The Concerns of a Citizen.* Putnam, 1968.

Romney, Mitt. *No Apology: The Case for American Greatness.* St. Martin's, 2010.

Romney, Mitt, with Timothy Robinson. *Turnaround: Crisis, Leadership, and the Olympic Games.* Regnery, 2004.

Romney, Thomas C. *Life Story of Miles P. Romney.* Zion, 1948.

Ronald Reagan Library. *Ronald Reagan: An American Hero : His Voice, His Values, His Vision.* Tehabi, 2002 (Limited Edition).Rosenfeld, Seth. *Subversives: The FBI's War on Student Radicals, and Reagan's Rise to Power.* Farrar, Straus and Giroux, 2012.

Rossum, Ralph A. *Antonin's Scalia's Jurisprudence: Text and Tradition.* University of Kansas, 2006.

Roth, David. *Sacred Honor: Colin Powell and the Insider Account of Life and Triumphs*. Zondervan, 1993.

Rove, Karl. *Courage and Consequence: My Life as a Conservative in the Fight*. Threshold, 2010.

Rumsfeld, Donald. *Known and Unknown: A Memoir*. Sentinel, 2011.

Russo, Gus. *Supermob: How Sidney Korshak and His Criminal Associates Became America's Hidden Power Brokers*. Bloomsbury, 2006.

Ryan, Cheyney. *The Chickenhawk Syndrome: War, Sacrifice, and Personal Responsibility*. Rowman and Littlefield, 2009.

St. Clair, Jeffrey, ed., with Joshua Frank, Kevin Alexander Gray, Kathy Kelly, Ralph Nader. *Hopeless: Barack Obama and the Politics of Illusion*. AK Press, 2012.

Sammon, Bill. *At Any Cost: How Al Gore Tried to Steal the Election*. Regnery, 2001.

Sanger, David E. *Confront and Conceal: Obama's Secret Wars and Surprising Use of American Power*. Crown, 2012.

Santorum, Rick. *It Takes a Family: Conservatism and the Common Good*. Intercollegiate Studies Institute, 2005.

————— *Rick Santorum*. Monument Press, 2005.

Saunders, Frances Stonor. *Cultural Cold War: The CIA and the World of Arts and Letters*. New Press, 2000.

Savage, Charlie. *Takeover: The Return of the Imperial Presidency and the Subversion of American Democracy*. Little, Brown, 2007.

Scahill, Jeremy. *Dirty Wars: The World Is A Battlefield*. Nation's Books, 2013.

Scheiber, Noam. *The Escape Artists: How Obama's Team Fumbled the Recovery*. Simon & Schuster, 2012.

Schoenfeld, Gabe. *Necessary Secrets: National Security, the Media, and the Rule of Law*. Norton, 2010.

Schroeder, Alice. *The Snowball: Warren Buffett and the Business of Life*. Bantam, 2008.

Schweizer, Peter. *Throw Them All Out*. Houghton Miflin Harcourt, 2011.

Schweizer, Peter, and Rochelle Schweizer. *The Bushes*. Doubleday, 2004.

Scott, Janny. *A Singular Woman: The Untold Story of Barack Obama' Mother*. Riverhead, 2011.

Scott, Peter Dale, and Jonathan Marshall. *Cocaine Politics: Drugs, Armies and the CIA in Central America*. University of California, 1998 (1992).

Scott, Ronald B. *Mitt Romney: An Inside Look at the Man and His Politics*. Lyons, 2012.

Shachtman, Tom. *Airlift to America: How Barack Obama, Sr., John F. Kennedy, Tom Mboya and 800 East African Students Changed Their World and Ours*. St. Martin's, 2009.

Shaffer, Anthony. *Operation Dark Heart: Spycraft and Special Ops on the Frontlines of Afghanistan — and the Path to Victory*. Thomas Dunne, 2012.

Shannon, Elaine, and Ann Blackman. *The Spy Next Door: The Extraordinary Secret Life of Robert Philip Hanssen, the Most Damaging FBI Agent in U.S. History*. Little, Brown, 2002.

Sharlett, Jeff. *C Street*. Little Brown, 2010.

————— *The Family*. Harper Collins, 2008.

Shipler, David K. *Rights at Risk: The Limits of Liberty in Modern America*. Knopf, 2012.

Skousen, W. Cleon. *The Naked Capitalist*. Buccaneer, 1970.

Sibley, Montgomery Blair. *Why Just Her: The Judicial Lynching of the D.C. Madam, Deborah Jeane Palfrey*. Full Court Press, 2009.

Sick, Gary. *October Surprise: America's Hostages in Iran and the Election of Ronald Reagan.* Crown, 1991.

Silverglate, Harvey A. *Three Felonies a Day: How the Feds Target the Innocent.* Encounter, 2009.

Simon, Jonathan. *Code Red: Computerized Elections and The New American Century.* Amazon Digital, 2012.

Simon, Paul. *Our Culture of Pandering.* Southern Illinois, 2003.

Smiley, Tavis, and Cornel West. *The Rich And The Rest Of Us: A Poverty Manifesto.* Smiley, 2012.

Smith, Adam, edited by R. H. Campbell and A. S. Skinner. *An Inquiry into the Nature and Causes of the Wealth of Nations.* Glasgow Edition of the Works and Correspondence of Adam Smith (2 vols.), Oxford University, 1976. First published in 1776.

Smith, Amanda. *Newspaper Titan: The infamous Life and Monumental Times of Cissy Patterson.* Knopf, 2011.

Smith, Jean Edward. *George Bush's War.* Henry Holt, 1992.

Smith, Sam. *Why Bother? Getting a Life in a Locked-down Land.* Federal House, 2001.

———— *Sam Smith's Great American Political Repair Manual.* Norton, 1997.

———— *Shadows of Hope: A Freethinkers Guide to Politics in the Time of Clinton.* Indiana University, 1994.

Solomon, Norman. *False Hope: the Politics of Illusion in the Clinton Era.* Common Courage, 1994.

Soufan, Ali H. *The Black Banners: The Inside Story of 9/11 and the War Against al-Qaeda.* Norton, 2012.

Spanier, John. *American Foreign Policy Since World War II.* Praeger, 1967.

Steele, Marta. *Grassroots, Geeks, Pros, and Pols.* Columbus Institute, 2012.

Stewart, David O. *American Emperor: Aaron's Burr's Challenge to Jefferson's America.* Simon & Schuster, 2011.

Stiglitz, Joseph E. *Globalization and Its Discontents.* Norton, 2002.

Stinnett, Robert B. *George Bush: His World War II Years.* Brassey's, 1992.

Stockman, David A. *The Great Deformation: The Corruption of Capitalism in America.* Public Affairs, 2013.

Stockwell, John. *In Search of Enemies: A CIA Story.* Norton, 1978.

Stone, Peter H. *Casino Jack and the United States of Money: Superlobbyist Jack Abramoff and the Buying of Washington.* Melville House, 2010.

Stuckler, David, and Sanjay Basu. *The Body Economic: Why Austerity Kills.* Basic, 2013.

Summers, Anthony. *Official and Confidential: The Secret life of J. Edgar Hoover.* Putnam's, 1993.

Summers, Anthony, and Robbyn Swan. *The Eleventh Day: The Full Story of 9/11 and Osama Bin Laden.* Ballantine, 2011.

———— *The Arrogance of Power: The Secret Life of Richard Nixon.* Viking, 2000.

Summers, Anthony, with Stephen Dorril. *Honeytrap.* Weidenfeld and Nicolson, 1987.

Suskind, Ron. *Confidence Men: Wall Street, Washington and the Education of a President.* HarperCollins, 2011.

———— *Price of Loyalty: George W. Bush, the White House, and the Education of Paul O'Neill.* Simon & Schuster, 2004.

Sutton, Antony C. *America's Secret Establishment: An Introduction to the Order of Skull & Bones.* TrineDay, 2004.

Swanson, David. *War Is a Lie.* Swanson, 2010.

———— *Daybreak: Undoing the Imperial Presidency and Forming a More Perfect Union.* Seven Stories, 2009.

Swarns, Rachel L. *American Tapestry: The Story of the Black, White and Multiracial Ancestors of Michelle Obama.* Amistad, 2012.

Tarpley, Webster G., and Chaitkin, Anton. *George Bush: The Unauthorized Biography.* Executive Intelligence, 1992.

Tarpley, Webster G. *Just Too Weird: Bishop Romney and the Mormon Takeover of America.* Progressive, 2012.

———— *Obama: The Postmodern Coup.* Progressive, 2008.

———— *Obama: The Unauthorized Biography.* Progressive, 2008.

Thomas, Clarence. *My Grandfather's Son: A Memoir.* HarperCollins, 2007.

Thomas, Helen, and Craig Crawford. *Listen Up, Mr. President.* Scribner / Simon & Schuster, 2009.

Tillman, Mary, with Narda Zacchino. *Boots on the Ground By Dusk: My Tribute to Pat Tillman.* Modern Times/Rodale, 2008.

Tonken, Aaron. *King of Cons: Exposing the Dirty Rotten Secrets of the Washington Elite and Hollywood Celebrities.* Nelson Current, 2004.

Timmerman, Kenneth R. *The Death Lobby: How the West Armed Iraq.* Houghton Mifflin, 1991.

Toobin, Jeffrey. *The Oath.* Random House, 2012.

———— *The Nine.* Anchor/Random House, 2008.

Trento, Joseph J. *Prelude To Terror: Edward P. Wilson and the Legacy of America's Private Intelligence Network.* Carroll and Graf, 2005.

———— *The Secret History of the CIA.* Basic, 2005.

Trento, Susan B. *The Power House: Robert Keith Gray and the Selling of Access and Influence in Washington.* St. Martin's, 1992.

———— *Unsafe at any Altitude: Failed Terrorism Investigations, Scapegoating 9/11, and the Shocking Truth about Aviation Security Today.* Steerforth, 2006.

Trepanier, Lee, and Lynita K. Newswander. *LDS in the USA: Mormonism and the Making of American Culture.* Baylor University, 2012.

Trippi, Joe. *The Revolution Will Not Be Televised.* ReganBooks, 2004.

Turner, Lisa Ray, and Kimberly Field. *Mitt Romney: The Man, His Values, and His Vision.* Mapletree, 2007.

Unger, Craig. *Boss Rove: Inside Karl Rove's Secret Kingdom of Power.* Scribner, 2012.

———— *House of Bush House of Saud: The Secret Relationship Between the World's Two Most Powerful Dynasties.* Scribner, 2004.

Unger, David C. *The Emergency State: America's Pursuit of Absolute Security at All Costs.* Penguin, 2012.

Van Buren, Peter. *We Meant Well: How I Helped Lose the Battle for the Hearts and Minds of the Iraqi People.* Metropolitan, 2012.

Van Wagoner, Richard S. *Mormon Polygamy: A History.* Signature, 1992.

Ventura, Jesse, and Dick Russell. *DemoCrips and ReBloodlicans: No More Gangs in Government.* Skyhorse, 2013.

———— *63 Documents the Government Doesn't Want You to Read.* Skyhorse, 2012.

————*American Conspiracies: Lies, Lies, and More Dirty Lies that the Government Tells Us.* Skyhorse, 2010.

Wallace, Irving. *The Prize.* Simon & Schuster, 1961.

Waller, Douglas. *Wild Bill Donovan: The Spymaster Who Created the OSS and Modern American Espionage.* Free Press, 2011.

Warren, Robert Penn. *All the King's Men*. Harcourt, Brace and Co., 1946.

Webb, Brandon, and Jack Murphy. *Benghazi: The Definitive Report*. William Morrow/HarperCollins, 2013.

Webb, Gary. *Dark Alliance: The CIA, the Contras, and the Crack Cocaine Explosion*. Seven Stories, 1998.

Wecht, Cyril H. *From Crime Scene to Courtroom: Examining the Mysteries Behind Famous Cases*. Prometheus, 2011.

——— *Mortal Evidence: The Forensics Behind Nine Shocking Cases*. Prometheus, 2003.

Wecht, Cyril H., Mark Curriden, and Benjamin Wecht. *Cause of Death: A Leading Forensic Expert Sets the Record Straight*. Dutton, 1993.

Wessel, David. *In Fed We Trust: Ben Bernanke's War on the Great Panic*. Crown Business, 2010.

Wicker, Tom. *George Herbert Walker Bush*. Viking, 2004.

Wilford, Hugh. *The Mighty Wurlitzer: How the CIA Played America*. Harvard University, 2008.

Wilson, Joseph C., IV. *The Politics of Truth: A Diplomat's Memoir: Inside the Lies that Led to War and Betrayed My Wife's CIA Identity*. Carroll & Graf, 2004.

Wilson, Valerie Plame. *Fair Game: My Life as a Spy, My Betrayal by the White House*. Simon & Schuster, 2007.

Winks, Robin. *Cloak and Gown: Scholars in the Secret War, 1939-1961*. William Morrow, 1987.

Wise, David. *Spy: The Inside Story of How the FBI's Robert Hanssen Betrayed America*. Random House, 2003.

Witcover, Jules. *Joe Biden: A Life of Trial and Redemption*. William Morrow, 2010.

Wolf, Naomi. *The End of America: Letter of Warning To a Young Patriot*, Chelsea Green, 2007.

Wolffe, Richard. *Renegade: The Making of a President*. Crown. 2009.

Woodward, Bob. *Bush at War*. Simon & Schuster, 2004.

——— *The Choice*. Simon & Schuster, 1996.

——— *The Agenda*. Simon & Schuster, 1992.

——— *Veil: The Secret Wars of the CIA, 1981-87*. Simon & Schuster, 1987.

Woodward, Bob, and Scott Armstrong. *The Brethren*. Simon & Schuster, 1979.

Worrall, Simon. *Cybergate: Was the White House Stolen By Cyberfraud?* Amazon Digital, 2012.

Zweigenhaft, Richard L., and G. William Domhoff. *Diversity in the Power Elite: How It Happened, Why It Matters*. Rowman & Littlefield, 2006.

Notes and Sources

Part I: How Our Imperial Presidency Imperils Us All

Chapter 1, Mitt Romney, Paul Ryan: Apprentice Oligarchs

[1] Jonathan Martin, Maggie Haberman, Anna Palmer, and Kenneth P. Vogel, "Herman Cain accused by two women of inappropriate behavior," *Politico*, October 31, 2011, http://www.politico.com/news/stories/1011/67194.html.

[2] Andrew Kreig, "Cain denies sexual harassment, touts tax plan, sings spiritual at Club luncheon," National Press Club, October 31, 2011, http://www.press.org/news-multimedia/news/cain-denies-sexual-harassment-touts-tax-plan-sings-spiritual-club-luncheon.

[3] Andrew Kreig, "Cain as Front Man for Billionaires is a Consumer Issue," Connecticut Watchdog, November 15, 2011, http://ctwatchdog.com/2011/11/15/cain-as-front-man-for-billionaires-is-a-consumer-issue.

[4] WAGA-TV via Huffington Post, "Herman Cain Suspending 2012 Campaign for President (VIDEO)," December. 3, 2011, http://www.huffingtonpost.com/2011/12/03/herman-cain-suspending-presidential-.campaign_n_1126331.html. See also, Sandhya Somashekhar, "Herman Cain says wife did not know of payments to alleged mistress Ginger White," *Washington Post*, December 1, 2011, http://www.washingtonpost.com/politics/herman-cain-says-wife-did-not-know-of-payments-to-alleged-mistress-ginger-white/2011/12/01/gIQAoQyLIO_story.html.

[5] The likely source for *Politico* was a rival GOP campaign for the nomination, not the 1990s victims under a non-disclosure agreement. Staff of the restaurant association (or their attorneys) had doubtless gossiped in confidence about the settlement for years. Washington opposition researchers make good livings warehousing that kind of information for sale at the right time to the right customer. Service typically includes help planting the story with a publication that will achieve wide display and will protect its source. Once the story was out, other women stepped forward, as this chronology indicates. However, there is no evidence that the two original litigants or any allies initiated the story. Staff Report, "Cain sells vision, denies harassment, sings spiritual," Herman Cain News Archive for Fall 2011, Justice Integrity Project, November 10, 2011, http://www.justice-integrity.org/faq/200-cain-sells-vision-denies-harassment-sings-spiritual.

[6] Clare O'Connor, "Herman Cain: I'm A Koch Brother From Another Mother," Forbes, November 4, 2011, http://www.forbes.com/sites/clareoconnor/2011/11/04/herman-cain-im-a-koch-brother-from-another-mother.

[7] Cain, Herman. *This is Herman Cain! My Journey to the White House*. Regnery, 2011.

[8] Chris Cillizza, "Herman Cain wins 'Worst week in Washington,'" *Washington Post*, November 19, 2011, http://www.washingtonpost.com/blogs/the-fix/post/herman-cain-wins-worst-week-in-washington/2011/11/19/gIQA63rPbN_blog.html.

[9] Amanda Terkel, "Sheldon Adelson Stands To Get $2 Billion Tax Cut If Mitt Romney Is Elected: Report," Huffington Post, September 11, 2012, http://www.huffingtonpost.com/2012/09/11/sheldon-adelson-2-billion-tax-cut-mitt-romney_n_1873683.html.

[10] Scott Douglas, "Paul Ryan Has Not Run Sub-3:00 Marathon," *Runner's World*, August 31, 2012, http://www.runnersworld.com/general-interest/paul-ryan-has-not-run-sub-300-marathon. The difference is between running at less than a seven-minute-per mile pace, or over nine-minutes-per-mile. Even for one mil, the difference is huge for most people.

[11] John Aravosis, "Paul Ryan may have lied about climbing 40 peaks of the Rockies," America's Blog, September 5, 2012, http://elections.americablog.com/2012/09/paul-ryan-may-have-lied-about-climbing-40-peaks-of-the-rockies.html.

[12] Tom Hamburger, "Romney's Bain Capital invested in companies that moved jobs overseas," *Washington Post*, June 21, 2012, http://www.washingtonpost.com/business/economy/romneys-bain-capital-invested-in-companies-that-moved-jobs-overseas/2012/06/21/gIQAsD9ptV_story.html; and Michael D. Shear, "*Washington Post* Rebuffs Romney on Retraction," *New York Times*, June 27, 2012, http://thecaucus.blogs.nytimes.com/2012/06/27/washington-post-rebuffs-romney-on-retraction.

[13] Michael McAuliff, "Scott DesJarlais, Pro-Life Republican Congressman And Doctor, Pressured Mistress Patient To Get Abortion," Huffington Post, October 10, 2012, http://www.huffingtonpost.com/2012/10/10/scott-desjarlais-abortion-pro-life_n_1953136.html.

[14] Justin Frank, M.D., "The Root of Mitt Romney's Comfort with Lying," *Time*, June 13, 2012, http://ideas.time.com/2012/06/13/the-root-of-mitt-romneys-comfort-with-lying.

[15] Religious necessity thus provides an excuse for a wide range of secrets and decisions that cannot be verified by voters or anyone else. In a widely published *Parade* interview just before the GOP 2012 convention, Romney cited his religion as yet another reason why he should not disclose more than two years of his tax returns." Lynn Sherr, "A Conversation with the Romneys," *Parade*, August 26, 2012, http://www.parade.com/news/2012/08/26-conversation-with-the-romneys.html.

[16] Brodie, Fawn M. *No Man Knows My History: The Life of Joseph Smith*. Vintage, 1995 (1945). Brodie's biography constructed vast numbers of early source materials into an authoritative history originally published in 1945. It has since widely reviewed, largely without serious attack on the work. See also, Kranish, Michael and Scott Helman. *The Real Romney*, Harper, 2012, 32-33.

[17] Brodie, *op. cit.*, 18. "For Joseph was not meant to be a plodding farmer, tied to the earth by habit or by love for the recurrent miracle of harvest."

[18] *People of the State of New York v. Joseph Smith*, March 20, 1826, as cited by Brodie, Ibid., 30, 427. A justice of the peace found Smith guilty of being a disorderly person and an impostor after a trial of allegations brought by a man from Bainbridge in Chenango County, New York. The complainant housed Smith for five months, and swore (as did other witnesses) that the defendant falsely claimed he could locate buried treasure by looking at a magical stone when placed in his hat.

[19] Brodie, *op. cit.*, Appendix C, "The Plural Wives of Joseph Smith," 457-88.

[20] Ibid., 263. "In January 1841 he presented to the church a revelation from God ordering the Saints to build a hotel…The extraordinarily mundane details in this commandment seem not to have troubled his people….The revelation then went on guilelessly to grant Joseph a suite of rooms in the hotel for himself and his posterity 'from generation to generation, for ever and ever.'"

[21] Kranish and Helman, *op. cit.*, 15.

[22] Questions arose only in passing in 2000 and 2008 about the presidential eligibility of GOP nominee John McCain, who was born in Panama in a hospital within the U.S. Canal Zone.

[23] Jaweed Kaleem, "Mitt Romney's French Mormon Mission Deepened His Faith In Jesus, Kept Him From Vietnam Draft," Huffington Post, August 30, 2012, http://www.huffingtonpost.com/2012/08/30/mitt-romney-vietnam-draft-french-mormon-mission_n_1838260.html.

[24] Nicholas Shaxson, "Where the Money Lives," *Vanity Fair*, August 2012, http://www.vanityfair.com/politics/2012/08/investigating-mitt-romney-offshore-accounts. See also, Joseph Cannon, "Bain, Romney, the CIA and (God help us) Howard Hughes," July 12, 2012, http://cannonfire.blogspot.com/2012/07/bain-romney-cia-and-god-help-us-howard.html, claiming that Bain resembled a money-laundering operation for certain of its early investors from prominent, CIA-linked families in Central America.

[25] Wikipedia, Robert C. Gay, http://en.wikipedia.org/wiki/Robert_C._Gay. See also, Huntsman-Gay Global Capital., http://www.hggc.com/team. The company's leaders include Jon Huntsman, former special assistant to President Nixon and father of 2012 GOP presidential candidate Jon Huntsman, Jr.; and former NFL football star J. Steve Young.

[26] Wikipedia, Frank William Gay, http://en.wikipedia.org/wiki/Frank_William_Gay.

[27] Wikipedia, Howard Hughes, http://en.wikipedia.org/wiki/Howard_Hughes.

[28] Brown, Peter Harry, and Pat H. Broeske. *Howard Hughes: The Untold Story*. De Capo, 2004, 130-31, 356.

[29] Anderson, Jack. *Confessions of a Muckraker*. Random House, 1979; and Brown and Broeske, *op. cit.*, 331-32, 380-83.

[30] Brown and Broeske, *op. cit.*, 380; and Tarpley, Webster Griffin. *Just Too Weird: Bishop Romney and the Mormon Takeover of America: Polygamy, Theocracy, and Subversion*. Progressive, 2012.

[31] Kranish and Helman, *op. cit.*

[32] Schweitzer, Albert. *The Mystery of the Kingdom of God: The Secret of Jesus' Messiahship and Passion*. Schocken, 1970 (first published in 1923). The African medical

missionary challenged his faith by examining whether the moral worth of charity is diminished if undertaken in hope of benefits, including salvation.

33 Gottlieb, Robert, and Peter Wiley. *America's Saints: The Rise of Mormon Power.* Harvest/HBJ, 1984.

34 Wikipedia, Brent Scowcroft, http://en.wikipedia.org/wiki/Brent_Scowcroft.

35 Denton, Sally, and Roger Morris. *The Money and the Power: The Making of Las Vegas and Its Hold on America.* Vintage, 2002.

36 Grace Wyler, "11 Surprising Things You Didn't Know About Mormons," Business Insider, June 24, 2011, http://www.businessinsider.com/11-surprising-things-you-didnt-know-about-mormons-2011-6?op=1. National Security Agency, "Utah Data Center," Government website (accessed June 12, 2013), http://nsa.gov1.info/utah-data-center. Andrew Kreig, "Daniel Ellsberg: Snowden's NSA Leak Was Heroic, Historic," Justice Integrity Project, June 10, 2013, http://www.justice-integrity.org/faq/490-snowden-s-nsa-leak-was-heroic-historic-ellsberg. James Bamford, "The NSA Is Building the Country's Biggest Spy Center (Watch What You Say)," *Wired,* March 15, 2012., http://www.wired.com/threatlevel/2012/03/ff_nsadatacenter.

37 Denton and Morris. *The Money and the Power, op. cit.,* 52.

38 David Corn, "Romney Invested in Medical-Waste Firm That Disposed of Aborted Fetuses, Government Documents Show," *Mother Jones,* July 2, 2012, http://www.motherjones.com/politics/2012/07/romney-bain-abortion-stericycle-sec.

39 Nick Baumann, "Romney Left Bain Later Than He Says, Documents Show," *Mother Jones,* July 2, 2012, http://www.motherjones.com/mojo/2012/07/romney-bain-about-when-romney-left-firm-documents-show.

40 Staff report, "2013's Top 20 Billionaires," *Forbes,* March 2013, http://www.forbes.com/pictures/mel45ghdi/charles-koch.

41 Jennifer Rubin, "Romney: Bold on spending cuts and entitlement reform," *Washington Post,* November 4, 2011, http://www.washingtonpost.com/blogs/right-turn/post/romney-bold-on-spending-cuts-and-entitlement-reform/2011/11/04/gIQAPmyUmM_blog.html.

42 Jane Mayer, "Covert Operations: The billionaire brothers who are waging a war against Obama," *New Yorker,* August 30, 2010, http://www.newyorker.com/reporting/2010/08/30/100830fa_fact_mayer?currentPage=all.

43 Paul Krugman, "An Unserious Man," *New York Times,* August 19, 2012. http://www.nytimes.com/2012/08/20/opinion/krugman-an-unserious-man.html?_r=1&partner=rssnyt&emc=rss.

44 Roger Stone, "The Paul Ryan Selection: The Koch Brothers Get Their Man," Stone Zone, August 17, 2012, http://stonezone.com/article.php?id=516.

45 Stone, "The Paul Ryan Selection," *op. cit.* See also, Joe Conason, "GOP Consultant: Koch Brothers Bought Ryan's Nomination With $100 Million Promise," National Memo, August 18, 2012, http://www.nationalmemo.com/gop-consultant-koch-brothers-bought-ryans-

nomination-with-100-million-promise. See also William E. Lewis Jr., "GOP Operative Roger Stone Defects to Libertarian Party, Red State," February 18, 2012, http://www.redstate.com/4billlewis/2012/02/18/gop-operative-roger-stone-defects-to-libertarian-party.

[46] Staff report, "The World's Billionaires," *Forbes*, Charles Koch and David Koch, " March 2012, http://www.forbes.com/lists/2010/10/billionaires-2010_Charles-Koch_Z9KL.html and http://www.forbes.com/profile/david-koch.

[47] Craig Unger, "Letter from Washington: Boss Rove," *Vanity Fair*, September 2012, http://www.vanityfair.com/politics/2012/09/karl-rove-gop-craig-unger, excerpted from, Unger, Craig. *Boss Rove: Inside Karl Rove's Secret Kingdom of Power.* Scribner, 2012 "The gist of the decision could be boiled down to two words: Anything goes."

[48] Wikipedia, Paul Ryan, http://en.wikipedia.org/wiki/Paul_Ryan.

[49] Brian Faler, "Ryan Health Plan Doesn't Give Constituents What He Gets," Bloomberg News, August 23, 2012, http://www.bloomberg.com/news/2012-08-23/ryan-plan-for-health-care-doesn-t-give-constituents-what-he-gets.html.

[50] Paul Krugman, "Ludicrous and Cruel," *New York Times*, April 7, 2011, http://www.nytimes.com/2011/04/08/opinion/08krugman.html?_r=2&smid=tw-NytimesKrugman&seid=auto.

[51] Charles Krauthammer, "After Ryan's leap, a rush of deficit demagoguery," *Washington Post*, April 7, 2011, http://www.washingtonpost.com/opinions/after-ryans-leap-a-rush-of-deficit-demagoguery/2011/04/07/AFUfOXxC_story.html.

[52] Editorial Board, "America's Health Disadvantage," *New York Times*, January 10, 2013, http://www.nytimes.com/2013/01/11/opinion/americas-health-disadvantage.html?partner=rssnyt&emc=rss&_r=0.

[53] Susan Heavey, "Study links 45,000 U.S. deaths to lack of insurance," Reuters, September 17, 2009, http://www.reuters.com/article/2009/09/17/us-usa-healthcare-deaths-idUSTRE58G6W520090917.

[54] Paul Craig Roberts, "America's descent into poverty," Institute for Political Economy, August 24, 2012. http://www.paulcraigroberts.org/2012/08/24/americas-descent-poverty-paul-craig-roberts. See also, Robert J. Samuelson, "'Saving' the middle class," *Washington Post*, August 26, 2012 http://www.washingtonpost.com/opinions/robert-samuelson-saving-the-middle-class/2012/08/26/0f5be24a-ef9a-11e1-adc6-87dfa8eff430_story.html.

[55] Richard Satran, "Stronger economy delivers smaller paystubs for most of us," NBC News, August 23, 2012, http://economywatch.nbcnews.com/_news/2012/08/23/13399710-stronger-economy-delivers-smaller-paystubs-for-most-of-us?lite.

[56] See, *e.g.* Paul Joseph Watson, "DHS to Purchase Another 750 Million Rounds of Ammo: Second massive ammunition buy this year fuels fears of civil unrest," Infowars.com, August 13, 2012, http://www.infowars.com/dhs-to-purchase-another-750-million-rounds-of-ammo. See also Department of Commerce, National Oceanic and Atmospheric Administration (NOAA), National

Weather Service, "Ammunition and Shooting Targets", FedBiz Opps, August 9, 2012, https://www.fbo.gov/index?s=opportunity&mode=form&tab=core&id=bfd95987a1ad9a6dfb22bca4a19150cb&_cview=0.Cited by CaptainKrunch, "Weather Service Buys 46000 Rounds of Illegal Hollow Point Bullets: NOAA Needs Hollow Points?" FreeRepublic.com, August 15, 2012, http://www.freerepublic.com/focus/f-bloggers/2918806/posts.

[57] Stephen Ohlemacher, "Social Security's Bullet Purchase Prompts Conspiracy Theories, Raises Eyebrows," Associated Press/*Huffington Post*, September 4, 2012, http://www.huffingtonpost.com/2012/09/04/social-security-bullet-purchase_n_1854121.html.

[58] David Edwards, "Romney says Obama is like a Roman emperor: 'Nero is fiddling,'" *Raw Story*, March 3, 2013, Raw Story, http://www.rawstory.com/rs/2013/03/03/romney-says-obama-is-like-a-roman-emperor-nero-is-fiddling/#.UTOiaMfuQ-E.facebook.

[59] Brodie, *op. cit.*, 423-25; and Kranish and Helman, *op. cit.*, 26, 72-73 186-87.

Chapter 2, Barack Obama: The President's Hidden History

[1] Some of my forebears from Bucks County in Pennsylvania had been lapsed Quakers named Doan, and were infamous during their Revolutionary Era as horse thieves, robbers and spies, with the era chronicled by another relative, the late historian E. Digby Baltzell, in *Puritan Boston and Quaker Philadelphia* (Transaction, 1996). See also McNealy, Terry A. *The Doan Gang: The Remarkable History of America's Most Notorious Loyalist Outlaws*, to be published by Westholme in 2013. The founder of Doane College helped vindicate the Doan(e) name by his good works later. These were part of my reflections on the day of President Obama's Inauguration in 2009 as I spoke with the Doane students – and currently, as I reflect for this book about the ongoing struggles — often in secret, of course — between plotters and patriots.

[2] Andrew Kreig, "Why the President 'Stepped Out' During His Inaugural Parade," Huffington Post, January 21, 2009, http://www.huffingtonpost.com/andrew-kreig/why-the-president-stepped_b_159875.html.

[3] Wolfgang Saxon, "Margaret B. Kreig, 76, Writer Who Warned of Drug Abuse, " *New York Times*, February 3, 1998, http://www.nytimes.com/1998/02/03/us/margaret-b-kreig-76-writer-who-warned-of-drug-abuse.html.

[4] Kreig, Margaret. *Green Medicine: The Search for the Plants that Heal*. Rand McNally, 1963, http://www.amazon.com/Green-medicine-search-plants-heal/dp/B0022FN968/ref=sr_1_3?s=books&ie=UTF8&qid=1356190382&sr=1-3.

[5] Kreig, Margaret. *Black Market Medicine: the Counterfeiting of Life-Saving Medications Dispensed by the Nation's Pharmacies*. Prentice Hall, 1967, http://www.amazon.com/MEDICINE-COUNTERFEITING-LIFE-SAVING-MEDICATIONS-DISPENSED/dp/B000LBQ96W/ref=sr_1_5?s=books&ie=UTF8&qid=1356190324&sr=1-5&keywords=margaret+kreig.

[6] House Government Operations Committee Hearings Transcript, "The Federal Effort against Organized Crime," 90th Congress, First Session, Part II, June 13, 20, and 27, 1967.

[7] Andrew Kreig, "Learning from Heroes Who Fought the Mafia," Justice Integrity Project, June 20, 2011, http://www.justice-integrity.org/faq/290-learning-from-eroes-who-broke-the-mafia.

[8] Wikipedia entry for J.C. King: http://en.wikipedia.org/wiki/J.C._King.

[9] John M. Crewdson and Joseph B. Treaster, "CIA established many links to journalists in U.S. and abroad," *New York Times*, December 27, 1977.

[10] Carl Bernstein, "The CIA and the Media, How Americas Most Powerful News Media Worked Hand in Glove with the Central Intelligence Agency and Why the Church Committee Covered It Up," *Rolling Stone*, October 20, 1977, http://www.carlbernstein.com/magazine_cia_and_media.php.

[11] Wayne Madsen, "Barack Obama's post-graduate CIA employment," Wayne Madsen Report, February 24, 2009 (Subscription only), http://www.waynemadsenreport.com/articles/20090224.

[12] Madsen, Wayne. *The Manufacturing of a President: The CIA's Insertion of Barack H. Obama, Jr. Into the White House.* WMR/Lulu, 2012.

[13] Crewdson and Treaster, "CIA Established Many Links To Journalists," *op. cit.*

Chapter 3, Hidden Evidence in Plain Sight

[1] Scott, Janny. *A Singular Woman.* Riverhead, 2011. Also, Janny A. Scott lecture, Barnes and Noble Bookstore, May 9, 2011 in Washington, DC.

[2] Remnick, David. *The Bridge: The Life and Rise of Barack Obama.* Knopf, 2010. Vintage, 2011.

[3] Remnick, *The Bridge*, 52. See also Obama, *Dreams from my Father*, 127.

[4] Wayne Madsen, "Part I: The Story of Obama: All in The Company," August 13, 2010; "Part II: History of Stanley Ann Dunham and Madelyn Dunham in CIA activities in Southeast Asia," August 16, 2010; "Part III: Add one more Obama Family Member to the CIA Payroll," August 19, 2010; "Part IV: More evidence surfaces on Obama's and his family's deep CIA links," August 25, 2010; and "Part V: Final Report," August 31, 2010 all available at www.waynemadsenreport.com (Subscription required). See also, Jerome R. Corsi, "Does WND reporting rule out an Obama Kenya birth?" World Net Daily, June 27, 2011, http://www.wnd.com/2011/06/316265.

[5] Maraniss, *Barack Obama, op. cit.*, 286-87. The description of Stanley as a struggling insurance salesman adds nuance, not contradiction to contentions that he was also a part-time or former part-time intelligence asset. Those in that field doing non-critical work were not necessarily well-paid. Even Ian Fleming, author of the James Bond books and himself a former high-ranking British intelligence executive, did not live like James Bond in a world of elegance.

[6] See, *e.g.*, the following columns, each published by Wayne Madsen in the Wayne Madsen Report, with the title, date and opening excerpt as follows: "Obama's 'Mommy Dearest' — targeting Indonesians for assassination," February 28, 2011. See also, "Obama's CIA brief: infiltrate the Marxist Left and "de-communize" it," December 14, 2010; "Link between Obama's CIA front

employer and mother's Asian work revealed," December 7, 2010;.; and "What was Obama's mother really doing in Ghana?" October 19, 2010.

7 A Columbia University undergraduate published a pioneering book on the student movement: Kunen, James Simon. *The Strawberry Statement: Notes of a College Revolutionary*. Avon, 1970, 130-31. Madsen cites Kunen as saying that Business International Corporation used money from Rockefeller interests to help fund a Students for Democratic Society (SDS) event in Chicago. Madsen, *The Manufacturing of a President, op. cit.*, 210-11. See also, Ayers, Bill. *Fugitive Days: A Memoir*. Beacon, 2001.

8 Dalton Tanonaka, "For Obama's Sister, Optimism Abounds in Jakarta Homecoming," *Jakarta Globe*, June 29, 2012, http://www.thejakartaglobe.com/lifeandtimes/in-the-first-sisters-jakarta-homecoming-theres-plenty-to-be-optimistic-about/527363.

9 Madsen, *The Manufacturing of a President, op. cit.*, 192-193 cites a formerly secret CIA memorandum of February 8, 1979 seen by this author describing a CIA recruitment trip to Occidental College that month that addressed 70 students. Obama enrolled in the school that fall.

10 Brzezinski, Zbigniew. *The Grand Chessboard*. Basic, 1998; and Brzezinski, Zbigniew. *Power and Principle: Memoirs of the National Security Adviser 1977-1981*. Farrar, Straus, Giroux, 1983.

11 Victor Marchetti, "The Spotlight," *Liberty Lobby*, August 14, 1978, available at New Combat, "Angleton's 1966 Memo to Helms re Hunt's presence in Dallas," September 9, 2007. The Marchetti article focused on a memo that James Jesus Angleton, the head of CIA counterintelligence during the agency's early decades, gave to Richard Helms as the latter assumed directorship of the agency in 1966. "The memo informs incoming director Helms that CIA has a problem: CIA officer E. Howard Hunt was in Dallas when JFK was shot."

12 Crewdson and Treaster, "CIA Established Many Links To Journalists," *op. cit.*

13 Maraniss, *op. cit., e.g.*, 471-82 and 490-507.

14 David Maraniss lecture, Politics and Prose bookstore, June 27, 2012 in Washington, DC.

15 Maraniss, *op. cit., e.g.*, at 478-79, 480.

16 Maraniss lecture, Politics and Prose bookstore, previously cited.

17 Hoover, J. Edgar. *Masters of Deceit: The Story of Communism in America and How to Fight It*. Henry Holt, 1958.

18 See, *e.g.*, Greene, Graham. *The Quiet American*. Penguin Classics, 2004 (1955); Perkins, John. *The Secret History of the American Empire: Economic Hit Men, Jackals, and the Truth about Global Corruption*. Dutton, 2007; and Lindner, Christoph. *The James Bond Phenomenon: A Critical Reader*. Manchester University, 2010, 220. In real life, Bond author Ian Fleming (1908-1964), a former Naval intelligence officer, had been an assistant to the chief of Great Britain's spy agency before he wrote the Bond series. The series has sold more than 100 million copies and fostered, along with films, the image of modern spycraft. "It is no coincidence," the critic Christoph Lindner wrote, "that Fleming housed his secret service in the offices of import/export company, and Bond often travelled under the guise of a salesman."

Chapter 4, Cold War, Hot Climates

[1] Harsh skeptics of the conventional Obama family history raise questions not just about Obama's birth record but also about such related matters as he marriage of Ann Dunham and Barack Obama Sr. *See, e.g.*, Jerome R. Corsi, *Where's the Birth Certificate: The Case that Barack Obama is Not Eligible to be President*, WND Books, 2011. In his June 27, 2012 lecture, *op. cit.*, David Maraniss dismissed the claim that Dunham and Obama were not officially married. Beyond that, these claims are beyond the scope of this book, which proceeds on the basis that Obama was born in Hawaii as the legitimate son of Ann Dunham and her husband, Barack Obama, Sr.

[2] George Orwell, "You and the Atomic Bomb," Tribune (London), October 19, 1945, http://tmh.floonet.net/articles/abombs.html. See also, Orwell, George. *Animal Farm.* 1945. Secker and Warburg, 1945 (United Kingdom); and Orwell, George. *1984.* Secker and Warburg, 1949 (United Kingdom).

[3] Council on Foreign Relations, http://www.cfr.org/about/index.html. The group cites membership of 4,700.

[4] Estulin, Daniel. *The True Story of the Bilderberg Group.* TrineDay, 2009, 137.

[5] Collier, Peter and David Horowitz. *The Rockefellers: An American Dynasty.* Holt, Rinehart & Winston, 1976. See also Harr, John Ensor and Peter J. Johnson. *The Rockefeller Conscience: An American Family in Public and in Private.* Charles Scribner's Sons, 1992; Harr, John Ensor and Peter J. Johnson. *The Rockefeller Century: Three Generations of America's Greatest Family.* Charles Scribner's Sons, 1988; Kert, Bernice. *Abby Aldrich Rockefeller: The Woman in the Family.* Random House, 1993; Morris, Joe Alex. *Those Rockefeller Brothers: An Informal Biography of Five Extraordinary Young Men.* Harper & Brothers, 1953; and Reich, Cary. *The Life of Nelson A. Rockefeller: Worlds to Conquer 1908-1958.* Doubleday, 1996.

[6] Ibid, 141.

[7] Tarpley, Webster G. *Obama: The Postmodern Coup.* Progressive, 2008.Tarpley, Webster G. *Obama: The Unauthorized Biography.* Progressive, 2008, 271.

[8] Tarpley, *The Unauthorized Biography, op. cit.*, 59-86.

[9] Harris, Frank. *My Life and Loves.* Grove, 1963, (1925), 781-82.

[10] *Loc. cit.* Harris was Irish-born, and educated in part in the United States and Germany. For many years, he was a leading newspaper and magazine editor in London. Also a society figure and powerbroker, he became notorious for his memoir, *My Life and Loves*, which was despised by the gentry on both sides of the Atlantic. On Cecil Rhodes: "I couldn't influence Rhodes; he talked to me repeatedly of Bartle Frere's idea: the British should possess Africa from the Cape to Cairo. 'They already own more than half of the Temperate Zone,' I said. 'Isn't that enough for them?'"

[11] Skousen, W. Cleon. *The Naked Capitalist.* Buccaneer, 1970, 26-31. Skousen, who died in 2006, was a popular author on historical, legal, and inspirational topics from a Mormon and extreme conservative viewpoint. A posthumously published book, written in 1994, predicted in religious terms a scourge that will depopulate the United States because of widespread sin. Skousen, W. Cleon. *The Cleansing of America.* Valor, 2010.

[12] Quigley, Carroll. *The Anglo-American Establishment.* G S G & Associates, 1981, 33-50; and *Tragedy and Hope: A History of the World In Our Time.* Angriff, 1966 available for free download at Carroll Quigley Books, http://www.carrollquigley.net/books.htm. See also Chatham House, http://www.chathamhouse.org ; the Rhodes Scholarship Trust, http://www.rhodesscholar.org; and, more generally, Chernow Ron. *The House of Morgan: An American Banking Dynasty and the Rise of Modern Finance.* Atlantic Monthly, 1990, 130-31, 206.

[13] Perloff, James. *The Shadows of Power: The Council on Foreign Relations and the American Decline.* Western Islands, 1988, 27. Wilson's campaign speeches, published after his election in book form, described unnamed powers who intimidated others in business. Wall Street was doubtless much on his mind, but he gave no specifics: "Since I entered politics, I have chiefly had men's views confided to me privately. Some of the biggest men in commerce and manufacture are afraid of somebody, are afraid of something. They know there is a power somewhere so organized, so subtle, so watchful, so interlocked, so complete, so pervasive, that they had better not speak above their breath when they speak in condemnation of it." Wilson, Woodrow. *The New Freedom.* Doubleday, 1913, 12-13, as cited by Perloff, Google Books, http://books.google.com/books?id=eifzgRKOZ_gC.

[14] Barksdale Maynard, "The Governor, The First Lady: And The Other Woman," *New Jersey Monthly,* October 11, 2010, http://njmonthly.com/articles/lifestyle/people/the-governor-the-first-lady-and-the-other-woman.html. Maynard, W. Barksdale. *Woodrow Wilson: Princeton to the Presidency.* Yale University, 2008.

[15] Link, Arthur. *Wilson and the Progressive Era.* Harper, 1954, 44-45. See generally, Wessel, David. *In FED We Trust: Ben Bernanke's War on the Great Panic.* Crown Business, 2010. Wikipedia, History of the Federal Reserve System, http://en.wikipedia.org/wiki/History_of_the_Federal_Reserve_System.

[16] Meyer largely hid his Jewish background, even from his children. They were reared as Protestants. The family had a pew in the president's church, St. John's Episcopal Church, across Lafayette Square from the White House. Graham, Katharine. *Personal History.* Knopf, 1997, 51-53. Her more than 600-page book mentioned none of the major secret or semi-secret global public affairs bodies such as the Bilderberg Group that *Post* owners have joined. She mentions the CIA just briefly, and revealed little of the family's close ties with Wall Street financiers aside from Warren Buffet, her close friend and a *Post* director.

[17] Clinton, Bill. *My Life.* Knopf, 2004, 77.

[18] Quigley, *op. cit.,* 1247-1248, cited in "Dr. Quigley's Tragedy and Hope reveals a call by Cecil Rhodes for an 'American Union,'" Jones Report, May 30, 2008, http://www.jonesreport.com/article/05_08/30quigley.html.

[19] Spanier, John. *American Foreign Policy Since World War II.* Praeger, 1967, 71.

[20] Ibid., 175.

[21] Morris, Richard B., ed., *Encyclopedia of American History Bicentennial Edition,* Harper and Row, 1976, 1018.

[22] Trento, Joseph J. *The Secret History of the CIA.* Basic Books, 2005, 44-45.

23 Trento, *The Secret History of the CIA, op. cit.*, 167.

24 Perkins, John. *Hoodwinked: An Economic Hit Man Reveals Why the World Financial Markets Imploded– and What We Need to Do to Remake.* Crown Business, 2011, 40-41; Trento, *The Secret History of the CIA, op. cit.*, 167; and De Bellaigue, Christopher. *Patriot of Persia: Muhammad Mossadegh and a Tragic Anglo- American Coup.* Harper, 2012.

25 Kitson, Frank. *Low Intensity Operations: Subversion, Insurgency, Peace-Keeping.* Faber and Faber, 1991 (1971 first edition).

26 Wikipedia, Jomo Kenyatta, http://en.wikipedia.org/wiki/Jomo_Kenyatta. "Jomo Kenyatta (c. 1890s – 22 August 1978) served as the first Prime Minister (1963–1964) and President (1964–1978) of Kenya. He is considered the founding father of his nation."

27 CIA "Current Intelligence Weekly Summary," November 19, 1959, as cited by Madsen, *op. cit.,* Part I: "The Story of Obama: All in The Company."

28 The *New Yorker's* Remnick describes Obama as "an aspiring economist with a rich, musical voice and a confident manner. " In 1959, Obama would become the first African student ever to attend the University of Hawaii. Remnick, *op. cit.,* 31-33.

29 Nkrumah was educated in the United States in the 1930s while Ghana (then known as the Gold Coast) was a British colony. He became Ghana's first prime minister upon its independence and evolved in his economic thinking to a philosophy of Marxism and non-alignment internationally. He met with President Kennedy in 1961 on apparently friendly terms. But the Soviet Union awarded Nkrumah its Lenin Prize that same year. He continued as Ghana's leader until his overthrow by the military in 1966. Wikipedia, Kwame Nkrumah, http://en.wikipedia.org/wiki/Kwame_Nkrumah.

30 Wikipedia, Patrice Lumumba, http://en.wikipedia.org/wiki/Patrice_Lumumba. I remember the news about Lumumba and several other African leaders from that time even though I was just a 12-year-old thinking mostly about playing baseball in the park. Those African developments were big news even though no hint of U.S. involvement was known or reported. Clearly, influential news editors knew the developments were important even if they could not be packaged in simplistic and entertaining ways.

31 Ibid., 67.

32 A secret CIA report dated February 8, 1962, now declassified, suggests that the CIA was working at the time with Mboya to isolate "old guard" leftists and former Mau Mau leaders. "Current Intelligence Weekly Summary," CIA, February 8, 1962 as cited by Wayne Madsen, "CIA invested heavily in Obama, Sr.'s mentor Tom Mboya in Kenya," September 28, 2010, www.waynemadsenreport.com (Subscription only).

33 These targets of the CIA included Kenyatta (a member of the Kikuyu tribe rivaling the Luo) and the nation's main leftist leader, Oginga Odinga, also a Luo but a rival to Mboya. Eric Ombok, "Kenya's Raila Odinga Sworn in as Prime Minister, Ending Crisis," Bloomberg, April 17, 2008, http://www.bloomberg.com/apps/news?pid=newsarchive&sid=abAJ_3lpr8 WA&refer=home.

34 Rosenfeld, Seth. *Subversives: The FBI's War on Student Radicals, and Reagan's Rise to Power.* Farrar, Straus and Giroux, 2012; and Rosenfeld, "Reagan's Personal Spying Machine," *New York Times,* September 1, 2012, http://www.nytimes.com/2012/09/02/opinion/sunday/reagans-personal-spying-machine.html?pagewanted=all&_r=1&and. See also, Andrew Kreig, "Two DC Media Ceremonies Contrast Courage, Comfort," Justice Integrity Project, April 30, 2013, http://www.justice-integrity.org/faq/471-two-dc-media-ceremonies-contrast-courage-comfort; Russo, Gus. *Supermob: How Sidney Korshak and His Criminal Associates Became America's Hidden Power Brokers.* Bloomsbury, 2006; and Moldea, Dan. *Dark Victory: Ronald Reagan, MCA, and the Mob.* Viking Penguin, 1986.

35 Sol Stern, with the special assistance of Lee Webb, Michael Ansara and Michael Wood, "A Short Account of International Student Politics and the Cold War with Particular Reference to the NSA, CIA, etc." *Ramparts,* March 1967, pp. 29-38, http://www.cia-on-campus.org/nsa/nsa.html. "Stearns and Groves pleaded that disclosure of the CIA relationship would be disastrous for NSA. It would put them in an awful political predicament. If they publicly admitted past CIA connections, it would tarnish NSA's image badly at home and abroad, and hurt its chances of receiving grants from other government agencies. NSA staff members also feared CIA retaliation, especially the loss of their draft deferments."

36 Morris, Roger. *Partners in Power: The Clintons and their America.* Henry Holt, 1996, 102-05, 406-15. See also, Maraniss, David. *First in His Class.* Touchstone/Simon & Schuster, 1995; and Jack Wheeler, "How the Clintons Will Destroy McCain," Free Republic, February 3, 2008, http://www.freerepublic.com/focus/f-news/1964221/posts.

37 Sol Stern, The *Ramparts* I Watched, *City Journal,* Winter 2010. http://www.city-journal.org/2010/20_1_ramparts.html. Stern's memoir described his regret at publishing his original revelations in 1967 about the CIA. He said he broke with the left primarily over policy on Israel, and came to believe as a conservative that the CIA needs to be able to operate in secrecy. Nonetheless, his contribution in 2010 describing Clinton's past underscores the ongoing tension between the demands of ideology and reporting.

38 Tom Ivancie, "Q&A With Christopher Hitchens," *Doublethink,* February 11, 2003, http://americasfuture.org/doublethink/2003/02/qa-with-christopher-hitchens. Ivancie: "You think Bill Clinton was recruited by the CIA? Hitchens: "Somebody was giving information to them about the anti-war draft resistors, and I think it was probably him."

39 Khrushchev's blunt criticisms of his predecessor leaders were regarded as so remarkable that a debate temporarily ensued over whether the memoirs were authentic. See Khrushchev, Nikita, with introduction, commentary and notes by Edward Crankshaw, translated and edited by Strobe Talbot. *Khrushchev Remembers.* Little Brown, 1970; and Khrushchev, Nikita, with introduction commentary and notes by Edward Crankshaw and Jerrold Schecter, translated and edited by Strobe Talbot. *Khrushchev Remembers: The Last Testament.* Little Brown, 1974. See also, Clinton, *My Life, op. cit.,* 162-63. He wrote: "I was especially fascinated to hear Strobe recount Khrushchev's tales of Kremlin

intrigue. Strobe's seminal book, *Khrushchev Remembers*, made a major contribution in the West to the understanding of the inner workings and tensions of the Soviet Union, and raised the hope that someday internal reform might bring more freedom and openness." Clinton's other roommate, Frank Aller, was a Rhodes Scholar who developed expertise on the Communist revolution in China. The situation was conducive to outreach by intelligence experts. Aller was an opponent of the Vietnam War who would kill himself in 1971 following a deep depression and a job offer to report on the war. *Ibid.*, 178.

[40] See, *e.g.*, Braestrup, Peter. *Big Story*. Anchor, 1978; and Halberstam, David. *The Coldest Winter: America and the Korean War*. Hyperion, 2007.

[41] Wikipedia, Sukarno, http://en.wikipedia.org/wiki/Sukarno. "Sukarno, born Kusno Sosrodihardjo, was the first President of Indonesia. Sukarno was the leader of his country's struggle for independence from the Netherlands and was Indonesia's first President from 1945 to 1967."

[42] Marilyn Berger, "Suharto Dies at 86; Indonesian Dictator Brought Order and Bloodshed," *New York Times,* January 28, 2008, http://www.nytimes.com/2008/01/28/world/asia/28suharto.html?pagewante d=all.

[43] Marchetti, Victor and Marks, John D. *The CIA and the Cult of Intelligence*. Knopf, 1974, 29. One author was Marchetti, a former special assistant to CIA Director Richard Helms. The other author was Marks, a former State Department analyst. I reviewed the book favorably for the *Hartford Courant* upon publication. On recently rereading it, I rediscovered this nugget: "As the Eisenhower years came to an end, there was still a national consensus that the CIA was justified in taking almost any action in that 'back alley' struggle against communism – this despite Eisenhower's clumsy effort to lie his way out of the U-2 shoot down, which lying led to the cancellation of the 1960 summit conference. Most Americans placed the CIA on the same above-politics level as the FBI, and it was no accident that President-elect Kennedy chose to announce on the same day that both J. Edgar Hoover and Allen Dulles would stay on in his administration."

[44] "Perhaps the prototype for CIA covert operations during the 1950s was the work of Air Force Colonel Edward Lansdale. His exploits under agency auspices, first in the Philippines and then in Vietnam, became so well known that he served as the model for characters in two best-selling novels, *The Ugly American*, by William J. Lederer and Eugene Burdick, and *The Quiet American* by Graham Greene. In the former, he was a heroic figure; in the latter, a bumbling fool." Marchetti and Marks, *op. cit.* 27.

[45] The Church Committee is the common term referring to the United States Senate Select Committee to Study Governmental Operations with Respect to Intelligence Activities, a U.S. Senate committee chaired by Senator Frank Church (D-ID) in 1975. http://en.wikipedia.org/wiki/Church_Committee.

[46] Stockwell, John. *In Search of Enemies: A CIA Story*. Norton, 1978, 105.

[47] Crewdson and Treaster, "CIA Established Many Links To Journalists in U.S. and Abroad," *op. cit.*

[48] Parry, Robert. *Fooling America: How Washington Insiders Twist the Truth and Manufacture Convention Wisdom.* Morrow, 1992,173-75. See also Parry's *Lost History: Contras, Cocaine, the Press & "Project Truth."* Media Consortium, 1999.

[49] Kreig, Andrew. *Spiked: How Chain Management Corrupted America's Oldest Newspaper.* Peregrine, 1987. Book details: http://andrewkreig.com/index.php/author.

[50] Parry, *Fooling America, op. cit.,* 313-15.

[51] Ibid., 55.

[52] Perkins, John. *Confessions of an Economic Hit Man,* Plume, 2006, 21-23. See also, Perkins, John. *Hoodwinked: An Economic Hit Man Reveals Why the World Financial Markets Imploded– and What We Need to Do to Remake.* Crown Business, 2011; Perkins, John. *The Secret History of the American Empire: Economic Hit Men, Jackals, and the Truth about Global Corruption.* Dutton, 2007. "By the time I enrolled in BU's [Boston University's] business school, a solution to the Roosevelt-as-CIA-agent problem had already been worked out. U.S. intelligence agencies – including the NSA – would identify prospective EHMs [Economic Hit Men], who could then be fired by international corporations. These EHMs would never be paid by the government; instead, they would draw their salaries from the private sector. As a result, their dirty work, if exposed, would be chalked up to corporate greed rather than government."

[53] Ralph L. Beals and Executive Board of the American Anthropological Association, "Background Information on Problems of Anthropological Research and Ethics," January 1967, http://onlinelibrary.wiley.com/doi/10.1525/an.1967.8.1.1/pdf.

[54] Wayne Madsen, "Obama's mother began her Indonesian field work at height of complaints about CIA involvement with foreign 'research,'" Wayne Madsen Report, March 28, 2011, www.waynemadsenreport.com. See also, McGehee, Ralph W. *Deadly Secrets: My 25 Years in the CIA.* Sheridan Square, 1983, 57-58, as cited in Madsen, *The Manufacturing of a President, op. cit.,* 63.

[55] In 1950, Braden became a leader in CIA covert action operations as head of the International Operations Division of the CIA's Office of Policy Coordination. In this post, he worked closely with CIA Director Allen Dulles and supervised Cord Meyer, head of the Operation Mockingbird program to influence journalists domestically and internationally. During World War II, Braden had courageously parachuted into France behind Nazi lines for the predecessor Office of Strategic Services and later became a prominent journalist with many high-level friends from both parties, including leaders of the Kennedy and Rockefeller families. See, Elaine Woo, "Tom Braden dies at 92; former CIA operative became columnist and talk show co-host." *Los Angeles Times,* April 4, 2009, http://www.latimes.com/news/obituaries/la-me-thomas-braden4-2009apr04,0,6736553.story; and Thomas W. Braden, "I'm glad the CIA Is 'immoral,'" *Saturday Evening Post,* May 20, 1967, http://www.cambridgeclarion.org/press_cuttings/braden_20may1967.html.

[56] Transcript, CNN "Crossfire," with Pat Buchanan, Tom Braden and guest Scott Stanley, Jr., editor of the John Birch Society's "Review of the News" and "American Opinion," September 15, 1983 via transcription by Radio TV Reports, Inc., 1-14, available via the National Archives, http://www.scribd.com/doc/113615488/CNN-Crossfire-Braden-Buchanan-

John-Birch-Society-s-Stanley. See also, *e.g.*, declassified memos from William J. Casey, cited by Wayne Madsen on the Wayne Madsen Report, June 11, 2013. One February 23, 1984 memo from a staffer reminded Casey of a Fuller briefing on Mideast issues just prior to Casey's meeting with President Reagan. Another memo from Casey on August 19, 1985 described the "Soviet Game Plan." Casey advised the National Intelligence Council vice chairman on work undertaken by Fuller, whom Casey clearly regarded as a trusted expert.

[57] Rove, Karl. *Courage and Consequence: My Life As a Conservative in the Fight.* Threshold / Simon & Schuster, 2010, 48-49.

[58] Unger, Craig. *House of Bush House of Saud: The Secret Relationship Between the World's Two Most Powerful Dynasties.* Scribner, 2004.

[59] Wikipedia, James A. Baker III, http://en.wikipedia.org/wiki/James_Baker.

[60] Baker, Russ. *Family of Secrets: The Bush Dynasty, America's Invisible Government, and the Hidden History of the Last Fifty Years.* Bloomsbury, 2009, 311.

[61] The *Washington Times* first reported the story. A follow up was: Staff report, with Jerry Seper, "Passports probe focuses on worker," *Washington Times*, March 22, 2008, http://www.washingtontimes.com/news/2008/mar/22/passports-probe-focuses-on-worker/?page=all. The story said only a AC employee accessed records of all three presidential candidates. However, two other suspects worked for a second private contractor, Stanley Inc., a 3,500-person technology firm that won a $570 million contract to continue providing passport services to the State Department.

[62] Ken Timmerman, "Obama's Intelligence Adviser Involved in Security Breach," *Newsmax*, January 12, 2009, http://www.newsmax.com/KenTimmerman/brennan-passport-breach/2009/01/12/id/337482.

[63] "Review of Controls and Notification for Access to Passport Records in the Department of State's Passport Information Electronic Records System (PIERS), AUD/IP-08-29," July 2008, http://epic.org/foia/EPIC_Passport_rpt.pdf, and "Special Briefing on the State Department Inspector General's Report on Passport Records Access," Principal Deputy Assistant Secretary of State for Consular Affairs Michael Kirby and Managing Director of Passport Services," Florence Fultz, July 3, 2008, http://2001-2009.state.gov/r/pa/prs/ps/2008/07/106518.htm.

[64] See for example, Department of Justice, "Former State Department Employee Sentenced for Illegally Accessing Confidential Passport Files," July 8, 2009, and Lynn Sweet, "State Department celebrity passport snooper sentenced," *Chicago Sun-Times*, December 9, 2009, http://blogs.suntimes.com/sweet/2009/12/state_department_celebrity_pas.html.

[65] Sundance, "President Obama: Part II – After High School Through College(s)," Conservative Treehouse, April 26, 2011, http://theconservativetreehouse.com/2011/04/26/president-obama-do-we-know-who-he-is-part-ii-after-high-school-through-colleges.

[66] O'Neil and Corsi, *Unfit for Command*, and Corsi, *Where's the Birth Certificate*, op. cit.

67 Jerome Corsi, "Did CIA pick sanitize Obama's passport records?" WND, January 8, 2013, http://mobile.wnd.com/2013/01/did-cia-pick-sanitize-obamas-passport-records.

68 Yogi Berra, the retired baseball star and manager born in 1925, jokes throughout his books that many pithy sayings are attributed to him in otherwise unrecorded conversations, and he's glad to take credit for them whether he remembers them or not. See Berra, Yogi. *Yogi: It Ain't Over.* Harper Paperbacks, 1989, 313.

69 Arthur Conan Doyle, "Silver Blaze," in *The Memoirs of Sherlock Holmes*, 1894.

70 Dwight Eisenhower and Nikita Khrushchev, as former World War II generals who had witnessed war's horrors first-hand, shared the goal of preventing reoccurrence — but needed to appear hard-line in public to maintain support from bellicose backers. Dickson, Paul. *Sputnik: The Shock of the Century.* 2001, Walker.

Chapter 5, Barack Obama: The President's Family Tree

1 Ogden, Christopher. *Life of the Party: The Biography of Pamela Digby Churchill Hayward Harriman.* Little, Brown, 1994.

2 Wikipedia, "Barack Obama," *op. cit.*

3 CIA covert intelligence officer Valerie Plame Wilson was publicly known as an import/export executive with a CIA front company, Brewster Jennings, in Boston. Vice presidential aide Lewis "Scooter" Libby disclosed her identity, thereby endangering her family, apparently as punishment for the unwillingness of her husband, former Ambassador Joseph Wilson, to lie to support the Iraq War. See Wilson, Joseph C., IV. *The Politics of Truth: A Diplomat's Memoir: Inside the Lies that Led to War and Betrayed My Wife's CIA Identity.* Carroll & Graf, 2004; Wilson, Valerie Plame. *Fair Game: My Life as a Spy, My Betrayal by the White House.* Simon & Schuster, 2007.

4 The basics of this family history in both Kenya and Kansas are drawn from standard sources, with the overall details not in dispute. The most thorough of the books on the future's president is Maraniss, *op. cit.*, which is also the most recent as of this writing and approximately the same length as that of Remnick, *op. cit.*, at some 600 pages, including notes. The works by Scott, *op. cit.*, Jacobs, *op. cit.*, and Obama, *op. cit.*, are especially valuable also for basic biographical information, of course. The utility of Obama's own books as reference sources is undermined by lack of reference notes and indices. Madsen's *The Manufacturing of a President, op. cit.*, covers basic family history in largely congruent terms as other books, but with far more interpretation of public policy implications.

5 Remnick, *op. cit.*, 32-33. In contrast to chronologies by many biographers, Obama was not part of the core, initial group of those first funded for the "Airlift" scholarships from Africa, according to Jerome Corsi' research. Instead, Obama travelled to the University of Hawaii in part on his own, relying on his own savings, a donation from Airlift supporters Helen Roberts and Elizabeth Kirk. See Shachtman, Tom. *Airlift to America: How Barack Obama, Sr., John F. Kennedy Tom Mboya and 800 East African Students Changed Their World and Ours*, St. Martin's, 2009, 6-9, 11, as cited by Corsi, *op. cit.*, 131-36.

[6] Maraniss, *op. cit.*, 150-51; Remnick, *op. cit.*, 30-41; Wikipedia, Barack Hussein Obama Sr., http://en.wikipedia.org/wiki/Barack_Obama,_Sr.

[7] Maraniss, Ibid.

[8] Kennedy, John F. *A Nation of Immigrants.* Harper Perennial, 2008 (1964, expanded from a 1958 treatise); Kennedy, John F. *Profiles in Courage.* Harper Perennial, 2006 (1955); and Kennedy, John F. *Why England Slept.* Harper Perennial, 2008.

[9] Scott, *op. cit.*, 77; Remnick, *op. cit.*, 30-41.

[10] Maraniss, *op. cit.*, 171-72.

[11] Marchetti and Marks, *op. cit.*, 114.

[12] Madsen's *The Manufacturing of a President, op. cit.*, 59. See also, as cited, CIA Directorate of Intelligence, Office of Research and Reports, Intelligence Brief, Confidential, "Impending Takeover of U.S. Rubber Estates in Indonesia," January 1965; and McGehee, Ralph W. *Deadly Deceits: My 25 Years in the CIA.* Sheridan Square, 1983, 57-58.

[13] Scott, *op. cit.*, 37; "President Obama: from Kansas to the capital," KAKE 10 News (ABC) (Wichita), http://www.kake.com/home/misc/38157259.html.

[14] Madsen believes standard biographies miss a time when the Dunham family lived in Lebanon in the early 1950s. Madsen, *The Manufacturing of a President, op. cit.*, 24-37.

[15] Maraniss, *op. cit.*, 155-57.

[16] Corsi writes in "Does WND's reporting rule out a Kenya birth?" *op. cit.*, that university records indicate that officials were concerned that Obama was pursuing multiple students romantically while he was listed in their records as married to a Kenyan. Corsi further reports that Obama and Dunham did not live together, and that immigration officials feared they had a sham marriage with the possible goal of advancing a path to U.S. citizenship for Obama, which he did not pursue. Additionally, Obama opponents have circulated photos of unknown authenticity purporting to be modeling photos of Ann Dunham.

[17] Remnick, *op. cit.*, 55. Barry Goldwater was born in Arizona when it was a United States territory. George Romney was born in Mexico. John McCain was born in the Panama Canal Zone within Panama. See Corsi, *Where's the Birth Certificate, op. cit.*, . Corsi, the most scholarly of the "Birther" critics, has compiled a useful history of similar controversies and of Obama failures to disclosure a variety of pertinent records, including of academic records. But the author ultimately fails to prove his point. This is in part because the book's overall tone. Corsi is a World Net Daily reporter who co-authored previous books in 2004 and 2008 attacking Democratic Presidential candidates. See O'Neill, John and Corsi, Jerome R. *Unfit for Command: Swift Boat Veterans Speak Out about John Kerry*, Regnery, 2004 and Corsi, Jerome R. *The Obama Nation: Leftist Politics and the Cult of Personality.* Simon & Schuster, 2008. In 2008, the Obama campaign issued a 40-page response, calling the Corsi book "unfit for publication." The campaign a press release said in part: "This book is nothing but a series of lies that were long ago discredited, written by an individual who was discredited after he wrote a similar book to help George Bush and Dick Cheney get re-elected four years ago."

[18] Ibid. 54." One of my sources, Alabama attorney Dana Jill Simpson, says she helped Karl Rove in 2000 develop on behalf of the Bush campaign material that could be used to attack rival John McCain's legitimacy because of his birth outside the United States but that the material was mothballed because of the McCain campaign's collapse. She suspects that following her split with GOP operatives a Rove-affiliated operative adapted the material to Obama. Interviews with Dana Jill Simpson, 2010-12. The GOP presidential candidacies by Barry Goldwater in 1964, George Romney in 1968 and John McCain in 2000 faced nothing similar, even though none of them was born in a state of the United States. That said, the prodigious research of the "Birthers" has unearthed important and otherwise unavailable material, and it is possible to see how some of them are energized with the same kind of motives as any political researcher.

[19] Obama, Barack. *Dreams from My Father*, Crown, 2004, 125-26. Compare with Jacobs, Sally H. *The Other Barack: The Bold and Reckless Life of President Obama's Father*. Public Affairs, 2011, 124, and Maraniss, *op. cit.*, 175. Obama's memoir does not clearly state a timeline that the couple lived together during the 1961-62 year. The book implies they did. Corsi demolishes that implication. Corsi, *Where's the Birth Certificate? op. cit.*, 116-17. "Now that we know that Obama has presented false information about his early life," Corsi writes, "we must reasonably ask if his entire official nativity story is likewise a fabrication."

[20] Obama, Barack. *Dreams from My Father*, *op. cit.*, 126. See also, Michiko Kakutani, "New President Found Voice," January 18, 2009, http://www.nytimes.com/2009/01/19/books/19read.html?_r=1&hp.

[21] Scott, *op. cit.*, 93.

[22] Madsen, *The Manufacturing of a President*, *op. cit.*, 31-37.

[23] Tarpley, Webster Griffin. *Obama: The Postmodern Coup: Making of a Manchurian Candidate*, Progressive, 2008. Based partly on Ann Dunham's relationships forged in Hawaii and expanded in Indonesia, Tarpley wrote repeatedly during the 2008 Presidential campaign that Obama was the secret choice of CIA and Wall Street to become president because, in his view, a gullible public would not suspect that a black "community organizer" would implement a craven, pro-corporate agenda.

[24] Tarpley, *Obama: The Postmodern Coup*, *op. cit.*, 5. The book jacket said in part: "Obama's economics are pure Skull & Bones / Chicago School austerity and sacrifice for American working families, all designed to bail out the bankrupt Wall Street elitist financiers who own Obama." See also, Tarpley, Webster G. *Barack H. Obama: The Unauthorized Biography*. Progressive, 2008.

[25] Angelo M. Codevilla, "The Chosen One," *Claremont Review of Books*, Summer 2011, July 13, 2011, http://www.claremont.org/publications/crb/id.1852/article_detail.asp.

[26] Lila Shapiro, "11 Most Paranoid Obama Conspiracy Theories," Huffington Post, March 18, 2010, http://www.huffingtonpost.com/2009/11/03/11-most-paranoid-obama-co_n_343771.html. (Updated and republished.

[27] Remnick, *op. cit.*, 94-97, 98.

[28] Tarpley, Webster Griffin. *Barack H. Obama: The Unauthorized Biography*. Progressive, 2008, 36-44.

29 Michael J. de la Merced, "With Citigroup Stabilized, Parsons Decides to Retire," *The New York Times*, Dealbook, March 2, 2012, http://dealbook.nytimes.com/2012/03/02/citigroup-said-to-name-new-chairman/?hp.

30 Paul Kengor. *The Communist: Frank Marshall Davis: The Untold Story of Barack Obama's Mentor.* Threshold/Simon & Schuster 2012. See also Remnick, *op. cit.*, 57. In the fall of 1982, Barack, Sr. died from crashing his car into a tree in Kenya while inebriated following celebration of successful workday.

31 Frank N. Trager, "The U.S. And Indonesia — A Tragedy In Diplomacy; The U.S. and Indonesia," *New York Times Magazine*, August 29, 1965, http://select.nytimes.com/gst/abstract.html?res=F20810FD3B591A7A93CB AB1783D85F418685F9. *See also,* "Howard P. Jones Is dead at 74; Envoy to Indonesia, 1958–65," *New York Times*, September 20, 1973.

32 Scott, *op. cit.*, 100.

33 Ibid., 57.

34 Remnick, *op. cit.*, 58-62. Maraniss, *Barack Obama, op. cit.*, 212-44.

35 Perkins describes the process as follows: Corrupt Indonesian leaders approved loans, which were on terms the country could never repay, in order to pay for hundreds of millions of dollars of U.S. contractor services. When the debt became too great financiers went after the host nation's collateral infrastructure. He says he and his colleagues used the process in many nations but excessive greed by his company led to its demise when it paid a huge bribe to win a contract in Indonesia but the bribe was so large it could not be hidden by standard accounting gimmicks. Perkins, John. *Confessions of an Economic Hit Man*, Plume, 2006, 24-39. Concerning his own mind-set as a young financier, Perkins wrote: "I was ready to rape and pillage when I headed to Asia in 1971. At twenty-six, I felt cheated by life. I wanted to take revenge. I am certain, in retrospect, that rage earned me my job. Hours of psychological testing by the National Security Agency (NSA) identified me as a potential economic hit man [EHM]. The nation's most clandestine spy organization concluded that I was a man whose passions could be channeled to help fulfill its mission of expanding the empire."

36 Perkins, John. *Hoodwinked: An Economic Hit Man Reveals Why the World Financial Markets Imploded — and What We Need to Do to Remake.* Crown Business, 2011, 21-22. "Although I had been an EHM for nearly seven year, I did not understand the profound implications of the system I was perpetrating until 1978. My job at the time was to convince Panama's chief of government, Omar Torrijos, to assume a huge World Bank loan....I am convinced that Omar's attempts to change the system cost him his life. He died when his private plane crashed in June 1981, an incident that much of the international press labeled a CIA assassination."

37 Ibid., 61.

38 Wayne Madsen, "Obama's 'Mommy Dearest' — targeting Indonesians for assassination," *op. cit.*; and Madsen, *The Manufacturing of a President, op. cit.*, 63-64.

39 Remnick, *op. cit.*, 73.

[40] Obama, *Dreams from My Father*, *op. cit.*, 77.-78. Madsen, based on extensive reporting by Jerome Corsi, says the bar was owned by William Lederer, the former CIA officer and co-author of *The Ugly American* and *A Nation of Sheep.* See Jerome R. Corsi, "Does WND reporting rule out an Obama Kenya birth?" World Net Daily, June 27, 2011, http://www.wnd.com/2011/06/316265.

[41] Maraniss, Politics and Prose lecture, *op. cit.*

[42] Remnick, *op. cit.*,73.

[43] Dunham, S. Ann (1992). *Peasant blacksmithing in Indonesia: Surviving against all odds.* Honolulu: University of Hawaii. The thesis was republished, *Surviving against the odds: village industry in Indonesia* by S. Ann Dunham, foreword by Maya Soetoro-Ng; afterword by Robert W. Hefner; edited and with preface by Alice G. Dewey & Nancy I. Cooper. Duke University Press, 2009.

[44] Remnick, *op. cit.*, 83.

[45] "The New Order in Indonesia," CIA Weekly Summary Special Report, August 11, 1967 as cited in Madsen, Part IV, "The Story of Obama," *op. cit.* His paraphrase is that Indonesia in 1966 re-aligned its economy in order to receive International Monetary Fund (IMF) assistance. The CIA reports it is happy with the new triumvirate ruling Indonesia in 1967. The report also rejoices in the outlawing of the PKI, but states it "retains a significant following in East and Central Java," where Ann Dunham Soetoro would largely concentrate her later efforts on behalf of USAID, the World Bank, and the Ford Foundation, all front activities for the CIA to "win the hearts and minds" of the Javanese farmers and artisans.

[46] Scott, *op. cit.*

[47] Wayne Madsen, "What was Obama's mother really doing in Ghana?" Wayne Madsen Report, October 19, 2010, www.waynemadsenreport.com.

[48] Ian Wilhelm, "Ford Foundation links parents of Obama and Treasury secretary nominee," *The Chronicle of Philanthropy*, December 3, 2008.

[49] Wayne Madsen has written the most thorough account in, "Feud between Emanuel and Netanyahu heats up," Wayne Madsen Report, August 3, 2009, http://www.waynemadsenreport.com/articles/20090802_4. My information comes from additional, unpublished sources.

[50] Carrick Mollenkamp, "Federal Reserve of New York Proposed Reforms for Libor Issues in 2007 to 2008," Reuters via Huffington Post, July 10, 2012, http://www.huffingtonpost.com/2012/07/10/federal-reserve-of-new-york-libor-scandal_n_1661268.html.

Chapter 6, Barack Obama: The Path to Power

[1] See especially, Maraniss, *op. cit.*, and Remnick, *op. cit.*

[2] Remnick, *op. cit.*, 99.

[3] Scott Helman, "Small college awakened future senator to service," *Boston Globe*, August 25, 2008, http://www.boston.com/news/politics/2008/articles/2008/08/25/small_college_awakened_future_senator_to_service/?page=full. (Subscription required).

[4] As cited in Madsen, *op. cit.*, "The Story of Obama: All in the Company," Part I: "The Story of Obama: All in The Company," August 13, 2010; Part II: "History of Stanley Ann Dunham and Madelyn Dunham in CIA activities in Southeast Asia," August 16, 2010; Part III: "Add one more Obama Family Member to the CIA Payroll," August 19, 2010; Part IV: "More evidence surfaces on Obama's and his family's deep CIA links," August. 25, 2010; and Part V: "Final Report," August 31, 2010, each available at www.waynemadsenreport.com (subscription required). But see, Cliff Kincaid, "Russian-Backed Propaganda Networks Claim Obama is a CIA Agent," Accuracy in Media, July 19, 2011, http://newswithviews.com/Kincaid/cliff537.htm.

[5] Remnick, *op. cit.*

[6] The programs included "Project Mockingbird," supervised by Cord Meyer, the ex-husband of former JFK lover Mary Meyer. Its purpose was to influence the domestic and global media with CIA assets working in journalism. Another such program was "MK-Ultra," which focused on mind-control. This at times involved doses of LSD to unsuspected targets to watch their reactions. At other times, the MK Ultra program was to lure targets into sex scandals.

[7] Sundance, "President Obama: Part II – After High School Through College(s)," Conservative Treehouse, April 26, 2011, http://theconservativetreehouse.com/2011/04/26/president-obama-do-we-know-who-he-is-part-ii-after-high-school-through-colleges.

[8] Arnold Dyre, "Last call for Bill's Bar," *Grenada Star*, February 2, 2010, http://www.grenadastar.com/v2/content.aspx?module=ContentItem&ID=164186&MemberID=1218, as cited by Madsen, *The Manufacturing of a President, op. cit.*, 29.

[9] Smith, Amanda. *Newspaper Titan: The infamous Life and Monumental Times of Cissy Patterson.* Knopf, 2011.

[10] Maraniss, *Barack Obama, op. cit.*, 428.

[11] Joseph Cannon, "Spies, lies, Barry and his mom," CannonFire, September 2008, http://cannonfire.blogspot.com/2008/11/spies-lies-barry-and-his-mom.html.

[12] Jerome R. Corsi, "Obama's 'missing year' at Columbia found? Clearinghouse claims its reports were wrong, transcript still under wraps," July 8, 2012, http://www.wnd.com/2012/07/record-shows-obama-at-columbia-only-1-year.

[13] Remnick, *op. cit.*, 103.

[14] Obama, *Dreams From My Father, op. cit.*, 133.

[15] D'Souza, Dinesh. *The Roots of Obama's Rage.* Regnery, 2010, 101-05.

[16] Interview, Wayne Allen Root, September 23, 2010.

[17] Judy Maltz, "Obama's Israeli Columbia classmates don't recall the young president," *Haaretz,* March 13, 2013, http://www.haaretz.com/weekend/week-s-end/obama-s-israeli-columbia-classmates-don-t-recall-the-young-president.premium-1.509648.

[18] Jason Kissner, "'Skeeterism' and Obama's Columbia Years," American Thinker, February 7, 2013,

http://www.americanthinker.com/2013/02/skeeterism_and_obamas_columbi a_years.html.

19 Michael Iachetta, "Reconstructing Obama's Columbia Transcript," American Thinker, February 11, 2013, http://www.americanthinker.com/2013/02/m-jason_kissner_recently_questioned_president.html.

20 Brzezinski, Zbigniew. *Power and Principle: Memoirs of the National Security Adviser 1977-1981*. Farrar, Straus, Giroux, 1983, 5.

21 Issacson, Walter. *Kissinger*. Simon & Schuster, 1992, 124-25. A top Rockefeller aide assembling the 1968 campaign team told Kissinger that Brzezinski could be the campaign's top foreign policy aide if Kissinger would not devote sufficient time to the work. The anecdote illustrates how Brzezinski, regarded throughout his career as a Democrat, may have been beyond those partisan concerns at times.

22 Ibid., 367. The former national security advisor to Carter states that he was "appalled" at Turner's "inept" analysis of Iran. Yet Brzezinski states memoirs (pages 515-16) that he was surprised at Carter's defeat after "a historically impressive record" in foreign affairs.

23 Sick, Gary. *October Surprise: America's Hostages in Iran and the Election of Ronald Reagan*. Crown, 1991, 3-36.

24 Wayne Madsen interview, March 4, 2013.

25 Sick, *October Surprise, op. cit.*,141-43. Robert Parry,"Second Thoughts on October Surprise," Consortium News, June 8, 2013, http://consortiumnews.com/2013/06/08/second-thoughts-on-october-surprise.

26 Carter, Jimmy. *White House Diary*. Farrar, Straus & Giroux, 2010, 24 and 375.

27 Maraniss, *Barack Obama, op. cit.*, 459. See also, Tarpley, *The Postmodern Coup, op. cit.*, 79. "It is plausible, although not yet proven, that Obama was discovered by the Brzezinskis [including son Mark, a member of the Clinton Administration's National Security Council] and created from the ground up starting in the early 1980s. Zbig taught at Columbia University from 1960 to 1989, and was the head of the head of the Institute for Communist Affairs, a nest of anti-Soviet ideologues. After two years at Occidental College in California, Obama transferred to Columbia for his junior and senior years, majoring in political science, with a specialization in international relations – Brzezinski's own bailiwick – and receiving a B.A degree in 1983." See also, *Power and Principle, op. cit.*, as quoted by Tarpley: "I remember discussing his [Carter's membership] with my two principal Trilateral Commission Colleagues, Gerard Smith and George Franklin….I then said, "Well, he's obviously our man.""

28 Ibid., 135.

29 Madsen, *op. cit.*, 222-23.

30 Obama, *Dreams from my Father, op. cit.*, 135-36.

31 Frazier, Mondo. *The Secret Life of Barack Hussein Obama*. Threshold/Simon & Schuster, 2011, 103-11.

32 Maraniss, *op. cit.*, 472.

33 Ibid., 140.

[34] Tarpley, *Barack H. Obama: The Unauthorized Biography, op. cit.*, 82.

[35] Ibid., 135.

[36] Ibid., 129-131. Wright's rhetoric from the pulpit in those years in the 1980s would severely harm the 2008 Obama campaign upon the media's discovery of audiotapes of such sermons as the one containing "God damn America" language. This posed a major challenge for the candidate. Obama finessed the problem with an eloquent speech and doubtless more private messages from his backers to the Rev. Wright on why he should keep quiet.

[37] Amy Sullivan, "The Origin of Obama Pastor Problem," *Time*, March 20, 2008, http://www.time.com/time/magazine/article/0,9171,1724383,00.html."

[38] Ayers, Bill. *Fugitive Days: A Memoir*. Beacon, 2001. See also, Jeffrey Ressner, "Ayers script hopes to gain from Obama," October 6, 2008, http://www.politico.com/news/stories/1008/14321.html.

[39] Cashill, Jack. *Deconstructing Obama: The Life, Loves, and Letters of America's First Postmodern President*. Threshold, 2009.

[40] Grathwohl's lecture was: "White Reds Exploiting Blacks: The Weather Underground, Barack Obama, and the Fundamental Transformation of the United States."

[41] As an editor of the *Cornell Daily Sun*, I helped cover one of the most notorious student occupations in the country, the armed takeover of Cornell University student union in 1969. For *A Century at Cornell*, a book published by the Sun in 1980 commemorating the university's centennial, *Sun* editors asked me to contribute a chapter on black power and anti-war protests, "The End of a Bizarre Era." That summer, I earned my first income as a journalist by providing information as a "stringer" to the *Chicago Tribune* and *Chicago Daily News* on the founding of "The Weather Underground," a breakaway faction of Students for a Democratic Society led by Ayres and Dorhn. A friend active in a Boston chapter of SDS loaned me a membership card, which was enough for me to be on the periphery of organizational issues briefly but not to obtain newsworthy information.

[42] Greene, *The Quiet American, op. cit.*

[43] *Somebody Up There Likes Me*, starring Paul Newman and directed by Robert Wise, is a 1956 film based on the life of hard-punching middleweight boxer Rocky Graziano. The movie, based on Graziano's memoir, exemplifies the underdog spirit and faith in higher power. Archive, *New York Times*, http://movies.nytimes.com/movie/45561/Somebody-Up-There-Likes-Me/details.

[44] Jack Cashill, "Saudi billionaire did help Obama into Harvard; Jack Cashill shares shocking secret president tried to keep under wraps," WND, September 23, 2012, http://www.wnd.com/2012/09/saudi-billionaire-did-help-obama-into-harvard; See also, E.R. Shipp, "E.R. Shipp Remembers Percy Sutton," *Harlem World Magazine*, January 19, 2010, http://harlemworldmag.com/2010/01/19/er-shipp-remembers-percy-sutton: and Ben Smith, "What Percy Sutton Might Have Been Talking About, Buzzfeed," September 24, 2012, http://www.buzzfeed.com/bensmith/what-percy-sutton-might-have-been-talking-about.

45 Douglas Martin, "Percy E. Sutton, Political Trailblazer, Dies at 89," *New York Times*, December 27, 2009, http://www.nytimes.com/2009/12/28/nyregion/28sutton.html?pagewanted=all&_r=0.

46 Katie Glueck, and Bobby Cervantes, "Donald Trump Obama announcement: Trump will give $5 million to charity if Obama releases records," *Politico*, October 24, 2012, http://www.politico.com/news/stories/1012/82810.html.

47 Wessel, David. *In FED We Trust: Ben Bernanke's War on the Great Panic.* Crown Business, 2010.

48 Author interviews with Dr. Randy Short, 2011 (various dates) and July 16, 2012, Washington, DC.

49 Jack Cashill, "Did Bill Ayers Write Obama's "Dreams"? (Part 1 of 3), World Net Daily, September 18, 2008, http://www.cashill.com/natl_general/did_bill_ayers_write_1.htm; and Cashill, Jack, *Deconstructing Obama, op. cit.*

50 Remnick, *op. cit.*, 253-255.

51 Conn Carroll, "The Obama you don't know: The myth of the 'rock-star professor'," *Washington Examiner*, September 20, 2012, http://washingtonexaminer.com/chapter-ii-the-myth-of-the-rock-star-professor/article/2508418#.UHXCgFHfJ8E.

52 Corsi, *Where's the Birth Certificate? op. cit.*, 324-5.

53 Corsi, *loc. cit.*

54 Kagan, Elena. "When A Speech Code Is A Speech Code: The Stanford Policy and the Theory of Incidental Restraints," 29 University of California at Davis Law Review 957 (1996); Kagan, Elena. "Private Speech, Public Purpose: The Role of Governmental Motive in First Amendment Doctrine," 63 University of Chicago Law Review 413 (1996); Kagan, Elena. "Confirmation Messes, Old and New," 62 University of Chicago Law Review 919 (1995) (book review); Kagan, Elena. "For Justice Marshall," 71 Texas Law Review 1125 (1993); Kagan, Elena. "A Libel Story: Sullivan Then and Now," 18 Law and Social Inquiry 197 (1993) (book review); Kagan, Elena. "Regulation of Hate Speech and Pornography After R.A.V," 60 University of Chicago Law Review 873 (1993); Kagan, Elena. "The Changing Faces of First Amendment Neutrality: *R.A.V. v St. Paul, Rust v Sullivan,* and the Problem of Content-Based Under inclusion," 1992 Supreme Court Review 29 (1992).

55 Mendell, *op. cit.*,103.

56 Remnick, *op. cit.*, 272.

57 Woods Fund, http://www.woodsfund.org/site/epage/61430_735.htm.

58 Mendell, *op. cit.*, 103.

59 Scott, *op. cit.*, 292. In 2009, the Duke University Press published the thesis as a book: Dunham, S. Ann. *Surviving Against the Odds: Village Industry in Indonesia.*

60 Remnick, *op. cit.*, 272. Jarrett's title was senior advisor and assistant to the president for Public Engagement and Intergovernmental Affairs. Earlier, she was co-chairperson of the Obama-Biden Transition Project. WhiteHouse.gov. "White House Staff," http://www.whitehouse.gov/administration/staff/valerie-jarrett.

[61] John M. Broder, "Powerful Shaper of U.S. Rules Quits, With Critics in Wake," *The New York Times*, August 3, 2012, http://www.nytimes.com/2012/08/04/science/earth/cass-sunstein-to-leave-top-regulatory-post.html.

[62] Power, Samantha. *A Problem From Hell: American and the Age of Genocide*. Perseus /Basic, 2002. Power was executive director of a human rights center at Harvard University before campaigning for Obama and joining his administration. Assisted by a grant from George Soros's Open Society Institute, her award-winning book is 610 pages. Despite its length, it had no room to address 1960s killings in Indonesia. The index does not mention Indonesia, Sukarno, or Suharto.

[63] Cass R. Sunstein and Adrian Vermeule, "Conspiracy Theories," Cass R. Sunstein & Adrian Vermeule, Harvard Law, and University of Chicago Law School Working Papers, January 15, 2008, http://papers.ssrn.com/sol3/papers.cfm?abstract_id=1084585.

[64] Jeff Zeleny, "After 'Monster' Remark, Aide to Obama Resigns," March 7, 2008, http://thecaucus.blogs.nytimes.com/2008/03/07/obama-aide-apologizes-for-calling-clinton-a-monster.

[65] Diana Johnstone, "The Good Intentions That Pave the Road to War," War is a Crime, February 5, 2013, http://warisacrime.org/content/good-intentions-pave-road-war; Chris Hedges, "The Hijacking of Human Rights," TruthDig/OpEd News, April 8, 2013. http://www.opednews.com/articles/The-Hijacking-of-Human-Rig-by-Chris-Hedges-130408-668.html.

[66] For criticism of the Sunstein working paper, see: Griffin, David Ray. *Cognitive Infiltration: An Obama Appointee's Plan to Undermine the 9/11 Conspiracy Theory*. Olive Branch, 2011; Glenn Greenwald, "Obama Confidant's Spine-Chilling Proposal," Salon, January 15, 2010, http://www.salon.com/news/op.inion/glenn_greenwald/2010/01/15/sunstein/index.html. For discussion of use of secret government payments to the key academic supposedly advocating the Obama health care plan from an independent perspective, see Clark Hoyt, "The Source's Stake In The News," *New York Times*, January 17, 2010, http://www.nytimes.com/2010/01/17/op.inion/17pubed.html; Glenn Greenwald, "Krugman, Gruber And Non-Disclosure Issues," Salon, January 16, 2010, http://www.salon.com/news/op.inion/glenn_greenwald/2010/01/16/krugman/index.html; Paul Krugman, "More On Jon Gruber," *New York Times*, January 15, 2010, http://krugman.blogs.nytimes.com/2010/01/15/more-on-jon-gruber. For a more general assessment on justice / death penalty issues, see, John J. Donohue III Lecture, "Powerful Evidence the Death Penalty Deters? Surely You Are Joking, Mr. Sunstein," Lecture at Yale Law School on appointment as Homer Surbeck Professor of Law, March 6, 2006, http://lawcasts.wordpress.com/2006/03/07/from-the-archives-john-donohues-inaugural-lecture-yale (must have account).

[67] Alice Palmer finished third in a primary won by Jesse Jackson, Jr. Embittered by Obama's role, she announced that she would not support Obama in the

general election. Mendell, *op. cit.*, 108-110. See also, Carol Felsenthal, "Barack Obambi? Not quite; just ask Alice Palmer," Huffington Post, July 1, 2008, http://www.huffingtonpost.com/carol-felsenthal/barack-obambi-not-quite-j_b_110297.html; and Christi Parsons, "Once Obama's mentor, Alice Palmer now campaigns for Clinton," *Chicago Tribune/Los Angeles Times*, April 26, 2008, http://latimesblogs.latimes.com/washington/2008/04/once-obamas-men.html.

[68] Dan Morain and Tom Hamburger, "Obama dogged by ties to donor," *Los Angeles Times*, January 23, 2008, http://articles.latimes.com/2008/jan/23/nation/na-rezko23. See also, James L. Merriner, "Mr. Inside Out," *Chicago Magazine*, November 2007, http://www.chicagomag.com/Chicago-Magazine/November-2007/Mr-Inside-Out/.

[69] Nomaan Merchant, "Tony Rezko Sentenced: Former Blagojevich Fundraiser Won't Serve More Time For New Conviction," Huffington Post, December 22, 2011. http://www.huffingtonpost.com/2011/12/22/tony-rezko-sentenced-blag_n_1165774.html.

[70] Jackie Calmes, "Statehouse Yields Clues to Obama; Sharp Elbows of Illinois Politics Taught Lessons In Art of Compromise," Wall Street Journal, February 23, 2007, http://online.wsj.com/article/SB117219748197216894.html

[71] Penny S. Pritzker, Biography, http://www.penny-pritzker.com/penny-pritzker-biography.html. See also, Wikipedia, Penny Pritzker, http://en.wikipedia.org/wiki/Penny_Pritzker.

[72] Greg Palast, "Billionaire Burglar Breaks into Obama's Cabinet, Pinch-Penny Pritzker pockets Commerce post," Truth-out, February 13, 2013, http://truth-out.org/opinion/item/14493-billionaire-banker-bandit-likely-commerce-secretary. See also, Shane Tritsch, "Tremors in the Empire," *Chicago Magazine*, December, 2001, http://www.chicagomag.com/Chicago-Magazine/December-2002/Tremors-in-the-Empire.

[73] Mendell, *op. cit.*, 171, 213-17.

[74] Jake Tapper, "Bill Seems Flustered," ABC News, January 8, 2008, http://abcnews.go.com/blogs/politics/2008/01/bill-seems-flus.

[75] Jake Tapper, "Was Hillary Dismissing MLK?" ABC News, January 7, 2008. http://abcnews.go.com/blogs/politics/2008/01/was-hillary-dis.

[76] Carl Hulse, "Civil Rights Tone Prompts Talk of an Endorsement," *New York Times*, January 11, 2008. http://www.nytimes.com/2008/01/11/us/politics/11clyburn.html?_r=1&scp=1&sq=clyburn. Clyburn went on to campaign for Obama, helping him secure victory in South Carolina and nationally. Once in office, Obama named Clyburn's daughter to become a member of the five-person Federal Communications Commission regulating the media and rest of the communications industry.

[77] YouTube, "Bill Clinton on Obama: Big Fairy Tale," uploaded by ScarceTV on January 8, 2008, http://www.youtube.com/watch?v=YLDx4NZr2u4.

[78] Andrew Gavin Marshall, "Barack O'Bilderberg: Picking the President," Global Research, June 9, 2008, http://www.globalresearch.ca/barack-o-bilderberg-

picking-the-president/9270. and Alyssa Farah, "Obama, Clinton Mum on Bilderberg," WND, June 7, 2008, http://www.wnd.com/2008/06/66442.

.[79] Wayne Madsen, "The Story of Obama, Part IV: More evidence surfaces on Obama's and his family's deep CIA links," Aug. 25, 2010; available at www.waynemadsenreport.com (Subscription required).

[80] Tarpley, Webster G. *9/11 Synthetic Terror*, Progressive, 2008. *See also*, Kay, Jonathan. *Among the Truthers: A Journey Through America's Growing Conspiracist Underground*. Harper, 2011, 87-88, 114-16. Kay is managing editor of Canada's National Post and a Yale Law School graduate who discussed his book as a 2011 guest on my weekly public affairs radio show, *MTL Washington Update*. See also, David Frum, "Among the Truthers and Other Conspiracists," Daily Beast, April 3, 2012, http://www.thedailybeast.com/articles/2012/04/03/among-the-truthers-and-other-conspiracy-theorists.html. The column indicated that CNN and *Newsweek* commentator Frum is a close friend of Kay's. Viewers may evaluable that discussion here: Book TV/ C-SPAN2, "C-SPAN 9/11 Debate: Webster Tarpley vs. Jonathan Kay," (Video, 1 hour, 42 minutes), Spy Museum, April 2, 2012, http://www.youtube.com/watch?v=-QMS0dMRz-o.

Chapter 7, Prescott Bush: The Roots of the Bushes

[1] Kelley, Kitty. *The Family: The Real Story of the Bush Dynasty*. Doubleday, 2004.

[2] Tarpley, Webster G. and Chaitkin, Anton. *George Bush: The Unauthorized Biography*. Executive Intelligence, 1992, 117-20.

[3] Samuel Russell became the largest American trader with China while cooperating with the British East India Company as it helped Britain balance its trade debt from tea and silk by exporting opium from India and Turkey into China against the desires of China's rulers. Fairbank, John King. *Trade and Diplomacy on the China Coast: The Opening of the Treaty Ports, 1842-1854*. Harvard University, 1953, 27-29; Linda Minor, "Why Would the Harvard Corporation Protect the Drug Trade?" Minor Musings, 2002, http://www.minormusings.com/Drugs/Delanos.html.

[4] Some of the initial members of Skull and Bones were from wealthy merchant families with pro-British sympathies, and later were from families harboring Confederate secessionist or similar opposition to the dominant United States government. These families included supporters of former U.S. Vice President Aaron Burr's failed effort to raise a private army to carve from U.S. southern and western territories a vast new empire that would be allied with Britain or Spain. Tarpley and Chaitkin, *Ibid*. See also, Stewart, David O. *American Emperor: Aaron's Burr's Challenge to Jefferson's America*. Simon & Schuster, 2011. The book does not discuss Yale or Skull and Bones, but is a lively description of a little-remembered era when Burr, who tied Thomas Jefferson in the Electoral College presidential vote of 1800, decided to raise a private army to carve from U.S. territories a new nation allied with European powers. As the publisher's blurb aptly states, "Stewart's vivid account of Burr's tumultuous life offers a rare and eye-opening description of the new nation's struggle to define itself."

[5] Robbins, Alexandra. *Secrets of the Tomb: Skull and Bones, the Ivy League and the Secret Paths to Power*. Back Bay, 2002, 3-4.

---

[6] Staff report, "High Military Honors Conferred on Capt. Bush; For Notable Gallantry When Leading Allied Commanders Were Endangered, Local Man Is Awarded French, English and U.S. Cross," *The Ohio State Journal* (Columbus), August 8, 1918, as cited in *Tarpley and Chaitkin, op. cit.*

[7] *Ibid.* 17-18.

[8] Rockefeller-controlled Remington Arms was the government's leading supplier. Bush worked for War Industries Board Chairman Bernard Baruch, a Wall Street financier who had made a fortune in the sugar market and also had close ties with, among others the railroad and financial magnates in the Harriman family. Tarpley and Chaitkin, *op. cit.,* 15.

[9] Ibid., 14.

[10] Ibid., 20.

[11] Ben Aris and Duncan Campbell, "How Bush's grandfather helped Hitler's rise to power," *The Guardian*, September 25, 2004, http://www.guardian.co.uk/world/2004/sep/25/usa.secondworldwar. See also, Thyssen, Fritz. *I Paid Hitler.* Kennikat, 1941, 133, as cited by Tarpley, *George Bush, op. cit.,* 26-42.

[12] Aris and Campbell, *op. cit.,* and Tarpley, *George Bush, op. cit.,* 30-33. Aris and Campbell wrote, "The Bush Family recently approved a flattering biography of Prescott Bush entitled *Duty, Honour, Country* by Mickey Herskowitz. The publishers, Rutledge Hill Press, promised the book would 'deal honestly with Prescott Bush's alleged business relationships with Nazi industrialists and other accusations.' In fact, the allegations are dealt with in less than two pages." Herskowitz, Mickey. *Duty, Honor, Country: The Life and Legacy of Prescott Bush.* Rutledge Hill, 2003.See also, Baker, *op. cit.,* 421-22, which describes the Prescott Bush book as an effort by the Bush Family to make-up for his work on an abortive campaign biography of George W. Bush in 1999 that threatened to disclose too much via George Bush interviews. Baker quoted Herskowitz, a well-known Houston sportswriter and author, as stating that a Bush campaign representative came to his home and "took his notes and computer files," thereby "removing all his documentation of Bush's thoughts." The incident shows the vast power of candidates compared to even well-established biographers and news reporters who need access to the candidates for material.

[13] As a Yale trustee and otherwise, Prescott Bush was prominent in birth control, eugenics and mind-control experimentation efforts housed at Yale Medical School and other Yale facilities. Among them was the Birth Control Society, renamed later as Planned Parenthood. These efforts more than his pre-war Nazi funding activities on behalf of Thyssen helped cause Bush's narrow loss in 1950 of his first race for a U.S. Senate seat. "Now in 1950, people who knew something about Prescott Bush knew that he had very unsavory roots in the eugenics movement. There were then, just after the anti-Hitler war, few open advocates of sterilization of 'unfit' or 'unnecessary' people." Tarpley and Chaitkin, *op. cit.,* 75.

[14] For discussion of Gray-led eugenics and sterilization efforts that evolved into the group Planned Parenthood, see Tarpley and Chaitkin, *George Bush, op. cit.,* 56-

62. See pages 76-82 for discussion of Gordon Gray's longstanding national security roles continuing into the Ford administration.

[15] For discussion of the close relationship between the Bush and Gray families, see Phillips, Kevin. *American Dynasty: Aristocracy. Fortune. And the Politics of Deceit in the House of Bush*. Viking, 2004, 196.

[16] Perlstein, Rick. *Before the Storm: Barry Goldwater and the Unmaking of the American Consensus*. Hill & Wang, 2001, available at George Mason University's History News Network, http://hnn.us/articles/203.html. See also, Mansfield, Stephen A. *The Faith of George W. Bush*. Strang, 2003.

[17] Baker, *Family of Secrets, op. cit.*, 166. Rockefeller, as president of Rockefeller Center housing the Radio City Music Hall, home of the Rockettes, was not without his own charms. The globe-trotting heir and high-ranking official had a famously warm smile, rivaling that of the Eisenhower's. Experienced New York City journalists regarded Rockefeller as an extreme philanderer, even by the standards of the *Mad Men* era, according to former NBC and CBS editor John Kelly.

[18] Ibid. See also, Loftus, John, and Mark Aarons, *The Secret War Against the Jews*. St. Martin's Press, 1994.

Chapter 8, George H. W. Bush: Poppy's Seed and Bitter Harvest

[1] "Nomination of George Bush To Be Director of Central Intelligence," *Congressional Record*, January 27. (1976).

[2] Bush, George H. W. *All the Best: My Life in Letters and Other Writings*. Touchstone / Simon and Schuster, 1999. See also, Bush, George with Victor Gold. *Looking Forward*. Doubleday, 1987; Bush, George with Doug Wead. *George Bush: Man of Integrity*. Harvest House, 1987; Bush, George H. W. and Brent Scowcroft. *A World Transformed*. Knopf, 1998. George H. W. Bush, Wikipedia: http://en.wikipedia.org/wiki/George_H.W.Bush.

[3] Greene, *The Quiet American, op., cit.*, 52. "I never knew a man who had better motives for all the trouble he caused," says the novel's narrator of Alden Pyle, a recent Harvard graduate sent from CIA headquarters to Saigon in the early 1950s. According to the novel: Pyle was a covert operative under the guise of an economic development planner. His mission was to create a dissension, including the bombing of a marketplace, during the French-Viet Minh war, thereby paving the way for an American presence when French colonial rule inevitably collapsed. The novel by Greene, an Oxford educated former British intelligence officer, has become a powerful metaphor for good intentions gone awry on the world stage.

[4] Baker, *op. cit.*, 72-73. See also, Douglass, James W. *JFK and the Unspeakable: Why He Died and Why It Matters*. Orbis, 2008, 47-49, 168. Douglass cited evidence that de Mohrenschildt kept in contact with the CIA while he helped Lee Harvey Oswald, and was rewarded with a $285,000 contract from Haiti's dictator for an oil exploration deal. Douglass argued that U.S. authorities secretly assigned Oswald, a former Marine, to suspicious undercover missions with leftists — and those missions led Oswald to become a patsy readily blamed for JFK's killing. Russell, Dick. *On the Trail of the JFK Assassins*. Skyhorse, 2008, 85-88, 133-38, is among others to probe such evidence.

[5] Bush, George and Victor Gold, *Looking Forward,* Doubleday, 1987, 36; Bush, George with Doug Wead. *George Bush: Man of Integrity,* Harvest House, 1987, 4-5; Stinnett, Robert B. *George Bush: His World War II Years.* Brassey's, 1992, 89; Hyams, Joe. *Flight of the Avenger: George Bush at War.* Harcourt, Brace Jovanovich, 1991; and Terrence Hunt, "Bush Praised for War Heroism," Associated Press, September 2, 1984.

[6] Allan Wolper and Al Ellenberger, "The day Bush bailed out," *New York Post,* August 12, 1988; and Associated Press, "Gunner in Squadron Disputes Bush on Downing of Bomber," *New York Times,* August 13, 1988.

[7] President's Commission on the Assassination of President John F. Kennedy (Warren Commission) (Full text), September 24, 1964, http://www.archives.gov/research/jfk/warren-commission-report/index.html and Warren Commission Hearings, http://www.history-matters.com/archive/contents/wc/contents_wh.htm. See also, Anthony Lewis, "Warren Commission Finds Oswald Guilty and Says Assassin and Ruby Acted Alone," *New York Times,* September 28, 1964; Bugliosi, Vincent. *Reclaiming History: The Assassination of President John F. Kennedy.* Norton, 2007, and Kelley, *op. cit.,* 97.

[8] Tarpley and Chaitkin, *op. cit.,* 116.

[9] Parmet, Herbert S. *George Bush: Life of a Lone Star Yankee.* Lisa Drew / Scribner, 1996.

[10] Two authors have attempted to establish the hundred wealthiest Americans, using as a rough measure estimated net assets as a comparison to gross national product. By this measure, John D. Rockefeller was the wealthiest American by a significant margin, with steel baron Andrew Carnegie the only other top-five member to survive into the Twentieth Century. Railroad tycoon Edward H. Harriman ranked number twenty-one in the list of all wealthy Americans, including those deceased before 1900. Financier J. Pierpont Morgan, whose achievements included organizing U.S. Steel Corp. and serving as exclusive bonds broker in the United States for Great Britain during World War I, ranked two spaces behind Harriman. Klepper, Michael and Robert Gunther. *The Wealthy 100: From Benjamin Franklin to Bill Gates-A Ranking of the Richest Americans, Past and Present.* Citadel, 1996. See also, J.D. Roth, "The Wealthy 100: A Ranking of the Richest Americans, Past and Present," Get Rich Slowly, July 29, 2006, Modified August 30, 2011, http://www.getrichslowly.org/blog/2006/07/29/the-wealthy-100-a-ranking-of-the-richest-americans-past-and-present.

[11] Phillips, *op. cit.,* 202-03.

[12] Ibid, 122; Tarpley and Chaitkin, *op. cit.,* 138-54.

[13] Ibid., 141. Several accounts claim that Neil Mallon (for whom George H.W. Bush named his son "Neil Mallon Bush") helped Prescott Bush display Geronimo's skull, stolen from a grave in Oklahoma, at Skull and Bones headquarters in New Haven. Ibid. 129-32. See also, Walter Pincus and Bob Woodward, "Bush Opened Up To Secret Yale Society," *Washington Post,* August 7, 1988; Walter Pincus and Bob Woodward, "Doing Well With help from Family, Friends," *Washington Post,* August 11, 1988; Scott Armstrong and Jeff Nason, "Company Man, " *Mother Jones,* October 1988.

[14] Tarpley and Chaitkin, *op. cit.*, 45.

[15] Ibid. Cockburn and St. Clair wrote: "That quintessential insider, Averell Harriman, was often to be seen at Mrs Graham's house in Georgetown, and it was Averell who once furnished a reminder of the journalistic facts of life so trenchant that every reporter and editor should have it tacked to their walls. Writing in 1943 to his friend James Lovett at the War Department, Harriman rasped his fury that *Newsweek* had dared question the efficiency of daylight bombing of Germany, a tactic devised by Lovett: "Tell Roland [Averell's brother, then a director of *Newsweek*, owned by Vincent Astor, who later sold it to Phil Graham] that I am in dead earnest and will brook no compromise."

[16] Estulin, Daniel. *The Bilderberg Group*. TrineDay, 2009, 28. See also his www.bilderbergbook.com. Thanks doubtless to Estulin's work, the Bilderberg Group discloses some of its activities on a website: http://www.bilderbergmeetings.org/index.html.

[17] Ibid., 95-99.

[18] "Hugh Liedtke, George H. W.'s principal partner from 1953 to 1959, besides being the Amherst and Harvard-educated son of Gulf Oil's chief counsel, was also a tax shelter whiz who began trading oil-producing properties in a way that permitted the eventual owner to defer his tax liabilities until the field was depleted, much like IRA accounts are deferred until someone's retirement." Phillips, *op. cit.*, 121-22. See also the role of oil expert Ray Kravis, father of future leveraged buy-out (LBO) mastermind Henry Kravis. "Firms like Brown Brothers Harriman, Goldman Sachs, and Bear Steams relied on [Ray] Kravis's ability to assess oil properties with a combined geological, accounting, and tax expertise. Clearly, Prescott Bush was well placed to put his son into the brainbox of the oil industry, not its toolshed, and that financial foundation always remained important during George H.W. Bush's stint as a Connecticut Yankee in King Petroleum's Court." Phillips, *op. cit.*, 122.

[19] Phillips, *op. cit.*, 200-08; Tarpley and Chaitkin, *op. cit.*, 150.

[20] William F. Buckley, "Who Did What?" *National Review*, November 1, 2005,. For context, see Melinda Pillsbury-Foster, "The Grand Pere of the NeoCons," Freedom's Phoenix, September. 22, 2007, http://www.freedomsphoenix.com/Article/024114-2007-09-23-how-the-rockefeller-republicans-raped-america-part-1-william-f.htm and Llewellyn H. Rockwell, Jr., "Before the Storm," *American Enterprise*, July 2001, http://www.lewrockwell.com/rockwell/before-storm.html.

[21] Buckley, "Who Did What?" *op. cit.*

[22] Joseph McBride, "Where Was George?" *Nation*, August 13, 1988, as quoted in Lane, Mark. *Plausible Denial: Was the CIA Involved in the Assassination of JFK?* Skyhorse, 2011 (1991), 376-78.

[23] Fred J. Cook, "The Warren Commission Report, Parts I and II," *Nation*, June 13 and June 20, 1966. My mother met Cook while undertaking mob and drug research in the 1960s, and praised him to me as the most courageous, honest reporter she had encountered in her long career. I never met him but corresponded with him on media issues in his later years. In his memoir, he described his ordeal for 18 months in finding a publisher for his criticism of the Warren Commission in the face of near-universal praise of its findings.

Even his wife opposed him for the first time in their life about one of his reporting decisions: "I explained my fear that an evil, dangerous precedent might have been set. 'Well, who are *you* to challenge the Warren Commission?'" Cook, Fred J. *Maverick: Fifty years of Investigative Reporting.* Putnam's, 1984, 271-291. See also, *Executive Action*, starring Burt Lancaster, Robert Ryan, and Will Geer, directed by David Miller, National General, 1973, http://www.amazon.com/Executive-Action-Burt-Lancaster/dp/B00005JMA5; Jarlett, Franklin. *Robert Ryan.* McFarland, 1990, 173; and Epstein, Edward J. *Inquest: The Warren Commission and the Establishment of Truth*, Viking, 1966. Written while Epstein was a graduate student at Cornell, the latter was the first book-length critique disputing some Warren Commission findings. In 1977, Epstein was taking a break from a multi-day interview of George de Mohrenschildt when the latter was found dead of a shotgun blast that was ruled a suicide.

[24] Prouty, L. Fletcher. *JFK: The CIA, Vietnam, and the Plot to Assassinate John F. Kennedy.* Skyhorse, 2011 (1996.), 334. Dr. Cyril Wecht, the first independent forensics expert to examine JFK's autopsy records, asserted the JFK assassination was an overthrow of the government: a "coup d'état in America." Cyril H. Wecht, JFK Archives, http://www.cyrilwecht.com/journal/archives/jfk/index.php.

[25] Bush, Barbara. *Barbara Bush: A Memoir.* Scribner, 1994; and Bush, Barbara. *Reflections.* Scribner, 2003.

[26] Monica Perin, "Adios, Zapata! Colorful company founded by Bush relocates to N.Y.," *Houston Business Journal*, April 25, 1999, http://www.bizjournals.com/houston/stories/1999/04/26/story2.html.

[27] Clay F. Richards, "George Bush: Co-President in the Reagan administration," United Press International, March 10, 1981.

[28] Staff report, "Alexander Haig," *Time*, April 2, 1984, http://www.time.com/time/magazine/article/0,9171,954230,00.html.

[29] Tarpley and Chaitkin, *op. cit.* 365, "Inexorably, the Brown Brothers Harriman / Skull and Bones network went into action against Haig. The idea was to paint him as a power-hungry megalomaniac bent on dominating the administration of the weak figurehead Reagan."

[30] Prescott Bush said he received excellent political advice from Luce's wife, Claire Booth Luce, a Connecticut congresswoman, ambassador and wife of *Time-Life* media magnate Henry Luce: "Three things to remember: claim everything, explain nothing, deny everything." Transcript of seven oral history interviews with Senator Prescott Sheldon Bush for Columbia University's oral history project on the Eisenhower administration, Dwight D. Eisenhower Library , http://research.archives.gov/description/732354.

[31] Arthur Wiese and Margaret Downing, "Bush's Son Was to Dine with Suspect's Brother," *Houston Post*, March 31, 1981.

[32] The NBC-TV comedy show *Saturday Night Live* led the way in portraying Bush as a "wimp," an image that carried over into the general media. See generally, John Solomon, "A Wimp He Wasn't," *Newsweek*, March 20, 2011, http://www.thedailybeast.com/newsweek/2011/03/20/a-wimp-he-wasn-t.html.

[33] "Bush-Ferraro Vice-Presidential Debate," The American Presidency Project, October 11, 1984.

[34] "The principal elements of scandal in Iran-Contra may be reduced to the following points: 1) the secret arming other Khomeini regime in Iran by the U.S. government, during an official U.S.-decreed arms embargo against Iran, while the U.S. publicly denounced the recipients of its secret deliveries as terrorist and kidnapper—a policy initiated under the Jimmy Carter presidency and accelerated by the Reagan-Bush administration; 2) the Reagan–Bush administration's secret arming of its "contract" for war against the Sandinista regime in Nicaragua, while such aid was explicitly prohibited under U.S. law; 3) the use of communist and terrorist enemies – often armed directly by the Anglo-Americans – to justify a police state and covert, oligarchic rule at home; 4) paying or and protecting the gun-running projects with drug-smuggling, embezzlement, theft, by diversion from authorized US programs and the "silencing of both opponents and knowledgeable participants in the schemes; and 5) the continual, routine perjury and deception of the public by government officials pretending to have no knowledge of these activities; and the routine acquiescence in that deception by Congressmen too frightened to oppose it." Tarpley and Chaitkin, *op. cit.*, 385. See also, Parry, Robert. *Secrecy & Privilege: Rise of the Bush Dynasty from Watergate to Iraq*, Media Consortium, 2004; Parry, Robert. *Lost History: Contras, Cocaine, the Press & "Project Truth."* Media Consortium, 1999; Webb, Gary. *Dark Alliance: The CIA, the Contras, and the Crack Cocaine Explosion.* Seven Stories, 1998; and Baker, *op. cit.*, 314-15; Dan Rather Interview of Vice President George H.W. Bush, CBS/YouTube, January 1988. (Nine minutes), http://www.youtube.com/watch?v=FqwQw3THRvU; Rather, Dan. *Rather Outspoken.* Grand Central, 2012, 157-61; Rogers, Toby. *Ambushed: Secrets of the Bush Family, the Stolen Presidency, 9-11, and 2004.* TrineDay, 2004.

[35] See also, Scott Armstrong, *The Chronology: The Documented Day-by-Day Account of the Secret Military Assistance to Iran and the Contras.* Warner Books, 1987; Walsh, Lawrence. *Firewall.* Norton, 1997. See also, Reagan, Ronald. *Ronald Reagan: An American Life.* Threshold / Simon & Schuster, 1990, 528-31. Reagan denied knowledge of a deal, and quoted his diary as stating, "This whole irresponsible press bilge about hostages and Iran has gotten totally out of hand. The media looks like it's trying to create another Watergate." On May 15, 2002, I attended the Congressional Gold Medal ceremony at the Ronald Reagan Center in Washington, DC to honor the Reagan Presidency and benefit his library. Each guest received a special edition book of photo highlights commemorating the Reagan life story: Ronald Reagan Library. *Ronald Reagan An American Hero: His Voice, His Values, His Vision.* Tehabi Books, 2002 (Limited Edition). The dinner featured remarks by former First Lady Nancy Reagan and presentation of the highest award by Congress. It convened a Who's Who of the nation's Republican leadership and corporate supporters. At a table near the front, I enjoyed an extensive conversation with Senate Energy and Commerce Committee Chairman Sen. Ted Stevens and his wife, for example. Personal contact is important in such a busy city. Years afterward, the Alaska Republican graciously helped the Wireless Communications Association I ran by sharing his views in keynoting our conference on homeland security. This

was one of the rare speeches he made outside of the Senate or Alaska in 2008. He faced reelection that year, and a trial on federal corruption charges, later vacated.

36 MacArthur, John R. *The Selling of "Free Trade": NAFTA, Washington, and the Subversion of American Democracy.* University of California, 2001; Pizzo, Stephen; Mary Fricker and Paul Muolo. *Inside Job: The Looting of America's Savings and Loans.* McGraw-Hill, 1989.

37 Andrew Kreig, "No Harm, No Foul," *Hartford Courant*, March 1978. See also Bork, Robert H. *The Antitrust Paradox. A Policy at War with Itself.* Basic Books, 1978.

38 Despite the many Republican attacks it took Kennedy's former chief of staff, himself tainted by federal convictions, to describe the worst allegations: many years of promiscuous sexual and drug-use escapades by the senator with staff and others. Burke, Richard E. *The Senator: My Ten Years with Ted Kennedy.* St. Martin's, 1993.

39 Kreig, *Spiked, op. cit.*

40 Klein, Naomi. *The Shock Doctrine: The Rise of Disaster Capitalism.* Picador, 2008. See also, Staff, "The Shock Doctrine," *Publisher's Weekly*, July 23, 2007, http://www.publishersweekly.com/978-0-8050-7983-8

41 Smith, Jean Edward. *George Bush's War.* Henry Holt, 1992.

42 Unger, Craig. *House of Bush, House of Saud: The Secret Relationship Between the World's Two Most Powerful Dynasties.* Scribner, 2004, 308.

43 Parry, Robert. *Fooling America: How Washington Insiders Twist the Truth and Manufacture Convention Wisdom.* Morrow, 1992, 148-70. Parry estimated that only about 80,000 of two million Kuwaiti residents could vote because of bans against women and male descendants of foreigners with no forbears in the country before 1920. Ibid, 151.

44 David Gergen, "The barbarities of Saddam Hussein, In Kuwait, 22 babies died when invaders stole their incubators," *US News & World Report*, September 30, 1990, http://community.seattletimes.nwsource.com/archive/?date=19900930&slug=1095812.

45 MacArthur, John R. *Second Front: Censorship and Propaganda in the 1991 Gulf War.* University of California, 1992, 43. Unger, *op., cit.*, 136-38; John Martin, ABC-TV, March 15, 1991.

46 Russ Baker, "War Syrian Style? Has Assad Ordered Mass Rapes?" WhoWhatWhy, July 24, 2012, http://whowhatwhy.com/2012/07/24/war-syrian-style-has-assad-ordered-mass-rapes.

47 Gray, Robert Keith. *Presidential Perks Gone Royal: Your Taxes Are Being Used for Obama's Re-election.* New Voices, 2012.

48 Gray had several longstanding personal and professional secrets, according to a husband-and-wife investigative team in separate books. Gray was a close business associate for many years of former CIA agent Edward P. Wilson, a major lobbyist who specialized in setting up CIA front companies and donating to members of Congress before he was convicted of illegally selling weapons to Libya. A federal judge vacated charges, thereby freeing Wilson

after 22 years in prison. Wilson believed Gray could have helped exonerate him from a frame-up allegedly led by former CIA spymaster Theodore Shackley, a business rival to Wilson. Trento, Joseph J. *Prelude to Terror: The Rogue CIA and the Legacy of America's Private Intelligence Network.* Carroll & Graff, 2005. Trento, with three decades experience covering the CIA, reported also that Gray was well-known in gay circles living in constant fear of exposure by the Washington media. *Prelude, op. cit.* 171. See also, Trento, *The Power House, op. cit.*, 94 and 176-84, describing how Gray used for his own purposes his significant power over many journalists and their organizations because he knew from his CIA contacts that they had been secret assets for the agency in ways that could prove embarrassing if disclosed.

[49] Phillips, *American Dynasty, op. cit.,* 258.

[50] George H.W. Bush, "Toward a New World Order," as cited by John B. Judis, "George Bush Meet Woodrow Wilson," *New York Times*, November 20, 1990, http://www.nytimes.com/1990/11/20/opinion/george-bush-meet-woodrow-wilson.html.

[51] Robertson, Pat. *The New World Order.* W Publishing, 1992, 92. Robertson is a graduate of Yale Law School. As the son of a well-connected U.S. senator, Roberts surely knew about The Order, although he was ineligible for membership in the undergraduate-only secret society. Henry Kissinger and Tony Blair repeatedly used the term in their foreign policy speeches. Rather than try to parse the meaning further, however, it is enough to say the term carries powerful authority for certain audiences.

[52] Ibid., 95-143.

[53] Ibid., 99-105.

[54] Philip Weiss, "Masters of the Universe Go to Camp: Inside Bohemian Grove," *Spy Magazine*, November 1989, http://www.scribd.com/doc/101806446/Weiss-Philip-Masters-of-the-Universe-Go-to-Camp-Inside-the-Bohemian-Grove-Spy-Magazine-Nov-1989-Pp-58-76.

Chapter 9, George W.: Shameless, Heartless, & Selected -Not Elected

[1] Sam Stein, "George W. Bush: The President Who Must Not Be Named At Republican Convention," Huffington Post, August 29, 2012, http://www.huffingtonpost.com/2012/08/29/george-w-bush-republican-convention_n_1838248.html.

[2] Kelley, Kitty. *The Family: The Real Story of the Bush Dynasty.* Doubleday, 2004, 99.

[3] Bush, Barbara. *Barbara Bush: A Memoir.* Scribner, 1994, 34.

[4] George W. *Decision Points.* Crown, 2010, 6; Barbara Bush, *op. cit.,* 45; Bush, Laura. *Spoken from the Heart.* Scribner, 2010, 276; Kelley, *op. cit.,* 127-43.

[5] Wikipedia, George W. Bush, http://en.wikipedia.org/wiki/George_W._Bush.

[6] Frank, Justin A. *Bush on the Couch Inside the Mind of the President.* HarperCollins, 2004, 3-6.

[7] Ibid., 232.

[8] Ibid. 151.

[9] Ibid. 232.

[10] "What Poppy had done quietly, even furtively, W. often did with the swagger of an entitled prince. The result was a government that in essence was not unlike those of third world oligarchs – a vehicle for military dominance and bounty for favored supporters and friends. The ruler would residence unchallenged. Dissonant truth would be suppressed, and the tellers of them banished." Baker, Russ. *Family of Secrets: The Bush Dynasty, America's Invisible Government, and the Hidden History of the Last Fifty Years.* Bloomsbury, 2009, 466. See also, Bugliosi, Vincent. *The Prosecution of George W. Bush for Murder.* Vanguard, 2008.

[11] Baker, Russ. *Family of Secrets: The Bush Dynasty, America's Invisible Government, and the Hidden History of the Last Fifty Years.* Bloomsbury Press, 2009, 36-57.

[12] Baker, *op. cit.,*407-22, 439-53.

[13] Mapes, Mary. *Truth and Duty: The Press, the President and the Privilege of Power.* St. Martin's/Griffin, 2006; Rather, Dan, with Digby Diehl. *Rather Outspoken: My Life in the News.* Grand Central Publishing, 2012.

[14] Bush, Laura. *Spoken from the Heart.* Scribner, 2010, 96.

[15] Large numbers of irregularities broke in Lyndon Johnson's favor, including late-discovered votes and a boss-run county that reported a voter turnout of 99.6 percent with more than 99 percent of those votes for Johnson. Perhaps most remarkable in the entire situation was that the incumbent failed to obtain redress in the press, courts or Senate despite powerful evidence of fraud. Caro, Robert A. *The Years of Lyndon Johnson: Means of Ascent.* Knopf, 1990, 303-17.

[16] Ibid. 316.

[17] Wikipedia, KBR (company), http://en.wikipedia.org/wiki/KBR_%28company%29.

[18] Ibid., 16. See also, Caro, Robert A. *The Years of Lyndon Johnson: The Master of the Senate.* Knopf, 2002, 427-29. "As soon as the LB J Ranch was in good enough shape to be shown to journalists from Washington and New York, Johnson began to invite them down....He wanted his image to be that of a westerner, or to be more precise a south westerner – a Texan."

[19] Harken had CIA connections via Thomas Devine, the co-founder of Zapata Offshore. Its investors included George Soros and Harvard University. Baker, *op. cit.,* 336-43, 349-57. The board member's fee provided critical financial help to George W. Bush, who described himself as, "I'm all name and no money." Kelley, *op. cit.,* 427. Unger, Craig. *House of Bush, House of Saud.* Scribner, 2004.

[20] Baker, *op. cit.,* 330-32.

[21] Baker, *op. cit.,* 365. Tom Schieffer helped make George president of the Texas Rangers baseball team and a viable candidate for governor. In a sweetheart arrangement for insiders, the value of Bush's team investment increased from $700,000 to $17 million by the time he cashed out. Meanwhile, CBS News anchor and managing editor Dan Rather was challenging Vice President George H.W. Bush on air in the iconic interview about whether Bush were implicated in Iran-Contra criminality. Not surprisingly, a grateful Bush administration would name Tom Schieffer ambassador to Australia and then to Japan. CBS later ousted Rather in a brutal, humiliating, and unjustified vendetta. The avuncular-sounding Bob Schieffer, Tom's brother, assumed

most of Rather's duties while the CBA parent company, Viacom, achieved regulatory successes at the Bush-run FCC.

[22] Baker, *op. cit.*, 376-78.

[23] In a 1999 profile, the conservative commentator Tucker Carlson wrote that candidate George W. Bush mocked Karla Faye Tucker, by pretending she was pleading "Please, don't kill me," after Bush signed her death warrant. Tucker Carlson, "Devil May Care," *Talk Magazine*, August, 1999. See also, Anthony Lewis, "Texas Executions: GW Bush Has Defined Himself, Unforgettably, As Shallow And Callous," *New York Times*, June 17, 2000. "There have been questions all along about the depth and seriousness of George W. Bush. They have been brought into sharp focus now by a surprising issue: the way the death penalty is administered in Texas. In his comments on that subject Governor Bush has defined himself, unforgettably, as shallow and callous. In his five years as governor of Texas, the state has executed 131 prisoners — far more than any other state. Mr. Bush has lately granted a stay of execution for the first time, for a DNA test." Conservative commentator Tucker Carlson aroused a nationwide furor by alleging that Bush in an interviewed mocked Karla Faye Tucker and her desire to live before she was executed, http://en.wikipedia.org/wiki/Karla_Faye_Tucker#cite_note-12.

[24] Bush, *Decision Points, op. cit.*, 95.

[25] Bush handlers spiked the proposed Bush biography as impolitic, but let Herskowitz as a consolation deal write an authorized biography of Bush's grandfather, Herskowitz, Mickey. *Duty, Honor, Country: The Life and Legacy of Prescott Bush*. Rutledge Hill, 2003.

[26] The interview is recounted in *Family of Secrets*, Baker, *op. cit.*, 423. Author Russ Baker wrote of Herskowitz's recollections of Bush: "He was thinking of about invading Iraq in 2000," Herskowitz told me in our 2004 interview, leaning in a little to make sure I could hear him properly. "It was on his mind. He said to me: 'One of the keys to being see as a great leader is to be seen as a commander in chief....' I'm not going to waste it. I'm going to get everything passed that I want to get passed, and I'm going to have a successful presidency.'" Baker, *loc. cit.*

[27] With no warning or appeal, the targeted voters were turned away from the polls, costing the Democratic candidate, Al Gore, an estimated 20,000 votes. Later recounts showed the governor's brother, George W. Bush, won by just over 200 votes, thus winning all of Florida's electoral votes and the U.S. Presidency. ChoicePoint, via its DBT subsidiary, earned $2 million from the state for its work. DBT/ChoicePoint replaced a $5,000 contractor apparently not able to deliver the state and the presidency to the Bush Family. For that price increase, Florida taxpayers helped the Bush Family get good value. See Palast, Greg. *The Best Democracy Money Can Buy*. Plume/Penguin, 2004, especially 1-7, 21-23, 26, 28-39, 56-59, 349-57; Palast, Greg. *Armed Madhouse*. Dutton, 2006.

[28] A contrary view is illustrated by Bill Sammon, the White House correspondent for the *Washington Times*. He authored a book of polemics that had no footnotes and addressed none of Palast's reporting. Sammon, Bill. *At Any Cost: How Al Gore Tried to Steal the Election*. Regnery, 2001.

[29] Andrew Kreig, "Cutting Through Hype, Hypocrisy of Vote Fraud Claims," Justice Integrity Project, August 13, 2011, http://www.justice-integrity.org/faq/267-cutting-through-vote-fraud-claims-hypocrisy.

[30] Lyndon Johnson's vote-theft won a 1948 election to the Senate representing Texas, as widely documented by Caro and others. LBJ, with his outsize personality and ambitions, would himself boast of the victory, in part to show that his power was invulnerable to criticism.

[31] Bugliosi, Vincent, and Gerry Spence. *The Betrayal of America: How the Supreme Court Undermined the Constitution and Chose Our President.* Nation, 2001.

[32] Clarke, Richard A. *Against All Enemies: Inside America's War on Terror.* Free Press, 2004.

[33] Greenwald, Glenn. *A Tragic Legacy: How a Good vs. Evil Mentality Destroyed the Bush Presidency.* Crown, 2007; and Greenwald, Glenn. *How Would a Patriot Act? Defending American Values from a President Run Amok.* Working Assets Publishing, 2006.

[34] Smith, Jean Edward. *George Bush's War.* New York: Henry Holt, 1992.

[35] Trento, Susan B. *The Power House: Robert Keith Gray and the Selling of Access and Influence in Washington.* St. Martin's, 1992. MacArthur, John R. *Second Front: Censorship and Propaganda in the Gulf War.* University of California. 1992.

[36] James Bamford, "The Man Who Sold The War," *Rolling Stone*, November 30, 2005, http://www.rollingstone.com/allaccess/search (Subscription required). "During the run-up to the Iraqi war, the Bush Administration hired "perception management" expert John Rendon to sell the public and journalists on the merits of the war. For $16 million, Rendon fed journalists, including Judith Miller of the *New York Times*, bogus intelligence about Iraq's WMD program."

[37] Blair, Tony. *A Journey: My Political Life.* Knopf, 2010 as cited by Robert Parry, "Blair Reveals Cheney's War Agenda," Consortium News, September 6, 2010. http://www.consortiumnews.com/2010/090610.html. Wesley Clark quoted a senior Pentagon official post-9/11 as telling him in 2001 to expect a campaign against seven Muslim nations. Clark, Wesley K. *Winning Modern Wars: Iraq, Terrorism, and the American Empire.* Public Affairs, 2003, 130.

[38] Bartlett, Bruce. *Imposter: How George W. Bush Bankrupted America and Betrayed the Reagan Legacy.* Doubleday, 2006. Hartmann, Thom. *Screwed: The Undeclared War Against the Middle Class – And What We Can Do About It.* Berrett-Koehler, 2006.

[39] O'Neill, John and Jerome R. Corsi. *Unfit for Command: Swift Boat Veterans Speak Out about John Kerry.* Regnery, 2004.

[40] Redstone's activities and focus were so wide-ranging that he omitted any mention of CBS News or its icons Dan Rather and Walter Cronkite in his 2001 autobiography: Redstone, Sumner with Peter Knobler. *A Passion to Win.* Simon & Schuster, 2001.

[41] Dan Rather, 1988 interview of Vice President George H.W. Bush, CBS via YouTube, http://www.youtube.com/watch?v=FqwQw3THRvU. See also, Peter Boyer, "Rather's Questioning of Bush Sets Off Shouting on Live Broadcast," New York Times, January26, 1988, http://www.nytimes.com/1988/01/26/us/rather-s-questioning-of-bush-sets-

off-shouting-on-live-broadcast.html. A Bush biographer described how the Bushes resented Rather for it years afterward. Mitchell, Elizabeth. *W— Revenge of the Bush Dynasty.* Hyperion, 2000, 230-31.

42 Wikipedia, Dan Rather, http://en.wikipedia.org/wiki/Dan_Rather. Rather, Dan, with Digby Diehl. *Rather Outspoken: My Life in the News.* Grand Central Publishing, 2012.

43 Wikipedia, Jessica Lynch, http://en.wikipedia.org/wiki/Jessica_Lynch.

44 Tillman, Mary with Narda Zacchino. *Boots on the Ground By Dusk: My Tribute to Pat Tillman.* Modern Times/Rodale, 2008. See also, Krakauer, Jon. *Where Men Win Glory: The Odyssey of Pat Tillman.* Doubleday, 2009.

45 See 2012 speech by Eileen Foster, recipient of annual Ridenhour "Truth Telling Award, National Press Club, http://www.ridenhour.org/prizes_truth-telling_2012b.html, as cited in Andy Breslau and Randy Fertel, May 4, 2012.

46 Abramoff, Jack. *Capitol Punishment: The Hard Truth About Washington Corruption From America's Most Notorious Lobbyist.* WND, 2011.

47 Roberts, Paul Craig and Stratton, Lawrence M. *The Tyranny of Good Intentions: How Prosecutors and Law Enforcement Are Trampling the Constitution in the Name of Justice.* Forum/Prima, 2000. Ackerman, Bruce. *The Decline and Fall of the American Republic,* Belknap/Harvard, 2010. Phillips, Kevin. *American Dynasty: Aristocracy. Fortune. And the Politics of Deceit in the House of Bush.* Viking, 2004., Dean, John. *Broken Government: How Republican Rule Destroyed the Legislative, Executive and Judicial Branches.* Viking, 2007; and Dean, John. *Conservatives Without a Conscience.* Viking, 2006.

48 See, *e.g.,* Paul Craig Roberts, "It Does Happen in America; The Political Trial of Don Siegelman," OpEdNews, February 28, 2008, http://www.opednews.com/articles/opedne_paul_cra_080301_it_does_happen_in_am.htm.

49 After 9/11, for example, I established a public safety committee in the association of industry leaders whose companies had played prominent roles in restoring communications in lower Manhattan following 9/11 disruption of wired communications. Broadband wireless was so significant that the Bush White House invited me to attend its first public-private partnership meeting at what would become the new Department of Homeland Security's command center on Nebraska Avenue in the city.

50 Dan Eggen and Paul Kane, "Justice Dept. Would Have Kept 'Loyal' Prosecutors," *Washington Post,* March 16, 2007, http://www.washingtonpost.com/wp-dyn/content/article/2007/03/14/AR2007031400519.html. Sampson, educated at Brigham Young University and the University of Chicago Law School, became a partner at the 800-attorney firm Hunton and Williams.

51 Iglesias, David with David Seay. *In Justice: Inside the Scandal that Rocked the Bush Administration.* Wiley, 2008, 195-213.

52 Glynn Wilson, "How the 2002 Election Was Stolen in Bay Minette," Locust Fork News-Journal, June 20, 2007, http://blog.locustfork.net/2007/06/how-the-2002-el.

53 Fitrakis, Bob and Harvey Wasserman, *How the GOP Stole America's 2004 Election & Is Rigging 2008,* Columbus Institute for Contemporary Journalism,

Wasserman.com, 2005. Fitrakis, Bob, Steve Rosenfeld, and Harvey Wasserman, eds. *Did George W. Bush Steal America's 2004 Election? Essential Documents*, Columbus Institute for Contemporary Journalism, 2005. Fitrakis, Bob, Steve Rosenfeld, and Harvey Wasserman, eds. *What Happened in Ohio: A Documentary Record of Theft And Fraud in the 2004 Election*. New Press, 2006.

54 Kreig, "Cutting Through Hype, Hypocrisy of Vote Fraud Claims," *op. cit.*, http://www.justice-integrity.org/faq/267-cutting-through-vote-fraud-claims-hypocrisy.

55 Harvey Wasserman, "Four Ways Ohio Republicans are Already Stealing the 2012 Election," OpEdNews/Free Press, August 26, 2012, http://www.opednews.com/articles/Four-Ways-Ohio-Republicans-by-Harvey-Wasserman-120824-129.html. See also, Russ Baker, "What Didn't Happen In Ohio," Tom Paine.com, May 5, 2005, http://www.russbaker.com/archives/TomPaine_com%20-%20What%20Didn%27t%20Happen%20In%20Ohio.htm.

56 Palast, Greg, Ted Rall and Robert F. Kennedy Jr. *Billionaires & Ballot Bandits: How to Steal an Election in 9 Easy Steps*. Seven Stories, 2012, http://www.amazon.com/Billionaires-Ballot-Bandits-Steal-Election/dp/1609804783/ref=sr_1_6?s=books&ie=UTF8&qid=1344532258&sr=1-6&keywords=greg+palast+books.

57 Bush, George W. *Decision Points*. Crown, 2010.

Part II: Romney Henchmen, Enablers and Fellow Puppets

Chapter 10, Karl Rove: A Frightening Fraud

1 Machiavelli, Niccolò. *The Prince and The Discourses*. Modern Library/Random House, 1950. See also, Alexander, Paul. *Machiavelli's Shadow*. Rodale, 2008.

2 Wikipedia, Karl Rove, Wikipedia. http://en.wikipedia.org/wiki/Karl_Rove. See also, Kenneth P. Vogel and Steve Friess, "Rove hits big: The birth of a mega-donor," *Politico*, July 13, 2012, http://www.politico.com/news/stories/0712/78466.html.

3 Unger, Craig. *Boss Rove: Inside Karl Rove's Secret Kingdom of Power*. Scribner, 2012, 20.

4 Moore, Wayne and James Slater. *Bush's Brain: How Karl Rove Made George W. Bush Presidential*. Wiley, 2004. See also Amy Goodman, "Rove's dirty tricks: Let us count the ways," *Seattle Post-Intelligencer*, August 15, 2007, http://www.seattlepi.com/local/opinion/article/Rove-s-dirty-tricks-Let-us-count-the-ways-1246665.php.

5 Rove, *Courage and Consequence, op. cit.*, 24.

6 Wikipedia, Terry Dolan, http://en.wikipedia.org/wiki/Terry_Dolan_%28activist%29.

7 Minutaglio, Bill. *First Son: George W. Bush and the Bush Family Dynasty*. Times/Random House, 1999, 166-67.

8 Cannon, Carl M., Lou Dubose and Jan Rein. *Boy Genius: Karl Rove, The Architect of George W. Bush's Remarkable Political Triumphs*. Public Affairs, 2005, 10-12.

9 Unger, *Boss Rove, op. cit.*, 29-30.

[10] Nicholas Lemann, "The Controller: Karl Rove Is Working to Get George Bush Elected, but He Has Bigger Plans," *New Yorker*, May 12, 2003, as cited by Unger, *op. cit.*, 30.

[11] Rove, *Courage and Consequence, op. cit.*, *56-57*. She would later say: "Karl has hundreds of friends and no one he's intimate with" outside their small family. Cannon, Carl M., Lou Dubose, and Jan Reid. *Boy Genius: Karl Rove, the Brains Behind the Remarkable Political Triumph of George W. Bush.* Free Press, 2003, 128.

[12] Scott Horton, "Boss Rove's Justice," *Harper's*, September 13, 2012, http://harpers.org/blog/2012/09/boss-roves-justice/.

[13] Ibid., 506. "For example, I had been involved in Alabama campaigns from 1994 to 2000."

[14] The title comes from a book by Texas journalists who covered Rove and Bush during the Bush gubernatorial era.

[15] Ron Suskind, "Why Are These Men Laughing?" *Esquire*, January 2003, http://www.ronsuskind.com/newsite/articles/archives/000032.html.

[16] Suskind, Ron. *Price of Loyalty: George W. Bush, the White House, and the Education of Paul O'Neil.* Simon & Schuster, 2004.

[17] Ron Suskind, "Faith, Certainty and the Presidency of George W. Bush," *New York Times Magazine,* October 17, 2004, http://www.nytimes.com/2004/10/17/magazine/17BUSH.html?_r=0.

[18] See, *e.g.*, Kaiser, Robert G. *So Damn Much Money: The Triumph of Lobbying and the Corrosion of American Government.* Knopf, 2009. Hettena, Seth. *Feasting on the Spoils: The Life and Times of Randy "Duke" Cunningham, History's Most Corrupt Congressman.* St. Martin's, 2007.

[19] Abramoff, *Capitol Punishment, op. cit.*

[20] Roger Shuler, "Rove Did NOT Deny Involvement In Siegelman Case," Legal Schnauzer, August 13, 2009, http://legalschnauzer.blogspot.com/2009/08/rove-did-not-deny-involvement-in.html; and Glynn Wilson, "Rove Issues Non-Denial Denial In Siegelman Case," Locust Fork News-Journal, August 12, 2009, http://blog.locustfork.net/2009/08/12/karl-rove-issues-non-denial-denial-of-involvement-in-siegelman-case; and Carrie Johnson, "Miers Told House Panel of 'Agitated' Rove," *Washington Post*, August 12, 2009, http://www.washingtonpost.com/wp-dyn/content/article/2009/08/11/AR2009081102104.html.

[21] Iglesias, David with David Seay. *In Justice: Inside the Scandal that Rocked the Bush Administration.* Wiley, 2008.

[22] Rove, *Courage and Consequences, op. cit.*, 493-503.

[23] Wikipedia, Alberto Gonzales, http://en.wikipedia.org/wiki/Alberto_Gonzales.

[24] Silverglate, Harvey A. *Three Felonies a Day: How the Feds Target the Innocent.* Encounter, 2009.

[25] Simpson says the chronology was that Madsen phoned her seeking news about the Siegelman case, and that she decided to one-up him by telling him about facts she had researched about his life in ways not reported in his articles and books. The books include: Madsen, Wayne. *Overthrow a Fascist Regime on $15 a Day: The Internet Irregulars vs. The Powers That Be!* Trine Day, 2008.

[26] Several others who provided especially notable coverage were Alabama-based Glynn Wilson of the Locust Fork News-Journal and Roger Shuler of Legal Schnauzer, Scott Horton of *Harper's Magazine*, and Adam Cohen of the *New York Times*.

[27] Andrew Kreig, "A Few Questions For Karl Rove On His Book Tour," Nieman Watchdog, May 27, 2010, http://www.niemanwatchdog.org/index.cfm?fuseaction=ask_this.view&askthisid=00458.

[28] Karl Rove, "'Closing in on Rove: Why John Conyers, the *New York Times* and the *Washington Post* owe me an apology,'" *Wall Street Journal*, August 19, 2011, http://online.wsj.com/article/SB10001424052970203550604574360500363745662.html. See also Roger Shuler, "Jill Simpson Fires Back at Rove and the *Wall Street Journal*," Legal Schnauzer, August 21, 2011, http://legalschnauzer.blogspot.com/2009/08/jill-simpson-fires-back-at-rove-and.html.

[29] U.S. House of Representatives, Committee on the Judiciary, September 14, 2007, Dana Jill Simpson interview with exhibits, http://www.clairepavlikpurgus.com/Schuster/docs/JillSimpsonInterviewWithExhibits.pdf.

[30] Unger, *Boss Rove, op. cit3*-6, 5, 6-8, 11, 204-06, 209-10, 211-12, et. seq.

[31] Carrie Levine, "Former Ogilvy Lobbyists Set Up New Shops," BLT / *Legal Times*, January 5, 2010, http://legaltimes.typepad.com/blt/2010/01/former-ogilvy-lobbyists-set-up-new-shops.html. "Lobbyists who left Ogilvy Government Relations over the past few weeks are setting up their own shops, even as Ogilvy changes its leadership."

[32] Unger, *Boss Rove, op. cit.*, Unger and other documentation of *Citizens United*. See also, Dylan Matthews, "Crossroads GPS and Priorities USA were created for the purpose of hiding donors," *Washington Post*, May 15, 2013, http://www.washingtonpost.com/blogs/wonkblog/wp/2013/05/15/crossroads-gps-and-priorities-usa-were-created-for-the-purpose-of-hiding-donors/?wprss=rss_national&tid=pp_widget.

[33] Karl Rove & Co., www.rove.com.

[34] Andrew Kreig, "Rove Suspected In Swedish-U.S. Political Prosecution of WikiLeaks," Huffington Post, December 19, 2010. http://www.huffingtonpost.com/andrew-kreig/rove-suspected-in-swedish_b_798737.html. See also, Andrew Kreig, "WikiLeaks Claims Secret U.S. Charges Against Assange," Justice Integrity Project, February 29, 2012.

[35] Wayne Madsen told me he declined an invitation to join the WikiLeaks founding board because he believed Assange formed the group to function under deep disguise as a government propaganda tool. See, more generally, evidence assembled on the same theme in Estulin, Daniel. *Deconstructing WikiLeaks*. TrineDay, 2012.

Chapter 11, David Petraeus: Revolt of the Generals

[1] Mikey Weinstein, "Petraeus, Supporter of Military's 'Spiritual Fitness' Program, Should Have Been Fired Years Ago," Truth-out/AlterNet, November 20,

2012, http://truth-out.org/opinion/item/12869-petraeus-should-have-been-fired-years-ago.

[2] *WCA 2005* was the annual convention of the Wireless Communications Association International held at the Marriott Wardman Park Hotel in Washington, DC from June 28 to July 1, 2005. It featured prominent U.S. government and private sector leaders, including the Iraq-based CEO of a WCA member operating a vital cellular network.

[3] See, for example, Alberts, David S., John J. Garstka, and Frederick P. Stein. *Network Centric Warfare: Developing and Leveraging Information Superiority.* Department of Defense Command and Control Research Program, 2003.

[4] Ricks, Thomas E. *The Gamble: General David Petraeus and the American Military Adventure in Iraq, 2006-2008.* Penguin, 2009, 94.

[5] Wikipedia, David Petraeus, http://en.wikipedia.org/wiki/David_Petraeus.

[6] Halberstam, David. *The Coldest Winter: America and the Korean War.* Hyperion, 2007, 105-114.

[7] Cohen, Eliot A. *Supreme Command: Soldiers, Statesmen, and Leadership in Wartime.* Free Press, 2002; Anchor, 2003. However, civilian leaders were the driving force in initiating the Iraq War during Cohen's own time.

[8] Ricks, *The Gamble, op cit.*, 98-99. Shortly after the Petraeus promotion in 2007, the Bush administration named Cohen as Department of State counselor.

[9] Rajiv Chandrasekaran and Greg Jaffe, "The four-style lifestyle," *Washington Post*, November 17, 2012, http://www.washingtonpost.com/world/national-security/petraeus-scandal-puts-four-star-general-lifestyle-under-scrutiny/2012/11/17/33a14f48-3043-11e2-a30e-5ca76eeec857_story.html?hpid=z2.

[10] The Obama administration appointed Holly Petraeus as assistant director for the Office of Servicemember Affairs at the new Consumer Financial Protection Bureau. The bureau was a concept of Harvard Law School professor Elizabeth Warren, established in 2011 over the strong opposition of Republicans.

[11] Vicky Ward, "Four-Star Scandal," *Town and Country*, March 2013. http://www.townandcountrymag.com/society/politics/jill-kelley-and-natalie-khawam-history. See also, Vicky Ward, "Jill Kelley: The Real Story Lies in Tampa," Huffington Post, February 5, 2013.

[12] Wayne Madsen, the former Navy intelligence officer, broke the story and introduced me to Massa. Madsen, "Which office do I go to .... to get my reputation back?" Wayne Madsen Report, November 3, 2011, http://www.waynemadsenreport.com/articles/20111103_3 (Subscription).

[13] House of Representatives, Final Roll Call on HR 3962, November 7, 20109, http://clerk.house.gov/evs/2009/roll887.xml.

[14] Massa, for example, sharply criticized U.S. purchases of Russian-made helicopters for the Afghan. Massa's district contained a plant manufacturing U.S. helicopters. The congressman threatened to call for hearings in which he would allege that the Russian helicopters were forbidden under a law against trading with Iran's suppliers. See Sharon Weinberger, "How to Do Business With a Blacklisted Russian Weapons Company," *Wired*, July 28, 2008, http://www.wired.com/dangerroom/2008/07/how-to-do-busin.

15 Tim Heffernan, "Staging a Coup? Petraeus Isn't Even Running for President," *Esquire*, May 24, 2010, http://www.esquire.com/blogs/politics/petraeus-2012-coup-052410.

16 Ryan D'Agostino, "Inside the Insane Saga of Congressman Eric Massa," *Esquire*, May 24, 2010, http://www.esquire.com/blogs/politics/eric-massa-esquire-052410.

17 Michael Hastings, "The Runaway General," *Rolling Stone*, July 8, 2010, http://www.rollingstone.com/politics/news/the-runaway-general-20100622.

18 *Washington Post*, "Transcript: Kathleen T. McFarland talks with Gen. David H. Petraeus," December 3, 2012, http://www.washingtonpost.com/lifestyle/style/transcript-kathleen-t-mcfarland-talks-with-gen-david-h-petraeus/2012/12/03/c0467cd4-3d8b-11e2-a2d9-822f58ac9fd5_story.html.

19 Rajiv Chandrasekaran, "Civilians held Petraeus ear in war zone," *Washington Post*, December 18, 2012, http://www.washingtonpost.com/world/national-security/civilian-analysts-gained-petraeuss-ear-while-he-was-commander-in-afghanistan/2012/12/18/290c0b50-446a-11e2-8061-253bccfc7532_story.html?hpid=z1.

20 Bob Woodward, "Fox News chief's failed attempt to enlist Petraeus as presidential candidate," *Washington Post*, December 3, 2012, http://www.washingtonpost.com/lifestyle/style/fox-news-chiefs-failed-attempt-to-enlist-petraeus-as-presidential-candidate/2012/12/03/15fdcea8-3d77-11e2-a2d9-822f58ac9fd5_story.html.

21 Andrew Kreig, "Petraeus Tape Reveals Disloyal Talks with Fox on Obama," Justice Integrity Project, December 4, 2012, http://www.justice-integrity.org/faq/231-petraeus-tape-reveals-disloyal-talks-with-fox-on-obama.

22 Wayne Madsen, "Petraeus affair known as early as 2004," Wayne Madsen report, February 7, 2013, (Subscription required) http://www.waynemadsenreport.com/articles/20130207_3.

23 Greg Jaffe and Anne Gearan, "Paula Broadwell's drive and resilience hit obstacles," *Washington Post*, November 15, 2012, http://www.washingtonpost.com/world/national-security/paula-broadwells-drive-and-resilience-hit-obstacles/2012/11/15/bf5989a2-2e94-11e2-89d4-040c9330702a_story.html?hpid=z2.

24 Douglas Lucas and Russ Baker, "Petraeus: the Plot Thickens," WhoWhatWhy, February 5, 2013, http://whowhatwhy.com/2013/02/05/petraeus-the-plot-thickens-1.

25 Joseph Straw , Jennifer H. Cunningham and Bill Hutchinson, "Paula Broadwell poses with submachine gun in tight jeans and leather boots on firing range," *New York Daily News*, November 20, 2012, http://www.nydailynews.com/news/national/paula-broadwell-poses-submachine-gun-article-1.1205335.

26 Ward, "Four-Star Scandal," *op cit.*

Chapter 12 Michael Leavitt: On a Mission from God

[1] George Romney named his first-born, "Willard" in honor of the future hotelier, according to the most authoritative biography of the 2012 GOP nominee. Kranish, Michael and Scott Helman. *The Real Romney*, Harper, 2012, 15.

[2] Philip Rucker, "Romney is hailed as 'ambassador' guiding Mormonism 'out of obscurity,'" *Washington Post*, September 2, 2012, http://www.washingtonpost.com/politics/romney-is-hailed-as-ambassador-guiding-mormonism-out-of-obscurity/2012/09/02/153181ee-f52a-11e1-a126-fc5f423715b5_story.html.

[3] Dan Eggen, "Romney picks Mike Leavitt to head transition team," *Washington Post*, June 3, 2012, http://www.washingtonpost.com/politics/romney-picks-mike-leavitt-to-head-transition-team/2012/06/03/gJQAdVZhBV_story.html.

[4] Ibid. See also Ben W. Heineman Jr., "Obama's Chief of Staff Will Be the Most Important Appointment of His Term," *Atlantic*, January 14, 2013, http://www.theatlantic.com/politics/archive/2013/01/obamas-chief-of-staff-will-be-the-most-important-appointment-of-his-term/267124.

[5] Mike Allen and Jim Vandehei, "Romney names Leavitt: Who's on the inside track for a Romney Cabinet," *Politico*, August 28, 2012, http://www.politico.com/news/stories/0812/80233.html.

[6] A vice president can be important or not as the president prefers. Mike Leavitt was far senior in experience and age to Paul Ryan. Leavitt would have begun a Romney presidency with the responsibility for staffing the administration. So there is no reason that the "strong" vice presidencies of the Biden, Cheney, Gore, and George H. W. Bush years would have occurred in a Romney-Ryan administration. Leavitt as chief of staff would be no less than the third most powerful official in the federal government because Congress deferred increasingly over the years to the Executive Branch when controlled by the same party.

[7] Grace, Wyler, "11 Surprising Things You Didn't Know About Mormons," Business Insider, June 24, 2011, http://www.businessinsider.com/11-surprising-things-you-didnt-know-about-mormons-2011-6?op=1. "Mormonism is one of the fastest-growing religions in the U.S. With 6 million members, Mormonism is now the fourth-largest religion in the United States, according to the most recent data from the Pew Research Center. The church claims to add about 1 million members every three years."

[8] Mansfield, Stephen. *The Mormonizing of America: How the Mormon Religion Became a Dominant Force in Politics, Entertainment and Pop Culture*. Worthy, 2012.

[9] Ibid., 114-16.

[10] Ibid., 258-59.

[11] Wikipedia, Michael Leavitt, http://en.wikipedia.org/wiki/Mike_Leavitt.

[12] University of Utah, "Utah and the Vietnam conflict," Utah History Encyclopedia. See also, Denny Roy, Grant P. Skabelund, and Ray C. Hillam. *A Time to Kill: Reflections on War* (1990).

[13] Kranish and Helman, *op. cit.*, 204-06.

[14] Brodie, *op. cit.*, 366.

[15] *People of the State of New York v. Joseph Smith,* March 20, 1926. A justice of the peace found Smith guilty after trial in Bainbridge, Chenango County, NY, as cited by Brodie, *No Man Knows My History, op. cit.,* 30, 426.

[16] Brodie, *op. cit.,* 31-32.

[17] Brodie, *op. cit,.* 32.

[18] Ancient Egyptian language was virtually unreadable in modern times until rediscovery in 1799 of the Rosetta Stone in Egypt by a French soldier. Wikipedia, Rosetta Stone, http://en.wikipedia.org/wiki/Rosetta_Stone

[19] Brodie, *op. cit,.* 416.

[20] Ibid., 194-99.

[21] Ibid., 214-16.

[22] Ibid., 237-48.

[23] Ibid., 309-33.

[24] Ibid., 280-82.

[25] Bennett, John C. *The History of the Saints, or an Exposé of Joe Smith and Mormonism.* Leland & Whiting, 1842, as cited by Brodie.

[26] Thomas Burr, "Romney candidacy has resurrected last days prophecy of Mormon saving the Constitution," *Salt Lake Tribune,* June 4, 2007, http://www.sltrib.com/lds/ci_6055090. "It's Mormon lore, a story passed along by some old-timers about the importance of their faith and their country. In the latter days, the story goes, the U.S. Constitution will hang by a thread and "a Mormon will ride in on a metaphorical white horse to save it. The Church of Jesus Christ of Latter-day Saints says it does not accept the legend — commonly referred to as the "White Horse Prophecy" — as doctrine."

[27] As noted in this book's first chapter, Fawn Brodie reported that Smith had 48 confirmed or strongly suspected plural wives aside from Emma Smith. Brodie's research expanded the list from the 27 ascertained by a church historian in 1887. Brodie, *op. cit.,* Appendix C, "The Plural Wives of Joseph Smith," 457-88.

[28] "Brigham Young proclaimed a revelation in which salvation was no longer available to the Gentiles, meaning Americans and other non-Mormons." Tarpley, *Just Too Weird, op cit.,* 119, citing contemporary historical sources.

[29] Tarpley, Webster G. *Just Too Weird. Bishop Romney and the Mormon Takeover of America: Polygamy, Theocracy, and Subversion.* Progressive. 2012, 85-86.

[30] Kranish and Helman, *op. cit.,* 39.

[31] Krakauer, Jon. *Under the Banner of Heaven: A Story of Violent Faith.* Doubleday, 2003, 207. "Through most of the twentieth century, African-Americans were strictly banned from the priesthood, and black-white marriages were considered an outrage against God. Then, in 1978, President Spencer W. Kimball had a revelation in which the Lord commanded that the LDS priesthood be open to males of all races, initiating a slow but profound shift in Mormon attitudes about race."

[32] .Krakauer, *op. cit.,* 208-27, 236-40 .

[33] Krakauer, *op. cit.,* 227.

[34] Ibid., 206

[35] Kranish and Helman, *op. cit.*, 40.

[36] Ibid., 47-48.

[37] Lee, John. *Mormonism Unveiled*, edited by Robert Grass Cleland and Juanita Leavitt Brooks, 1870, as cited by Krakauer, *op. cit.*, 247-48.

[38] Doyle, Arthur Conan, with annotations by Leslie S. Klinger. *The New Annotated Sherlock Holmes: The Novels (A Study in Scarlet, The Sign of Four, The Hound of the Baskervilles, The Valley of Fear.* W.W. Norton, 2005. *A Study in Scarlet* was first published in *Beeton's Christmas Annual* magazine in 1887, and as a book in 1888.

[39] Kranish and Helman, *op. cit.*, 46.

[40] The 2002 kidnapping of Elizabeth Smart, age nine, from a Salt Lake City street by LDS fundamentalist Brian D. Mitchell, 49, was one of the more notorious crimes chronicled by Krakauer in his book on the topic, *Under the Banner of Heaven, op. cit.* A book by the victim's parents provides little of that context and instead focuses heavily on the family's religious faith that their daughter would return safe. Smart, Ed and Lois, with Laura Morton. *Bringing Elizabeth Home.* Doubleday, 2003.

[41] Kranish and Helman, *op. cit.*, 44-45.

[42] Ibid., 46.

[43] Ibid., 48.

[44] Kranish, Michael and Scott Helman. *The Real Romney*, Harper, 2012.

[45] Mahoney, Tom. *The Story of George Romney: Builder, Salesman, Crusader.* Harper, 1960; and Romney, George W. *The Concerns of a Citizen.* Putnam, 1968.

[46] Ibid. Tarpley extensively cites source materials, including such previous authors as Fawn Brodie in ways that needed not be replicated here. In sum, Tarpley's perspective is highly one-sided but with substantial evidence.

[47] Krakauer, Jon. *Under the Banner of Heaven: A Story of Violent Faith.* Doubleday, 2003, 2008.

[48] Greg Burton "Descended From Proud Polygamists." *Salt Lake Tribune*, as cited by Frank Kirkman's Mountain Meadows Site in the Dudley Leavitt section, http://1857massacre.com/MMM/leavitt.htm.

[49] Robert Gehrke, "Utah Gov. Clarifies Polygamy Views," Associated Press, August 1, 1998, http://www.skeptictank.org/mormnut3.htm.

[50] Wikipedia, Thuggee, http://en.wikipedia.org/wiki/Thuggee. Thugee, also known as tuggee or simply thugs, was a religious cult and an organized gang of professional assassins who traveled in groups across India for several hundred years until elimination under British colonial rule.

[51] Christopher Smith, "Unearthing Mountain Meadows Secrets: Backhoe at a S. Utah killing field rips open 142-year-old wound," *Salt Lake Tribune*, March 14, 2000, as cited on the website, *We Won't Forget,* http://1857massacre.com/MMM/142-year-old-wound.htm. The website also quoted a descendant of the murdered families, Scott Fancher, president of the Mountain Meadows Monument Foundation in Arkansas, as saying, "There's a sense among some of our members it's like having Lee Harvey Oswald in charge of JFK's tomb." As a contrary view: "It would be unfortunate if this sad moment in our state's history, and the rather good-spirited attempt to put

it behind us, was highlighted by controversy," Leavitt wrote state antiquities officials shortly before LDS Church President Gordon B. Hinckley presided over a ceremony at Mountain Meadows.

52 Krakauer, *op. cit.*, 209-25.

53 Christopher Smith, *op. cit.* "The Aug. 3, 1999, excavation of the remains of at least 29 of the 120 emigrants slaughtered in the Mountain Meadows massacre eventually prompted Gov. Mike Leavitt to intercede. He encouraged state officials to quickly rebury the remains, even though the basic scientific analysis required by state law was unfinished."

54 Webster Tarpley, the presidential biographer, alleged during the 2012 campaign that empowerment of Leavitt would endanger the public. "He is corrupt. He is dirty," wrote Tarpley, who described Leavitt as, "The right-hand man" who would distribute all federal jobs under Romney. Webster G. Tarpley, "Romney's Top Aide Mike Leavitt Implicated in Olympic Corruption, Toleration of Polygamy, Mountain Meadows Massacre Coverup," September 6, 2012, http://tarpley.net/2012/09/06/romneys-top-aide-mike-leavitt-implicated-in-olympic-corruption-toleration-of-polygamy-moutain-meadows-massacre-coverup.

55 Robert Gehrke, "Did Gov. Leavitt cross the line? Governor and his top advisers had 'seminary' meetings to discuss the role of LDS teachings in government," *Salt Lake Tribune*, December 30, 2007, as cited by http://www.rickross.com/reference/mormon/mormon464.html.

56 Wayne Madsen, "Mitt Romney hardly lifted a finger to save Winter Games," Wayne Madsen Report, September 6, 2012, http://www.waynemadsenreport.com/articles/20120906.

57 Howard Berkes, "Leavitt Charity's $500,000 Returns, in the Form of Rent," National Public Radio, July 28, 2006, http://www.npr.org/templates/story/story.php?storyId=5590281.

58 Berkes, *op. cit.*

59 Ibid. "The Insurance Industry: Can Leavitt Leave It?" Center for American Progress, January 18, 2005, http://www.americanprogress.org/issues/open-government/news/2005/01/18/1291/the-insurance-industry-can-leavitt-leave-it.

60 Aliza Marcus, "Sebelius Confirmed as Health Chief, Completes Cabinet," Bloomberg, April 28, 2009, http://www.bloomberg.com/apps/news?pid=newsarchive&sid=aiBDawmVSDBQ.

61 Charles E. Johnson, The Leavitt Group, http://leavittpartners.com/team/charlie-johnson.

62 F. William Engdahl, "Is Avian Flu another Pentagon Hoax?" Global Research, October 30, 2005, http://www.globalresearch.ca/is-avian-flu-another-pentagon-hoax.

Chapter 13, Big Brothers for Romney — and Us?

[1] Robert Parry, "Romney's Jaw-Dropping Incoherence," OpEdNews, September 14, 2012, http://www.opednews.com/articles/Romney-s-Jaw-Dropping-Inco-by-Robert-Parry-120913-262.html.

[2] Ibid. "However, to make his point stick, Romney had to reverse the actual chronology of events." As the attacks unfolded, Romney quickly issued a statement, based on the response of the US embassy in Egypt, accusing Obama of "sympathiz[ing] with those who waged the attacks" (the Obama White House repudiated the statement from the embassy in Cairo). The chairman of the GOP, Reince Preibus, unloaded on the world this disgusting tweet: "Obama sympathizes with attackers in Egypt. Sad and pathetic."

[3] David Remnick, "Neocon gambits," *New Yorker*, September 12, 2012, http://www.newyorker.com/online/blogs/newsdesk/2012/09/have-benjamin-netanyahus-attacks-on-obama-gone-too-far.html. See also, Glenn Greenwald, "The tragic consulate killings in Libya and America's hierarchy of human life," OpEdNews, September 14, 2012, http://www.opednews.com/articles/The-tragic-consulate-killi-by-Glenn-Greenwald-120914-771.html. John Heilemann, "Don't Say 'Desperate,'" *New York Magazine*, Sept. 14, 2012. http://nymag.com/news/politics/powergrid/mitt-romney-middle-east-unrest-2012-9.

[4] Laura Rozen, "Mitt Romney announces his foreign policy team," The Envoy, Yahoo News, October 6, 2011, http://news.yahoo.com/blogs/envoy/mitt-romney-announces-foreign-policy-team-171303969.html. See also, National Journal Staff report, "Obama's and Romney's Key Foreign Policy Advisers," August 22, 2012 (updated from May 18, 2012), http://www.nationaljournal.com/pictures-video/obama-s-and-romney-s-key-foreign-policy-advisers-pictures-20120518, and Laura Hughes, "Mitt Romney Foreign Policy Team: 17 of 24 Advisors Are Bush Neocons," Policy Mic, July 2012, http://www.policymic.com/articles/11219/mitt-romney-foreign-policy-team-17-of-24-advisors-are-bush-neocons.

[5] Tommy Christopher, "Norah O'Donnell Decimates Mitt Romney Foreign Policy Argument With Great Journalism," Mediaite, August 29, 2012, http://www.mediaite.com/tv/norah-odonnell-decimates-mitt-romney-foreign-policy-argument-with-great-journalism. "Rice was unable to name a single foreign policy failure of President Obama's, and was hard-pressed to explain what, exactly, Mitt Romney would do differently."

[6] Staff report, "Who Are Obama's and Romney's Key National Security Advisers?" The *National Journal*, June 8, 2012, http://www.nationaljournal.com/pictures-video/who-are-obama-s-and-romney-s-key-national-security-advisers-pictures-20120608, See also, Mark Landler, "On Foreign Policy, Romney Breaks With Advisers," *New York Times*, January 20, 2012, http://thecaucus.blogs.nytimes.com/2012/01/20/on-foreign-policy-romney-breaks-with-advisers.

[7] This is not simply a United States problem, of course, as indicated by a major investigation in the British media. Nicky Robinson, "Arms firms call up

'generals for hire,'" *Sunday Times*, October 14, 2012,
http://www.thesundaytimes.co.uk/sto/news/insight/article1147765.ece.
"Top-ranking retired military officers have been secretly filmed boasting about
lobbying to win multi-million-pound defence deals for arms firms in breach of
official rules."

[8] Greenwald, "The tragic consulate killings in Libya," *Guardian, op. cit.*," Here, they
had a real political opportunity to attack Obama — if US diplomats are killed
and embassies stormed, it makes the president appear weak and ineffectual —
but they are so drowning in their own blinding extremism and hate-driven bile,
so wedded to their tired and moronic political attacks (unpatriotic Democrats
love America's Muslim enemies!), that they cannot avoid instantly self-
destructing. Within a matter of hours, they managed to turn a politically
dangerous situation for Obama into yet more evidence of their unhinged,
undisciplined radicalism."

[9] Bamford summarizes the law concisely, "The FISA act says if you want to
eavesdrop on what they call 'a U.S. person,' you get a warrant from the FISA
court. You don't bypass it. That's a felony. You can get five years in prison."

[10] Wikipedia: Michael Hayden, http://en.wikipedia.org/wiki/Michael_Hayden.

Targeting Americans

[11] Orwell, George. *1984, op. cit.* See also, Chris Hedges, "A Brave New Dystopia,"
Truth Dig, December 27, 2010. "The two greatest visions of a future dystopia
were George Orwell's 1984 and Aldous Huxley's Brave New World. The
debate, between those who watched our descent towards corporate
totalitarianism, was who was right. Would we be, as Orwell wrote, dominated
by a repressive surveillance and security state that used crude and violent forms
of control? Or would we be, as Huxley envisioned, entranced by entertainment
and spectacle, captivated by technology and seduced by profligate
consumption to embrace our own oppression? It turns out Orwell and Huxley
were both right. Huxley saw the first stage of our enslavement. Orwell saw the
second."

[12] Bamford, James. *Body of Secrets: Anatomy of the Ultra-Secret National Security Agency*.
Anchor / Random House, 2002, 82-91, 300-01; *The Puzzle Palace: Inside the
National Security Agency, America's Most Secret Intelligence Organization*. Houghton
Mifflin /Penguin, 1982; and *The Shadow Factory: The Ultra-Secret National Security
Agency from 9/11 to the Eavesdropping on America*. Anchor / Random House,
2009. See also, James Bamford, "Big Brother Is Watching," Lecture, the
Independent Institute, June 6, 2002, Oakland, CA,
http://www.independent.org/events/transcript.asp?eventID=8. Douglass
cites Northwoods as among JFK's concerns leading to his assassination.
Douglass argues throughout his book, *JFK and the Unspeakable, op. cit.*, that
Oswald, a former Marine, was a secret U.S. intelligence asset assigned to left-
wing roles, framed as a patsy, and then set up for his murder by Jack Ruby to
prevent trial. Prouty would have known about Northwoods as a top aide to the
Joint Chiefs. But Prouty published the first edition of *JFK* before Northwoods
details became public in Bamford's book. So, Prouty cited other specifics as
evidence for what he called a "High Cabal" conspiracy to use CIA-trained

gunmen to kill the president in a coup and falsely blame Oswald as a lone assassin, Prouty, *op. cit.*, 119, 317-18.

[13] Wikipedia, United States Foreign Intelligence Surveillance Court, http://en.wikipedia.org/wiki/United_States_Foreign_Intelligence_Surveillance_Court. The court is authorized under 50 U.S.C. § 1803, Pub.L. 95-511, 92 Stat. 1788, enacted October 25, 1978 by the Foreign Intelligence Surveillance Act of 1978. The court oversees requests for surveillance warrants against suspected foreign intelligence agents inside the United States by federal law enforcement agencies, primarily the FBI.

[14] "On February 27, 2001, two weeks after Qwest inaugurated local broadband service in Washington and Baltimore, Nacchio and the new head of Qwest's government business unit, James F.X. Payne, arrived at the NSA. They had come to present their proposal to become part of the Groundbreaker project....Neither, however, was prepared for the agency's counteroffer: to give the NSA secret, warrantless access to Qwest's database containing the calling records of its millions of American customers. And possibly later, to give Nacchio's blessing to installing monitoring equipment on the company's Class 5 switching facilities, the system over which most of the company's domestic traffic flows." Bamford, *The Shadow Factory, op. cit.*, 173.

[15] Ibid., 173. "No doubt to Hayden's surprise, despite Nacchio's penchant for risk-taking, he declined to have anything to do with the agency illegally installing its monitoring equipment on the company's switching facilities. Although some international traffic passed through the switches – the traffic Hayden was interested in – they primarily transmitted only localized calls, such as neighborhood to neighborhood. While he never flatly said no, Nacchio wanted no part of the operation. Having spent his entire career in the long distance telephone business, he felt such an agreement would be illegal – a view shared by his in-house attorneys in Denver. They believed any such cooperation – even if limited to email – would violate the Electronic Communications Privacy Act."

[16] Nacchio's appellate attorney was Maureen Mahoney, the Bush administration's deputy solicitor general and one of the nation's most respected Supreme Court advocates. "I am deeply disappointed by the court's decision," she said of the Court's rejection of Nacchio's appeal, "because I am convinced that he is innocent and did not receive a fair trial." Nacchio's petition to the court was based on technical arguments, but pleadings before lower courts raised the surveillance issues.

[17] Two former high-level executives working with Nacchio told me they believed he was prosecuted because of the surveillance issues. See also, Andrew Kreig, "Bush-Era Mississippi, Qwest Prosecutions Still Making News," Justice Integrity Project, See also, "In New Jersey, imprisoned former Qwest CEO Joseph Nacchio sued his politically well-connected former lawyer, Herbert Stern, on grounds of ineffective legal work during Nacchio's prosecution on insider trading charges – despite Stern's $25 million in legal fees." Andy Vuong, "U.S. Supreme Court denies Nacchio review," *Denver Post*, October 5, 2009, http://www.denverpost.com/nacchio/ci_13488938 See also, Ashby Jones, "Mahoney Delivers Again, this Time for Joe Nacchio," *Wall Street*

Journal, March 17, 2008, http://blogs.wsj.com/law/2008/03/17/donut-lover-mahoney-delivers-again-this-time-for-joe-nacchio.

18 Drake Materials Andrew Kreig, "Justice Advocate Radack Authors Courageous, Powerful Memoir," Justice Integrity Project, http://www.justice-integrity.org/faq/66-justice-advocate-radack-authors-courageous-powerful-memoir.

19 Klein, Mark. *Wiring Up the Big Brother Machine…And Fighting It.* Booksurge, 2009.

20 Risen, James. *State of War: The Secret History of the CIA and the Bush Administration.* Free Press / Simon & Schuster, 2006.

21 Kiriakou, John. *The Reluctant Spy: My Secret Life in the CIA's War on Terror.* Bantam, 2010.

22 Michael Collins, "9/11 Prediction Revealed at Susan Lindauer Hearing on Competence," Scoop Independent News, June 19, 2008, http://www.scoop.co.nz/stories/HL0806/S00263.htm.

23 Andrew Kreig, "Press Probes 'Obama's War on Leaks,'" Justice Integrity Project, May 2, 2012, http://www.justice-integrity.org/index.php?option=com_content&view=article&id=129:anibal-acevedo-vila&catid=56:leading-cases.

24 Charlie Savage, "Former CIA Operative Pleads Guilty in Leak of Colleague's Name," *New York Times*, October 23, 2012, http://www.nytimes.com/2012/10/24/us/former-cia-officer-pleads-guilty-in-leak-case.html?_r=0. "Less than two months after the Justice Department announced that it would not charge Central Intelligence Agency officials who participated in the brutal interrogation of detainees during the Bush administration, prosecutors on Tuesday won the conviction of a former CIA counterterrorism operative who told a reporter the name of a covert CIA officer involved in the program."

25 Michael S. Schmidt, "Ex-Officer for CIA Sentenced to 30 Months in Leak Case," *New York Times*, January 25, 2013, http://www.nytimes.com/2013/01/26/us/ex-officer-for-cia-is-sentenced-in-leak-case.html?emc=eta1&_r=0.

26 James Nye, "CIA agents in Benghazi twice asked for permission to help Ambassador Chris Stevens as bullets were flying and twice were told to 'stand down,'" *Daily Mail*, October 25, 2012, http://www.dailymail.co.uk/news/article-2223747/CIA-agents-Benghazi-twice-asked-permission-help-Ambassador-Chris-Stevens-bullets-flying-twice-told-stand-down.html?ITO=1490.

27 Webster G. Tarpley, "Webster Tarpley: CIA Has Fingerprints All Over Benghazi Assault," Alex Jones Show, October 20, 2012, http://www.prisonplanet.com/webster-tarpley-cia-has-fingerprints-all-over-benghazi-assault.html.

2008 Telecom Immunity Kills Public Protections for Privacy

28 Andrew Kreig, "Senator's Lonely Battle For Public's Privacy Rights," WhoWhatWhy, August 6, 2012.

http://whowhatwhy.com/2012/08/06/senators-lonely-battle-for-publics-privacy-rights.

9/11, Anthrax and the Patriot Act

29 National Commission on Terrorist Attacks Upon the United States, http://www.9-11commission.gov/report/index.htm.

30 Joint Inquiry into Intelligence Community Activities, http://www.gpo.gov/fdsys/search/pagedetails.action?browsePath=107/HRP T/%5B700%3B799%5D&granuleId=CRPT-107hrpt792&packageId=CRPT-107hrpt792. See also, generally, Richard F. Grimmett, "Terrorism: Key Recommendations of the 9/11 Commission and Recent Major Commissions and Inquiries," Congressional Research Service, August 11, 2004, http://www.au.af.mil/au/awc/awcgate/crs/rl32519.pdf; Summers, Anthony and Robbyn Swan. *The Eleventh Day: The Full Story of 9/11 and Osama Bin Laden.* Ballantine, 2011; and Coll, Steve. *The Bin Ladens: An Arabian Family in the American Century.* Penguin, 2008.

31 Wikipedia, 2001 Anthrax Attacks, http://en.wikipedia.org/wiki/2001_anthrax_attacks.

32 Wikipedia, Steven Hatfill, http://en.wikipedia.org/wiki/Steven_Hatfill.

33 Wikipedia, Bruce Ivins, http://en.wikipedia.org/wiki/Bruce_Edwards_Ivins.

34 Andrew Kreig, "Doubts Raised on Probe of Anthrax Killer," Justice Integrity Project, July 20, 2011. http://www.justice-integrity.org/faq/276-did-fbi-find-killer-in-dc-anthrax-attacks

35 Andrew Kreig, Senate Renews FISA Procedures, Justice Integrity Project, December 28, 2012, http://www.justice-integrity.org/faq/239-senate-renews-fisa-procedures.

From Langley, With Love

36 The rivalry and Donovan's dalliances are extensively reported by the spy chief's leading biographer. Waller, Douglas. *Wild Bill Donovan: The Spymaster Who Created the OSS and Modern American Espionage.* Simon & Schuster, 2011.

37 Trento, Joseph J. *The Secret History of the CIA.* Basic, 2005, 121-22. James J. Angleton, CIA counterintelligence chief for many years, was among those who entrusted Trento with his confidences and papers to assist book research.

38 *Spiked, op. cit.,* 106. The leading criticism of *Spiked* was that included a phrase describing a prominent, married publisher, Michael Davies, has having the nickname "Motel Mike" when he published a self-righteous column criticizing Gary Hart for lack of morals. In fact, the column understated the criticism of the publisher, who later lost his job as editor and publisher of the Baltimore Sun because of a sex scandal.

39 Trento, Susan B. *The Power House: Robert Keith Gray and the Selling of Access and Influence in Washington.* St. Martin's, 1992, 306. See also Kelley, *op. cit.,* whose index lists Jennifer Fitzgerald a dozen times; and Joe Conason, "1,000 Reasons Not To Vote for George Bush," *Spy,* August 1992. One of the author's reasons: "He cheats on his wife." Via email, Gray denied to me the validity of Susan Trento's reporting about him, or the Fitzgerald-Bush claim. The former

president's wife enied the latter also. Bush, Barbara. *A Memoir.* Scribner, 1994, 240.

[40] Paula Chin, "George Bush Confronts a Rumor; New Claims Surface about An Alleged Extramarital Affair," *People,* August 24, 1992, http://www.people.com/people/archive/article/0,,20108467,00.html.

[41] John LeBoutillier, "Why The Bushes Will Never Hire Linda Tripp," February 12, 2001, http://www.sarasotasailingsquadron.com/JenniferFitzgerald_Bush.htm.

[42] Staff at one major network tried to disregard the junior Bush's command by reporting that his father used to meet his lover at the posh Jefferson Hotel near the White House. But network higher-ups killed the story, according to my source.

[43] Central Intelligence Agency Inspector General Report of Investigation Improper Handling of Classified Information by John M. Deutch, February 18, 2000, http://www.fas.org/irp/cia/product/ig_deutch.html; See also, WikiPedia, John M. Deutch, http://en.wikipedia.org/wiki/John_M._Deutch.

[44] Wikipedia, Porter Goss, http://en.wikipedia.org/wiki/Porter_Goss; Hettena, Seth. *Feasting on the Spoils: The Life and Times of Randy "Duke" Cunningham, History's Most Corrupt Congressman.* St. Martin's, 2007, 252-53.

[45] Office of Congressional Ethics, http://oce.house.gov/porter-goss.html. See also, Scott Bronstein, Joe Johns, and Rachel Solomon, "Congressional ethics investigators could soon be silenced," CNN, December 29, 2012 (Video). "The Office of Congressional Ethics was created in 2008 amid a wave of scandals. If it's not reauthorized soon, it could be shut down. It has investigated 100 instances of possible misconduct by members of Congress."

[46] A recent sample of such tales includes: McEwen, Lillian. *DC Unmasked and Undressed.* TitleTown Publishing, 2011. Sibley, Montgomery Blair. *Why Just Her: The Judicial Lynching of the D.C. Madam,* Deborah Jeane Palfrey. Full Court Press, 2009. Bryant, Nick. *The Franklin Scandal: A Story of Powerbrokers, Child Abuses and Betrayal.* TrineDay, 2009. Baron, Lisa .*The Life of the Party: A Political Press Tart Bares All.* Citadel, 2011. An older book examines an iconic 1960s scandal in London involving Lord John Profumo. Summers, Anthony with Stephen Dorril. *Honeytrap.* Weidenfeld and Nicolson, 1987.

[47] One source who corresponded with Palfrey is Robin Head of Las Vegas, a native of Texas who served eight years in prison on organized crime charges. She contends that federal authorities unfairly targeted her because she refused to cooperate with the FBI and CIA by using her Playboy Escorts service for sexual entrapment and blackmail schemes. Her website http://vegasmadam.wordpress.com features allegations of sexual blackmail by authorities against political leaders in seldom-reported ways.

[48] Fuller, Jack. *The News about the News.* University of Chicago, 2010, 25-26. Fuller, former CEO of the Tribune Companies and a former Justice Department executive, argued that his scientific research showed why the human-mind is hard-wired to seek lessons from what snobs might deride as "gossip."

[49] Sibley, Montgomery. *Why Just her: The Judicial Lynching of the D.C. Madam. Deborah Jeane Palfrey.* Full Court Press, 2009. Janovic, Matthew Henry. *Let the Dead Bury the Dead: A DC Madam Account.* Trithemius, 2012.

50 The Madam scandal had far more importance than the prosecution abuses against Palfrey, her tawdry death, and her clientele even though it clearly exposed as Palfrey customers and hypocrites three high-ranking "Family Values" Republicans who advocated harsh government crusades against women's reproductive choices. The scandal, which threatened many more revelations that were suppressed, also overlapped with major lobbying scandals of national and global significance.

51 Grof, Stanislav. *Beyond the Brain: Birth, Death, and Transcendence in Psychotherapy.* State University of New York, 1985. Grof cites, "A Sexual Study of Men in Power" by Janus, Bess, and Saltus (1977), a study of the clientele and practices of high-priced call girls, based on 700 hours of interviews focused on clients. The author's research for *Presidential Puppetry* has tended to confirm those themes. This research was primarily through attorneys who have represented sex workers serving high-paying customers, and through a former madam seeking to expose physical dangers for sex workers, even those serving VIP clients.

52 Norm Pattis, "Anna Gristina prosecution exposes tawdry truth about justice," Litchfield (Connecticut) Register-Citizen, November. 21, 2012. http://www.registercitizen.com/articles/2012/11/21/opinion/doc50ad161d3 7508806331455.txt.

Meet Holly Weber, and Beware

53 Andrew Kreig, "Feeling Friendly This Week? Beware," OpEd News, August 22, 2011, http://www.opednews.com/articles/Feeling-Friendly-This-Week-by-Andrew-Kreig-110822-684.html. The *CSI* Hollywood actress, Holly Weber, had nothing to do with the scam, which used an avatar of someone else. HB Gary declined comment. See also, Lee Fang, "US Chamber's Lobbyists Solicited Hackers To Sabotage Unions, Smear Chamber's Political Opponents," Think Progress, February 10, 2011. http://thinkprogress.org/economy/2011/02/10/143419/lobbyists-chamberleaks; Glenn Greenwald, "The leaked campaign to attack WikiLeaks and its supporters," Salon, February 11, 2011. http://www.salon.com/2011/02/11/campaigns_4; Eric Lipton and Charlie Savage, "Hackers Reveal Offers to Spy on Corporate Rivals," *New York Times*, February 11, 2011, http://www.nytimes.com/2011/02/12/us/politics/12hackers.html?_r=2&hp & and Lee Fang, "Revealed: Fake Facebook Identity Used By Military Contractors Plotting To Hack Progressive Organizations," Think Progress, August 18, 2011, http://thinkprogress.org/politics/2011/08/18/298081/hbgary-federal-us-chamber-persona/?mobile=nc .

54 Glenn Greenwald, "NSA collecting phone records of millions of Verizon customers daily," *Guardian*, June 4, 2013. http://www.guardian.co.uk/world/2013/jun/06/nsa-phone-records-verizon-court-order; and Glenn Greenwald, Ewen MacAskill and Laura Poitras, "Edward Snowden: the whistleblower behind revelations of NSA surveillance,"*Guardian*, June 9, 2013, http://www.guardian.co.uk/world/2013/jun/09/edward-snowden-nsa-

whistleblower-surveillance. See also the news roundup in Andrew Kreig, "Snowden's NSA Leak Was Heroic, Historic: Daniel Ellsberg," Justice Integrity Project, June 10, 2013, http://www.justice-integrity.org/faq/490-snowden-s-nsa-leak-was-heroic-historic-ellsberg.

55 The Chertoff Group. http://www.chertoffgroup.com. Michael V. Hayden, "Birthers, Truthers and Interrogation Deniers," *Wall Street Journal,* June 2, 2011.
http://online.wsj.com/article/SB10001424052702303745304576359820767777538.html.

56 *See, e.g.,* Andrews, Lori. *I Know Who You Are and What You Did.* Free Press / Simon & Schuster, 2012.

57 *Clapper v. Amnesty International USA*, Case No. No. 11-1025. A friend of the court brief by the Electronic Privacy Information Center (EPIC) and 32 legal scholars and other experts (including Mark Klein and Thomas Drake) argues that members of the public should have standing to litigate surveillance and privacy issues. http://www.jdsupra.com/legalnews/brief-of-amici-curiae-electronic-privacy-98235.

58 Kevin Gosztola, "Supreme Court Rules Warrantless Wiretapping Law Cannot Be Challenged Without Proof of Secret Surveillance," FireDogLake, February 26, 2013, http://dissenter.firedoglake.com/2013/02/26/supreme-court-rules-warrantless-wiretapping-law-cannot-be-challenged-without-proof-of-secret-surveillance.

59 Tucker Reals, "Ex-CIA chief Michael Hayden: 'Only the U.S.' can strike Iran nuclear sites effectively," CBS News, September 4, 2012, http://www.cbsnews.com/8301-503543_162-57505379-503543/ex-cia-chief-michael-hayden-only-the-u.s.-can-strike-iran-nuclear-sites-effectively.

60 Fareed Zakaria, "'Red line' folly," *Washington Post*, September12, 2012, http://www.washingtonpost.com/opinions/fareed-zakaria-the-folly-over-red-lines-for-iran/2012/09/12/119a6a62-fd10-11e1-8adc-499661afe377_story.html.

Robert Kagan: Fearless Fighter for a Nation's Chickenhawks

61 Wikipedia, Neoconservative, http://en.wikipedia.org/wiki/Neoconservatism.

62 Wikipedia, Project for a New American Century, http://en.wikipedia.org/wiki/Project_for_the_New_American_Century.

63 Wayne Madsen, "Retaliation against Siegelman has roots in Bush '41 crimes," Wayne Madsen Report, Sept. 4, 2012, http://www.waynemadsenreport.com/articles/20120904. The re-imprisonment of former Alabama Democratic Governor Don Siegelman by George W. Bush-appointed U.S. Judge Mark E. Fuller is part of a political retaliation process that has its roots in the Iran-contra scandal, according to a high-level WMR source.

64 Donald Kagan formerly taught at Cornell University when I was a student. I phoned him at his Connecticut home in 2010 after the nomination of Elena Kagan to the Supreme Court to learn if she was related to him. He denied any relationship. In the course of an engaging conversation, he informed me that

his son, Frederick, was named after the late Cornell History Department Chairman Frederick Marcham, who had been my student advisor in college. The main point in sharing this anecdote, however, is to illustrate that dangerous policy can be advocated by individuals who are extremely well-educated and personally congenial.

65 American Enterprise Institute, Frederick W. Kagan, http://www.aei.org/scholar/frederick-w-kagan.

66 Wikipedia, Robert Kagan, http://en.wikipedia.org/wiki/Robert_Kagan.

67 She obtained the post after her predecessor, former Admiral P.J. Crowley, was forced out when he mentioned during what he thought was an off-the-record Harvard seminar his opinion that accused leaker, Private Bradley Manning, was being treated too harshly in pre-trial solitary confinement. Wikipedia, Philip J. Crowley, http://en.wikipedia.org/wiki/Philip_J._Crowley.

68 Among many other situations: Romney foreign policy adviser Daniel Senor, former spokesman for the Iraq Provisional authority, is married to CNN anchor Campbell Brown. Bush White House Communication is Director Catherine Martin is married to Federal Communications Commission Chairman Kevin Martin. Her job was to influence the media, and his was to regulate it. Newsweek/Daily Beast Washington Bureau Chief Howard Kurtz, also host of CNN's Reliable Sources program and formerly a longtime reporter on the media for the *Washington Post*, is married to Sherry Annis, a public relations consultant and speechwriter, primarily for conservative public policy positions. On the Democratic side, Washington Post editorial board member Ruth Marcus (specializing in legal affairs) is married to Jon Liebowitz, the first Federal Trade Commission chairman for the Obama administration. This is just a sample of a long list. To be sure, each person might be able to describe a firewall on any particular matter. But the essence is overlapping relationships and conflicts on an ongoing basis involving core functions.

69 Ryan, Cheyney. *The Chickenhawk Syndrome: War, Sacrifice, and Personal Responsibility.* Rowman and Littlefield, 2009.

70 Bugliosi, Vincent. *The Prosecution of George W. Bush for Murder.* Vanguard, 2008. Fein, Bruce. *The American Empire Before The Fall.* CreateSpace, 2010. Hastings, Michael. *The Operators: The Wild and Terrifying Inside Story of America's War in Afghanistan.* Blue Rider, 2012. Parry, Robert. *Secrecy & Privilege: Rise of the Bush Dynasty from Watergate to Iraq,* Media Consortium, 2004. Tillman, Mary with Narda Zacchino. *Boots on the Ground By Dusk: My Tribute to Pat Tillman.* Modern Times/Rodale, 2008. Van Buren, Peter. *We Meant Well: How I Helped Lose the Battle for the Hearts and Minds of the Iraqi People.* Metropolitan, 2012. Wilson, Joseph C., IV. *The Politics of Truth: A Diplomat's Memoir: Inside the Lies that Led to War and Betrayed My Wife's CIA Identity.* Carroll & Graf, 2004. Wilson, Valerie Plame. *Fair Game: My Life as a Spy, My Betrayal by the White House.* Simon & Schuster, 2007.

71 Laurie Bennett, "Robert Kagan, neocon listened to by both presidential candidates," *Foreign Policy,* August 27, 2012, http://news.muckety.com/2012/08/27/robert-kagan-neocon-listened-to-by-both-presidential-candidates/38081. See also, Josh Rogin, "Obama embraces Romney advisor's theory on 'The Myth of American Decline,'" *Foreign Policy,*

January 26, 2012,
http://thecable.foreignpolicy.com/posts/2012/01/26/obama_embraces_rom
ney_advisor_s_theory_on_the_myth_of_american_decline.

[72] Olivier Knox, "Obama: Does Romney want 'to start another war' in Middle East?" Yahoo News, September 23, 2012,
http://news.yahoo.com/blogs/ticket/obama-does-romney-want-start-
another-war-middle-014855301—election.html.

Michael Chertoff: Marketing Fear

[73] Wikipedia, Patriot Act, http://en.wikipedia.org/wiki/Patriot_Act.

[74] Radack, Jesselyn A. *Traitor: The Whistleblower and the "American Taliban."* Whistleblower, 2012.

[75] Edmonds, Sibel. *Classified Woman, The Sibel Edmonds Story: A Memoir*, Boiling Frogs, 2012.

[76] Andrew Kreig, "Former NSA Analyst, Secret Service Agent Speaks Out On Scandals," Justice Integrity Project, April, 19, 2012, http://www.justice-
integrity.org/135-former-nsa-analyst-secret-service-officer-speaks-out-on-
scandals.

[77] Wilson, Joseph C., IV. *The Politics of Truth: A Diplomat's Memoir: Inside the Lies that Led to War and Betrayed My Wife's CIA Identity.* Carroll & Graf, 2004. Wilson, Valerie Plame. *Fair Game: My Life as a Spy, My Betrayal by the White House.* Simon & Schuster, 2007.

[78] Other prominent examples include former Senate Majority Leader and U.S. District Judge George Mitchell, former Texas Supreme Court Justice and Bush Attorney General Alberto Gonzales, former U.S. District Judge and Bush Attorney General Michael Mukasey, and former District of Columbia Superior Court Judge and Obama Attorney General Eric Holder.

[79] "A Failure of Initiative: The Final Report of the Select Bipartisan Committee to Investigate the Preparation for and Response to Hurricane Katrina," Chairman Tom Davis, R-VA, February 16, 2006,
http://www.katrina.house.gov/full_katrina_report.htm.

[80] Also, the administration and media soon identified a convenient scapegoat, Michael Brown, the Federal Emergency Management Administration director. Only later and soon forgotten would it emerge that Brown, despite his posturing bringing ridicule, had actually warned higher-ups to take better preparations, but to no avail.

[81] Wikipedia, Umar Farouk Abdulmutallab
http://en.wikipedia.org/wiki/Umar_Farouk_Abdulmutallab.

[82] Paul Craig Roberts, "How Liberty Was Lost," Institute for Political Economy, April 23, 2012, http://www.paulcraigroberts.org/2012/04/23/how-liberty-
was-lost.

[83] Ron Paul, "Enough is enough," House of Representatives Speech, November 17, 2010, as cited in Andrew Kreig, "Terror and TSA," Huffington Post, November 22, 2010, http://www.huffingtonpost.com/andrew-kreig/terror-
tsa-and-the-sheepl_b_786434.html. See also, Paul Joseph Watson, "Ron Paul Unleashes On TSA: 'Enough Is Enough,'" Alex Jones, Info Wars, November

18, 2010, http://www.infowars.com/ron-paul-unleashes-on-tsa-enough-is-enough.

[84] Andrew Kreig, "TSA Boondoggle Defies Logic, Decency," Justice Integrity Project, November 26, 2010, http://www.justice-integrity.org/faq/384-tsa-boondoggle-defies-logic-decency.

[85] Brian Doherty, "TSA's Intrusions on American Dignity," *Reason,* January 5, 2011, http://reason.com/blog/2011/01/05/new-at-reason-brian-doherty-on.

[86] FireDogLake, "Rape Victim Arrested by TSA for Refusing Groping, Michael Whitney, December 24, 2010, http://my.firedoglake.com/michaelwhitney/2010/12/24/rape-victim-arrested-by-tsa-for-refusing-groping/#comments.

[87] Jeff Plungis, "Naked-Image Scanners to Be Removed From U.S. Airports," Bloomberg, January 18, 2013, http://www.bloomberg.com/news/2013-01-18/naked-image-scanners-to-be-removed-from-u-s-airports.html ; and Stephen Colbert, "Rapiscan Scanners," Colbert Report, January 28, 2013, http://www.colbertnation.com/the-colbert-report-videos/423267/january-28-2013/rapiscan-scanners.

[88] "At least 90 officials at the Department of Homeland Security or the White House Office of Homeland Security — including the department's former secretary, Tom Ridge; the former deputy secretary, Adm. James M. Loy; and the former undersecretary, Asa Hutchinson — are executives, consultants or lobbyists for companies that collectively do billions of dollars' worth of domestic security business. More than two-thirds of the department's most senior executives in its first years have moved through the revolving door." Eric Lipton, "Former Antiterror Officials Find Industry Pays Better " *New York Times,* June 18, 2006, http://www.nytimes.com/2006/06/18/washington/18lobby.html?pagewanted=all, as cited in Trento, Susan B. *Unsafe at Any Altitude: Failed Terrorism Investigations, Scapegoating 9/11, and the Shocking Truth about Aviation Security Today.* Steerforth, 2006, 225.

[89] Kaiser, *So Damn Much Money, op. cit.*

[90] Ashley Halsey III, "TSA to pull revealing scanners from airports," *Washington Post,* January 18, 2013, http://www.washingtonpost.com/local/trafficandcommuting/tsa-to-pull-revealing-scanners-from-airports/2013/01/18/1b7d5d22-6198-11e2-9940-6fc488f3fecd_story.html?hpid=z3.

[91] Baker, Russ. *Family of Secrets: The Bush Dynasty, America's Invisible Government, and the Hidden History of the Last Fifty Years.* Bloomsbury Press, 2009, 470.

Chapter 14, Probing the 2012 Voting Schemes

[1] Black Box Voting, www.blackboxvoting.org.

[2] Richard Charnin, "Updated Daily: Presidential True Vote/Election Fraud Forecast Model," Richard Charnin.com, October 26, 2012, http://richardcharnin.wordpress.com/2012/10/17/update-daily-presidential-true-voteelection-fraud-forecast-model. See also, Richard Charnin, "Election Fraud: An Introduction to Exit Poll Probability Analysis," Richard Charnin's Blog, June 23, 2012,

http://richardcharnin.wordpress.com/2012/06/25/election-fraud-an-introduction-to-exit-poll-probability-analysis.

3 See also, Michael Collins, "Rigged Elections for Romney?" OpEdNews, October 22, 2012, http://www.opednews.com/articles/Rigged-Elections-for-Romne-by-Michael-Collins-121022-13.html.

4 Andrew Kreig, "NBC's Todd Mocks Election Fraud Critics, Wins Washington Applause," Justice Integrity Project, January 30, 2013, http://www.justice-integrity.org/faq/432-nbc-s-todd-mocks-election-fraud-critics-wins-washington-applause.

5 Rove, *Courage and Consequence, op. cit.*, 505-11. I have requested comment from Rove via his spokeswoman several times without success.

6 Unger, Craig. *Boss Rove: Inside Karl Rove's Secret Kingdom of Power.* Scribner, 2012, 249-50.

7 Sheelah Kolhatkar, "Forget Mitt Romney, Karl Rove's Eyes Are on the Senate," Bloomberg BusinessWeek, September 10, 2012, http://www.businessweek.com/articles/2012-09-06/forget-mitt-romney-dot-karl-roves-eyes-are-on-the-senate.

8 Keith Thomson, "Could Romney-Linked Electronic Voting Machines Jeopardize Ohio's Vote Accuracy?" Huffington Post, October 26, 2012, http://www.huffingtonpost.com/keith-thomson/romney-electronic-voting-machines_b_2025490.html.

9 James Rosen, "Closing arguments set for South Carolina voting case," *Washington Post*, September 24, 2012, http://www.washingtonpost.com/politics/decision2012/closing-arguments-set-for-south-carolina-voting-case/2012/09/23/fb0eb190-0589-11e2-a10c-fa5a255a9258_story.html

10 Wayne Madsen, "A 'Price Tag' October Surprise in September for Obama." Strategic Culture Foundation, September 20, 2012, http://www.strategic-culture.org/news/2012/09/20/a-price-tag-october-surprise-in-september-for-obama.html.

11 Schroeder, Alice. *The Snowball: Warren Buffett and the Business of Life.* Bantam, 2008. The 800-page book mentions neither Hagel nor American Information Systems in its various names.

12 Alexander Cockburn and Jeffrey St. Clair, "She Needed Fewer Friends: The High Life of Katharine Graham," *Counterpunch*, July 25, 2001. http://www.counterpunch.org/2001/07/25/the-high-life-of-katharine-graham. It begins: "Mrs Graham sustained her fatal fall during an annual confab of the nation's biggest media and e-billionaires, organized by the investment banker Herb Allen and held in Sun Valley, Idaho. In truth it was a richly symbolic setting for Mrs Graham's exit. Sun Valley was developed as a resort by the Harrimans, starting with that ruthless nineteenth century railroad king, E.H. Harriman."

13 Office of Ethics in Government, Charles T. Hagel letter, January 22, 2013, http://www.oge.gov/DisplayTemplates/201_Form/FilerDetail.aspx?id=8589935521. The brief letter offers minimal disclosure. See also, LegiStorm, for Senate disclosure documents, www.LegiStorm.com.

[14] Harris, *Black Box Voting, op. cit.*, 38-39. See also, Miller, Mark Crispin. *Fooled Again: How the Right Stole the 2004 Election and Why They'll Steal the Next One Too (Unless We Stop Them)*. Basic Books, 2005, 194-95.

[15] Don Smith, "Cover-ups concerning former Republican Senator Chuck Hagel," June 27, 2011, OpEdNews, http://www.opednews.com/articles/Coverups-concerning-former-by-Don-Smith-110627-384.html. See also Harris, Bev. *Black Box Voting*. Plan Nine, 2003, 11-32.

[16] Gerry Bello and Bob Fitrakis, "Vote counting company tied to Romney," Free Press, September 28, 2012, http://www.freepress.org/departments/display/19/2012/4725.

[17] Andrew Kreig, "Rove Vote-Switching 'Empire' Alleged to Threaten Nov. 6 Results," Justice Integrity Project, November 4, 2012, http://www.justice-integrity.org/faq/176-rove-vote-switching. See also, Jeff Ostrowski, "Boca Raton database pioneer Hank Asher dead at 61," *Palm Beach Post*, January 11, 2013, http://m.palmbeachpost.com/news/business/boca-raton-database-pioneer-hank-asher-dead-at-61/nTtM2.

[18] Cliff Arnebeck, "Rove Taunts Bring Simpson Back in the Ring," Election Protection Action, November 1, 2012, http://electionprotectionaction.org/4/post/2012/11/rove-taunts-bring-simpson-back-to-the-ring.html.

[19] Jim March, Jill Simpson, and Dana Siegelman with Clifford Arnebeck and Andrew Kreig (moderators), "Karl Rove's election fraud empire," News conference, National Press Club, October 24, 2012.

[20] Andrew Kreig, "Cutting Through Hype, Hypocrisy of Vote Fraud Claims,"Justice Integrity Project, August, 14, 2010 (later updated), http://www.justice-integrity.org/faq/267-cutting-through-vote-fraud-claims-hypocrisy.

[21] The Justice Integrity Project published several columns on election fraud books, allegations, rebuttals in the fall of 2012. The most comprehensive was, "Election Fraud Critics Seek Halt To Ohio's Secret Software In GOP Plan," November 5, 2012, http://www.justice-integrity.org/faq/39-election-fraud-critics-seek-halt-to-ohios-secret-software-in-gop-plan.

[22] *King Lincoln Bronzeville Neighborhood Association et al. vs. Ohio Secretary of State Jennifer Brunner* [originally Kenneth Blackwell], *et al.*, U.S. District Court for the Southern District of Ohio (2006), Civil Action No. C2-06-645. Wikipedia, *King Lincoln Bronzeville v. Blackwell,*

[23] Unger, *op. cit.*, 35-49, 176-78.

[24] Baker, *op. cit.*, 331-32.

[25] Ibid., 176-78.

[26] Ibid., 176-179. See also, Ney, Robert W. *Sideswiped: Lessons Learned Courtesy of the Hit Men of Capitol Hill*. Changing Lives, 2013, 172-78.

[27] Ibid., 85.

[28] Ibid., 48-49.

[29] Free Press, "Does the Romney family now own your e-vote?" Gerry Bello, Bob Fitrakis & Harvey Wasserman," October 18, 2012, http://freepress.org/departments/display/19/2012/4748. "Through a closely held equity fund called Solamere, Mitt Romney and his wife, son and brother

are major investors in an investment firm called H.I.G. Capital. H.I.G. in turn holds a majority share and three out of five board members in Hart InterCivic, a company that owns the notoriously faulty electronic voting machines that will count the ballots in swing state Ohio November 6."

30 Scytl, http://www.scytl.com/company/about-scytl/index.html

31 Black Box Voting, www.blackboxvoting.org. See also, Harris, Bev, with David Allen. *Black Box Voting: Ballot-tampering in the 21st Century.* Plan Nine Publishing, 2003.

32 Scytl Management Team, http://www.scytl.com/company/management-team/index.html.

33 Michelle M. Schaffer, Scytl, director of communications and government relations, email: "Scytl USA provides electronic ballot delivery solutions for military and overseas voters. SOE Software, a subsidiary of Scytl USA provides election management software solutions that increase productivity and efficiency for states and local jurisdictions. These solutions include Election Night Reporting, Voter Education Web Portals, Online Training for Poll workers and Asset Tracking. Election Night Reporting should not in any way be interpreted as ballot tabulation. SOE does not provide ballot tabulation solutions. Scytl no longer has an office in Virginia. Scytl USA's headquarters are based in Baltimore, MD and SOE Software's offices are based in Tampa, Florida. See our website at http://www.scytl.com/en/contact-c-6.html. Combined, the company has over 50 U.S. based employees. Like many companies, some of our employees are based remotely within the U.S., but most work from either our Baltimore or Tampa offices." The above website has changed to http://www.scytl.com/contact/index.html.

34 Gerry Bello, "Who owns Scytl? George Soros isn't in the voting machines, but the intelligence community is," Free Press, September 18, 2012, http://www.freepress.org/departments/display/19/2012/4719.

35 Greg Palast, MTL Washington Update, interview by author, October 4, 2012.

36 Editorial Board, "The toothless watchdog FEC," *Washington Post*, December 29, 2012, http://www.washingtonpost.com/opinions/toothless-election-oversight/2012/12/29/f535949c-4958-11e2-820e-17eefac2f939_story.html.

37 Juliet Lapidos, "The Ron Paul Revolt," *New York Times*, August 28, 2012, http://takingnote.blogs.nytimes.com/2012/08/28/the-ron-paul-revolt. See also, Michael Collins, "Rigged Elections for Romney?" OpEdNews, October 22, 2012, http://www.opednews.com/articles/Rigged-Elections-for-Romne-by-Michael-Collins-121022-13.html. "A group of independent researchers caught a pattern of apparent vote flipping during the 2012 Republican primaries that consistently favored Mitt Romney."

38 Parallel problems exist in other threats to consumers, such as hacking, identity theft, and spam attacks. Individuals and most corporations are over-matched by adversaries using guerrilla tactics. Yet governments provide only modest consumer-friendly services, and in some cases are suspected of helping hacker attacks or even funding false identity social media plans, as indicated by these columns: Andrew Kreig, "Feeling Friendly This Week? Beware," Justice Integrity Project, August 22, 2011, http://www.justice-integrity.org/faq/264-feeling-friendly-this-week-beware. See also, Lee Fang, "US Chamber's

Lobbyists Solicited Hackers To Sabotage Unions, Smear Chamber's Political Opponents," Think Progress / Center for American Progress, February 10, 2011, http://thinkprogress.org/economy/2011/02/10/143419/lobbyists-chamberleaks/?mobile=nc. Glenn Greenwald, "The leaked campaign to attack WikiLeaks and its supporters," Salon/Unclaimed Territory, February 11, 2011, http://www.salon.com/2011/02/11/campaigns_4.

[39] Brad Friedman, "NBC News Election Expert Chuck Todd: Voting Machine Concerns are 'Conspiracy Garbage,'" BradBlog, October 21, 2012, http://www.bradblog.com/?p=9651. Todd is represented by one of the nation's top speaker bureaus: Leading Authorities, Chuck Todd, http://www.leadingauthorities.com/speaker/chuck-todd.aspx. The fees he charges groups are undisclosed. But, the fees charged by other media personnel, the payments almost inevitably create a conflict of interest. Ohio Secretary of State Jon Husted, for examples, serves on the executive committee of the group that invited Todd to speak at the convention.

[40] Andrew Kreig, "NBC's Todd Mocks Election Fraud Critics, Wins Washington Applause," OpEdNews, January. 29, 2013. http://www.opednews.com/articles/NBC-s-Todd-Mocks-Election-by-Andrew-Kreig-130129-725.html.

[41] Kreig, "Cutting Through Hype, Hypocrisy of Vote Fraud Claims," *op. cit.*

[42] Simon, Jonathan D. *Code Red: Computerized Election Theft and the New American Century.* Election Defense Alliance, 2012.

[43] I referred the professor to Jonathan Simon for details on how election fraud occurs. He is the leader of the civic group Election Defense Alliance (www.ElectionDefenseAlliance.org).

[44] Andrew Kreig, "Siegelman Deserves New Trial Because of Judge's 'Grudge', Evidence Shows....$300 Million in Bush Military Contracts Awarded to Judge's Private Company," Huffington Post, May 15, 2009, http://www.huffingtonpost.com/andrew-kreig/siegelman-deserves-new-tr_b_201455.html. The judge has repeatedly declined my requests for comment, but did deliver a 2012 lecture on judicial ethics at the University of Alabama School of Law, his *alma mater*. During the lecture, Fuller told the students he properly conducted himself at all times, a view challenged by one of the students, Joseph Siegelman, son of the defendant. Later, the judge was revealed to have been having a long-running affair with his court-clerk, prompting divorce actions by the spouses of both lovers.

[45] Andrew Kreig, "GOP Former Congressman Decries Injustice for Siegelman," Justice Integrity Project, November 27, 2012. http://www.justice-integrity.org/faq/228-gop-former-congressman-decries-injustice-for-siegelman.

[46] Andrew Kreig, "Siegelman's First Trial Judge Blasts U.S. Prosecutors, Seeks Probe of 'Unfounded' Charges," May 21, 2009, Huffington Post http://www.huffingtonpost.com/andrew-kreig/siegelmans-first-trial-ju_b_206546.html. See also a video of 13 speakers, including retired judge Clemon, at a forum I organized. C-SPAN cablecast the three-hour event in its entirety. "Prosecutorial Misconduct Forum At National Press Club," June 26,

2009 (3 hours, 4 minutes), Video: C-SPAN http://www.c-spanvideo.org/program/287304-1.

47 The essence of the prosecution was that Siegelman reappointed to a state board Richard Scrushy, a donor to the non-profit Alabama Education Foundation. Prosecutors claimed that a jury could find a *quid pro quo* sufficient for theft of honest services convictions, even though no direct evidence of a deal was offered and three previous governors had appointed Scrushy to the unpaid state board after his contributions to their campaigns.

48 Andrew Kreig, "Siegelman Sentence Cements Judicial Scandal In History," Justice Integrity Project, August. 4, 2013, http://www.justice-integrity.org/faq/75-siegelman-sentence-cements-judicial-scandal-in-history.

49 Andrew Kreig, "Inside Story on DoD's Boeing Air Force Tanker Deal," Connecticut Watchdog, February 25, 2011, http://ctwatchdog.com/2011/02/25/inside-story-on-dods-boeing-air-force-tanker-deal-opinion-analysis. See also Andrew Kreig, "Famed Editor Sir Harold Evans Reflects on Investigative Reporting Threats," Justice Integrity Project, February 22, 2012, http://www.justice-integrity.org/faq/159-sir-harold-evans-describes-threats-to-investigative-reporting; and "Rothschild Loses Libel Suit In 'Puppet-Master' Regulatory Scandal," Justice Integrity Project, February 17, 2012, http://www.justice-integrity.org/faq/163-rothschild-loses-libel-suit-in-puppet-master-regulatory-scandal; and Tom Peck, "Rothschild loses libel case, and reveals secret world of money and politics," *Independent* (United Kingdom), February 11, 2012. http://www.independent.co.uk/news/uk/home-news/rothschild-loses-libel-case-and-reveals-secret-world-of-money-and-politics-6720015.html.

50 Dan Froomkin, "Karl Rove's Donor Plan Could Run Afoul Of IRS, Congressional Report Suggests." Huffington Post, August 1, 2012, http://www.huffingtonpost.com/2012/08/31/karl-roves-donor-plan-afoul_n_1847834.html?utm_source=Alert-blogger&utm_medium=email&utm_campaign=Email%2B.

51 Michael D. Shear, "Obama's Lawyer Demands Information on Group's Donors," *New York Times*, June 19, 2012, http://thecaucus.blogs.nytimes.com/2012/06/19/obamas-lawyer-demands-information-on-groups-donors/. Sam Stein, "Bob Bauer, Obama Campaign's Top Lawyer, Demands Retraction From Karl Rove," Huffington Post, June 21, 2012, http://www.huffingtonpost.com/2012/06/21/bob-bauer-obama-campaign-karl-rove_n_1616021.html.

52 Greta Van Susteren, "Rove: Obama campaign trying to intimidate my Crossroads GPS group with 'thuggish behavior,'" Fox News / On the Record interviews Karl Rove, June 20, 2012, http://www.foxnews.com/on-air/on-the-record/2012/06/21/rove-obama-campaign-trying-intimidate-my-crossroads-gps-group-thuggish-behavior.

53 The announced goal by Florida's legislature and Secretary of State Kathleen Harris (also co-chair of the Bush-Cheney campaign in Florida) ostensibly was to eliminate felons. The purge was vastly overbroad, eliminating many eligible voters in a state that conveniently lists voters by party and race. Governor Jeb Bush's administration paid the contractor $2 million for work the previous

contractor had performed for $5,000. Palast, *The Best Democracy Money Can Buy*, *op. cit.*

54 Dan Froomkin, "Pennsylvania Voter ID Law Ruling: Judge Halts Enforcement Of Law For Election," Huffington Post, October 2, 2012, http://www.huffingtonpost.com/2012/10/02/pennsylvania-voter-id-ruling_n_1919187.html?utm_source=Alert-blogger&utm_medium=email&utm_campaign=Email%2BNotifications.

55 Fund, John. *Stealing Elections: How Voter Fraud Threatens Our Democracy.* Encounter, 2008.

56 Elizabeth Drew, "Voting Wrongs," *New York Review of Books*, September 21, 2012, http://www.nybooks.com/blogs/nyrblog/2012/sep/21/voting-wrongs. "The Republicans' plan is that if they can't buy the 2012 election they will steal it."

57 Brad Friedman, "NC GOP Joins FL in Firing RNC's Romney-Tied Voter Registration Firm Accused of Fraud," Brad Blog, September 27, 2012, http://www.bradblog.com/?p=9592.

58 Bill Moyers, "ALEC: The Scheme to Remake America, One State House at a Time," Huffington Post, September 26, 2012, http://www.huffingtonpost.com/bill-moyers/alec-the-scheme-to-remake_b_1916171.html.

59 Elizabeth Drew, "Voting Wrongs," *New York Review of Books*, September 21, 2012, http://www.nybooks.com/blogs/nyrblog/2012/sep/21/voting-wrongs. The Republicans' plan is that if they can't buy the 2012 election they will steal it."

60 Ian Gray, "Jim Greer, Ex-Florida GOP Chair, Claims Republican Voting Laws Focused On Suppression, Racism," Huffington Post, November 26, 212. http://www.huffingtonpost.com/2012/11/26/jim-greer-florida-voting-laws_n_2192802.html.

61 Staff reports, "Fox News Hosts Mock Desiline Victor, 102 Year Old Woman Who Waited Three Hours To Vote," Huffington Post/Media Matters/Fox News, February 14, 2013, http://www.huffingtonpost.com/2013/02/14/fox-news-hosts-desiline-victor_n_2688111.html.

62 Scott Shane, "Ex-Officers Attack Obama Over Leaks on Bin Laden Raid," *New York Times*, August 15, 2012, http://www.nytimes.com/2012/08/16/us/politics/ex-military-and-cia-officers-attack-obama-over-bin-laden-leaks.html?_r=0.

63 Special Operations (OPSEC), http://opsecteam.org. "Mission Statement: STOP the politicians, President Obama and others, from politically capitalizing on US national security operations and secrets!"

64 Karl Rove, "'The Road We've Traveled' With Obama," *Wall Street Journal*, March 21, 2012, http://online.wsj.com/article/SB10001424052702304724404577295601147645884.html.

65 Simpson emails and Black Box Voting internal memo made available to author.

66 Staff report, "Pastor Terry Jones *vs.* the Muslims," American Free Press, September 23, 2012, http://americanfreepress.net/?p=6226#more-6226.

67 Wikipedia, Special Operations OPSEC Education Fund, http://en.wikipedia.org/wiki/Special_Operations_OPSEC_Education_Fund.

[68] Mark Hosenball, "Obama campaign accuses Republicans of smear tactics over bin Laden, leaks," Reuters, August 15, 2012, http://www.reuters.com/article/2012/08/15/us-usa-campaign-binladen-ad-idUSBRE87E01F20120815.

[69] Scott Shane, "Ex-Officers Attack Obama Over Leaks on Bin Laden Raid," *New York Times*, August 15, 2012, http://www.nytimes.com/2012/08/16/us/politics/ex-military-and-cia-officers-attack-obama-over-bin-laden-leaks.html?_r=0.

[70] Ibid.

[71] See, generally: Graham, Bob. *Intelligence Matters: The CIA, The FBI, Saudi Arabia, and The Failure of America's War on Terror*. Random House, 2004.Coll, Steve. *The Bin Ladens: An Arabian Family in the American Century*. Penguin, 2008; and Roxane Farmanfarmaian, "Redrawing the Middle East map: Iran, Syria and the new Cold War," Al Jazeera, November 15, 2012, http://www.aljazeera.com/indepth/opinion/2012/11/2012111311424048459.html.

[72] Tabassum Zakaria, Susan Cornwell and Hadeel Al Shalchi, "For Benghazi diplomatic security, U.S. relied on small British firm," Reuters, October 17 2012, http://www.reuters.com/article/2012/10/18/us-libya-usa-bluemountain-idUSBRE89G1TI20121018.

[73] U.S. Department of State, "Briefing on the Accountability Review Board Report," William J. Burns, Ambassador Tom Pickering, and Admiral Michael Mullen, December 19, 2012, http://www.state.gov/r/pa/prs/ps/2012/12/202282.htm. See also, "Accountability Review Board Report," http://www.state.gov/documents/organization/202446.pdf; and U.S. Senate Committee on Homeland Security and Governmental Affairs, "Flashing Red: A Special Report on the Terrorist Attack at Benghazi," Chairman Joseph I. Lieberman and Ranking Member Susan M. Collins, December 30, 2012, 112thCongress, http://www.collins.senate.gov/public/_cache/files/81d5e2d9-cc8d-45af-aa8b-b937c55c7208/Flashing%20Red-HSGAC%20Special%20Report%20final.pdf.

[74] Webb, Brandon, and Jack Murphy. *Benghazi: The Definitive Report*. HarperCollins, Kindle Edition, 2013.

[75] Peter Schworm and John R. Ellement, "Winchester native among Libya attack victims," *Boston Globe*, September 13, 2012, http://www.bostonglobe.com/metro/2012/09/13/winchester-native-one-four-americans-killed-libya-consulate-attack-benghazi/cBPcnSCVqmEDJA7ewADhVK/story.html.

[76] Ibid. See also, Wikipedia, 2012 Benghazi Attack, http://en.wikipedia.org/wiki/2012_Benghazi_attack.

[77] Ibid., Kindle Locations, 604-607.

[78] Fund, John. *Stealing Elections: How Voter Fraud Threatens Our Democracy*. Encounter, 2008.

[79] In September 2012,Greg Palast published *Billionaires and Ballots*. It explains what election thieves are planning in the November elections — and how voters can fight back. Palast, Greg, with comics by Ted Rall and introduction by Robert F. Kennedy, Jr. *Billionaires and Ballots: How To Steal An Election in 9 Easy Steps.* Seven Stories, 2012. See also, Palast, Greg. *The Best Democracy Money Can Buy.* Plume/Penguin, 2004.

[80] Craig Unger, "Boss Rove," *Vanity Fair*, September 2012, http://www.vanityfair.com/politics/2012/09/karl-rove-gop-craig-unger.

[81] Amanda Terkel, "Project ORCA: Mitt Romney Campaign Plans Massive, State-Of-The-Art Poll Monitoring Effort," Huffington Post, November 1, 2012. http://www.huffingtonpost.com/2012/11/01/project-orca-mitt-romney_n_2052861.html.

[82] Sasha Issenberg , "Obama's White Whale How the campaign's top-secret project Narwhal could change this race, and many to come," Slate, February 15, 2012, http://www.slate.com/articles/news_and_politics/victory_lab/2012/02/project_narwhal_how_a_top_secret_obama_campaign_program_could_change_the_2012_race_.html.

Part III: The 2012 Contenders

Chapter 15, Paul Ryan: Killing Us Softly....

[1] Office of Hon. Paul Ryan, "Rep. Paul Ryan Selected to be Ranking Member of House Budget Committee," December 7, 2006, http://paulryan.house.gov/news/documentsingle.aspx?DocumentID=246834.

[2] As a member of the House Republican leadership, Ryan had a good read on how Republicans were going to vote. Party leaders conduct secret tallies before each major legislative vote. Ryan had to know that House Republicans were in full revolt. On September 29, 133 of 198 House Republicans voted against the proposal. Along with 95 Democrats, members from the Republican Party formed a 225-member majority to defeat the bailout.

[3] Carl Hulse and David M. Herszenhorn, "House Rejects Bailout Package, 228-205; Stocks Plunge," *New York Times*, September 29, 2008, http://www.nytimes.com/2008/09/30/business/30bailout.html?pagewanted=all Edmund L. Andrews, "Vast Bailout Proposed by U.S. in Bid to Stem the Financial Crisis," New York Times, September 18, 2008, http://www.nytimes.com/2008/09/19/business/19fed.html?_r=0&adxnnl=1&pagewanted=all&adxnnlx=1350274674-cbDkVK1vfvXocddaMO4E1w.

[4] Lynn Stuart Parramore, "The Paul Ryan Insider Trading Story Won't Die Because It's Legitimate," AlterNet, August 17, 2012. http://www.alternet.org/election-2012/paul-ryan-insider-trading-story-wont-die-because-its-legitimate Editor's note; and Paul Jay, "Paul Ryan â Insider Trading and Attack on Medicare; Tom Ferguson Interview," Real News Network, August 17, 2012, http://therealnews.com/t2/index.php?Itemid=74&id=31&jumival=8710&option=com_content&task=view. But see Benjy Sarlin, "Paul Ryan Insider Trading Rumor Quickly Debunked," Talking Points Memo, August 13, 2012,

http://2012.talkingpointsmemo.com/2012/08/paul-ryan-insider-trading-rumor-quickly-debunked.php

5 Steve Kroft, "Congress trading stock on insider information," *60 Minutes,* CBS News, November 12, 2011, http://www.cbsnews.com/8301-18560_162-57323527/congress-trading-stock-on-inside-information/?tag=contentMain;contentBody.

6 Eric Zuesse, "Did Mitt Romney Commit a Crime Punishable by Prison?" Huffington Post, August 21, 2012, http://www.huffingtonpost.com/eric-zuesse/did-mitt-romney-commit-a-_b_1819061.html.

7 Michael Cohen, "Did Republicans deliberately crash the US economy?" *Guardian,* June 9, 2012. http://www.guardian.co.uk/commentisfree/2012/jun/09/did-republicans-deliberately-crash-us-economy.

8 Robert Kuttner, "Thank you, Paul Ryan," Huffington Post, September 16, 2012, http://www.huffingtonpost.com/robert-kuttner/thank-you-paul-ryan_b_1888870.html.

9 Michael Shear and Michael Barbarosa, "In Video Romney Calls 47% 'Dependent' and Feeling Entitled', *New York Times,* September 17, 2012, http://thecaucus.blogs.nytimes.com/2012/09/17/romney-faults-those-dependent-on-government.

10 David Corn, "Romney '47 Percent' Fundraiser Host: Hedge Fund Manager Who Likes Sex Parties," *Mother Jones,* September 17, 2012, http://www.motherjones.com/mojo/2012/09/romney-secret-video-marc-leder-sex-parties.

11 Dan Gross, "Sixers co-owner Marc Leder is a party animal, paper reports," Philly.com, September 19, 2012, http://www.philly.com/philly/blogs/entertainment/celebrities_gossip/Sixers-co-owner-Marc-Leder-is-a-party-animal-paper-reports.html.

12 "Presidential campaigns wallow so tediously in pseudo-events and manufactured outrage that our senses can be numbed to the appearance of something genuinely momentous. Mitt Romney's secretly recorded comments at a fund-raiser are such an event — they reveal something vital about Romney, and they disqualify his claim to the presidency. To think of Romney's leaked discourse as a "gaffe" grossly misdescribes its importance." Jonathan Chait, "The Real Romney: A Sneering Plutocrat," *New York Magazine,* September 18, 2012, http://nymag.com/daily/intel/2012/09/real-romney-is-a-sneering-plutocrat.html.

13 Heather, "Mary Matalin Equates Those Using 'Poverty Programs' to 'Parasites,'" Crooks and Liars, September 18, 2012 (video), http://videocafe.crooksandliars.com/heather/mary-matalin-equates-those-using-poverty-p.

14 Michael Collins, "Questions for The Money Party: Why Negative Job Growth for 11 Years?," OpEdNews, June 22, 2011, http://www.opednews.com/articles/Michael-Collins-Questions-by-Michael-Collins-110622-31.html.

15 Sally Kohn, "Ryan Didn't Build That," Salon, April 14, 2012, http://www.salon.com/2012/08/14/paul_ryan_didnt_build_that.

[16] Sarah Jones, "Busted: Paul Ryan Left $1-5 Million Trust Off Disclosure Forms Until He Was Vetted," PoliticsUSA, August 16, 2012, http://www.politicususa.com/busted-paul-ryans-1-5-million-trust-left-disclosure-forms-vetted.html.

[17] Staff report, "14 things you probably don't know about Paul Ryan," http://now.msn.com/facts-you-might-not-know-about-romneys-vp-pick; and Matthew DeLuca, "7 Fun Facts About Paul Ryan," Daily Beast, August 11, 2012, http://www.thedailybeast.com/articles/2012/08/11/7-fun-facts-about-paul-ryan.html.

[18] Albert R. Hunt, "Paul Ryan's Role Model Was Jack Kemp," Bloomberg News/New York Times, August 12, 2012, http://www.nytimes.com/2012/08/13/us/13iht-letter13.html?_r=0.

[19] Adam Smith, *The Wealth of Nations*. Book 1, Ch. 8, http://www.econlib.org/library/Smith/smWN.html.

[20] Cantor, Eric, Paul Ryan, and Kevin McCarthy, *Young Guns: A New Generation of Conservative Leaders*. Threshhold, 2010.

[21] Matthew O'Brien, "Mitt Romney Would Pay 0.82 Percent in Taxes Under Paul Ryan's Plan," *Atlantic*, August 11, 2012, http://www.theatlantic.com/business/archive/2012/08/mitt-romney-would-pay-082-percent-in-taxes-under-paul-ryans-plan/261027.

[22] John Aravosis, "Paul Ryan may have lied about climbing 40 peaks of the Rockies," America's Blog, September 5, 2012, http://elections.americablog.com/2012/09/paul-ryan-may-have-lied-about-climbing-40-peaks-of-the-rockies.htm. See also, Bob Somerby, "How Ryan got to be honest!" Daily Howler, September 3, 2012, http://dailyhowler.blogspot.com/2012/09/how-ryan-became-honest-man.html, and Krugman, "Rosie Ruiz Republicans," *op. cit.*

[23] Felicia Sonmez, "Charity president unhappy about Paul Ryan soup kitchen 'photo op,'" *Washington Post*, October 15, 2012, http://www.washingtonpost.com/blogs/election-2012/wp/2012/10/15/charity-president-unhappy-about-paul-ryan-soup-kitchen-photo-op.

[24] Wikipedia, Ayn Rand, http://en.wikipedia.org/wiki/ayn_rand.

[25] Tim Mak, "Vice president nominee Paul Ryan's love-hate with Ayn Rand," *Politico*, August 11, 2012 http://www.politico.com/news/stories/0812/79597.html#ixzz29F6zbjwc.

[26] Mark Ames, "Paul Ryan's Guru Ayn Rand Worshiped a Serial Killer Who Kidnapped and Dismembered Little Girls," Naked Capitalism, August 12, 2012, http://www.nakedcapitalism.com/2012/08/mark-ames-paul-ryans-guru-ayn-rand-worshipped-a-serial-killer-who-kidnapped-and-dismembered-little-girls.html.

[27] Rand, Ayn. *Atlas Shrugged*. Signet/Penguin, 1992 (First edition, 1957); Wikipedia, *Atlas Shrugged*, http://en.wikipedia.org/wiki/Atlas_Shrugged; Paul Krugman, "Galt, Gold and God," *New York Times*, August 23, 2012, http://www.nytimes.com/2012/08/24/opinion/krugman-galt-gold-and-god.html?_r=1&smid=tw-NytimesKrugman&seid=auto.

[28] Alan Greenspan published a 1957 letter to the *New York Times* as follows "*Atlas Shrugged* is a celebration of life and happiness. Justice is unrelenting. Creative individuals and undeviating purpose and rationality achieve joy and fulfillment. Parasites who persistently avoid either purpose or reason perish as they should." Burns, Jennifer. *Goddess of the Market*. Oxford University, 2009. See also Harriet Rubin, "Ayn Rand's Literature of Capitalism," *New York Times*, September 15, 2007, http://www.nytimes.com/2007/09/15/business/15atlas.html?em&ex=11900 01600&en=2959fe5398fc21f5&ei=5087%0A&_r=0.

[29] Tim Mak, "Vice president nominee Paul Ryan's love-hate with Ayn Rand," *Politico*, August 11, 2012, http://www.politico.com/news/stories/0812/79597.html.

[30] Jason Linkins, "Paul Ryan Will Battle Paul Krugman To The Death To Defeat 'Keynesian Economics,'" Huffington Post, March 13, 2013, http://www.huffingtonpost.com/2013/03/13/paul-ryan-paul-krugman_n_2869126.html?utm_hp_ref=politics.

[31] Paul Krugman, "Pink Slime Economics," *New York Times*, April 1, 2012, http://www.nytimes.com/2012/04/02/opinion/krugman-pink-slime-economics.html?_r=0; and Michael Collins, "Killing Us Quickly - Ryan's Medicare Proposal," OpEdNews, April 15, 2011 http://www.opednews.com/articles/Killing-Us-Quickly---Ryan-by-Michael-Collins-110415-38.html.

[32] Wikipedia, Paul Ryan, http://en.wikipedia.org/wiki/Paul_Ryan.

[33] Julian Brookes, "The Koch Brothers – Exposed!" *Rolling Stone*, April 20, 2012, http://www.rollingstone.com/politics/blogs/national-affairs/the-koch-brothers-exposed-20120420#ixzz1sh6wmhis.

Chapter 16, Mitt Romney: The Prophet of Profit

[1] Ryan Grim and Matt Sledge, "Romney Video Offends Liberals and Conservatives Alike, Receives Negative Press Response," Huffington Post, September 18, 2012, http://www.huffingtonpost.com/2012/09/18/mitt-romney-video-offends_n_1893343.html?ncid=edlinkusaolp0000000.

[2] Jason Cherkis and Ryan Grim, "Scott Prouty, '47 Percent' Filmmaker, Reveals Identity On 'The Ed Show,'" Huffington Post, March 13, 2013. http://www.huffingtonpost.com/2013/03/13/scott-prouty-47-percent_n_2870837.html?1363219207&ncid=edlinkusaolp00000009.

[3] David Corn, "Secret Video: Romney Tells Millionaire Donors What He REALLY Thinks of Obama Voters, Mother Jones, September 17, 2012, http://www.motherjones.com/politics/2012/09/secret-video-romney-private-fundraiser.

[4] Jesse Drucker, "Romney Avoids Taxes via Loophole Cutting Mormon Donations," Bloomberg, October 29, 2012, http://www.bloomberg.com/news/2012-10-29/romney-avoids-taxes-via-loophole-cutting-mormon-donations.html and RenoBerkeley, "Harry Reid Was Right: Mitt Romney Paid No Taxes for 15 Years," Politics, October 29, 2012,

http://politics.gather.com/viewArticle.action?articleId=281474981730200#co
mments.

5 Greg Palast, "Mitt Romney's Bailout Bonanza," *Nation*, October 18, 2012,
http://www.thenation.com/article/170644/mitt-romneys-bailout-bonanza.

6 Palast, Greg. *Vultures Picnic: In Pursuit of Petroleum Pigs, Power Pirates, and High-Finance
Carnivores*. Dutton, 2011.See also Greg Palast, "Romney's Billionaire Vulture
Paul Singer, the GOP's Baddie Sugar Daddie," February 3, 2012,
http://www.gregpalast.com/romneys-billionaire-vulturepaul-singer-the-gops-
baddie-sugar-daddie.

7 Webster G. Tarpley, "Romney campaign, CIA Mormon Mafia both responsible for
Benghazi attack," Press TV, October 14, 2012,
http://www.presstv.ir/detail/2012/10/14/266560/benghazi-attack-cia-mafia-
in-action. See also, Tarpley, "Romney Campaign, CIA Mormon Mafia, John
Bolton's Islamophobia Network Stir Middle East Chaos to Get October
Surprise Against Obama," Info-Wars/Tarpley Net, September 16, 2012,
http://tarpley.net/2012/09/16/john-boltons-islamophobia-network-stir-
middle-east-chaos-to-get-october-surprise.

8 Wikipedia, October Surprise, http://en.wikipedia.org/wiki/October_surprise.

9 Reports by Webster Tarpley received minimal follow-up from the mainstream
media. Conventional reporters freeze-out Tarpley especially from any notice, in
part because he once worked for Lyndon LaRouche's publications and in part
because Tarpley's current outlets include alternative or international outlets.
Yet any experienced reporter will admit in private that conventional
Washington sources provide incomplete or inaccurate information.

10 Michael Collins, "Romney's Albatross," OpEdNews, August 23, 2012,
http://www.opednews.com/articles/Romney-s-Albatross-by-Michael-Collins-
120823-242.html

11 Mann, Thomas E., and Norman J. Ornstein. *It's Even Worse Than It Looks: How the
American Constitutional System Collided with the New Politics of Extremism*. Basic
Books, 2012.

12 Paul Craig Roberts, "America's descent into poverty," Institute for Political
Economy, August 24, 2012.
http://www.paulcraigroberts.org/2012/08/24/americas-descent-poverty-paul-
craig-roberts.

13 William, like his brother, Frederick, sold his Koch Industries interest shares to
Charles and David Koch, but remains active in political and philanthropic
causes. Forbes, *op. cit*. See also, Philip Rucker, "Mitt Romney reveals a literary
connection with a Koch brother," *Washington Post*, August 22, 2012,
http://www.washingtonpost.com/politics/mitt-romney-reveals-a-literary-
connection-with-a-koch-brother/2012/08/22/292a2090-ebff-11e1-a80b-
9f898562d010_story.html?wpisrc=emailtoafriend.

14 Koch also faced a legal problem. Julia Filip, "Koch Employee Says Billionaire
Kidnapped & Interrogated Him," Courthouse News, October 12, 2012,
http://www.courthousenews.com/2012/10/12/51239.htm. See also, Ryan
Grim and Nick Wing, "William Koch, Billionaire Koch Brother, Accused of
Imprisoning Executive," Huffington Post,

http://www.huffingtonpost.com/2012/10/13/william-koch-kirby-martensen_n_1962400.html?1350135562&ncid=edlinkusaolp00000009.

[15] Ibid.

[16] Ryan, Cheyney. *The Chickenhawk Syndrome, op cit.* See also, Sherr, "The Romneys," *op. cit.*, and Juan Cole, "Col. Wilkerson on Romney's Chickenhawk Advisors: They 'make me sick,'" Informed Comment/Op Ed News, Oct. 21, 2012, http://www.opednews.com/populum/linkframe.php?linkid=157495.

[17] Rucker, *op. cit.*

[18] Erin Emery, "AFA ends 'Bring Me Men' era; Longtime Sign Falls in Shake-up at Academy," *Denver Post*, March 29, 2003. "With the clinking of hammers, one of the most recognizable images in Colorado disappeared Friday. It was only 10 letters, each of them two feet tall: 'Bring Me Men'....After women came to the academy in 1976, the sign was viewed by some as chauvinistic, an outdated symbol that showed disrespect to female cadets who met the rigorous academic, athletic and character standards at the academy."

[19] Diana Jean Schemo, "Rate of Rape at Academy Is Put at 12% in Survey," *New York Times*, August 28, 2003, http://www.nytimes.com/2003/08/29/national/29ACAD.html?th.

[20] Charles P. Pierce, "What Democrats *Should* Be Talking about at the DNC," *Esquire*, September 2012, http://www.esquire.com/blogs/politics/voting-rights-dnc-12353394#ixzz26Tf5vz37. See also, Natasha Khan and Corbin Carson, "Comprehensive Database of U.S. Voter Fraud Uncovers No Evidence That Photo ID Is Needed," News 21/ Walter Cronkite School of Journalism and Mass Communication at Arizona State University, http://afgedefendsdemocracy.wordpress.com/2012/09/04/from-news21-comprehensive-database-of-u-s-voter-fraud-uncovers-no-evidence-that-photo-id-is-needed/.

[21] Ibid. Calhoun's eloquence on behalf of a bogus history brought a rebuke in the 1830s from Constitution drafter James Madison, a Virginia-born two-term president.

[22] Jon Cohen and Rosalind S. Helderman, "Poll shows a widening racial gap in the presidential election," Washington Post, October 25, 2012, http://articles.washingtonpost.com/2012-10-25/politics/35500866_1_white-voters-exit-poll-president-obama. "The 2012 election is shaping up to be more polarized along racial lines than any presidential contest since 1988, with President Obama experiencing a steep drop in support among white voters from four years ago."

[23] Similoluwa Ojurongbe, "Ohio voter fraud billboard accused of intimidating black voters," The Grio, October 5, 2012, http://thegrio.com/2012/10/05/ohio-voter-fraud-billboard-accused-of-intimidating-black-voters; and Richard Myers, "Does Romney's Bain Capital Support Voter Suppression," Daily Kos, October 10, 2012, http://www.dailykos.com/story/2012/10/10/1142856/-Does-Romney-s-Bain-Capital-Support-Voter-Suppression. Amy Goodman, "Clear Channel Rejects Times Square Peace Billboard Timed for RNC," Democracy Now!, July 145, 2012, http://www.democracynow.org/2004/7/14/clear_channel_rejects_times_square_peace.

[24] Krissah Thompson, "2008 voter-intimidation case against New Black Panthers riles the right," *Washington Post*, July 15, 2010, http://www.washingtonpost.com/wp-dyn/content/article/2010/07/14/AR2010071405880.html. See also, more generally, Fund, John. *Stealing Elections: How Voter Fraud Threatens Our Democracy.* Encounter, 2008.

[25] Wendy Gittleson, "Follow The Money – Bain Capital Owns Most Conservative And Some Liberal Radio Stations," Addicting Info, January 13, 2012, http://www.addictinginfo.org/2012/01/13/follow-the-money-bain-capital-owns-most-conservative-and-some-liberal-radio-stations.

[26] Chris Brunner, "Mitt Romney's VC Firm to Buy Clear Channel," LRC Blog, December 14, 2007, http://www.lewrockwell.com/blog/lewrw/archives/017694.html.

[27] Amy Goodman, "Clear Channel Rejects Times Square Peace Billboard Timed for RNC," Democracy Now!, July 145, 2012, http://www.democracynow.org/2004/7/14/clear_channel_rejects_times_squ are_peace.

[28] Rashad Robinson, "Tell Clear Channel: Take Down These Billboards," Color of Change.org, October 13, 2012, http://act.colorofchange.org/sign/billboards?akid=2684.1453335.MNnEVq& rd=1&t=3.

[29] Those involved could resolve the issue by making the district part of a nearby state for voting purposes, or by passing a Constitutional amendment. Few want to make even a serious effort.

[30] Ryan Grim and Matt Sledge, "Romney Video Offends Liberals And Conservatives Alike, Receives Negative Press Response," Huffington Post, September 18, 2012, http://www.huffingtonpost.com/2012/09/18/mitt-romney-video-offends_n_1893343.html?ncid=edlinkusaolp0000000

[31] Romney, Mitt. *No Apology: The Case for American Greatness.* St. Martin's Press. 2010.

[32] Jacob Weisberg, "Romney's Religion A Mormon president? No way," Slate, December 20, 2006, http://www.slate.com/articles/news_and_politics/the_big_idea/2006/12/ro mneys_religion.html.

[33] Daniel Burke, "Mormon church lashes back at magazine over portrayal of prophet and profits," Religion News Service/*Washington Post*, July 13, 2012, http://www.washingtonpost.com/national/on-faith/mormon-church-lashes-back-at-magazine-over-portrayal-of-prophet-and-profits/2012/07/13/gIQAMmsbiW_story.html.

[34] See, for example, Jason Horowitz, "When is Mormonism fair game?" *Washington Post*, June 1, 2012, http://www.washingtonpost.com/opinions/is-mitt-romneys-mormonism-fair-game/2012/06/01/gIQAhDo56U_story.html Sandhya Somashekhar, "Romney's faith tangles with history," *Washington Post*, May 20, 2012, http://www.washingtonpost.com/politics/mitt-romneys-mormon-faith-tangles-with-a-quirk-of-arkansas-history/2012/05/20/gIQAKHVFeU_story.html; Jason Horowitz, "Reluctant Romney found his footing at BYU," *Washington Post*, February 18, 2012., http://www.washingtonpost.com/politics/mitt-romney-as-a-student-at-a-

chaotic-time-for-byu-focused-on-family-church/2012/02/17/gIQABaWaMR_story.html.

[35] Richard Packham, "Why I left the Church," Ex Mormon Foundation, 1998, http://www.exmormonfoundation.org/stories.html

[36] Richard Packham, "Mitt Romney's Mormon Secrets," Yahoo Voices, March 13, 2012, http://voices.yahoo.com/mitt-romneys-mormon-secrets-11070962.html?cat=9.

[37] Jamie Reno, "Exclusive: Brigham Young's Great-Great-Granddaughter [Sue Emmett] on Mormonism and Mitt Romney," August 7, 2012, http://www.thedailybeast.com/articles/2012/08/07/exclusive-brigham-young-s-great-great-granddaughter-on-mormonism-and-mitt-romney.html.

[38] Michael L. (Mikey) Weinstein, "The Darkest of All Lies," Huffington Post, October 10, 2012, http://www.huffingtonpost.com/michael-l-weinstein/mitt-romney-libya_b_1955396.html.

[39] Oren Kessler, "Why do Mormons Love Israel?" World News Daily, July 30, http://www.informationclearinghouse.info/article32020.htm.

[40] John F. Kennedy, "Transcript: JFK's Speech on His Religion," Greater Houston Ministerial Association, September 12, 1960, as published by National Public Radio, 2007, http://www.npr.org/templates/story/story.php?storyId=16920600.

[41] Alford, Mimi. *Once Upon a Secret: My Affair with President John F. Kennedy and Its Aftermath*. Random House, 2012.

Chapter 17, Mitt Romney: Going For the Gold

[1] Naifeh, Steven and Gregory White Smith. *The Mormon Murders: A True Story of Greed, Forgery, Deceit, and Death*. St. Martin's, 1988. But see, Charlie Rose, Gayle King and Armen Keyteyian, "Doing Business the Mormon Way," CBS News, April 17, 2012,http://www.cbsnews.com/video/watch/?id=7405692n&tag=mg%3Bmostpopvideo Author Jeff Benedict talks about Mitt Romney, Mormonism, and his book, *The Mormon Way of Doing Business*, Business Plus, 2008.

[2] Ryan Grim, "Mitt Romney Started Bain Capital With Money From Families Tied To Death Squads," Huffington Post, August 8, 2012, http://www.huffingtonpost.com/2012/08/08/mitt-romney-death-squads-bain_n_1710133.html; and Amy Goodman, "Romney's Death Squad Ties: Bain Launched with Funds from Oligarchs Behind Salvadoran Murders," Democracy Now! August 10, 2012, http://www.democracynow.org/2012/8/10/romneys_death_squad_ties_bain_launched.

[3] Philip Rucker, "1984 Bain Capital money photo captured Romney on eve of major success," *Washington Post*, June 19, 2012, http://www.washingtonpost.com/politics/1984-bain-capital-money-photo-captured-romney-on-eve-of-major-success/2012/06/19/gIQAXvt2oV_story.html.

[4] Kranish and Helman, *op. cit.*, 153.

5 Paul Krugman, "Mitt's Gray Areas," *New York Times*, July 8, 2012.
http://www.nytimes.com/2012/07/09/opinion/krugman-mitts-gray-areas.html?_r=4&ref=opinion.

6 David A. Farhenthold and Tom Hamburger, "Both parties struggling with how to talk about private-equity industry," *Washington Post*, May 22, 2012, http://www.washingtonpost.com/politics/both-parties-struggling-with-how-to-talk-about-private-equity-industry/2012/05/22/gIQAedlCjU_story.html.

7 Tom Hamburger, "Romney using ethics exception to limit disclosure of Bain holdings," *Washington Post*, April 5, 2012, http://www.washingtonpost.com/politics/romney-using-ethics-exception-to-limit-disclosure-of-bain-holdings/2012/04/05/gIQARcVmxS_story.html.

8 Baumann, "Romney Left Bain Later Than He Says," *op. cit.*

9 Nicholas Shaxson, "Where the Money Lives," *Vanity Fair*, August 2012, http://www.vanityfair.com/politics/2012/08/investigating-mitt-romney-offshore-accounts.

10 Matt Taibbi, "Politics: Greed and Debt: The True Story of Mitt Romney and Bain Capital," *Rolling Stone*, September 13, 2012, http://www.rollingstone.com/politics/news/greed-and-debt-the-true-story-of-mitt-romney-and-bain-capital-20120829.

11 Andrew Kreig, "U.S. Judge Criticized By Bankruptcy Lawyers," *Hartford Courant*, June 11, 1978, as formerly cited on the Schuster Institute for Investigative Journalism website at Brandeis University

12 Ron (RMuse) Bynum, "Was Mitt Romney Running His Own Bankruptcy Ring?" Politics USA, September 12, 2012, http://www.politicususa.com/romney-bain-capital-bankruptcy-ring.html, "Romney's record reveals that much of his wealth came from leveraging companies with crushing debt and using a team of trusted specialists who mastered the art of manipulating bankruptcies that left investors and creditors with little or nothing."

13 David Corn, "Romney Invested in Medical-Waste Firm That Disposed of Aborted Fetuses, Government Documents Show," *op. cit.*

14 *In re eToys et al.*, Cases No. 01-706 thru 01-709 (MFW),U.S. Bankruptcy Court, District of Delaware.

15 Haas notes that his legal complaints to federal authorities on alleged improprieties often fell into the jurisdiction of Delaware's Bush-appointed U.S. Attorney, Colm Connolly. Connolly was an MNAT partner during the time covered by Haas complaints, circa 2000.

16 Brown, *Howard Hughes, op. cit.*

17 Marc Hosenball, "Romney staff spent nearly $100,000 to clear computer records," Reuters, December 6, 2011, http://www.reuters.com/article/2011/12/06/us-usa-campaign-romney-computers-idUSTRE7B500X20111206.

18 John Cook, "The Bain Files: Inside Mitt Romney's Tax-Dodging Cayman Schemes," Gawker, August 23, 2012, http://gawker.com/5936394.

19 Jesse Drucker, "Romney 'I Dig It' Trust Gives Heirs Triple Benefit," Bloomberg News, September 27, 2012, http://www.bloomberg.com/news/2012-09-27/romney-i-dig-it-trust-gives-heirs-triple-benefit.html.

20 Jillian Berman, "Mitt Romney After Bain Capital: Leaked Documents Connect Candidate To Adelson, Casinos, Cigarettes," Huffington Post, August 23, 2012. http://www.huffingtonpost.com/2012/08/23/mitt-romney-bain-capital-leaked-documents_n_1825466.html.

21 Carol D. Leonnig, "Judge releases Romney testimony from Staples founder's divorce trial," *Washington Post*, October 25, 2012, http://www.washingtonpost.com/politics/decision2012/judge-to-release-romney-testimony-from-staples-founders-divorce-trial/2012/10/25/2db37c9a-1eb0-11e2-ba31-3083ca97c314_story.html.

22 Romney for President, http://www.mittromney.com.

23 Annie-Rose Strasser, "Moody's Chief Economist On Romney's Tax Plan: 'The Arithmetic Doesn't Work,'" Think Progress, October 12, 2012, http://thinkprogress.org/economy/2012/10/12/1004921/zandi-romney-tax-plan.

24 Josh Barro, "The Final Word on Mitt Romney's Tax Plan," Bloomberg News, October 12, 2012, http://www.bloomberg.com/news/2012-10-12/the-final-word-on-mitt-romney-s-tax-plan.html.

25 David Dayen, "New Joint Committee on Taxation Study Shows Futility of Base-Broadening to Pay for Massive Tax Rate Cuts," FireDogLake, October 13, 2012, http://news.firedoglake.com/2012/10/12/new-jct-study-shows-futility-of-base-broadening-to-pay-for-massive-tax-rate-cuts.

26 Corn, "Romney '47 Percent' Fundraiser Host: Hedge Fund Manager Who Likes Sex Parties," *op. cit.*

27 Ahmed Shihab-Eldin and Ryan Grim, "Scott Prouty, Mitt Romney 47 Percent Filmmaker, Tells All," (Video), March 13,2013. http://www.huffingtonpost.com/2013/03/14/scott-prouty-mitt-romney-n_2876373.html.

28 Paul Craig Roberts, "America R.I.P.," Institute for Political Economy, October 16, 2012, http://www.paulcraigroberts.org/2012/10/16/america-r-i-p.

29 Rubin, *op. cit.*, "The spending and entitlement plan Romney presents embodies a great many of the ideas that Ryan, chairman of the House Budget Committee, has laid out in his original 'Roadmap for America's Future' (on Social Security) and in his 2012 budget….The big news here is on entitlements. No longer is Romney hiding behind generalities. He's staked his flag in the ground on Social Security and tweaked the Ryan plan with an approach that defuses some of the political toxicity."

30 Robert Parry, "Is Mitt Romney a Racist?" OpEdNews, August 25, 2012, http://www.opednews.com/articles/Is-Mitt-Romney-a-Racist-by-Robert-Parry-120825-723.html.

31 Robert Frank, "Romney's Top 10 Wealth Gaffes," *Wall Street Journal* , February 28, 2012, http://blogs.wsj.com/wealth/2012/02/28/romneys-top-10-wealth-gaffes.

32 Staff report, "Ann Romney: We've Given 'All You People Need To Know' About Family Finances," Associated Press/ Huffington Post, July 19, 2012, http://www.huffingtonpost.com/2012/07/19/ann-romney_n_1685735.html. See also, Matthew Mosk, "Does Mitt Romney Have an In-Law Problem?"

ABC-TV, October 18, 2012, http://abcnews.go.com/Blotter/mitt-romney-law-problem/story?id=17506248#.UIBm6YbfJ8F.

[33] John M. Broder, "NAACP Offers Chilly Response to Perot Speech," *Los Angeles Times*, July 12, 1992, http://articles.latimes.com/1992-07-12/news/mn-4266_1_ross-perot.

[34] McKay Coppins, "News Outlets Send Letter To Romney Campaign Contesting Expenses," BuzzFeed, December 17. 2012, http://www.buzzfeed.com/mckaycoppins/news-outlets-send-letter-to-romney-campaign-contes.

[35] Regarding Rove's upbringing, see: Rove, *Courage and Consequence, op. cit.*, 15; and Cannon, Carl M., Lou Dubose, and Jan Rein. *Boy Genius: Karl Rove, The Architect of George W. Bush's Remarkable Political Triumphs.* Public Affairs, 2005, 7.

[36] Unger, "Letter from Washington: *Boss Rove*," *op. cit.*

[37] Hedges, Chris. *American Fascists: The Christian Right and the War on America.* Free Press, 2006.

[38] Hedges, *op. cit.*, ix-xiv, citing Umberto Eco, "Eternal Fascism: Fourteen Ways of a Looking at a Blackshirt."

[39] Hedges, *op. cit.*, 89. "All those who do not subscribe to this male fantasy, or who were born female or gay, must be pressured to conform. By disempowering women, by returning them to their 'proper' place as a subservient partner in the male-dominated home, the movement creates the larger paradigm of the Christian state."

[40] Ibid., 183.

[41] Jan Mickelson WHO (Des Moines, Iowa), "Mitt Romney speaking about Mormon faith," YouTube, August 2007, http://www.youtube.com/watch?v=okLAi3rpb_U "I'm not running to talk about Mormonism." See also, Dominique Mosbergen, "Mitt Romney Talks Mormonism, YouTube Clip From 2007 Interview Goes Viral (VIDEO), November 5, 2012. A video showing Mitt Romney discussing his Mormon faith has become a viral sensation in the days leading up to the election., http://www.huffingtonpost.com/2012/11/05/mitt-romney-mormon-video_n_2077433.html; and Katie Glueke, "Radio host defends Mormon video," Politico, November 6, 2012, http://www.politico.com/news/stories/1112/83389.html?hp=l8.

Part IV What's To Be Done?

Chapter 18, Joseph Biden: When the Smiling Stops

[1] As of 2012, those who rival Biden in terms of years in office and the stature of the offices include: U.S. Senator Daniel Inouye, a Democrat elected in 1962 to represent Hawaii, and two Michigan Congressman, John Dingell, who was elected in 1955, succeeding his father, and Dingell's former aide, John Conyers, elected to an adjoining district west of Detroit in 1964.

[2] Tim Mark, "Joe Biden favorability in the negative, poll says," *Politico*, May 23, 2012, http://www.politico.com/news/stories/0512/76683.html. See also, Christian Heinze, "Polls: Ryan beats Biden in popularity," *The Hill*, September 12, 2012,

http://thehill.com/blogs/ballot-box/christian-heinze/248891-polls-ryan-beats-biden-in-popularity.

3 Vice President Joseph Biden's Convention Speech, National Public Radio and Federal News Service, September 6, 2012, transcript and audio (38 minutes, 24 seconds), http://www.npr.org/2012/09/06/160713378/transcript-vice-president-bidens-convention-speech.

4 See also David Firestone, "Joe Biden's Speech," *New York Times*, September 6, 2012, http://takingnote.blogs.nytimes.com/2012/09/06/joe-bidens-speech.

5 Koszczuk, Jackie and Martha Angel, editors. *Politics in America, Congressional Quarterly Staff*, Congressional Quarterly, 2008.

6 Ibid. That description was published in 2008. After the election victory Biden and his second wife, Jill, a teacher, moved to traditional vice presidential residence near the Naval Observatory in Northwest Washington, DC.

7 The White House, Vice President Joe Biden, http://www.whitehouse.gov/administration/vice-president-biden.

8 Biden Jr., Joseph R. *Promises to Keep*. Random House, 2007. See also, Wikipedia, Joseph Biden, http://en.wikipedia.org/wiki/Joe_Biden.

9 Koszczu and Angel, *op. cit.*

10 Witcover, Jules. *Joe Biden*. William Morrow, 2010, 186-91.

11 Among other examples of misleading incidents that supposedly reveal essential qualities of presidential candidates: In 1972, Democratic Senator Ed Muskie, a front-runner, was portrayed as crying during a New Hampshire campaign speech. This created so much ridicule that Muskie quit the race that he once led. In reality, melted snowflakes, not tears, may have glistened from Muskie's cheeks, according to recollections later by the *Washington Post's* David Broder, who broke the original story. Somewhat similarly, Republican President Gerald Ford was lampooned for years on *Saturday Night Live!* as a clumsy buffoon after he once slipped while descending a flight of steps from an airplane. In real life, the still-trim 1976 GOP nominee had been an All-America football player drafted by the Chicago Bears, and also was a graduate of Yale Law School. Finally, Vice President Al Gore did not claim upon beginning his 2000 presidential campaign to have "invented" the Internet. Instead, he responded to a CNN question about his legislative accomplishments by accurately describing his lead role in the Senate to advocate for federal funding. Gore's claim was so clearly true that it received no news coverage. Then GOP operatives persuaded a gullible Associated Press reporter to publish GOP claims that Gore claimed to have "invented" the Internet. This triggered many stories during the campaign portraying Gore as a vain blowhard for trivial or even hoked-up occurrences, much like the coverage that Biden received in 1988.

12 Ibid.

13 In November 2007, Senator Joe Biden stated during his campaign for the Democratic presidential nomination that he would move to impeach President Bush if he were to bomb Iran without first gaining congressional approval. See, Adam Leech, "Biden: Impeachment if Bush bombs Iran," Seacoast Online, November 29, 2007,

http://www.seacoastonline.com/apps/pbcs.dll/article?AID=/20071129/NEWS/71129018.

14 McEwen, Lillian. *D.C. Unmasked and Undressed. TitleTown, 2011.*

15 Witcover, *op. cit.* 282-83.

16 Ibid.

17 Roberts, Paul Craig and Lawrence M. Stratton. *The Tyranny of Good Intentions: How Prosecutors and Law Enforcement Are Trampling the Constitution in the Name of Justice.* Three Rivers/Crown, 2008.

18 The White House, Vice President Joe Biden, http://www.whitehouse.gov/administration/vice-president-biden.

19 Jonah Goldberg, "Big &#%!ing Joker: On the comedy routine that is Joe Biden's Vice Presidency," *National Review*, April 30, 2012, https://www.nationalreview.com/nrd/articles/295963/big-ing-joker (Subscription only). See also, Peter Wallsten and David Nakamura, "Ryan Pick Presents New Challenge: Blunt-spoken defense of Obama faces a seasoned lawmaker," *Washington Post*, August 16, 2012, http://www.washingtonpost.com/politics/ryan-pick-presents-new-challenges-for-biden/2012/08/15/a8db838a-e707-11e1-8f62-58260e3940a0_story.html. Unlike four years ago, when Biden squared off against an unknown and largely untested Sarah Palin, the vice president is competing against a longtime congressman known for being a quick-minded policy expert. Now, unlike then, Biden must defend the Obama record while, associates say, keeping an eye on a potential 2016 White House bid of his own.

20 Witcover, *op. cit.*

21 Wolffe, Richard. *Renegade: The Making of a President.* Crown, 2010, 216-17. See also, Heilemann, John and Mark Halperin. *Game Change: Obama and the Clintons, McCain and Palin, and the Race of a Lifetime.* HarperCollins, 2010.

Chapter 19, Barack Obama: The President as Performer

1 In May 2012, Barack Obama began his 2012 re-election campaign in Ohio by decrying Republican attacks on the Social Security and Medicare safety net programs for the elderly. Taxpayers legitimately expect leaders to honor expectations that payroll taxes already extracted will provide the benefits promised in old age. Obama has wavered on that commitment, as illustrated by his October debate performance. This may be the most important economic issue of our time. Michael Collins, "Obama Embraces Populist Themes in Ohio," OpEdNews, May 7, 2012, http://www.opednews.com/articles/Obama-embraces-populist-th-by-Michael-Collins-120507-314.html.

2 Paul Krugman, "Romney's Sick Joke," *New York Times*, October 4, 2012, http://www.nytimes.com/2012/10/05/opinion/krugman-romneys-sick-joke.html.

3 Dana Milbank, "Obama pays price for ducking the questions," *Washington Post*, October 4, 2012, http://www.washingtonpost.com/opinions/dana-milbank-president-obama-doesnt-meet-the-press/2012/10/04/ac688c8a-0e78-11e2-bb5e-492c0d30bff6_story.html.

4 Madsen, *The Manufacturing of a President, op. cit.*

5 There were undoubtedly multiple reasons for Obama's debate performance. Romney's relentless attacks were a factor. Another was Obama's obviously inadequate debate preparation. Obama's training partner in mock debate was, of all people, Senator John Kerry, the 2004 Democratic nominee who had failed to respond effectively during his own campaign to Swift Boat attacks. Many presidents, Obama included, are so used to deferential treatment from the White House press corps that criticism is genuinely surprising.

6 Stewart, David O. *American Emperor: Aaron's Burr's Challenge to Jefferson's America.* Simon & Schuster, 2011.

7 Andrew Kreig, "Election Fraud Critics Seek Halt To Ohio's Secret Software In GOP Plan," November 5, 2012, http://www.justice-integrity.org/faq/39-election-fraud-critics-seek-halt-to-ohios-secret-software-in-gop-plan and " Rove Vote-Switching 'Empire' Alleged to Threaten Nov. 6 Results," November 4, 2012, http://www.justice-integrity.org/176-rove-vote-switching, both published by the Justice Integrity Project with extensive appendices of related news clippings.

8 Andrew Kreig, "Did Expert Witness, Activists Thwart a Rove Ohio Vote Plot?" Justice Integrity Project, November 14, 2012, http://www.justice-integrity.org/index.php?option=com_content&view=article&id=691:did-expert-witness-activists-thwart-a-rove-ohio-vote-plot&catid=44:myblog.

9 I had been asked to moderate an October 25th news briefing at the National Press Club featuring Clifford Arnebeck, Dana Jill Simpson, Jim March and Dana Siegelman. That involved additional discussions with attorneys, journalists and other experts in the election integrity movement focused especially on swing states.

10 Alexander Abad-Santos, "Romney Finally Captures 47% of America," *Atlantic*, November 26, 2012. http://www.theatlanticwire.com/politics/2012/11/mitt-romney-47-percent-popular-vote/59327.

11 Jerry Markon and Karen Tumulty, "Romney: Obama's gift giving led to loss," *Washington Post*, November 14, 2012, http://www.washingtonpost.com/politics/romney-obamas-gift-giving-led-to-loss/2012/11/14/c8d7e744-2eb7-11e2-89d4-040c9330702a_story.html.

12 Philip Rucker, "A detached Romney tends wounds in seclusion after failed White House bid," *Washington Post*, December 1, 2012 http://www.washingtonpost.com/politics/a-detached-romney-tends-wounds-in-seclusion-after-failed-white-house-bid/2012/12/01/4305079a-38a9-11e2-8a97-363b0f9a0ab3_story.html.

13 Wikipedia, The Fox and the Grapes, http://en.wikipedia.org/wiki/The_Fox_and_the_Grapes.

14 Michael Kranish, "The story behind Mitt Romney's loss in the presidential campaign to President Obama," *Boston Globe*, December 22, 2012, http://www.boston.com/news/politics/2012/president/2012/12/23/the-story-behind-mitt-romney-loss-the-presidential-campaign-president-obama/2QWkUB9pJgVIi1mAcIhQjL/story.html. Tagg Romney's comment is so strange on the surface that it raises the possibility it has a deeper meaning. One possible meaning might be that his father had felt an obligation to run.

15 Kevin Hechtkopf, "Obama, Clark Kellogg Play Basketball at White House," (Video) CBS News, April 3, 2010, http://www.cbsnews.com/8301-503544_162-20001717-503544.html; Glenn Greenwald, "Obama's terrorism speech: seeing what you want to see," *Guardian*, May 27, 2013. http://www.guardian.co.uk/commentisfree/2013/may/27/obama-war-on-terror-speech?.

16 Public Religion Institute, "Post-Election Survey: Changing Religious Landscape Challenges Influence of White Christian Vote," November 15, 2012, http://publicreligion.org/research/2012/11/american-values-post-election-survey-2012.

17 Chris Cillizza, Aaron Blake and Sean, "The Fix's first rankings of the 2016 Republican presidential field," *Washington Post*, February 8, 2013, http://www.washingtonpost.com/blogs/the-fix/wp/2013/02/08/the-fixs-first-rankings-of-the-2016-republican-presidential-field/?hpid=z4; Michael D. Shear, "Jeb Bush Enters Debate, and Possibly 2016 Race," *New York Times*, March 5, 2013, http://www.nytimes.com/2013/03/06/us/politics/jeb-bushs-rocky-re-entry-in-immigration-debate.html; and Neil King Jr., "In GOP, All Eyes on Jeb Bush," *Wall Street Journal*, January 6, 2012. http://online.wsj.com/article/SB100014241278873242966045781775513314 38098.html.

18 Elise Foley, "Jeb Bush Book: Undocumented Immigrants Should Be Ineligible For Citizenship," Huffington Post, March 4, 2013, http://www.huffingtonpost.com/2013/03/04/jeb-bush-book_n_2806602.html?ref=topbar. Much of the mainstream media accorded the Bush family highly flattering coverage by the spring of 2013 in tandem with the opening of the Bush Presidential Library and Museum at Southern Methodist University in Dallas. See, Mark K. Updegrove, "President and Mrs. Bush," *Parade*, April 21, 2013.

19 John LeBoutillier, "The Jeb Bush Illegal Drug and Liquor Distributorship at Andover," Boot's Blasts January 24, 2013. http://leboutillier.blogspot.com/search?q=jeb+bush+illegal+drug+and+liquor&submit=Search The former New York congressman, author and Fox News commentator described hearing the Bush story at a Harvard reunion.

20 Wayne Madsen, "Jeb Bush and the crimes of Brickell Avenue," March 20, 2013, http://www.waynemadsenreport.com/articles/20130320 and, Wayne Madsen, "Phil Marshall's 'docu-novel' cites Poppy and Jeb Bush as villains in Iran-contra," March 18, 2013, Wayne Madsen Report (Subscription),. http://www.waynemadsenreport.com/articles/20130316.

21 Sari Horwitz and Greg Miller, "FBI probe of Petraeus triggered by e-mail threats from biographer, officials say," *Washington Post*, November 10, 2012 http://www.washingtonpost.com/world/national-security/fbi-probe-of-petraeus-triggered-by-e-mail-threats-from-biographer-officials-say/2012/11/10/d2fc52de-2b68-11e2-bab2-eda299503684_story.html. Joby Warrick, Ernesto Londoño and Kimberly Kindy, "With Paula Broadwell, David Petraeus let his security down," *Washington Post*, November 10, 2012 http://www.washingtonpost.com/world/national-security/with-paula-broadwell-gen-david-petraeus-let-his-guard-down/2012/11/10/f54d3f38-2b8b-11e2-bab2-eda299503684_story.html?tid=pm_world_pop.

22 Craig Whitlock, "FBI probe widens to second general." *Washington Post*, November 13, 2012, http://www.washingtonpost.com/world/national-security/scandal-probe-ensnares-commander-of-us-nato-troops-in-afghanistan/2012/11/13/a2a27232-2d7d-11e2-a99d-5c4203af7b7a_story.html.

23 Sari Horwitz, Kimberly Kindy and Scott Wilson, "Petraeus didn't plan to resign from CIA," *Washington Post*, November 12, 2012. http://www.washingtonpost.com/politics/petraeus-told-biographer-to-stop-harassing-family-friend-officials-say/2012/11/12/6ccb325c-2d00-11e2-a99d-5c4203af7b7a_story.html?hpid=z1.

24 George Stephanopoulos, "Obama Leaves Door Open (a Bit) On Prosecuting Bush Officials," ABC News, January 11, 2009, http://abcnews.go.com/blogs/politics/2009/01/obama-leaves-do.

25 Denton and Morris, *op. cit.*

26 Andrew Kreig, "Obama Team Feared Coup If He Probed War Crimes, Justice Integrity Project," September 7, 2011. http://www.justice-integrity.org/faq/261-obama-team-feared-coup-death-if-he-prosecuted-war-crimes

27 University California at Berkeley Law School Dean Christopher Edley's description of the transition team's fear of revolt against Obama arose at a school legal forum. Susan Harman, a retiree, protested the law school's decision under Edley to rehire John Yoo, a former professor who had been the Bush Justice Department lawyer who had authored the notorious "torture memo." Ibid. Courts later dismissed suit against Yoo, who maintained he did nothing wrong. David Kravets, "U.S. Appeals Court Clears Torture Memo Author," *Wired*, May 2, 2012, http://www.wired.com/threatlevel/2012/05/yoo-torture-lawsuit.

28 Raymond McGovern, "Doubting Obama's Resolve To Do Right," WBAI-FM Interview of former CIA Analyst, Michael Smith and Michael Ratner, June 3, 2013, http://lawanddisorder.org. More generally, I published many round-ups of disturbing Obama-era due process shortcomings on the Justice Integrity Project site and elsewhere, such as, "Complaints About Justice Department Go Nowhere," May 27, 2011. http://www.justice-integrity.org/faq/299-complaints-about-justice-department-go-nowhere and "Obama DOJ Continues War Against Bush Prosecution Victims," May 13, 2011, http://www.justice-integrity.org/faq/303-obama-doj-continues-war-against-bush-prosecution-victims.

29 Sam Stein, "Robert Draper Book: GOP's Anti-Obama Campaign Started Night Of Inauguration," Huffington Post, April 25, 2012, http://www.huffingtonpost.com/2012/04/25/robert-draper-anti-obama-campaign_n_1452899.html.

30 Andrew Kreig, "Bush Frame-Up Still Festers in Mississippi," Justice Integrity Project, January 11, 2013 http://www.justice-integrity.org/faq/424-bush-frame-up-still-festers-in-mississippi

31 Walter Gibbs, "From 205 Names, Panel Chose the Most Visible," *New York Times*, October 9, 2009, http://www.nytimes.com/2009/10/10/world/10oslo.html?_r=2&hp&; and

Wikipedia, 2009 Nobel Peace Prize.,
http://en.wikipedia.org/wiki/2009_Nobel_Peace_Prize#cite_note-9.

[32] James Taranto, "Most Embarrassing Moment: The Norwegian Nobel Committee makes President Obama look ridiculous, *Wall Street Journal,* October 9, 2009, http://online.wsj.com/article/SB10001424052748703746604574463171820234630.html.

[33] *Hoodwinked: An Economic Hit Man Reveals Why the World Financial Markets Imploded — and How To Fix It.* Crown Business, 2011, 214.

[34] Roger Shuler, "Prosecutors Used 'Sex Scandal' to Intimidate Key Witness in Siegelman case," Legal Schnauzer, July 21, 2009, http://legalschnauzer.blogspot.com/2009/07/prosecutors-used-sex-scandal-to.html.

[35] Jacob Soboroff, "Free Don Siegelman," HuffPost Live (Video), December 10, 2012, interview with Don Siegelman daughter Dana Siegelman, GOP former Congressman Parker Griffiths of Alabama, GOP former Arizona Attorney General Grant Woods (former co-chair of the 2008 McCain for President Campaign), actress Mimi Kennedy, and law professor Scott Horton, http://live.huffingtonpost.com/r/segment/pardon-don-siegelman%2C-don-siegelman-clemency/50a59f2602a76032d20000b2.

[36] Andrew Kreig, "Presidential Clemency System Broken, Experts Say," Justice Integrity Project, December 11, 2012. http://www.justice-integrity.org/faq/235-presidential-clemency-system-broken-experts-say.

[37] Andrew Kreig, "Stevens Misconduct Report Targets Mid-Level DOJ Officials," Justice Integrity Project, March 18, 2012.

[38] Andrew Kreig, "CIA Torture Investigator Plays Powerful But Mysterious Role," Justice Integrity Project, July 2, 2011. Andrew Kreig, "New Questions Raised About Prosecutor Who Cleared Bush Officials in U.S. Attorney Firings," Nieman Watchdog, July 25, 2010, http://www.niemanwatchdog.org/index.cfm?fuseaction=ask_this.view&askthisid=00469.

[39] The Justice Department did bring a half dozen civil suits through its frauds unit. See, for example, Danielle Douglas and Brady Dennis, "Wells Fargo accused of mortgage fraud," *Washington Post* , October 10, 2012, http://www.washingtonpost.com/business/economy/government-sues-wells-fargo-for-reckless-lending-practices/2012/10/09/28db64c4-124b-11e2-a16b-2c110031514a_story.html. However, a vast discrepancy generally exists between prosecution standards of protected categories of defendants and those targeted politically for similar conduct.

[40] Suskind, Ron. *Confidence Men: Wall Street, Washington and the Education of a President.* HarperCollins, 2011; and Dave Lindorff, "Obama Dumped by the Money Men," *Counterpunch,* October 12-14, 2012, http://www.counterpunch.org/2012/10/12/bankers-man-in-2008-obamas-been-dumped-by-the-money-men.

[41] Lindorff, *op. cit.,* "Meanwhile, GE's chairman and CEO, Jeffrey Immelt, who famously exported thousands of GE jobs abroad, was given the post of White House Jobs 'Czar.'… Open Secrets reports that this year there is only one Wall Street bank listed among Obama's top 20 largest donors: Wells Fargo, which

only gave the president's re-election campaign a scant $202,000, less than half what the smallest of his top 20 donors gave four years ago. Over all, big banks gave Obama over $4 million in 2008, and only $200,000, or just five percent as much, in 2012."

42 Ibid., 72.

43 Ian Wilhelm, "Ford Foundation Links Parents of Obama and Treasury Secretary Nominee," *The Chronicle of Philanthropy*, December 3, 2008, http://philanthropy.com/blogs/government-and-politics/ford-foundation-links-parents-of-obamatreasury-secretary-nominee/10851, as cited by Wayne Madsen, *The Manufacturing of a President, op. cit.* Remarkably few other biographical accounts mention the family tie between the president and such an important cabinet member, whose office was especially newsworthy during the Obama administration because of the economic collapse and responses.

44 Estulin, Daniel. *The True Story of the Bilderberg Group.* TrineDay, 2009.

45 Glenn Greenwald, "Democrats and Bain," Salon, May 21, 2012, http://www.salon.com/2012/05/21/democrats_and_bain_2/singleton.

46 Robert Gates, who holds a doctorate degree, rose from being a CIA intelligence officer during the Vietnam War to his current post as chancellor of his undergraduate university. College of William and Mary, Robert M. Gates, http://www.wm.edu/about/administration/chancellor/index.php.

47 Madsen, Wayne. *L'Affair Petraeus.* WMR/Lulu, 2012, 6-7.

48 Glenn Greenwald, "The war on WikiLeaks and why it matters," Salon, March 27, 2010, http://www.salon.com/2010/03/27/wikileaks/The U.S. government escalates its campaign to harass and destroy a key whistle-blowing site, citing CIA via WikiLeaks, "Afghanistan: Sustaining West European Support for the NATO-led," (Classified as Confidential / No Foreign Nationals), March 11, 2010, http://wikileaks.org/file/cia-afgthanistan.pdf.

49 Sunstein and Vermeule, *op. cit.;* Paul Krugman, "More On Jon Gruber," *New York Times* January 15, 2010, http://krugman.blogs.nytimes.com/2010/01/15/more-on-jon-gruber. Clark Hoyt, "The Source's Stake In the News," *New York Times*, January 17, 2010, http://www.nytimes.com/2010/01/17/opinion/17pubed.html; and Glenn Greenwald, "Krugman, Gruber And Non-Disclosure Issues," Salon, January 16, 2010, http://www.salon.com/news/opinion/glenn_greenwald/2010/01/16/krugman/index.html.

50 Robert Corsini, House Special Hearing: "Costs of Broken Health Care System, Benefits of Public Option," Aboriginal Media, October 27, 2009. U.S. Rep. Sheila Jackson Lee opened the proceedings: http://www.youtube.com/watch?v=BQM40cCNfok (Video: 4:43 minutes).

51 Andrew Kreig, "Fans of House Health Option Cite Rights, Hopes, But Risk Big Defeat, Huffington Post, November 4, 2009, http://www.huffingtonpost.com/andrew-kreig/fans-of-house-health-opti_b_346117.html.

52 Robert Corsini and Natalie Noel, video interview of House Judiciary Chairman John Conyers, Aboriginal Media and Goddess Strides Productions, October

27, 2009. Part I, http://www.youtube.com/watch?v=Sij3OxxwHfs; and Part II, http://www.youtube.com/watch?v=zzDH8-J7cdk.

[53] The communications directors for Conyers and Lee did little to publicize the hearings.

[54] Ed White, "Monica Conyers, Wife To John Conyers, Sentenced To 3 Years In Prison For Detroit Bribes," Associated Press / Huffington Post, May 10, 2010, http://www.huffingtonpost.com/2010/03/10/monica-conyers-wife-to-jo_n_494305.html. See also Colbert I. King, "A different kind of black-and-white issue," *Washington Post*, February 23, 2013, http://www.washingtonpost.com/opinions/colbert-king-jesse-jackson-and-misbehaving-politicians/2013/02/22/65ddf592-7c5b-11e2-9a75-dab0201670da_story.html.

[55] Jordan Weissmann, "The Recession's Toll: How Middle Class Wealth Collapsed to a 40-Year Low," *Atlantic*, December 4, 2012, http://www.theatlantic.com/business/archive/2012/12/the-recessions-toll-how-middle-class-wealth-collapsed-to-a-40-year-low/265743.

[56] Among the topics that remain *verboten* are: Financial incentives to move well-paid United States manufacturing jobs offshore and other "free trade" policies; the excessive costs of the country's health care system (more than double those of every other Western nation, with no improvement in quality); employer complicity in the time-bomb of illegal immigration, helping create a near-unemployable underclass of American-born workers; and the undercount of the workforce, which makes the most widely reported unemployment statistics unduly small. Paul Craig Roberts, "More Phony Employment Numbers," December 8, 2012, http://www.paulcraigroberts.org/2012/12/08/more-phony-employment-numbers.

[57] Brendan DeMelle, "Study Confirms Tea Party Was Created by Big Tobacco and Billionaire Koch Brothers," Desmogblog/Huffington Post, February 11, 2013, http://www.huffingtonpost.com/brendan-demelle/study-confirms-tea-party-b_2663125.html?utm_source=Alert-blogger&utm_medium=email&utm_campaign=Email%2BNotifications.

[58] Naomi Wolf, "Revealed: how the FBI coordinated the crackdown on Occupy," *Guardian*, http://www.guardian.co.uk/commentisfree/2012/dec/29/fbi-coordinated-crackdown-occupy. New documents prove what was once dismissed as paranoid fantasy: totally integrated corporate-state repression of dissent.

[59] Wikipedia, John Warner, http://en.wikipedia.org/wiki/John_Warner.

[60] David Dayen, "The Lasting Impact of 2010 Election: Redistricting Cementing Republican House Majority," FireDogLake, October 25, 2012, http://news.firedoglake.com/2012/10/25/the-lasting-impact-of-2010-election-redistricting-cementing-republican-house-majority.

[61] Dana Milbank, "In the House, a deck stacked for Republicans," *Washington Post*, Dana Milbank, January 4, 2013. http://www.washingtonpost.com/opinions/dana-milbank-republican-gerrymandering-makes-the-difference-in-the-house/2013/01/04/f6e9bd1e-56a4-11e2-8b9e-dd8773594efc_story.html.

62 Will Femia, "Republicans reap the fruits of redistricting," Maddow Blog, December 13, 2012, http://maddowblog.msnbc.com/ news/2012/12/13/15876038-republicans-reap-the-fruits-of-redistricting?lite.

63 Bob Somerby, "Turse and Moyers discuss our "forbidden history!" Daily Howler, February 11, 2013, http://dailyhowler.blogspot.com/2013/02/turse-and-moyers-discuss-forbidden.html.

64 I moderated a panel at the conference featuring Alabama's former governor, who told the audience of his conversation with Valerie Jarrett at the event. *Netroots Nation*, "Reporting DoJ Misconduct Scandals: "Why Netroots Remains Last Hope for Justice," Don Siegelman, Dr. Cyril Wecht, Jerry McDevitt, Gail Sistrunk, Andrew Kreig, August 15, 2009, Pittsburgh, PA, Video: http://blip.tv/netroots-nation/netroots-nation-2009-reporting-doj-misconduct-scandals-why-netroots-remains-last-hope-for-justice-2556820 Gail Sistrunk, "Prosecutorial Injustice & Misconduct: We Need To Be Outraged," OpEd News.

65 For details on how Zell financed the purchase, see a three-part series, "The Story Behind Tribune's Broken Deal," Michael Oneal and Steve Mills, "Part one: Zell's big gamble," *Chicago Tribune/Hartford Courant*, January 13, 2013, http://articles.chicagotribune.com/2013-01-13/business/ct-biz-trib-series-1-20130113_1_sam-zell-randy-michaels-big-gambleError! Hyperlink reference not valid.

66 Andrew Kreig, "PBS Report on Murdoch Shows How 'Hacking' Led to Political Blackmail," Justice Integrity Project, March 30, 2012; See also, Troy McMullen, "Murdoch UK Hacking Scandal Comes to America," ABC-News, April 12, 2012, http://abcnews.go.com/Business/british-hacking-scandal-suits-filed-us/story?id=16124049.

67 Michael J. Copps, "Promises To Keep," Benton Foundation, December 2, 2012, http://benton.org/node/140512.

68 Frank, Justin A. *Obama on the Couch: Inside the Mind of the President*. FreePress, 2011, 85-87.

69 Ibid., 220.

70 The most notorious jackal is undoubtedly the Venezuelan-born Marxist Ilich Ramírez Sánchez, now serving a life sentence in France. Wikipedia, Carlos the Jackal, http://en.wikipedia.org/wiki/Carlos_the_Jackal. See also, Perkins, John. *The Secret History of the American Empire: Economic Hit Men, Jackals, and the Truth about Global Corruption, op. cit.*; *Confessions of an Economic Hit Man*. Penguin, 2004. Plume, 2006; and *Hoodwinked, op. cit.*

71 Such was the case for the affair between President John F. Kennedy and Mary Meyer, former wife of the high-ranking CIA executive Cord Meyer. See Janney, Peter. *Mary's Mosaic: The CIA Conspiracy to Murder John F. Kennedy, Mary Pinchot Meyer, and Their Vision of World Peace*. Skyhorse, 2012. Whether or not one accepts the theory stated by the book's subtitle, the book's evidence is important. It shows that *Newsweek/Washington Post* legend Ben Bradlee covered-up parts of his murdered sister-in-law-'s affair and diary. This illuminates our understanding of the *Washington Post's* operations in modern

times. The book also presents, for example, a document indicating that Bradlee was a CIA liaison early in his career.

[72] Most in the public, for example, would have regarded Commission Member Allen Dulles rather simply as the eminent former CIA -- and thus far more expert in investigations than the political appointees to the commission. Not widely known until years after the Commission report was how Kennedy had forced Dulles to resign from the CIA following the botched CIA-planned Bay of Pigs invasion of Cuba.

[73] Bob Graham and Sharon Premoli, "Re-Open the 9/11 Investigation Now," Huffington Post, September 11, 2012, http://www.huffingtonpost.com/bob-graham/911-saudi-arabia_b_1868863.html. See specifically the editor's note.

[74] Graham, Bob. *Keys to the Kingdom*. Vanguard, 2011; and *Intelligence Matters: The CIA, The FBI, Saudi Arabia, and The Failure of America's War on Terror*, Random House, 2004. See also, Andrew Kreig, "Ex-Senators, Reporters Again Question Saudi Innocence in 9/11 Attacks," Justice Integrity Project, March 21, 2012.

[75] Kay, Jonathan. *Among the Truthers: A Journey America's Growing Conspiracist Underground*. Harper, 2011. Kay is a Yale Law graduate, and is a managing editor of Canada's *National Post*. He was a 2012 guest on my radio show, *MTL Washington Update*. He failed then, in his 340-page book, and at a lecture/debate I watched at the Spy Museum in Washington, DC to address in any depth the arguments of his book's subjects. Instead, Kay's method was largely to deride his targets in brief portraits, conveyed with his scorn at their gall in questioning findings by official bodies.

[76] Perkins, *Hoodwinked, op. cit.*

[77] Wikipedia, Omar Torrijos, http://en.wikipedia.org/wiki/Omar_Torrijos.

[78] Wikipedia, John F. Kennedy Jr. Plane Crash, http://en.wikipedia.org/wiki/John_F._Kennedy,_Jr._plane_crash.

[79] Joe Lauria, "Democracy on the Ballot," Consortium News, November 5, 2012, http://consortiumnews.com/2012/11/05/democracy-on-the-ballot.

[80] Andrew Kreig, "Comparing Presidential Results, Polls, Predictions and Pundits," Justice Integrity Project, November 7, 2012.

[81] Public Policy Institute, "Congress somewhere below cockroaches, traffic jams, and Nickelback in Americans' esteem," January 8,2013, http://www.publicpolicypolling.com/main/2013/01/congress-somewhere-below-cockroaches-traffic-jams-and-nickleback-in-americans-esteem.html; The results were comparable to a Gallup poll finding that just 10 percent of Americans believe members of Congress have high or very high honesty standards. Greg Giroux, "Voters Throw Bums In While Holding Congress in Disdain," Bloomberg, December 13, 2012, http://www.bloomberg.com/news/2012-12-13/voters-throw-bums-in-while-disdaining-congress-bgov-barometer.html.

[82] Stephen Braun and Jack Gillum, "2012 Presidential Election Cost Hits $2 Billion Mark," Associated Press/Huffington Post, December 7, 2012. http://www.huffingtonpost.com/2012/12/06/2012-presidential-election-cost_n_2254138.html.

[83] A new law required federal spending for pre-election transition planning by the Romney team in case it won. Katy Steinmetz, "The Cost of Romney's Government-Assisted Transition: $8.9 Million," *Time*, December 19, 2012, http://swampland.time.com/2012/12/19/the-cost-of-romneys-government-assisted-transition-8-9-million.

[84] Peter H. Stone, "Sheldon Adelson Spent Far More On Campaign Than Previously Known," Huffington Post, December 3, 2012. http://www.huffingtonpost.com/2012/12/03/sheldon-adelson-2012-election_n_2223589.html.

[85] Staff report, "2013's Top 20 Billionaires," *Forbes*, March 2013, http://www.forbes.com/pictures/mel45ghdi/sheldon-adelson.

[86] Kim Barker, "Karl Rove's Dark Money Group Promised IRS It Would Spend 'Limited' Money on Elections," ProPublica, December 14, 2012, http://www.propublica.org/article/what-karl-roves-dark-money-nonprofit-told-the-irs.

[87] *Washington Post* Staff, "Run: An American Election," http://www.washingtonpost.com/supergrid/run.

[88] Amanda Terkel, "Florida's Long Lines On Election Day Discouraged 49,000 People From Voting: Report," Huffington Post, December 29, 2012, http://www.huffingtonpost.com/2012/12/29/floridas-long-lines-election-voting_n_2381482.html.

[89] Sean Gallagher, "Inside Team Romney's whale of an IT meltdown; Orca, the Romney campaign's 'killer' app, skips beta and pays the price," Ars Technica, November 9, 2012, http://arstechnica.com/information-technology/2012/11/inside-team-romneys-whale-of-an-it-meltdown.

[90] Alexis C. Madrigal, "When the Nerds Go Marching In," *Atlantic*, November 16, 2012, http://www.theatlantic.com/technology/archive/2012/11/when-the-nerds-go-marching-in/265325/2. For a round-up of tech-oriented articles comparing the performances, see John Mancini, "Big Data Operation Narwhal, Project Orca and the Election of a President," Digital Landfill, December 5, 2012, http://www.digitallandfill.org/2012/12/big-data-operation-narwhal-project-orca-and-the-election-of-a-president.html.

[91] Marc A. Thiessen, "Obama's 'Moneyball' campaign," *Washington Post*, November 12, 2012, http://www.washingtonpost.com/opinions/marc-thiessen-how-obama-trumped-romney-with-big-data/2012/11/12/6fa599da-2cd4-11e2-89d4-040c9330702a_story.html.

[92] Thom Hartmann and Sam Sacks, "Anonymous, Karl Rove and 2012 Election Fix?" Truthout, November 19, 2012, http://truth-out.org/news/item/12845-anonymous-karl-rove-and-2012-election-fix.

[93] Roger Shuler, "Did A Progressive Firewall Keep Karl Rove And Co. From Stealing The 2012 Presidential Election?" Legal Schnauzer, November 20, 2012, http://legalschnauzer.blogspot.com/2012/11/did-progressive-firewall-keep-karl-rove.html.

[94] Looking ahead, an additional unanswered question after the election is: Who owns and/or gets to use the best databases from the campaigns? The information and procedures are valuable for future elections. The Obama campaign could

provide the information widely to other Democrats, or use it as a political tool to help allies especially in future elections.

[95] Richard Charnin, "2012 Election Fraud: A True Vote Model Proof," Richard Charnin's Blog, January 2, 2013, http://richardcharnin.wordpress.com/2013/01/02/2012-election-fraud-a-true-vote-model-proof.

[96] Andrew Kreig, "Did Expert Witness, Activists Thwart a Rove Ohio Vote Plot?" Justice Integrity Project, November 14, 2012.

Chapter 20, A Petraeus Betrayal?

[1] Larry Margasack, "David Petraeus Testifying About Benghazi Attacks On Capitol Hill," Associated Press/Huffington Post, November 16, 2012. http://www.huffingtonpost.com/2012/11/16/david-petraeus-benghazi_n_2143447.html.

[2] Eli Lake, "David Petraeus's Secret Trip to Libya After the Benghazi Attack," Daily Beast, November 13, 201,. http://www.thedailybeast.com/articles/2012/11/13/david-petraeus-s-secret-trip-to-libya-after-the-benghazi-attack.html.

[3] Ronald Kessler, "Kessler: FBI Investigation Led to Petraeus Resignation," Newsmax, November 9, 2012, http://www.newsmax.com/Headline/petraeus-resigns-cia-affair/2012/11/09/id/463573#ixzz2BpwPcpg0; and "Ron Kessler on Petraeus Resignation: There Are Several Cover-ups Going On" (Video), Fox News, November 9, 2012, http://www.thegatewaypundit.com/2012/11/ron-kessler-on-petraeus-resignation-there-are-several-cover-ups-going-on-video.

[4] Perez, Gorman and Barrett, "FBI Scrutinized on Petraeus; Complaints by Female Social Planner Led to Email Trail That Undid CIA Chief," *op. cit.*, http://online.wsj.com/article/SB100014241278873240735045781134608523 95852.html.

[5] James Risen described how he had undergone years of financially damaging federal investigation and potential imprisonment for refusing to reveal his government sources. Justice Integrity Project, "Press Club Forum Probes 'Obama's War On Leaks,'" Andrew Kreig, May 2, 2012. http://www.justice-integrity.org/faq/129-press-club-forum-probes-obamas-war-on-leaks.

[6] See also, more generally, my column for the Justice Integrity Project, "DC News Workshop Preserves Lost Era of Press That Protected Public," April 26, 2012. This report about a separate event at the National Press Club commemorated in video a fast-disappearing era of aggressive investigative reporting by mainstream media.

[7] Rank has its privileges, as the saying goes. The Obama administration, like its Bush predecessors, could be extraordinarily ruthless and indeed cruel in enforcing discipline against whistleblowers. Among the targets have been former CIA officer John Kiriakou and Army Private Bradley Manning, just as the Bush administration prosecuted low-ranking personnel in the Abu Ghraib torture scandal.

8 Silverglate, Harvey A., with Foreword by Alan M. Dershowitz. *Three Felonies a Day: How the Feds Target the Innocent.* Encounter, 2009.

9 Bush, *All the Best, op. cit.* One of Bush's former presidential aides, a friend of mine, recalls a number of warm memories of his personal thoughtfulness.

10 Separately, Wayne Madsen reported a tip that Petraeus met Broadwell in 2004. If true that would discredit the conventional timeline of their meeting as beginning in 2006. See Wayne Madsen Report, February 7, 2013 (Subscription required), http://www.waynemadsenreport.com.

11 Eric Schmitt, Helene Cooper and Michael S. Schmidt, "Deadly Attack in Libya Was Major Blow to CIA Efforts," *New York Times,* September 23, 2012, http://www.nytimes.com/2012/09/24/world/africa/attack-in-libya-was-major-blow-to-cia-efforts.html?pagewanted=all&_r=0.

12 Staff report, "Security chiefs resign over Benghazi probe that blamed 'grossly poor' security and State Department's 'systematic failures' for attack that killed U.S. ambassador," *Daily Mail,* December 18, 2012, http://www.dailymail.co.uk/news/article-2250347/Eric-Boswell-Charlene-Lamb-Security-chiefs-resign-probe-Benghazi-strike-death-Christopher-Stevens.html.Congress moved in early 2013 to authorized $2 billion more for diplomatic security worldwide, thereby illustrating how the Republican attempt to pin the Benghazi deaths entirely on the Obama administration was an obvious partisan talking point.

13 Aaron Klein, "Media ignore Hillary's bombshell Benghazi claim; Secretary insists she did not know about gun-running at U.S. mission," January 24, 2013, http://www.wnd.com/2013/01/media-ignore-hillarys-bombshell-benghazi-claim.

14 Ibid.

15 Bob Somerby, "Idiocracy Benghazi Style," Daily Howler, November 3, 2013, http://dailyhowler.blogspot.com/2012/11/idiocracy-benghazi-style-you-may-live.html. As often the case, it was an unpaid blogger writing a daily column who took the trouble to read the relevant transcripts and write more than a dozen columns pointing out what the professionals were missing. An inspector general's report and emails show that the CIA drafted talking points for Rice and that former Defense Secretary Robert Gates, a Republican, was among those asserting that the military determined that a rscue could not occur in time. Scott Wilson and Karen DeYoung, "Obama administration releases e-mails detailing agencies' debate over Benghazi," *Washington Post,* May 15, 2013. http://www.washingtonpost.com/politics/obama-administration-releases-e-mails-detailing-agencies-debate-over-benghazi/2013/05/15/e177cc80-bda8-11e2-9b09-1638acc3942e_story.html; David Ignatius, "The Benghazi e-mails' backside-covering," *Washington Post,* May 17, 2013. http://www.washingtonpost.com/opinions/david-ignatius-the-benghazi-e-mails-backside-covering/2013/05/17/8a4f6fa2-be62-11e2-97d4-a479289a31f9_story.html. See generally, Andrew Kreig, "Obama Battered By DOJ, IRS, State Revelations," Justice Integrity Project May 14, 2013. http://www.justice-integrity.org/faq/481-obama-civil-rights-image-battered-by-irs-doj-cia-revelations.

[16] Scott Wilson and Karen DeYoung, "Petraeus had key role in Benghazi talking points," *Washington Post*, May 21, 2013. http://www.washingtonpost.com/politics/petraeuss-role-in-drafting-benghazi-talking-points-raises-questions/2013/05/21/db19f352-c165-11e2-ab60-67bba7be7813_story.html?hpid=z1: Kevin Drum, "Looking For a Benghazi Talking Points Villain? It Was David Petraeus, Not Barack Obama, *Mother Jones*, May 21, 2013, http://www.motherjones.com/kevin-drum/2013/05/looking-benghazi-talking-points-villain-it-was-david-petraeus-not-barack-obama; and Michael Hirsh, "Five myths about Benghazi,"Washington Post, May 16, 2013, http://www.washingtonpost.com/opinions/five-myths-about-benghazi/2013/05/16/3baac71c-bcd1-11e2-9b09-1638acc3942e_story.html?hpid=z6.

[17] Victoria Kim, "'Innocence of Muslims' filmmaker gets a year in prison," *Los Angeles Times*, November 7, 2012, http://latimesblogs.latimes.com/lanow/2012/11/innocence-muslims-filmmaker-sentenced.html.

[18] Greg Miller and Julie Tate, "CIA's Global Response Staff emerging from shadows after incidents in Libya and Pakistan," *Washington Post*, December 26, 2012. http://www.washingtonpost.com/world/national-security/cias-global-response-staff-emerging-from-shadows-after-incidents-in-libya-and-pakistan/2012/12/26/27db2d1c-4b7f-11e2-b709-667035ff9029_story.html.

[19] Schmitt, Cooper and Schmidt, "Deadly Attack in Libya Was Major Blow to CIA Efforts," *op. cit.*

[20] Craig Unger, "Karl Rove's October Surprise: Can a Desperate 'Jimmy Carter Strategy' Make Obama Look Weak on Terrorism, Libya?" Salon, October 1, 2012, http://www.bossrove.com/news/frame/72c086211bf0eaaf8a9480034bf27f8a.

[21] Webster G. Tarpley, "Romney campaign, CIA Mormon Mafia both responsible for Benghazi attack," Press TV, October 14, 2012, http://www.presstv.ir/detail/2012/10/14/266560/benghazi-attack-cia-mafia-in-action.

[22] Wikipedia, *Seven Days in May*, http://en.wikipedia.org/wiki/Seven_Days_in_May. "The story is said to have been influenced by the right-wing anti-Communist political activities of General Edwin A. Walker after he resigned from the military. President John F. Kennedy had read the novel and believed the scenario as described could actually occur in the United States."

[23] Even high-ranking government leaders do not name all their staffers. Some are recommended by administration or power-brokers, and thus can constitute a potentially disloyal force in an office. Also, underlings can provide deniability to leaders by shielding them from direct discussions of the specifics of disreputable matters. Only aggressive investigations of scandals can ferret out the facts, including the relative culpability of leaders and staff.

[24] Webb and Murphy. *Benghazi, op cit.* Authors Webb and Murphy run SOCREP.com, a website and organization that reports on former special operations personnel. In 2010, Webb coauthored a book with his friend, Glen Doherty, a fellow former SEAL who was killed while working as a CIA contractor during the

Benghazi massacre. The Webb-Murphy book reported on resentment by special operations personnel against Petraeus and the Obama administration.

[25] William Kristol, "Petraeus Throws Obama Under the Bus," *Weekly Standard*, October 26, 2012, http://www.weeklystandard.com/blogs/petraeus-throws-obama-under-bus_657896.html.

[26] Dana Milbank, "Letting us in on a secret," *Washington Post*, October 10, 2012, http://articles.washingtonpost.com/2012-10-10/opinions/35501217_1_benghazi-darrell-issa-security-lapses.

[27] Christopher Ruddy, "A Tale of the Two Obamas," *Newsmax*, August 2, 2012, http://www.newsmax.com/Ruddy/obama-romney-/2012/08/02/id/447391.

[28] Dana Milbank, "Petraeus's behavior is no scandal," *Washington Post*, November 20, 2012. http://www.washingtonpost.com/opinions/dana-milbank-petraeuss-behavior-is-no-scandal/2012/11/20/7a3357c4-334c-11e2-bfd5-e202b6d7b501_story.html. See also, Kaplan, Fred. *The Insurgents: David Petraeus and the Plot to Change the American Way of War.* Simon & Schuster, 2013, 267-68, a flattering portrayal of Petraeus and his historical role that treats his resignation briefly.

[29] James Petras, "Elite Intrigues and Military Purges: It's Not About Sex, Stupid!" Global Research, November 22, 2012, http://www.globalresearch.ca/elite-intrigues-and-military-purges-its-not-about-sex-stupid/5312591. Petras, a retired university professor and author of 64 books, suggested that Petraeus policies caused his career implosion. Petras nonetheless discounts the official version from the White House as incredible.

[30] Anne Gearan, "Review of Benghazi attack faults 'grossly' inadequate security, leadership failures," *Washington Post*, December 18, 2012, http://www.washingtonpost.com/world/national-security/benghazi-panel-presents-findings-to-lawmakers-makes-recommendations/2012/12/18/9ada6032-495c-11e2-b6f0-e851e741d196_story.html?hpid=z.

[31] Josh Gerstein, "Report: Leon Panetta revealed classified SEAL unit info," *Politico*, June 5, 2013, http://www.politico.com/story/2013/06/leon-panetta-seal-leak-92263.html. The agency cooperated with a Hollywood version of the raid, and later attacked its storyline. Connor Simpson, "The CIA Is Not Too Happy with 'Zero Dark Thirty,' *Atlantic*, December 22, 2012, http://news.yahoo.com/cia-not-too-happy-zero-dark-thirty-152018214.html.

[32] Craig Whitlock and Ernesto Londoño, "Pentagon reviewing legal, ethical conduct of senior officers," *Washington Post*, November 15, 2012

[33] Wayne Madsen, "Post-Benghazi purges continue," Wayne Madsen Report, December 2012, http://www.waynemadsenreport.com/articles/201212201.

[34] Presidential Memorandum, "National Insider Threat Policy and Minimum Standards for Executive Branch Insider Threat Programs," White House Briefing Room, November 21, 2012, http://www.whitehouse.gov/the-press-office/2012/11/21/presidential-memorandum-national-insider-threat-policy-and-minimum-stand.

[35] Wayne Madsen, "Sex, Lies, and Audiotapes — The right-wing plot against Obama," Wayne Madsen Report, November 12, 2012 (Subscription required)

http://www.waynemadsenreport.com/articles/20121112_1; Madsen, Wayne, L'Affaire Petraeus: The Benghazi Stand-down and the Plot To "Carterize" Obama. Lulu, Dec. 5, 2012.

36 Gareth Porter, "Broadwell Defended Petraeus' Village Destruction Policy," IPS News, November 15, 2012. http://www.ipsnews.net/2012/11/broadwell-defended-petraeus-village-destruction-policy; Ray McGovern, "Good Riddance Petraeus," OpEd News, November 10, 2012. http://www.opednews.com/articles/Pundit-Tears-for-Petraeus-by-Ray-McGovern-121110-349.html; Robert Parry, "Behind Petraeus's Resignation," Consortium News, November 10, 2012. http://consortiumnews.com/2012/11/10/behind-petraeuss-resignation.

37 Webster G. Tarpley, "CIA Mormon Mafia, Neocons, Netanyahu to Carterize Obama," Press TV, September 15, 2012, http://tarpley.net/2012/09/15/cia-mormon-mafia-neocons-netanyahu-to-carterize-obama.

38 Michael Collins, "What Did Petraeus Know and When Did He Know It?" OpEdNews, November 15, 2012. http://www.opednews.com/articles/What-Did-Petraeus-Know-and-by-Michael-Collins-121115-283.html.

39 Webb and Murphy. Benghazi: The Definitive Report, op. cit. as cited by. Michael Zennie, "David Petraeus was brought down after betrayal by vengeful CIA agents and his own bodyguards who made sure his affair was exposed, claims new book," Daily Mail, February 10, 2013, http://www.dailymail.co.uk/news/article-2276139/David-Petraeus-CIA-directors-bodyguards-exposed-affair-Paula-Broadwell-claims-Benghazi-The-Definitive-Report.html.

40 Bob Woodward, "Fox News chief's failed attempt to enlist Petraeus as presidential candidate," Washington Post, December 3, 2012, http://www.washingtonpost.com/lifestyle/style/fox-news-chiefs-failed-attempt-to-enlist-petraeus-as-presidential-candidate/2012/12/03/15fdcea8-3d77-11e2-a2d9-822f58ac9fd5_story.html.

41 Andrew Kreig, "Petraeus Tape Reveals Disloyal Talks With Fox on Obama," Justice Integrity Project, December 4, 2012, http://www.justice-integrity.org/faq/231-petraeus-tape-reveals-disloyal-talks-with-fox-on-obama.

42 McFarland denied that she was the source of the tape or that the conversation was serious. Her claims illustrate the difficulties of sourcing military/political intrigues and motives, even with a tape-recording as a basis. Kathleen McFarland, "My Petraeus interview firestorm silly, off-base," FoxNews.com, December 4, 2012, http://www.foxnews.com/opinion/2012/12/04/my-petraeus-interview-firestorm-silly-off-base.

43 Carl Bernstein, "Why the US media ignored Murdoch's brazen bid to hijack the presidency; Did the Washington Post and others underplay the story through fear of the News Corp chairman, or simply tin-eared judgment?" Guardian, December 20, 2012. http://www.guardian.co.uk/commentisfree/2012/dec/20/bernstein-murdoch-ailes-petraeus-presidency. "The Ailes/Petraeus tape made clear to many that Murdoch's goals in America have always been nefarious. So now we have it: what appears to be hard, irrefutable evidence of Rupert Murdoch's ultimate and most audacious attempt to hijack America's democratic

institutions on a scale equal to his success in kidnapping and corrupting the essential democratic institutions of Great Britain through money, influence and wholesale abuse of the privileges of a free press. In the American instance, Murdoch's goal seems to have been nothing less than using his media empire – notably Fox News – to recruit, bankroll, and support in secret the presidential candidacy of General David Petraeus in the 2012 election."

[44] Ibid.

[45] Jonathan Cook, "Why the *Washington Post* killed the story of Murdoch's bid to buy the US presidency, " OpEd News, December 21, 2012. http://www.opednews.com/articles/Why-the-Washington-Post-ki-by-Jonathan-Cook-121221-969.html.

[46] Lorna Aldrich, "NPC Luncheon with Leon Panetta," National Press Club," December 18, 2012, (63-minute video), http://www.press.org/news-multimedia/videos/npc-luncheon-leon-panetta. Panetta responded to a question on why Petraeus had to resign.

[47] Harry S. Truman Library, "'The Buck Stops Here' Desk Sign," http://www.trumanlibrary.org/hstpaper/svp.htm. The library has adopted the practice of placing a period after the middle initial of Truman's name. Truman had no middle name, only an initial.

[48] Tom Murphy, "David Petraeus To Head Private Equity Firm KKR's New Global Institute," AP via Huffington Post, May 30, 2013. http://www.huffingtonpost.com/2013/05/30/david-petraeus-kkr_n_3358253.html; Ewen MacAskill, "David Petraeus to apologize for affair in comeback speech," *Guardian*, March 26, 2013. http://m.guardiannews.com/world/2013/mar/26/david-petraeus-general-apologise-affair.

Chapter 21, Planning a Second Obama Term

[1] Andrew Kreig, "Economists Warn of Near Treason In DC Policies," Justice Integrity Project, March 5, 2013. http://www.justice-integrity.org/faq/447-economists-warn-of-near-treason-in-dc-policies.

[2] Paul Krugman, "The Deal Dilemma," *New York Times*, December 18, 2012. http://krugman.blogs.nytimes.com/2012/12/18/the-deal-dilemma. "First things first: cutting Social Security benefits is a cruel, stupid policy — just not nearly as cruel and stupid as raising the Medicare eligibility age." See also, Paul Krugman, "Ben Bernanke, Hippie," *New York Times*, February 28, 2013. http://www.nytimes.com/2013/03/01/opinion/krugman-ben-bernanke-hippie.html?hp&_r=1&.

[3] Morris, *Encyclopedia of American History, op. cit.*, 1061-62; Perloff, *Shadows of Power, op. cit.*, 28; Seymour, Charles, ed. *The Intimate Papers of Colonel House.* Houghton Miflin, 1926, vol. I, 126, Wikipedia, Edward M. House, http://en.wikipedia.org/wiki/Edward_M._House.

[4] Zweigenhaft, Richard L., and G. William Domhoff. *Diversity in the Power Elite: How It Happened, Why It Matters.* Rowman & Littlefield, 2006.

[5] Rob Kall, "Susan Rice for Secretary of State? Very Bad For Liberals and Progressives," OpEdNews, December 2, 2012,

http://www.opednews.com/articles/Susan-Rice-for-Secretary-o-by-Rob-Kall-121202-105.html. See also, Ray McGovern, "Hillary Clinton, Brutality and Hillary Clinton — A Year Later," OpEdNews, February 19, 2012. http://www.opednews.com/articles/Brutality-and-Hillary-Clin-by-Ray-McGovern-120218-940.html.

6 Scott Dodd, "Secretary of State Candidate Has a Major Financial Stake in Canadian Tar Sands," On Earth, November 28, 2012, http://www.onearth.org/article/susan-rice-obama-secretary-state-tar-sands-finances. The prospective nominee and her husband has millions invested in other Canadian companies arguably relevant also to the $7 billion Keystone XL pipeline.

7 John M. Broder, "Report May Ease Path for New Pipeline," *New York Times*, March 1, 2013, http://www.nytimes.com/2013/03/02/us/us-report-sees-no-environmental-bar-to-keystone-pipeline.html?ref=us&_r=0.

8 Mills, C. Wright, *The Power Elite*. Oxford University, 1956, as cited by Ben Schreiner, "Washington's Strategic Policy Shift on Syria: Edging Closer to Direct Military Intervention?" Global Research, February 28, 2013, http://www.globalresearch.ca/washingtons-strategic-policy-shift-on-syria-edging-closer-to-direct-military-intervention/5324606.

9 One source was Wayne Madsen, who published, "Hagel-DoD *quid pro quo*," Wayne Madsen Report, December 18, 2012 (Subscription required), http://www.waynemadsenreport.com/articles/20121218_1. Others with independent information sources prefer to remain anonymous.

10 Joseph Spectoron, "NY State Board of Elections has no investigators," News from Underground, January 7, 2013, http://markcrispinmiller.com/2013/01/ny-state-board-of-elections-has-no-investigators.

11 Wikipedia, Al Waleed bin Talal, http://en.wikipedia.org/wiki/Al-Waleed_bin_Talal.

12 Berens, Charlyne. *Chuck Hagel: Moving Forward*. University of Nebraska, 2006.

13 Danny Hakim, "Obama's Treasury Nominee Got Unusual Exit Bonus on Leaving N.Y.U." *New York Times*, February 25, 2013, http://www.nytimes.com/2013/02/26/nyregion/lew-treasury-nominee-got-exit-bonus-from-nyu.html?_r=1&.

14 Editorial, "Jack Lew's Golden Parachute: His Citigroup contract paid him a bonus for returning to government, *Wall Street Journal*, February 24, 2013, http://online.wsj.com/article/SB10001424127887323384604578244428305470044.html?mod=WSJ_Opinion_LEADTop.

15 Kevin Roose, "Did Citigroup Pay Jack Lew a Government-Job Bounty?" *New York Magazine*, http://nymag.com/daily/intelligencer/2013/02/did-citi-pay-jack-lew-a-government-job-bounty.html.

16 Scott Wilson, "Obama turns to like-minded allies, advisers to fill out his second-term Cabinet," *Washington Post*, January 10, 2013, http://articles.washingtonpost.com/2013-01-10/politics/36272420_1_president-obama-jack-lew-chief-counterterrorism-adviser.

17 Russ Baker, "NYT's Rhodes to Nowhere: A Cipher in the Oval Office," WhoWhatWhy, March 21, 2013. http://whowhatwhy.com/2013/03/21/nyts-rhodes-to-nowhere-a-cipher-in-the-oval-office. As it turns out, Rhodes was one of three high-ranking Obama aides who were siblings of network television presidents, illustrating the tight ties at the top. Noel Sheppard, "Presidents of ABC and CBS News Have Siblings Working at White House With Ties to Benghazi," News Busters interview of Richard Grenell, May 11, 2013, http://newsbusters.org/blogs/noel-sheppard/2013/05/11/fox-abc-and-cbs-news-presidents-have-siblings-working-white-house-tie#ixzz2WaWFyRc0.

18 Coll, Steve. *The Bins Ladens: An Arabian Family in the American Century.* Penguin, 2008, 74-75. Osama Bin Laden, reared as a Sunni, was born to a Syrian mother from an Alawite region.

19 Ray McGovern, "John Brennan's Heavy Baggage," Consortium News, March 11, 2013, http://consortiumnews.com/2013/03/11/john-brennans-heavy-baggage.

20 Rachel Bade, "Dems seize on re-issued CRS tax report," Politico, December 13, 2012, http://www.politico.com/story/2012/12/dems-seize-on-re-issued-crs-tax-report-85067_Page2.html; and David Dayen, "CRS Resurrects Report Showing No Correlation Between Low Tax Rates on the Wealthy and Economic Growth," December 14, 2012, http://news.firedoglake.com/2012/12/14/crs-resurrects-report-showing-no-correlation-between-low-tax-rates-on-the-wealthy-and-economic-growth.

21 Meg Fowler, "From Eisenhower to Obama: What the Wealthiest Americans Pay in Taxes," ABC News, January 24, 2011, http://abcnews.go.com/Politics/eisenhower-obama-wealthy-americans-mitt-romney-pay-taxes/story?id=15387862#1.

22 Jordan Weissmann, "The Recession's Toll," *op cit.*

23 AP Staff Writer, "U.S. CEOs push plan to raise full retirement age to 70," CBS News/Associated Press, January 16, 2013, http://www.opednews.com/Quicklink/U-S-CEOs-push-plan-to-rai-in-Best_Web_OpEds-130118-113.html.

24 Mike Lux, "He's Only Stuck If He Lets Himself Be," Huffington Post, December 11, 2012, http://www.huffingtonpost.com/mike-lux/hes-only-stuck-if-he-lets_b_2271053.html?utm_source=Alert-blogger&utm_medium=email&utm_campaign=Email%2BNotifications.

25 David Dayen, "Though Liberals Carp at Chained CPI, Pelosi Says She Could Live With It," FireDogLake, December 18, 2012., http://news.firedoglake.com/2012/12/18/though-liberals-carp-at-chained-cpi-pelosi-says-she-could-live-with-it.

26 Robert Reich, "Cliff Hanger: The President's Unnecessary and Unwise Concessions," Huffington Post, December 20, 2012, http://www.huffingtonpost.com/robert-reich/cliff-hanger-the-president_b_2338483.html.

27 Patrick Temple-West, Marcus Stern, and Susan Cornwell, "Corporate Tax Breaks Included In Fiscal Cliff Deal Thanks To White House Urging," Reuters/Huffington Post, January 8, 2013,

http://www.huffingtonpost.com/2013/01/08/corporate-tax-breaks-fiscal-cliff_n_2430580.html.

28 Jonathan Chait, "Why Is Obama Caving on Taxes?" New York Magazine, December 31, 2012, http://nymag.com/daily/intelligencer/2012/12/why-is-obama-caving-on-taxes.html; DS Wright, "Obama Caves On Taxes While House Prepares To Vote On Deal," FireDogLake, January 1, 2012, http://news.firedoglake.com/2013/01/01/obama-caves-on-taxes-while-house-prepares-to-vote-on-deal.

29 Matt Stoller, "Eight Corporate Subsidies in the Fiscal Cliff Bill, From Goldman Sachs to Disney to NASCAR," Naked Capitalism, January 3, 2012. http://www.nakedcapitalism.com/2013/01/eight-corporate-subsidies-in-the-fiscal-cliff-bill-from-goldman-sachs-to-disney-to-nascar.html.

30 Eric Lipton and Kevin Sack, "Fiscal Footnote: Big Senate Gift to Drug Maker," New York Times, January 19, 2013, http://www.nytimes.com/2013/01/20/us/medicare-pricing-delay-is-political-win-for-amgen-drug-maker.html?ref=opinion&_r=0. See also, Johnston, David Cay. Perfectly Legal: The Covert Campaign to Rig Our Tax System to Benefit the Super Rich, and Cheat Everybody Else. Portfolio, 2003; and Ryan Grim and Paul Blumenthal, "Orrin Hatch Defends Costly Amgen Provision In Fiscal Cliff Deal," Huffington Post, February 2, 2013, http://www.huffingtonpost.com/2013/02/02/fiscal-cliff-deal-amgen-hatch_n_2607175.html.

31 Jonathan Weisman, "Lines of Resistance on Fiscal Deal," New York Times, January 1, 2013, http://www.nytimes.com/2013/01/02/us/politics/a-new-breed-of-republicans-resists-the-fiscal-deal.html?_r=2&.

32 Jonathan Chait, "Why Is Obama Caving on Taxes?" New York Magazine, December 31, 2012, http://nymag.com/daily/intelligencer/2012/12/why-is-obama-caving-on-taxes.html; Paul Krugman, "That Bad Ceiling Feeling," New York Times, January 2, 2013, http://krugman.blogs.nytimes.com/2013/01/02/that-bad-ceiling-feeling/?smid=tw-NytimesKrugman&seid=auto.

33 Paul Krugman, "Battles of the Budget," New York Times, January 3, 2013. http://www.nytimes.com/2013/01/04/opinion/kurgman-battles-of-the-budget.html?hp&_r=0. Many economic arguments for austerity relied upon a major academic study whose results were based on mistaken data entries. See Paul Krugman, "The Jobless Trap," New York Times, April 22, 2013, http://www.nytimes.com/2013/04/22/opinion/krugman-the-jobless-trap.html?ref=paulkrugman&_r=1&.

34 Peter Schroeder, "Dark mood casts a pall on big day," The Hill, January 21, 2013, www.thehill.com.

35 John Nichols, "This President Can — and Must — Claim a Mandate to Govern," Nation/OpEdNews, January 20, 2013. http://www.opednews.com/articles/This-President-Can--and-by-John-Nichols-130120-96.html.

36 Michael McAuliff, "Tom Harkin: Filibuster Reform Failure Hamstrings Obama Agenda," Huffington Post, January 25, 2013,

http://www.huffingtonpost.com/2013/01/24/tom-harkin-filibuster-reform_n_2544153.html.

[37] Andrew Kreig, "Let Us Now Praise (and Appraise) Our Famous President," Justice Integrity Project, January 23, 2013, http://www.justice-integrity.org/faq/430-let-us-now-praise-and-appraise-famous-presidents.

[38] Bruce A. Dixon, "Symbols Are All We Need: Four More Years of Black Silence, Irrelevance," Black Agenda Report Radio, January 23, 2013.

[39] Robert Reich, "The End of the Recovery That Never Really Began," Huffington Post, February 1, 2013, http://www.huffingtonpost.com/robert-reich/january-jobs-numbers-economic-recovery_b_2599098.html. See also, Jim Tankersley, "Shift to a service-driven economy delays job recovery," *Washington Post,* May 3, 2013 http://www.washingtonpost.com/business/economy/shift-to-services-delays-job-recovery/2013/05/03/a78ec0f0-b3f3-11e2-9a98-4be1688d7d84_story.html.

[40] Paul Craig Roberts, "The Missing Recovery," Institute for Political Economy/OpEdNews, March 1, 2013, http://www.opednews.com/articles/The-Missing-Recovery-by-Paul-Craig-Roberts-130301-410.html. See also, Roberts, "Another Phony Jobs Report," June 7, 2013. http://www.paulcraigroberts.org/2013/06/07/another-phony-jobs-report-from-a-government-that-lies-about-everything-paul-craig-roberts. But see Jeffrey A. Miron, "The Sequester Will Be Good for the Economy," Cato Institute/*Daily Caller,* February 28, 2013, http://www.cato.org/publications/commentary/sequester-will-be-good-economy. Miron, a well-credentialed economist, nonetheless relied heavily on straw man arguments and cherry-picked examples.

[41] Steven T. Dennis and Daniel Newhauser, "Obama's Lost Leverage," *Roll Call,* March 1, 2013, http://www.rollcall.com/news/obamas_lost_leverage-222792-1.html?ET=rollcall:e15254:115837a:&st=email&pos=eam.

[42] Sam Stein, "Obama Budget: Administration Explains Why It Started With A 'Compromise Proposal,'" Huffington Post, April 5, 2013. http://www.huffingtonpost.com/2013/04/05/obama-budget_n_3019281.html. Michael Collins, "Cave in: Obama puts Social Security and Medicare in budget deal," OpEdNews, March 22, 2013, http://www.opednews.com/articles/Cave-in-Obama-puts-Social-by-Michael-Collins-130322-842.html."

[43] David Brown and Sean Sullivan, "Ryan calls for both Obamacare repeal and finding 'common ground' in budget fight," *Washington Post,* March 10, 2013. http://www.washingtonpost.com/politics/ryan-calls-for-both-obamacare-repeal-and-finding-common-ground-in-budget-fight/2013/03/10/db2c7cd2-89b3-11e2-8d72-dc76641cb8d4_story.html.

[44] Editorial Board, "Repairs to Medicare," *Washington Post,* January 6, 2013, http://www.washingtonpost.com/opinions/repairing-medicare/2013/01/06/1646366c-56a3-11e2-a613-ec8d394535c6_story.html.

[45] Paul Krugman, "Ben Bernanke, Hippie," *New York Times,* February 28, 2013. http://www.nytimes.com/2013/03/01/opinion/krugman-ben-bernanke-hippie.html?hp&_r=1&.

[46] Roberts, "The Missing Recovery," *op. cit.*

[47] "The President's Plan" foresaw $130 billion in Social Security savings as cited by Jennifer Palmieri, "A Balanced Plan to Avert the Sequester and Reduce the Deficit," White House Blog, February 21, 2013, http://www.whitehouse.gov/blog/2013/02/21/balanced-plan-avert-sequester-and-reduce-deficit. See also Dean Baker, "Macho Men, Social Security, and the Chained CPI," Truthout/Huffington Post, February 25, 2013, http://truth-out.org/news/item/14764-macho-men-social-security-and-the-chained-cpi.

[48] Roberts, "The Missing Recovery," *op. cit.*

[49] Morris, Richard B., ed., *Encyclopedia of American History Bicentennial Edition.* Harper and Row, 1976, 980-81. See also Mitchell Schlimer, "Entrepreneurs Hall of Fame: Phineas Taylor Barnum," Let's Talk Business Network, http://www.ltbn.com/hall_of_fame/Barnum.html.

[50] Barnum's successes included an exhibition in the nation's capital and elsewhere of an exotic horse, supposedly captured on a California expedition by Col. John C. Fremont, the era's greatest war hero and explorer. Barnum advertised the "woolly horse" as part elephant, camel, buffalo, and horse. At a site two blocks from my office, a U.S. senator paid 25 cents to see the creature, then unsuccessfully sought Barnum's federal prosecution for fraud. Barnum, Phineas T. *The Life of P. T. Barnum.* 1855.

[51] Wayne Madsen, "Michelle Obama honors CIA film while paying homage to her husband's first year with the agency," Wayne Madsen Report, February 26, 2013, http://www.waynemadsenreport.com/articles/20130226_1.

[52] The high-dollar event was at the home of Reed Hundt, former chairman of the Federal Communications Commission under President Clinton and later a leader in the Obama transition.

[53] Morgenson, Gretchen, and Joshua Rosner. *Reckless Endangerment: How Outsized Ambition, Greed and Corruption Led to Economic Armageddon.* Times, 2011, xi. "Josh and I felt compelled to write this book because we are angry that the American economy was almost wrecked by a crowd of self-interested, politically influential, and arrogant people who have not been held accountable for their actions." Ibid., xiv-xv.

[54] Jim Vandehei and Mike Allen, "Behind the Curtain: The 'hell no' caucus," *Politico,* January 8, 2013 http://www.politico.com/story/2013/01/behind-the-curtain-the-hell-no-caucus-85872.html.

[55] Michael Collins, "Debt Ceiling Disaster - Crazy or Criminal?" OpEd News, January 9, 2013. http://www.opednews.com/articles/Debt-Ceiling-Disaster--Cr-by-Michael-Collins-130109-8.html.

[56] Smiley, Tavis, and Cornel West. *The Rich and The Rest Of Us: A Poverty Manifesto.* Smiley, 2012.

[57] Dorgan, Byron L. *Take this Job and Ship It: How Corporate Greed and Brain-Dead Politics Are Selling Out America.* St. Martin's, 2006. See also, Klein, *Shock Doctrine, op. cit.*

[58] Andrew Kreig, "Hard Times and Horsemeat: Coming Here?" Justice Integrity Project, February 17, 2013, http://www.justice-integrity.org/faq/439-hard-times-and-horsemeat-coming-soon.

[59] Andrew Kreig, "Disturbing Developments for Democracy Wind Up Year," Justice Integrity Project, December 23, 2012. http://www.justice-integrity.org/faq/238-disturbing-developments-for-democracy-wind-up-year.

[60] Andrew Kreig, "Mr. Drake Goes To Washington," Justice Integrity Project, March 21, 2013. http://www.justice-integrity.org/faq/455-mister-drake-goes-to-washington.

[61] Albert Alschuler, Gregory Craig, Robert Ehrlich, Jr., Margaret Love, Paul Rosenzweig, "Clemency: Old Problems and New Solutions," (one hour video), Heritage Foundation, December 10, 2012, http://www.heritage.org/events/2012/12/clemency, as cited in Andrew Kreig, "Presidential Clemency System Broken, Experts Say," Justice Integrity Project, December 11, 2012, http://www.justice-integrity.org/faq/235-presidential-clemency-system-broken-experts-say.

[62] David Dayen, "Obama campaign reluctant to give up database," FireDogLake, December 5, 2012, http://news.firedoglake.com/2012/12/05/obama-campaign-reluctant-to-give-up-database.

[63] Silverglate, Harvey A. *Three Felonies a Day: How the Feds Target the Innocent.* Encounter, 2009; Greenwald, Glenn. *With Liberty and Justice for Some.* Metropolitan, 2011; Fein, Bruce. *The American Empire Before The Fall.* CreateSpace, 2010; and Roberts, Paul Craig, and Lawrence M. Stratton. *The Tyranny of Good Intentions: How Prosecutors and Law Enforcement Are Trampling the Constitution in the Name of Justice.* Forum/Prima, 2000.

[64] Justice Integrity Project, www.justice-integrity.org. Monthly news archive: http://www.justice-integrity.org/news-reports.

[65] Neil King Jr., "Romney Planning to Rejoin National Dialogue," *Wall Street Journal,* May 30, 2013, .Zeke J. Miller, "Mitt Romney Inc.: The White House That Never Was," *Time,* June 2, 2013, http://swampland.time.com/2013/06/02/mitt-romney-inc-the-white-house-that-never-was; Murphy, "David Petraeus To Head Private Equity Firm KKR's New Global Institute," *op. cit.;*Andrew Kreig, "Obama's FBI Nominee Deserves Tough Scrutiny....That He Won't Get," Justice Integrity Project, June 2, 2013. http://www.justice-integrity.org/faq/484-obama-s-fbi-nominee-deserves-tough-scrutiny-that-he-won-t-get.

[66] Rick Wiles, "Muslim Marxist in the White House posing as the president," TruNews, May 2, 2013. http://www.trunews.com/Audio/5_2_13_thursday_trunews2.mp3; and Andrew Kreig, "Obama Battered By DOJ, IRS, State Revelations," Justice Integrity Project, May 14, 2013. http://www.justice-integrity.org/faq/481-obama-civil-rights-image-battered-by-irs-doj-cia-revelations.

[67] David Stuckler and Sanjay Basu, "How Austerity Kills," *New York Times,* May 12, 2013, http://www.nytimes.com/2013/05/13/opinion/how-austerity-kills.html?pagewanted=all&_r=1&; Jason Linkins, "Michael Kinsley Feels Your Austerity Pain, Middle Class," May 18, 2013. http://www.huffingtonpost.com/2013/05/18/michael-kinsley-

austerity_n_3295664.html?utm_source=Alert-
blogger&utm_medium=email&utm_campaign=Email%2BNotifications; and
Sarah Kliff, "Cancer Clinics Turn Away Patients," *Washington Post*, April 3,
2013,
http://www.washingtonpost.com/blogs/wonkblog/wp/2013/04/03/cancer-
clinics-are-turning-away-thousands-of-medicare-patients-blame-the-
sequester/?hpid=z1.

[68] Shaxson, "Where the Money Lives," *Vanity Fair. op. cit.*

[69] Rosenfeld, *Subversives, op. cit.*

[70] "The print and TV media and many Internet sites got the message: Serve
Washington's agenda, and will you will prosper. Advertisers and the CIA will
pump money into your coffers." Paul Craig Roberts, "You Are The Hope,"
Institute for Political Economy, May 1, 2013.
http://www.paulcraigroberts.org/2013/05/01/you-are-the-hope-paul-craig-
roberts.

[71] Kelly, Tom. *The Imperial Post*. William Morrow.1983, 115-16.

[72] Quigley, *The Anglo-American Establishment, op. cit*, 100-39, 197, 309

[73] Graham, *Personal History, op. cit.*, 259-67.

[74] Kelly, *op. cit.*, 115,

[75] Ray McGovern, "Are Presidents Afraid of the CIA?" Consortium News,
December 29, 2009, http://www.consortiumnews.com/2009/122909b.html.

[76] Ibid. See also, Douglass, *JFK and the Unspeakable, op. cit.* 332-33.

[77] Marc Fisher, with 11 colleagues reporting, "Portrait of a Faded American Dream,"
Washington Post, April 27, 2013.
http://www.washingtonpost.com/sf/feature/wp/2013/04/27/the-tsarnaev-
family-a-faded-portrait-of-an-immigrants-american-dream.

[78] Russ Baker, "Bombing Story Mysteries," WhoWhatWhy, May 14, 2013,
http://whowhatwhy.com/2013/05/14/who-in-boston-bombing-story-
mysteries/10599209-spider-web-illustration-for-background.

[79] Wayne Madsen, "Uncle Ruslan's former father-in-law was a right-hand man of Bill
Casey," Wayne Madsen Report, June 12, 2013,
http://www.waynemadsenreport.com/articles/20130611_2 (subscription
only). "Previously classified couments obtained by WMR show that Graham
Fuller was a right-hand man of CIA director William Casey. Tsarni, when he
used the last name Tsarnaev, helped raise the deceased accused bomber
Tamerlan Tsarnaev in Kyrgyzstan, after his brother and sister-in-law, Anzor
and Zubeidat Tsarnaev fled Kyrgyzstan to the United States with their young
son, Dzhokhar Tsarnaev, in 2002." See also, Wayne Madsen, "America's
support network for Chechen and North Caucasus included Tsarnaev fronts,"
Wayne Madsen Report, April 28, 2013 (subscription),
http://www.waynemadsenreport.com/articles/20130428; Daniel Hopsicker,
"'Uncle Ruslan' aided terrorists from CIA official's home," MadCow News,
April 29, 2013, http://www.madcowprod.com/2013/04/29/uncle-ruslan-aid-
to-terrorists-from-cia-officials-home.

[80] Ibid. See also, Laura Rozen, "Former CIA officer: 'Absurd' to link uncle of
Boston suspects, Agency," Al Monitor, "April 27, 2013,

http://backchannel.al-monitor.com/index.php/2013/04/5090/former-cia-officer-absurd-to-link-uncle-of-boston-suspects-agency-over-daughters-brief-marriage/#ixzz2Tgk5T9XP. Rozen is a well-established reporter writing also for *Foreign Policy*, which is owned by the *Washington Post*.

[81] Anastasia Kashevarova and Julia Choi, "Tamerlane Tsarnaeva recruited via the Georgian Foundation, Izvestia, April 24, 2013, as translated by Google, http://translate.googleusercontent.com/translate_c?depth=1&ei=Ggp4UaiIOsPW2AXi3IHYCw&hl=en&prev=/search%3Fq%3D. Cited by Kurt Nimmo, "Tamerlan Tsarnaev was radicalized by the CIA," Infowars.com, April 24, 2013. http://www.infowars.com/tamerlan-tsarnaev-attended-cia-sponsored-workshop. See also, Staff report, "A Welcome Wagon for Defectors," *Newsweek*, June 25, 1984, a document in sanitized CIA files.

[82] Madsen, "America's support network for Chechen and North Caucasus," *op. cit.;* Jamestown Foundation, Wikipedia, http://en.wikipedia.org/wiki/The_Jamestown_Foundation.

[83] Xiamiam, "It is very odd that Rusian (sic) Tsarni was married to Graham Fullers daughter," Democratic Underground, April 29, 2013, http://www.democraticunderground.com/?com=view_post&forum=1002&pid=2772321.

[84] J. Michael Springmann, "Boston Baked BS: It Goes So Well With Turkeys When They've Come Home To Roost," Foreign Policy Journal, May 10, 2013, http://www.foreignpolicyjournal.com/2013/05/10/boston-baked-bs-it-goes-so-well-with-turkeys-when-theyve-come-home-to-roost. See also, more generally, Ray Locker, Kevin McCoy and Gregg Zoroya, "Russia's Chechnya, Caucasus: A breeding ground for terror," *USA Today*, April 19, 2013. http://www.usatoday.com/story/news/world/2013/04/19/russia-chechnya-terror-caucasus/2095995.

[85] James C. Goodale, "Only Nixon Harmed a Free Press More," *New York Times*, May 21, 2013. http://www.nytimes.com/roomfordebate/2013/05/21/obama-the-media-and-national-security/only-nixon-harmed-a-free-press-more. For more general roundups, see my Justice Integrity Project columns and appendices, "Free Press Expert Goodale Warns Against Obama DOJ's Abuses," May 24, 2013 "Obama Doubles Down on National Security Strategy" and "California Senator Rejects Criticism of Privacy Violations, Husband's Deal," each on June 7, 2013 at www.justice-integrity.org.

[86] Ron Unz, "Our American *Pravda*," *American Conservative*, April 29, 2013. http://www.theamericanconservative.com/articles/our-american-pravda. Unz later amplified his themes on my weekly radio show. "'American Conservative' Publisher Decries Major Media Conventional Wisdom, Cover-ups," Justice Integrity Project, June 7, 2013. http://www.justice-integrity.org/faq/489-american-conservative-publisher-decries-major-media-conventional-wisdom-cover-ups.

[87] On March 26, 2013, Nader spoke to the McClendon Group, which for a quarter of a century has provided a forum for alternative speakers at the National Press Club. Among his relevant commentaries are: *The Good Fight: Declare Your Independence and Close the Democracy Gap*, HarperCollins; 2004; and Libby Casey,

"Ralph Nader on Income Inequality and the Minimum Wage," C-SPAN, http://www.c-spanvideo.org/program/311703-4.

[88] Nader, Ralph. *The Seventeen Traditions*. Harper Collins, 2007, 39-45, "The Tradition of the Family Table."

Chapter 22, Next Steps

[1] Louis D. Brandeis Fund for Social Justice, Brandeis University, http://www.brandeis.edu/legacyfund/bio.html.

[2] Estulin, *The Bilderberg Group, op. cit.*, 24.

[3] Lord, Winston. *Aid & Abet*, Vol. II, 7, as cited in Estulin, *op., cit.*, 65. See also, Domhoff, William G. *The Higher Circles*. Vintage, 1971. See also Estulin, *op. cit.*, 86-87 for an extensive discussion drawn from participants and scholars of elite foundations and similar groups on how they coordinate with governmental bodies for action.

[4] Greenwald, MacAskill and Poitras, "Edward Snowden: the whistleblower behind revelations of NSA surveillance," *op. cit.* Kreig, "Snowden's NSA Leak Was Heroic, Historic: Daniel Ellsberg," *op. cit.*; and Michael Riley, "U.S. Agencies Said to Swap Data With Thousands of Firms," Bloomberg, June 13, 2013, http://www.justice-integrity.org/faq/495-backfgrounder-on-obama-s-big-data-domestic-spying-system, noting especially James Bamford, "Connecting the Dots on PRISM, Phone Surveillance, and the NSA's Massive Spy Center," *Wired*, June 6, 2013, http://www.wired.com/threatlevel/2013/06/nsa-prism-verizon-surveillance.

[5] Andrew Kreig, "Jesse Ventura: Fighting for Freedoms, Against Both Parties," Justice Integrity Project, June 14, 2014, http://www.justice-integrity.org/faq/494-jesse-ventura-fighting-for-freedoms-against-both-parties. Ventura, Jesse. *DemoCrips and ReBloodLicans: No More Gangs in Government*. Skyhorse, 2013.

[6] Robin Bravender, "Running Tally of Republican Mega-donors," *Politico*, August 7, 2012, http://www.politico.com//gallery/2012/08/the-billion-dollar-buy-2012-mega-donors/000332-004274.html and "Running Tally of Democratic Mega-donors," *Politico*, August 7, 2012, http://www.politico.com/news/stories/0812/79414.html.

[7] Ibid. "Adelson has already given about three times as much as the previous record-holder, hedge fund manager George Soros, who dropped $24 million to try to defeat President George W. Bush in 2004. And Adelson has already given about one-third of the amount that Sen. John McCain (R-Ariz.) spent on his entire campaign in 2008."

[8] Mike Allen, "Sheldon Adelson: Inside the mind of the mega-donor," September 23, 2012, http://www.politico.com/news/stories/0912/81588.html.

[9] Ibid.

[10] Ibid. See also, Peter H. Stone, "Sheldon Adelson's Woes Mount With Grand Jury In Las Vegas Sands Money-Laundering Probe," Huffington Post, June 5, 2013. http://www.huffingtonpost.com/2013/06/05/sheldon-adelson-grand-jury-money-laundering_n_3381628.html.

[11] Jesse Drucker, "Romney Avoids Taxes via Loophole Cutting Mormon Donations," Bloomberg, October 26, 2012,

http://www.bloomberg.com/news/2012-10-29/romney-avoids-taxes-via-loophole-cutting-mormon-donations.html. Mitt Romney used the tax-exempt status of a charity — the Mormon Church, according to a 2007 filing — to defer taxes for more than 15 years.

12 To be clear, I have no information specifically linking Adelson to such practices. The general patterns have been reported by many, including me.

13 *The Godfather: Part II* (Paramount, 1974) dramatized an extreme, fictionalized example of such a situation when a mob lawyer tells Nevada's U.S. Senator Pat Geary that his supporters in the gaming industry will erase a prostitution/murder scandal, "and all that will be left is our friendship."

14 Abramoff, *Capitol Punishment, op. cit.* Abramoff amplified the book's description to me during Q&A at an event, and in conversation later.

15 Greg Palast, "Mitt Romney's Bailout Bonanza," *op. cit.*

16 *See, e.g.,* Peterson, Peter G. *Running on Empty: How the Democratic and Republican Parties Are Bankrupting Our Future and What Americans Can Do about It.* Picador, 2005.

17 Peter G. Peterson, *America Works Summit, Atlantic,* December 10, 2012.

18 Wikipedia, George Soros, http://en.wikipedia.org/wiki/George_Soros.

19 Krugman, Paul. *The Accidental Theorist and Other Dispatches from the Dismal Science.* Norton, 1999, 160.

20 Dana Milbank, "Where money talks," *Washington Post,* May 24, 2013. www.washingtonpost.com/opinions/dana-milbank-where-money-talks/2013/05/24/d6d64afe-c47e-11e2-8c3b-0b5e9247e8ca_story.html.

21 Al Gore, "False Spontaneity of the Tea Party," Huffington Post, February 14, 2013, http://www.huffingtonpost.com/al-gore/tea-party-koch-brothers-big-tobacco_b_2689380.html.

22 Biographer Robert Caro, among others, has written extensively about Johnson's canny reasons for bragging about his voting frauds and similar deceptions.

23 Hillel Aron, "Are the Koch Brothers Trying to Buy the Los Angeles Times?" *LA Weekly,* March 12 2013, http://blogs.laweekly.com/informer/2013/03/will_koch_brothers_buy_la_times.php.

24 Wikipedia, Richard Mellon Scaife, http://en.wikipedia.org/wiki/Richard_Mellon_Scaife.

25 For Murdoch companies, political favoritism primarily benefited Republicans and (in the United Kingdom) Conservatives. Labor Prime Minister Tony Blair was a major exception, and Blair repaid the debt with an administration that approved major expansion of Murdoch holdings despite antitrust concerns.

26 Palast, Greg, with 48-page comics insert by Ted Rall and Introduction by Robert F. Kennedy, Jr. *Billionaires and Ballots: How to Steal an Election in 9 Easy Steps.* Seven Stories, 2012.

27 Victoria Ward, "Nathaniel Rothschild loses High Court libel battle," *Daily Telegraph,* a (10 February 10, 2012, http://www.telegraph.co.uk/news/politics/9073717/Nathaniel-Rothschild-loses-High-Court-libel-battle.html, "Nathaniel Rothschild, the billionaire

financier, has lost a High Court libel action over a claim that he was the 'puppet master' behind a deal involving Lord Mandelson and a Russian oligarch."

28 Luisa Kroll, "Inside the 2013 billionaires list," *Forbes*, March 4, 2013, http://www.forbes.com/sites/luisakroll/2013/03/04/inside-the-2013-billionaires-list-facts-and-figures; and Russell Adams, "Carlos Slim Boosts Stake In *New York Times* Again," *Wall Street Journal*, October 6, 2011. http://online.wsj.com/article/SB10001424052970203388804576615123528159748.html.

29 Wikipedia, Al-Waleed bin Talal, http://en.wikipedia.org/wiki/Al-Waleed_bin_Talal.

30 For the inside story, see, for example. Goodwin, Jan. *Price of Honor: Muslim Women Life the Veil of Silence on the Islamic World*. Plume, 1995; and Coll, Steve. *The Bin Ladens: An Arabian Family in the American Century*. Penguin, 2008.

31 Wikipedia, David Rockefeller, http://en.wikipedia.org/wiki/David_Rockefeller.

32 Bremer, L. Paul III. *My Year in Iraq: The Struggle to Build a Future of Hope*. Simon & Schuster, 2006.

How To Change History

33 C-SPAN, "*Citizens United*: What Happened? What Now?" Featuring John Samples, Robert Bauer, Bradley Smith, Ray LaRaja, Michael Malbin, Don McGahn, Federal Election Commission; and Lawrence Lessig, January 23, 2013, http://www.cato.org/events/campaign-finance-after-citizens-united-what-happened-what-now.

34 Lessig, Lawrence. *Republic, Lost: How Money Corrupts Congress — -and a Plan to Stop It*. Twelve, 2011.

35 Smith, Sam. *Why Bother? Getting a Life in a Locked-down Land*. Federal House, 2001, 1.

36 Mann, Thomas E., and Norman J. Ornstein. *It's Even Worse Than It Looks: How the American Constitutional System Collided with the New Politics of Extremism*. Basic, 2012.

37 Nietzsche, Friedrich, translated by Adrian Collins. *The Use and Abuse of History*. The Library of Liberal Arts/Bobbs Merrill, 1957, 35. The quotation is from my tattered copy of Nietzsche's powerful monograph, which conservative scholar Alan Bloom assigned in the 1960s at Cornell University. Bloom described Nietzsche as one of the most important political intellectuals in Western history. More generally, however, Nietzsche was falsely attacked after his death as a madman, anti-Semite, and ultra-nationalist. Walter Kaufmann, who converted to Judaism in Nazi Germany in the 1930s and then became an eminent cultural scholar based at Princeton University, almost single-handed rectified the record. His pivotal treatment was, *Nietzsche: Philosopher, Psychologist, Antichrist*. Princeton University, 1975 (Fourth edition). Kaufmann researched and wrote his revisionist appraisal during the World War II era at the peak of anti-German, anti-Nazi opinion.

³⁸ Based on my recent encounters with them or their writing, I believe each would concur with this characterization of their views. None has seen this book, and so I do not presume to ascribe any concurrence with its material.

Appendix: Reform Resources

¹ Radio guest and listener information: http://www.justice-integrity.org/articles.

² Rob Kall, "Beyond Demonstrations, Beyond Civil Disobedience," OpEdNews, February 21, 2013, http://www.opednews.com/articles/Beyond-Demonstrations-Bey-by-Rob-Kall-130221-133.html.

³ Justice Integrity Project and Sarah McClendon Group, "Prosecutorial Misconduct Forum," C-SPAN, June 26, 2009 (3 hours, 4 minutes), http://www.c-spanvideo.org/program/287304-1

⁴ Corsini, "The Rev. Fauntroy," *op. cit.*, http://www.youtube.com/watch?v=P6GrY3zEXI4.

Index

About the Author

Washington, DC-based Andrew Kreig directs the Justice Integrity Project (www.justice-integrity.org) and three other organizations in business and civic affairs. He is an attorney, author, and public affairs strategist who has been listed in *Who's Who in the World* and *Who's Who in America* since the mid-1990s. He has lectured on government and business issues on five continents, including as co-keynoter at the annual *Futures Summit* of the National Association of Broadcasters. In recent years, he has been a research fellow affiliated with two universities.

From 1996 to 2008, he was the president/CEO of the Wireless Communications Association in its worldwide advocacy to create a wireless broadband industry. Earlier, he was the association's vice president/general counsel after working as an attorney with a national law firm and as law clerk to a prominent federal judge in Boston.

In 1987, he authored *Spiked: How Chain Management Corrupted America's Oldest Newspaper*, which was widely reviewed as a pioneering case study of the damage that news industry profiteering inflicts on the public.

Reared in Chicago, Arkansas, and on the West Side of Manhattan, he won scholarships to attend Collegiate School, founded in 1628 and now the nation's oldest educational institution. He holds law degrees from Yale Law School and the University of Chicago School of Law, and a history degree from Cornell University, where he was a student newspaper editor, rowing team member, and Golden Gloves boxer.

CPSIA information can be obtained at www.ICGtesting.com
Printed in the USA
LVOW080555050713

341506LV00003B/76/P